Complex
Human
Behavior

Complex
Human
Behavior

A Systematic Extension
of Learning Principles

Arthur W. Staats and Carolyn K. Staats
ARIZONA STATE UNIVERSITY

HOLT, RINEHART AND WINSTON
New York · *Chicago* · *San Francisco* · *Toronto* · *London*

To Jennifer and Peter

Preface

THE PURPOSE of this book is to explore various experimental and naturalistic observations of complex human behavior in terms of learning principles and thereby to offer a relatively general conception of how the physical and social environments may shape human behavior.

The strategy is to employ an integrated set of learning principles that seem to have "heavy-weight" effects. There is no attempt to give an exhaustive account of learning principles or to consider the controversies and on-going research concerned with those that are presented. In extending the principles to complex human behavior, areas of application are sometimes reached that have not yet been sufficiently subjected to experimentation. Nevertheless, there appears to be enough support of the basic principles as well as a sufficient number of demonstrations of the relevance of their extrapolations to consider a learning conception of complex human behavior to be a powerful approach.

Certain aspects of the strategy of the book emerged from the experience of teaching general psychology to a population of students that included both psychology and education majors and general education students. It was found that lectures which presented a selected set of behavior principles were much more meaningful and interesting to the students when they were presented in simple form and the possible extensions to human behavior were outlined in some detail. It was concluded that for the student who will take only one or two courses in psychology the interpretive application of learning principles can yield a practical type of knowledge and yet remain consistent with a scientific approach. For the major in psychology, on the other hand, this approach seemed capable of leading the student to think of human behavior in terms of experimentally derived principles and to appreciate the technical research underlying the establishment of such principles.

It will be recognized that the systematic orientation of the present book is coincident with other efforts to extend learning principles to complex human behavior. It does attempt, however, to give a more central position to description of the development and function of language. This is possible because of recent theoretical and experimental extensions of learning principles to this area. The present interpretation also brings together the conceptions of a number of learning psychologists and in so doing attempts to abstract congruent principles rather than indicate conflicts. The most influential conceptions have been those of B. F. Skinner, and F. S. Keller and W. N. Schoenfeld, on the one hand, and J. Dollard and N. E. Miller, C. L. Hull, O. H. Mowrer, C. E. Osgood, and K. Spence on the other.

While the book that has developed from these considerations is in the same tradition as that of previous extensions of learning principles to human behaviors, it does have a new format and does incorporate relatively new theoretical and experimental developments. As such, teaching uses for the book can be suggested only tentatively. Thus, the book could be used in general psychology where the instructor is interested in the systematic presentation of a set of learning principles applied to various areas of human behavior, rather than with a survey of approaches and experiments in psychology. To the extent that the instructor wishes to emphasize learning, the book might also find use in specific courses in the area of general psychology, such as child psychology, personality, the psychology of language, and human learning.

The book also seems appropriate in a similar sense for students of education and educational psychology. In this field one is concerned primarily with human learning, and the various chapters deal with human behaviors that are significant to the educational enterprise. Furthermore, the growing extension of experimental methods and principles of learning to some of the problems of education enhances the need for an understanding of the approach and its applications.

The point in the student's career at which the individual instructor might wish to introduce such a book may be expected to vary. The book is intended to be self-contained and to depend upon no prior special training in psychology. In this sense it could be thought of as introductory. On the other hand, the student who already has a background in the basic principles may find it productive to consider complex human behavior in terms of these principles.

Although the authors interchanged comments and suggestions on all chapters and worked and re-worked the expressive aspects throughout, some of the chapters were individually and some jointly composed. Chapters 1, 3, 4, 5, 6, 9, and 11 were composed by A.W.S., and chapters 2, 7, 8, and 10 were jointly composed.

It was in the conduct of research supported by several governmental agencies that some of the conceptions basic to the book began to develop. For this support, appreciation is extended to the Office of Naval Research for a continuing research project on the psychological processes in language and communication; to the National Institute of Mental Health for a project to study personality and verbal response classes; and to the Office of Education, Cooperative Research Branch, for support of several preliminary experiments investigating certain aspects of the acquisition of reading as discrimination learning. A.W.S. is also grateful for a National Science Foundation Faculty Fellowship for the first term of 1961–1962, spent at Maudsley Hospital of the University of London, and for a sabbatical leave from Arizona State University for both terms of that year—both of which contributed to the present project.

The authors also wish to express appreciation to several individuals who read the book in whole or in part and contributed valuable suggestions: Albert Bandura, Dale Harris, John L. Michael, and Richard E. Schutz. In addition, Judson R. Finley and Karl A. Minke gave helpful assistance in the physical preparation of the manuscript.

November 1963 A.W.S.
Tempe, Arizona C.K.S.

Contents

1

Introduction

It is evident from an even cursory look at the course of man's acquisition of knowledge of the world and ability to deal with the world that certain methods of making progress have been more successful than others. The methods of investigation that are called science, or scientific, have been singularly successful.

Fundamental to scientific activity is its empirical basis (Braithwaite, 1955). The scientist may observe without the aid of instrumentation, or he may construct advanced apparatus for this purpose. His observations may be quantified and thus susceptible to mathematical treatment, or they may be very gross. The observations may be well controlled in the precision of the laboratory, or they may be naturalistic observations obtained in the field. Relationships between observations may be noted or single observations studied. Regardless of these differences, statements within a science are, in general, accepted or rejected on the basis of their observational support.

It may be said, however, that especially useful types of observations made by a scientist are those which show the lawful relationships existing between the events in which he is interested and the conditions which determine those events. In everyday language it would be said that the scientist is looking for the "cause" of events.

The term "cause," however, has come to have philosophical meanings that extend beyond scientific considerations, and today it is preferable to use the term "functional" rather than "causal" in describing these types of relationships. In any event, the scientific investigator looks for observable events which are related in such a way that if the first event occurs, the second event also occurs. If the first event does not occur, neither does the second. More precisely, the occurrence of the second event may be termed a function of the first. This type of functional relationship constitutes an explanation of the second event; it answers the query concerning why the second event occurred. For example, a scientific explanation of a sort became available in answer to the question why tides occur when it was observed that certain positions of the moon are lawfully related to the tidal event.

Once statements based upon observed functional relationships have been made, they have very useful products. If the occurrence or nonoccurrence of the first event is known, then the occurrence of the second event can be predicted. In addition, if the first event can be manipulated (that is, altered), then the second event can be controlled. If, for example, the second event depends upon the occurrence of the first, and the occurrence of the first event can be prevented, then the second event can be prevented.

Of course, to get these important advantages of scientific statements, the observations upon which they are based must be reliable and as precise as possible. If someone reports an event as occurring when in actuality no such event occurred, then statements based upon this will be in error—and be likely to lead to erroneous predictions. Although at this sophisticated stage of scientific development there are many ways to make observations reliable—that is, to guarantee that what is said is based upon observable events in a precise way—one very general injunction is that observations must be public and repeatable (Stevens, 1939). The history of knowledge has indicated that if an event can be observed by only one individual or if it is in any manner not repeatable, it cannot be considered a reliable observation and cannot lead to statements from which prediction and control may be obtained.

This is a very short statement about certain aspects of a very important activity—science. However, this will suffice at present and will be expanded in the second chapter. The point which should be stressed now is that these methods of observation were not always accepted as a legitimate way of generating and evaluating statements about the events of the world. At one time, statements did not have to have public and repeatable verification. Individual claims to subjective observations were accepted without public validation or the possibility of repetition. As a matter of fact, at one time systematic observation was eschewed as a method, and competitive statements were favored that derived from authority, tradition, or dogma. Failure to abide by this approach, that is, challenge of dogmatic or authoritative statement, was dealt with severely (see White, 1899).

However, public and repeatable observations that were made, often surreptitiously, showed regularity and lawfulness of natural events and thus yielded predictions. That is, once the relationship between observations had been firmly established and a scientific law stated, it became possible to forecast one event from knowledge of the other. The assumption of such lawfulness in new areas of study resulted in further accumulation of observations, further successful predictions, and so on. New statements based upon observations began replacing those based upon authority in many areas of study.

Because the scientist tests statements with observations, the scientific method may be said (1) to be sceptical of statements of authority, tradition, or dogma; (2) to assume that the events of the world are natural and lawful, thus knowable through observational methods; and (3) since new evidence leads to revision when it conflicts with the old, to be tolerant of change.

When the empirical approach, even in the face of competing statements of tradition and dogma, had proven its value and was finally accepted, it became possible to move from naturalistic observations in the field into more detailed, systematic, and reliable study in the laboratory. Laboratory study may be considered to be a way of observing an event by eliminating the interference of those disturbing variables that occur in naturalistic circumstances. Sometimes apparatus may be used to aid in observing these events; however, most importantly, the laboratory experiment may be considered to be a situation in which control of irrelevant variables or events is obtained. In other words, if one wishes to study the effects of one event upon a later event, he must be sure that the later event is not being affected by other variables which, in this instance, are extraneous. Thus, the movement to the laboratory yielded an increase in control over the effects of irrelevant events upon those that were being observed, and resulted in more reliable observations.

The greater the experimental control, however, the further the events seemed to be from real life occurrences. Feathers in real life may fall gently to the ground or even swoop into the air, whereas in the experimental control established by a vacuum chamber they behave quite differently. Laboratory work appears on face value to be artificial and impractical. As a result, the scientist is often denigrated as "ivory towerish" and impractical. Sometimes this characterization is accepted by the man of science himself, who values his work as "pure," as opposed to "applied," science.

It was a long time before the practical results of scientific activity were recognized, perhaps not self-consciously until the time of Bacon.

Thus, Bacon symbolizes, even though he obviously did not initiate, a very profound change in the attitude of man toward knowledge. In the past, science had been primarily concerned with the search for law and order. It was theoretical rather than practical—an adornment of life. After Bacon, knowledge increasingly became an instrument to achieve mastery over nature. First in the Western countries, then all over the world, this attitude became identified with progress and civilization (Dubos, 1961, pp. 1207–1208).

The ivory-tower conception of science is thus the reverse of actuality. The potentialities of the prediction and control of natural events is of immense practical significance. The scientist and his findings are, and have been, of the greatest utility in achieving control over events of the natural world. This is possible because his statements, more than any others', correspond to reality, to what is observed. They are weighed in terms of the extent to which they can be validated by the occurrence of observable events. In this way, the scientist is less likely to make statements that are not related to actual worldly events.

Because this is so, the accumulation of laboratory-established principles that emerges in the later stages of the development of a science may receive wide application and solve problems that in the past had appeared insoluble. When this has occurred, the methods of observation of that science and its basic concepts and statements are publicly acclaimed. In due time some of these concepts and statements are assimilated into the common language and are accepted by people in general. The value of the general activity becomes recognized and is encouraged, at least for that particular area of study.

Psychology

The subject matter of psychology is the behavior of organisms; these are the events in which psychology is interested, and the task is to observe them in detail as well as to find the events which determine them. "Like every other science, psychology conceives its problem as one of establishing the interrelations within a set of variables, most characteristically between response variables on the one hand and a manifold of environmental variables on the other" (Bergmann and Spence, 1941, pp. 9–10). By human responses, or behavior, we mean all the activities of the human being—such disparate events as walking, talking, fighting, laughing, thinking, learning to read, as well as simple muscle and glandular responses.

The previous characterization of the development of certain aspects of a science is useful in describing the development of the study of man's behavior. At first the statements in this area of study were of the traditional and dogmatic kind. All behavior, for example, was thought at one time to be spontaneous or the work of capricious spirits, demons, and other supernatural entities. In such an atmosphere the observational study of human behavior was discouraged. Certainly, if the causes of behavior were unpredictable and uncontrollable, little could be accomplished by empirical investigation. Coleman (1950), for example, relates the following in the area of abnormal behavior.

References to mental disorders in the early writings of the Chinese, Egyptians, Hebrews, and Greeks make it clear that they too attributed such disorders to demons which had taken possession of the individual. This is not surprising when we remember that "good" and "bad" spirits were widely used to explain lightning, thunder, earthquakes, storms, fires, sickness, and many other events which primitive men did not understand. . . . Moses is quoted in the Bible as saying "The Lord shall smite thee with madness." Apparently this primarily involved the withdrawal of God's protection, and the abandonment of the individual to the forces of evil. For example, Saul presumably disobeyed God with the result that the spirit was thereby permitted to enter. In such cases every effort was made to rid the patient of the evil spirit. Christ reportedly cured a man with an "unclean spirit" by casting out the devils that plagued him into a herd of swine who in turn became possessed and "ran violently down a steep place into the sea" . . . (p. 23).

Such conceptions of the determinants of human behavior also dictated the type of treatment applied. Thus, the common treatment for unusual behavior was exorcism of the offending spirits and demons, by methods that ranged from prayer and incantation to flogging and starving. In addition, interpretations of human behavior in terms of these supernatural forces were strongly adhered to. "Any criticism or questioning of the theological doctrine of demonology during the Middle Ages was made at the risk of life itself" (Coleman, p. 32).

Later, however, naturalistic observations accumulated that contradicted the interpretation of the capriciousness of behavior as determined by spirits and demons. A conception of abnormal behavior as "mental illness" emerged. Freud, as an important example, in observing and working with patients who came to him for help, developed a conception of the lawfulness of human behavior, the conception that human behavior was determined by natural events, not supernatural ones. These statements competed very successfully with those derived from tradition and dogma. That is, the statements derived from clinical observation were more helpful in solving life problems than were the traditional statements. Many other valuable observations about man's behavior have been derived from naturalistic and clinical settings.

The experience of other experimental sciences and their observational methods have also had an impact upon psychology, beginning with the advent of psychology as a self-conscious science about 1880 (see Boring, 1950). Since that time a major portion of psychology has been concerned with laboratory methods and can be called experimental psychology.

While discovery of some of the basic principles of behavior occurred around the turn of the century, the early stages of experimental psychology have been restricted to simple situations and, usually, simple organisms. Most of the studies used the white rat or some other lower organism, in restricted laboratory situations. By this means, as with other experimental sciences, it was possible to gain control of or eliminate some of the irrelevant variables so that reliable observations could be made of certain behaviors as they were affected by certain determining events.

As a result, however, the experimental study of behavior principles took on the isolated, artificial, impractical appearance that has been described. Even among professional psychologists concerned with human problems, experimental psychology has been considered of negligible relevance to an understanding of complex human behavior. "Rat" and "brass-instrument" psychology was derogated as divorced from practical realities.

And, to an extent, this was true. Investigators interested in a scientific approach to behavior first had to work with simple situations to find the principles relating environmental variables to behavioral variables. This consumed most of their efforts. Before the everyday case could be dealt with in all its complexity, a system of reliable behavior principles had to be established. During its time of "restriction" to the laboratory, however, such a system of behavior principles was emerging. The work of Pavlov, Watson, Thorndike, Hull, Skinner, Spence, and many others has contributed most effectively to this scientific conception of behavior.

It appears at this time, however, that psychology is on the threshold of the stage of development where its methods and its products, the principles, may be extended to life occurrences and by their success replace older methods. Extensions of behavior principles to complex human behavior by such men as Miller and Dollard, Osgood, Mowrer, Keller and Schoenfeld, and Skinner and his associates, and the substantiating research that has relatively recently begun to accumulate, provide evidence to support this contention. While the progress of psychology as an experimental science is far from ended, these extensions indicate that a set of experimentally derived behavior principles is already available which, when organized into a conception of human behavior, may profitably replace the conceptions of man which have been formulated from previous traditional approaches or from naturalistic clinical observations. Although such conceptions or interpretations have to extend beyond their experimental foundations, the general outlines of empirical support for such extrapolations have to some extent been laid down, and relevant experiments are accumulating at an accelerating rate. Such conceptions, stemming from laboratory principles, should have an increased likelihood of yielding improved prediction and control of human problems.

Moreover, in addition to prediction and control, the general conception of man's behavior which is implied by a set of principles is of practical importance, for it determines in many cases how we react to various social problems. The previous example of demonology is one illustration, but there are many examples of a more subtle nature in our everyday lives. We take many actions, ranging from deciding whether a movie is appropriate for our children, through voting on the advisability of capital punishment, to our considerations of international problems; which may all rest upon our conception of man's behavior.

In addition, work in other behavioral science areas (such as sociology, anthropology, economics, political science, and history) is frequently based upon a conception of human behavior. In the absence of an acceptable conception derived from experimental principles of behavior, these areas have often utilized conceptions based upon naturalistic or clinical observations. The same is true of applied areas of psychology in clinical, industrial, and educational settings.

The present book attempts to take some of the established principles of behavior and to organize them into a schema that is capable of dealing with human behavior in complex situations. It is not the first of these attempts (see Dollard and Miller, 1950; Keller and Schoenfeld, 1950; Miller and Dollard, 1941; Mowrer, 1950; Skinner, 1953). Like some of its predecessors, it assumes that in order to deal with the complexity of human behavior as it is encountered in naturalistic situations the principles must include a rather complete account of language development and function. This seems necessary since most of man's behavior involves or depends upon language.

Thus, the book will first present the methodology of an experimental approach to behavior as well as the experimental principles that have been derived from such an approach. With these principles, bulwarked by relevant experimental and naturalistic evidence, various types of complex human behaviors will be treated in the following chapters, beginning with discussions of the development and function of language.

2

The Method

MAN HAS been seeking explanations of the world about him, including the behavior of other men, for a very long time. The superiority of scientific explanations of nature to prescientific approaches is well documented in all areas of modern life. Our present task is to examine some of the distinctive methods generally used by science to achieve its enormous predictive power so that we may determine what aspects of the method are significant for understanding human behavior. How does one go about establishing a science of human behavior? How do scientific accounts of human behavior differ from nonscientific accounts? The present chapter seeks to discuss in summary fashion some of the questions involved. The discussions are fundamental to those in later chapters of the book.

Observation, Description, Classification

The enormous power over the events of nature that scientific study has provided springs in large part from empirical observations. Because the products of a science—the ability to predict and control—heavily involve observation, the state of development of the observations in a field helps determine the quality and quantity of these products. "[W]e find in the end that discrimination, or differential response, is the fundamental operation [in science]. . . . [T]wo people . . . find that unless they can each discriminate the same simple objects or read the same scales they still will not agree" (Stevens, 1939, p. 228). To appreciate this fully, we now need to examine in greater detail the function of observation in science.

A public record of a simple observation of an event could be said to constitute the first stage in the development of knowledge about the event. When the record of observation is made by using verbal symbols we have a description. Observation and description are thus closely related; description provides a convenient means of permanently recording and publicly communicating our observations. When observation is detailed and systematic, it is possible to prepare detailed and systematic description.

Detailed description, in turn, can be very useful, both in its own right and as a step toward the classification of events. In discussing the importance of classification in science Stevens (1939) points out again that classification depends upon the fundamental operation of discrimination. "If we can discriminate crucial differences between Dobbin and other animals we have named horses, we reject Dobbin as something not horse. In other words, we 'correlate' our discriminations—those made on Dobbin with those made on other objects—and the 'goodness' of the correlation determines where we shall classify the beast" (p. 233).

Let us look at some examples of how this has worked out in practice. Botany is a science in which observation, description, and classification have played an important role. In botany the events of interest are plant life. Important knowledge is derived by accurately observing and describing the characteristics of different plants. The gross events that were of original interest can be seen to consist of finer parts. Detailed descriptions based upon such observation may be organized so that fine similarities and differences (discriminations) are noted and a "class" of plants identified. In this way we now talk about "Eucalyptus, Ash, and Elm" rather than merely about "trees." Thus, detailed observation and description enable us to make comparative examination of the fine parts of which the whole events are constructed, and systematic classification of those parts.

The mere systematic recording and classification of observations is an improvement on nonscientific interest, since it enables observers to notice relationships that would never be apparent on the basis of casual observation. For example, although the conception of the evolution of living organisms had been suggested by Greek philosophers (Reichenbach, 1951, pp. 196–197), it was only after Darwin and others had systematically described many plants and animals and noted their similarities and differences that the concept of the progression which takes place in the evolution of living matter was given a solid foundation. Thus, observation and description may serve an important function by opening the door for a step toward further knowledge.

In addition, however, simple observation and description may have another productive result. Returning to botany as the example, we find that the botanist, in constructing a classification system, may take into consideration physical and functional characteristics of plants. Plants are assigned to a family on the basis of such physical aspects as leaf shape, root type, and flower, as well as on such behavioral characteristics as soil requirements, blooming season, pollination method, etc. Now, with such a classification system, suppose a botanist traveling through foreign terrain comes across a new plant he has not seen before. Upon careful observation, he sees that the plant has certain physical characteristics similar to those

of a plant family with which he is familiar. Knowing the characteristics of
the general class, he may make predictions about the specific case. He may
predict that it will pollinate in the same manner, bear flowers in a certain
season of the year, and so on.

Thus, such classification systems may have important practical as well
as scientific utility. Knowledge of the general class of events defined by
similarities and differences in the observed events may allow prediction
about the new individual case. The statements involved in this logic may
be put into syllogistic form and have been described as rules of class
inference (see Reichenbach, 1951, pp. 215–216). For example, the case
we have cited could be put in the following form.

> *All plants in class x bear flowers in the spring.*
> *This new plant is a member of class x.*
> *The new plant will bear flowers in the spring.*

Much of our knowledge in other areas has been developed and is
employed in an analogous fashion. Medicine contains many such examples,
for medical diagnosis has typically leaned heavily on this methodology.
Having himself observed and described a number of cases of a certain
constellation of symptoms, or having studied descriptions made by other
qualified observers, a physician includes each new patient who demonstrates a similar symptom pattern in the general class. He now expects the
same behaviors in the individual patient that he has found in the general
class, and he expects treatments that have been successful for the general
class to be successful for the individual case.

The same methodology underlies the efforts expended on observation
and classification of abnormal human behavior. It was believed that
adequate description of the general class of "schizophrenia," for instance,
would enable the clinical psychologist to deal successfully with the individual "schizophrenic."

Detailed observation and comparative description can therefore be a
source of powerful information for dealing with new events that man may
encounter in life. The novice scientist who inherits someone else's classificatory system is much better able to cope with new events than is the
layman who does not have this knowledge.

A word should be said about the importance of the public nature of
observations. As was mentioned in the first chapter, it has been found that
descriptions based upon public and repeatable observations are the ones
which produce the productive fruits of a science. In the history of human
knowledge about the natural world there have been many statements based
upon "observations" that were neither public nor repeatable. Such state-

ments, however, have not yielded the products—such as prediction—that science has to offer.

Since science is based upon observations, it is of the utmost importance that the observations be reliable. Reliable observations are those that can be obtained again under the same conditions. In the development of a science the search for reliability usually leads to a movement from observations of the event in its natural state to observations in very controlled circumstances—in other words, to the experiment. In addition, there is a movement away from the individual scientist as the "observing instrument," with all his frailties as such an instrument, to the use of mechanical and electronic instruments for observing and recording events.

Furthermore, complex logical methods for deciding whether an observation is reliable have been constructed. Thus, statistical analysis of recorded observations can be used to indicate whether under the same circumstances the same observations would be made, or whether the event was actually due to some uncontrolled factors.

These and other developments are all concerned with insuring that reliable observations are made. Statements about natural events cannot ordinarily include less error than the observations upon which they are based.

Operational Definitions

Science is not an individual matter; it is a social endeavor involving many people. "Science, as we find it, is a set of empirical propositions agreed upon by members of a society" (Stevens, 1939, p. 227). What one observes is significant when it is presented to others. This involves words, as the term "description" implies. The observing behavior of the scientist is important when he responds in some verbal form, which can then affect other people. In order for this to occur, however, his verbal behavior must be very precise. He cannot, for example, report things that are not there or have not occurred. He must respond with the same term to only one object or event. If he responds in the same way to two different events, ambiguity exists. These may seem like commonplace injunctions, but the history of science indicates that they are not, as will be seen. The precise use of terms is very important in scientific endeavor.

Real difficulty is encountered when the terminology used in description is so loose and ambiguous that one cannot be sure what was observed. Greater difficulty is involved when terms occur for which there are no physical counterparts, although they purport to refer to physical events. Descriptions which include ambiguous or empty definitions must be revised so that they use only terms which have been adequately defined. To avoid this methodological difficulty scientists have become very partic-

ular about the terminology used in describing events and have established
definite criteria for the acceptability of a term.

In psychology one is concerned with the problem of terminology at
every stage, but particularly when one seems to be getting away from
directly observable events. When we talk about behavior we mean that
which man does: the walking, talking, swimming; the being anxious or
bright or loyal, and so on, that is observed in men and that behavioral
scientists are interested in describing and explaining. The terms "anxious,"
"bright," and "loyal," however, may not appear to refer to observable behavior in the same direct way as do "walking," "talking," and "swimming."
Nevertheless, as long as these former terms are thought of as nothing
more than "shorthand" labels for classes of behavior—"anxious" behavior, "loyal" behavior, and so on—we are on safe ground. Unfortunately, in
everyday thinking, people commonly act as if the "real" thing to study is
not the behavior itself, but rather some inner entity, "anxiety" or "loyalty,"
which accounts for the behavior observed. Many times, however, no such
inferred inner entity is adequately specified by observations. Thus, such an
approach may violate a basic scientific dictum that the events of interest
must be observable by any investigator sufficiently trained to observe them.

Psychologists have found the logic of *operationism* useful in avoiding
this kind of confusion in terminology. *Operational definitions* allow scientists to successfully pursue their activity by providing a framework within
which the terms they use in communication are explicitly defined by
observable events. A term, accordingly, *means* nothing more than the
observations to which the term is attached. An operational definition, in
its simplest form, specifies the observational operations used to identify
phenomena. As long as these observational operations themselves meet the
criteria of the scientific approach, the term introduced may enter into
further scientific statements. The canon of operational definition of terms
prevents us from composing statements which give the impression that
something is being said about empirical events when the statement is
really empty of such meaning.

As an example, let us look at a concept that is frequently used, the
concept of "emotional maturity." Can this term be appropriately used?
As long as the term means only certain observations, the answer might be
affirmative. It might be said, for instance, that a child is emotionally
mature if he studies by himself without being coerced, if he is not overly
demanding, if he has good relationships with other children, etc. On the
other hand, a child who does not study well by himself, who is disruptive
in his demands, who does not get along with other children, who has
temper tantrums, and so on, might be termed "emotionally immature."
At this point the term "emotional maturity" is defined in terms of a num-

ber of observable responses. The single term "emotional maturity" now stands for all these separate behaviors that seem to occur concomitantly. As such, it is simply a shorthand label for an elaborate set of observations.

When the definition of a concept consists of the observations that are made and labeled by the concept, the concept is said to be operationally defined. It is necessary to remember, however, that an operational definition is, after all, only a definition; it has no more scientific status than the behaviors observed and described. To attach the label "emotional maturity" to a diverse set of responses is useful only as a classificatory device; it merely classifies many different acts into a single category that may be used in communicating with others who follow the same convention. Operational definitions, then, do not explain the phenomena under consideration. The primary importance of an operational definition is to insure that persons interested in a certain set of phenomena are all talking about the same events (see Mandler and Kessen, 1959, for a discussion of the unambiguous use of terms in psychology). In actual practice, the term "emotional maturity," for example, has been used with a variety of meanings and as a consequence has not acquired much scientific utility.

To summarize, since the events in the natural world are so complex, the conceptual (or symbolic or verbal) terms that are used to stand for the observations will also become quite complex. Because of this, a good deal of attention must be paid to the conceptual, or verbal, tools in a science, in other words, to the way a term is to be introduced, its relations to other terms, and so on. The standards of operational definition help in keeping the conceptual tools distinct. The criteria that a concept must meet in order to gain admission to scientific parlance should be clearly understood. It must be defined by observations that are unique to this term and to no other.

Having arrived at satisfactory observations, then, we are ready to search for explanation; in our terms, to relate the phenomena to the variables of which they are a function. An operational definition is a way of evaluating the terms in the system, of eliminating terms which overlap, and of excluding those which are "fictional," that is, have no observational counterparts. We are still forced, however, to look for those prior conditions that determine the behavior defining the term if explanatory statements concerning the behavior are to be established.

Description as Pseudo Explanation

Solely on the basis of observation and operational definition of the terms, the events in which we are interested may not be fully explored. Although the physician may have learned a description of a certain disease and may be able to treat the individual case on this basis, this is not to say that he has made any explanatory statement about the disease. For example, it has been observed that individuals sometimes exhibit a series of symptoms: the first stage being marked by restlessness, apprehension, and obvious ill health; the second by hyperactivity and spasms of the muscles of swallowing and respiration; and the third by a general paralysis ascending the spinal column and final death. This set of observations, let us say, defines the term "rabies." On observing these symptoms in an individual a physician may accurately label the behavior and consequently state that there is nothing that can be done for the victim. He can then predict the victim's eventual demise. With only this knowledge, however, the physician is incorrect if he says that the patient is going to die *because* he has rabies; with only a classificatory scheme of diseases he has nothing to explain the death. He can legitimately only describe the disease itself rather than speculate about its "causes."

It is easy, however, to fall into the trap of treating a descriptive term as a pseudo cause. In the field of abnormal psychology, investigators have been concerned with classifying and categorizing different classes of deviant behavior. These classification systems have proved useful for reasons already discussed. One such class includes the behaviors of suspiciousness, envy, extreme jealousy, and stubbornness, as well as delusions of persecution and/or grandeur, and so on. These types of behavior seem to appear together in many cases, and a term has been defined by these observations: *paranoia*. On observing this set of behaviors, the psychologist is in a position to state that the individual concerned is "paranoid," or may be labeled "paranoid." The danger enters when either he or his audience think that the undesirable behavior has been explained, *when indeed it has only been named*. The explanatory step of specifying why the individual acts as he does has not yet been taken. There is only a single set of facts: the observations of the behavior of the individual.

Perhaps a diagram will illustrate the faulty logic involved in substituting labeling for explaining. It was said that a certain set of behaviors may be named by one term, "paranoia," because they are related:

$$\left.\begin{array}{l} \text{Beh}_1 \text{ (suspiciousness)} \\ \text{Beh}_2 \text{ (envy)} \\ \text{Beh}_3 \text{ (stubbornness)} \\ \text{Beh}_4 \text{ (delusions)} \end{array}\right\} \text{Paranoia}$$

The incorrect step in thinking occurs when it is stated that the individual behaves in such fashion because he is "paranoid," inferring now some internal entity "paranoia" to *account* for the behavior. In diagrammatic form it can be seen that in this misuse of the term, "paranoia" is inferred to be inside the organism (as indicated by the circle) and comes before —"causes"—the observed behavior:

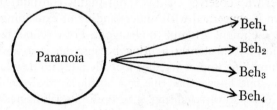

The circularity of this type of thinking is apparent when we ask the investigator, "How do you know that this person is paranoid?" and the answer is, "See how he behaves." The behavior is fallaciously *explained* in terms of the concept, and the concept is verified by the behavior.

Spence (1944) calls such terms "animistic conceptions," [1] and Skinner (1953) points to this specious substitution of a definition for a "cause" in his discussion of traits:

> Trait-names usually begin as adjectives—"intelligent," "aggressive," "disorganized," "angry," "introverted," "ravenous," and so on—but the almost inevitable linguistic result is that adjectives give birth to nouns. The things to which these nouns refer are then taken to be the active causes of the aspects. We begin with "intelligent behavior," pass first to "behavior which *shows* intelligence," and then to "behavior which is the *effect* of intelligence." Similarly, we begin by observing a preoccupation with a mirror which recalls the legend of Narcissus; we invent the adjective "narcissistic," and then the noun "narcissism," and finally we assert that the thing presumably referred to by the noun is the cause of the behavior with which we began. But at no point in such a series do we make contact with any event outside the behavior itself which justifies the claim of a causal connection (p. 202).

In our everyday thinking, we can find numerous examples of such faulty explanations. For example, it is observed that people in a situation of danger usually behave in a manner which has the effect of saving their own lives, and this behavior is named "self-preservation." Later, we attempt to explain this behavior with the assertion that all people have an instinct of self-preservation.

In a less dramatic context, the behavior of an individual who spends a large portion of his time practicing the violin may be observed. Consistent, strong, tenacious behavior of this sort has been labeled "interest." A perfect

---

[1] Terms that are inadequately defined and that suggest unobservable internal processes of a causative nature have been discussed extensively in psychology. See, for example, the discussion of hypothetical constructs by MacCorquodale and Meehl (1948).

circle in thinking is completed, however, when it is said that the individual plays the violin *because* of his interest.

The teacher who observes eight-year-old Jimmy constantly fighting with other children is concerned with understanding or explaining his behavior in order that she might attempt to change it. For a school psychologist to say that Jimmy is constantly fighting because he is a hostile-aggressive child may sound very impressive, but it really adds no new knowledge, for if we ask how one knows that this is a hostile-aggressive child, the reply is that the child is always fighting. The term "hostile-aggressive," then, is only another name for "one who is always fighting." It does not explain the behavior or indeed add any new information, if the only ways of observing "hostility" are in the behavior itself. In the end, the statement that "Jimmy fights because he is hostile-aggressive" proves to be a tautology: "Jimmy fights because he fights."

Functional Relationships

Now that a type of pseudo explanation has been discussed, we may go on to discuss adequate explanation in psychology that yields the products of scientific laws in general. Explanation in psychology, as in other sciences, is developed upon the basis of systematic observation. That is, when systematic observation of some phenomenon has been made, the second stage in the development of a science may begin: the search for the cause of the phenomenon, or, more accurately, the specification of some independently observed prior event to which it is related.

The stuff out of which the lawful relationships are found are the *observations* of the events in which the scientist is interested and the *independent observations* of the conditions that determine these events. In order to explain an event, then, something more than observing and describing similar events must be done. The *antecedent* conditions under which the event will occur must be known, as well as those conditions under which it will not occur. That is, the relationships between the event of concern and the events determining it must be established.

Let us refer once more to the field of medicine for an example. When it was discovered that infection with a certain virus resulted in the symptoms called rabies, then an explanatory statement of a sort had been made. This is an example of a lawful relationship and may be schematized as follows:

Introduction of $\longrightarrow$ Symptoms of

virus into body   rabies

Although this case may seem simple, this is the type of lawful relationship that science seeks to discover. The symptomatic behavior termed

rabies has been observed to follow upon the independently observed introduction of certain viruses into the body. When it is discovered that the
two events are lawfully related, the requirements for a scientific law have
been fulfilled.

That this is, in essence, a fundamental task of all science may be shown
by examining examples of primitive "laws" from different areas of study.
In physics, for example, there was interest in explaining events such as
changes in the state of water. It may be observed, on the one hand, that
water changes from a liquid to a solid state under certain conditions. It
may also be observed, aided by a very simple instrument (a thermometer)
that atmospheric temperatures vary. These observations are independent
of each other; it is not necessary to see water to know that the temperature
has changed, nor is a thermometer necessary in order to observe that water
has become solid. However, when it is found that the two events are indeed
reliably related, we have the substance of a scientific law. The explanation
of the change in state of water is to be found in temperature variations.

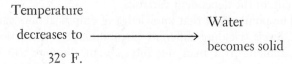

Temperature
decreases to ⟶ Water
32° F. becomes solid

Turning to biology and the science of genetics, we find the task to be
the same: that of finding the relationship between certain events in which
one is interested and the events that determine them. Relationships have
been found in genetics between certain physical characteristics of the
organism and the physical characteristics of its parents. After each phenomenon has been independently observed, the further observation that
they are generally related constitutes an empirical law. In genetics one
possible lawful relationship might be between certain eye colors of parents
and the eye colors of their offspring.

Both parents have ⟶ Offspring has
blue eyes blue eyes

Having found a lawful relationship between two events, one preceding
the other in time—in common-sense terms a "cause"—two powerful products of science may be obtained. First, if the occurrence of event$_1$ is reliably
followed by (lawfully related to) event$_2$, knowledge of event$_1$ gives knowledge of what event$_2$ will be. If it can be determined whether or not the
particular filterable virus has been introduced into the body of an individual, whether or not the individual will display the symptoms of rabies
may be predicted. Thus, when a person is bitten by a dog, the dog is exam-

ined to see if it could have transmitted the virus. If the virus has been transmitted, it can be predicted that unless preventive action is taken, rabies symptoms will in due course appear in the person.

In addition to the power of prediction, empirical laws may also yield control. Interest in a particular natural event is often accompanied by an interest in influencing or controlling its occurrence. Now, if there is a lawful relationship between event$_1$ and event$_2$, the second event can be predicted from the first. Moreover, if event$_1$ can be manipulated so that it either does or does not occur, then the control of event$_2$ is achieved. In the above example, if the first event, the introduction of rabies into the body, can be manipulated, then the second event, the occurrence of the disease, can be controlled. (For the sake of simplicity other determining factors have been ignored, such as the treatment that can be inserted between event$_1$ and event$_2$.)

In later discussions event$_1$ will be called the independent variable, or antecedent condition or event. Event$_2$ will be called the consequent condition or event, or the dependent variable.

It should be pointed out that knowledge of empirical laws can take place at different levels, yielding different possibilities for prediction and control. The statement "If a 'mad' dog bites a man, the man will later display the symptoms of rabies" constitutes an important empirical law, yielding the products of prediction and control as discussed. This is a valid and useful empirical law in itself, even though there is no knowledge of the physiological and bacteriological events involved. More detailed observation has, however, indicated that the brain of a "mad" dog contains a certain virus strain which, if injected into the blood of another mammal, results in the occurrence of rabies symptoms in this animal. This constitutes another empirical law, yielding additional products of prediction and control. Applying these empirical laws and others, scientists may develop vaccines for rabies, methods of treatment, and so on. Thus, each empirical law is itself important, but finer and finer detail in the lawful structure should also be sought.

To obtain prediction, one must possess information concerning the *occurrence* of the specific determining event or events, as well as of the lawful relationships involved. If this information is not available prediction is not possible, even though the underlying empirical law is available. For example, the physicist who knows what events determine how a body will fall through space is in a position to predict the course of the fall of a specific body *only* if he is given access to information about the determining events in this case. It is for this reason that the trained physicist may be as helpless in predicting the flight of a stray feather through the air as is the layman. The layman knows neither the determining events nor the laws relating these events to the flight of the feather. The physicist knows the laws relating the events, but without information concerning the occurrence of the actual determining events he is just as powerless as the layman to make predictions.

The psychologist faces the same problem when dealing with the individual case. Although he may be aware of the functional relationships existing between certain behavior and certain environmental conditions, he is powerless to predict the development of the behavior if he is uninformed of these environmental conditions in the life history of a specific individual. It should be emphasized, however, that in many cases the potential for the control of determining events is present but is not utilized because the relationships to the phenomena under consideration have not yet been discovered. Thus, the discovery of empirical laws may have extremely important consequences.

Determinants of Behavior

To explain behavioral phenomena, the task is once more to observe the relationship of the determining events to the behavior of interest. What kinds of events are determinants of behavior? Of course, the first criterion is that the determinants must be independently observable. It is possible, however, to classify the determinants of behavior into two general categories of events acting upon the individual: biological and environmental.

The relationship between behavior and its general determinants can be depicted using a diagram similar to the previous examples. On the one hand there is the biological history of the individual, which may be further subdivided into the individual's membership in a particular species and his personal biological history, such as the genetic endowment determined by his particular parental background. At the same time additional determinants are to be found in the environmental events acting upon, or having acted upon, the individual. The environmental conditions related to behavior start with the prenatal conditions in which the child begins life and continue throughout life. This, of course, includes a great quantity of events that have a determining action upon the behavior of the individual.

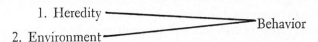

Some disciplines of behavioral science are concerned primarily with heredity and the biological determinants of behavior, while others are interested primarily in environmental determinants. For example, physical anthropologists look for explanations of behavior in the history of the species. Physiological psychologists study behavior as a function of the nervous system, the actions of muscles and glands, and so on. On the other hand, social psychologists, sociologists, and cultural anthropologists are interested in the behavior of man in groups and seeks explanations for this behavior in a person's group memberships, the institutions that affect him, the "beliefs" and "attitudes" of the culture in which he is raised, and so on.

Psychology is interested in any lawful relationships involving behavior that may be discovered. However, at present, there is relatively little that can be done to manipulate the hereditary or biological events which affect the type of complex behavioral skills we shall be discussing. In attempting to deal with the behavior that is of everyday significance, we are largely restricted to working with environmental variables. For this reason, the present book is concerned with laws involving environmental rather than biological determining events, although it is recognized that the search for lawful relationships between biological events and behavior is very important.

S–R Laws

The independent events we shall be concerned with will be environmental events, to be called stimuli, and behavioral events, to be called responses. As a consequence of this interest in stimulus (S) and response (R) events, psychology has been concerned with making reliable observations of both. There are therefore operationally defined terms whose referents are observations or measurements of stimulus events, and there are operationally defined terms whose referents are observations of response events.

In addition, there are terms whose operational referents consist of S–R relationships. That is, the term may actually be defined by an S–R law. Such concepts seem even one step further from our original statement that *observability* is the crucial criterion for a term in science. It should be recognized, however, that a term may label a relationship between a set of observable stimulus conditions and a set of observable response conditions. The operational definition of the term in this case is simply the relationship between the two events.

Numerous terms of this sort will be dealt with in this book, but again, we must be sure that they fulfill the essential requirements of scientific methodology before they are accepted. Examples of such terms that are important in psychology are "learning" and "motivation."

Let us examine the concept "learning," for example. In everyday language it is said that a child has "learned" if he is observed to be correctly reciting a poem or if he earns a high mark on an arithmetic test or if he swims with ease and speed. But actually, only a number of different responses have been observed in these cases. Correct use of the term, however, would involve stating the events or conditions that determine these behaviors. For example, if it was pointed out that the child was using a cue card to read the poem or that he copied the answers to the arithmetic problems, one would hardly be satisfied with the statement that he had "learned" the observed adequate responses. In other words, the appropriate behavior by itself is not what is meant by "learning," but rather it is a relationship between a class of antecedent (stimulus) conditions on the one hand and a class of response conditions (behavior) on the other hand that defines the term.

In every-day language, one of the stimulus conditions leading to the "learned" type of behavior described is practice, the repeated presentation of some stimulus material, such as the words in a poem. An oversimplified definition of learning which can be used as an example at this point is that "learning is a relatively permanent change in behavior which occurs as a result of practice." Thus, neither the stimulus conditions alone nor the response conditions alone define the term. Learning is thus defined by *both* a set of stimulus conditions (repeated presentation of stimulus material) and a set of response conditions (the acquired behaviors). This could be called an operational definition of learning.

In the general case, then, concepts are also acceptable in a science when they are defined by an empirical relationship between events—in psychology between stimulus conditions and response conditions. In a diagram form the concept of learning is shown below as such a concept.

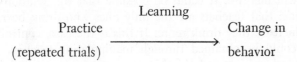

Of course, the most important aspect of the process for the behavioral scientist is that the relationship between stimulus and response conditions has been observed. Adding the term "learning" has really added nothing of explanatory value. Regardless of the term used, the business of the scientist remains the same—to discover relationships between the events of interest and the events that determine them. The concept is useful, however, as a sort of "shorthand" device. Rather than saying that "the child's behavior has changed as a result of practice," it is simply said that "the child has learned." As a shorthand device, the term allows for the designation of entire sets of stimulus conditions, entire sets of response conditions, and all the relationships between them, with a single term. In the example, all the numerous relationships between the very great number of "practice"

situations and the innumerable forms of the consequent permanent changes of behavior have been reduced to a manageable, coherent statement. It must be emphasized, however, that the *only* meaning possessed by the concept as used in this manner is the relationship of the stimulus and response variables.

This type of term, or rather the relationship that defines it, yields the same products as do empirical laws in other sciences. That is, when an S–R law has been found, knowledge of the S conditions will enable the R to be predicted. It may be predicted that if there has been no presentation of the poem stimulus materials, the unprompted recitation behavior will not occur. Or, if the repetitions of the presentation have been few the recitation behavior will be poor, and so on. In addition, the S–R law offers the possibility of the control of behavior. As the presentation of the stimulus material is manipulated, the recitation behavior will vary. The principles to be presented in the next chapter are examples of S–R laws.

R–R Laws

It should be pointed out that there are independently observed events which, although lawfully related, do not provide the possibility of control. Consider, for example, the relationship between teachers' salaries and beer consumption in the United States. As it happens, years in which teachers' salaries are high are also years when beer consumption is high.

Since these two independently observed events are lawfully related, once it is discovered that teachers' salaries are up, it can be predicted that beer consumption will increase. It could be possible that this relationship is a determining one; that teachers are the only ones who drink beer, and as their salaries increase they drink more. If this is the case, control of beer consumption could be obtained through manipulating teachers' salaries.

On the other hand, the relationship may not be a determining one. Economic conditions in the country may be the actual independent variable and both teachers' salaries and beer consumption the dependent variables. Thus, manipulation of economic conditions would result in changes in both teachers' salaries and beer consumption. While these latter two events are, as a consequence, related, they are not in an independent-dependent relationship and are not explanatory in terms of the determining relationships discussed.

There are empirical laws of this sort in psychology also. For example, lawful relationships may exist between two responses of the same person at different times (Spence, 1944). That is, it may be observed that the behavior an individual displays at time$_1$ is related to the behavior he dis-

plays later at time$_2$. It might be found, for example, that if an infant displays temper tantrums at time$_1$, the same individual as a school-age child at time$_2$ will periodically explode into "rages."

Sometimes R–R relationships can be found between verbal behavior and subsequent motor behavior, between what a person says at time$_1$ and what he does at time$_2$. Recognizing this relationship, psychologists have attempted to describe verbal behavior precisely, to quantify it, and to relate it to later overt behavior of various kinds. When such a relationship is discovered an observation of behavior made at time$_1$ may be used to predict behavior at time$_2$.

Paper and pencil tests may be considered to be measures of verbal behavior that have been found to be related to other behaviors of the individual. For example, obtaining a high score on a test of personality maladjustment (the R_1) might be found, let us say, to be related to other aggressive behaviors (the R_2) (Kimble, 1956).

S–R and R–R Laws Compared

As we have seen, an antecedent event in a functional relationship may be either a stimulus event or a response event. These two types of empirical laws yield different products, however. To illustrate the comparison, the previous example of a boy who fights a great deal in school will be used. Let us assume for a moment that two relationships between fighting behavior and antecedent events had been discovered; one might be a hypothetical S–R relationship. This might consist of the observation that when fighting behavior is rewarded (S) in the home the child will fight (R) in other situations. The R–R relationship might be that a high score on the Rotten Kid Adjustment Test (R_1) is related to frequent fighting behavior (R_2). In either case, the teacher has quite a bit of information. Applying the general S–R law, it is known that if Jimmy comes from a home in which fighting is rewarded he is likely to become engaged in frequent battles. Applying the R–R law yields the same prediction. In other words, having discovered either an S–R or an R–R law one is in a position to predict behavior (Kimble, 1956).

If one is concerned only with predicting behavior, then both types of law might satisfy the purpose equally well. The criterion for choosing between them would then simply be the amount of error involved in the particular statements, the ease of application of the law, and so on. For example, testing the child might be more practicable than observing home training procedures. In one particular situation it may be the S–R law that is more precise; in another situation it may be the R–R law.

The usefulness of the two types of laws can be further contrasted, however. Is the teacher satisfied simply to predict which child will be aggressive?
Probably, it is also important to prevent the undesirable behavior by
modifying the conditions that lead to it. With Jimmy, the teacher might,
on the basis of the S–R law, have a talk with his parents, explain the situation to them, and suggest other ways of dealing with Jimmy that will have
a more desirable effect. If the parents will cooperate, the fighting behavior
can be controlled. The R–R law, on the other hand, would be of no help
in controlling Jimmy's fighting. Although it may be that when Jimmy makes
a certain score on the personality test his behavior is likely to be belligerent,
we know too that preventing him from taking the test will hardly prevent
the behavior of fighting from occurring. Thus, if we are interested not only
in predicting, but also in controlling human behavior, we must search for
S–R laws (Kimble, 1956; Spence, 1944).

Unfortunately, the properties of the two kinds of laws are sometimes
confused. Although the R–R law is of no value in exercising control of
behavior, this is not always clearly understood, and it also may be thought
that such a law by itself has this type of explanatory power. Suppose, for
example, that an investigator develops a "personality test" which will
predict which children are in need of psychological help; he has demonstrated an R–R relationship. At about this point questions of "causation"
may arise that are similar to those in our previous discussion of pseudo
explanation. It is obvious, of course, that the test behavior (R_1) cannot be
regarded as the determinant of R_2, the later maladjustive behavior. Instead
of recognizing the limitation of R–R laws and launching a search for S–R
relationships, however, there may be in more subtle cases a tendency to
infer some causal entity from the test, R_1, which is then thought to *determine* R_2. Following our example, an entity called "weak ego structure"
might be inferred from a low score on the personality test, and then the
assumption made that a "weak ego" determines the poor behavior in later
situations, as in the following diagram. If the term was based solely on
the observation of responses, on an R–R relationship itself, a spurious
causative event would in this way be invented.[2] While this example quite
obviously involves improper methods and would be unlikely to actually
occur, misuses do occur in real-life cases where the circumstances are more
complicated.

R–R laws by themselves simply do not provide information concerning
independent variables that offer controlling possibilities. Although it may

------

[2] A justifiable basis for introducing explanatory terms intervening between stimuli and
responses—*intervening variables*, terms which may enter into controlling as well as
predictive statements—will be mentioned in general significance in the next section and
discussed more fully in Chapter 3.

appear that something has been gained by adding the "weak ego" between R_1 and R_2, no information has actually been gained. The only means of identifying this supposed weak ego is to administer the personality test.

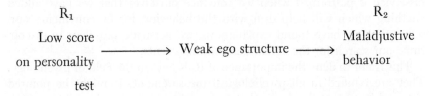

$$R_1 \qquad\qquad\qquad\qquad\qquad\qquad R_2$$

Low score $\qquad\qquad\qquad\qquad$ Maladjustive

$\qquad\qquad\longrightarrow$ Weak ego structure $\longrightarrow$

on personality $\qquad\qquad\qquad\qquad\qquad$ behavior

test

"Weak ego," then, is nothing more than another name for "low score on personality test." That is, while it is said that the individual has a "weak ego" when he has a low score on the personality test and that the weak ego is the source of his later maladjustive behavior, actually only a single functional relationship has been established, not the two that the previous statement implies.

R–R laws alone always leave unanswered questions concerning the "cause" or "causes" of both R_1 and R_2. In order to answer these questions it is necessary to establish the relationship between antecedent conditions, which are often stimulus events (S), and both R_1 and R_2.

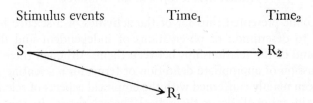

Stimulus events $\qquad\qquad$ Time$_1$ $\qquad\qquad$ Time$_2$

$$S \longrightarrow R_2$$
$$\searrow R_1$$

As the diagram indicates, the reason why a lawful relationship exists between R_1 and R_2 may be that they are both determined by the same stimulus conditions. Returning once more to the example of Jimmy's fighting, one of the possible lawful relationships may be diagrammed in the following manner:

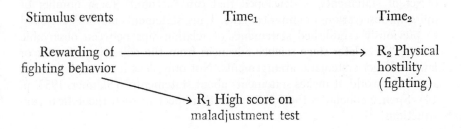

Stimulus events $\qquad\qquad\qquad$ Time$_1$ $\qquad\qquad\qquad$ Time$_2$

Rewarding of $\longrightarrow$ $\qquad\qquad\qquad\qquad\qquad$ R_2 Physical
fighting behavior $\qquad\qquad\qquad\qquad\qquad\qquad$ hostility
$\qquad\qquad\qquad\qquad\qquad\qquad\qquad\qquad$ (fighting)
$\qquad\qquad\searrow R_1$ High score on
$\qquad\qquad\qquad$ maladjustment test

To infer an explanatory concept from R_1 to explain R_2, however, is no improvement over an ad hoc explanation of R_1. It is as circular as the substitution of a label for an explanation, as we showed earlier. Moreover, a disservice is performed when we convince ourselves that we have added anything which will help deal with the behavior, for by convincing ourselves that we have found explanations, we persuade ourselves to discontinue our search for the actual determining events.

This is not to deny the importance of R–R laws in the field of psychology. They are typified in all psychological measurement. It might be pointed out in this context, however, that tests and testing procedures have sometimes fallen into disrepute due to a misunderstanding of the nature of R–R statements. Since tests do not enter into S–R relationships, they cannot be used to manipulate behavior. From R–R laws *alone* no knowledge of how to teach a child arithmetic or how to prevent him from becoming maladjusted in adulthood can be derived. Thus, it is important to use the information yielded by R–R relationships to the full extent possible in prediction, but at the same time their limitations when it comes to explanation (and control) must be recognized and care taken not to infer improperly referenced causal entities.

Additional Aspects of Science

The account presented thus far of the activities of a science has stayed very close to description of observations of independent and dependent variables, and of the relationships between them. Although there has been some discussion of appropriate definition of terms for a scientific language, we have been mainly concerned with the empirical aspects of science rather than with its rationalistic or theoretical characteristics. In this section a few matters will be discussed that are relevant to theory in science and that also have significance for the present book.

Theory in Science

In the advanced stages of a science statements are often made concerning the complex interrelations of empirical laws, or a general statement, or set of statements, is developed that can "account" for a number of different observations or empirical laws. Thus, statements may be developed to previously established statements of relationships between observable events. "In a later stage science advances from the collection of rules or laws to larger systematic arrangements. Not only does it make statements about the world, it makes statements about statements" (Skinner, 1953, p. 14). Spence concludes the following with respect to such theoretical constructions.

The physicist is able to isolate, experimentally, elementary situations, i.e., situations in which there are a limited number of variables, and thus finds it possible to infer or discover descriptive, low-order laws. Theory comes into play for the physicist when he attempts to formulate more abstract principles which will bring these low-order laws into relationship with one another. Examples of such comprehensive theories are Newton's principle of gravitation and the kinetic theory of gases. The former provided a theoretical integration of such laws as Kepler's concerning planetary motions, Galileo's law of falling bodies, laws of the tides and so on. The kinetic theory has served to integrate the various laws relating certain properties of gases to other experimental variables (1944, pp. 47–48).

When such an advanced stage of a science is reached the theoretical body may instill much confidence by being well verified observationally. And it may allow one to predict diverse happenings as well as to control those happenings. Much of the advancement in the science may then come in further developments in these theoretical, or higher-level, statements—in reorganizations of these statements that better incorporate the various empirical laws and observations. The spectacular results of such reorganizations in being better able to account for past observations, and in suggesting new ones, and in solving various problems hitherto unsolved, elevates these theoretical activities of science to a lofty perch and tends to make less lofty-seeming the original observations and empirical laws upon which the higher-level theoretical statements were based. Some philosophers of science have thus given precedence to "rational" or theoretical elements in science rather than to the empirical elements and have considered the sciences that have attained this advanced stage as the model for all sciences. It would seem, however, that both types of activity, empirical and theoretical, if they indeed are separable, are productive (see Reichenbach, 1951).

According to Spence (1944), psychology has not yet reached that stage of development where there is a body of higher-level theoretical statements. Perhaps it is thus less important in the present context to describe in detail the features of such theoretical constructions. Notwithstanding this, there are some considerations that should be indicated, which are relevant for "theory" within psychology, as well as significant for the general approach or strategy of this book.

Generalization or Extension of Principles

First, whenever a general statement is made on the basis of a limited number of observations, the general statement has less than perfect probability of being correct, and in this sense has a theoretical or hypothetical quality. For example, a lawful relationship found for a single observation of one animal has a relatively low probability of holding for all animals of the same species.[3] Thus, it might be found that injecting a white rat with a certain drug was followed by the disappearance of certain disease symptoms. A general statement based upon this observation, however, would have the characteristics of a hypothesis—to which each successful repetition with a new animal would add support. The validity of the general statement would increase with each verification with a new case, but unless all possible cases were examined (usually an impossibility) there would never be perfect proof of the generality of the law (see Braithwaite, 1955), although with sufficient repetition the probability of validity would become quite high.

In the example described, the extension of the original empirical statement was to very similar circumstances—let us say to members of the same species under as nearly identical conditions as possible. The extension, or generalization, of such a statement, however, may be further afield, for example, to other organisms, under different conditions. The more the conditions have changed from those under which the generalization is made, the lower is the probability that the hypothesis will hold true. Let us say, as an example, that the statement relating the drug administration to disappearance of symptoms in the rat is extended to another organism, such as man. The extension would again be in the nature of a hypothesis, with a reduced probability of holding true.

Each time a statement is extended to a new set of conditions and is verified, however, the statement gains in generality and may be said to have a higher probability of being "true."

Extension with Indirect Verification

As Spence (1944) points out, theory may also play a role in psychology in the process of finding the relationships between stimulus and response events. As will be discussed in the next chapter under the heading of "Intervening Variables," there are some behaviors of interest in psychology that are not directly capable of observation. In this case theoretical terms may play a part if they are correctly specified with indirect methods of observation. At this time, however, it will be worth while describing analogous procedures that occur in other sciences.

Lachman (1960) states, in a context which is meaningful for psychology, that statements which derive from observations of relationships between events may be extended to new conditions which involve the consideration

---

[3] This is not meant to imply that reliable observations which produce statements having general characteristics cannot be established with single organisms. Methods for obtaining reliable observations with one organism will be mentioned in Chapter 10. See also Sidman (1960a).

of some events not directly observable. Lachman gives as an example the previously mentioned gas laws, in which the term "model" is the theoretical set of statements that is extended as a hypothesis to a consideration of the observed effects of gases.

> Let us first observe the pictorial model of the kinetic theory in its most limited form. A gas is represented by this initial model as consisting of minute invisible particles (molecules or atoms) in incessant motion, colliding with one another and with the walls of any restricting container; at a given instant, most of the particles are separated by vacant space (1960, p. 118).

As Lachman goes on to show, by extending statements that have been derived from observing the movements of large objects to the inferred, unobservable gas particles, the principles (knowledge) already gained can be applied. "Here, the gas particles are conceived as behaving analogously to medium sized bodies such as billiard balls, rocks, or planets: the laws of classical mechanics governing the motions of the latter and the principles of dynamics describing their energy states are ascribed, approximately, to the motions and energy states of the imaginary gas particles . . ." (Lachman, 1960, p. 118). As a consequence of this generalization, extension, or hypothecation, new implications (predictions) can be derived concerning the manner in which gases should behave with respect to effects that are directly observable (such as the temperature and pressure of the gas as a function of volume). The validity of a set of statements extended from a set of observable events to a set of events that are not directly observable is to be assessed, it should be remembered, by the extent to which this extension suggests additional correct prediction and control of the observable events involved.[4] (In Chapter 3 analogous extensions of statements established with observable events to events not directly observable will be described as they are relevant to psychology. See "Implicit Responses as Intervening Variables.") As with any extension, until the extended statement has been found to make correct predictions, it is of the nature of a hypothesis that requires considerable support before it generates much confidence.

---

[4] There are, in addition, sophisticated questions concerning whether such inferences, when they do lead to correct prediction and control, also "prove" the existence of the unobservable events involved in the statements (see Toulmin, 1953). For example, when statements considering gases as collections of small particles lead to correct prediction and control, does this also prove the existence of the unobserved particles, or does this merely validate the usefulness of applying the set of statements to this new area of study. These, however, are questions that need not concern us at this time.

Indirect Verification in the Extension of Sets of Principles

As the preceding example involving the gas laws implies, sometimes the extension into a new area may involve a set of principles, not merely one principle. This may be true when the extension is being made from statements involving observable events to a new realm of observable events, or as in the last example, to a realm of unobservable events. In any case, there are some important considerations that should be mentioned in the "theoretical" extension of a *set* of principles—since this is particularly relevant to the present project.

We have previously mentioned that a scientific theory may consist of related statements, some of which are in a hierarchical relationship. That is, a higher-level statement may relate to two or more lower-level empirical laws. A theory may thus be composed of a set of higher-level statements of this kind as well as their lower-level statements. Braithwaite (1955, pp. 12–21) points out that support for such a theoretical system is given in several ways. First, a higher-level statement (or hypothesis) might receive support directly. In addition, however, whenever a lower-order hypothesis receives empirical support, this also constitutes indirect support for the higher-level hypothesis. Furthermore, whenever one of the related statements or hypotheses in the set forming the theoretical system receives empirical verification, the other principles in the system also receive such indirect support. Let us say, following an earlier example, that it has been found that a *group* of chemically related drugs has certain disease-combating effects with rats. The *set* of empirical laws derived from the observation of each relationship between drug and disease-cure would constitute the "theoretical" system when applied to a new organism. Let us say that one begins the study of the resulting set of principles with man. As each drug is tested with humans it would represent a single hypothesis. Each time one of these hypotheses is confirmed, it would receive support itself in this new realm of observations. In addition, however, the general set of principles involving the applicability of the *various* drugs would receive indirect support—and we would have more confidence that the chemically related drugs found to work with rats will function similarly with humans.

Implications for the Extension of Behavior Principles

This brief discussion can by no means be considered to cover what is meant by scientific theory. However, it does abstract some points that are important for considering some of the general features of the present project. The strategy to be followed will be to present first a set of behavioral principles or laws in the next chapter. Many of these principles were originally established with lower organisms in simple situations, although many have already been verified in studies of simple behaviors with humans. This set of statements may, then, be considered as a related set of hypotheses, or a theory, which in the rest of the book is extended to the consideration of man's complex behavior. Nevertheless, as will be indicated, this extension is not without support of the types that have been mentioned. There are various experiments that have already been conducted that substantiate the validity of the individual behavior principles (or hypotheses) with the types of human behavior to be discussed. Each of these validations may be thought to support the extension of the individual behavior principle, as well as to substantiate the related set of behavior principles as a general conception or theory of the human behavior involved.

It is therefore important for the student to keep in mind the characteristics involved in the extension of empirical statements in one area or set of circumstances to the events in another area or set of circumstances. Until verified in the new conditions, the extension inspires less confidence that the statements will hold. Moreover, as we shall see in discussing intervening variables in the next chapter, even some of the basic principles are, in the present case, still in the nature of hypotheses—in other words, have not received enough verification to have a high probability of validity. In addition, if the discussions of some of the principles were made in great enough detail, the student would also see that there are still areas of controversy over some of the principles.

This is stated in negative terms at the beginning so that the reader may keep in mind the tentative nature of the extension of principles as he peruses the book. However, it should also be remembered, lest the reader make the error of over scepticism, preferring to retain the conception of human behavior he has already acquired, perhaps on a common-sense basis, that there are *two* types of error involved in the type of venture proposed in this book. Statements may be extended to a new area and accepted, but be shown by later evidence to be false. On the other hand, the extended statements, after premature rejection, may receive more definite support from later evidence; or competing common-sense principles may be retained instead of better-verified newly proposed principles. While one does not wish to accept a conception that has insufficient support, to retain a competing conception which has significantly less support is a greater error. Various conceptions or theories of human behavior are available. The problem of the interested person is to examine the principles involved in each theory and to utilize, at least until new evidence changes the situation, the set that has the most support. Each competing conception of human behavior must be examined *by the same criteria*—by establishment of the extent to which its principles and their implications have been observationally verified with complex human behavior. It is because the principles to be presented have, in the authors' opinion, the greatest support for considerations of the relevant aspects of complex human behavior, that the following extensions are made.

The Relationship between Conceptions and Actions

Use of the scientific method has established lawful statements important in everyday life, and the approach and methods seem equally important in understanding actual human behavior. This section will show, in general terms, why a scientific approach to human behavior would be expected to pay practical dividends. Let us consider for a moment how an understanding of the laws underlying phenomena affects the approach to practical problems in other areas of study. Medicine, the applied science built upon the biological sciences of zoology, biochemistry, physiology, botany, and so forth, provides clear illustrations of the relationship between the level of understanding of the laws of the science and the uses to which such understanding can be put. For example, prior to the discovery of the lawful relationship between virus or bacterial infection and the development of certain disease symptoms, there was no understanding of the determinants of disease. Until a patient developed symptoms, therefore, there was no way to predict or control a particular disease. Ignorant of the lawful relationships involved, man had no ability to deal with the events of concern, the occurrence of disease. As is often the case, when people are ignorant of the actual determinants of an event, incorrect conceptions of the determining events arose. These incorrect conceptions then provided a basis for action which, rather than leading to the prediction and control of the events in question, actually compounded the error. Lacking knowledge that explained illness, man attempted to control disease by praying to various gods, by offering sacrifice, by drawing blood from the afflicted, by wearing "protective" garments or jewelry, and so on. For example, the Jivaro Indians of South America are to this day not acquainted with the lawful relationship between antecedent biological events of infection and the resulting illness. They are therefore still unable to deal effectively with disease. To make matters worse, they accept inappropriately defined conceptions which state that illness and death occur because another person directs evil spirits to attack the victim. Because of this conception of death or illness resulting only from evil spirits, when an individual dies or becomes ill the family of the victim attempts to find the responsible evil-doer, and this often results in further occasion for sorrow among the population. The concepts one accepts, good or bad in terms of observational definition, will determine what is done about the event in question.

Let us now turn to human behavior. Here, too, the general system of explanation incorporated into one's thinking helps determine how one deals with practical problems. For example, at one time it was thought that an individual who behaved abnormally was possessed by the devil. This conception led to ways of treating abnormally behaving individuals that are now recognized as inefficient, if not detrimental to advantageous behavior change. At that time, the objective of treatment was to convince the devil that a given body was not a fit place for him to inhabit—that it was too uncomfortable. To prove the point to the devil, "therapy" involved whipping the person, burning him, immersing him in ice water, casting him into a snake-pit, and so on. The treatment was, of course, in line with the prevalent conception of the source of abnormal behavior; it was assumed that the devil would choose to vacate this particular body, and the individual would be "cured."

Today, once again in accord with the prevalent conception of the source of abnormal behavioral phenomena, individuals who behave abnormally are treated as sick people; their behavior is explained in terms of mental illness rather than in terms of possession by the devil. Because of this "illness" concept, mental "hospitals" are provided, drugs that will help an individual regain his "health" are sought, and people are taught to be as kind and thoughtful with the "mentally ill" as with any person suffering from ill health. That this conception may not lead to effective treatment in some cases will be shown in later chapters.

This example illustrates the intimate relationship between the system we use to explain behavior and our reactions to other people. The common-sense conceptions we hold concerning behavior also determine how we respond to others. If our common-sense conceptions correspond to empirical laws concerning behavior, we tend to respond appropriately. If the conceptions are poor, our responses may be inadequate.

The reader should now be able to see the value of establishing empirical laws, whether he be psychologist, parent, teacher, or merely interested in understanding human behavior. Each person's conception of human behavior helps dictate his actions toward others, young and old. For example, a teacher who accepts the premise that the young "mind" must be disciplined like an immature musculature may spend much time drilling on difficult material, regardless of its practicality. On the other hand, a teacher who has been trained in concepts of learning drawn from Gestalt theory will say that drill on individual skills is less important than holistic experiences of a naturalistic sort. In the same way, a parent whose explanatory system involves the terms "personality" and "character" defined as inherited and immutable entities will respond differently to children than will another parent who defines the same terms as a function of the child's past experience and the type of situations with which he is presently confronted. When one's conception of human behavior coincides with the events involved—and, as we have shown, scientific concepts are constructed to do just this—then his actions should in this sense be "good" ones. When the concepts are awry, the actions should be awry.

The set of principles to be presented in the next chapter, based upon the approach that has been described, provides a conceptual framework that we hope will dictate improved ways of dealing with other people's behavior even in areas where the principles have not yet been so firmly established as to allow precise prediction or control. Since any interpretation or conception of behavior that we hold will dictate our social behaviors, it would seem advantageous to develop an interpretation based upon experimentally established behavior principles.

3

Relevant Principles
of Behavior

IT IS the purpose of this chapter to introduce the experimental principles
with which to interpret the development and maintenance of significant
aspects of human behavior. Although it will be worth-while to describe
some of the original laboratory experiments whereby these principles were
discovered, it must be remembered that each principle is presented solely
because it is considered by the authors to be important for understanding
human behavior. In most cases, the principle will be presented and then
an example will be described of a human behavior that might function
according to that principle. This will be done to give a general conception
of how human behavior might be learned—more comprehensive and detailed applications of the principles to human behavior will come later.
The principles presented in this chapter form the foundation of the book.

Since the later chapters in the text are concerned with complex human
behaviors, the experiments cited there usually employ human subjects.
In the present chapter many of the experiments cited will use animals as
subjects. As this indicates, most of the principles have been derived from
experiments utilizing simpler situations and organisms, illustrating the
continuity between more basic research and its extensions. From the
reader's point of view the simplicity of the animal experiments also will
enable the principle illustrated to be portrayed in simple terms.

Respondent or Classical Conditioning

This first principle can be introduced through an example involving
behavior in an everyday situation. At one time or another nearly every
child is taken to a physician's office for a vaccination or inoculation of
some sort. Over a number of such visits, systematic changes might be
observed in the child's behavior. On the first visit the child cries when the

"painful" injection is administered. Painful stimuli elicit this type of response. On succeeding visits, however, it may be observed that the child does not wait until the needle is presented before beginning to cry. On the second or third visit it might be observed that the child howls at the sight of the physician. If the visits are extended, the child might even begin crying upon entering the outer office.

Several aspects of this example should be particularly noted. Originally, the physician—or, more precisely, the visual stimulus that he constitutes —was neutral with respect to crying. The painful stimulus provided by the needle jab, on the other hand, reliably elicits crying behavior. After the sight of the physician has been followed by the painful stimulus one or more times, the formerly neutral stimulus acquires the characteristics of the painful stimulus, and the sight of the physician itself elicits crying behavior.

This sequence of events illustrates the general principle originally called conditioning and now frequently termed "respondent conditioning," or "classical conditioning." If a stimulus, originally neutral with respect to a particular response, is paired a number of times with a stimulus eliciting that response, the previously neutral stimulus itself will come to elicit the response. This principle has wide generality. Many different types of behavior are acquired as a result of this process, not just "negative" behaviors, such as crying. The principle of classical conditioning is of great importance in understanding how language is learned, how communication occurs, and how attitudes develop, as the reader will see in later chapters.

Actually, it has been recognized in a vague way for a long time that things which occur together tend to become associated. A song that has been repeatedly played during a certain period of one's life will later tend to arouse the same responses that occurred at the earlier date. If the responses were "pleasant" ones, the song will later elicit "pleasant" responses —and the converse is also true. Though the process of "association" has long been recognized, it was not systematically explored until recent times. People were content with naturalistic observations and the subjective interpretation that intangible "mental" events become associated when they occur together. Systematic and objective accounts of the process of association awaited the activity of laboratory workers, one of the first of whom was Ivan Pavlov. His experiments began to show how the environment molds or shapes the behavior of the organism and thus opened the way for understanding the great complexities of human behavior that cannot be accounted for on the basis of biological factors alone.

As is customary in an initial investigation of an area, Pavlov restricted his study to a simple situation in which as many extraneous factors as possible could be controlled. Basically, this is what constitutes an experiment in any area of study. Controlling for various factors that might affect the behavior of his experimental animal, in this case a dog, he manipulated one variable and observed the effect upon the animal's behavior. This variable consisted of confronting the dog with two environmental stimuli presented in contiguity. One of the stimuli elicited a certain response at the beginning of the experiment; the other stimulus did not elicit this response. After presenting the two stimuli together a number of times, the latter stimulus also came to elicit the response.

More specifically, the dog was strapped into a harness in a sound-proofed room. An auditory stimulus was presented, and shortly afterward a bit of meat powder was placed on the dog's tongue. The meat powder, of course, elicited a salivary response. Apparatus was used to observe precisely the amount of the dog's salivation, the time of the presentation of the auditory stimulus, and the amount of food given the dog.

The auditory stimulus and the food stimulus were presented in close order a number of times. It was found that if the auditory stimulus was finally presented alone the dog would salivate. The extent of salivation proved to be in part a function of the number of times the sound had been paired with the meat powder. The more times the auditory stimulus was paired with the meat stimulus, the greater was the salivary response to the sound, until the dog was maximally conditioned. The time interval between the presentation of the sound stimulus and the presentation of the meat stimulus proved also to be an important variable. When the sound preceded the meat powder by approximately one half a second, the strongest conditioning was produced. Longer or shorter intervals decreased the amount of conditioning.

Since we will refer to the principle of respondent conditioning many times, it is important that the reader learn the proper terms for the different aspects of the conditioning process. The stimulus, the sound in this case, that does *not* at first elicit the response is called the *conditioned stimulus* (abbreviated CS). The stimulus, the meat powder in this case, that initially elicits the response is called the *unconditioned stimulus* (abbreviated UCS). The process of classical conditioning can be schematized as in Figure 3.1.

The principles of classical conditioning have been validated using other organisms and other types of responses. Experiments with human subjects were necessary to demonstrate that the principles apply to man. These experiments also were made as simple as possible and thus involved simple responses that could be easily measured and recorded. With humans, the eyelid response to a puff of air, acceleration in heartbeat to a UCS of electric shock, and many other behaviors have been conditioned.

Razran (1939a, 1939b, 1949) has conducted several experiments that

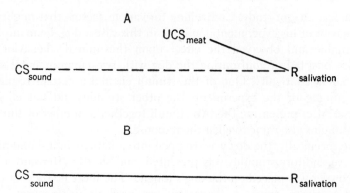

Fig. 3.1. The process of classical or respondent conditioning. Each time the CS is presented with the UCS, which already elicits the R, the tendency for the CS also to elicit the R is increased. After a number of such pairings of CS and UCS (conditioning trials), the CS will itself elicit the R. The extent to which the CS elicits the R is indicated by the heaviness of the line; after the first trial the weak conditioning is indicated by the broken line. After many trials the stronger conditioning is indicated by the heavier line. This convention will be followed in later figures.

demonstrate the process of conditioning in humans in a rather interesting way, which is analogous to the original experiments of Pavlov. Razran used different types of food (such as pretzels, tea, sandwiches, or candy) as the UCS, in the same way that meat powder was used with Pavlov's dogs. When various types of stimuli were presented as CSs while the subjects were eating or drinking, it was found that the CS would later elicit salivation by itself. The extent of salivation to the CS was measured by placing a standard-size roll of cotton in the subject's mouth for a specified period of time, where it absorbed any saliva that was secreted. The cotton was weighed following this procedure to obtain a measure of the extent of salivation.

Razran's procedure has been schematized in Figure 3.2, primarily to illustrate a refinement of the general classical conditioning principle. Not all the response elicited by the UCS is conditioned to the CS. Only certain portions of the total response become conditioned. For example, the food UCS in the experiment elicits many responses: grasping the solid food objects, putting them in one's mouth, chewing, salivating, and so on. Only parts of this total response become conditioned to the CS—for example, the salivary response in the diagram. The CS will never elicit chewing responses, or at any rate, such conditioning quickly disappears.

Much experimental work has been conducted to determine precisely how respondent conditioning occurs and what factors affect the process. For the purposes of this book it is not necessary to go into these details.

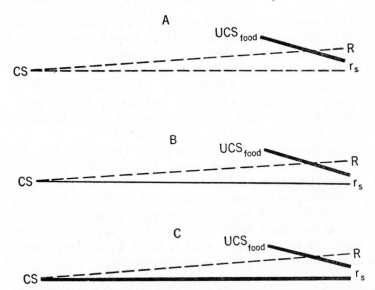

Fig. 3.2. The CS is paired with the UCS a number of times. The response is shown as having two parts—r_s, the part that is conditionable (for example, salivation), and R, the part that is not easily conditionable (grasping, chewing, and so on). The strength of the association between the CS and r_s increases with each trial, as is shown by the increased heaviness of the line. The strength of the association between the CS and R, on the other hand, increases very little, as is shown by the unchanged line between the two.

It should be noted, however, that a conditioned response can occur in different strengths. Response strength may be measured in several ways: intensity of the response; the interim period between the presentation of the CS and the occurrence of the response—that is, the latency of the response; and the frequency with which the organism responds to the CS, since he may respond on some presentations and not others. Stronger conditioning yields more intense and more frequent responses, and shorter latencies.

Higher-Order Conditioning

Further experiments conducted by Frolov in Pavlov's laboratory indicated that the effects of environmental events on behavior are even more far-reaching than those involved in *simple* classical conditioning. Frolov found that after stable conditioning had been produced, the CS could be used as the "unconditioned stimulus" in conditioning the response to yet a new stimulus. That is, a response which had come to be elicited by one stimulus through conditioning could then be "transferred" to a new stimulus.

The actual experiment was performed with a dog as the subject, using first the sound of a metronome as the CS and meat powder as the UCS. After a number of trials in which the meat powder was paired with the sound of the metronome, the metronome elicited a strong conditioned response of salivation. Later, a black square, which did not elicit salivation, was used as a new conditioned stimulus and paired with the metronome as the UCS. After a number of these paired trials the black square came to elicit the salivary response (Hull, 1943, p. 85).

The entire two-stage process is depicted in Figure 3.3. Part A of the figure shows the first-order conditioning. Part B shows the second-order conditioning. It has proved difficult to extend the process beyond third-order conditioning in a laboratory situation. Osgood (1953) states, "This process is certainly greatly extended in human learning, however, especially in the area of language behavior" (p. 316). Evidence will be presented in later chapters to indicate the manner in which higher-order conditioning seems to apply to human learning involving language.

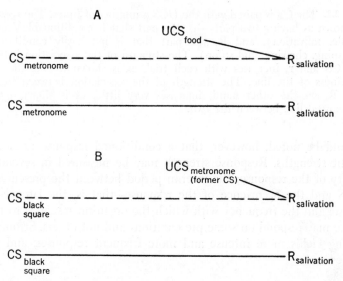

Fig. 3.3. In part A the CS, the sound of a metronome, is paired with the UCS, food. After a number of trials the salivary response is stably conditioned to the sound of the metronome. At this point, as is depicted in part B, the sound of the metronome is used as the UCS, since it now elicits the salivary response, and is paired with a new CS—the visual stimulus of a black square. After a number of pairings of the black square and the metronome, the new CS also comes to elicit the conditioned response.

Summary

We may summarize the principles of classical or respondent conditioning in the following way. Whenever a stimulus which does elicit a response occurs in close contiguity with a stimulus which does not, there results an increase in the tendency for the new stimulus to elicit that response. The stimulus that will initially elicit the response to be conditioned is called the UCS. The stimulus which is paired with UCS so that it too will later elicit the response is called the CS. Some responses condition more easily than other responses. Thus, if several responses elicited by a UCS occur in contiguity with a stimulus, there is a greater tendency for the conditioned stimulus to elicit some responses than others.

When the CS will stably elicit the conditioned response, one may go on to use the CS as a UCS in bringing the response under the control of other neutral stimuli. This latter process is called higher-order conditioning and is very important for human language learning and communication.

Operant or Instrumental Conditioning

The account of respondent conditioning just presented involves a basic principle of behavior that has great generality. We shall now look at another principle which has the same universality in that it is involved in the acquisition of many different behaviors by many different organisms.

In an every-day situation, a child is often given a cookie when he begins to whine or to fuss in order to "pacify" him. The cookie frequently accomplishes its objective in a limited way since the child is occupied for a time in eating and playing with the cookie. However, if one were systematically to observe the future behavior of the child, it would be seen that he tends to whine and fuss more frequently. That is, receiving the cookie tends to increase, or strengthen, the frequency of the whining type of behavior on later occasions.

Abstracting from this example, it can be stated generally that the consequences which follow a particular behavior affect the future occurrence of that behavior. Some consequences, which are called "rewards" in common-sense language, serve to strengthen behavior. Although it is usually difficult to observe this principle, due to the complexity of most human behavior, the results are often so strong that even casual observations yield some hint of its operation. Thus, one may see in prescientific attempts to explain man's behavior concepts that indicate some understanding of this principle, such as hedonism. Until relatively recent times, however, this understanding was poorly developed, its general significance not seen, and interpretations of the principle not scientifically acceptable.

Edward L. Thorndike was the first investigator to explore the principle of instrumental conditioning systematically. On the basis of his experiments, Thorndike concluded that behavior which was followed by a "satisfying" state of affairs would be more likely to occur again, in comparison to behavior which was not followed by such a state of affairs. On the other hand, Thorndike first thought that behavior which was followed by a "dissatisfying" state of affairs would be weakened. The terms "satisfying" and "dissatisfying" themselves add nothing to the account of the principle. The basic observations are that behavior is stronger in the future when it is followed by certain stimuli, that is, certain environmental occurrences, which in everyday life we call "rewards."

B. F. Skinner has been most influential in emphasizing the importance of this principle, in systematically studying its details, and in making applications of the findings to complex human behavior. Skinner and his associates have developed a number of ingenious techniques and instruments for studying instrumental conditioning—or operant conditioning, as he prefers to call the process. The principle of reinforcement can most easily be demonstrated using one of these types of operant conditioning apparatus. As with all experimental apparatus, its purpose is to enable the experimenter to isolate and reliably observe the event of interest while uncontrolled factors are kept at a minimum. A picture of an operant conditioning chamber for rats is shown in Figure 3.4. The apparatus has been constructed so that one type of behavior, the pressing of a bar which projects into the chamber, can be observed in isolation from other behaviors. According to the principle of reinforcement, the bar-pressing response should increase in strength if it is followed by certain consequences. Food is such a consequence to a hungry animal. Thus, if a hungry rat is supplied with a bit of food after it presses the bar, this response should occur more frequently; it should become a stronger response in this situation compared with the other responses that might be emitted by the animal.

This prediction with respect to the bar-pressing response has been experimentally confirmed many times. The principle also holds for other responses that are treated in the same manner. All that is necessary in order to increase the strength of a response in an operant conditioning apparatus is to follow the response with an appropriate stimulus object. Figure 3.5 presents a graph of the increase in strength of a reinforced response in the situation described. An automatic device attached to the bar produces such graphs, called "cumulative records," by recording the number of times the bar is pressed. As time passes, a line is recorded horizontally, from left to right. Each time the bar is pressed the line makes a step upward. Thus, when the line goes up steeply it means the animal is pressing the bar very rapidly. When the line moves only in a horizontal direction it means the

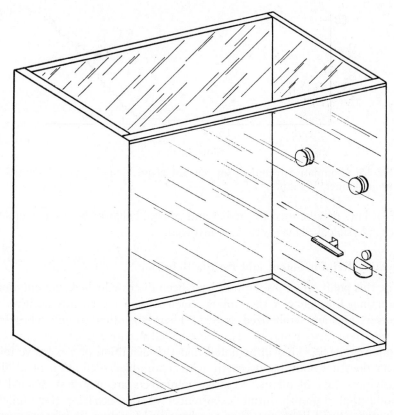

Fig. 3.4. An operant conditioning chamber for rats. The bar is located below the lights in the center of the panel and the food tray is located in the lower right-hand corner. The lights and food-delivery mechanism are operated by automatic programing equipment, and bar-pressing responses are automatically recorded.

animal is not pressing the bar at all. That is, the strength of the bar-pressing response can be seen from the slope of the line. This graph shows that the bar-pressing response was weak at first, but that it became stronger as it was reinforced, just as would be predicted from the principle of reinforcement.

Questions are sometimes raised concerning why some stimuli are reinforcing. The physiology of the principle of reinforcement is an important issue and one that numerous researchers in physiological psychology are actively investigating, although these accounts are incomplete at the present time. An understanding of the physiological basis of reinforcement should eventually contribute to a better understanding of behavior. However, as has been elsewhere discussed in detail (Sidman, 1960a; Skinner,

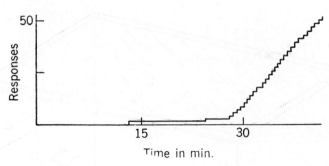

Fig. 3.5. Cumulative record of an operant acquisition situation (adapted from Skinner, 1938, p. 68)

1953), laws may be used to predict and control behavior without reference to the physiological events that are involved.

Negative Reinforcement and Escape Behavior

To this point only those stimuli have been discussed whose *presentations* strengthen the behavior they follow. Such stimuli are termed positive reinforcers and are symbolized as S^{R+}. There are other stimuli whose *removal* strengthens behavior. These are called negative reinforcers and are symbolized as S^{R-}. It will be noted that this definition of a negative reinforcer does not correspond exactly with Thorndike's definition of a "dissatisfying" state of affairs. Negative reinforcers are not best defined as stimuli that diminish future occurrences of the behavior they follow, although, as will be shown, they also have this function. It is easy to confuse these two possible operations, even on an observational level. However, the principle of negative reinforcement can be illustrated as follows. If a rat is put into a Skinner box where the floor is electrified so that he is continuously being shocked, and if pressing the bar turns off the shock for a time, the rat will soon increase his rate of bar pressing. This type of behavior may be termed escape behavior, since the behavior results in escape from (or removal of) the electric shock.

There are numerous examples of the action of negative reinforcers in everyday life. For example, in a very noisy place the response of putting one's hands over one's ears is strengthened by the elimination (or diminution) of the aversive sound stimulus. Although we are tempted to say that this occurs because we know the sound will be lessened if we hold our ears, this is an incorrect analysis. We hold our ears because in the past this action has been strengthened by the removal of the sound stimuli. Actually, it is also because of our past experience that we "know"—can report—that this action will be effective in reducing the stimulus.

We do many things that in the past have had the effect of ridding us of aversive stimuli. We learn to go into the shade from the hot sun, reinforced by the reduction in heat. A husband performs a task in the house that terminates (removes) his wife's nagging. A student studies hard when this behavior is reinforced by the diminution of his unpleasant "thinking" about a test.

The Presentation of Aversive Stimuli

The operation just discussed concerns the removal of certain stimuli (which in everyday life would be called "painful," "unpleasant," or "aversive") contingent on the performance of certain responses. A stimulus that when removed strengthens a response is called a negative reinforcer. This same stimulus, however, also can affect behavior through another operation, the operation of *presenting* the stimulus. That is, if a response occurs and is followed by the presentation of that type of stimulus, which will be called an *aversive stimulus* in this context, the response will not occur as frequently for a time or may be completely suppressed. This operation fits closely what in everyday life is called punishment. A more detailed analysis of this process will be presented in a later section.

One point is worth making explicit here. The same "painful" stimulus, to use a common-sense word, may function both as a negative reinforcer (whose removal strengthens behavior), and as an aversive stimulus (whose presentation weakens behavior). The terms *negative reinforcer* and *aversive stimulus* will be considered as synonyms, although it should be remembered that the stimulus can function in two different ways: (1) when it follows behavior it will weaken future occurrences of that behavior, and (2) when it is removed following a behavior it will strengthen future occurrences of that behavior.

Reinforcement and Adjustment

From an evolutionary point of view it is eminently reasonable that the positive or negative consequences of behavior should mold future behavior. If organisms did not function according to the principle of reinforcement, it is difficult to see how they could survive. Organisms, for example, whose behavior was strengthened by injurious consequences (negative reinforcers) would soon die, and their species would become extinct.

Other Variables in Operant Conditioning

Much experimentation has been conducted to determine the effects of various factors involved in the principle of reinforcement, such as the type of reinforcer, the time between the response and the reinforcer, the effortfulness of the response. For precise prediction and control of behavior, it is important to have detailed knowledge of the effects of all these variables. For the present purposes, however, where only the main principle itself is of major concern, it should be emphasized that reinforcement must follow the response *immediately* to have its greatest effect. The positive reinforcement of an "A" test paper would seem to more greatly reinforce the studying behavior involved the more quickly it was returned to the student.

Erroneous Interpretations of Reinforcement Effects

The importance of the principle of reinforcement in shaping the behavior of organisms is not generally appreciated. Instead of utilizing the principle in our everyday language, we typically attempt to account for behavior by assuming internal, subjective states, which are never observed, to be the determining events. We say that a trained dog sits because he "wants" a piece of food or because he "knows" that if he does so he will get a piece of food. But we do not specify the antecedent conditions for the behavior, and our statements are thus empty of explanatory value. It could be said, rather, that the dog sits because this type of behavior has been strengthened in the past by following it with reinforcers (food).

A reward, or reinforcer, is often called a goal, and we may make the mistake of concluding that a future goal determines the organism's behavior, in other words, that the goal has an attractive force for the behavior of obtaining the goal. However, something that has not yet happened cannot determine something that occurs before it in time. This error is not made when we realize that what determines the organism's behavior in the present is not a future occurrence (a goal) but the fact that that behavior has been strengthened by past reinforcers.

A simple experiment may be used as an analogy. If a rat is put into a runway that forks into two separate paths and is reinforced with a bit of food each time it goes to the right, the animal will soon go to the right when it is put into the runway. It would be incorrect to say, when the animal runs down the runway and into the pathway leading to the right, that the food goal determines its behavior. The food might or might not be there; a cat might even be there, and the rat would still run down the right pathway. It could be said that the rat runs to the right because in the past this type of behavior has been strengthened by being followed with reinforcing stimuli.

In making the mistake of considering the nature of behavior as "purposive," we often find incomprehensible certain types of behavior. For example, a person does something that results in self-harm, in the extreme case "martyring himself for some cause." We consider such behavior abnormal, for even though the final consequence was death the person continued his behavior. When it is seen that the consequence does not determine the behavior which precedes it, then this self-harmful type of behavior becomes understandable. It must be the individual's *past* history of reinforcement that explains his intensely strong behavior—that is, past reinforcement would account for standing by certain principles. The fact that this time such action eventuated in death is irrelevant as a determinant of his behavior.

One of the reasons it may be so difficult for us to feel that our behavior results from past conditions is that many times we go through a chain of "thinking" responses (language responses) before doing something, and the thinking pertains to future events. These thinking responses that occur in the present may mediate what we finally do. For example, a student may read in the paper some evening that an excellent movie is showing at the neighborhood theater. He then goes through a chain of language responses involving the remoteness of the next test in school, how caught-up he is with his schoolwork, and so on. This chain of responses, in turn, may mediate either his going to the movie or staying home and studying. It would seem insufficient in this example to say that he goes to the show because he wants to (assuming he does go), that he goes because he decided to go, or even that the future movie or test determines his behavior. The "wanting to go" or the "deciding to go" may also be considered to be sequences of behavior that are themselves determined by the individual's past history. Thus, past determinants could account for wanting and deciding behaviors as well as the going to the show. For this reason we must be concerned both with the way in which the individual's past experience affects his deciding or reasoning behavior and also with the way in which this latter type of behavior mediates other behaviors. These topics will be discussed in detail later.

Of course, introspection on the nature of one's own "reasoning" responses does not meet the criteria of a science; observations must be public and repeatable. In order to study the characteristics of such implicit processes one must use other subjects and specify the characteristics of the implicit processes through observational studies of the antecedent environmental occurrences and the consequent overt behavior. An appropriate experimental method for the study of such implicit processes will be presented in the later section dealing with intervening variables.

Summary

The principle of reinforcement has great generality and plays a most significant role in the molding of human behavior. The principle may be simply stated as follows. When certain stimuli closely follow a certain behavior they increase the probability of that behavior occurring again in the future. Stimuli that serve this function are called positive reinforcers,

S^{R+}. Other stimuli increase the probability of behavior occurring again when their removal closely follows that behavior. These stimuli are called negative reinforcers, S^{R-}.

Conditioned Reinforcement

Our examples to this point have been limited to naturally reinforcing stimuli whose reinforcing effects were not acquired. Stimuli such as these affect the behavior of the organism the first time they are applied. A wide range of stimuli, however, *acquire* reinforcing properties in the course of the organism's experience. These learned reinforcers are perhaps of greater importance than natural reinforcers in molding the behavior of human beings. Learned reinforcers are called conditioned or secondary reinforcers to distinguish them from the primary or unconditioned reinforcers that are reinforcing from the beginning.

After early childhood at least, it is commonly observed that such things as the presentation of food and water or the removal of painful stimuli (all primary reinforcers), seem to become increasingly less and less important for shaping human behavior. As the child grows older, stimuli that are social in nature gain greater prominence: the way other people respond to us with smiles, frowns, affectionate behavior; the things they say to us, such as praise, criticism, derogatory remarks; the social rewards that are presented to us such as money, grades, honors. These are only a few of the important consequences that markedly affect the behavior they follow.

Traditionally, such things as affection and social approval were considered intangibles that were not subject to an objective, scientific study. However, we now possess experimentally derived principles that appear to account with a great depth of understanding for the reinforcing value of social stimuli. The explanation for the development of "social rewards" seems to lie in the principle of conditioned reinforcement.

The principle of conditioned reinforcement refers to the operations through which a stimulus may acquire reinforcing properties. Experimentally, the principle may be easily demonstrated. We described in the last section how an animal could be operantly conditioned to press the bar in an operant conditioning chamber through the use of food pellets as a primary reinforcer. Let us assume now that the operation of the feeding mechanism produces a noticeable click each time a food pellet is delivered and that the click as a stimulus has no reinforcement value for the animal at first. We would observe that after the click had preceded the appearance of the food a number of times, the click itself would become a reinforcing stimulus. That is, the click alone would now strengthen behavior. For example, a new behavior of the rat such as standing up on its hind legs could be conditioned by presenting the click alone after occurrences of the behavior. It has been experimentally shown by Zimmerman (1957) that, under the appropriate conditions, a conditioned reinforcer will retain its reinforcing value long after it is no longer paired with the primary reinforcer.

Thus, the general principle of conditioned reinforcement may be stated as follows: a stimulus that does not have reinforcing properties will gain these properties if it is repeatedly paired with a reinforcing stimulus. The corollary principle holds for conditioned negative reinforcers. A neutral stimulus that is paired with a primary negative reinforcer acquires negative reinforcement value. For example, a rat might be placed in an operant conditioning chamber that had a floor that could be electrified. A buzzer might be sounded each time the animal was shocked by electrifying the floor. Electric shock is a primary negative reinforcer; its removal will strengthen any response that it follows. Now, after a number of pairings of the buzzer and shock, it would be found that removal of the buzzer stimulus also strengthens behavior. That is, if the buzzer were connected to the bar in the chamber so that a bar-pressing response would turn the buzzer off, the animal could be conditioned to press the bar with this reinforcement alone (see Miller, 1948a).

Conditioned Aversive Stimuli

It should be noted that the same operation—pairing a neutral stimulus with a negatively reinforcing stimulus—changes the neutral stimulus so it will function as a conditioned aversive stimulus as well as a conditioned negative reinforcer. Thus, in the experimental situation we have just described, the buzzer would also become an aversive stimulus for the rat. Whenever the buzzer was *presented* it would weaken any ongoing behavior, as well as serve as a negative reinforcer and strengthen any behavior that resulted in its removal.

Social Stimuli as Reinforcers

There is ample opportunity during human infancy and childhood for the systematic pairing of many kinds of social stimuli with primary reinforcers. The infant is completely helpless for a long period of time during which the presentation of all positive primary reinforcers and the removal of all negative reinforcers is accompanied by social stimuli—the sight, sound, touch, and so on, of parents, siblings, relatives, and friends. Through the paired presentation of these originally neutral stimuli with primary reinforcers, social stimuli become reinforcers themselves.

On first presentation, the sight or sound of other humans has no reinforcing value, but they develop into very strong reinforcers. It may be commonly observed, for example, that many young children develop very strong "attention-getting" behavior and may be observed on occasion to demand of their parents, "Look at me." Because this type of behavior has been so widely observed, it was suggested by early investigators that everyone has an "inborn need" for attention. When it is understood, however, that the stimuli of someone looking at us or listening to us become reinforcing through the operation of the principle of conditioned reinforcement, the inference of an "inborn need" becomes an unnecessary concept. It may be said that being looked at and listened to is reinforcing because in our past histories these stimuli have been presented along with primary reinforcers. It is when the mother is "paying attention" to the child that he is fed, uncomfortable pins are removed, warmth is provided, and so on. Each situation pairs the "attention" with primary reinforcement. Thus, the "attention" of other people should become a very strong secondary or conditioned reinforcer. It may then be observed that behavior which is followed by the attention of others (which "gets attention") is strengthened. It is interesting to note in this connection that the phrase "to attend to" may mean to take care of someone as well as to "pay attention" to him.

Imagine, however, a child for whom attention was always accompanied by the presentation of aversive stimuli, in other words, where punishment was delivered each time other people attended to him. Later in life this child's behavior would not be strengthened by "attention." He would not be likely to have a strong response of saying, "Look at me." Rather, this child's behavior would be reinforced by the removal of attention because attention for him would be a conditioned negative reinforcer. Attention would also function as an aversive stimulus in weakening some action of the child when attention was given. Of course, this history of experience is not likely to occur, at least not in quite such a one-sided manner. Unless the infant is provided with a certain number of primary positive reinforcers by parents he will not survive, since he cannot obtain these for himself. The more usual case is that the presence of others is paired with both positive and negative reinforcers, although more often with the former. Because of the duality of this experience, attention of others becomes both positively and negatively reinforcing. That is, in the individual's past history, being looked at when the "looker" is smiling, nodding, and so on, has been accompanied by positive reinforcers such as good things to eat and drink, complimentary words, and other conditioned reinforcers. On the other hand, when the "looker" is frowning, shouting, snarling, and so on, aversive stimuli have usually been present.

Thus, though simply being looked at usually becomes a positive conditioned reinforcer, "social approval" usually becomes an even stronger positive reinforcer, and "social disapproval" becomes a strong negative reinforcer. Involved in this development is the process of discrimination, which will be described in detail in a later section.

Since positive reinforcers are usually dispensed in the presence of others, people in general become strong positive reinforcers. The so-called "gregarious instinct" in man, as well as in many lower animals, may be accounted for in this way. Of course, as in all the examples discussed so far, each person has a different history with respect to reinforcement in the presence of other people. For this reason, individual differences would be expected in "gregariousness," that is, in the extent to which the general presence of other people is reinforcing.

Vocal responses of other people are auditory stimuli that also become very strong positive or negative reinforcers because they are systematically paired with reinforcing events. That is, such statements as "You're a good boy," "You've done a good job," "You are very bright," are typically accompanied by positive reinforcement. On the other hand, such verbal stimuli as "You have been very bad," "You are acting stupidly," "I'm going to punch you in the nose," are likely to be followed by aversive stimuli.

Tokens as Conditioned Reinforcers

Other conditioned reinforcers are also very important in molding behavior. The term *tokens* has been applied to one class of these. Examples of the class are money, grades, diplomas, and medals. Of these, money is perhaps the most important. Although money has no more reinforcing value to the very young child than any other comparable object, it acquires strong reinforcing value as the child grows older because it is so reliably paired with other positive reinforcers. Fortunately for the educator, scholastic grades are also usually paired with positive reinforcers, both social approval of various kinds and primary reinforcers. In some circles, however, good scholastic marks may not be paired with positive reinforcers. For individuals with this kind of history, good marks would not be expected to have positive reinforcing value.

Another class of tokens is developed as conditioned negative reinforcers and conditioned aversive stimuli. In most cases, for example, poor grades are paired with aversive stimuli and become conditioned negative reinforcers. The same is true of overdue bills, traffic tickets, and so on.

Complications in the Use of Negative Reinforcers

Because negative reinforcement properties also "rub off" on the person applying aversive stimuli, one must be aware of the possible side effects of their use. For example, an adult who frequently applies aversive stimulation to a child in an attempt to manipulate the child's behavior must realize that in so doing he should become a conditioned negative reinforcer. Each time the adult punishes the child, he acquires to some extent negative reinforcement value himself (or at least weakens himself as a positive reinforcer). If the adult does this frequently enough he may become a strong conditioned negative reinforcer. It will then be found that *his* removal from the presence of the child is reinforcing. In other terms, the behaviors of the child which remove him from the adult are strengthened, sometimes to the extent that the child avoids the adult completely, in other words, "runs away."

The same general principle holds for any situation involving negative reinforcers. A parent may be anxious to train his child to perform a certain skill—to play tennis, for example. If the parent is impatient, however, and chides the child, criticizes him severely, and in general profusely uses these verbal stimuli as conditioned aversive stimuli or negative reinforcers, it will soon be found that the child may avoid the training situation entirely. The situation itself may become a strong conditioned negative reinforcer. Then, unless the parent wishes to apply even stronger aversive stimuli for avoiding the situation than those which occur in the situation, the training will come to a halt. The same principles may be expected to apply to any human interaction, including the educational situation.

For this reason, the use of aversive stimuli in the training of a child is complex. Although the use of punishment may have instantaneous results in suppressing undesirable behavior, and so strengthen the parent's use of such methods, a by-product may be that the adult becomes a less effective positive reinforcer in the future and may find it more difficult to train the child. That is, some of the positive reinforcement value the adult has built up will be depleted. This is not to say that aversive stimuli have no place in the training of the child, as will be discussed later. However, the adult who administers them should be aware of the complicated learning that results.

S–R Principles Involved in Conditioned Reinforcement

A number of the variables in the acquisition of conditioned reinforcement are like the variables involved in the learning of any association between a stimulus and a response, for example, the number of times the to-be-conditioned reinforcing stimulus is paired with the reinforcing stimulus, the time interval between the stimuli, and so on. It has also been stated (Hull, 1943; Mowrer, 1960a; Osgood, 1953) that a stimulus comes to be a conditioned reinforcer when it has been respondently conditioned to elicit a part of the same response which another reinforcing stimulus elicits on an unconditioned basis.

Figure 3.1 may be referred to as an example. A sound is presented to the dog and is followed by the presentation of meat powder. The meat powder elicits a salivary response. After a number of these pairings the sound also comes to elicit a salivary response. Because the sound, the CS, now elicits the salivary response and perhaps other responses, through this process of classical conditioning, it is suggested that the CS becomes a conditioned reinforcer (see Mowrer, 1960b, p. 8). That is, it would be expected that any response of the animal followed by presentation of the sound stimulus would be strengthened.

The same holds for conditioned negative reinforcers. Aversive stimuli, such as electric shocks, elicit certain respondents in the organism: for example, changes in heart-rate and GSR alterations. To use common-sense terms, these responses could be called "pain" responses or "fear" responses. Since they are responses to aversive stimuli, they may be called "aversive" responses. When the aversive stimuli are paired with neutral stimuli (CSs), the neutral stimuli will come to elicit the "aversive" responses according to the principles of classical conditioning. According to this conception of conditioned reinforcers, it is this process that gives the neutral stimuli the function of negative conditioned reinforcers, as well as of conditioned aversive stimuli. Thus, presentation of these stimuli will weaken behavior that is then occurring, indicating their function as conditioned aversive stimuli. In addition, they will function as conditioned negative reinforcers since their removal will strengthen any response that precedes the removal. These "aversive" responses, when conditioned, have been called "anxiety" or "anxiety responses" (Dollard and Miller, 1950; Mowrer, 1950; Osgood, 1953).

It should be pointed out that, although positive and negative conditioned reinforcers may be considered to be formed on the basis of respondent conditioning, not all respondent conditioning would be expected to lead to the formation of conditioned reinforcers. There are some stimuli that are neither positive nor negative reinforcers but that are nevertheless unconditioned stimuli for some response. Thus, a light stimulus will elicit a pupillary response in the organism. The light, however, may not be a reinforcing stimulus. As a consequence, although a neutral stimulus when paired with the light will come to elicit the pupillary response, the neutral stimulus will not through this process become a conditioned reinforcer.

Conditioned Reinforcing Value Acquired
from Other Conditioned Reinforcers

There is one other point which should be made concerning secondary reinforcement that follows from the previous section. Any stimulus that itself has acquired reinforcement value (is a secondary reinforcer) may impart this reinforcing value to still another stimulus with which it is paired. Hull states, for example, that "secondary reinforcement may be acquired by a stimulus from association with some previously established secondary reinforcement . . . " (1943, p. 97). As an example, smiling may acquire reinforcing value because it occurs when primary positive reinforcers are presented to the child. Later, however, certain words may acquire positive reinforcing value because they occur when people are smiling. It is in part because of the far-reaching extensions of this type of learning that the experience of the individual is so important. Not only does the individual's experience directly shape his responses, but experience also effects what stimuli will be effective in further shaping his responses.

Summary

Most of the occurrences that strengthen our behavior as adults are social reinforcers that have acquired their reinforcing properties from other reinforcers. The general principle underlying this phenomenon is that any neutral stimulus which is paired with a stimulus having reinforcing value will, through repeated pairings, acquire reinforcing value itself. In the history of an individual, with his long period of helplessness and dependency in childhood and infancy, there is ample opportunity for various types of social stimuli to acquire reinforcing value. Ordinarily, the following social stimuli become strong positive reinforcers: attention, that is, the visual stimulus of someone looking at us or responding to our behavior; approval, such as the visual stimulus of people smiling and nodding at us; verbal approval, in the form of various kinds of complimentary words spoken to us; affection, physical or verbal responses of "endearment," stroking, patting, snuggling, and verbal counterparts; tokens, such as money, honors, medals, good grades; the sheer presence of other people; group approval, such as applause, group laughter, group attention.

Ordinarily, through being paired with aversive stimulation, the following social stimuli become strong conditioned negative reinforcers and conditioned aversive stimuli: disapproval, or the visual stimulus of people frowning at us; verbal disapproval, such as the auditory stimulus of various deprecating words; harsh tones, threats, criticism, derision; negative tokens, in the form of bad grades, traffic tickets; group disapproval, such as silence, booing, catcalls, heckling.

The foregoing are some examples of stimuli that have acquired reinforcement value and are very important in molding human behavior; they do not, of course, systematically cover all the social stimuli that determine our behavior.

One further point was discussed. A stimulus has been considered to become a conditioned reinforcer or conditioned aversive stimulus when it elicits a portion of the same responses that are elicited by the reinforcing stimulus with which it is paired.

Extinction

It has been noted that a response which is followed by a positively reinforcing stimulus is more likely to occur in the future. A good deal of the adaptability of living organisms seems to be a result of the action of this principle. If, in a particular situation, one response is habitually followed by a reinforcing stimulus and another response is not, it will be seen that the first response becomes relatively more frequent.

Actually, two things are occurring in this example. One response increases in frequency due to reinforcement. At the same time the other response decreases in frequency of occurrence, due to nonreinforcement. That is to say, whenever an instrumentally conditioned response is continuously emitted without being followed by reinforcement, the response decreases in frequency of occurrence. The process of weakening a response by not following it with reinforcement is called extinction.

Earlier in the chapter we suggested, through an illustrative example, that a mother might inadvertently develop a whining and fussing child by giving him a cookie each time he engaged in this kind of behavior. On the other hand, extinction of this response to its original strength would occur if the mother made sure that she did not give the child a cookie or other reinforcement when he whined or fussed.

The effects of extinction can readily be shown in an operant conditioning chamber. On the commencement of the extinction procedure, when the bar-pressing response is no longer followed by reinforcement, the animal may press the bar somewhat more rapidly at first. However, each nonreinforced occurrence decreases the probability of the response; the rate of bar pressing diminishes and finally stops, or reverts to the preconditioning level.

The same process of extinction would be expected to occur where the response had been conditioned under the action of negative reinforcement. Thus, when the response was no longer effective in removing the negative reinforcer, the behavior would weaken to its preconditioning strength.

Extinction in Classical Conditioning

Responses that have been acquired through respondent conditioning also extinguish in a manner analogous to extinction in operant conditioning. Extinction of a classically conditioned response occurs when the CS is presented but is not followed by the UCS. The CS alone will continue to elicit the response for a time, but each nonreinforced trial (when the UCS is absent) will weaken the CS–R association.

For example, a child that has been startled by a dog's sudden appearance and barking may be conditioned to cry upon the sight of the dog. However, if the sight of a dog, the CS, occurs a number of times without a repetition of the UCS, the sudden barking, the crying response will extinguish.

In the remaining discussions of the principles of response acquisition and change either respondent (classical) conditioning or operant (instrumental) conditioning examples may be described, although some psychologists make a clear distinction between these two types of conditioning (Holland and Skinner, 1961; Keller and Schoenfeld, 1950). This will be done in the interest of simplicity and because in general the same principles hold for both respondent and operant conditioning.

Resistance to Extinction and Extent of Conditioning

In discussing respondent conditioning it was stated that the number of conditioning trials is related to the subsequent frequency of emission of the response, the amplitude of response, and the latency of the response. Resistance to extinction also is affected by the extent of conditioning. A response that has been established in many respondent conditioning trials will continue to be elicited for many trials when the CS is presented alone. The same is true for operantly conditioned responses. When a response has in the past been followed by reinforcement many times, it will continue to be emitted often even though it is no longer reinforced, as opposed to a response which has only been reinforced a few times. As an illustration, a child who has often been allowed to stay up late when he cries will continue to cry at bedtime long after the response is no longer reinforced. If this response has been reinforced only a few times, it will not occur frequently and will also extinguish rapidly.

"Emotional" Responses and Extinction Trials

It is interesting to note that the withdrawal of reinforcement after the organism has had a history of being reinforced for some response produces certain responses of a type which may in common-sense terms be *described* as "hostile" or "emotional." That is, in the operant conditioning chamber, the animal is likely to bite the bar, tug at it, and so on, when extinction commences. It may also be observed that the animal is likely to urinate and defecate at such times; that is, he may show other evidence of physiological responses which have been called "emotional."

In everyday life we see many analogous examples. Everyone has seen someone playing a game, only to make a "poor shot" that was not followed by reinforcement, in other words, was not successful. In such circumstances the golfer may break his club, the tennis player may slam the ball into the fence, the poker player may throw his cards on the table with undue force. Children are even more likely than adults to display this type of behavior. If reinforcement is not presented following behavior that is customarily reinforced, the young child typically cries or displays other "emotional" behavior. Continued experience in life tends to extinguish this type of behavior because it is usually not reinforced as the child grows older. In addition, the adult is usually conditioned to emit socially approved responses in lieu of "emotional" behavior. When these responses become strong and the emotional responses become weak, we say that a person is a "good loser."

Extinction and Forgetting

It is important to note that the weakening of a response that occurs in the process of extinction is not the same as the weakening that occurs in what is commonly called forgetting. Where nonreinforced trials have not occurred, conditioned responses are retained at the same strength for long periods of time. A conditioned response does not gradually weaken as a function of time itself. For example, Skinner (1953) has demonstrated that pigeons operantly conditioned to peck in an appropriate operant conditioning chamber retained this response in good strength for several years if they were presented no nonreinforced trials in the interim. It might thus be said that a conditioned behavior will continue in good strength until it is subjected to one or more of the effective weakening operations.

The Weakening Effect of Punishment

Weakening a response through nonreinforcement and through the application of aversive stimuli (punishment) are often considered to be similar. These are, however, different processes. Extinction in operant behavior refers only to the permanent weakening that a response undergoes when it occurs and is no longer followed by reinforcement. Punishment will also suppress a response, as will be discussed more fully in a later section, but there are differences in the effects of punishment and extinction. For example, a rat that has been reinforced for bar pressing will develop a strong bar-pressing response. If, however, the animal is then given a strong shock when it presses the bar, it will be observed that the response no longer occurs. If the animal is left in the operant conditioning chamber, however, it may approach the bar tentatively again and again and finally press the bar. If there is no shock the animal will resume its bar pressing. In this type of situation the punishment effects are thus temporary, whereas full weakening of the response through extinction would be permanent.

There are several factors that may decrease the frequency of a response besides the processes of extinction and punishment—fatigue and motivational factors, for example. Extinction refers only to the weakening of a response through nonreinforced occurrences of the response in either instrumental or classical conditioning situations.

Conditioned Reinforcement and Extinction

We have already described the way in which conditioned reinforcing stimuli are developed according to the principles of classical conditioning. Since this is the case, it might be expected that conditioned reinforcers could also be "unlearned" or rather, extinguished. Such a process does occur. Although a neutral stimulus acquires reinforcing value when it accompanies a reinforcing stimulus, its reinforcing properties are extinguished to some extent when it is presented to the organism without the support of the reinforcing stimulus. Complete extinction does not occur with only one unsupported presentation, of course.

The extent to which the reinforcing properties of a secondary reinforcer resist extinction depends upon a number of factors. For example, in the same way that the *number* of times a response occurs and is reinforced determines in part the resistance of the response to extinction, the number of times the neutral stimulus and reinforcing stimulus are paired determines to some extent the ease with which the reinforcement value of a stimulus extinguishes. If the number of pairings has been large, the secondary reinforcer may be very resistant to extinction.

Summary

After a response has been strengthened through conditioning, nonreinforcement trials will weaken the response. The process of weakening a response through nonreinforcement is called extinction. This occurs both in operant and in respondent conditioning. In operant conditioning, extinction occurs when the response is not followed by a reinforcing stimulus. In respondent conditioning extinction takes place when the CS occurs and it is not followed by the UCS.

Resistance to extinction depends upon how strongly the response has been conditioned. Thus, in general, the greater the number of reinforced trials the greater the resistance to extinction.

When an organism has been reinforced continuously for a particular response, cessation of reinforcement for this response customarily produces nonadaptive behavior that may be described as "emotional."

The weakening of a response through extinction is not the same as the weakening of a response through "forgetting." When nonreinforced trials have not occurred, conditioned responses are retained in the same strength for long periods of time.

When a response is punished the response may also be weakened. This, however, is a different process from extinction. Still other factors, such as motivational and fatigue factors, may be involved in weakening a response and these processes also are different from extinction.

The acquisition of conditioned reinforcement takes place in the manner of the classical conditioning of a response, and the process of extinction of conditioned reinforcement value seems to follow the principles of extinction of classically conditioned responses.

Schedules of Reinforcement

The schedule of reinforced and nonreinforced trials in a learning situation is an important factor in maintaining a response in strength. In everyday life it usually happens that a given response is reinforced on some occasions and not on others. Sometimes we catch a whole string of fish in our favorite stream. At other times we catch nothing. It has been found (Ferster and Skinner, 1957) that a wide number of different reinforcement schedules have systematic effects on the emission of the response and on the characteristics of the response in the process of extinction.

The importance of reinforcement schedules may be illustrated by looking at two rats with different histories of reinforcement. Let us say that each rat was placed alone in an operant conditioning chamber and the first fifty responses of pressing the bar were reinforced each time with a pellet of food. At this point, however, the two animals were treated differently. Both animals received fifty more reinforcements, but rat A was reinforced only for every other response, while rat B remained on the 100 percent reinforcement schedule. The next time the animals were run, rat A was reinforced every third time, while rat B again received "continuous" reinforcement. Let us say that rat A was finally brought to the point where it received reinforcement for only every twentieth response, while rat B continued to receive reinforcement for each response. Notice, however, that the total number of reinforcements for each animal was kept equal.

After this difference in past history of reinforcement for the behavior under study, wide differences in the behavior of the animals would be evident. Rat A, the intermittently reinforced animal, would display a much stronger response, as measured by the rate of pressing the bar. He would be a very hard-working animal and one that persistently pressed the bar rapidly. Rat B, on the other hand, would be much less "ambitious." He would work at about the same rate as after the first day's conditioning.

Moreover, rat A would be much more "persevering" than rat B when the animals are no longer reinforced for their efforts. In addition, rat B would also be more "emotional." When extinction trials were begun, he would exhibit the typical extinction emotionality. He would press the bar more rapidly for a short time, bite the bar, and so on, but would quickly discontinue working at the bar. Rat A, on the other hand, would not display the "emotional" behavior and would continue to work very hard pressing the bar for a much greater number of non-reinforced responses.

The terms "hard working," "persevering," and "emotional" were purposely used in this discussion. The reader may not be particularly interested in the factors underlying the rate and resistance to extinction of a bar-pressing response, but he is probably interested in whether organisms (especially humans) are hard-working and persevering, or emotional in the face of nonreward. Schedules of reinforcement are extremely important in developing and maintaining vigorous and persistent behavior in all organisms, including human beings. When we say a person is interested, ambitious, motivated, tenacious, and so on, we are usually referring to behavior that is strong in terms of the vigor and frequency with which it occurs and in terms of its resistance to extinction. For example, we want to know why some pupils study hard, or, as we say, are "interested" in school, while others are not. Thus, principles concerning the vigor and persistence of behavior are extremely important to our understanding of human behavior.

We have the same interest in what we have called "emotional" behavior. In every-day terminology, when a person is no longer reinforced for something and then engages in "disturbed" or "emotional" behavior that is nonadaptive, it may be said that he is "frustrated." It can be seen in the example of the rats that rat A "tolerates frustration" to a greater extent that does the continuously reinforced animal. Again, these terms are used purposely because we are interested in why some children become "frustrated" in the face of failure and others continue making adjustive responses, even though they are not always reinforced or the reward is long delayed. In common-sense terms it is described as "emotionally mature" when a child can continue to work in the face of long-postponed goals or when he does not display nonadjustive "emotional" behavior when confronted with failure. Almost everyone has had experiences with people who "could not abide" even trivial cases where reinforcement was not forthcoming or would be delayed. For example, some people display unusual emotional behavior when losing in a game, whereas most other people, in the same situation, act as if the event is unimportant.

These are indeed types of behavior in which we are interested and which it is suggested may be rooted in the individual's past history of reinforcement.

Types of Schedules of Reinforcement

There are many different ways in which schedules of reinforcement can vary, and each type of schedule produces predictable effects upon the behavior concerned. Several of the main types of schedules will be discussed.

Fixed-Ratio Schedule

In the example used above, the final schedule of reinforcement used with rat A may be termed a fixed-ratio schedule, in other words, it was reinforced each time for the twentieth response from the last reinforcement. The general effects of fixed-ratio schedules should be considered more closely, as should the details of these schedules that produce the effects.

It is important to note that the rat was not introduced to the 1:20 ratio immediately. It was first reinforced after each response, then every other time, every third time, and so on. The steps for advancing the ratio must be fairly small. If an animal is placed on too high a ratio schedule immediately, its bar-pressing response will extinguish. For example, if rat A had been reinforced fifty times and then placed on a 1:100 fixed-ratio schedule, his behavior would extinguish before the schedule could come to control his behavior as it could if the steps were more gradual. This is also true of other partial, or intermittent, reinforcement schedules. In order to produce, as in the example, a hard-working, persevering animal, the organism must be introduced to the program gradually.

A closer look at the fixed-ratio schedule gives a better understanding of some of the factors that produce the vigor of responding. The rate at which the animal responds does, of course, vary from time to time. Sometimes it presses the bar rapidly, sometimes relatively slowly. Under a ratio schedule the more rapidly the animal presses the bar, the more immediately it is reinforced. Therefore, it would be expected, according to the principle of operant conditioning, that rapid responding would be strengthened to a greater extent than slow responding. And that is what fixed-ratio schedules produce.

On the other hand, on a schedule of 1:20, just following the appearance of the food pellet the probability of the rat being reinforced for pressing the bar is zero; the first response following the receipt of reinforcement is never reinforced. Nor is the second, and so on. Reinforcement occurs only after an extended period of responding. The animal's behavior also reflects these contingencies. After a reinforcement, the cumulative record shows a pause in responding. This is indicated in Figure 3.6 for a situation similar to the one we have been discussing. This record was obtained utilizing a pigeon as the responding animal, since scheduling principles have been most completely studied using this organism.

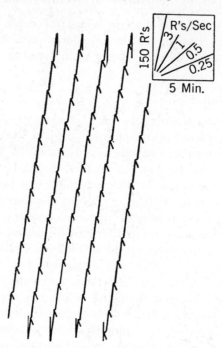

Fig. 3.6. Cumulative curve generated by a pigeon under a fixed-ratio 1:90 reinforcement schedule (adapted from Ferster and Skinner, 1957, p. 111)

An analogy of the fixed-ratio schedule is the case when workers are paid on a piecework basis. In this system the worker is paid according to how many parts he makes; he might be given a certain amount of money for every ten completed parts.

Fixed-Interval Schedule

This schedule is another type of intermittent reinforcement procedure. In the laboratory study of this reinforcement schedule the experimenter sets a time limit within which the organism is not reinforced for responding. The first response emitted at the end of the limit, however, is reinforced. Thus, a one-minute fixed-interval schedule would be one in which the organism is reinforced for responding, but is not given more than one reinforcement per minute.

This type schedule lawfully produces a certain type of behavior: the organism responds quite slowly when it has just received a reinforcer, but as the end of the time interval approaches, the organism's rate of responding steadily increases until the organism is again reinforced (see Figure 3.7). This again shows how the contingencies of reinforcement shape the organism's behavior. Immediately following a reinforcement there is a zero probability of a response being followed by a reinforcer, and a response in the presence of these stimulus conditions is weakened by this extinction. However, later, when the taste of the food, and so on, has disappeared and several responses have been made, there is a much higher probability that the response will be reinforced. Thus, these stimuli come to control stronger responding. There may be a tendency to say at this point that the organism, even if it is a rat or a pigeon, "knows" when the reinforcer will be given, and this accounts for its behavior. This is a nonexplanatory statement, however, and quite misleading. The explanatory statement relates the schedule of reinforcement to the regularly produced type of behavior. A later section of the present chapter, on discrimination, will discuss in detail how a stimulus can come to control an organism's behavior—in other words, how the stimuli involved with just having eaten a reinforcer can control nonresponding.

In every-day life a fixed salary system, in which the worker is paid every week, for example, roughly resembles a fixed-interval schedule of reinforcement. The behavior of coming to work and working is reinforced only periodically and at fixed times.

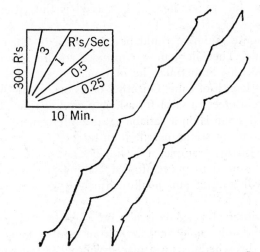

Fig. 3.7. Cumulative curve generated by a pigeon on a fixed-interval 4-minute reinforcement schedule (adapted from Ferster and Skinner, 1957, p. 245)

Variable Schedules

There are also schedules in which reinforcement is not administered in any regular pattern, in terms either of a regular interval of time or of a regular proportion of responses. Such variable schedules probably occur more generally in real life than do fixed schedules. Most social reinforcement is not delivered in a fixed fashion but is irregular. We behave verbally and motorically in many ways, and every once in a while we experience a compliment, a smile, attention, a token, and so on. The fisherman and farmer bring in good "crops" in an irregular fashion.

In general, there is an irregular schedule to match each of the two types of fixed schedules. The irregular ratio schedule is called the *variable-ratio schedule*. In this schedule, the organism is reinforced for a certain proportion of his responses, but the proportion is randomly varied about some value. For example, an organism could be gradually introduced to a variable-ratio 20 schedule. The 20 stands for the average number of responses per reinforcement. However, the ratio might randomly vary between 1:1 and something like 1:40. This type of schedule has equal probabilities of reinforcement for each response no matter how many non-reinforced responses have preceded it. Thus, the response should be at equal strength regardless of the number of nonreinforced responses preceding it, and responding should assume a more stable rate than that which occurs in fixed-ratio schedules—and that is what happens.

As in the fixed-ratio schedule, rapid responding is more immediately reinforced than slow responding, and "speed" is thus strengthened (see Figure 3.8).

A house-to-house salesman could be considered to be on this type of variable schedule. The salesman is reinforced for his selling behavior in an unsystematic way. Sometimes, he may make several sales in a row or in a fairly short length of time. On other occasions selling behavior is not followed by a reinforcer (a sale) for a long period of time. The selling behavior of the salesman is on a variable-ratio reinforcement schedule, since the greater the rate of seeing potential customers, the more likelihood of making a sale. In this example, it is also interesting to speculate that if the ratio of reinforced to nonreinforced "selling" responses is too great, the behavior will weaken and finally extinguish—the salesman will quit his job.

The variable-interval schedule is like the fixed-interval, except that the intervals are randomly varied in length from zero to some maximum interval. Because this schedule is irregular, it will not strengthen the behavior in a cyclical manner, as does a fixed-interval schedule. Rate of responding is equally strengthened for all responses, irrespective of the other responses

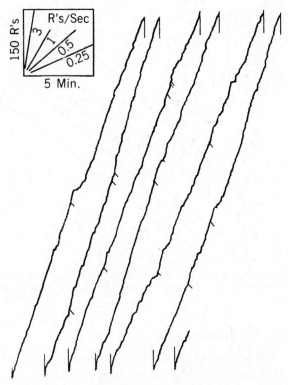

Fig. 3.8. Cumulative curve generated by a pigeon on a variable-ratio 1:360 reinforcement schedule (Ferster and Skinner, 1957, p. 393)

of the organism and the period of time elapsing since the last reinforcement. Thus, a stable rate of response is produced, in contrast to the marked cyclical rate produced in the fixed-interval schedule. (See Figure 3.9.)

A final but important point should be made with respect to specific schedules of reinforcement. Not only do these intermittent schedules produce characteristically different rates of maintenance of the response, but, in addition, once reinforcement has been discontinued, different extinction rates are also produced. Of particular significance to the control of behavior is the finding that intermittent schedules yield behavior which is more resistant to extinction than behavior which has been continuously reinforced. This finding has been established with many different types of responses under many different circumstances. In addition, variable schedules yield behavior that is more resistant to extinction than behavior that has been subjected to fixed or periodic reinforcement schedules.

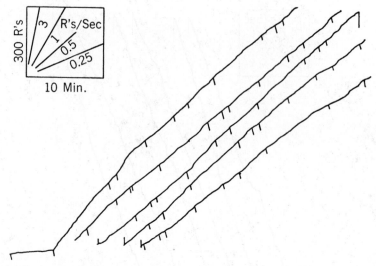

Fig. 3.9. Cumulative curve generated by a pigeon on a variable-interval 2-minute reinforcement schedule (adapted from Ferster and Skinner, 1957, p. 330)

Other Schedules of Reinforcement

Although a full account of the research on schedules cannot be presented here, many other important effects have been established (see Ferster and Skinner, 1957). For example, in the same way that a fixed-ratio schedule can produce rapid responding, there are schedules which shape slow behavior, or even not responding! In addition, various combinations of the above schedules have been studied in the laboratory to ascertain their systematic effects upon behavior. It is to be expected that such research will yield valuable information pertinent to understanding human behavior.

Effect of Scheduling on the Extinction of Conditioned Reinforcers

The schedule by which a neutral stimulus and a reinforcing stimulus are paired is also very important. Although it may seem paradoxical to common-sense expectations, a neutral stimulus that has sometimes been paired with a reinforcing stimulus and sometimes not will continue to function as a reinforcer for a longer period of time after it is no longer paired with the reinforcing stimulus than will a neutral stimulus that has been continuously paired with the reinforcing stimulus. Thus, if one wished to produce a conditioned reinforcer that would be very resistant to extinction, that is, would continue to act as a reinforcer for a long period of time with no support from a primary reinforcer, he would insure that in the original conditioning of the stimulus as a conditioned reinforcer some schedule of intermittent reinforcement was followed.

In a laboratory experiment, Zimmerman (1957) created conditioned reinforcers that could be used to condition other behaviors of rats long after these secondary reinforcers were no longer paired with primary reinforcers. The investigator paired a buzzer with the delivery of water to thirsty animals, first on a continuous schedule. That is, if the animal went to a water delivery dipper at the time the buzzer sounded, it received a small amount of water. The buzzer would sound at various times, but never when the animal hovered over the water delivery dipper. After the animal reliably went to the water upon the sound of the buzzer, the water was given only on alternate soundings of the buzzer, that is, on a 1:2 fixed-ratio schedule. Then the ratio was both gradually increased and randomly varied until finally a variable-ratio schedule was established. The longest ratio was 1:14, with a mean ratio of 1:10. Even though the pairing of buzzer (neutral stimulus) with the primary reinforcer was of fairly low probability, the animal nevertheless presented itself at the dipper whenever the buzzer sounded.

After this training, it was found that the buzzer had become a strong conditioned reinforcer and was very resistant to extinction. The buzzer could now be used as a reinforcer to operantly condition other responses of the animals. For example, a bar was set into the box and whenever the bar was pressed by the animal, the buzzer was sounded—no water was given at all. The buzzer was sufficient reinforcement to condition the animal to press the bar and to maintain this response in good strength. When the buzzer no longer followed pressing the bar, the bar-pressing response extinguished. When the buzzer was again made contingent upon bar pressing, the response was reconditioned. The buzzer had become a strongly established conditioned reinforcer that was highly resistant to extinction.

Thus, the prior experience of the animal had made its behavior modifiable without the use of primary reinforcers such as food and water. A previously neutral sensory stimulus had come to have reinforcing value for the animal and, when appropriately applied, molded new behaviors. It would have been possible to maintain the buzzer as a reinforcer indefinitely if occasionally the buzzer and water had again been made to occur together.

This training is analogous to that which typically occurs in every-day situations. The stimuli of attention, certain words, approval, and so on,

which are originally neutral with respect to reinforcement value, come to
have positive reinforcement value because they have in the past been
paired with positive primary reinforcers. The schedule for the pairing of
these stimuli with the primary reinforcers, however, would seem to be
intermittent, and these social stimuli thus come to be conditioned reinforcers which are very resistant to extinction. For this reason, social reinforcers could in this way come to be largely "independent" of support
by other primary reinforcers. Although attention is first almost always
paired with positive primary reinforcers, it increasingly seems to occur on
a more extended intermittent reinforcement schedule. People look at and
listen to the child many times when no positive reinforcement is being
delivered. However, from time to time, attention is paired with positive
reinforcement, and, in this way, it should become a strong conditioned
reinforcer, quite resistant to the extinction process.

Adaptiveness and Reinforcement, Extinction, and Scheduling Principles

Organisms, including humans, function according to principles that
allow for a great deal of modifiability and consequent adjustment to environmental occurrences. It was seen that behavior which is followed by
certain consequences (positive reinforcers) increases in strength, that is,
is more likely to reoccur. It is not surprising that organisms have evolved
in this manner, since a species of organisms which did not function according to this principle would not be likely to survive. An organism that took
one branch of a winding path and found water and became less likely
to make that same response might not live to reproduce its kind. It seems
that it is only because the consequences of an organism's behavior affect
its later behavior in a certain way that an organism adapts to its environment and survives.

Sometimes, however, the environment changes. Although a certain type
of behavior may have been reinforced at one time, later this type of behavior may no longer be reinforced—the water hole may dry up. It is,
therefore, also important for the adaptability of the organism that, even
though a response has become strong, it is not immutable. When a
response ceases to be reinforced, it becomes weaker. After the response
occurs a number of times without reinforcement, it will return to its
original level of strength.

Further, the adaptability of the organism to the conditions of reinforcement in the environment can be seen perhaps from the effects of intermittent reinforcement. Different schedules of reinforcement have specifically different and lawful effects upon the behavior of the organism. It is

important to see that behavior makes very sensitive adjustments to the reinforcing contingencies in the environment. As the reinforcing contingencies in the environment vary, distinct and lawful effects are imposed on the characteristics of the emission of a response and the extinction process.

It has been pointed out that the principles by which organisms behave are those of adaptability to environmental events, and that this adaptability must have been necessary for the survival of individual and species— thus, perhaps, the learning characteristics of living organisms arise in biological evolution. This is not to say, however, that organisms are perfectly adjustable or that behavior is always perfectly adjustive. The circumstances of reinforcement at one period of an organism's development could produce behavior which was very maladjustive at a later period under changed environmental circumstances. And this maladjustive behavior could be very resistant to change. Although an animal's behavior conditioned under a schedule of variable-ratio reinforcement becomes quite vigorous, if the reinforcement is withdrawn for good, it means that the animal will persevere for a very long period of time and "waste" much time and effort. Although it is adjustive when the intervals between reinforcements are lengthened, when the reinforcement ceases altogether, the longer resistance to extinction is maladaptive. It is important to point out that human behavior may also be maladaptive, since humans may, because of their past history of reinforcement, persist in behaviors which have long since ceased to be functional—ceased to be followed by reinforcement.

Summary

In every-day life, it is usual that a particular response will be reinforced sometimes but not other times. The schedule by which a response is operantly conditioned and maintained is important to the vigor, rate, and resistance to extinction of that response.

There are various types of schedules of reinforcement. When an organism receives reinforcement for a fixed proportion of its emissions of a certain response, it is said to be under a fixed-ratio schedule. Before such a schedule can be introduced, the organism must first be reinforced each time it emits the response until the response involved becomes strong. Then the ratio of nonreinforced to reinforced trials can be increased. This schedule produces rapid responding with a pause after delivery of a reinforcer. The behavior is more resistant to extinction than when continually reinforced.

When a response is not reinforced for a certain fixed period of time following the last reinforcement, the schedule is termed fixed-interval. The intervals must be short at first, so as not to extinguish the response. The behavior produced is quite cyclical; it is weak just after a reinforcement, but becomes stronger as the interval progresses. Again, these responses are more resistant to extinction than are continuously reinforced responses.

Irregular schedules occur when reinforcement does not occur according to any regular pattern. When the intervals or ratios vary, schedules of variable-interval and variable-ratio result. Variable-interval schedules customarily produce very stable rates, and variable-ratio schedules produce rapid responding; both schedules produce behavior that is highly resistant to extinction.

Various mixtures of the above schedules can be studied in the laboratory and probably have their counterparts in everyday life.

Scheduling affects also the resistance to extinction of conditioned reinforcers. If the conditioned reinforcer has in the past continuously been paired with the reinforcement, it will not be maximally resistant to extinction. However, if it was at first always paired with a reinforcer but later on was gradually paired with the reinforcer less and less often, then the conditioned reinforcer will remain effective when it is no longer paired with the stimulus from which it acquired its reinforcing properties. Most of the secondary reinforcers that are effective for humans seem to have this type of development. In adult life, they may only infrequently be paired with other reinforcers, and they become seemingly "independent" rewards. It is this quality, perhaps, which, in part, makes social reinforcers seem to be the result of "inborn needs."

The marvelous characteristic of organisms to reflect happenings in the environment is shown by the facts of classical and instrumental conditioning and by the change in behavior that occurs when reinforcement ceases. This adjustability may be seen also in the sensitivity of the behavior of organisms to schedules of reinforcement.

Generalization and Discrimination

The principle of stimulus generalization refers to the fact that a response which has come, through conditioning, to be elicited by a particular stimulus will also be elicited by similar stimuli. For a first illustration of the principle of generalization let us hark back to Pavlov's classical conditioning experiments in which a bell was presented to a dog and shortly followed by the presentation of food powder. After a number of such conditioning trials it will be found that presentation of the bell alone elicits a salivary response. In addition, however, it will be found that other sounds similar to the bell also elicit the salivary response. For example, if the original CS has been a sound of 1200 cycles per second, it will be found that other tone frequencies elicit the response to the extent that they are like the original sound. A sound of 1150 cycles per second will elicit a vigorous response, a sound of 1050 a less vigorous response, a sound of 1000 still less, and so on. The same will hold for sounds of greater frequency than the original CS— the greater the difference between the sound and the original CS the weaker the tendency to respond. Generalization can take place along any effective stimulus dimension: size, shape, color, sound frequency, loudness, smell, taste, and so on.

An every-day situation was described earlier in which a physician was the CS, a painful hypodermic injection was the UCS, and crying was the conditioned response. After a few shots the child cried simply on seeing the physician. Now, the stimulus of the physician is a complex one: a man of a certain size, shape, sound, smell, and so on, covered with a white coat. It will be found that the crying response conditioned to the physician will generalize to similar stimuli which differ somewhat along the various dimensions. It might be found, for example, that the child will cry the next day on entering the barber shop and seeing a different man wearing a somewhat different white coat.

The principle of stimulus generalization holds for operant as well as for respondent conditioning. In an experiment by S. H. White (1958) children were given sixteen reinforced trials of pulling a lever during a presentation of a colored visual stimulus. The children were reinforced in this experiment by the delivery of a marble when the response was performed. Later, the children were presented with visual stimuli that were similar to the original one but that differed in varying degrees from the original in either hue or brightness. In general, the expected generalization gradient occurred for both stimulus dimensions. That is, a test stimulus that was different from the original in hue controlled the lever-pulling response, but to a less extent than the original stimulus. The same was true of test stimuli that differed from the original stimulus on the brightness dimension.

It is easy to see examples of stimulus generalization in every-day life, where it is an important principle of behavior. The following illustration is such an example. The parents of a young child first hear the child say DADDY and make a good deal of fuss over the child, in other words, reinforce the child's verbal behavior. After a number of such reinforcements the child begins to say DADDY more frequently. Reinforcement of this response originally occurs when the child says the word in the presence of his father in the household situation. As a result of this reinforcement history, the child comes to say DADDY when the father comes home from work, and so on. It may be observed in the early stages of the child's language development, however, that he says the word at other times: for example, to the milkman when he comes to the house to collect his bill or perhaps to the grocery clerk when the mother takes the child shopping. This is an example of generalization. The verbal response that was first conditioned to the complex stimulus of the father is controlled by other stimuli with similar properties along some of the original stimulus dimensions.

Another every-day example of generalization is the common experience of speaking or waving to someone only to discover that this person is not the friend we had expected. The person we have "mistaken" for our friend will turn out to be someone who is in some way similar to the person we have been reinforced for greeting.

The foregoing examples of the principle of generalization have all involved inappropriate behavior. Actually, however, the principle has an extremely important adaptive function. Because behavior generalizes, organisms do not have to relearn behavior in each new situation. No two stimulus situations are ever precisely the same. If a child had to start from scratch learning to respond to every slightly different situation, he would never progress. Take the simple motor behavior of moving out of the way of an approaching object. Having been bruised by one object, the child will avoid its approach in the future. Moreover, he will not have to relearn this response with each new approaching object, as behavior that is acquired through reinforcement in one situation will also occur in similar situations. It is not specific to the first situation only.

Although it may be essential that responses generalize, it is also apparent from the examples that inappropriate behavior does sometimes result. That is, behavior which is strengthened through reinforcement in one situation may not be reinforced in a similar situation; it may even be punished. For example, a child may have attended family gatherings, drive-in movies, and parties where fairly boisterous, playful, affectionate behavior among the children and adults was positively reinforced. However, on the child's first day in church, a very similar situation with respect to the group membership, the same behavior may not be positively reinforced at all. In common-sense terms, it could be said that the principle of generalization indeed "steered the child wrong."

Although the principle of stimulus generalization accounts for our responding to new but similar situations with appropriate behavior, nevertheless situations which are only slightly different from ones experienced in the past may be quite the reverse in terms of the type of behavior which is reinforced in that stimulus situation. For this reason it is important that there is a counteractive process to generalization. This is called discrimination.

Discrimination

Although the child who has been reinforced for saying DADDY in the presence of his father will also say DADDY to other similar stimuli, other experiences result in discrimination, so that he now says DADDY to his father but not to other people. This comes about through differential reinforcement. While looking at his father the child is reinforced when he says DADDY. When looking at the grocery clerk the child also says the word, but he is not reinforced. Thus, in the presence of stimuli other than his father, the response of saying DADDY will eventually extinguish altogether. However, saying DADDY in the presence of his father continues to be reinforced by at least the occasional attention of the father.

To describe the operations involved in the principle of discrimination more precisely, let us return to the simple situation of the rat in an operant conditioning chamber. Let us assume we have operantly conditioned a rat to press the bar frequently. We now change the situation by turning on a 60-watt light bulb near the box. If the rat now presses the bar in the presence of this stimulus, a food pellet is delivered. The light is left on until the rat presses the bar and is then turned off. If the rat presses the bar when the light is off reinforcement is not delivered, and the light will remain off until the animal does not press the bar for thirty consecutive seconds. After thirty seconds of no bar pressing, the light turns on again, and the animal is reinforced when it presses the bar.

Thus, the presence of the light is the occasion on which the response is reinforced. This stimulus constellation is called the S^D (ess-dee), or discriminative stimulus. The absence of the light, on the other hand, is never an occasion for reinforcement. The situation without the light is called the S^Δ (ess-delta). In this situation the light soon comes to control the animal's bar-pressing behavior. After sufficient training, when the light goes on (S^D) the animal will immediately press the bar. However, when the light goes off (S^Δ) the animal will not press the bar or will do so very infrequently; in other words, the stimulus situation without the light comes to control "cessation" behavior.

Generalization could now easily be demonstrated in this situation. If the 60-watt light were changed to one of 50-watts, the smaller bulb, too, would result in bar-pressing behavior, but not as strongly as would the 60-watt bulb. The response would also generalize to other intensities of light to the extent that they were similar to that of the 60-watt bulb.

The animal's responsiveness to light stimuli could be narrowed by further discrimination training. For example, the experimenter could decide to turn on lights of various wattage from time to time—but to reinforce only responses to the 60-watt light. Then when the animal would press the bar when the 60-watt light is present he would receive reinforcement. However, when, let us say, a 20-watt light or a 100-watt was presented, the response would not be reinforced, and reinforcement would be postponed until the animal has 30 seconds of nonresponding in the presence of the light. Under this regimen of reinforcement it would be found that the rate of the animal's response to the two lights other than the 60-watt light would eventually decrease, and he would come to respond only to the 60-watt light. This discrimination between light intensities could be continued to the point where the sensory capacity of the animal to respond differently to light stimuli was exceeded.

Thus, we see that even though an organism responds in the same way to similar situations, the generalization process continues only if its responding continues to be reinforced in the new situation. If the organism's response is not reinforced in the new situation, it will extinguish. The response will occur only in situations where it has been reinforced. This stimulus situation will then control the response.

Much of our behavior has come under the control of certain environmental stimuli because in the past it has been reinforced in the presence of those stimuli. Certain types of behavior are positively reinforced in the presence of certain people. As a result, individuals as stimulus objects gain control over our behavior, in other words, become discriminative stimuli. This is why we behave differently in the presence of different types of people. For example, we will behave differently in the presence of a teacher, friend, maiden aunt, priest, or police officer, because different types of verbal and motor behavior have been reinforced in the presence of each person.

Words that other people say to us also become discriminative stimuli. In the past history of each of us, the phrase, PASS THE SALT, PLEASE, has been the occasion on which, if we pass the salt, our behavior is reinforced. Thus, we pass the salt in the presence of this stimulus, but not in its absence. In common-sense terms, one would say that one passes the salt because he "knows that the person requesting it wants the salt." This is again an example, however, of the nonexplanatory value of many common-sense statements about human behavior. The salt is passed because in the past, in the presence of those auditory stimuli, salt-passing behavior has been reinforced.

A common example of a child's behavior in the presence of a stranger may serve to illustrate the process of discrimination of verbal stimuli. The child may bring the visitor some household object such as an ash tray. The visitor will usually thank the child elaborately and give him a good deal of attention. The attention reinforces the preceding behavior, and the child is soon actively bringing the visitor all kinds of things. At this point no fine discriminative stimulus has been established for this type of behavior, the visitor himself is the discriminative stimulus. After the child has made a nuisance of himself by bringing things, however, the visitor may withhold reinforcement, or even provide some aversive stimuli. As the child grows older, his "bringing" behavior will customarily be reinforced only in the presence of certain additional stimuli other than the sheer presence of people, such as BRING ME AN ASH TRAY, PLEASE. These types of verbal stimuli thus typically come to control this type of behavior. This is the legitimate scientific explanation of the individual's response to the stimulus, PLEASE BRING ME SUCH AND SUCH. Because of our past histories of reinforcement in the presence of such stimuli, these stimuli have come to control certain behavior.

As shall be more completely described in a later chapter, many verbal stimuli come to control one's behavior because they have come to be discriminative stimuli. This is one of the important aspects of language.

"Abstractions," a Form of Discrimination

The same general procedures could also define another type of discrimination learning—the acquisition of an abstraction. The term *abstraction* has been used technically to describe the process where a response comes under the control of a single stimulus element that is common to many stimuli but that does not exist except as part of those stimuli (Holland & Skinner, 1961). More specifically, any stimulus object may be considered to be made up of a number of elements or to have several properties, such as size, shape, and color. It has already been stated that generalization may take place along any of these stimulus dimensions when a response is reinforced in the presence of the object. The term *abstraction* or *abstract response* may be used when control is acquired by one of the stimulus elements regardless of the object that is involved, and when other properties of each specific stimulus become S^{Δ}s.

Suppose, for example, that a child was reinforced upon saying RED in the presence of a red car. In the future, according to the principle of generalization, this response might be expected to be emitted in the presence of any car (as well as, to some extent, any red object, and so on). However, if the response RED were emitted in the presence of a car of another color, reinforcement would not follow and a simple discrimination might begin to be formed. In the future, red cars would control RED but other cars would not. Red cars would then be S^Ds for the response RED while all other cars would become S^{Δ}s for this response.

In addition, of course, the response RED would also be reinforced in the presence of red dresses, red road signals, red blocks, and so on, and extinguished in the presence of other colored dresses, blocks, or green signals. Finally all other colors and all other stimulus elements would become S^Δs for the response RED. The child would be said to have acquired the abstraction "red." The response RED would now be under the control of redness, a single property of many diverse stimulus objects.

Generalization of Conditioned Reinforcers

In general, it could be said that the principles of stimulus generalization and discrimination hold for whatever functions the stimulus has. Thus, it should be pointed out that the acquired conditioned reinforcement value of a stimulus may also generalize to similar stimuli. That is, when a stimulus becomes a conditioned reinforcer because it has been paired with another reinforcer, other stimuli which are similar to the new conditioned reinforcer also tend to acquire conditioned reinforcing properties. If, as in Zimmerman's study, a sound of a certain frequency was made a secondary reinforcer, it would be found that other similar sounds would also be reinforcing.[1]

The generalization of conditioned reinforcers can be seen frequently in every-day life. Because parents provide positive primary reinforcers to infants, the parents become secondary reinforcers. This reinforcement value will generalize to other similar stimulus objects, that is, other people. The more similar these other people are to the parents, the greater will be their effect as conditioned reinforcers. The parents' voices likewise become conditioned reinforcers, and similar auditory stimuli consequently also have reinforcement value.

As another example, a child who has been positively reinforced during his early years in school will find books, teachers, studying, and so on, positively reinforcing when he goes to a new school. That is, the behavior of going to school and spending time there will be strengthened by the presence of the conditioned reinforcers of the sight of the school, teacher, and so on. The reinforcement value acquired by his first school will generalize, and other similar situations, that is, other school environments, will be positive reinforcers.

It would also be expected that discriminations among similar conditioned reinforcers could be established.

---

[1] It should be stated that the acquisition of conditioned reinforcement value is considered by some investigators to be itself a process of discrimination learning. Keller and Schoenfeld (1950), for example, conclude that conditioned reinforcers are developed only in this manner. That is, as a stimulus becomes an S^D, it also acquires reinforcing properties.

Summary

When a stimulus, through respondent or operant conditioning, has come to elicit [2] a response, this response will be elicited by other stimuli to the degree to which they are similar to the original stimulus. This is the principle of stimulus generalization. If the original stimulus has complex stimulus dimensions, generalization will take place along each of the dimensions. Because of generalization, organisms do not have to relearn appropriate responses in every situation. If a new situation is similar to those that have occurred in the past, then behavior that has been reinforced in the previous situations will tend to occur in the new situation.

Although this principle of behavior enables adjustive behavior to generalize to new situations, it can result in maladjustive behavior in these new situations, that is, it may lead to behavior which is not followed by positive reinforcement in the presence of these new stimuli. When this occurs, the animal adjusts to the new reinforcement contingencies; it discriminates. That is, if behavior is reinforced in the presence of one stimulus situation but not in a similar stimulus situation, the behavior will come to occur only in the presence of the former stimulus condition. The stimulus situation in whose presence the behavior is reinforced is called a discriminative stimulus. In a sense, discriminative stimuli come to control that behavior, since a given response occurs in its presence but not in its absence. It is in this way that various aspects of the environment, including social aspects, come to control people's behavior.

The conditioned reinforcing properties of a stimulus also generalize. When a stimulus becomes a reinforcer through conditioning, stimuli that are similar to the reinforcing stimulus also acquire reinforcing value.

Differentiation and Successive Approximation

If a response must be made before it can be strengthened with reinforcement, the reader may have wondered how new, original responses are developed. The principles of behavior now to be discussed make it possible for reinforcement contingencies in the environment to "produce" behavior that would not ordinarily occur except for those contingencies.

---

[2] It is customary (Holland and Skinner, 1961; Keller and Schoenfeld, 1950), in the process of distinguishing between operant and respondent conditioning, to speak of the organism "emitting" a response in the presence of a stimulus when speaking of operant conditioning. The term "elicit" is reserved for respondently conditioned responses. However, the first usage above is cumbersome, and "elicit" will be applied to both operantly and respondently conditioned responses.

(Discussions in later chapters will describe additional ways in which novel responses may occur when complex human behavior is involved.)

As an example, let us use a behavior of a pigeon described by Skinner (1953, pp. 63 ff.). Ordinarily it would be quite unusual for a pigeon to walk around with its head held as high in the air as possible. If one were to wait until this response occurred so that it could be reinforced, the delay might be interminable. However, the pigeon can be gradually conditioned to perform the response. Actually, if we were to observe him locomoting about his cage, we would notice some variation in the bobbing of the pigeon's head. If only the most extreme cases of head-bobbing were reinforced, we would find that the "head-raising" response would increase in frequency.

These operations could be facilitated by using an electronic device. An invisible light beam could be flashed across the cage. Whenever the beam was broken by the pigeon's head, the animal could be reinforced with a bit of food. At first the light beam could be focused at a low level so that slight "bobs" of the pigeon's head would break the light beam. Since these responses would be strengthened by reinforcement, they would occur more frequently—the pigeon would be bobbing its head, on the average, at a greater height than it did before. At this point the light beam would be raised so that only a few of the pigeon's head-bobbings would now break the beam; when this occurred, the pigeon would again be reinforced. Thus, since only higher head-bobbings would be followed by reinforcement, it would be expected that after a period of time the pigeon would more frequently be bobbing its head even higher.

Through this gradual procedure of successive approximation to the final response desired, the pigeon could finally be operantly conditioned to emit a response that would never ordinarily occur. A person seeing the pigeon for the first time after the completion of conditioning would find its behavior quite unusual, and, in ignorance of the events molding its behavior, might consider the action "abnormal."

The principles involved in the foregoing illustration may be abstracted as follows. Behavior normally occurs with certain slight variations. These variations of a response constitute a class where reinforcement of one variation will strengthen other variations in the class. If only certain variations of a class of responses are reinforced, then the constitution of the class will change in that direction. This process is called the differentiation of a response, in other words, the differential reinforcement of certain variations of a response class will "differentiate out," or, more precisely, will condition those variations, while other variations represented in the response class will extinguish.

There still will be variations of response, but they will now vary from a different position in the behavior class. If only extreme variations at one end of the distribution of responses are reinforced, then these cases will occur more frequently and the cases at the other extreme will occur less frequently. In essence, the class of responses will drift toward the extreme that is reinforced. If this is done in a gradually increasing manner, the organism can soon be conditioned to respond in a very extreme manner, which otherwise would not occur. A series of such differentiations is called successive approximation.

There is no difficulty in finding illustrations of the principles of differentiation and successive approximation in everyday life. For example, crying in early infancy seems to be a natural response to certain aversive stimuli. Later, however, learning seems to be involved. As the infant grows older he is reinforced for crying by the attention and solicitation of his parents and other adults and his behavior seems to be shaped by this experience (see Chapter 9). By the time the child reaches school age, crying is usually considered to be an undesirable type of behavior—particularly when it occurs in what are considered to be inappropriate situations. Thus, at a certain age most parents try to "discourage" crying behavior in their children. The parents may ignore the youngster when he cries inappropriately or may even admonish the child (in our terms, withhold reinforcement or apply aversive stimuli). Sometimes, inadvertently, the following happens and may produce the behavior of a temper tantrum.

Let us say, for example, that the parents observe that their child at a certain age cries too frequently in too many situations. Perhaps they even decide to ignore the child's crying, "hoping" that it will cease. If reinforcement were consistently withheld for all crying responses, it would be expected that extinction would to some extent take place. However, in the process some parents may inadvertently reinforce the child on the basis of how hard he cries.

Suppose that, in the present example, if the child cries with enough intensity, his parents finally reinforce him—"give him what he asks for," and so on. In temporarily ignoring the child or refusing his request, they would have produced more extreme crying, since withholding reinforcement from an organism that has customarily been reinforced for a certain behavior will at first produce more extreme behavior of the same sort. When the parents then reinforce extreme crying, it would be expected that this type of behavior would be more likely to occur in the future. After this happens several times it would be observed that the child is crying intensely on each occasion. At some point the parents might again try to discourage crying by ignoring the behavior. They might even say to themselves that they will not give the child attention unless it is really a serious matter. That is, they refuse to reinforce the child unless he cries even harder. When again they withhold reinforcement, the child would be expected to cry even harder, and so on.

By gradually raising the level of intensity at which the child must cry before reinforcement is given, crying tantrums could be shaped up that would never otherwise occur. The situation could also be complicated somewhere along the line by the use of punishment. In the midst of an extended crying session, the father might suddenly "explode" and punish the child to make him stop crying. The punishment, however, would be an unconditioned stimulus for crying, and the child would cry even more intensely. Then, if the mother steps in and comforts this extreme case of crying, this type of behavior would be further strengthened. It is suggested that this type of history of reinforcement may shape up "temper tantrums" so extreme as to seem incomprehensible to the casual observer (see Ferster, 1961, p. 445). Such behaviors are then likely to be classified as "abnormal." In general, it is suggested that such histories of reinforcement must always be considered when dealing with behavior that is so extreme that it appears to involve principles different from those which have been shown to operate with "normal" people.

However, the operation of the principles of differentiation and successive approximation is not limited to maladjustive behaviors; they are equally important in "shaping" behavior significant for normal adjustment. Many adjustive human behaviors seemingly would never be acquired if reinforcement was postponed until the behaviors appeared in precise form. If, for example, parents waited until a word was perfectly articulated by their child before they reinforced the child, the child's language development would be severely retarded. Further examples of important behaviors shaped through successive approximation will be given after the process has been discussed in greater detail.

Response Class

An experiment by Verplanck (1956) illustrates the operation of successive approximation in shaping up behavior in humans. The experimenter gave the subjects points (which they recorded) as reinforcers. Using these conditioned reinforcers, it was possible to shape up a variety of behaviors in the college students used as subjects, such as scratching one's ear with the right hand, smiling, facial mannerisms, and saying certain classes of words. This example may be used to discuss further the topics of differentiation and successive approximation. Responses may be considered to be in the same response class when the reinforcement of one of the responses in the class strengthens all the other responses in the class, and conversely when nonreinforcement of one of the responses weakens all the other responses in the response class.

For example, if one wished to strengthen another person's response of scratching his right ear, as in Verplanck's experiment, the experimenter would first reinforce any movement of the subject. The subject might first shift in his chair—not moving his arms at all. Reinforcement of this response would strengthen the whole class of "movement" responses. The subject would now be more likely to move an arm, leg, hand, head, or shoulder, and so on, than he would have been prior to reinforcement. Thus, "movements in general" could constitute a class of responses for the individual, since reinforcement of one movement strengthens other movements of the body.

For a time, the experimenter would strengthen this general class of movement responses by reinforcing any movement the person might make. This would, among other things, raise the probability of the person moving his right shoulder. When this occurred, the experimenter would reinforce this response as he did the others, and right shoulder movements would now occur more frequently. At this point differentiation (selective reinforcement and extinction) could commence in shaping the behavior of the individual. The experimenter could begin reinforcing the movements of the subject's right shoulder, but not other movements.

However, since nonreinforcement of some movements will also weaken all the responses in the class, the experimenter must be careful not to allow too many nonreinforced responses. Otherwise, the total class of behaviors may extinguish while he waits for another right shoulder movement. To maintain the movement class of responses in good strength he may have to reinforce other responses besides the right shoulder movement. He should attempt to reinforce only the more pertinent movements, such as movements of the upper body, especially those on the right side. Responses that are clearly not in the direction of the desired response, such as a left shoulder or left arm movement, should not be reinforced. By maintaining the strength of the general class of movement responses the experimenter could insure the occurrence of right shoulder movements along with the other responses in the movement class. Since right shoulder responses would always be reinforced and some of the other responses would not, movements of the right shoulder and side would eventually become dominant.

The shift in response frequencies has important consequences. While movements of the right arm might be very weak or infrequently occurring members of the "general movement" class of responses, they would probably be strong members of the "right shoulder" subclass of movements. Thus, strengthening right shoulder movements would raise the probability of occurrence of right arm movements.

The process of strengthening the right arm class of responses could begin when a member of this subclass of responses first appeared. Reinforcement would then strengthen the class of arm movements, and they should occur more frequently. Again, since they would still occur infrequently, the experimenter would want to continue to reinforce right shoulder movements and even other body movements to insure that the general class of movement responses did not extinguish. On the other hand, the experimenter would also attempt to withhold reinforcement for movements which were the farthest removed from the right arm movement, that is, the movements of the lower limbs and body, movements on the left side of the body, and movements above the shoulders.

Thus, right arm movements would be reinforced every time, and other responses would slowly be subjected to an increasing proportion of extinction trials. When the class of arm movements had been sufficiently strengthened to occur frequently, movements of the arm toward the head would be continuously reinforced, other arm movements would be allowed to weaken, and other body movements would no longer be reinforced. Through succeeding differentiations, the original class of general movements would be broken down into a subclass of right side movements, then a further subclass of right shoulder and arm movements, then a further subclass of right arm movements, then a further subclass of right arm movements extending upward to the head, and so on.

The principles of this process can now be summarized. (1) A response class forms a functional unity in the following way. Reinforcement of one response in the class strengthens the other responses in the class. Nonreinforcement of one response in the class weakens the other responses in the class. (2) The functional unity of the response class can be altered through the differential reinforcement of some members of the class. That is, if some members of the class are reinforced and not others, those responses will be strengthened and the others weakened. (3) Strengthening a particular response strengthens similar responses more than it does dissimilar responses and the converse for extinction. (4) The differentiating process must not be carried out too rapidly; that is, the general class of responses must be maintained in good strength until those which are to be reinforced begin to occur frequently enough. If too large a step is made toward the final response desired, the first general class of behaviors may extinguish before the desired behavior has had a chance to be strengthened. Thus, an appropriate ratio of reinforcement-to-work must be maintained. (5) A progressive series of differentiations can produce a terminal response that is quite different from any of the responses previously exhibited in the original class.

Differentiation and successive approximation appear to have an extremely important adaptive function in all educational training situations. Several generalizations on the basis of laboratory work seem warranted. If the end objective is to produce a skilled motor behavior, for example, the first step may be to reinforce any kind of general movement or merely general attendance and participation. Only gradually should the parent or coach withhold reinforcement for certain members of the general response class and begin reinforcing only "better" responses. If one attempts to reinforce only the desired responses before they begin to occur in abundance, the training will at the very least be set back. The general class of behavior may even extinguish, and competing responses occur; for example, the child may do something else or have to be restrained from leaving the situation. If that occurs, the coach or the parent will have to give up the enterprise or go back and start over again, reinforcing the more general class of grosser responses. The "skilled" coach is perhaps one who is sensitive to the strength of behavior and never begins nonreinforcement of the less desirable members of the response class until there is a sufficient number of desirable responses to reinforce. On the other hand, a coach can move too slowly, that is, he can continue to reinforce poor responses in a class when there are enough occurrences of good responses, which, if reinforced, would maintain the general class of behaviors as well as continue the progress toward terminal expertness. Poor responses that are unnecessarily reinforced would in this case be strengthened and compete with preferred responses and later would be harder to extinguish—making the task more difficult.

The process of successive approximation seems to occur in much expert coaching, where finer and finer responses are differentiated out of the former class of grosser variations. The same principles appear to be involved in the acquisition of verbal "intellectual" skills. First, relatively gross responses may require reinforcement. For example, the ancient Hebrews were said to put a coin on the page of the book the first time the child came to learn to read. This would be expected to strengthen the general response of coming to the book, and so on. When such general responses become strong, more precise skills may be differentiated out of the class of responses through the selective use of reinforcement. It should be emphasized that the progress and final achievement of skilled performance may depend upon the excellence of the teacher, parent, or coach in discriminating what is preferred performance and in his ability gradually to reinforce these behaviors and extinguish the less desirable ones, maintaining the class of relevant behaviors in good strength at all times. (See Holland and Skinner, 1961, as well as later chapters of this book, for further discussion of the principles and applications of such behavioral shaping.)

Awareness and the Shaping of Behavior

When evidence, such as Verplanck's experiment, is presented that human behavior can be gradually molded under the action of differential reinforcement, the reader may have a tendency to explain the subject's behavior by saying that the subject finally "got the idea" as to what the experimenter "wanted" and then started doing it. To say this would, according to the present interpretation, be ignoring the actual explanation of the subject's behavior. A more satisfactory explanation would be thought to involve the history of reinforcement that gradually strengthened a certain type of behavior, and the principles that have just been discussed. This explanation is supported by the fact that many of the subjects in Verplanck's experiment were never aware of what was taking place in the experiment, that is, they never could verbalize which of their specific responses were followed by reinforcement (how they obtained their points). Subjects were less likely to be aware when the response that was shaped was subtle, such as a smile or a facial mannerism. (Verplanck, 1962, has further discussed "awareness" in terms of conditioning principles.)

Differentiation of Speed and Force of Behavior

It may have occurred to the reader that a fixed-ratio reinforcement schedule has elements which are very similar to our description of differentiation. Under a fixed-ratio schedule the organism is reinforced for responding rapidly. The more rapidly he responds, the more frequently he is reinforced. Rapid responding is reinforced more quickly and is thus strengthened more than slow responding (Keller and Schoenfeld, 1950). The schedule, therefore, differentiates rapid responses out of a class of varied "rate" responses.

It would be possible to arrange conditions even more precisely to differentiate out rapidity as a response. For example, if apparatus was set up to gauge rapidity instantaneously and to reinforce rapid responses, rapid responding could soon be strengthened precisely. Then the experimenter would have only to increase the number of rapid responses emitted prior to reinforcement in order to produce long sequences of rapid responding.

The possibility of conditioning rates of responding has been described here because rapidity of response is important in general work and in study habits. Other things being equal, the person who works rapidly will be a much higher achiever. It should be pointed out that the converse of rapidity, slowness, also can be strengthened through reinforcement (see Ferster and Skinner, 1957).

Forcefulness of response is subject to differentiation (Keller and Schoenfeld, 1950) in the same manner as other responses. The force with which a response occurs is subject to variation, and "force" responses constitute a class of behavior. It is possible to differentiate out responses of a certain degree of force by reinforcing only that type of response. In everyday life, we meet some people who characteristically behave very forcefully. They speak forcefully, shake hands forcefully, they open doors forcefully, and so on. This "trait" can in part be interpreted in terms of a past history of differential reinforcement for forceful responses in a variety of situations. It is certainly true that parents differ in the extent to which they reinforce calm, slow, and gentle behavior or, conversely, vigorous, aggressive, forceful behavior.

Differentiation and Discrimination

The terms *differentiation* and *discrimination* frequently are confused when the principles are first learned. For this reason, the distinction should be particularly noted. Differentiation denotes the change that takes place in the variations of a class of responses through the selective reinforcement of some of the variations. The stimulus situation is not a variable in this process.

Discrimination, on the other hand, involves different stimuli and a constant response. That is, once a response has come to be elicited by a particular stimulus, it will also be elicited by similar stimuli. If that response is then reinforced only in the presence of one of those stimuli, however, it will come to be emitted only in the presence of that stimulus. This is the process of discrimination.

Actually, these two processes may take place at the same time, and in every-day life they seem to be inextricably interwoven. For example, the case of temper tantrums that has been described as a series of differentiations actually illustrates both principles. The parents continually raised the level of crying that was necessary to procure reinforcement and eventually shaped up temper tantrums. Such a process would take place over an extended period of time, during which the process of discrimination would also be occurring. Reinforcement by the parents of the child's crying behavior will strengthen the tendency of the child to cry in the presence of similar stimuli, such as other adults. When the parents strengthen extreme cases of crying, this behavior will also generalize to similar adults. However, if the child cries in the presence of these adults and is not reinforced, a discrimination will occur; the child will come to have temper tantrums in the presence of the parents, but not other people. This might bewilder the parents, but would actually be quite lawful.

The independent operation of these two processes is difficult to observe in every-day life situations, such as the above, but simple to observe in the laboratory. This is a good illustration of the necessity for laboratory experimentation in establishing basic principles. In real life, they are often intermingled in such complex ways that they cannot be isolated.

Summary

No response occurs in exactly the same way each time it is emitted. There are slight variations in the response each time it occurs. It is therefore necessary to consider classes of responses. Certain members of a response class can be strengthened without strengthening other members of the class by reinforcing only the former. When this occurs, those responses in the class that have been reinforced are said to be differentiated out of the class. There will still be variations among the discrete differentiated responses, and thus a response class will still exist. However, the variation will now be around a new point in the class of responses. When the more extreme members of a response class are reinforced, the class shifts in that direction. By successively differentiating out only the extreme members of a class of responses, a response class can be obtained that is markedly different from the original class and would otherwise never have arisen. A series of such differentiations is called successive approximation and can finally result in a distinctly novel response. This process seems to be involved in the training of novel, complex, and important human behavior.

Sequences or Chains of Responses

To illustrate the foregoing principles in as "pure" a form as possible, we have so far used examples involving fairly discrete S–R relationships. In every-day situations, however, one observes that the behavior of organisms appears to be a continuous on-going sequence, with one response leading smoothly to another. Hull (1930) has described the principles by which such behavioral sequences are developed and function.

An experimental prototype of this kind of behavior can be seen in the responses of a rat traversing a maze that includes a number of choice points. Originally, the rat's responses are elicited by the specific stimuli impinging upon it at each choice point. After the animal has traced the shortest path to food a number of times, the specific responses are "chained," resulting in a smooth performance in which one response elicits the next. (See Figure 3.10.)

Actually, it is not a response itself that comes to elicit the next response in a sequence, but the stimuli the first response produces. To understand how this can happen, it is necessary to point out that each response an individual makes produces certain internal, implicit stimuli, since there are sensory receptors in each muscle and tendon that are sensitive to movement. Each time the individual moves, certain of these sensory receptors

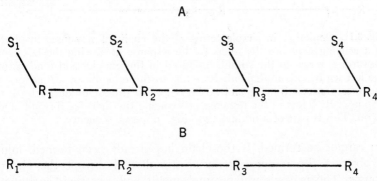

Fig. 3.10. Development of a sequence of responses involving an animal traversing a maze. The stimuli S_1 to S_4 represent choice points in the maze. At first each choice-point stimulus controls each response in the sequence, as is indicated in part A of the figure. Part A also indicates that associations are beginning to form between the responses, as indicated by the dotted lines. In part B the response chain is fully formed and may function without the support of the original eliciting stimuli. For example, if at this point the animal's senses of hearing, vision, and smell were totally obstructed, the organism would still be able to trace its way through the maze to the food.

are activated. The stimuli arising from such movements will differ, depending on the position of the muscle or tendon. These stimuli are customarily called proprioceptive stimuli (Keller and Schoenfeld, 1950).

It is because of these internal sources of stimulation that we can report where our limbs are at any moment without looking at them—just as we can respond to external sources of stimulation, such as light rays, sound waves, and tactual and taste cues. Without response-produced stimuli, it would be impossible to respond to our own movements in a normal manner.

The response chain involved in a simple motor behavior such as walking is schematized in Figure 3.11, indicating how the internal stimuli are produced by a response and enter into a sequence of responses. The first response produces stimuli that elicit the next response. This second response, in turn, produces new stimuli that lead to the next response, and so on.

When, because of disease or injury to the spinal cord, the sensory receptors in the muscles and tendons are obstructed from providing stimuli, an individual is not able to develop the chain of behavior involved in walking in the manner just described. Even though he can still move his limbs, no stimuli arise from the movement. Consequently, as is shown in Figure 3.12, part A, one response does not elicit the next, and a response

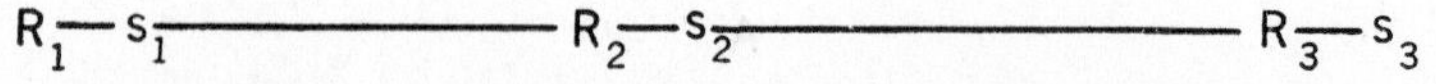

$$R_1 - s_1 \text{——————} R_2 - s_2 \text{——————} R_3 - s_3$$

Fig. 3.11. Depiction in simple terms of the chain of responses involved in a walking sequence. R_1 refers to the response of moving the left foot forward; s_1 refers to the stimuli produced in the muscles and tendons of the left leg by this movement. R_2 refers to the response of lifting up on the toes of the left foot, and s_2 refers to the stimuli produced by this response. R_3 refers to the response of swinging the right leg forward, and so on. This is part of a normal "walking" response sequence.

chain cannot be formed. If the chain has already been formed, injuries that obstruct the response-produced stimuli will disrupt the chain of responses. The person's walking movements will lose their coordination unless the response chain is maintained through some other source of stimulation. Such individuals must look at their limbs as they walk; the

A

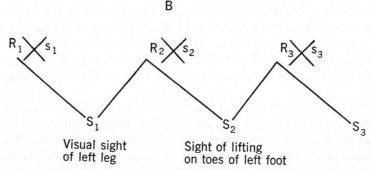

B

Visual sight   Sight of lifting
of left leg   on toes of left foot

Fig. 3.12. The breakdown of the "walking" response chain is depicted in part A. Through disease or injury no stimuli are produced by the various responses. As a consequence each association is broken, and there is no longer a smooth walking chain. Part B shows how visual stimuli may replace the internal response-produced stimuli that no longer occur to mediate the walking sequence. In this case, the sequence is now possible because the individual looks at the position of his limbs. The movement of lifting up on the toes of the left foot, for example, will then depend upon seeing where the left leg is.

visual stimuli replace the lost internal sources of stimulation in the response chain. The substitute chain of responses involving visual stimuli is schematized in Figure 3.12, part B.

The description of response chains has so far involved only proprioceptive stimuli. It should be indicated, however, that other types of stimuli may be involved in chaining, some of which are internal to the organism and some of which are external. In the former case, there are internal stimuli arising, for example, from the intestines and glands. In addition, a response may produce external stimuli as was the case in the relearning of walking on the basis of response produced visual stimuli. Movements—walking, running, driving—also result in the occurrence of new visual stimuli from the environment which may control a response chain. Thus, the rat's smooth performance in the maze was also a result of visual stimuli, in addition to the chaining effected by proprioceptive stimuli. In this case, each turning response would bring the animal to the next visual stimulus (choice point) which would come to control his next response.

Responses may also result in other stimuli such as smells, tastes, and sounds. For example, talking consists of muscular movements with each vocal response producing a sound stimulus. These sound stimuli are important in maintaining sequences of speech responses and disruption of these stimuli disrupts one's vocal chains (see Goldiamond, 1962, p. 307, for this example). Thus, any stimulus that a response produces may come to control the next response in a sequence and be part of a response chain.

Change in Stimulus Control of Response Chains

Many behavior sequences are originally formed by each response being elicited by some environmental stimulus. For example, when a person is learning to drive a car his responses are dependent upon external stimuli (usually verbal instruction), such as PUT IN THE CLUTCH . . . PUT IT IN LOW GEAR . . . LET OUT THE CLUTCH SLOWLY AND PRESS UPON THE ACCELERATOR AT THE SAME TIME, and so on. Each verbal stimulus elicits a motor response, and the pupil haltingly drives the car. After a number of such trials, however, it would be expected that the stimuli produced by the preceding response would elicit the next response, and the smooth sequence which marks the expert driver would result. This process is schematized in Figure 3.13.

The example illustrates several important points. Behavior sequences may originally parallel sequences of environmental stimuli because each stimulus elicits a response. However, once a chain has been formed the response sequence can occur independently of the original eliciting stimuli. The response sequence then may anticipate the verbal stimulus sequence. At some point the driving instructor says PUT IN THE CLUTCH, and

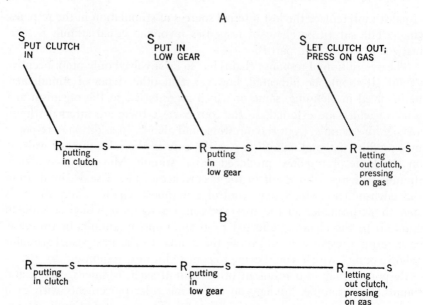

Fig. 3.13. Formation of an automobile-driving sequence of responses. In part A, the figures shows how each verbal stimulus elicits the appropriate motor response. The series of responses is under the control of the series of verbal stimuli. Part B indicates how each response becomes conditioned to the stimuli produced by the preceding response, resulting in a smooth performance where each response elicits the next and where other sources of stimulus control are no longer necessary.

before he can complete the other instructions the pupil already has the car in motion. (See Prediction and Control, pp. 246 ff., for further discussion.)

Many other types of human behavior seem to be coordinated in response chains. When first playing a new piece a pianist who reads music will follow the music note by note and each time respond by striking the correct key. After a number of times, however, his sequence of responses becomes independent of the external stimuli (the marks on the sheet of music) that originally elicited the responses.

Analogous operations are involved in memorizing a passage of poetry or learning the alphabet. One begins by responding to each visual stimulus. Finally, after a number of repetitions, the stimuli produced by each response elicit the next, and the sequence becomes flawless. Since "alphabet responses" are not usually elicited in reverse order, this sequence of responses is not as strongly formed, and recitation of the alphabet in reverse order is not a smooth chain of responses.[3]

---

[3] Osgood (1957) has suggested that chaining can also take place in the central nervous system and that rapid chains of responses do not depend upon proprioceptive stimuli.

The Principles Involved in Strengthening Response Chains

The explanation of how chains of responses are strengthened becomes quite complicated. In some cases it would seem that simple contiguity of the S–R components, as occurs in classical conditioning, is sufficient. In other cases, reinforcement, as it occurs in operant conditioning, is obviously involved.

Implicit Responses

It was indicated in the preceding discussion that the stimuli produced by responses may be implicit; that is, they may occur without being readily observable using casual, every-day methods. Responses, too, may occur on an implicit level. For instance, implicit responses are involved when we say that a person is talking to himself. At these times the individual is making verbal responses, but they are not overt and thus not readily observable. Although we may sometimes see the individual moving his lips, these verbal responses are usually entirely covert, at least by readily available observational methods.

Implicit responses, such as talking to oneself, however, seem to enter into extended chains of responses and in the end may produce a stimulus for an overt motor response. Dollard and Miller (1950) assume the occurrence of such verbal responses as well as their function of producing stimuli that mediate other responses. Much important human behavior seems to be of this type. Thus, the mediation of overt behavior by implicit verbal responses may be considered an extremely important mechanism.

An experiment performed by Miller (1935) demonstrates how "thinking" responses follow the same principles as overt verbal responses—that is, how covert verbal responses can mediate overt responses. In this experiment a *galvanic skin response* or GSR (a response of the sweat glands in the skin to certain stimuli) was conditioned to saying the letter "T." This was done by presenting sometimes the letter "T" and sometimes the figure "4," with the subject required to pronounce each as it appeared. Each time "T" was presented and pronounced the subject was given an electric shock that elicited the galvanic skin response. Thus, the stimuli produced by the response of saying "T" constituted the CS. The shock was the UCS. According to the principles already discussed, the GSR elicited by the shock was classically conditioned to the stimuli produced by the response of saying "T." The conditioning process is schematized in Figure 3.14, part A.

Next the subject was presented with a series of dots, one at a time, and asked to think *to himself* of "T" when one dot was presented and FOUR when the next dot was presented, and so on, in an alternate manner.

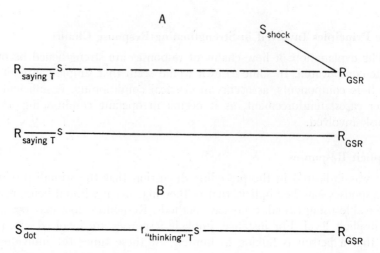

Fig. 3.14. When the response of saying the letter "T" is paired with a shock, the stimuli produced by the speaking response come to elicit the GSR elicited originally only by the shock. This process is shown in part A of the figure. Later, as depicted in part B, when the subject is instructed to think of "T" when a dot is presented, the S_{dot} elicits the "thinking" response, and the stimuli produced by this response then elicit the GSR.

Records were kept of the subject's GSR. It was found that to every other dot (those to which the subject has been instructed to think "T") he responded with a conditioned GSR. This part of the process is shown in part B of Figure 3.14.

> In other words, the involuntary conditioned galvanic responses, which the subject did not know he was making, generalized from the cues produced by pronouncing the words aloud to those produced by thinking them. This would seem to indicate a considerable degree of similarity between the cues produced by saying and thinking the same words (Dollard and Miller, 1950, p. 205).

Implicit Responses as Intervening Variables

It was strongly emphasized in the first two chapters that scientific terms must be established on the basis of observation. Observations of stimulus events (the independent variable) can serve to define a term, as can observations of response events (the dependent variable). Other terms are defined by the relationship between the two. The reader must by now be asking, however, if science is interested only in observables, how does it deal with events that are not directly observed, such as proprioceptive stimuli, and thinking and other implicit responses? Some psychologists have tended to avoid consideration of implicit responses, at least on a formal basis. However, even casual consideration seems to indicate that some of our most important responses are not directly observable. The problem facing the scientist is that in order to work with such behaviors it must be possible in some way to make them observable—or rather, their characteristics must be established by observations.

The term "thinking response" is at best an example of a term not defined by a directly observable event. We cannot look into the subject to see if somewhere such a response has indeed been made. Nor is the term defined by a simple stimulus–response relationship. However, there is another type of scientific term (of which "thinking" is an example) that will be introduced here in addition to the three types of operationally defined terms already discussed in Chapter 2. Such terms are called *intervening variables*, since they refer to variables intervening between the observable independent and dependent variables (for example, between stimulus variables and response variables).

In Miller's experiment the dot stimulus may be considered to elicit the thinking response, and the thinking response, through its stimuli, to elicit the overt response. The definition of the intervening variable therefore involves two functional relationships. On the one hand there is the functional relation between the independent variable and the thinking response; the second relation is between the stimulus produced by the thinking response and the dependent variable.

It is this two-stage process that differentiates the intervening variable from a term defined by a straight S–R relationship. As it can be seen in the case of the present intervening variable, two "learnings" are involved: that between the observable stimulus and the thinking response and that between the stimuli of the thinking response and the overt response. This is depicted in general terms in Figure 3.15.

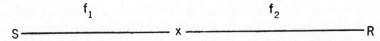

Fig. 3.15. An intervening variable in psychology. The stimulus (S) has a certain functional relationship to the intervening term (x), and the intervening term, or process, has a functional relationship to the consequent response (R).

The characteristics of an intervening variable must, then, be established by observation, albeit indirect observation. Miller's experiment indicates that at least this type of "thinking process" has the characteristics of a response in that it produces stimuli to which other responses can be conditioned. It also indicates that the process is likely to be a response process, because the GSR was actually conditioned initially to the overt response. In addition, instructions that would ordinarily act as stimuli eliciting overt speech responses, such as instructions to say the letter "T" when a dot is presented, also functioned in the same way with the thinking response.

However, these particular indirect observations would by themselves not be considered to completely establish the detailed characteristics of this type of intervening variable. If thinking does indeed have the characteristics of responses, then it should also follow in other respects the laws that have been established for responses. For example, if the "thinking response" actually is a response, then its relationship to the stimulus should be the same as those of other responses of its type, for example, the greater the number of trials the stronger should be the conditioning. The same should hold true for the second relationship. Since the thinking response, like other responses, would have stimulus characteristics, its relationship to the GSR should display all the characteristics of S–R relationships. In fact, all the characteristics of the establishment and maintenance of responses that have previously been found in dealing with observable responses should apply to these implicit "thinking responses."

These characteristics must, of course, be established by experimentation. For example, conditions would have to be varied for different subjects so that the stimulus elicited the overt speech response (and thus the covert thinking response) in different strengths and then it could be observed how this affected the elicitation of the GSR by the stimulus. During such an experiment the strength of the tendency of the thinking response to elicit the GSR would be kept constant. The same type of experimentation would have to be conducted to establish the functional relationships between the thinking response and the overt response it elicits.

If many of these experiments were conducted with positive results, the characteristics of the implicit process would be even more soundly established. The term "thinking response" would then be well defined, although in this indirect manner. The term could be called an intervening variable because its referent intervenes between the independent variable (the observable stimulus) and the dependent variable (the observable response).

The same types of prediction and control should be possible from the application of intervening variable terms as from straight S–R laws. When the two functional relationships shown in Figure 3.15 have been established, then the final prediction and control of the overt response is possible. Whether or not, for example, the individual will respond with a GSR in the experimental example used will depend upon whether the stimulus elicits the implicit "thinking response" and whether this thinking response has in the past been paired with electric shock.

Summary

In the normal human being every overt response produces stimuli. Such stimuli can come to elicit other responses in the same way that any stimulus does. Since response-produced stimuli may elicit another response, which in turn may produce the stimuli for yet another response, sequences of responses may be formed. Much of our ordinary behavior is made up of such chains of responses. Most skilled actions are not one individual response but are rather a series of responses. A skill as simple as tying one's shoelace is composed of a series of responses that were originally not linked together so as to unfold one after the other in a smooth chain. Originally, tying one's shoes was a difficult and halting task. Behavior chains, once formed, can be independent of the environmental stimuli that first were necessary to elicit each response in the chain.

Language behavior as well as physical skills depends heavily upon response chains. Such sequences can easily be demonstrated in the memorization of passages of verbal material. Sequences of language responses may be quite complex and may enter into complex human activities such as thinking, reasoning, foresight, problem-solving, and communication, topics that will be discussed in detail in later chapters.

In the same way that the stimuli produced by a response may be implicit (such as proprioceptive stimuli), so may responses themselves be implicit. That is, the organism makes many responses which are not customarily observed by the casual observer. In every-day language, for example, it is said that people "talk to themselves." This "talking" can be considered to be a series of implicit responses. Like overt responses, implicit responses produce stimuli. Thus, there may be chains of implicit responses, the end members of which produce stimuli for overt physical or verbal responses. This occurs when a person "thinks" (performs implicit verbal responses) before speaking or doing.

In studying implicit responses as inferred processes, the observable antecedents and observable consequences of the inferred processes must be used to define the characteristics of the process. Thus, the relationship of the antecedent stimulus events to the inferred process must be established as well as the relationship of the inferred process to the consequent behavioral events. A term defined by two such functional relationships may be called an intervening variable.

"Self"-Reinforced Behavior

The concept of the response-produced stimulus has implications in addition to those involved in the formation of extended response sequences.

In every-day life it may be noticed that behavior which is originally re-ported as "hard work" or "unenjoyable" may, after a long time of being reinforced, be reported as "pleasant." An individual who as a young man was "reluctant" to work may behave as if an important source of reinforce-ment has been removed when he is finally retired from the same job. In common-sense terms, he would say that he just "enjoyed doing the work."

This type of occurrence may be considered in terms of the response-produced stimulus. Each time a response occurs it produces its character-istic stimuli. If this response is followed by a positive reinforcer, it would be expected that the response elicited by the reinforcer would be condi-tioned to the response-produced stimuli. These response-produced stimuli would therefore become conditioned reinforcers. Thus, the stimuli pro-duced by a response can function as conditioned positive reinforcers and serve to strengthen the response that produces them.[4] This process is schematized in Figure 3.16.

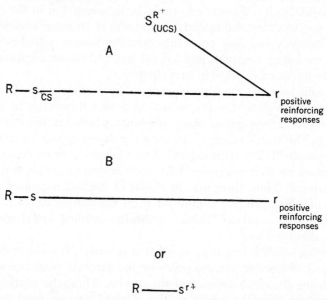

Fig. 3.16. As depicted in part A, when a response occurs it produces a stimulus that, in this case, will have the function of a CS. This response is followed by the presentation of a positive reinforcer which functions as a UCS in that it elicits positively reinforcing responses. Part B shows that these are conditioned to the response-produced stimuli and give those stimuli conditioned reinforcing value.

---

[4] It is interesting to note that Mowrer (1960a) has suggested that the basis for habit-formation, that is, the strengthening of a response, lies in this process whereby the stim-uli produced by a response acquire reinforcing properties.

As an illustration, let us say that a rat was reinforced by a bit of food when it sat up. The salivary response, for example, elicited by the food would be conditioned to the stimuli produced by sitting up. When the animal would sit, it would also salivate. Thus, it would be expected that, as a consequence of responses elicited by food being conditioned to stimuli produced by the sitting response, the response-produced stimuli would become conditioned reinforcers.

Conditioned Aversive Response-Produced Stimuli

In the same way that a response may come to have positive reinforcing properties through the stimuli which it produces, a response also could come to have aversive properties. When a response is followed by the presentation of an aversive stimulus, the "aversive" responses elicited by the stimulus will be respondently conditioned to the stimuli produced by the aversively treated response. These response-produced stimuli, since they now elicit these conditioned aversive responses, should be conditioned negative reinforcers (Mowrer, 1960a).

What is commonly called "anxiety" or "guilt" may be considered in terms of conditioned aversive responses. A situation paired with a stimulus that elicits an aversive response will come to elicit parts of this response. This situation will thus come to elicit "anxiety," or rather, an anxiety response, in the individual. Thus, as Osgood (1953) points out, when a rat is presented with a buzzer sound paired with electric shock, the shock produces jumping and squeaking responses as well as autonomic responses (changes in blood pressure, heart rate, GSR, and so on). Some of these autonomic responses will be conditioned to the buzzer and will constitute the "anxiety," or anxiety response, which the buzzer will elicit.

The same process may be thought to be involved when the stimulus that comes to elicit the conditioned anxiety response is the stimulus produced by another preceding response of the organism. In this case performance of this response would elicit the anxiety response in the manner suggested by Mowrer. Thus, when an individual reports that when he does such and such it makes him feel "anxious" or "guilty," this may be interpreted as a report that performing the certain response elicits conditioned aversive or anxiety responses in the individual.

Punishment: A Weakener of Responses

In a previous section dealing with negative reinforcers (aversive stimuli) it was said that such stimuli could strengthen "escape" behaviors which were followed by the removal of the stimuli. However, the presentation of aversive stimuli following the occurrence of a response, in other words, punishment, and the resultant weakening of that response on future occasions has only briefly been mentioned. The effects of punishment can be more fully described by using the principle of conditioned reinforcement and the concept of the response-produced stimulus to indicate how punishment may weaken behavior through the strengthening of an "escape" response.

When the stimuli produced by a response have acquired negative reinforcing properties, that is, elicit conditioned aversive or anxiety responses, performance of the response produces conditioned aversive stimuli. As a consequence, if the organism "stops emitting that response," or responds in a different way, the response-produced stimuli cease, and the aversive stimuli are removed. Therefore, "stopping that response" or responding in another manner is strengthened. Thus, it may only appear that punishment following the undesirable response has weakened that response. Actually, it could be said that punishment has made that response aversive, and "not doing" that response or "doing something else" is consequently strengthened. As a result, when an individual reports that doing something makes him feel "anxious" or "guilty," the emission of a different (non-punished) response should reduce the anxiety and thus be strengthened (Dollard and Miller, 1950; Mowrer, 1950).

Following the earlier discussion of the side-effects of punishment, it should be remembered that the aversive responses elicited by the punishment also become conditioned to all other stimuli which are present—for example, to situational stimuli, including those of a social nature, and to internal stimuli, including those which are response-produced. One further point concerning punishment: Holland and Skinner (1961) and Mowrer (1960a) consider the removal of a positive reinforcer also to have the properties of aversive stimulation. Thus, the removal of a positive reinforcer contingent upon some response may be considered as a punishment of that response.

Mediated Generalization

It was stated in the section on generalization and discrimination that a response which has been conditioned to a particular stimulus will also be elicited by similar stimuli—stimuli which are close to each other on some stimulus dimension. This type of generalization, consequently, is termed primary stimulus generalization to indicate that the basis for this generalization is the similarity of the stimuli involved.

Now that the concept of the response-produced stimulus has been presented it is possible to indicate the conditions under which generalization may take place between two stimuli which have no physical similarity. That is, two stimuli which are unlike in their physical properties may nevertheless be "similar" if they have both been conditioned to elicit the same response.

As an example, a visual stimulus (a flash of light) and a tactual stimulus (a tap to the cheek) are not similar. They are not even on the same physical stimulus dimension, as is shown in Figure 3.17, part A. It would, therefore, not be expected that a response which was conditioned to one of them would generalize to the other. Let us say, however, that they both elicit the same response, perhaps through conditioning, shown as r_x in part B of the figure. In this respect the two stimuli could be considered similar, since the response that both elicit produces a characteristic stimulus, s_x.

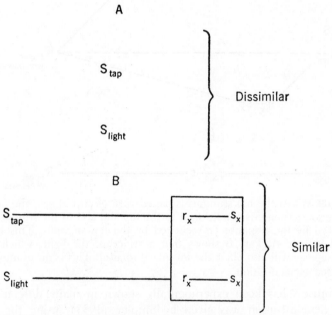

Fig. 3.17. Two physically different stimuli are depicted in part A. These stimuli can become "similar" if they both elicit the same response, however. This is depicted in part B, where both stimuli are shown to elicit the response r_x, which produces the stimulus s_x.

On this basis, whenever either the tap or the light is presented as a CS in an experiment, it would be expected that the response elicited by the UCS would be conditioned to the stimulus used, but, in addition, the response would be conditioned to the stimulus (s_x) produced by the response (r_x) which both stimuli elicit. An example is shown in Figure 3.18, part A. If, for example, the tap stimulus (CS) was paired with an electric shock (UCS), which elicited a finger-withdrawal response, the finger withdrawal would be conditioned to the tap stimulus. In addition, however, the finger withdrawal would also be conditioned to the stimulus (s_x) produced by the response (r_x) elicited by the tap stimulus.

The finger-withdrawal response should now generalize to the flash of light also, mediated by the r_x–s_x that the light elicits. That is, when the light is presented it elicits r_x. The response r_x produces the stimulus (s_x) that has been conditioned to elicit the finger withdrawal. This type of generalization is depicted in part B of Figure 3.18.

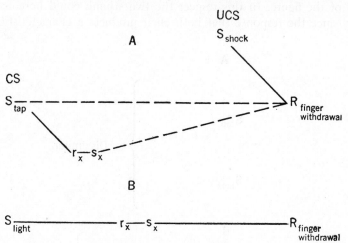

Fig. 3.18. When the tap stimulus is paired with electric shock, the finger-withdrawal response is conditioned to the tap and also to the stimuli (s_x) produced by the response (r_x) elicited by the tap stimulus. This is depicted in part A. Part B shows that a stimulus, the light, which also elicits r_x–s_x, will also elicit the finger withdrawal. This is an example of mediated generalization.

This process has been experimentally shown in many different ways. A clear demonstration was given by Shipley (1933), using the stimuli involved in the above example. He made sure that the light stimulus and the tap stimulus both elicited the same response by pairing the two in a respondent conditioning process with the light as the CS and the tap as the UCS. The tap elicited an eye-blink response which was conditioned to the light. Thus, in the manner depicted in part B of Figure 3.17, both the light and the tap stimulus elicited the same response, the eye-blink. The former elicited the response on a conditioned basis, the latter on an unconditioned basis.

In the second part of the experiment, Shipley presented the tap stimulus as a CS along with the UCS of shock to the finger. The finger-withdrawal response was conditioned to the tap stimulus. In addition, the eye-blink

(r_x) elicited the finger withdrawal. This would be analogous to the process depicted in Figure 3.18, part A.

As a result of this conditioning, the light stimulus also elicited the finger-withdrawal response, mediated by the eye-blink response, as is shown in Figure 3.18, part B. The light, when presented, elicited the eye-blink, and this response produced stimuli that elicited the finger withdrawal. This occurred even though the light had never been paired with the shock. In general terms, any stimulus that elicited the eye-blink response would now elicit the finger withdrawal. Stimuli that were on different physical dimensions could be "similar" in this respect. A response conditioned to one of them would be elicited by all of them, mediated by the common eye-blink response. This process is called response-mediated, or just mediated, generalization. As will be shown later, the process is very important in language function.

Response Hierarchies

Even with the elaboration of the chaining of responses, the discussion so far has been concerned with the elicitation of single responses by stimulus situations. Yet learning customarily occurs with greater complexity than that. It has probably occurred to the reader that human behavior is often not so simple that a stimulus situation tends to elicit only one response or one chain of responses. Sometimes the same stimulus situation tends to elicit several responses or chains from the individual.

Due to his past history a person may have tendencies to respond in several ways when he encounters a situation. The individual who goes to a party (considering this as a complex stimulus) where there are a number of people may have tendencies to approach some people, avoid others, dance with some, speak with others, approach the refreshment counter, and so on. The student whose study is interrupted by a call from a friend inviting him to attend a movie is likewise faced (or at least should be faced) with competing response tendencies—studying or attending the movie. The operations through which one situation acquires tendencies to elicit a repertoire of competing responses from an individual deserves further discussion.

To illustrate the principle that seems to be involved here we shall again describe the behavior of a simple organism in a simple situation. If a rat is introduced into an operant conditioning chamber containing a horizontal bar and is reinforced by a pellet of food upon pressing the bar, it will in a short time acquire a strong "bar-pressing response." Let us suppose that the animal is then put into another operant conditioning chamber in which the former horizontal bar requiring a downward pressure has been replaced by a vertical bar which must be pressed sideways. If the rat is reinforced for pushing this bar, the organism will acquire this type of response. If the animal is now put into a special chamber containing two bars, one vertical and one horizontal, he will have two response tendencies to the same stimulus situation. The animal will tend to press one bar down and the other bar sideways. This is schematized in Figure 3.19.

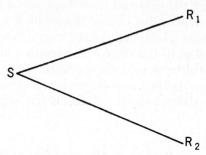

Fig. 3.19. A simple hierarchy of responses. In one stimulus situation, the organism has tendencies to respond in two different ways. The relative strengths of the two responses is indicated by the numbers assigned to the responses: thus, (1) is the stronger response and (2) is the weaker.

Hull (1939) has shown that the strength of the tendency to press each bar is a function of the organism's past history of reinforcement in the two separate stimulus situations. To demonstrate this principle Hull trained his experimental rats to press one bar (say the horizontal) but only allowed them a few reinforced trials. He then reinforced pressing the vertical bar a large number of times in the other box. When both bars were presented at the same time, Hull found that the animals initially performed the response for which they had been reinforced the greater number of times: they pressed the vertical bar.

In a situation that elicits several competing responses, only one of which can occur at a time, the strongest response will occur at first, as is shown by the numbers assigned to the responses in Figure 3.19. Together the responses form a simple hierarchy in terms of response strength.

A response hierarchy is involved each time an individual is confronted with a situation that tends to elicit two or more responses. In such a situation the strongest response in the hierarchy will be the dominant response and will occur first.

Response Hierarchies and "Trial-and-Error" Learning

Such a hierarchy of responses, however, can undergo changes as a result of the conditions of reinforcement in the situation. Hull states in the same experimental paper that "trial-and-error" learning is the rearrangement of the relative strengths of the responses in a hierarchy under the action of the conditions of reinforcement and extinction in the situation. In his experiment the animals were not reinforced when their strongest response (the vertical bar press) was emitted. After a time nonreinforcement weakened the response below the strength of the other response, and the animal emitted the formerly weaker response (the horizontal bar press). Since this response was followed by reinforcement it finally became the stronger response in the situation containing the two response alternatives.

In general, if the dominant response in a hierarchy is not reinforced in the particular situation it will finally extinguish to the point that the next strongest response becomes dominant. The second response will then occur. If it is not reinforced, it too may extinguish to a point where either the first response, or one of the others, becomes dominant. The process of the shift in response strength continues until a response is followed by reinforcement. The reinforcement will serve to strengthen that response and increase its dominance in the hierarchy.

The individual's repertoire of responses when confronting a situation is, therefore, a function of past conditioning in that situation (or similar situations). However, the course of his behavior in the situation will be determined by the conditions of reinforcement and extinction in that situation also. A situation in which a dominant response is extinguished and a weak response is reinforced and becomes dominant has been called trial-and-error learning, although only the principles of operant conditioning are involved. It can be seen, at any rate, that in such a situation the behavior of the organism is not haphazard but instead is a lawful reflection of past and present conditions.

Response Hierarchies in Every-day Life

Most situations humans meet involve response hierarchies. Each situation tends to elicit a repertoire of responses rather than a single response. The response that is elicited will depend upon the past conditions of strengthening for each response. Thus, in order to predict whether or not a given response will occur, we not only need information concerning its reinforcement history but also must know the strength of the other responses the situation tends to elicit.

A child, for example, hears an ice cream man when in the presence of his parents. He responds first by asking the parents for an ice cream cone; next by whining that he is hungry; next by saying he will be a good boy if he can have a cone; and finally by crying. This would be the expected sequence of behaviors if the child had received the greatest number of reinforcements for quiet asking behavior, the next greatest for whining behavior, the next for promising things, and the least for crying. However, if the parents wait until the crying occurs before they reinforce the child by buying the ice cream cone, then crying will be strengthened, and the other responses will be weakened by nonreinforcement. If the effect of this reinforcement is great enough, it may be seen that on future occasions the child cries sooner in such a situation, in other words, the hierarchy has been changed.

Additional Variables Underlying the Order in Response Hierarchies

Which will be the strongest response in the hierarchy, the next strongest, and so on, depends upon the same variables that determine the strength of responses in general. Not only is the number of reinforced responses important; other aspects of the reinforcement contingencies also play a part. For example, other things being equal, it would be expected that a response that had in the past been followed by large amounts of a reinforcer would be stronger than a response reinforced with smaller amounts. In addition, a response which had been reinforced more quickly would also dominate over one for which reinforcements had been delayed.

Response Hierarchies in Language

Hierarchies of responses occur frequently in language behavior in a way that should be mentioned briefly at this time. Whenever two words occur in contiguity with each other there should be, according to the principles already discussed, a tendency for the first word, when presented as a stimulus, to elicit the second word. For example, if the subject were frequently presented with words in pairs it would be expected that the presentation of the first word of the pair would come to elicit the next one. This happens in everyday life repeatedly. Each of us has been presented with the words SALT and PEPPER in close contiguity a large number of times. Because of this experience, it would be expected that if a group of people were asked to write down the first word that the word SALT made them think of, most people would respond with PEPPER. Thus, SALT should function as a stimulus word, and the response of the person should be to write PEPPER. Not everyone should respond with PEPPER, however, for each of us has also had the word SALT paired with other words, though not usually as frequently as the word has been paired with PEPPER. For example, since the word SALT has occasionally been paired with the word SUGAR, when SALT is presented as a stimulus word many people should respond by saying SUGAR. In addition, SALT WATER is a frequent pair in our language experience, and an association would be expected here which will sometimes result in the response WATER when the word SALT is presented as a stimulus. If SALT–PEPPER has occurred more frequently than SALT–SUGAR, which has occurred more frequently than SALT–WATER for an individual, then when presented with the stimulus SALT the individual should respond first with PEPPER, next with SUGAR, and lastly with WATER. This may be considered as an example of a verbal response hierarchy, as illustrated in Figure 3.20.

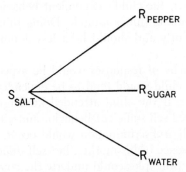

Fig. 3.20. Presentation of SALT as a stimulus will have tendencies to elicit PEPPER, SUGAR, and WATER as responses. As is shown by the position of the responses in the figure, however, PEPPER is the strongest response, SUGAR the next strongest, and WATER the weakest.

Stimulus Generalization and Response Hierarchies

When discussing simple S–R relationships, we stated that a response conditioned to one stimulus situation would be elicited by similar stimulus situations. The same is true in the case of response hierarchies. When a stimulus situation has tendencies to elicit a hierarchy of conditioned responses, a similar stimulus situation will also elicit the hierarchy of responses to the extent of its similarity to the original stimulus situation.

Of course, if the conditions of reinforcement are different in the new situation, the hierarchy of responses will undergo the kinds of changes that were demonstrated in Hull's experiment.

Discrimination and Response Hierarchies

Even though a response elicited by one stimulus will generalize to similar stimuli, a discrimination may be formed if the response is reinforced only in the presence of the one stimulus. In the same manner a discrimination can be formed when the hierarchy of responses elicited by a stimulus generalizes to other similar stimuli.

For example, a mother might tend to reinforce "dependent behavior" more strongly than "self-sufficient behavior." Whenever the child behaved in such a way as to indicate locomotion toward an object, the mother might get the object for the child. In time the child should become strongly conditioned only to indicate moving toward something (either physically or by saying he wanted the object), rather than to get it himself. If the object was not immediately received, the child might cry until it was given. With such a history of reinforcement, it would be expected that in the presence of the mother, the child's dependent behavior would be stronger than his behavior of doing things himself. Doing things himself would be reinforced less frequently and should be a less dominant response in the hierarchy.

This type of hierarchy of responses would be expected to generalize to other people and the child would tend to be dependent when anyone else was present. However, if the child attended kindergarten with a teacher who strongly reinforced self-sufficient behavior and allowed the dependent behavior to extinguish, a discrimination would occur. The child would be dependent in the presence of his mother, but self-sufficient in the presence of the teacher. These principles could underly the common phenomena of mothers saying, "It's so strange. With her my child does things for himself, but when he's at home he expects me to do everything."

Summary

In the previous section on generalization and discrimination, it was stated that several stimuli may have tendencies to elicit the same response. It is also true that one stimulus, or stimulus situation, may acquire the tendency to elicit several mutually exclusive, or incompatible, responses. Each response in the hierarchy can be thought to have a certain strength, based upon its past history of reinforcement (and other variables). Being mutually exclusive, if one response occurs the others cannot simultaneously occur. Thus, in any situation, the strongest response of those in the hierarchy will occur first.

If the first occurring, or dominant, response is not reinforced it will extinguish to some extent each time it occurs. When it has weakened to a point below the strength of the next strongest response, then the second response will occur. If this response is not reinforced, it too will undergo weakening until one of the other responses, possibly the response that was originally dominant, is strongest and occurs. The process of the rearrangement of the various responses in a response hierarchy through the action of reinforcement and extinction is sometimes referred to as "trial-and-error" learning, although, as has been shown here, the behavior is far from random.

Response hierarchies seem in part to account for the flexibility and variability of behavior that is observed in everyday life. It is also true that conditions of reinforcement at one stage of life may be altered at another stage and thus result in the change of response hierarchies.

The principles of generalization and discrimination operate to modify and extend the function of response hierarchies.

Motivation

Our previous discussion of both classical and instrumental conditioning principles has involved an implicit assumption which we are now prepared to make explicit. We have been assuming in each case that a "motivated" organism was involved. It is time to give more operational meaning to the general term *motivation* or to its specific cases, which are called drives.

We have made frequent illustrative use of an animal whose bar-pressing responses were reinforced with food. In so doing, we assumed that the animal would first have undergone a certain period of food deprivation. Without such prior deprivation the food pellets would not strengthen the behavior of pressing the bar. This suggests that in order to predict and control behavior, we must have knowledge of another variable over and above the knowledge of those previously discussed.

For example, one may observe a little boy walk through a park, turn the handle of a drinking fountain, and drink. Knowledge of his past history of reinforced drinking responses would certainly seem important in predicting whether on any specific occasion the boy will stop at the drinking fountain on his way through the park. But information concerning the past history of reinforcement is only one of the variables involved in predicting the boy's behavior. One must also know how long the boy has been deprived of water. If he has just had a long drink—that is, if deprivation is zero—the boy will be unlikely to drink, even if he has been reinforced for the response many times. In fact, he will be less likely to drink than a boy who has had fewer reinforced "drinking responses" but who has been deprived of water or other liquid for some time.

Appetitive Drives

This simple example leads to a definition of a drive. One type of drive can be defined in terms of the *relationship* between (1) the deprivation of a stimulus object and (2) certain lawful effects upon the behavior of the organism so deprived. Several aspects are involved. First of all, it is the operation of deprivation of a stimulus that makes the stimulus an effective reinforcer. In other words, the organism does not consume food unless it has been deprived of food for a certain length of time, and this kind of relationship is involved in a definition of "hunger drive." Deprivation of food makes food a reinforcer, and behavior that is followed by food is strengthened.

It should be stated, however, that deprivation of the stimulus alone does not define a drive. It is important to note that one may deprive an organism of a stimulus and yet find that this has no effect upon the organism's behavior; in other words, the stimulus does not become a reinforcer, and following a response with the stimulus will not strengthen the behavior. For example, depriving a rat of the stimulus of classical music will not result in classical music becoming a reinforcer for the animal. Depriving an infant of books will not make the presentation of a book reinforcing.

Neither is the behavior of the organism alone sufficient to define a drive, for example, the fact that the person eats does not indicate that deprivation has made the food reinforcing. A person might eat when he had not been deprived and food was not reinforcing. Although it would be unusual, a person might eat under coercion; he might also eat if such behavior was strengthened by reinforcers other than food, such as social reinforcement. Although the person might under these circumstances eat lustily, this alone would not indicate that food was reinforcing because of previous deprivation. This type of drive, which will be referred to as an appetitive drive, is appropriately defined only by the relationship between the occurrence of deprivation and the consequent effects of the deprived stimulus upon behavior.

In addition to making a stimulus an effective reinforcer, the operation of deprivation has another important effect upon behavior. It has been said that under deprivation conditions the vigor of the organism's responding increases (Hull, 1943; Spence, 1956).[5] The infant who has not been fed may become more and more active, until it breaks into vigorous squalling. The child who has not eaten breakfast may move around uneasily in his seat just before the noon bell and may be too squirmy to attend to the teacher's instruction. The adolescent who is deprived of a sexual object may be fidgety, that is, more active. These examples may be considered in terms of a deprivation-strength of behavior relationship.

Deprivation of a stimulus object may thus be considered to have these two effects: it may result in more vigorous behavior, and it makes presentation of the deprived stimulus reinforcing. Using this definition, it might be said that there are as many appetitive drives as there are defining operations. For example, depriving an organism of food has the two effects on its behavior just mentioned. These relationships between events define the term "hunger drive." In a similar way a "thirst drive," a "sex drive," and so on, may be operationally defined. This is diagrammed in Figure 3.21.

---

[5] There is not complete agreement on this point, however (see Mowrer, 1960a).

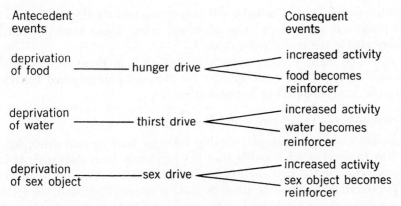

Fig. 3.21. Operations by which the terms "hunger drive," "thirst drive," and "sex drive" may be defined. Each term is defined by the relationship between the observed antecedent and consequent events.

Aversive Drives

There is another operation that has similar effects upon the behavior of organisms and thus comes under the heading of motivation. In the case of appetitive drives, it is the continued absence of certain stimulus objects that affects the organism's behavior. However, certain stimuli have a similar effect upon behavior when they are *presented*. It is this kind of relationship that defines an aversive drive.

For example, if a very intense light is directed into the living quarters of a rat, the general activity level of the animal would be expected to increase. In addition, the operation of presenting the intense light would establish the removal of the stimulus as a reinforcing condition. That is, any response followed by the cessation of the light stimulus would be strengthened.

There are many aversive stimuli in everyday life whose presentation seems to result in increased general activity and whose *removal* acts as a reinforcement. Any intense stimulus—sound waves, light waves, strong tactile stimulation (such as a spanking)—could result in the effects upon behavior necessary to define a drive. For example, it sometimes happens that a radio or television set is turned on with the volume at full blast. The intense auditory stimulus will result in a sudden increase in activity on the part of the organisms within its range of stimulation. A baby will become active and finally begin to cry. A sleeping dog will awaken, become active, and leave the room. The adult will make vigorous movements that bring him to the blaring set to turn it down. When the volume goes down it will be observed that the activity of the organisms decreases to the prestimulation level. The baby will stop crying and the dog will return to its place and go to sleep. The adult will relax. These examples can be interpreted in terms of aversive drives.[6]

Although many primary aversive stimuli such as these are potentially available, people in our culture have for the most part acquired behaviors that effectively dissipate such stimulation.

Relationship between Drive and Learning

Before elaborating the relationship between learning and drive, let us return to another relationship that has previously been discussed. It has already been stated that the frequency with which a response occurs and is reinforced determines the strength of the response. In general, the greater the number of reinforced trials, the stronger will be the response. (Actually, the increase does not continue indefinitely, but tapers off to a small unit increase after a great number of trials.) It is this relationship between reinforced trials and strength of response that defines operant learning.

In addition, appetitive drive has been defined in terms of the relationship between deprivation and general activity level, or strength of response. It might be said more specifically that the greater the period of deprivation, the stronger will be the responses emitted by the organism. This has been referred to as the "energizing" function of a drive.

Thus, it can be seen that these two different types of conditions (drive and learning) both determine the strength of the organism's response. Since they are different variables it is essential that they be distinguished. For example, the vigor of responding has been discussed as an important aspect of human behavior. Our common language has many terms to describe this—hard-working, ambitious, interested, eager, and so on. However, to understand why a person is vigorous in his behavior, the conditions that give rise to his behavior must be known.

For example, a hungry individual may walk home more rapidly than one who has just eaten. But a man who has been reinforced for vigorous behavior of this type in the past will also walk more rapidly than one who has not been so reinforced. Thus, since the individual's past learning history is also important, it might be past reinforcement conditions that are responsible for vigorous behavior rather than the conditions of motivation.

To adequately account for behavior it is necessary to specify (1) the separate effect of the past history of reinforcement (learning) upon behavior and (2) the separate effect of conditions of deprivation (drive)

---

[6] This type of occurrence could also be considered in operant conditioning terms as the result of "escape" training, where the individual has learned certain responses that remove aversive stimuli. The best way of conceptualizing these observations, as in some other cases, remains to be established.

upon behavior. As will be discussed in a later chapter, the topic of human motivation often erroneously describes the strength of the behavior involved. That is, the contribution of the independent variables of learning conditions and deprivation conditions are sometimes not separated as they should be.

The Guiding Function of Drive

In addition to the previous operational definition involving the lawful relationship between deprivation and the two immediate effects upon behavior ("energizing" effects, and establishment of the deprived stimuli as reinforcers), some of the characteristics of drive as an internal process have been considered by psychologists. For instance, it has been stated that drive states have stimulus properties (Hull, 1943; Osgood, 1953; Spence, 1956).

Following this interpretation, it could be said that specific drive stimuli should be capable of controlling specific responses. This could come about in the ordinary process of discrimination learning, with the drive stimulus becoming the S^D. For example, when the organism has been deprived of food, the deprivation, let us say, produces internal stimuli (such as stomach contractions). Let us also say that the situation as well as the deprivation result in the emission of a repertoire of responses. If a response in the repertoire occurs and is followed by food, then the response that has been reinforced in the presence of the drive-produced stimuli should come under the control of those stimuli, in other words, when those stimuli occur again the organism will tend to respond in that particular way.

Let us suppose that a child goes to the kitchen water faucet when deprived of water and to the refrigerator when he has not eaten for a while. This could occur because in the past when he has not eaten and internal "drive" stimuli have been present he has gone to the refrigerator and been reinforced; the drive stimuli subsequently disappear. If other responses had occurred and were not reinforced, the drive stimuli would have persisted, and the child would have remained active. Thus, the drive stimuli would become discriminative stimuli for going to the refrigerator. In the same way, when the child has been deprived of water for some time and has a dry throat and mouth, he has been reinforced for going to the water faucet, not the refrigerator, and so on. After the latter experience, upon awakening at night with a dry throat, the child would immediately go for water.

Figure 3.22 shows the way in which internal stimuli produced by water deprivation might come to be discriminative stimuli for a particular response. The principle depicted corresponds to the common-sense notion that occurrences internal to our bodies also dictate our behavior. That is, behavior seems not to be solely a function of external stimuli. People seem

to say and do things because of internal stimuli also, some of which arise
through deprivation operations.

Water_____S—————————R_____S R
deprivation   dry   taking glass   Water
                                                 throat   to water faucet

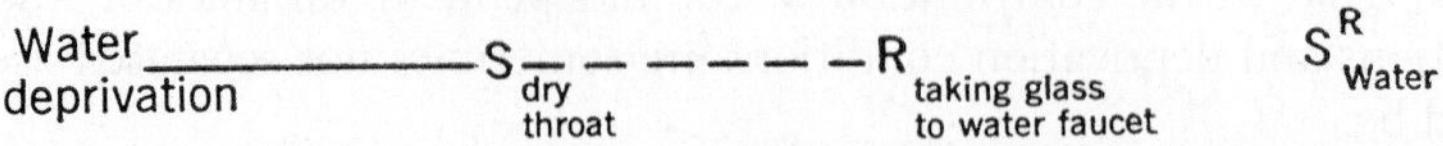

Fig. 3.22. In the presence of a dry throat due to water deprivation the
response of getting a glass and going to a water faucet is strengthened
by the attainment of water as a reinforcer.

Learned Drives

The discussion to this point has dealt with motivation that derives from
the biological structure of the organism. These drives, which do not depend
upon the learning of the individual, are termed *primary* drives to distinguish them from *learned* or *secondary* drives. The conception of learned
drives has been described by various theorists, such as Dollard and Miller
(1950), Gewirtz (1956), and Osgood (1953).

Because individuals in our culture are rarely under primary drive conditions for any length of time, it might be mistakenly concluded that
drive-inducing variables are unimportant to human behavior. It is true
that people in our society are rarely deprived of food for long periods and
are rarely confronted with intense aversive stimulation such as extreme
auditory, visual, or tactile stimuli. On the other hand, the fact that we are
usually under some moderate deprivation or are presented with slight
aversive stimulation is no doubt significant in some of our behaviors.
Moreover, especially at certain ages, deprivation of sexual objects in our
culture is common and produces marked effects upon behavior. In addition
to these effects, a large part of human behavior may be a function of
secondary drives (Dollard and Miller, 1950).

In discussing primary and learned drives, it will be helpful to return for
a moment to the earlier discussion of reinforcers. The deprivation operations necessary to establish a primary appetitive drive must involve certain
types of stimuli that have previously been called primary positive reinforcers. The presentation of unconditioned aversive stimuli is in the same
way necessary to establish a primary aversive drive.

The question thus arises, do the same drive effects on behavior occur
when secondary rather than primary reinforcers are involved? Although it
would be desirable to have more complete evidence in the case of appetitive drives, for our purposes we may consider learned drives in the same
terms as are primary drives, with conditioned reinforcers being involved in
the operations rather than primary reinforcers. It appears that the operations involving conditioned reinforcers, such as deprivation, do have the
effects upon behavior which define the two types of drive.

A study by May (1948) may be cited to demonstrate the formation of a conditioned negative reinforcer and its "energizing" effects upon behavior. First, a group of rats were individually placed in a box in which each side of the floor could be independently electrified. When one side of the box was electrified, the animal became more active and finally went to the other side of the box. Since there was no shock there, the negative reinforcer was withdrawn, and the behavior of running to the other side was strengthened as a consequence. The animals were next individually confined in a box where the total floor could be electrified. In this situation the sound of a buzzer was paired with the presentation of electric shock and thus acquired secondary negative reinforcing properties. Consequently, the presentation of the buzzer would be expected to have the same "energizing" and "guiding" effects upon the behavior of the animals as the primary negative reinforcer, the shock itself. This prediction was experimentally confirmed. The animals were again placed in the divided box, and the buzzer was sounded but no shock given. The rats crossed the box just as they had done when the shock was presented. A control group of animals that had learned to cross the grid to shock but had not later had the buzzer paired with shock did not cross the box when the buzzer was presented. Thus, the experiment demonstrated that a previously neutral stimulus, when paired with a negative reinforcer, could also energize and guide behavior and so define an aversive drive.

Many stimuli in every-day life seem to affect behavior in an analogous manner because these stimuli have in the past been paired with other aversive stimuli, either primary or secondary. Many of these "drive-inducing" stimuli are verbal. That is, people may say things to us which energize our behavior until the verbal stimuli are removed. The wife's critical words energize the husband's behavior and this continues until the negatively reinforcing stimuli are removed. As final examination day approaches, a student's studying behavior becomes more active, as does perhaps his general behavior. These are but two every-day life examples of secondary aversive drives.

There also seem to be learned appetitive drives, although the evidence on this is quite sparse. When a neutral stimulus is paired with a primary positive reinforcer, it too becomes a positive reinforcer. After these operations, deprivation of the conditioned reinforcer should have the same effects on behavior as when the organism is deprived of primary reinforcers.

One result of the deprivation of a secondary reinforcing stimulus should thus be the enhancement of the reinforcing value of the stimulus. An experiment by Gewirtz and Baer (1958) indicates that this is indeed the case. In this study children were introduced to a two-response game of dropping marbles into a machine. Approving verbal responses of the adult experimenter were applied to reinforce one of the two responses. The deprivation history of the children was varied by dividing them into three groups and subjecting the groups to different degrees of deprivation of the conditioned positive reinforcer. One group of subjects, the socially deprived group, played alone in a room for twenty minutes prior to the test situation. A second group of subjects played the game immediately after the school class—this condition was intermediate between deprivation and satiation. The third group of children in the experiment spent the preexperimental twenty minutes drawing and cutting out designs while the experimenter talked to them and approved of their designs and statements in an appropriate manner—this was the group satiated for social contact and approval. On the basis of the foregoing principles it would be expected that greater deprivation would make the positively reinforcing stimulus a more effective reinforcer of the response. This is what did indeed occur. The socially deprived group was most affected by the approval of the experimenter (that is, his approval was more reinforcing), the nondeprived group was next, while the satiated group was least affected. In the authors' words, "Thus, a reinforcer appearing to be typical of those involved in children's social drives appears responsive to deprivation and satiation operations of a similar order as those controlling the effectiveness of reinforcers of a number of the primary appetitive drives" (1958, p. 172).

Although this experiment appears to indicate that deprivation of a conditioned reinforcer increases its reinforcing effect, which is one definition of a drive, the other definitions of a drive are not demonstrated.

Summary

There are two types of drives. The term *appetitive drive* refers to the fact that an organism which is *deprived* of stimuli having positive reinforcing properties becomes more active generally, and more likely to respond in specific ways which in the past have obtained the reinforcers. In addition, the reinforcing value of such a stimulus is increased by deprivation operations.

The term *aversive drive* refers to the fact that certain other stimuli, aversive stimuli, have an analogous effect upon behavior when they are *presented*.

Drives may also be learned. That is, conditioned aversive stimuli when presented seem to have effects upon behavior which define a drive. There is some evidence that there are also learned appetitive drives.

4

Language Development

The Development of Speech

IT HAS often been said that it is language which most distinctly sets man apart from other organisms. In considering an individual's vast history of educational experiences during his lifetime, one could not place too much emphasis upon the role of language. Certainly almost all education is concerned with or based upon language behavior. O. H. Mowrer, in his presidential address to the American Psychological Association, states very forcefully the place of language in cultural transmission.

> . . . [It is] language [that] makes it possible for its users to have *vicarious experience*, to learn through and from the learning of others—and this, as I see it, is the essence of education. Culture, in both its technological and socially regulatory aspects, is what our forebears have been taught and have confirmed or modified on the basis of their own experience, which they then pass on to us, and which we, in turn, transmit to our children and students. While the power of example, as opposed to precept, is not to be underrated, yet there seems to be no serious dissent from the assumption that this continuous, never-ending flow of knowledge and belief which we call culture occurs mainly through the medium of language and that without it, the cultural stream would quickly shrink to the veriest trickle (1954, p. 684).

In general, complex human behavior seems to involve language so predominantly that a central consideration should be given to the manner in which language behavior develops and functions. The following account of language will be derived from the principles of behavior already presented. Then, both the general behavior principles themselves and the principles of language behavior will together form the basis for further extensions into other complex areas of behavior.

In presenting the principles of language, this chapter may appear to be following a developmental approach, commencing with the initiation of speech. Actually, some of the other processes introduced later in the chapter seem to develop concurrently with speech. The separation of the discussion into different sections is simply for didactic purposes—it is not possible to talk about all the principles at the same time, even though the behaviors may develop and function that way.

Early Development of Speech Responses

For the most part, babies during the first month of life do not make vocal sounds that resemble speech; vocalizations include crying, a few squeaks and clucks, and so on. In the first several months, however, the infant will produce varied sounds that have duplicates in human speech.

The extent to which the first behavioral development of this kind is due to maturational factors and the extent to which it is due to the effects of reinforcement history need not concern us here. It is important to note, however, that this type of behavior can be operantly conditioned, even at an early age, under the action of an adult's social response as the reinforcer. A study by Rheingold, Gewirtz, and Ross (1959), using 21 three-month-old infants as subjects, appears to demonstrate this. First, a preconditioning baseline tabulation of vocal responses was made for each infant. During this period the experimenter was in view of the infant but maintained an expressionless face. During the conditioning phase of the experiment the experimenter reinforced vocal responses by smiling, clucking, and lightly squeezing the infant's abdomen. In the third phase of the study, extinction, the experimenter again did not reinforce the speech responses. The results of the study showed that (1) mean vocalizing rate was higher during conditioning than during baseline and higher than during extinction; and (2) mean rate was higher during the second than during the first conditioning day. The authors therefore concluded that operant conditioning of a component of social responsiveness was demonstrated, with an adult's social response serving as a reinforcer.

Thus, it appears that the principles of reinforcement apply to this important human behavior even when the level of development of the behavior is still very primitive. When it is realized that primitive speech behavior is the basic class of behaviors from which more and more precise speech responses may be differentiated, the significance of this conclusion becomes quite clear.

The study also suggests that individual differences in children's speech development must, to some extent, be dependent upon the conditions of reinforcement. To the extent that parents differ in their responses made contingent upon the child's speech responses, it would be expected that the early speech development of their children would differ.

A further implication is thus that the systematic and educated application of reinforcement, even at an early age, could produce earlier and more proficient speech development in the child. If the short period of conditioning applied in the study had a significant effect, the opportunities available to the parent for shaping this type of behavior could produce far larger effects. (See Chapter 10 for further discussion of the application of operant conditioning principles to original language learning in children.)

Sources of Reinforcement

Before discussing further the development of speech, the types of reinforcers that seem to be effective in shaping early vocal behavior should be elaborated. One type of reinforcement is that delivered by the parents. This could involve primary reinforcers such as food, relief from pain, or secondary reinforcers such as the smiles of the parents, the sounds they make, and so on. This was the type of reinforcer presented in the study by Rheingold, Gewirtz, and Ross. When the infants vocalized, the experimenters presented reinforcing stimuli: they smiled, clucked, and squeezed the children's abdomens.

Another important source of reinforcement involved in the child's language development appears to be sounds the child himself produces. Mowrer (1950) and Miller and Dollard (1941) have described the manner in which the sounds produced by the child may be reinforcing and may shape early language development.

> Since the mother talks to the child while administering primary rewards such as food, the sound of the human voice should acquire secondary reward value. Because the child's voice produces sounds similar to that of his mother's, some of this acquired reward value generalizes to it. . . . From this hypothesis it may be deduced that children talked to while being fed and otherwise cared for should exhibit more iterative and imitative babbling than children not talked to while being rewarded (Miller and Dollard, 1941, p. 277).

In the terms that have been developed in the preceding chapters, the parents' voices become conditioned or secondary positive reinforcers because these sound stimuli have been paired with other positive reinforcers. The principle of stimulus generalization is also important here. Since the child's voice varies along many of the same stimulus dimensions as do the voices of the parents, acquisition of secondary reinforcement value by the parents' voices should generalize to the sound produced by the child's own vocal responses. On this basis it would be expected that a response on the part of the child which produced a sound in some way similar to sounds produced by the parents would be strengthened and would occur more frequently.

Further Developments in Early Speech

On the basis of recordings made of a child's vocalizations during the first year of life, Osgood (1953) has concluded that infants make ". . . all of the speech sounds that the human vocal system can produce, including French vowels and trills, German umlaut and guttural sounds, and many that are only describable in phonetic symbols. This is in flat contradiction to the notion that the infant gradually 'becomes capable' of making various sounds" (p. 684). Evidently present in the infant are the structures and muscular flexibility with which he can produce many different sounds— many more than he will eventually make habitually.

Even though the infant may make all types of speech sounds, as development proceeds the frequency of emitting particular sounds undergoes a change. The child's vocal behavior becomes increasingly like the vocal behavior of the adults in the child's environment (Irwin, 1948, 1952). Sounds like those produced in his language environment increase in frequency, and sounds that do not occur in his language environment drop out—even though these sounds may be dominant in a different language community.

Although it is important to describe the course of language development, it is even more important to emphasize the variables that control this process. In the present case, the principles whereby certain sounds may become conditioned reinforcers seem to be relevant. To illustrate such an explanation, consider a child raised in an English-speaking home. The language environment of such a child would consist of syllable sounds like BA, MA, DA, KEE, LO, FOO, and so on. These sounds would occur frequently in the speech of the parents and in the presence of positive reinforcers administered by the parents; the sounds would become conditioned positive reinforcers. In this manner, therefore, vocal responses by the child that produced similar sounds would immediately be reinforced. However, a child raised in a situation where these sounds did not occur in the presence of positive reinforcers would not be reinforced when he produced such sounds, and the responses involved would not be strengthened. (See Mowrer, 1952, for a fuller discussion of the acquisition of speech through the conditioned reinforcing properties of sounds.)

Thus, it may be concluded that the child emits a very extended class of speech responses. The early development of speech consists of the differential reinforcement of certain members of this class; some of these speech responses may be reinforced by other people and some by the sounds they produce. This has the effect of differentiating these response members out of the more general class of vocal responses.

By the age of five to seven months, after a series of such differentiations, the child's speech consists of syllables more and more like the syllables that occur in adult speech in that language community. This type of verbal behavior is called babbling. Many of the sounds produced by the vocal responses of the child at this time approximate word and phrase responses emitted by the parents. An example of syllabic babbling observed by Shirley (1933), which is similar to a phrase probably said frequently by parents, is the response AWOOH–AWAH, a good approximation of ARE YOU AWAKE? The development of this sound as a reinforcer for the child could easily occur. The parent might make such sounds as he approached the child's crib. The sight of the parent is a strong positive reinforcer, since it has been paired with many primary reinforcers. As a consequence, the contiguous occurrence of this particular speech sound and the sight of the parent would make this sound especially reinforcing (Osgood, 1953, p. 688).

It is interesting to note that deaf children do not progress into the babbling stage of vocal development. This would be expected on the basis of the previous analysis. Since the deaf child is not sensitive to auditory stimuli, speech sounds cannot become conditioned reinforcers. Thus, vocal responses of the deaf child that sound like those of its parents will not be strengthened in this manner.

Progression from the babbling stage to the development of the first few speech responses appropriately emitted involves continued differentiation of the class of babbling responses; in other words, the speech of the normal child develops through successive approximation to the point where the sounds he produces are quite like the sounds produced by adults. When the child finally begins to utter its first clearly recognizable words in the proximity of the parents there is customarily immediate and strong reinforcement, and the child's verbal behavior enters a new phase of more rapid shaping. At this point the parents' direct and immediate reinforcement of speech responses probably assumes a more important role in the shaping of the child's speech than the self-reinforcement provided by saying words like those of the parents—although the latter type of reinforcement still continues to be effective. The parents, as well as other members of the verbal community who have contact with the child, may now become more attentive to the speech responses of the child and reinforce the approximations to English words. Speech responses like WAHWAH may be reinforced with a drink of water, and DA may be reinforced by the presentation of the child's toy dog. In this manner, a rudimentary repertoire of speech responses can be further differentiated out of the large class of vocal responses formerly made by the child.

Shaping of Speech through Successive Approximation

However, WAHWAH, WAHDA, WATA, WATAH, and so on, are not examples of the precise speech sound WATER made in the English speech community. Although the parents may reinforce these other speech responses, they also recognize them as somewhat sloppy. Further successive approximation under several types of reinforcement acts to gradually shape the speech responses of the child to more and more precise duplicates of adult speech.

If, when the first approximations to the sound WATER are made, the parents reinforce these responses, a general class of verbal behaviors whose members may differ in a number of ways or combinations is strengthened. This is probably a most important function of the parents' direct and immediate reinforcement—making more frequent those classes of verbal responses that grossly approximate English equivalents. Finer shaping of these classes through differentially reinforcing only some of the responses is probably not often done by the parents, although such a method could prove to facilitate this stage in a child's speech development. Most parents do not withhold the drink of water for certain words in the class and give the water only upon the better pronunciations. However, the same effect is achieved when, because of his own training, the parent can respond more quickly to the better speech responses of his child. This means the child is reinforced more quickly for his better responses, and the sooner the reinforcer follows the response the greater the consequent strengthening. Immediate reinforcement, for example, of the better WATER-responses in the class and somewhat delayed reinforcement of the less standard responses would greatly strengthen the precise response and yet maintain the whole class in sufficient strength.

The process of differential reinforcement of better verbal responses in a class can probably be attributed to other people as well as the child's parents. The parents become familiar with the child's idiosyncratic verbal responses and may tend to reinforce the poorer responses in the class as well as the better responses. However, adults or other children, less familiar with the child's speech, may not respond at all to his grosser verbal responses and may thus reinforce only the better pronunciations. For example, if when the child says WOOK to the parent, the parent turns and looks at the child, this verbal response is reinforced. However, when the child emits this response in the presence of the children next door, he may well be ignored. Only when his verbal response more closely approximates the English equivalent do the children reinforce his behavior by looking at him. WAHWAH may immediately produce water in the home, but when the child is visiting it results in a greater delay in getting water than would the response WAHTA, WAHTAR, or WATER. When the child emits a verbal response and is asked WHAT DID YOU SAY, reinforcement is postponed and a further response is required; this verbal response thus receives less strengthening than one to which the listener immediately makes an appropriate response. The fact that a question such as WHAT DID YOU SAY? is nonreinforcing can easily be seen in the "emotional" responses often displayed by adults as well as children following such a reply.

Experimental Demonstrations of Continued Shaping of Speech

Thus, more and more precise classes of speech responses may be gradually shaped up through successive approximation until the child readily emits the speech units involved in everyday language, in other words, finally acquires a repertoire of correct speech responses. Once these units of speech have been developed, the conditions of reinforcement continue to operate, shaping speech in various other ways. A number of studies have shown, for example, that already formed speech responses in adult subjects may be manipulated through differential reinforcement.

The general method for studying the conditioning of verbal behavior in humans was used first by Greenspoon (1950). In this method the subject was given simple instructions to say different individual words and not to use sentences, phrases, or numbers. The experimenter then proceeded to reinforce only certain classes of word responses, which consequently became more dominant. For example, plural noun responses were reinforced by the experimenter saying MMM–HMM and this increased the subject's frequency of emitting responses in this class. The subjects were conditioned without becoming aware of the relationship between their verbal behavior and the reinforcement conditions.

It has been shown that various classes of word responses are subject to operant conditioning, in other words, that following a word response with reinforcement, as in the Greenspoon experiment, will increase the strength of other word responses in the class. Continued reinforcement of the various word responses in a class will increase the frequency of emitting those word responses. This has been done for travel words and living-thing words (Wilson and Verplanck, 1956), animal words (Ball, 1952), action words (Wickes, 1956), and so on.

In a somewhat different method, Cohen, Kalish, Thurston, and Cohen (1954) operantly conditioned the use of I and WE pronouns in composing sentences. The experimenter in this study presented the subject with a card on which was printed six personal pronouns and a verb. The instructions were to compose a sentence using one of the pronouns and the verb.

Use of certain pronouns was operantly conditioned by following the sentences that included these pronouns with the reinforcement of the experimenter saying GOOD.

Using points as the reinforcer, Verplanck (1956) has shown that certain speech responses may be strengthened in an experimental situation through the process of successive approximation. He states,

> Verbal behavior is readily conditioned. . . . Almost invariably, in this case, shaping is necessary unless S has been instructed to "say words," or unless the verbal response is saying numbers, such as "two," "twenty-five," and so on. When E shapes verbal behavior he should pre-select verbal responses that can be unequivocally identified in a stream of language, as for example, saying *"aunt," "uncle,"* or *the name of any member of a family*, or *saying names of books and authors* (even in a particular field, as E chooses). By reinforcing sentences containing these words, E achieves control of a topic of conversation. . . . The E may also bring S to say, and to say repeatedly, particular quasi-nonsense sentences, such as: "I said that he said that you said that I said so." The Ss may be conditioned to count, to count by threes, or backwards by sevens, and so on, when shaping is used (p. 76).

To illustrate the process and the principle involved the procedure could be characterized as follows. If the experimenter decided to condition the subject to say words referring to a member of the subject's immediate family, the experimenter might start out by reinforcing any verbal behavior of the subject. When this class of behaviors had been sufficiently strengthened so that it occurred frequently, the experimenter could commence the successive approximation. He could begin gradually reinforcing two subclasses of word responses, one subclass having to do with people and the other having to do with home. At the same time, he could gradually start withholding reinforcement when the word responses were too deviant from those he finally wanted to condition. Raising the class of word responses involving people as well as the class involving things about the home would raise the probability that the subject would emit a "relative" word response. Reinforcement of this response upon its emission would raise its strength, as well as the strength of all words in the "relative" subclass, and they should all occur more frequently. By differentially reinforcing these responses and, finally, the "close relative" responses, the final subclass could be made the most dominant, and the subject's conversation would involve primarily those word responses.

Figure 4.1 shows the cumulative number of responses for a subject who was conditioned to name book titles or authors. As the figure indicates, successive approximation was necessary to bring about the emission of the correct response; once the response occurred, continuous reinforcement of the response ensued. The curve shows a decidedly upward slope at this point, and the rate of emitting the correct response was maintained until extinction was commenced.

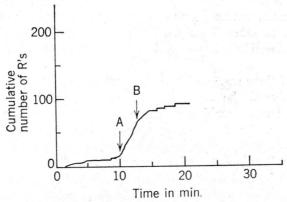

Fig. 4.1. Cumulative number of responses for a subject conditioned to name book titles or authors (adapted from Verplanck, 1956, p. 76). Successive approximation was given to point A, then continuous reinforcement to point B, where extinction was introduced.

Formation of Verbal Discriminations

Matching

In addition to the procedure of gradual successive approximation through differential reinforcement, there is another process involved in the development of precision in speech. Conditions are arranged so that the child learns to "match" his behavior to that of others—or, more precisely, to match the stimuli his responses produce to the stimuli produced by someone else. Basically, the principles involved in matching behavior are stimulus discrimination and the conditioning of reinforcers.

It will be remembered that a response reinforced in the presence of a particular stimulus will come under the control of that stimulus. That is, the organism will discriminate the particular stimulus from other similar stimuli and will respond only in the presence of that one. For example, Ferster (1960) has shown that pigeons can be conditioned to peck a key which matches another key in color. It would be expected that on the basis of this type of training, matching stimuli would become conditioned reinforcers as well as S^Ds. It should be possible to establish a variable stimulus and a standard stimulus such that a matching of the variable stimulus to the standard would constitute an S^D and a missmatch an S^Δ.

In addition, if a rat was reinforced when two white circular forms of equal size were presented and not when one of the forms deviated from the other in size, the animal would soon discriminate two matching circles from two nonmatching circles. In fact, if presented with a device constructed so that the variable circle could be adjusted by the rat himself, he could be trained to adjust the variable circle until it equaled the other one by presenting reinforcement only when the rat had adjusted the circles to match one another. Thus, the rat should be able to learn to match a stimulus produced by his own responses to a stimulus produced by someone else.

In both of these suggested types of training, the visual stimulus of the equal circles would be expected to become a conditioned reinforcer because the organism would receive reinforcement in the presence of this stimulus. Thus, after this training it would be expected that it would be reinforcing for the organism to match the circles, even if no other reinforcement was made contingent upon the act.

It seems that children normally learn to match their speech responses to the speech responses of others in an analogous manner. When the parent states, SAY WATER, a response which produces a sound like that made by the parent is reinforced immediately. If a different sound is emitted, however, the request is repeated and reinforcement delayed. In other words, in the presence of matched imitated sounds, one of which he has produced himself, the child receives reinforcement—but no reinforcement is forthcoming in the absence of matched sounds. It is suggested that the child thus comes to discriminate matched from unmatched sounds.

This process as described would mean that each new word the child became able to match would involve an elaborate conditioning process. This process of successive approximation could be short-circuited, however, if the child had already acquired the necessary response *units* under the control of the appropriate speech sound.

An analogy for this type of training may be seen in the suggested example of the rat producing matching white circles of equal size. It would be expected that not only could matched circles become reinforcing for the animal, but the specific responses involved in producing the matched stimuli could come under the control of the stimuli themselves. For example, under the action of the reinforcement, the rat could come to make one type of response if the variable circle was smaller than the standard, and another type of response if the variable circle was larger than the standard. That is, in time, the disparity of the stimuli would immediately elicit the response appropriate to the direction of the disparity.

In a similar manner, it would seem that the child learns many matching responses in units so that later the successive approximation required in the original matching training is no longer necessary. Skinner (1957) calls these discriminated verbal behaviors "echoic" responses.

An echoic repertoire is established in the child through "educational" reinforcement because it is useful to parents, teachers, and others. It makes possible a short-circuiting of the process of progressive approximation, since it can be used to evoke new units of response upon which other types of reinforcement may then be made contingent. The educational reinforcement is usually supplied with the aid of . . . *Say* "X" where a listener, becoming a speaker, is reinforced if his response yields the sound pattern "X" (p. 56).

Echoic behaviors seem to be capable of division into units smaller than a whole word. That is, having learned to discriminate the various vowel and consonant sounds and to make responses that produce those sounds, the child is then prepared to learn new word responses simply on the basis of matching the sound produced by an adult. Thus, the child, when told SAY DAUGHTER, will be able to do so more quickly if he has already been trained to match his responses to the sounds /D/OG and W/ATER/ produced by adults.

The first echoic operants acquired by a child tend to be fairly large integral patterns, and they are of little help in permitting him to echo novel patterns. A unit repertoire at the level of separable "speech-sounds" develops later and often quite slowly. Small echoic responses may be reinforced by parents and others for the express purpose of building such a repertoire. The child is taught to repeat small sound-patterns such as *ä*, *sp*, and so on. Such a basic echoic repertoire may be acquired at the same time as other forms of verbal behavior or even larger echoic units. The child may emit responses as large as syllables, words, or even sentences as unitary echoic operants. For help in echoing a novel stimulus, however, he falls back upon the single-sound repertoire. . . .

An educational program which emphasizes minimal correspondences between verbal stimulus and verbal response is not necessary in developing a basic echoic repertoire. Minimal echoic operants seem to become functional as a matter of course when larger correspondences have been set up. Having acquired a dozen complex echoic responses all of which begin with the sound *b*, the child may correctly echo a thirteenth pattern which begins with *b* to the extent of beginning the larger response with *b* also. When this happens, we must recognize the functional independence of an echoic operant as small as *b* (Skinner, 1957, pp. 62–63).

After the various response units have been formed, and matching has become reinforcing, it will be easier for a child to be helped in developing precise speech by the "coaching" given to him by adults and other children who have more precise speech. When the child has emitted some speech response and has been instructed in a more precise pronunciation, it will be reinforcing for him to repeat the word. The closer the match, the more the response will be reinforced.

As an aside, it may be of interest to note that people differ with respect to their ability to discriminate slightly different speech mannerisms and to match their own speech to that of others. Some people are said to be very sensitive to slightly different speech mannerisms and can imitate many different types of speech well. It would seem that, in part at least, these differences are due to different opportunities for hearing diverse types of speech as well as to the different training with respect to discriminating and matching these speech sounds. In general, a child reinforced gradually for closer and closer approximations to adults' speech would finally speak more precisely. In addition, however, this child would be more sensitive to differences in speech sounds than one who had not undergone such precise training. (See Skinner, 1957, for a discussion of mimicry in terms of echoic behavior.)

The principle of discrimination learning is involved further in language development, however. Acquisition of speech includes not only the development of speech responses, but also the emission of these responses under appropriate stimulus conditions. In order to present the different principles clearly, the process of shaping correct speech responses was separated from the processes involved in the emission of these responses at the proper time and place—that is, the processes whereby speech comes under the control of the appropriate stimuli. Actually, the child is learning both simultaneously. He is trained to make "good" speech responses at the same time that he is trained to respond only under certain circumstances. The proper circumstances for emitting speech responses are of several types, which will be discussed separately in the next two sections.

Verbal Behavior under Environmental Control

Skinner (1957) has described in detail the manner in which speech responses may come under the control of an environmental stimulus. The principle involved is that of discrimination.

When the child first says DADDY, or an approximation, the child's parents generally reinforce this response, whether or not the father is present or the child is looking at the father. This experience strengthens the response DADDY, but in the presence of many different stimuli. The response is thus not under specific stimulus control. The child may say DADDY when the mother is caring for the child, when other adults and children are present, and so on. Once this speech response has been strengthened to the point where it occurs frequently, even to inappropriate stimuli, the discrimination training customarily starts. Reinforcement does not occur when the child says DADDY in the absence of father. When, however, the child says DADDY in the presence of the father, the father may go to the child, look at the child, or emit some such response; at any rate, the child's response is consequently reinforced.

At this point the response still might not be precisely under the control of the appropriate stimulus. For example, it might be found that the child, because of its previous training, says MAMA in the presence of mother and DADDY in the presence of father but also says DADDY in the presence of stimulus objects similar to father, such as other males with their characteristic attire. For example, a salesman calling in the afternoon, when father usually comes home, may be greeted by the child's response DADDY. This is, of course, an illustration of the simple principle of stimulus generalization.

The child will not be reinforced for this generalized response, however, and in due time his speech response will come under the precise control of the stimulus object, father. Skinner calls such a discriminated speech response a *tact*.

> A tact may be defined as a verbal operant in which a response of given form is evoked (or at least strengthened) by a particular object or event or property of an object or event. We account for the strength by showing that in the presence of the object or event a response of that form is characteristically reinforced in a given verbal community (1957, pp. 81–82).

After the basic sounds involved in English speech have increased in frequency and after the child is able, within limits, to produce sounds that match those produced by someone else, rapid vocabulary growth is possible. The mother holds a ball and says BALL. When the child produces a reasonable match by emitting a vocal response while looking at the ball, the mother might hug the child, thus reinforcing the behavior. Later, when the mother holds the ball and says WHAT IS THIS? and the child says BALL or some facsimile, the mother may again reinforce the tact. Later, the father may hand the ball to the child, and if the child emits the response BALL, reinforcement again will follow. (The social reinforcement administered by the parents may, of course, vary widely in terms of frequency as well as type of reinforcer used.)

This response will generalize to other stimulus objects of a similar nature. Sometimes the response will be reinforced, as when the object is another ball; sometimes it will not be reinforced, as when the object is an orange, egg, and so on. Through these experiences the particular vocal response of the child comes under the control of certain stimulus objects in his environment.

Numerous experiences of this type seem to occur. When the child goes on an automobile ride with his parents, for a walk, to the store, and so on, there are many occasions upon which the child looks at an object or event at the same time as the appropriate word is presented. The child is asked to repeat the word, and the response is reinforced. Thus, the child acquires tacts to a variety of environmental events.

For example, in the presence of a moving automobile the child might be told that it is moving. When the child says MOVING in the presence of something moving, the response is reinforced. A moving object thus becomes the discriminative stimulus for that speech response. If an automobile is also a discriminative stimulus for the response AUTOMO-BILE, then in the presence of a moving automobile, the child will tend to emit the response AUTOMOBILE MOVING, or some such statement. Through this training the child may be thought to learn both simple and complex speech responses to many events.

The child may also learn to tact various actions of other organisms in a similar manner. In the presence of certain visual and auditory stimuli occurring when father is angry, such as scowling facial expressions or a loud voice, the child may be told DADDY IS ANGRY, and reinforcement follows if he repeats ANGRY. In this way the child would be operantly conditioned to make the appropriate speech response in this particular stimulus situation. Other verbal responses will ordinarily be conditioned in this manner to other stimulus situations that involve various postures and movements of people and animals.

The learning of tacts seems also to be carried on in great detail in ordinary language training. Although at first reinforcement may follow upon saying AUTOMOBILE in the presence of the total stimulus object, eventually reinforcement may be made contingent upon emitting the appropriate speech responses with various parts of the object serving as the discriminative stimuli. In other words, the child may be put through very detailed discrimination training in the presence of subaspects of the total stimulus. The acquisition of each new speech response involves the same principles.

The detail with which the discrimination of verbal behavior takes place with respect to complicated stimulus objects or events has a great deal of significance, as we shall see in later sections. However, the parallel between the development of verbal discriminations and what was previously described as one activity of science—observation and description—may be briefly noted at this point. In Chapter 2 it was pointed out that sheer detailed observation and description is important to the development of a science. In an analogous manner, detailed training in tacting is important for the scientist. Before he can respond differentially to complex stimuli and to slight differences in such stimuli, the individual must have undergone complex discrimination training. The responses involved in this type of training are usually verbal. Thus, one aspect of becoming expert in a particular field is the acquisition of appropriate tacts to the objects and events with which that field is concerned. The botanist acquires his special repertoire of speech responses to certain objects, as does the biologist or physicist, or the physician or lawyer.

It is also to be expected that a parent or teacher who himself has been trained to respond discriminatively to fine details of his environment will be able to apply finely detailed discrimination training to the child. The child on a hike with the ordinary parent, for example, will receive verbal discrimination training in the presence of trees, bushes, flowers, and so on. The child of the parent whose verbal responses are in addition under the control of different types of trees, etc., as well as the various parts and functions of these stimulus objects, will undergo a greatly expanded form of discrimination training. This child will consequently emerge with a much finer set of verbal discriminations.

It is certainly unlikely that one individual would be capable of acquiring all the tacts which man, through specializing in particular areas, has been able to establish. However, other things being equal, in the formal education of the child a finely discriminated repertoire of tacts to objects, events, and individual and group behaviors is no doubt advantageous. Since one of the functions of formal schooling is to extend this repertoire, the teacher may be considered, in part, analogous to the parent in the preceding example, who is prepared, by reason of his own education, to provide the child with finer and more detailed discrimination training.

Perhaps a word could be said about the amount of detailed training that should be presented to a child in any particular area. If the aim is to instruct the child in general broad areas, with a great deal of flexibility and adaptability, then one would not wish to carry tacting training to a point where specialized training in one area detracted from general language development. It would seem, however, that in most cases children do not approach the full development of verbal discrimination of which they would be capable under the proper conditions.

Verbal Behavior under Internal Stimulus Control

Skinner (1957) has presented in detail the way in which certain speech responses may come under the control of drive-producing conditions. He calls such verbal responses *mands* and defines them in the following manner: "A 'mand' . . . may be defined as a verbal operant in which the response is reinforced by a characteristic consequence and is therefore under the functional control of relevant conditions of deprivation or aversive stimulation" (pp. 35–36). The following discussion utilizes Skinner's concept of mands plus the concept presented in Chapter 3 that deprivation produces internal stimuli which can come to function as discriminative stimuli and control responses, in this case verbal responses.

It was stated in Chapter 3, under "The Guiding Function of Drive," that if a certain response is reinforced in the presence of internal stimuli produced by deprivation, that response will come under the control of those stimuli. As an illustration, it was shown how the responses of finding a glass and pouring some water would be reinforced when the child had been deprived of liquids for some time. In the future, the stimulus of a dry throat would control that response.

It is suggested that speech behavior may also come under the control of this type of stimulus. Using the same example, when the child has been deprived of water and says WATER! in the presence of a dry throat and when this verbal response is followed by the receipt of water, the deprivation-produced stimuli would be expected to gain control of that verbal response—the mand. This is schematized in Figure 4.2.

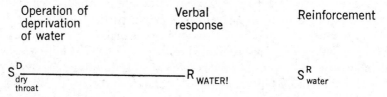

Fig. 4.2. Certain stimuli, such as a dry throat, are elicited by water deprivation. If the verbal response WATER! is made in the presence of these stimuli and is reinforced by the presentation of water, then the stimuli come to control this speech response, called a *mand*.

Many verbal responses seem to be controlled by such internal stimuli. It should be remembered that a long history of such training is necessary before the correct verbal responses come under the control of the appropriate stimulus, according to the principles set forth. Since there are a great many different stimuli produced by deprivations of various sorts and since stimulus generalization is probably involved as well, it would be expected that fine and extended verbal discrimination training must take place for every child. For example, it is likely that deprivation of milk would produce stimuli similar to those which through past experience have come to control the speech response WATER. Thus, there would be a tendency for the child to say WATER when deprived of milk. However, this response will not be reinforced by the presentation of milk. In this manner, a fine discrimination between the stimuli produced by milk deprivation and those produced by water deprivation could perhaps be established.

The manner in which speech responses come under the control of the appropriate internal (drive) stimuli is probably much less time-consuming than the successive approximation training necessary in establishing echoic and tacting responses as presented in previous sections. After speech-matching behavior has been acquired by the child, *mands* may be developed much more easily. For example, the mother who is aware of the child's preceding deprivation conditions may say ARE YOU HUNGRY? when the child is fretful or grouchy. When the child echoes and says HUNGRY, reinforcement follows, and the tendency for the internal stimuli produced by food deprivation to control the verbal response HUNGRY is increased. The same process may occur for innumerable deprivation conditions and the stimuli they produce. The reader can no doubt supply many examples of *mands* and can probably reconstruct the experiences through which they were learned. Much of our verbal behavior consists of *mands* controlled by deprivation operations.

There is an analogous process for aversive drive stimuli. The presentation of aversive stimuli may come to control verbal responses because the verbal behavior has in the past been reinforced by the removal of the aversive stimulation. We learn to say WOULD YOU PLEASE TURN THE RADIO DOWN because in the presence of the aversive auditory stimulation this speech response has been followed by the reinforcement of the diminution of the stimulus. Toilet training of a child seems to involve the same principle. In the presence of a distended bladder or rectum, which produces aversive stimulation, the child is reinforced by being helped to reduce that stimulation if he says POTTY or some similar speech response. When these internal stimuli come to control the child's verbal and overt behavior, then the child is toilet-trained. A fuller account of this training will be given later.

A similar type of training seems to be involved in the development of another type of very important verbal response, "the ability to report internal conditions." Unlike adults, young children, prior to the requisite training, are not able to "tell you what is wrong with them." A young child may cry and fret and in general give the impression that something is wrong, but make no specific speech response. Until the appropriate training has occurred, the many internal stimuli which for an adult control certain verbal responses will not control the child's verbal behavior in that way.

Eliminating crying as a verbal response, an example of a first speech response which seems to come under the control of painful stimuli, especially as the result of an accident, might be the word HURT. In the same manner as described in the discussion of tacting, this single response to a constellation of stimuli will be elaborated into a large vocabulary of speech responses under the control of internal stimuli. When the child comes to the mother and says HURT, the mother will respond WHERE? Although the child has an earache, these stimuli will only elicit the response HURT even though the child may have the speech response EAR in his repertoire. The mother may notice, however, that the child is rubbing an ear and asks, DOES IT HURT IN YOUR EAR? When the child nods, the mother says, YOU HAVE AN EARACHE. The child repeats EAR-ACHE, and the mother's attention and the administration of medicine reinforces the child's behavior, including the speech response EARACHE, in the presence of the appropriate internal stimuli.

Each child normally receives this type of training in the presence of a multitude of internal stimuli. When the child's verbal responses come under the control of specific aversive internal stimuli, it is often possible to reduce this aversive stimulation. Again, the more detailed the child's ability to respond discriminatively to these stimuli, the more appropriate the possible treatment. Ordinarily, fine discriminations will occur to different types of internal aversive stimuli such that discriminated verbal operants as IT BURNS, IT THROBS, IT IS A DULL ACHE, IT IS A SHARP PAIN, and so on, will be formed.

There are many other internal stimuli besides those produced by responses to injury or illness to which the child may be trained to respond discriminatively with different speech responses. In the presence of the stimuli resulting from deprivation, the child will learn to say I WANT SUCH AND SUCH. In the presence of the same stimuli, but also in the presence of failure to obtain the object, the individual will learn to emit such speech responses as I AM FRUSTRATED BECAUSE I CAN'T GET SUCH AND SUCH, and so on. The individual seems to receive training through which the verbal responses, I AM HAPPY, I HATE TO WORK, I LOVE YOU, I AM JEALOUS, I DESIRE THIS, I'M IMPA-TIENT, and so on, come under the control of the appropriate internal stimulation. In all probability this discussion oversimplifies the complex learning involved here. It is suggested, however, that this type of learning is involved in the child's acquisition of verbal statements made to some of his own body sensations.

Another situation in which verbal behavior should come under the control of internal stimuli according to the principles of operant discrimination learning involves the formation of verbal discriminations to one's own overt behaviors. In the same manner that a child may learn to tact an event, he may learn to tact the event of his own behavior—again, on the basis of the stimuli it produces. For example, the child may be prompted to echo the word RUNNING while looking at a boy running and be reinforced when he says the word. After this, the child would be likely to emit the speech response RUNNING in the presence of the visual stimulus of a running boy (or man, girl, dog, for that matter, according to the principle of stimulus generalization). In the same manner, the child may be prompted to emit the response RUNNING in the presence of the stimuli produced by his own running, and the verbal response would thus come under the control of these stimuli. This stimulation would include the internal stimuli produced by the rapid muscular and tendon movements, as well as external stimuli such as visual stimuli.

The child will normally learn verbal discriminations to many of his movements; for example, in the presence of the stimuli produced by his lifted arm, he will have some tendency to say I LIFTED MY ARM. Such discriminations may be formed far past the point usually required under average circumstances, although normally this requires a specially trained parent, coach, or teacher. We would find, for example, that an expert diver, ballet dancer, boxer, or violinist would have a repertoire of discriminated speech responses to different movements that are much more finely detailed in certain ways than are the responses of people in general; these discriminations would also differ from one of these experts to another. These discriminations, as we shall see later, may be very important in the further learning of the individual.

The developing child will learn speech responses not only to the stimuli produced by specific movements, but also to the complex stimuli of various kinds produced by certain of his own complex acts. For example, if a child strikes another and the other child cries, an adult may respond with YOU SHOULDN'T DO THAT and prompt the child to repeat the phrase I WAS MEAN, I SHOULDN'T DO THAT, reinforcing the child upon the emission of that response. In this way a child seems to learn speech responses to his own behavior and its effects upon others. That is, the stimuli produced by his own behavior and the behavior of those he effects will come to control certain speech responses. The individual thus learns a whole repertoire of verbal responses descriptive of his own behavior and the responses of others to this behavior. In various situations the child learns to say I WAS MEAN, I WAS KIND, I WAS AMUSING, I WAS SUCCESSFUL, I BEHAVED LIKE AN IDIOT, I WAS SOCIABLE, and so on.

These are only examples of the types of stimuli that are thought to come to control particular speech responses of the individual according to learning principles. They are so common that it could be said that this discussion belabors the obvious. However, there are practical reasons why it is important to understand that these discriminations which are "so much a part of us" appear to come about only through a long and gradual process of detailed training. Common-sense knowledge does not tell us how these speech responses come under the appropriate stimulus control. And, without knowledge of the principles and processes involved, it is not possible to systematically effect the training.

In addition, these verbal responses enter significantly into other behaviors of the individual and help determine the individual's adjustment. In order to understand how language functions in this manner, it is necessary to understand thoroughly the development of the specific behaviors involved.

Discrimination of Speech Responses
to Visual Verbal Stimuli

It is important that speech responses be brought under the control of appropriate external and internal stimulation. In addition, it is very important that speech responses come under the control of one particular form of external stimulus—appropriate visually presented verbal stimuli. In Skinner's terminology this is called *texting*. A textual response is a speech response under the control of the appropriate visually presented verbal stimulus. The closest common term to this is *reading*.

Textual behavior is formed in a manner similar to that involved in learning a repertoire of speech responses to other types of stimuli. Ordinarily, however, by the time training in textual behavior commences the individual has acquired the speech responses involved and is able to match his speech responses to the prompting of the person guiding the instruction. Thus, a simple model for training a textual response might be to present the written verbal stimulus to the child, say the word aloud, and have the child emit a response that matches the sound—an echoic response.

For example, let us say that the word *dog* is presented to the pupil or group of pupils, and the teacher says DOG. The pupil responds by repeating DOG while looking at the word stimulus. Later, the stimulus word *dog* is presented, and the pupil says DOG with no prompting. When the visually presented stimulus word elicits the appropriate speech response the child is said to be able to read the word. Figure 4.3 shows this process.

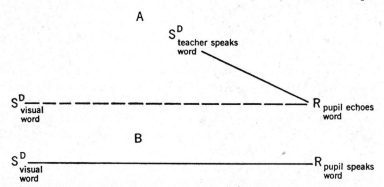

Fig. 4.3. In the presence of a visual word stimulus the student is prompted to say the word by the teacher, as depicted in part A. Following a number of such trials, the pupil responds with the appropriate word to the visual stimulus in the absence of the teacher's prompting. This may be called *texting* and is shown in part B of the figure.

Textual word responses may be acquired in units finer than whole words, either through the practice of the child or through formal training (see Skinner, 1957). The units of which stimulus words are composed will come to control unitary speech responses of which word responses are composed. The child will come, under similar circumstances, to emit the correct syllabic speech response in the presence of the syllabic units and single letters of which the words are composed. When this type of finer discriminative control of textual behavior has been conditioned, the acquisition of speech responses to novel stimulus words may take place. That is, the pupil is capable of self-learning of a textual response if he is already familiar with the auditorily presented verbal stimulus. By responding successively to the syllables of the stimulus word he finally makes the total speech response. Then the total speech response will be under the discriminative control of the whole stimulus word.

An example of the acquisition of a total speech response when the units of that response are already discriminated responses occurs in "sounding out" a new word, such as *familiar*. As shown in Figure 4.4, to the syllabic units of the word, the child makes the correct speech responses. At the end of the sequence the child hears the word FAMILIAR, which matches an already learned vocal response. This matching sound constitutes the reinforcement, so that finally the entire word response comes under the control of the word stimulus as a single unit.

Novel speech responses may also be acquired through responding successively to the syllabic units in a stimulus word. In this manner the novel speech response will be under the control of the appropriate visual stimulus word and would be one of the speech responses in the repertoire

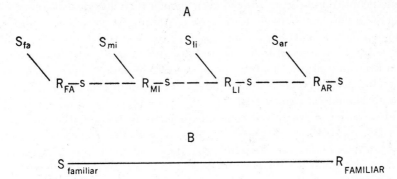

Fig. 4.4. In part A the child makes the correct speech responses to the various syllabic units of the printed word *familiar*. Following this sequence the child hears the already learned verbal response FAMILIAR and thus is reinforced. Therefore, the entire word response, as a unit, comes under the control of the word stimulus. This is depicted in part B.

of the individual. However, the word response would not be under the control of other stimuli and would not, consequently, occur in appropriate circumstances; nor, as we shall see, would such a word be meaningful.

Comparison of Speech and Reading Development

Interesting comparisons may be made between the learning of verbal responses to nonverbal stimuli and the learning of those same responses to visual verbal stimuli, in other words, texting. The same principles seem to be involved in both types of learning; both are essentially problems of establishing verbal responses under stimulus control. Virtually every intact individual acquires adequate speech behaviors, yet there are many individuals who, although they display adequate vocal behaviors, are seemingly unable to learn to read, or do so only with great difficulty.

It is commonly suggested that such uneven development is a result of some biological defect, such as neurological impairment. However, unless there is some independent observation of a defect, this type of conclusion may simply be *ad hoc*. If the child is capable of acquiring differential speech responses to ordinary visual stimuli in a normal manner, then it should be possible for visual verbal stimuli to also come to control the verbal responses. There is certainly no obvious difference in the stimuli themselves, since both are visual and both are complex. Ordinary language behavior requires that verbal responses be under the control of very subtle aspects of one's stimulus environment. The same thing is true of reading, that is to say, the stimuli are no more complex.

On the other hand, on the basis of the present analysis, it would seem that, exclusive of personal defect, there are some very real reasons why some people do not learn to read even though their speech development is otherwise normal. Actually, for everyone, learning to read is accomplished only with great difficulty in comparison to the acquisition of speech under the control of other stimuli. To indicate the reasons, several important characteristics of the acquisition of speech responses, and the process whereby speech responses come under the control of external and internal stimuli should be emphasized.

First, as has been implicit in the previous discussion, the process of speech acquisition is very gradual. Beginning with the strengthening of the general speech class in early infancy, more and more precise speech responses are gradually shaped up until the exact word responses of the language community occur. These responses are only gradually brought under the control of the appropriate stimulus objects in a long program of training. Learning sessions occur intermittently and are dispersed throughout the day. In addition, new objects are introduced over a period of years in building up verbal discriminations.

Secondly, there are strong sources of reinforcement involved. When the child first says WAHTAR the strong reinforcer of a cup of water is presented. When the child says BAYBEE the strong reinforcer of a baby doll is presented. In addition, strong reinforcers are abundantly available in the attention and approval of people in the environment. When the child says LOOK and another child responds by looking, this is a reinforcer for the verbal response.

Thirdly, these strong reinforcers are individually applied, and they are applied immediately following the speech behaviors involved. As has been discussed, it is most important that the reinforcing stimulus be presented quickly after a response has occurred. If no reinforcer is presented, or if the lag is too great, the response will not be strengthened.

Intensity of training in reading.—Comparing these characteristics with those involved in the acquisition of reading behavior, it becomes obvious that the learning of reading would be more difficult for everyone. Unlike speech behavior itself, and speech behavior under the control of other types of stimuli, reading is not gradually acquired in the preschool years. It is customary to introduce training in the acquisition of speech responses to visually presented verbal stimuli only when the child enters school. Although there is some attempt to make this more gradual through the use of nursery schools, kindergartens, and reading readiness programs, in comparison to the learning of speech responses the onset of reading training is sudden and intensive.

This major difference between speech and reading learning has important consequences. For example, intensive periods involving the acquisition, or the performance, of responses may be considered to have aversive characteristics. It has been shown that discriminative stimuli acquire aversive characteristics after an extended period of "working" in the presence of the stimuli, even when the responses involved are reinforced. That is, another response which will remove the discriminative stimulus will be maintained in some strength. Furthermore, the more intensive the "work" is (that is, the greater the ratio of responses to reinforcement), the more aversive the discriminative stimulus becomes (Azrin, 1961).

Naturalistic observations also suggest that the intensive rather than gradual training of reading has aversive aspects. Many children describe school and school activities as "work," and in aversive terms. Although the language learning which takes place prior to school training is just as complex, and in these terms just as difficult to acquire, it is not described as being trying or difficult to the same extent as is formal training. The child does not say that he is having, or has had, a difficult time in learning to speak—or learning his extensive repertoire of discriminated verbal operants.

In addition, to the extent that the school situation is aversive, it will be reinforcing to "escape" the situation. Any behavior that removes the child from the aversive situation will be strengthened. Thus, behaviors such as talking to other pupils, cutting up, doodling and playing quiet games, teasing other pupils, or daydreaming, will be strengthened by providing an escape from the aversive training situation. Of course, it is possible to make the behavior of leaving the situation in these ways more aversive through punishment and, in this manner, maintain good participation in learning. Education in former times utilized these methods.

It would seem, then, that there might be two ways to deal with the problems introduced by so intensive a training program. First, it should be possible to reduce the aversive nature of the onset of formal training by having it introduced considerably more gradually. In addition, the introduction of positive reinforcers into such an intensive program would change the situation in the direction of making it more positively reinforcing. To some extent, both of these developments have occurred in American education. Nursery schools, kindergartens, and reading readiness programs do make the training somewhat more gradual. In addition, an attempt has been made to make learning more gamelike, lifelike, or "interesting" (reinforcing) and less worklike (aversive). These methods have sometimes been identified by the term "progressive" education. Unfortunately, it is well established that the acquisition of reading still forms a problem of training; the corrective measures taken thus far have not been adequate.

Sources of reinforcement for reading in the school situation.—A closer look at some of the sources of reinforcement available in the early school situation will indicate some of the remaining difficulties. To an extent dependent upon the child's past history, the acquisition of a new behavior (learning) may itself become reinforcing. That is, the stimuli produced by studying something and acquiring new "knowledge" (verbal behaviors) or "skills" (motor behaviors) will become secondary reinforcers if positive reinforcers have been frequently paired with them in the past. It is traditionally assumed that this type of reinforcement should be present for all students, witness the old saw, "Learning is (or should be) its own reward." Again, however, this cannot be counted upon. Many children do not have a past history that has made learning itself reinforcing. When this is the case, it is ineffective to simply invoke the plea that learning *should* be reinforcing.

The same thing occurs in making educators and their approval secondary reinforcers. For some children the teacher's attention and approval are strong reinforcing stimuli. Since these are learned reinforcers, the extent to which they function as reinforcers will depend upon the past history of the child. If the child comes from a home that has not paired learning with reinforcing stimuli, where education and educators have not become secondary reinforcers, he would be said to have little "value" for education. The teacher's approval would have scant reinforcing properties in such a case. Unfortunately, many children would be expected to have ineffective histories in this respect.

In addition to the inadequacy of the teacher's approval as a positive reinforcer for some children, there are other restrictions upon the effectiveness of this source of reinforcement. In the school situation, reading training involves a group of children. To a large extent, this makes impossible the presentation of the reinforcement immediately contingent upon the behavior of the individual child. Only when the child recites individually may his behavior be immediately reinforced by other persons, and, of course, only a small proportion of school time will be occupied with the behavior of any one child. Much of the work takes place in group study or group recital where no extrinsic reinforcement is involved.

There are other reinforcers in the school program, such as grades, special privileges, games, recesses, and the approval of other students. In kindergarten the children are provided with toys, snacks, rest periods, television, and so on. These stimuli undoubtedly act as reinforcers for some children. However, these reinforcers are seldom presented contingent upon correct reading behavior, and even when contingent they are not immediately delivered. In addition, most of the available reinforcing stimuli are heavyweight reinforcers that are delivered all at one time, whereas the behavior involved consists of numerous responses, a good proportion of which should be individually reinforced.

The reinforcers available in the school situation may vary from child to child. And for some children there may be only weak reinforcers that are made contingent upon his reading behavior. In addition, there is a "snowballing" effect, since the child for whom there are only weak reinforcers in the school situation learns to read very slowly. Because he accomplishes little he receives less reinforcement contingent upon his classroom performance, and his behavior becomes relatively weaker. It may be concluded that, as compared to speech learning in everyday life, learning to read occurs in a situation much less favorable in terms of the application of reinforcement principles. It would thus be expected that many failures would occur in the development of this vital repertoire of behaviors.

One final point: if positive reinforcers available in the school situation are weak or ineffectively applied, then the behaviors that are prerequisites to the acquisition of reading will not be maintained. To acquire reading behavior the child must respond first by looking at the words and letters and then by making the appropriate verbal responses to the prompts of the teacher. If these prerequisite behaviors, which in everyday terms are called the attention of the child, are extinguished through lack of sufficient reinforcement, then further progress in learning to read ceases. Such a child would not acquire proper reading behavior even though present in class during appropriate training. It would certainly be erroneous to conclude in such a case that the child had some physical defect.

A summary of the important points involved in this section might be as follows. First, the onset of an intensive training program in reading is relatively sudden and may involve a good deal of aversiveness. In addition, there are only weak sources of reinforcement for many children in the training situation. Furthermore, the reinforcers that are available are not made immediately contingent upon the many reading responses involved. Finally, if adequate reinforcement for the child is not available in the reading program, the behaviors that are prerequisites for the acquisition of reading may extinguish. If this happens, progress in learning to read will cease. There will be further discussion of the acquisition of reading in Chapter 10.

This analysis of textual behavior provides several important practical implications for the training of verbal responses under control of visually presented stimuli. In the chapter on educational psychology we shall again deal at some length with both the analysis and its implications for teaching.

Development of Word Meaning

So far the discussion has concerned only the development of speech responses and the manner in which they come to be controlled by stimuli. However, in the development of speech, other processes also are important to the individual's language behavior. For example, in the preceding section it was shown that after the correct speech units have come under the control of visually presented syllables, the child can sound out a new word. In this way the new word may come under the control of the appropriate visual verbal stimulus. However, if this word is entirely new, it will be "meaningless." In our everyday language we would say the child can "read" the word but does not "understand" it.

Meaning is a term, common in our everyday language, that has long been discussed in a nonobjective manner. These discussions amounted to philosophical arguments concerning the term and did not contribute to a scientific understanding of the processes involved in the formation of word meaning. Nor did these accounts describe the importance of word meaning in the operation of verbal behavior. With the growth of a scientific account of human behavior, however, it has become possible to consider meaning in objective terms.[1] Such considerations, founded upon experimentation, have been developing rapidly.

The principles involved in the learning of word meaning appear primarily to be those of classical conditioning, discussed earlier. In classical conditioning an originally neutral stimulus, one which does not elicit a particular response, may come to do so if it is paired repeatedly with a stimulus that does elicit the response. The originally neutral stimulus is the CS, while the stimulus that originally elicits the response is the UCS. The process of classical conditioning, thus, rests upon the repeated pairing of two stimuli, only one of which initially elicits the response.

When we direct our attention to certain aspects of language learning we find an analogous process. Osgood (1953), for example, has stated that the meaning of a word (or sign) arises from the sign being paired with the stimulus object. "A minimal but distinctive portion of the total behavior . . . originally elicited by an object . . . come[s] to be elicited by another pattern of stimulation . . ." (p. 697). Certain verbal stimuli (word sounds) are systematically and repeatedly paired with certain other stimuli. An example might be when the mother says BALL many times as the child gazes at the stimulus object, a ball. The mother also says CAT in the presence of a cat. The mother says NO and forcefully pulls the child away from something or slaps the child's hand. In each of these cases, there is a systematic pairing of two stimuli, one of which is a verbal stimulus.

Let us examine more closely what should occur during these systematic pairings in terms of the principles of classical conditioning. The auditory stimulus NO may be considered a neutral stimulus the first time it is presented with respect to the response of withdrawing one's hand. A slap on the hand, however, may be considered an unconditioned stimulus for hand withdrawal. A few pairings of these two stimuli will result in NO becoming an effective stimulus for hand withdrawal. Later, when the child begins to tug on a television dial the word NO will result in immediate withdrawal—without the support of an accompanying slap. The observer of the appropriate response to the verbal stimulus would say, in common-sense terms, that the child has learned the meaning of the word.

In a similar manner, many words are paired with UCSs that elicit other

---

[1] It should be pointed out here that the following discussions of word meaning are based upon the type of indirect observation discussed in Chapter 3, and the term may be considered a type of intervening variable. Until the characteristics of such a term have been more completely established, the same confidence cannot be placed in the term as in principles or terms derived from direct observations. However, a number of experiments have accrued that through indirect observation seem to be adequately establishing some of the characteristics of the term, and a number of learning theorists use it in their formulations (e.g., Mowrer, 1954, 1960b; Osgood, 1953, 1957).

types of responses; later, the child's response to these words may be described as meaningful. The word BAD, for example, is systematically paired with a variety of stimuli that have in common aversive characteristics. Some of these stimuli are delivered as punishments and elicit crying responses. Other examples of such stimuli are spoiled food and annoying behaviors of other children. In the case of these stimuli the response conditioned may not be as immediately observable as hand withdrawal—at least without the aid of special apparatus. An aversive stimulus customarily results in certain autonomic responses; for example, heart rate, blood pressure, and sweat gland activity (GSR) change when such a stimulus is presented. A neutral verbal stimulus, paired with an aversive UCS, through conditioning comes to elicit these physiological responses. Again, the formerly neutral verbal stimulus will be responded to in a manner appropriate to the stimulus with which it is systematically paired. It could now be said that the verbal stimulus "stands for" the actual aversive stimulus, in other words, means the same thing as does the aversive stimulus (see Osgood, 1953).

An experiment conducted by Staats, Staats, and Crawford (1962) may be used to illustrate this process. A list of words was presented orally to both an experimental and a control group of subjects. These subjects were instructed to learn the list of words. The subjects in the experimental group were given a shock or presented with a loud, harsh sound after each presentation of the word LARGE, which appeared a number of times in the list. These aversive stimuli, as UCSs, elicited a palmar sweat gland reaction (GSR). The control group also received the shock and sound, but never in contiguity with the word LARGE. During this process a record of the subject's palmar sweat gland activity was kept. At the end of this procedure the word LARGE was presented without shock or sound, and the GSR to the word alone was recorded. In addition, subjects were asked to rate the "pleasantness" of the meaning of some of the words presented them in the word list, including the word LARGE. The results of the GSR recordings and the word-meaning ratings indicated that (1) pairing the word LARGE with shock and noise had changed the rated meaning of the word and made it more unpleasant; (2) the procedure also conditioned the GSR response to LARGE; and (3) the intensity of the rated meaning of the word was significantly related to the intensity of the conditioned GSR, in other words, subjects conditioned to respond with a stronger GSR to the word were also conditioned to respond with a more intense unpleasant meaning rating to the word.

The results of this study suggest that word meaning may be classically conditioned in the same manner as other responses, and thus word meaning may be considered a response. In addition, the findings indicate that conditioned autonomic responses may, at least in part, constitute the meaning of a word.

Perhaps other responses may also be conditioned to a word to form its meaning. Many stimulus objects may be considered UCSs in terms of the sensory responses they elicit. For example, a visual stimulus may be considered to elicit a "seeing" response in the individual in the sense that seeing the object is a response. An auditory stimulus may be considered to elicit a "hearing" response, a tactual stimulus to elicit a "feeling" response, and so on.

Several studies (for example, Leuba, 1940; Lipton and Blanton, 1957; Phillips, 1958) indicate that portions of such sensory responses may be conditioned. Skinner (1953) has discussed how sensory responses can come to be elicited by formerly neutral stimuli on the basis of classical conditioning.

> A man may see or hear "stimuli which are not present" on the pattern of the conditioned reflex: he may see X, not only when X is present, but when any stimulus which has frequently accompanied X is present. The dinner bell not only makes our mouth water, it makes us see food (p. 266).

Mowrer (1960b) has also discussed the conditioning of sensations.

> . . . [W]e may confidently assume that the light . . . produces a light *sensation* . . . which is conditionable in the form of a light *image*. Such a reaction, to be sure, is central or "cognitive," rather than overt, behavioral . . . (p. 282).

Thus, as in the example already given, when a mother shows her child an object, such as a ball, and says BALL, this may be regarded as a conditioning trial in the classical conditioning of a meaning response to a verbal stimulus. The ball elicits a sensory response, part of which may be conditioned to the verbal stimulus, becoming its meaning. This is depicted in Figure 4.5. This sensory response can be considered to be only a portion of the total sensory response elicited by the object itself, not a precise duplicate, and this has probably led to the descriptive label *image*.

It is thus suggested that word meaning may be classically conditioned through pairing a word stimulus with another stimulus—specifically, a UCS for some response. Since the conditioned response is the word meaning, it may be called a conditioned "meaning" response. Considered in this manner, it would be expected that the various principles which apply to the conditioning of responses in general would also apply to the acquisition of word meaning, for example, the greater the number of pairings of the word stimulus and the UCS, the stronger the meaning (see Staats and Staats, 1959a).

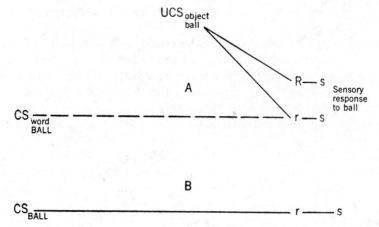

Fig. 4.5. A ball, as a stimulus object, may be considered a UCS for a sensory response (R—s), a portion of which (r—s) may be conditioned to other stimuli. When the word BALL, as a CS, is paired with the object ball, as in part A, the word comes to elicit a portion of the sensory responses elicited by the ball, constituting the meaning of the word. This is depicted in part B.

As was stated earlier, it should be emphasized that the meaning response conditioned to a word stimulus may be different from the total response which the stimulus object itself elicits. For example, a stimulus such as a very hot object may elicit a violent motor response (such as hand withdrawal), while the word HOT, through pairing with the object, comes to elicit only part of the motor response elicited by the object. Although at first the response made to the word may be like that produced by the object, in time the meaning response customarily is considerably reduced and may not be observable.

Osgood (1953) stresses the distinction between the responses elicited by the stimulus object and those finally elicited by the word. Those responses that occur only when the stimulus object is itself stimulating the organism he calls "object-tied," while those that were initially elicited by the stimulus object but can occur without the object's presence are called "detachable" responses. As an example, he discusses the distinction between the motor responses elicited by a hammer as a stimulus object and those elicited by the word HAMMER. "The stimulus-object, a heavy thing having certain visual characteristics and certain tactual and proprioceptive effects, elicits in the young child . . . a total pattern of behavior, including grasping and pounding movements" (p. 697). Of this total pattern, only certain "detachable" responses become conditioned to the word. As Osgood points out, with conditioned motor responses the process of reduction is especially important. ". . . [O]bviously, overt movements of the hands will interfere with other on-going instrumental behaviors and therefore tend to be extinguished. A young child, however, may actually be observed to clench his hand and move it up and down when asked for 'hammer' " (p. 697). The same is true, however, of conditioned autonomic responses and conditioned sensory responses that become the meaning of words; only portions of the total response elicited by the object may be stably conditioned to a word and form its meaning.

It should also be pointed out that a word stimulus may be conditioned to elicit more than one type of meaning response. For example, the word HOT, as described above, would be conditioned to elicit motor, autonomic, and sensory meaning responses through its pairing with a hot object.

Meaning Responses and Speech Responses

Combining this interpretation with some of the language principles already presented, let us look again at the various associations that would be expected to form in the language training of the child. The meaning responses discussed will be sensory responses, since this provides the simplest description. It should be kept in mind, however, that the processes involving motor and autonomic responses are essentially the same.

The first process in this interpretation is that whenever a stimulus object is presented, it elicits a sensory response, part of which is conditionable (see Figure 4.5).

In addition, this sensory response, like any other response, produces a characteristic stimulus, as is also represented in Figure 4.5. Thus, not only may a sensory response be conditioned to another stimulus, but other responses also can be conditioned to the sensory response—or rather, to the stimuli produced by the sensory response.

Both these types of associations would be important in language learning. As has been described, the conditionable components of sensory responses elicited by an object may be conditioned to a word stimulus to form the word's meaning. In addition, speech responses can be conditioned to the sensory responses. Thus, in the process of tacting, a speech response is actually reinforced in the presence of the sensory response (and its stimuli) elicited by the object. This forms an association between the sensory response elicited by the object and the speech response. This is depicted in Figure 4.6.

For example, as shown in Figure 4.7, part A, the mother says BALL as the child observes a ball—that is, makes a sensory response to the ball. Part of this sensory response, $rm_b—s$, is classically conditioned to the word BALL.

In addition, since the mother at other times also reinforces the child's

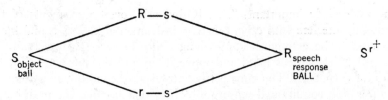

Fig. 4.6. When a child says BALL in the presence of the stimulus object ball and is reinforced, the word BALL becomes conditioned to the stimulus properties of the sensory responses elicited by the ball.

saying BALL while he is responding to the object, an association would be established between the sensory responses to the ball and the speech response BALL. In this way the speech response BALL would come to be evoked by the sensory response, rm_b—s, as shown in Figure 4.7, part B.

Thus, through classical conditioning, the conditionable sensory responses elicited by the ball, rm_b—s, would be conditioned to the speech response BALL. In addition, when the child is reinforced for saying BALL while looking at the ball, the speech response would be conditioned to the same sensory response, rm_b—s. In this manner the speech response, $R_{\overline{BALL}}$s, would

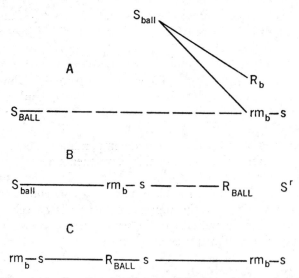

Fig. 4.7. Part A depicts the classical conditioning of part of the sensory responses, rm_b—s, elicited by the stimulus object, S_{ball}, to the contiguously presented verbal stimulus, S_{BALL}. Part B depicts the reinforcement of the speech response, R_{BALL}, in the presence of S_{ball}, which elicits the sensory response rm_b—s. As a result, as depicted in part C, rm_b—s comes to elicit $R_{\overline{BALL}}$s, and $R_{\overline{BALL}}$s comes to elicit rm_b—s as well.

tend to elicit rm$_b$—s, but rm$_b$—s would also tend to elicit the speech response (Figure 4.7, part C).

It could be said that the meaning of a word would through this experience tend to elicit the word response in the child; but, in addition, the word response emitted by the child or by someone else would come to elicit the meaning of the word in the child.

Semantic Generalization

Word-Object Semantic Generalization

From this interpretation of word meaning the manner in which the response to a word comes to be appropriate to the object which the word "stands for" can be considered. This may be thought to occur because the word actually comes to elicit part of the response the object itself elicits. Moreover, on this basis it would be expected that behavior conditioned to a word would generalize to the objects denoted by the words. The interpretation of how experience with words can affect our behavior toward the referents of the words seems important in understanding the part that words, and thus language, can play in the learning history of a human being.

A number of experiments dealing with a phenomenon termed semantic generalization establish a base for this interpretation; later considerations of communication will enlarge upon this base. The experimental facts of semantic generalization studies involve the following: if in an experiment a word is used as a CS and a response is conditioned to it, this new conditioned response will also be elicited by the object referred to by the word. For example, if the word BLUE was used as a CS and a response was conditioned to it, the response would also be elicited, without further conditioning, by a blue light. Since there is no physical similarity between a word and the object it denotes, one cannot explain this occurrence on the basis of primary stimulus generalization.

The conditioning of implicit meaning responses, however, constitutes a basis for semantic generalization. As an example, in the usual training of the child the word BLUE is often paired with blue light emanating from many different sources. As a consequence, it would be expected that part of the sensory response made to the blue light would be conditioned to the word stimulus BLUE. As a result both the blue light and the word BLUE would elicit an identical response. This is schematized in Figure 4.8.

On the basis of this original conditioning any new behavior conditioned to the word would generalize to the light, that is to say, if another response was conditioned to the word BLUE, the response would also be elicited by

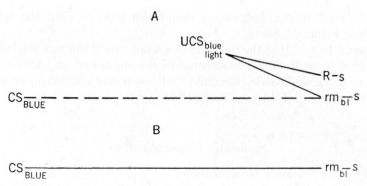

Fig. 4.8. When the word BLUE is often paired with a blue light, as depicted in part A, a part of the sensory response (rm_{bl}—s) made to the blue light becomes conditioned to the word BLUE. This is shown in part B. When this occurs, both the blue light and the word BLUE elicit an identical response (rm_{bl}—s).

a blue object. For example, if the word BLUE was repeatedly presented along with a mild electric shock, the GSR elicited by the shock would come to be elicited when the word alone was presented. This process would actually involve also the meaning of the word, rm_{bl}—s. Each time the word BLUE is presented it elicits the sensory response conditioned to it. By pairing the shock with the word stimulus, the GSR elicited by the shock would be conditioned to the meaning of the word, rm_{bl}—s. This is depicted in part A of Figure 4.9.

Since any blue light also elicits rm_{bl}—s, the blue light would now also elicit the GSR—presentation of the light would elicit rm_{bl}—s, and rm_{bl}—s

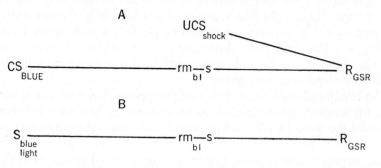

Fig. 4.9. In part A the word BLUE, eliciting the sensory response conditioned to it, is paired with an electric shock, which elicits a GSR. Thus, the stimuli produced by the sensory response (rm_{bl}—s) also come to elicit the GSR. Therefore, when later a blue light is presented, which also elicits rm_{bl}—s, the GSR also occurs; this is depicted in part B. This phenomenon is called semantic generalization.

would elicit the GSR. Thus we can see how the pairing of the word BLUE with shock will result in the autonomic response being elicited by the blue object, through the mediation of the response rm_{bl}—s that both the light and the word elicit. The generalization of the response conditioned to the word to the stimulus object itself is shown in part B of the figure.

Basically, this seems to be one of the primary functions of language: on the basis of experience involving language, the individual comes to respond differently to various environmental occurrences. We see in this example how a stimulus, the blue object, although never paired with the stimulus (shock) that elicits the response (GSR), may nevertheless come to elicit that response. Since the individual responds to the object as he does to the shock, it would appear as if, in the person's experience, the blue object and the shock had been paired with each other. Thus, simply on the basis of experience involving a word, the individual's response to the environment has been changed. (See Cofer and Foley, 1942; and Osgood, 1953 for more detailed accounts of semantic generalization. The significance of this interpretation for understanding communication has been elaborated by Mowrer, 1954, and will be discussed in the next chapter.)

Object-Word Semantic Generalization

In the same manner, it would be expected that the reverse type of generalization would also occur. That is, if a blue object was the CS and a GSR was conditioned to it by pairing it with shock, a later presentation of the word BLUE would also elicit the GSR. The processes involved would be the same. The blue object elicits a certain sensory response, rm_{bl}—s, which has stimulus characteristics. When the blue object is paired with the shock stimulus, the GSR elicited by the shock is conditioned to the "blue" sensory response. Later, when the word is presented it too will now elicit the GSR, mediated by its meaning, rm_{bl}—s, which elicits the GSR.

Word-Word Semantic Generalization

When two words in the same language have the same meaning, or almost the same meaning, we call them synonyms. The concepts of language already presented provide an account of synonymity. A word becomes "meaningful" by being paired with another stimulus that elicits a certain response. Often in our language learning it happens that two or more words will be systematically paired with the same, or similar, stimulus objects. As a result, these words will come to elicit the same, or similar, conditioned meaning responses. Thus, we will respond to these words in a similar manner and say that these words mean the same thing or are synonyms. For example, CAR and AUTOMOBILE are synonyms because they have been paired with similar stimulus objects and are thus conditioned to elicit similar meaning responses.

Since synonyms elicit similar meaning responses, generalization from one to the other would be expected on the same basis as that which accounts for other cases of semantic generalization. Using the previous example, pairing the word BLUE with electric shock would condition the GSR to the meaning of the word. Since AZURE would elicit the same meaning response, the GSR would now be elicited by AZURE. Thus, any behavior conditioned to the one word stimulus would generalize to the other.

An experiment by Phillips (1958) may be used to indicate more specifically the process of synonym development and the way in which word-word semantic generalization may take place. The materials used were five Turkish words (unfamiliar to the subjects, thus meaningless) and five different shades of gray, varying on a continuum from light to dark. In much the same fashion as a child learns to name objects, the subjects were trained to respond with a particular word to a particular shade of gray and to point to the proper shade of gray when the word was presented. It would be expected that this training would condition the image (conditionable sensory response) of the shade of gray to the stimuli produced by the word response, forming the meaning of the word. (In addition, though this is not of concern now, the speech response would be brought under the control of the appropriate shade of gray.) Thus, each word would come to elicit a gray conditioned sensory response, and each of the responses would, to varying degrees, be similar to the others. This is schematized for the first Turkish word in Figure 4.10. Figure 4.11 shows each Turkish word stimulus eliciting a conditioned meaning response. Since all the meaning responses are similar, the stimuli that they produce would be expected to vary along a common stimulus gradient.

At this point the five word stimuli could be termed synonyms of one another, that is, they should all elicit similar conditioned sensory responses, or, in common-sense terms, the words should have similar meanings. As a consequence, it would be expected that semantic generalization from one word to the others would occur. The greatest generalization would be expected to occur among the words that were closest to each other in meaning.

The second part of the experiment tested this expectation. The Turkish word that had come to elicit the darkest gray image as its meaning was paired with a loud sound; thus, through conditioning, this Turkish word came to elicit a GSR. The experimental hypothesis was that this GSR would be elicited by the other Turkish words to the extent that their meanings (conditioned sensory responses) were similar to the meaning of the

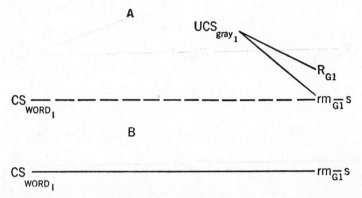

Fig. 4.10. The first Turkish word is paired a number of times with the first shade of gray, which elicits a particular sensory response (R_{G1}) in the individual. This is depicted in part A. Thus, the Turkish word now comes to elicit a portion of the sensory response (rm_{G1}—s) made to the shade of gray; this is depicted in part B.

CS Turkish word. The rationale for this expectation could be stated in the following manner. Each time the Turkish word was presented it would elicit its conditioned sensory response. When the loud noise occurred shortly afterward, eliciting a GSR, the GSR would be conditioned to the stimuli produced by the conditioned sensory response. Since the other words also elicited similar conditioned sensory responses, they would also elicit the GSR to a degree varying with their similarity in meaning to the CS word. In general, the predictions were borne out by the results. This process is depicted in Figure 4.12.

Fig. 4.11. Each Turkish word elicits a conditioned meaning response. Since these meaning responses are similar, the stimuli they produce should vary along a common stimulus gradient.

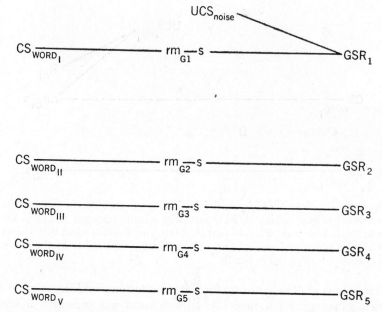

Fig. 4.12. When the first Turkish word is followed by a loud noise, the GSR the noise elicits becomes conditioned to the stimulus properties of the conditioned sensory response elicited by the word. This is depicted in part A. Then, since the other words also elicit similar conditioned sensory responses, they also elicit the GSR to a degree varying with their similarity in meaning to the CS word, as shown in part B.

Thus, when any two words are synonymous, that is, elicit similar meaning responses, experience with one of the words should generalize to the other. According to this interpretation words might elicit similar meaning responses to varying degrees. At one extreme two words could be systematically paired with exactly the same stimulus objects and would be expected to come to elicit precisely the same conditioned meaning response. On the other hand, two words could come to elicit conditioned meaning responses that were similar in certain ways and dissimilar in others. For example, the words BITTER, DIRTY, SICK, and FAILURE would be judged as having a negative, or unpleasant, meaning by most people, presumably because the various stimuli with which these words are habitually paired elicit a common or similar negative meaning response. As a consequence it would be expected that the autonomic responses elicited by these stimuli and conditioned to the words to form part of their meanings would have a certain degree of similarity. To this extent the words would be synonymous. On the other hand, the stimuli with which the words are paired also are dissimilar in many ways and elicit dissimilar responses (different sensory responses). The words should thus be dissimilar to the extent that these dissimilar responses are conditioned to the words to form a part of their meaning. Although ordinarily the term *synonym* is reserved for words which elicit meaning responses very similar to each other, it is suggested that the degree of synonymity constitutes a dimension.

Verbal Habit–Families

In discussing synonyms, the way in which words, or word responses, might be related to one another was suggested. Actually, a somewhat more detailed extension of this interpretation is relevant for additional aspects of cognitive organization that have long been of concern to students of human behavior, such as concept formation and function.

In the child's language learning, in the presence of a spherical object, the child will be reinforced if he says IT IS ROUND; but he will also be reinforced if he uses the words SPHERICAL and CIRCULAR. And, depending upon what the spherical object is, he may be reinforced for using the word MELON, BALL, ORANGE, and so on. In this type of experience, according to the previous interpretation, two types of associations should be formed: (1) the conditionable sensory responses elicited by the "round" objects should be conditioned to the various speech responses, forming part of their meaning, and (2) the speech responses should also be conditioned to the same sensory response of "roundness."

All of these various associations, when depicted together, may be termed a verbal habit-family, using the theoretical concept "habit-family" developed by Hull (1930). In simple terms, a verbal habit-family is said to exist when a stimulus will elicit a conditionable meaning response (in this case a conditionable sensory response) which has tendencies to elicit a number of speech responses, each of which will also elicit that same meaning response. The verbal habit-family for "roundness" is depicted in Figure 4.13.

After the associations in a verbal habit-family have been formed, any stimulus that elicits a particular common meaning response would be expected to tend to elicit the various word responses conditioned to that meaning response. For this example, such a stimulus might be any round object. Which word is elicited by the meaning response will depend upon the relative strength of the various associations (see the section on response hierarchies in Chapter 3). In addition, the emission of any of the word responses in the habit-family would elicit the meaning response and so tend to elicit all of the words in the verbal habit-family (Staats, 1961).

The verbal habit-family for "roundness," diagrammed in Figure 4.13, would ordinarily be called a concept (the concept of "roundness"), and it is suggested that the processes which have been discussed actually repre-

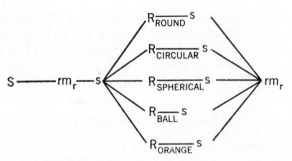

Fig. 4.13. Some stimulus elicits the "roundness" meaning response (rm_r—s), the stimulus properties of which tend to elicit a number of words, each of which tends to elicit the "roundness" meaning response. This represents the verbal habit-family for roundness.

sent concept formation. A concept may be considered as a verbal habit-family formed on the basis of learning principles.

Much of the organization that occurs in language behavior may be due to such verbal habit-families or concepts. When an individual has been instructed to SAY ALL THE ROUND WORDS YOU CAN THINK OF, it will be observed that he immediately emits a series of "round" words. It is suggested that this occurs because the instructions will elicit in the individual the meaning response for "roundness" and that, in turn, will tend to elicit each of the words in the "roundness" habit-family. Other naturalistic examples of the functioning of these principles might be seen in the fact that different broad classes of verbal responses tend to occur in different stimulus situations. That is, since church, burlesque shows, wrestling matches, parties, and the presence of one's boss, and so on, would elicit different characteristic meaning responses, different verbal habit-families would be aroused in these situations.

The concept of the verbal habit-family has been discussed, in part, to illustrate the possible complexities of language behavior. Later sections of the book will frequently simplify language habits in order to expand the principles involved. It should thus be kept in mind that verbal habit-families may be involved where only simple verbal responses are being discussed.

Verbal Conditioned Reinforcers and Meaning

It has been suggested that a word can become a secondary reinforcer. That is, if a word stimulus is paired with a reinforcing stimulus, the word will also become a reinforcer. In addition, the manner in which a word may come to elicit a meaning response has also been suggested. If the word is paired with a stimulus which elicits a response, the word will come to elicit part of that response; the response conditioned to the word is thought to constitute the meaning of the word.

As can be seen, the same operations are involved both in the establishment of a word as a secondary or conditioned reinforcer and in the development of a word's meaning. In both cases the result seems to depend upon the pairing of the word with other stimuli. Basically, the relationship between these two phenomena was already indicated in Chapter 3, where it was suggested that a stimulus becomes a conditioned reinforcer when, through conditioning, it elicits the same response as is elicited by a reinforcing stimulus.

Not all word stimuli that come to elicit conditioned meaning responses would be expected to become secondary reinforcers, however. Although many sensory, autonomic, and muscular responses may be conditioned to words and establish their "meaning," it would be thought that only some of these conditioned responses would have reinforcing properties. A meaning response that would be expected to have conditioned reinforcing value may be termed "evaluative." Thus, it may be said that a word which is a positive reinforcer is one which elicits a positive evaluative meaning response, and a word which is a negative reinforcer is one which elicits a negative evaluative meaning response. A number of studies (see Krasner, 1958; and Salzinger, 1959) have shown that words such as GOOD may serve as reinforcers to strengthen responses they follow.

While this evaluative dimension of meaning may be only one of an almost infinite number of possible meaning-response dimensions, it nevertheless appears that this one is most important and widespread. Osgood and Suci (1955) found, for example, that evaluative meaning is the most general and strongest type of word meaning. This finding has been supported by studies in a number of languages (Kumata, 1957; Kumata and Schramm, 1956; Suci, 1960; Triandis and Osgood, 1958). Since what is spoken of as the positive and negative evaluative meaning of a word may also be interpreted as indicating the positive or negative reinforcing value of the word stimulus, this finding suggests that the great number of words found to be evaluative in meaning can be considered to have reinforcing properties.

Some of the words that were found by Osgood and Suci to have strong positive evaluative meaning—in our terms, to elicit strong conditioned reinforcing responses—were GOOD, BEAUTIFUL, SWEET, CLEAN, TASTY, VALUABLE, KIND, PLEASANT, HAPPY, SACRED, NICE, FRAGRANT, HONEST, FAIR, HEALTHY, FRESH, BRIGHT,

BRAVE, and PEACEFUL. Words that elicited negative meaning responses were also established. In addition, there would seem to be many, many other word responses that elicit either positive or negative meaning responses.

Thus, it can be considered that there is an exceedingly large verbal habit-family involving each of these types of meaning. Figure 4.14 depicts part of the verbal habit-family for negative evaluative meaning. A naturalistic observation of such a habit-family can be obtained by asking someone to describe a person using negative evaluative terms, for example. These directions should elicit the negative meaning response, and the stimulus properties of this response should tend to elicit part of the large class of negative words.

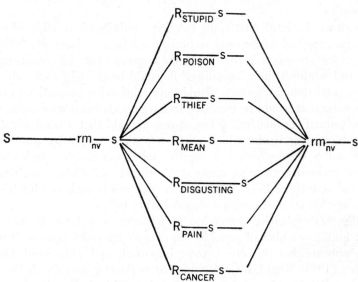

Fig. 4.14. This depicts part of the large verbal habit-family of negative meaning word responses. The figure indicates that when a stimulus elicits the negative meaning response, rm_{nv}, the stimuli produced by this response will tend to elicit a large class of word responses, all of which themselves elicit the same negative meaning response.

The fact that a great many words may be considered to have reinforcing properties on the basis of eliciting an evaluative meaning component seems quite reasonable in view of the interpretation that a word may be conditioned to elicit more than one meaning response. Through classical conditioning, a word might come to elicit not only a conditioned sensory response, but also a conditioned evaluative response—establishing its reinforcing properties. For example, the words FRIEND, VACATION,

MONEY, CANDY, and MOTHER would all be expected to be positive reinforcers because they have been paired with other stimuli that are positive reinforcers. Thus, the words share the same quality in that they elicit the same "reinforcing" meaning response. However, these word stimuli should also elicit additional conditioned meaning responses (sensory, autonomic, or motor responses) which are quite different.

Some words are frequently paired with many stimuli, all of which are reinforcers but which would be expected to elicit quite varied responses in other respects. As a result, these varied responses would compete with each other (inhibit each other) and the word paired with them would come to elicit strongly only the "reinforcing" meaning response. NICE, GOOD, FINE, and PLEASANT seem to be examples of such words. The only strong meaning response elicited by these words seems to be the one that establishes their positive reinforcing value. The only difference between the words lies in the intensity of their reinforcing value and the situations in which they are likely to occur. An experimental demonstration of the development of such meaning will be given in the next chapter.

Thus, it is thought that many words, both by themselves and in conjunction with other words in sentences, become conditioned or secondary reinforcers by being paired with other positive reinforcers. Many words come to be negative reinforcers in the same manner, that is, by being paired with an aversive stimulus the word comes to elicit parts of the same response elicited by the aversive stimulus. In common-sense terms these words might be said to elicit an "anxiety" response or to arouse "anxiety."

At any rate, one of the greatest sources of reinforcement for shaping behavior is the application and withdrawal of positive and negative word reinforcers. For this reason the principles that are involved in words becoming secondary reinforcers should be well understood. The effect of word reinforcers upon the development of specific behaviors will be covered more fully when those behaviors are the subject of discussion. It will suffice to say at this time that if language is to become an effective means of controlling behavior, many words must become adequate secondary reinforcers.

Development of Word Associations

Concern with "mental" associations, like the interest in meaning, predates the development of scientific psychology by several centuries. It was not, however, until late in the nineteenth century that experimental work on word association was begun. Prior to that time the philosophers' contributions to knowledge were based largely upon introspection of their own experiences. Throughout this long history of Associationism the philosophers and psychologists were interested in these considerations only as a device for analyzing the "mind." They were not concerned with establishing relationships between independent variables and the consequent behavior they produce.

During the latter part of the nineteenth century, systematic observations of variables that effect word associations were begun. Since that time innumerable laboratory studies have been conducted to establish the way in which sequences of verbal responses are formed. The details of these studies are not relevant to this book, since our interest is largely with those relationships that lead to prediction and control of events in life situations. In this interest we are concerned not only with the independent variables that determine the formation of word associations, but especially with how such associations function in the complex behaviors of the individual. While laboratory studies have been quite successful in isolating in considerable detail those variables involved in the acquisition and maintenance of word-response chains, there has been little systematic effort to analyze how such chains are formed in the individual's every-day experience and to relate the function of word-response chains to other complex behaviors. For example, Underwood (1959), one of the outstanding investigators in the field of verbal learning, states, "It is a fact that some of the phenomena dealt with in the laboratory studies of verbal learning are so small in magnitude and so highly dependent upon a specific set of conditions that they would probably be judged of little or no consequence for the school situation" (p. 108). This is not to say, Underwood continues, that the "small" phenomena may not have large scientific significance, or even, it might be added, that they may not be shown in the future to have practical significance. However, it might be suggested that although a great deal more study is necessary in these areas, it would be important to analyze the great wealth of findings already available in terms of their importance for understanding complex human behavior. Only a brief outline of some general principles in this area of study will be presented in this section. An attempt will be made to apply some of these principles later.

Serial Learning

In a common laboratory study, a list of nonsense syllables or words may be presented in series (*serial learning*) in the window of a device called a memory drum. On first presentation the subject simply reads the list. On later trials the subject, upon seeing one syllable, must correctly say what the next one will be before it is presented. This procedure is continued until the whole list is correctly anticipated—until when each stimulus syllable is shown the correct syllable response is made. Let us say that the following six nonsense syllables are presented in that manner: YOF, GAX, LEC, XEM, LUJ, JID. When the stimulus YOF is presented the correct response is GAX. When GAX is shown the correct response is LEC, and so on. When the subject does not respond, or does so incorrectly, the response-syllable is presented and he reads it. This process is shown in Figure 4.15. In part A, depicting the beginning of the learning task, the syllables are individually presented, and the subject reads them aloud. Part B depicts the learning that takes place. Each response produces its characteristic stimuli (such as auditory stimuli, produced by the vocal motor responses) that come to elicit the next response. After a sufficient number of trials, the result is a smooth serial chain of verbal responses as shown in part C. In every-day life an example of serial learning would be involved in alphabet learning, learning a poem, memorizing a shopping list, and so on.

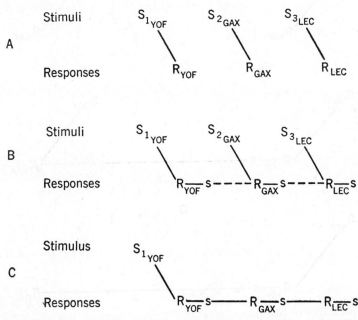

Fig. 4.15. At the beginning of the serial learning task each syllable is individually presented, and the subject responds to each of them separately; this is depicted in part A. Part B illustrates the formation of the serial chain. Each response produces its characteristic stimuli, which come to elicit the next response. After a number of trials a smooth serial chain of verbal responses is established and may be elicited even in the absence of the supporting stimuli, as in part C of the figure.

Paired-Associate Chaining

In a method called *paired-associate learning* another type of verbal learning is studied by presenting stimulus syllables in pairs, the subjects' task being to give the response-syllable when each stimulus-syllable is presented. This is depicted in Figure 4.16 for one word association.

This paradigm is exemplified in foreign language learning, where when a word is presented in one language, its equivalent in another language is the appropriate response to be elicited. The procedure is, however, theoretically very similar to that of serial learning, except that associations are estab-

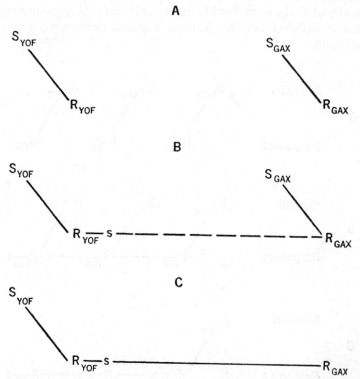

Fig. 4.16. On the first presentation of the paired-associate learning task the two syllables are presented, and the subject responds to each of them, as indicated in part A. Later, however, the subject is instructed to read the first syllable and respond with the second syllable. The stimulus properties of the "reading" response to the first syllable (the reading response may also be implicit) come to elicit the second response. The formation of this association is depicted in part B. After a number of such trials the subject gives the second response when only the first word is presented, as shown in part C.

lished most strongly between two syllables rather than among a number of syllables in a continuous chain. Both types of procedures have been used to study a number of variables concerned with simple verbal learning and retention. In general, it could be said that the S–R principles presented in Chapter 3 are relevant to both serial and paired-associate verbal learning —for example, the greater number of trials the stronger the learning. Moreover, a great many studies have been concerned with the effects of a wide range of additional variables upon this type of learning. For example, once a list is learned, how will retention of the list be affected by learning another list? Or, what effect does the familiarity or the meaningfulness of the list items have upon learning? These are only examples of the many complex variables that have been studied.

Word-Response Hierarchies

In addition to single verbal S–R associations, more than one response can be associated to the same verbal stimulus to form a word-response hierarchy (Staats and Staats, 1959b; Staats, Staats, Finley, and Heard, in press). For example, the syllable XEM as a stimulus could be paired with both the syllables LUJ and LEC as responses in two paired-associate learning tasks. In time, both responses would tend to be elicited by XEM (or rather, by the stimulus properties of the response to the syllable). Thus, when the subject said XEM both LEC and LUJ would tend to be elicited. Which response occurred first or more frequently would depend upon the strength of the conditioning involved. This process is shown in Figure 4.17, along with the resulting word-response hierarchy. The strength of the word responses in the hierarchy would be expected to depend upon the usual conditioning variables, such as number of trials, as well as upon some other variables that have been studied extensively in the field of verbal learning, such as similarity of the word responses.

The Formation of Verbal Response
Chains in Everyday Life

Procedures analogous to those producing serial word chains, word associates, and word-response hierarchies seem to take place in every-day life to form the type of verbal chains just illustrated. We have already discussed how single speech responses are operantly conditioned. It is not a complicated extension to see how a simple speech response chain may be established. Let us say the child at first is reinforced when he simply says MILK. After a time, however, his mother may instruct him, PLEASE, SAY PLEASE, and withhold reinforcement until the child says MILK PLEASE. After such training the child would be expected to follow MILK with PLEASE. This is, of course, merely a little more complicated example of

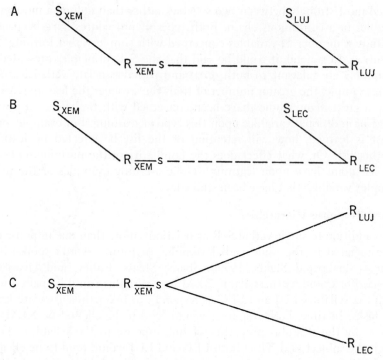

Fig. 4.17. The syllable XEM is paired first with the syllable LUJ (part A) and then with the syllable LEC (part B), in a paired-associate learning task. Later, the stimulus properties of the implicit response to XEM will tend to elicit both the syllables LUJ and LEC, and a simple word response hierarchy is formed (part C).

acquiring a mand. However, two speech responses are involved instead of merely one, and each repetition of the responses together would strengthen their association.[2] In the course of the child's development, more and more extended sequences of speech may be required in any situation before reinforcement is given. Each time multiple speech responses are treated in this manner, it would be expected that one response would elicit the next, and so on. Many word associations seem to be acquired in this manner.

It is suggested, in addition, that whenever the subject responds to sequences of written verbal stimuli with an appropriate sequence of word responses, the result will also be the formation of tendencies for each response to elicit the next. These chains seem even more closely analogous to what occurs in the experiments on serial learning summarized above, that is to say, when the child reads he is forming chains of word responses.

---

[2] Skinner (1957) calls such associations intraverbal responses or intraverbals.

For example, each word in the sentence NOW IS THE TIME FOR ALL GOOD MEN TO COME TO THE AID OF THEIR PARTY may be considered a verbal stimulus that elicits a word response (overt or covert). Since each response produces stimuli, repetitions of the sentence will form associations between the responses, and a verbal chain will result. This is shown in Figure 4.18. Thus, each time an individual reads a newspaper or novel or comic book such associations should result. The same should also be true when the verbal stimuli are presented in auditory fashion. Listening to (making verbal responses to) someone else's speech also would be expected to produce the type of word associations discussed. Thus, our casual conversations with others, the movies we attend, the televised programs we listen to, and so on, should also produce word associations.

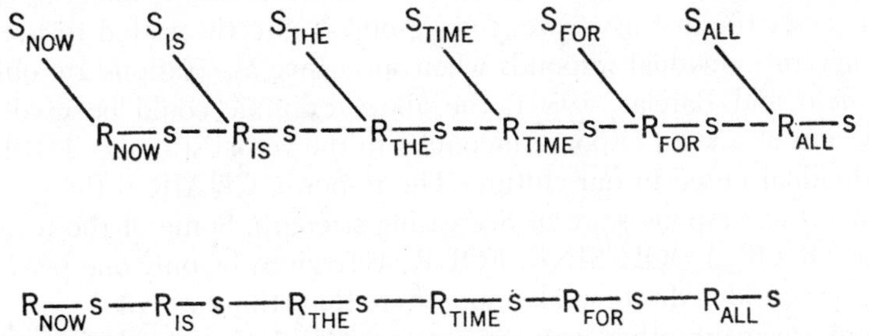

Fig. 4.18. As the individual reads the sentence each word elicits a word response. Since each word response has stimulus properties, after a number of readings there will be associations formed between the responses, and a verbal chain will be established.

Furthermore, it is suggested that these complex interassociations are also formed when single environmental stimuli which control single verbal responses (tacts) occur together in the same general stimulus situation, and the verbal responses are then elicited together. (See the section on originality in the next chapter for further discussion of these associations.) Since they are contiguous in complex ways, they would be expected to become associated in complex ways. In this manner, amongst others, occurrences in the environment could put their stamp upon the individual's verbal behavior, that is, upon his "thinking," "mentality," or "consciousness." In other words, to the extent that a person's personal experiences elicit verbal responses in him, word-response associations would be expected to be formed.

Measurement of Word Associates

The word associations that are formed as a result of the individual's experiences have been surveyed by several investigators (Bousfield *et al.*,

1961; Deese, 1959; Kent and Rosanoff, 1910; Russell and Jenkins, 1954) for use in other experiments. A method for doing this is to present a series of words, one at a time, to a large group of subjects, and have them write down the first word they "think of" (the first word response they make). These responses can then be tabulated over the group of subjects, and the word associates of each stimulus word as well as the strength of each word associate can be determined. Ordinarily, it will be found that many different subjects respond with the same associate, fewer subjects respond with another associate, fewer yet with a third, and so on.

For example, when the first word response to the stimulus TABLE was obtained from 1008 college students, 840 gave CHAIR, 41 FOOD, 21 DESK, 15 TOP, 11 LEG, 9 EAT, 8 CLOTH, 7 DISH, 6 WOOD, and so on (Russell and Jenkins, 1954). Since it has been shown that the relative frequency of the first associates for a group is directly related to the order in which an individual responds when successive associations are obtained (Bousfield and Barclay, 1950), the above example could be used as an illustration of a word-response hierarchy to the verbal stimulus TABLE for an individual raised in our culture. The response CHAIR is the strongest, and the other responses are of decreasing strength. Some of the responses, such as DOOR, POOL, SINK, FOUR, were given by only one person and would be considered very weak responses to that stimulus.

There are many other very strong associations that can be observed to occur in the speech customs of every-day life, and there are many weaker associations that, although not as obvious, nevertheless determine what our next response will be following a particular response. Many of the associations between word responses are of a complex relationship. For example, the word stimulus MUSIC elicits as responses SWEET and SOFT (Russell and Jenkins, 1954), but SWEET and SOFT also elicit MUSIC. The word LOUD, although not directly elicited by MUSIC, is elicited by SOFT. Thus, LOUD would tend to occur as a response to MUSIC, since it is mediated by the response SOFT. Furthermore, LOUD as a stimulus word has as its associates a number of responses that are also direct associates to MUSIC, as well as the word MUSIC itself. This complex network of inter-related associations is illustrated in Figure 4.19. If complete word association norms were available for these words, additional interassociations would no doubt be seen (Staats, Staats, Finley, and Minke, 1961).

Up to this point, the word response made to a single verbal stimulus has been discussed. There is evidence to show, however, that in a verbal chain it is not just one word which influences the response which is elicited but, rather, multiple preceding words. Howes and Osgood (1954) demonstrated that the response made to a stimulus word when it is preceded by three other words may be different from the response to the word alone or to

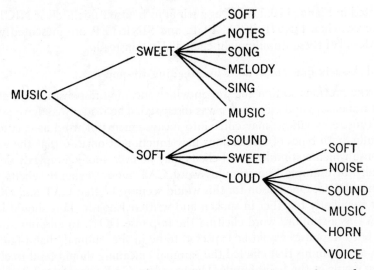

Fig. 4.19. Some of the interassociations established between the word associates to MUSIC.

the word when it is preceded by other words. As an example, the word response to DARK alone would be different from the response elicited if DARK was preceded by the words DEVIL, FEARFUL, SINISTER. Thus, several word stimuli may severally elicit a particular word response—in a manner analogous to a reversed hierarchy of responses. For example, as is

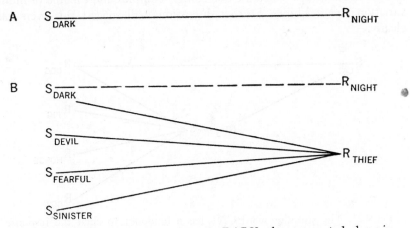

Fig. 4.20. The most probable response to DARK when presented alone is NIGHT, as depicted in part A. However, when DARK is presented along with DEVIL, FEARFUL, and SINISTER as in part B, the response elicited is THIEF.

depicted in Figure 4.20, DARK as a stimulus by itself might elicit NIGHT. However, when DEVIL, FEARFUL, and SINISTER are presented with DARK, all of these stimuli might elicit THIEF instead.

Word Associations Influenced by Meaning Responses

In the previous section the way in which meaning responses could elicit word responses (and vice versa) was discussed. The reader may have asked how those associations may enter into measurements of word associations. Actually, both types of associations may function at once so that the word response which a stimulus word elicits may be even more complexly determined. For example, the stimulus word CAT most frequently elicits the response DOG. One reason for this would seem to be that CAT and DOG occur frequently together in spoken and written English. This should lead to CAT as a stimulus word eliciting the response DOG. In addition, however, both responses would be expected to be in the "animal" habit-family. Thus, any stimulus that elicited the "animal" meaning should tend to elicit all the words in the habit-family. Hence, when CAT is presented it might be expected to elicit the animal meaning that would tend to elicit DOG, among other animal words. This situation is diagrammed in Figure 4.21.

It must be evident to the reader at this point that the number and complexity of language associations is extremely large and much more complicated than has been described. It is suggested that even though the stimulus–response principles which seem to be involved are relatively simple, the various experiences of an individual can produce combinations of S–R relationships which are exceedingly complex and capable of infinite variation and flexibility. Further discussions will suggest this even more clearly.

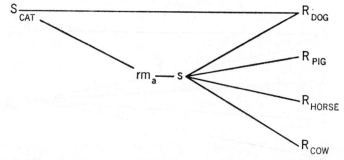

Fig. 4.21. The stimulus word CAT has a tendency to elicit the response DOG because in the past the words CAT and DOG have occurred many times in contiguity. In addition, however, the word CAT, as a member of the "animal" habit-family, elicits the "animal" meaning response, which, in turn, elicits, among other animal words, the word DOG.

Function of Word Associations

The next chapter will deal with the function of various language behaviors in the adjustment of the individual. However, there is an experiment that demonstrates in the laboratory the effect which word associations may have upon behavior and that will help to introduce the later discussions of the function of word associations.

The fact that a particular word response may come to elicit another word response as well as the manner in which norms for these word associations may be established has already been discussed. Furthermore, in order to demonstrate the functioning of a series of word associations in a learning task, Russell and Storms (1955) devised the following experiment. First, by consulting the word association norms, they found a word B that would elicit word C as an associate. Word C, in turn, elicited D as a word associate when C was presented as a stimulus. An example is the following: STEM (B) elicits FLOWER (C), which itself will elicit SMELL (D). Ten such chains (B–C–D) of word associates were constructed. Thus, on the basis of these chains alone, it would be expected that there would be a tendency for B to elicit D, mediated by the intervening response C.

The expectation that word associations would function as mediators of later responses was tested in the experiment proper. In a learning task subjects were first required to learn a list of A–B pairs (for example, YOF–STEM), where the A terms were nonsense syllables and the B terms were the initial members of the association chains. Then, in the test situation, the subjects learned another list consisting of half A–D (YOF–SMELL) and half A–X pairs (YOF–JOY). The D terms were the final members of the word association chains, but the X terms were unrelated to the chains, in other words there was no chain of word responses mediating the association between A and X as there was between A and D. It was found that the subjects learned the pairs in the test situation which were linked by the type of chaining described (the A–D pairs) more rapidly than they learned the unconnected pairs (the A–X pairs). Moreover, since the B–C links in the chain did not appear—that is, were never presented to the subjects during the experiment—the subjects were not even aware that there was any "connection" between the A and D members of the word pairs.

Figure 4.22 depicts the manner in which the word-association chains functioned. For example, in part A of the figure the subject must learn the $S_{\overline{YOF}}$——R_{SMELL} association. Since S_{YOF} elicits the implicit word associate $r_{\overline{STEM}}s$ that elicits $r_{\overline{FLOWER}}s$ and this in turn, elicits R_{SMELL}, some tendency for S_{YOF} to elicit R_{SMELL} is already present. Thus, relatively few pairings of S_{YOF} and R_{SMELL} should be necessary. This is not true for subjects required to learn an $S_{\overline{YOF}}$—R_{JOY} association. There are still tendencies for S_{YOF} finally to elicit R_{SMELL}, but this does not aid the acquisition of the $S_{\overline{YOF}}$—R_{JOY} association.

These results indicate that word-response chains may function to determine an individual's overt, observable behavior. Because the individual, through his past experiences, has had certain word associations formed, he is better able to learn, to "solve a problem," or to "adjust" in a new situation. The ease of establishing new associations may depend upon the previous establishment of other associations.

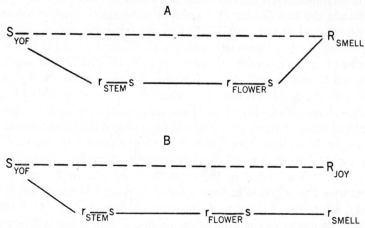

Fig. 4.22. As shown in part A, S_{YOF} already has tendencies to elicit R_{SMELL}, mediated by the word association chain S_{YOF}, $r_{\overline{STEM}}s$, $r_{\overline{FLOWER}}s$, and R_{SMELL}. This is not the case with $S_{\overline{YOF}}$—R_{JOY}, as depicted in part B. consequently the $S_{\overline{YOF}}$—R_{SMELL} association is acquired much more easily.

A further point of this important study is that these association chains took place implicitly. That is, the subjects did not emit the chains of responses aloud; in fact, they were not aware of the fact that they were responding in that manner at all.[3] The fact that the subjects were unaware of their own implicit responses indicates not only that people may respond without awareness of the response, but also that they may be unaware of what the independent variables are which determine those responses or how those responses function in determining other important aspects of their behavior.

---

[3] The reader may recognize this experiment as another example of the way in which the characteristics of events which are not directly observable may be established by indirect observation. That is, the experiment indirectly established the manner in which implicit response chains function without directly observing the intervening responses in the chain.

In the next section, as well as the next chapter, the manner in which chains of word responses may function in reasoning and problem-solving will be described. The study of Russell and Storms, however, may be considered to be a laboratory experiment that produces basic principles relevant to these topics.

Learning and Grammatical Habits

In discussing word-association functioning in language we focused on customary usages. It is suggested that because of an individual's history of conditioning associations are formed which determine his word responses. Grammatical usages may be considered to be in part such learned habits. It would seem that certain word responses come to follow other word responses because in the spoken and written customs of a language community those words as stimuli occur in that order. A suggested mechanism is that verbal behavior which parallels these customs is reinforced; behavior which does is not is not reinforced. Each individual has a long history, for example, in which his "tacts" and "mands" are reinforced if they are in a certain *order*. Osgood (1957) gives the following as evidence of grammatical habits.

> Wilson Taylor . . . , using his "cloz" procedure in which the subject fills in the gaps in mutilated messages, finds that with both sides of the gap given as in his method structural determinism is almost perfect (for example, in filling in "the old man _____ along the road," all subjects will fill in a verb form even though they vary semantically in what verb they choose). Miller and Selfridge . . . and others have demonstrated that ease of learning and retention of meaningful materials varies with the degree of approximation to English structure. Along similar lines . . . [Swanson] compared the ease of learning nonsense sequences that retained the structure of the English sentences from which they were derived, for example,
>
> The maff vlems oothly um the glox nerfs
>
> with matched materials in which the grammatical cues had been eliminated, for example,
>
> maff vlem ooth um glox nerf.
>
> Despite the greater absolute amount of material in the structured forms, they were learned significantly more easily than the matched strings of nonsense items (p. 88).

Such evidence suggests that grammatical usage in speech is acquired according to the principles of learning and that the product is an extremely complex repertoire of verbal habits. If that is indeed the case, it would seem that a better understanding of grammatical usage would result from a more detailed S–R analysis of the topic.

Acquisition of Simple Grammatical Habits

Although it is not possible herein to attempt a complete analysis of complex grammatical language behaviors, several studies may be described in terms of behavior principles to suggest that such an analysis would be productive.

The work of Brown and Fraser (1961) and Brown and Berko (1960) constitutes a most important step in bringing together the methodology and principles of the linguist with some of the experimental methods of psychology. For example, in discussing an analysis of parts of speech, Brown and Berko make the following point.

> The linguistic scientist defines the parts-of-speech in purely syntactic or formal terms. He has shown that the English teacher's semantic definitions (e.g., "a noun is the name of a person, place, or thing") are imprecise approximations to the underlying but less obvious syntactic facts. The noun, in descriptive linguistics, is a class of words having similar "privileges of occurrence." Nouns are words that can follow articles and can occur in subject and object positions and, in this respect, are distinct from such other classes of words as the verb, adjective, and adverb (1960, p. 2).

As an example, Brown and Fraser show how "count nouns" may be defined in the following description.

> Hearing *car* as a new word in the sentence: "See the *car*" a child could use this context as a basis for listing *car* with count nouns and so be prepared to hear and say such additional sentences as: "I own a *car*"; "The *car* is new"; "This *car* is mine." And a multitude of others. Of course the particular sentence uttered on a given occasion would depend on semantic and motivational factors, but the population of sentences from which the particular could be drawn would be established by the syntactic kinship linking *car* with *house, barn, table,* and *fence* (1961, pp. 7–8).

This type of analysis seems to provide an excellent systematic description of certain language behavior that can serve as the basis for an investigation in terms of learning principles. For example, the term "privileges of occurrence" seems to refer to the fact that certain groups of words occur in certain circumstances, or rather, in a certain relationship to other words. That is, what a child reads and hears and what he is reinforced for saying will be of a certain form. From our knowledge of S–R principles of word associations, it could be said in general that such experiences should produce a systematic set of language habits.

If that is the case it should be possible to discover the principles and the particular controlling variables underlying the formation of these classes

Brown and Fraser describe. The following fairly complicated set of S–R mechanisms is offered to explain the finding that having heard SEE THE CAR, a child can then emit the response CAR in other syntactically appropriate sentences, such as I OWN A CAR, THE CAR IS NEW, and THIS CAR IS MINE.

First, let us say that the responses THE, A, and THIS, among others, have each come to have extensive associations with many words. For example, the child has heard, read, and been reinforced for saying THE HORSE, THE HOUSE, THE DOG, THE TABLE, and so on. The stimuli provided by the vocal response THE should come as a consequence (according to the principles of conditioning) to tend to elicit many word responses.

In turn, however, one could expect THE to be elicited by the stimuli produced by many other word responses. SEE, OWN, WHAT, for example, should all come to elicit THE through being in contiguity with THE in sentences such as SEE THE BLANK, I OWN THE BLANK, DO YOU KNOW WHAT THE BLANK IS?, and so on.

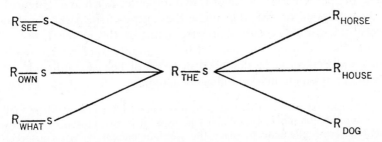

Fig. 4.23. In the individual's experience the responses SEE, OWN, and WHAT, among others, are paired with the response THE and come to elicit this response. In the same manner the response THE comes to elicit HORSE, HOUSE, DOG, and so on.

Thus, let us say, the word THE is elicited by many words and tends to elicit many other words. This is depicted in Figure 4.23. The term "privileges of occurrence" may be thought to refer to the learning conditions that produce such hierarchies of responses. It is suggested that as a consequence of these associations, formed through conditioning during one's extensive language experience, an individual will say such things as SEE THE HORSE but not HORSE THE SEE.

The generality of word usage Brown and Fraser describe would be expected to occur according to this interpretation, on the basis of such S–R mechanisms. That is, a new word, through being paired with THE, would become associated with THE, in other words, THE would tend to elicit the new word.. The sentence SEE THE CAR, for example, would establish the sequence THE CAR. As a consequence, the response CAR would tend to occur in all situations that elicited THE—for example, I OWN THE CAR. The key to the syntactically appropriate emission of CAR would depend upon the association $R_{\overline{THE}}$ s———R_{CAR}. Any time THE would be elicited, one of the words it would tend to elicit would now be CAR.

However, let us say that in addition to these associations, the child also forms associations between THE, A, and THIS, among others.[4] As a consequence, any one of these word responses would have a tendency to elicit either of the other two. With these associations added, Figure 4.23 would be much more complicated.

Moreover, there would be even greater generality of usage due to this training, produced by the associations between THE, THIS, and A. It would be expected that when CAR is associated to THE it would also become associated with THIS and A, among other words. Thus, any time THIS or A is elicited in the individual, CAR would also tend to occur.

These, of course, would constitute the syntactic associations. In the emission of any particular sequence of verbal responses (such as a sentence) the specific words emitted would be under the control of the particular stimulus objects and stimulus events that were acting at the moment.

With these concepts in hand, the important experimental results of Brown and Berko can be described in terms of behavior principles. They discuss the research in the following manner.

> The general plan of this test is to introduce to S a new word (actually a pronounceable nonsense syllable) by using it in two sentences. The two sentences are adequate to place the word in one of six parts-of-speech: the count noun, mass noun, transitive verb, intransitive verb, adjective, or adverb. After this introduction to the word, S was asked to use it in sentences of his own creation, and these were scored as correct if the new word was used as it ought to be in view of the part-of-speech implied by the introductory sentences.
>
> As "new words" 12 nonsense syllables were used. . . . There were 12 problems in all with two syllables assigned to each of the six parts-of-speech. . . .
>
> For each problem, S was shown a colorful picture of either a girl, a boy, a man, a woman, a cat, or a dog, and E read text of the following kind: "Do you know what a *wug* is? This is a picture of a little girl thinking about a *wug*. Can you make up what that might mean?" This was the presentation identifying *wug* as a count noun. Where *wug* was to be identified as an intransitive verb, E would say: "Do you know what it means to *wug*? This is a picture of a little boy who wants to *wug*." With

---

[4] A more complete analysis of this would involve the implicit elicitation of all three of these responses by stimuli like SEE, OWN, and WHAT. As a consequence of this implicit elicitation, the words THE, A, and THIS are contiguous and become associated.

wug as a mass noun there would be such sentences as: "This is a cat thinking about some *wug*." With *wug* as a transitive verb such a sentence as this was used: "This is a woman who wants to *wug* something." Where *wug* was to be identified as an adverb E spoke of a dog thinking of doing something *wuggily* (1960, p. 6).

Actually, all these cases may be considered in terms of S–R mechanisms that are very similar to the one already described. The analysis of the first case, concerning the count noun, seems to be precisely the same. WUG is conditioned to A, let us say, and the type of generalization already described should take place. The same is true of the mass noun. When WUG is conditioned to SOME, any set of verbal stimuli that will elicit SOME should now tend also to elicit WUG. It would be expected that the child, after being told THIS IS A CAT THINKING ABOUT SOME WUG, would say such things as I WOULD LIKE SOME WUG, WHEN DO I GET SOME WUG, EVERYONE ENJOYS SOME WUG, and so on. The same is true of the intransitive verb. The sentences should produce in the child the response sequence $R_{\overline{TO}}$ s————R_{WUG}. Thus, whenever a set of verbal stimuli that will elicit TO is presented, it will tend also to elicit WUG. After having heard such sentences, the child would be likely to say, I LIKE TO WUG, MY SISTER TRIES TO WUG, WHERE DO YOU GO TO WUG? As the reader will be able to see by this time, a similar analysis can be made for the transitive verb, the adverb, and the adjective.

This interpretation may also be used to consider the additional important result of Brown and Berko's experiment that children showed an ability, increasing with age, to construct grammatically correct sentences using new words. This finding would be expected on the basis of the behavioral analysis. Since the S–R mechanisms involved seem quite complex, it would be expected that many conditioning trials would be required to establish all the associations involved. Ordinarily, the older the child, the more such trials he would have an opportunity to experience.

Development of Syntactical Habits

The relationship of age to syntactical usage—that is, to the learning of syntactical habits—should be considered in somewhat greater detail. Such consideration should help specify the results of the process of "privileges of occurrence."

For example, on the basis of the foregoing analysis, certain systematic changes would be expected in word-association norms as a function of age. Thus, responses given to a stimulus word should change as new verbal associations were formed. It has long been known that children's associations differ in a systematic manner from those of adults (Woodrow and

Lowell, 1916). And Ervin (1957) has shown that there are changes in word responses as a function of children's ages. Moreover, she found that the grammatical nature of the responses differed systematically—that is, older children tended to give as a word response the same part of speech as the stimulus word.

Brown and Fraser (1961) have also systematically observed and described the natural speech habits of children between the ages of 24 and 36 months of age. They found that the number of word responses included in each separate sentence (complete sequence of verbal responses) increased as the children grew older. In addition, they noticed that the speech of these young children was systematically abbreviated, and the extent of abbreviation was related to the number of word responses they produced in their average utterance. Children who produced a low average number of word responses per complete utterance tended to say I GOING TO TOWN rather than the complete I AM GOING TO TOWN.

These investigators further studied the abbreviation effect by having the children match, or echo, sentences produced by the experimenter. They found that with increasing age the match made by the child included more of the individual words presented by the experimenter. In addition, when words were excluded, they tended to be the less essential words: ". . . words that occur in intermediate positions in the sentence, words that are not reference-making forms, words that belong to such small-sized grammatical categories as the articles, modal auxiliaries, and inflections; words that are relatively predictable from context and so carry little information, and words that receive the weaker stresses in ordinary English pronunciation" (pp. 37–38). This led the authors to describe the speech of the children as "telegraphic English" and to attribute the increased ability to match sentences to an increase in "memory span."

Although these authors interpret their findings in these other terms, an analysis of children's speech development in terms of behavior principles suggests the determinants of the "telegraphic English," as well as the development of the increased ability to repeat sentences ("memory span").

As an example, let us say that a young child has just been conditioned to say the single word BALL as a tact, a mand, or an echoic response. The child, of course, will not be able to repeat the sentence GIVE ME THE RED BALL solely on the basis of this training. In time, however, the child should, by the same type of training, be able to tact, mand, or echo the response sequence RED BALL. Each time he does this the tendency for the first response to elicit the second would be strengthened. In time the child will also, through conditioning, come to make the response GIVE and thus to be able to emit the sequence GIVE RED BALL. In further training the child will be prompted to repeat THE RED BALL instead of the simpler phrase, and when he makes the complete response he is more heavily reinforced. Finally, articles and pronouns would be expected to be habitually included in such verbal response sequences, and the child comes to say GIVE ME THE RED BALL. These various word response sequences are depicted in Figure 4.24, part A.

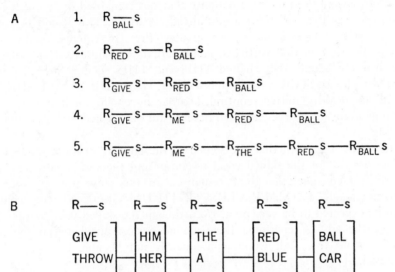

Fig. 4.24. Part A depicts the step-by-step acquisition of a verbal response sequence. The simple response is established first, and later, with more conditioning trials, more complicated sequences are established. Part A, line #5 indicates a five-link verbal response sequence. Similar experiences with different words produce the sequence of response hierarchies depicted in part B. For the sake of simplifying the figure, words which all tend to elicit a word (or words) are bracketed together. In addition, when a set of words all tend to be elicited by a previous word (or words) the set is bracketed. Such sequences provide the flexibility of grammatical speech seen in every-day language behavior.

This training seems to take place over a period of years, starting from the conditioning of simple responses up to the formation of the complex response sequence. At the same time, other responses also would be reinforced in combination with each other and would acquire tendencies to elicit each other in certain orders. That is, not only would GIVE come to elicit ME, but so would other responses—THROW, PUSH, and so on. In addition, not only would ME come to be elicited by those verbs, but so would HIM and HER, etc. It is suggested that at each point in the response sequence there would be a hierarchy of responses which would tend to be elicited, and these hierarchies would in many cases be extremely large. It can be seen that the possible combinations for even this simple sentence on the basis of the existing associations would be extremely numerous. These sequences of hierarchies of responses are depicted in Figure 4.24, part *B*.

After such hierarchies of responses had been formed the child would find no difficulty in echoing a sentence that was composed of any of these alternatives; the associations would already be there. This would be true even though the new sequence of responses (the new sentence) had never occurred before in that particular combination. As long as GIVE tended to elicit HER and HER elicited THIS and THIS elicited SMALL and SMALL elicited SHIRT, the sentence GIVE HER THIS SMALL SHIRT could be readily emitted, controlled either by environmental or verbal stimuli, even though the child had never heard or repeated such a sentence before.

It is thus suggested that the source of the child's "memory span" for words consists of the skilled vocal responses and the various associations between (sequences of) these responses. In the same way an adult's "memory span" for MAFF VLEM OOTH UM GLOX NERFS would also be expected to be very poor. Even though the skilled vocal responses are in the adult's repertoire, there are no associations between the responses, and the adult would consequently not be able to repeat the material.

Another example of syntactic training seems to reveal another S–R mechanism that functions to produce grammatical verbal response sequences. It has already been suggested that the child, in the course of his language training, will go through a large number of similar experiences involving word-response sequences which are in part the same and in part different—THE GIRL IS FAT, THE DOG IS RUNNING, THE CAR IS BIG.

As a consequence of this type of experience, the word response IS should, in part, come to be elicited by the stimuli produced by the response THE—but not *solely* by these stimuli. That is, in the presence of the stimuli produced by THE, plus the stimuli produced by another word response following THE, the word response IS would be reinforced. However, in the presence of THE and the absence of another word response, the response IS would not be reinforced. The controlling stimuli for IS, in this case, would thus come to be those produced by the response THE *plus* another word response, such as THE BALL, THE GIRL, or THE HOUSE. The combined stimuli would have strong tendencies to elicit IS, whereas THE alone would not.

It would be expected on the basis of this interpretation that THE plus the stimuli produced by a novel (therefore, nonsense) word response would tend to elicit the response IS. For example, if subjects were given the stimulus THE WUH in a word-association task it would be expected that the response IS would (among others) tend to occur. The stimulus properties produced by THE and another word response would tend to elicit IS on the basis of stimulus generalization. It is suggested that it is this type of word association which accounts for the fact that THE MAFF VLEMS OOTHLY UM THE GLOX NERFS is more easily learned than MAFF VLEM OOTH UM GLOX NERFS. That is, THE plus a word response has been paired with verbs such as SWIMS, CLIMBS, SUMS, SLUMS, BUMS, RAMS, JAMS, and as a result tends to elicit responses ending in the vocal response MS. If that is the case there would already be associations between THE MAFF VLEMS; on this basis, learning this sequence *should* require fewer trials than verbal response sequences which are completely unconnected. The same type of mechanism would operate in other parts of this sequence. The previously described experiment of Russell and Storms suggests that implicit response chains of this type could mediate our learning, or, in this instance, our "memory span."

Word Endings as a Function of S–R Associations

It is also suggested that grammatical word endings depend upon the formation of the appropriate response associations. However, in this case, vocal responses that form parts of words seem to be involved. Let us take plural endings as an example.

> The rule in English is: a word ending in a voiceless consonant forms its plural with the voiceless sibilant . . . as in *cats, cakes,* and *lips;* a word ending in either a vowel or a voiced consonant forms its plural with the voiced sibilant . . . as in *dogs, crows,* and *ribs;* a word ending in the singular with either /s/ or /z/ forms its plural with /z/ plus an interpolated neutral vowel as in *classes* and *poses.* We all follow these rules and know at once that a new word like *bazooka* will have, as its plural, bazooka/-z/, even though most speakers of English will never know the rule in explicit form (Brown and Fraser, 1961, pp. 5–7).

The word "rule" as used here can only be thought of as a descriptive term; a person does not ordinarily say things *because* he is following a rule. Actually, in this case the S–R account is rather simple. It is suggested that the stimuli which come to control the voiceless sibilant /-s/ vocal response are, for example, the plural stimulus object and the tacting response which ends in the voiceless consonant. After the child has had many, many trials where he is reinforced for the sibilant /-s/ following the voiceless consonant, this stimulus would elicit the appropriate response. After the appropriate associations have been formed between the ending of a word and the "plural" response, the appropriate ending would be expected to occur even when a novel word was introduced. Berko (1958) showed this to be the case by constructing a figure of an imaginary animal, for example, and showing it to a child with the instructions, THIS IS A WUG. NOW THERE ARE TWO _____? The child's task was to supply the word response, including its plural ending, and would usually do this correctly by responding WUG/-Z/. The child's ability to do this could be accounted for on the basis of word associations.

Grammatical Responses Based upon Meaning Responses

These examples suggest that one of the determinants of verbal response sequences are the grammatical habits acquired on the basis of conditioning principles. This is not to say that all the various grammatical forms of verbal responses are a function of word association sequences, however. Some "grammatical" differences in verbal behavior may result from processes involved in the learning of meaning. In the child's training the verbal response IS tends to occur in contiguity with an ongoing stimulus event or a present stimulus object, as when the response HE IS HERE occurs in the presence of some stimulus object. On the other hand, WAS tends to occur after the stimulus object was present or the event has taken place—HE WAS HERE, THE DOG WAS PLAYING, and so on. As a consequence, the unconditioned stimuli with which these verbal stimuli of different tense are systematically paired are different and should elicit different responses in the individual. Thus, it would be expected that the meaning responses conditioned to these two different verbal stimuli would be different in certain features. Since the unconditioned stimuli, although different, would nevertheless be similar in certain respects, the meaning responses of the different verb forms would also share common features.

In addition, as was discussed in the section on the conditioning of meaning responses, the different stimulus conditions and the responses they produce would be expected to come to elicit the correct speech response. That is, speech responses of one verb form would be reinforced in the presence of the event or object and speech responses of the other under circumstances involving a time interval following the occurrence of the event or the presence of the stimulus object.

There are also grammatical usages that seem to involve word associations as well as control by external stimuli (actually, the responses they produce). For example, in the presence of two people as a stimulus the verbal responses THEY ARE will be reinforced. In the presence of only one man the verbal responses HE IS will be reinforced. This type of experience should yield the following S–R processes. The sensory responses elicited by two (or more) people would come to control both the verbal response THEY and the verbal response ARE. In addition, portions of these sensory responses would be conditioned to the stimuli produced by the verbal responses (in the case of ARE this experience is modified by the fact that this verbal stimulus is also paired with singular stimulus objects—YOU ARE). Finally, the word response ARE would be conditioned to the stimulus produced by THEY. Thus, the word association THEY ARE would be formed. These three S–R events are schematized in Figure 4.25.

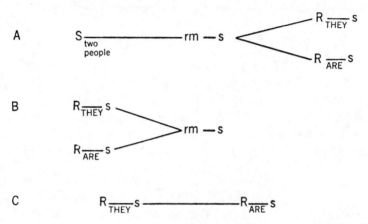

Fig. 4.25. In the presence of two people the verbal responses THEY ARE will be reinforced, and thus the sensory responses elicited by the two people will come to control both verbal responses. This is depicted in part A. Further, portions of these sensory responses will become conditioned to the two words, as shown in part B. Finally, as in part C, the response ARE is conditioned to the stimuli produced by THEY, and the word association THEY ARE is formed.

These types of "grammatical" habits would be expected to contribute to the multiple determination of verbal behavior.

Development of Verbal-Motor Behavior Associations

It is often said that verbal knowledge alone is not sufficient, that the child must learn to put what he "knows" into practice. Another familiar statement is the admonition to "learn by doing." Both statements reflect the observation that a person can have the correct verbal sequences without having acquired the parallel correct overt motor behavior.

In a similar manner, people often say the right things and yet behave in other ways that are quite contradictory. Not always is verbal behavior an indicator of what the individual's motor behavior will be. These considerations merely reflect the very general proposition that one's verbal behavior must in certain cases be "connected" to one's motor behavior to complete the function of verbal behavior. Many times verbal behavior is not in itself significant; it is only what the verbal behavior will lead someone to *do* that is important.

The way in which verbal behavior seems to come under the control of other stimuli has already been discussed. The way in which motor behavior comes under the control of verbal stimuli seems to involve the same principles—the principles of discriminated operants. Early in the development of the child's language he customarily receives training in "following instructions." At the earliest level this might involve something like the following. A father might call to a baby of perhaps even seven or eight months of age, COME TO DADDY, while holding in his hand an attractive toy. When the child responds by crawling to the father in the presence of the verbal stimulus and is reinforced for this by the toy, the verbal stimulus COME TO DADDY would start to become a discriminative stimulus for the response. This same verbal stimulus, or similar ones, seem to occur frequently when the approaching response is reinforced, and it is suggested that as a consequence they come to control the behavior of the child. Many of these conditioning trials would be expected to occur in the ordinary play of parent and child, where the reinforcement is a hug or a toss into the air or some other conditioned reinforcer.

As another example, a little later on, in the presence of the auditory stimulus of mother saying DRINK YOUR MILK, the child is reinforced if he indeed drinks his milk. This is diagrammed in Figure 4.26. In these examples behaviors not appropriate to the verbal statement will not be reinforced.

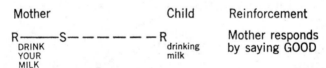

Fig. 4.26. When the child drinks his milk in the presence of the verbal stimulus DRINK YOUR MILK, he is reinforced by his mother saying GOOD. Thus, the verbal stimulus comes to elicit the milk-drinking response.

The pattern of setting up verbal stimuli as discriminative stimuli for some motor behavior seems to occur repeatedly in the child's history. The child brings the parent an ash tray even though it is unsolicited, and reinforcement may follow. It is then likely that the child will bring the parent other objects. However, the parent soon withholds reinforcement for this behavior unless he has previously presented the appropriate verbal stimulus, such as BRING ME THE ASH TRAY PLEASE. Repeatedly in the child's history the behavior of bringing something to the parent will be reinforced

—but only in the presence of certain auditory, verbal stimuli (of course, the same process of training would be expected to bring the individual's behaviors under the control of visually presented verbal stimuli also).

We do not usually think of such behavior in these terms. If someone were to be asked why he passed the salt when asked for it at the dinner table, he would probably state that he did so because the other person wanted the salt. This does not seem to be the explanation. It is suggested that the reason the verbal stimulus PASS THE SALT PLEASE controls our "salt-passing" behavior is because of our long history of operant conditioning—because in the past our response has been reinforced in the presence of that stimulus, but not in its absence. In general, the appropriateness of our response to verbal discriminative stimuli seems to depend upon this type of training.

During the course of a child's training a large repertoire of behavioral *units* comes under the control of appropriate verbal stimuli. For example, in the presence of auditory stimuli such as OPEN YOUR EYE, EXTEND YOUR TONGUE, BEND YOUR LEG, PUT YOUR RIGHT FOOT FORWARD, PRESS WITH YOUR INDEX FINGER, the person is reinforced for making the correct response. As a result of this, it is suggested, the individual acquires a repertoire of response units under the control of appropriate verbal stimuli. It seems that after a suitable repertoire of responses to verbal stimuli has been established, novel skills involving chains of motor behavior can be produced entirely on a verbal basis. An athlete or dancer, for example, acquires many new skills and sequences on the basis of such verbal-motor associations. A choreographer needs only to present a verbal sequence to a trained dancer, each stimulus unit in the sequence controlling a response unit. As a result, the response sequence will be acquired. The dancer, of course, has acquired a much more extensive repertoire of such verbal-stimuli–movement associations than the nontrained individual and thus can much more quickly learn new sequences of dance steps. A good example illustrating this mechanism was given in Chapter 3 (see Figure 3.13) concerning the acquisition of a car-driving sequence of motor responses. This process seems to be an important part of communication and the general "socialization" of the individual and will be discussed in the next chapter.

Motor Behavior Controlled by Our Own Verbal Behavior

The process whereby one's motor behavior comes under the control of one's own verbal behavior seems to be similar in many ways to the process just discussed. In the usual case, the child is positively reinforced for doing what he says he will do, in other words, specific motor behaviors are reinforced in the presence of the individual's own speech. In many cases the parents will attempt to train their child to "keep his word." There seem to be many cases where the child is reinforced if he follows his own verbal behavior with a specific motor response. When in reply to his mother's urging the child says I WILL DRINK MY MILK, positive reinforcement follows if he performs the appropriate response. When the child states that he will mow the lawn, the behavior of doing so is reinforced, or punishment may follow if he does not do so. The formation of this type of learning is illustrated in Figure 4.27.

Fig. 4.27. When the child says I WILL MOW THE LAWN and subsequently does indeed mow the lawn, he is reinforced, and this verbal response of the child now comes to control his motor behavior.

For almost every individual, training is given in which verbal stimuli (produced by others or by oneself) come to control motor behavior. However, this seems to be done in ways that differ in the detail and intensity of the training and also in its efficacy. It is suggested that for this reason wide differences exist in the extent to which individuals' motor behavior is controlled by appropriate verbal stimuli. These differences will be the subject of later sections that deal with the behavior involved.

Motor Behavior Controlled by Word-Meaning Responses

The way in which meaning responses are classically conditioned to words has been described. In addition, the manner in which meaning responses, or the stimuli they produce, come to elicit a group of word responses has also been described. It is suggested that responses other than word responses are also conditioned to meaning responses. As a result, words, through meaning responses, would come to control hierarchies of motor responses. Further description of this suggested S–R mechanism and its importance will be made in a later section, when attitude formation and function are discussed.

Summary

This chapter has been concerned with the formation of certain crucial stimulus—response relationships that appear to yield the various language associations so important to human adjustment. The summary of this interpretation will set forth, in a very abbreviated manner, the various types of language associations that have been described.

1. Various environmental stimuli come to control certain specific speech responses.

2. Internal drive stimuli come to control certain speech responses.

3. The stimuli produced by one's own responses come to control speech responses.

4. Printed and written verbal stimuli come to control the appropriate speech responses.

5. Verbal stimuli (or speech responses) come to elicit implicit responses through classical conditioning. These implicit responses may be called meaning responses.

6. These meaning responses produce stimulus characteristics that come to elicit speech responses having a similar component of meaning.

7. Word stimuli (or speech responses, through the stimuli they produce) come to elicit other word responses. Sequences of speech responses may be formed in this manner.

8. Verbal stimuli (written, auditory, and those produced by one's own speech responses), as well as the stimuli produced by meaning responses, come to control certain motor behaviors.

9. The child acquires vocal responses that produce sound stimuli that "echo" or "match" those produced by an authority source, as well as other types of verbal "matching" responses. The matching stimuli that result become conditioned reinforcers.

The discussions in this chapter must certainly give the impression that complex variables underlie the language behavior of an individual, even at any particular moment. Since verbal behavior is characterized by both great complexity and great flexibility, this would indeed be expected. It is probably because of the complexity of the behavior as well as its determinants that some people feel that one's language behavior is "free," undetermined by natural factors. A less extreme conclusion might question the possibility of ever having useful knowledge concerning language behavior, since it is so complex, in other words, the possibility of predicting or controlling what someone will say or think. Perhaps it can be said that no one is in possession of knowledge of the past events that will determine what a friend's next verbal response will be. But this problem is no different from that which occurs in other sciences. The determining variables in any case must be discovered in simple situations, and the variables must be capable of relatively simple manipulations. A physicist might not be able to predict with exactitude which way a feather will fall because of the complex combination of variables that are involved—but knowing the principles he can manipulate variables that will produce what he wants in other situations. In an analogous manner, we might not be able to predict what a person will say next, but from a knowledge of the principles of language learning, we should be able to arrange situations so that a child will have experiences that will produce the type of knowledge (verbal behavior) the culture feels is valuable and which, as we shall show, may enable him to solve important problems of various kinds.

5

Language Function

THE TITLES of the present and preceding chapters imply that the manner in which verbal behavior develops will first be presented, and then, in a clear separation, the function of this verbal behavior in the individual's total behavior will be discussed. Although there is enough didactic advantage to warrant the imposition of this type of organization, the reader will recognize that some aspects of language function were discussed in the preceding chapter, and some aspects of language development will be discussed in the present chapter. Nevertheless, the activities of communication, reasoning, mathematical learning, originality, composition, and scientific behavior involve previously acquired verbal behavior even though new verbal learning may also be occurring.

COMMUNICATION

Communication Involving Transfer of Meaning

In very general terms, communication may be considered as written or vocal speech emitted by one individual that results either in the establishment of new S–R mechanisms in another individual or in the elicitation of S–R mechanisms that have been previously acquired.

Under the rubric *communication* it is customary to discuss several phenomena that may be analyzed in terms of diverse types of S–R mechanisms. As will be shown, both respondent and operant conditioning are involved.

Mowrer's Conception of Communication

Mowrer (1954) has described communication as the higher-order conditioning of meaning. The principle involved was discussed in Chapter 3, where it was pointed out that a stimulus which has become a CS in a first-order classical conditioning procedure may serve as a UCS when later paired with a neutral stimulus. Thus, a stimulus which has come, through conditioning, to elicit a response may "transfer" this response to yet other neutral stimuli with which it is paired.

In extending this process to communication, Mowrer used as an example the sentence TOM IS A THIEF. In this example, Mowrer considered TOM as the CS, and THIEF as the UCS eliciting a certain type of meaning response. When the sentence is presented, the meaning elicited by THIEF is conditioned to the word TOM. This is depicted in Figure 5.1.

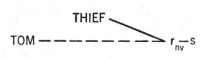

CS   UCS

THIEF

TOM — — — — — — — — $\longrightarrow$ r_{nv}—s

Fig. 5.1. The higher-order conditioning of a negative meaning response (r_{nv}) to TOM through the sentence TOM IS A THIEF.

This is seemingly a straightforward instance of second-order conditioning: By first-order conditioning some part of the total reaction elicited by real thieves gets shifted to the word, "thief," and by second-order conditioning of the type provided by the sentence, this same reaction, with some attenuation or weakening, gets further transferred or shifted to the word "Tom" (p. 667).

Empirical support for this paradigm has been provided by the present authors and associates (Staats and Staats, 1957; Staats, Staats, Heard, and Nims, 1959). The experimental procedure involved pairing a nonsense syllable with many different words, all of the words having, however, an identical meaning component. For example, the words PRETTY, SWEET, and HEALTHY have in common a positive evaluative meaning component (although they are quite different in meaning otherwise). In the actual experiment, one nonsense syllable was always paired with words of positive evaluative meaning, another syllable with words eliciting negative evaluative meaning responses. After a number of such pairings, the subjects rated the nonsense syllables on a semantic differential scale of "pleasantness–unpleasantness." As predicted, the nonsense syllable paired with positive evaluative words was rated "pleasant" relative to the syllable paired with the negative words. It was thus concluded that pairing the nonsense syllable many times with the same meaning response conditioned the response to the syllable.

Other studies have shown that other meaning responses also could be conditioned to nonsense syllables. In one study (Staats, Staats, and Heard, 1961), denotative meanings were conditioned using the same method. That is, it was possible to condition "round" meaning using UCS words such as GLOBE, BULB, and MARBLES, and "angular" meaning using UCS words such as BOX, ROOF, and ZIGZAG. Furthermore, it was shown (Staats and Staats, 1959a) that the strength of the conditioned meaning depends upon the number of language-conditioning trials. The greater the number of trials, the more intense is the meaning response conditioned.

An interesting example of communication through the conditioning of meaning responses is given by Dodge (1955). The communication took place through the reading of stories modeled after those appearing in *The National Geographic Magazine*. In the stories fictitious tribes of people were described, such as the "Meblu" tribe, as though the author were taking a trip through an unfamiliar area. The stories then proceeded to pair this nonsense name with meaningful words. For example, in one story the phrase the *friendly Meblu* was presented several times. It would be expected that each time this phrase occurred, the positive evaluative meaning elicited by the word *friendly* would be conditioned to *Meblu*. The results of the study supported this and indicated again that the strength of the conditioning was a function of the frequency with which the meaningful word was paired with the nonsense name.

From these studies, it appears that language conditioning, that is, the higher-order conditioning of meaning responses, involves the same paradigm as does the conditioning of simple responses in simple organisms. In the first place, words seem to come through conditioning to elicit meaning responses. Once a word does elicit meaning, it can function to condition this meaning response to any stimulus with which it is paired. This conditioning seems to occur automatically (without the subject's awareness), and yet may be quite effective.

To return to the analysis of the sentence TOM IS A THIEF, however, Mowrer also points out that this sentence results in products of communication in addition to the fact that the word TOM now elicits the meaning of THIEF. For example, on the basis of the sentence, the listener would also respond differently to his acquaintance Tom.

> . . . [I]n order for the sentence completely to fulfill its intended function there must also be the phenomenon of response mediation . . . , whereby the new meaning which thus gets connected to the sentence subject can generalize, or transfer, to the thing thus symbolized (p. 673).

This would occur on the basis of the following processes. Prior to the exposure to the sentence and because of the past experiences of the listener with Tom himself, the word TOM has acquired a meaning, in other words, it elicits a meaning response. Let us say that the experiences have been of a simple sensory sort so that pairing the word TOM with Tom himself has conditioned a particular sensory meaning response to the word. This is depicted in Figure 5.2, part A.

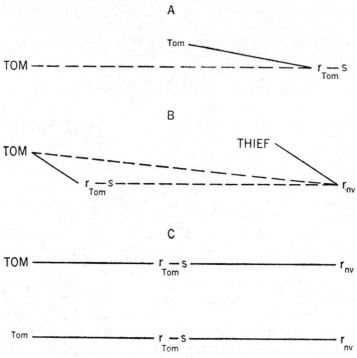

Fig. 5.2. In part A the word TOM acquires a particular sensory meaning response through its association with the person Tom. In part B this meaning response, as well as the word TOM, acquires the negative meaning response (r_{nv}) elicited by THIEF when the sentence TOM IS A THIEF is presented. In part C Tom the person, since he elicits the same response as has been conditioned to the word TOM, elicits through semantic generalization the negative meaning response appropriate to THIEF.

When the person is told that TOM IS A THIEF the meaning response of THIEF is thus elicited in contiguity not only with the word TOM, but with the meaning response which is elicited by TOM as well. The meaning response of THIEF is thus conditioned to the stimuli produced by the meaning response elicited by TOM. This process is depicted in Figure 5.2, part B.

Now the word TOM elicits its former meaning response, but in addi-

tion this meaning response elicits the meaning of THIEF. It will be recalled that Tom himself elicits the same response as does the name TOM.
Thus, according to the principles of semantic generalization discussed in
Chapter 4, Tom will now elicit the meaning response of THIEF. This is
depicted in Figure 5.2, part C. The sight of Tom elicits a characteristic
response, and the stimuli produced by this response elicit the meaning of
THIEF.

Empirical support for Mowrer's analysis was gained from the following
experiment. Staats, Staats, and Heard (1959), using the method of conditioning meaning responses to words already described, showed that a meaning response could be conditioned to a meaning response. In the
experiment, a meaning response was conditioned to the word ROCK, and
presumably to the meaning of ROCK. Since the word STONE elicits the
same meaning as ROCK, the conditioned meaning should also be elicited
by STONE, and the results supported this expectation.

Thus, it seems that the meaning of Tom the person could change solely
on the basis of language experience. The discussion of verbal habit-families
or concepts is useful to consider in this context. It will be remembered that
a meaning response component may have tendencies to elicit a number
of different word responses. When the meaning of THIEF is conditioned
through the communication TOM IS A THIEF, that meaning will have
tendencies to elicit a number of word responses. That is, the question
WHAT KIND OF PERSON IS TOM? would have tendencies to elicit
word responses such as DISHONEST, CRIMINAL, UNTRUST-
WORTHY, DANGEROUS, or BAD. The conditioning of a single meaning response component will associate also all the word responses the
meaning response tends to elicit. This is depicted in Figure 5.3 for the
example used.

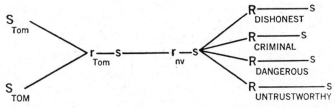

Fig. 5.3. Both Tom the person and the name TOM elicit the meaning
response appropriate to Tom, to which has been conditioned the "thief,"
or negative evaluative, meaning response. The stimuli produced by this
response would be expected to elicit the verbal habit-family of negative
evaluative words.

In addition, through conditioning, the negative meaning response of
THIEF will ordinarily have come to elicit other responses. For example,

after the THIEF meaning had been conditioned to TOM, if the listener was asked to rank his friends in order of preference, he would rank Tom lower than he would have previously. In a face-to-face situation with Tom himself, it would be found that this person would tend to a greater extent to avoid Tom. In the terms already described, the THIEF meaning which had been conditioned to the meaning of TOM (and Tom himself) would have associations with a hierarchy of "negative" responses ranging from negative words describing the person to negative ratings or judgment responses, motor avoidance responses, motor aggressive responses, and so on. Which of the responses in the hierarchy was elicited would seem to depend upon other stimulus conditions in the total situation. This type of communication is relevant to attitude formation and function and will be discussed in this context in Chapter 8.

Meaningful Words with No Empirical Referents Established through Communication

On the basis of the previous section, one may see how it is possible for a word to become very meaningful, how it may even appear to stand for some real object or event while it actually has no objective counterpart. For example, let us suppose that the word DEVIL has been considered by some persons (at least in the past) to be the name for some real entity or process of an "evil" nature. Following the present interpretation, the word must have elicited complex meaning responses of both a connotative (evaluative) and denotative (sensory) type to function in this manner. But of course, there is no environmental stimulus that can serve as the unconditioned stimulus to establish vivid sensory meanings to the word (assuming also that pictures are not involved). In other words, there is no being who carries a spear, is bright red, has a pointed tail, horns, or whatever the physical characteristics of the devil might be considered to be.

After the previous discussion, however, it should be recognized that although the meaning of the word could not have been gained on a primary conditioning basis with an actual devil stimulus object, it could have been acquired through higher-order conditioning. Simply by pairing DEVIL with appropriate words that already elicited meaning responses, the word DEVIL could come to elicit vivid meaning responses.

There seem to be many words in our language that because they elicit intense meanings seem to refer to "real" objects while in actuality, since no such objects exist, they have gained their meanings solely through pairing with other words (or perhaps other conditioned "reality" stimuli such as pictures). This is pointed out because, among other implications, it indicates that the interpretations of meaning presented in this text do not rest upon the criterion that there be a referent object for every meaningful word in our language. In addition, it indicates that the meaning of any single word may have been conditioned in different and complex ways. Many words, for example, seem to have some meaning that has been conditioned on a primary basis and some meaning that has been conditioned on a higher-order basis, in other words, through communication (Staats, 1959; Staats, 1961). The following is an interpretation of the differences in the meaning of certain words as a function of differences in the higher-order conditioning of the meanings of the words.

> . . . [I]n a cross-cultural experiment, Triandis and Osgood . . . found that the word STRAIGHT was favorably evaluated as compared with the word CURVED for Greek students but not for Americans. To help explain this difference they quote from D. D. Lee . . . concerning Greek culture, "the beloved is commonly likened to a tree . . . slim, straight, tall, hard." Here we can see the development of the dual processes of first-order and higher-order conditioning in practice. The word STRAIGHT is presented in the presence of the stimulus objects tree, ruler, straight lines, etc., and gains a portion of its meaning directly from the responses elicited by these environmental objects. This portion of the meaning of the word would be the same for all language users everywhere. But in Greek speech, the word BELOVED (which has itself become positive in evaluative meaning through contact with certain aspects of the natural environment) is paired with the word STRAIGHT, and the positive evaluative meaning elicited by BELOVED is conditioned to the word STRAIGHT, until it too becomes positive in connotation. In the future, the Greek responds to the word STRAIGHT . . . in terms of the evaluative meaning as well. Thus, although each of the component responses was initially elicited by the natural environment, when conditioned in combination, the explanation of the resultant response need not be tied to the environment any longer (Staats, 1959, pp. 5–6).

The foregoing implies that word meaning formed through communication may or may not be equivalent in all essentials to meaning formed on a first-order basis, that is to say, as if the word has been paired with the stimulus object itself. It should be recognized that on the basis of communication of this type (on the principle of higher-order language conditioning), word meanings might be established which are different, or even antagonistic, to the meanings which would have been conditioned through pairing the word with the object. For example, even though Tom is not a thief, the sentence TOM IS A THIEF would be expected to be effective in establishing a new and "unrealistic" meaning response to TOM.

Development of Secondary Reinforcers
through Communication

The process through which a word can become a conditioned reinforcer has been discussed briefly in previous sections. This occurs when a word is paired with other stimuli that are reinforcers—with positive or aversive stimuli. Thus, the words NO or BAD may be paired with aversive stimuli such as slaps or spankings or the removal of positive reinforcers. As we have pointed out earlier, under this circumstance two processes would be expected to occur: the responses made to the original aversive stimuli become conditioned to the words and form the meaning of the words and the words as a consequence become conditioned negative reinforcers. The same holds true for positive conditioned reinforcers. Conditioning a word so that it has positive evaluative meaning also makes the word a positive reinforcing stimulus. Thus, the process of establishing a conditioned reinforcer may be considered the same as making the stimulus a CS in a classical conditioning sense.

Of special importance, however, in discussing the reinforcing properties of words, is the possibility that a word can gain its evaluative meaning (reinforcing value) on the basis of communication. It is not thought necessary, for example, that a word be paired with primary aversive stimuli in order to become aversive itself. Once a word through classical conditioning has come to elicit a negative evaluative meaning, and thus has become a conditioned negative reinforcer, it should function in a higher-order conditioning sense and "transfer" its evaluative meaning response to new words, as well as to other objects and events. This seems to be one of the powers of language. Many words, objects, and events may come to be positive or negative reinforcers on the basis of the higher-order conditioning of meaning.

As an example, a child could be presented with many experiences in which the word SEX was paired with words of negative evaluative meaning (negative reinforcers or aversive stimuli), such as FILTHY, EVIL, HARMFUL. In this manner, the word SEX could come to elicit a negative evaluative meaning response. This child would as a consequence learn to escape situations in which the word SEX was present. On the basis of semantic generalization the child would later also find actual experiences of a sexual nature aversive. In addition, the word SEX would be paired in the individual's experience with many other words, and these too would come to be aversive on the basis of the same principles.

Although the example given is a simple one, this is a very important aspect of communication. As shall be described in later chapters, the formation of attitudes and values may also take place through the processes discussed.

Reading and the Elicitation and Transfer of Meaning

In the preceding chapter reading (or texting) was discussed as the control of verbal responses by specific visually presented verbal stimuli. One of the examples used suggested that a visual verbal stimulus could control a verbal response even though neither the verbal stimulus nor the response itself was "meaningful," that is, elicited a meaning response. In other words, after syllable responses have come under the control of the appropriate visually presented verbal stimuli, a child can "sound out" many words with which he is otherwise unfamiliar.

However, it is often only the visual verbal stimulus that is unfamiliar; the word response itself (or, rather, the auditory stimulus it produces) has come to elicit a meaning response on the basis of previous classical conditioning procedures. When this occurs the meaning response elicited by the verbal response itself will be conditioned to the "meaningless" visual verbal stimulus. Henceforth, the word stimulus should, according to this interpretation, directly elicit the meaning response.

Let us suppose that a child has been conditioned to make the proper unitary syllabic vocal responses to certain visual verbal stimuli. To the stimulus *cho* he responds CHO, to *co* he responds CO, to *late* he responds LATE. However, let us say the printed stimulus *chocolate* is meaningless to him since it is entirely novel. On the other hand, the child has acquired a meaning response to the auditory presentation of the verbal stimulus (in other words the verbal stimulus has many times in the past been paired with the candy). Now when the printed stimulus *chocolate* is presented the child makes syllabic responses CHO–CO–LATE and the auditory stimulus that is produced serves to elicit the meaning of the word. The meaning response thus elicited will be conditioned to the visual stimulus of the word, and thereafter the visually presented word stimulus will itself elicit the meaning response. The process is schematized in Figure 5.4.

When the child is originally taught to read, the verbal *responses* involved are customarily those that already elicit meaning responses. The process of learning to read thus involves bringing the verbal response under the control of the visual verbal stimulus. In addition, it is suggested that the meaning response already elicited by the verbal response must come to be elicited by the visual verbal stimulus—a second aspect of the learning. When the meaning response has been strongly conditioned to the visually presented word, reading might be expected to occur more rapidly. That is, if the visual stimulus itself elicits the meaning response, the delay required for the individual to completely emit the word response may not be necessary.

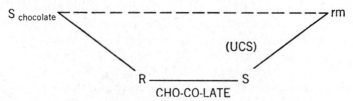

Fig. 5.4. The written word *chocolate* is an S^D that controls the word response CHO-CO-LATE. The written word, as a CS, acquires the meaning response elicited by the auditory stimulus CHO-CO-LATE. In the future the written stimulus *chocolate* will directly elicit the meaning response.

The manner in which the visual verbal stimulus may come to elicit the meaning response is thus also a case of the higher-order conditioning of meaning. In addition, the higher-order conditioning of meaning that Mowrer calls communication should also take place through reading. If the sentence *Tom is a thief* were read, it would be expected to have its same effect. However, in this case the meaning of *thief* would be conditioned to the visual stimulus *Tom* as well as to the auditory stimulus TOM.

Additional S–R Processes in Communication

Communication through Controlling Verbal Stimuli

In addition to communication involving meaning responses, there are forms of communication that involve other types of verbal responses. For example, it may be said that communication has occurred when after person A says something, person B responds in an appropriate overt manner. When a mother says CLOSE THE DOOR, PLEASE to a child and the child gets up and closes the door, the mother can be said to have "communicated" with the child.

This will be recognized simply as a situation in which a verbal stimulus, in this case auditory, has become a discriminative stimulus for a particular motor response. The example here is a little more complicated because two controlling verbal stimuli are involved. The communication rests upon the previous establishment of CLOSE as an S^D for the motor behavior of closing something, and of THE DOOR as an S^D for a response to a particular environmental stimulus, the door.

The above example is a simple one. Much more complex examples are quite familiar in every-day life. The mother might have said GO INTO

THE KITCHEN PLEASE AND PUT A SAUCEPAN OF WATER ON THE RANGE TO BOIL. Again, this act of communication would rest upon the previous establishment of the verbal stimuli as S^Ds. When the number or complexity of these S^Ds has passed a certain point, however, the communication involves another process now to be discussed.

The Role of Word-Response Sequences in Communication

Many communication stimuli are simply too long or too complicated to result in the immediate elicitation of appropriate behavior. In addition, frequently the communication stimulus is presented at one time, but only considerably later can the motor behavior occur. Under these two circumstances, an intervening step in the communication is often required—a word-response sequence must be established to mediate between the communication stimulus and the overt behavior.

Let us suppose, for example, that a novice golfer consults a manual to improve his game. The following is taken from a book by Ben Hogan on golf (1957) and contains systematic instructions for the appropriate way to "waggle" one's club prior to addressing the ball in earnest.

EACH TIME YOU WAGGLE THE CLUB BACK, THE RIGHT ELBOW SHOULD HIT THE FRONT PART OF YOUR RIGHT HIP, JUST ABOUT WHERE YOUR WATCH POCKET IS. WHEN THIS TAKES PLACE, THE LEFT ELBOW, AS IT MUST, COMES OUT SLIGHTLY, THE LOWER PART OF THE ARM FROM THE ELBOW DOWN ROTATES A LITTLE, AND THE LEFT HAND MOVES THREE INCHES OR SO PAST THE BALL TOWARD THE TARGET. AS THE HANDS MOVE BACK TO THE BALL ON THE FORWARD WAGGLE, THE LEFT HAND ALSO MOVES AN INCH OR TWO PAST THE BALL TOWARD THE TARGET (pp. 66–67).

As can be seen from this excerpt, even the instructions on "waggling" are quite complex for the novice—too complex to elicit immediately the appropriate sequence of motor responses. The novice golfer would have to refer back to the instructions in parts, that is, individually respond to each specific instruction (verbal S^D), or he would have to make textual responses to the passage until a verbal response chain was formed which could then control the motor behavior. In common-sense terms it would be said that he would have to memorize the passage. Then later, with club in hand and the ball in front of him, this verbal response sequence could act as a chain of S^Ds for the appropriate motor behaviors. It would be thought that many important communication acts involve the establishment of word-response sequences which later control overt behaviors significant to the individual or society.

There are times, however, when the *sole* effect of communication stimuli is to produce the verbal response chain itself. Much of the verbal material in the school situation can be considered of this sort. The verbal material is presented. If it occurs frequently enough the student forms verbal response chains. The chains of responses may not mediate any motor behavior whatsoever; the sole function of the sequence may be as an appropriate response to certain situations, such as classroom tests or drawing room conversation. For example, in a history class the student may be presented with the communication stimulus THE BATTLE OF HASTINGS WAS FOUGHT IN 1066 AND WON BY THE NORMAN FORCES. The word responses to this sequence may form a verbal response chain although this verbal chain may not elicit any particular motor behavior on the part of the student. The chain itself may be elicited by a class test question such as WHAT DO YOU KNOW ABOUT ANGLO–SAXON HISTORY?, and the major function of the chain may be its occurrence in such situations.

Thus, many communications may be effective only in establishing word-response chains. There are many people in our society whose function it is to provide such verbal stimulus sequences for others. That is, even though these people themselves have the verbal response sequences, the sequences do not have the function of mediating important overt behaviors in them. In fact, the important mediated behaviors may not even be in their repertoires. It may only be when these people establish such sequences *in others* that the important behaviors occur—that the function of the communication is achieved. For example, the pure mathematician has many verbal response sequences but these sequences may never elicit instrumental behaviors, such as building a bridge, constructing a missile, or solving problems in theoretical physics. His response sequences are reinforced by society because he can provide the appropriate verbal stimuli for students who, when they have the verbal response sequences, and also the other responses involved, *will* build bridges, and so on.

Role of Supporting Stimuli in Communication

The verbal stimuli of the communication may not be the only determinant of the recipient's behavior. Frequently the appropriate motor response will not be elicited until a later time when other S^Ds in the situation also support this behavior. The following example taken from a text on communication will illustrate. The writer is discussing a North Korean soldier who had surrendered.

> He said that when he picked up the leaflet, it actually made him fight harder. It rather irritated him, and he didn't like the idea of having to

surrender . . . [T]he message actually aroused a lot of aggression in him. Then the situation deteriorated. His division was hit hard and thrown back, and he lost contact with the command post. He had no food, except what he could find in the fields, and little ammunition. What was left of his company was isolated by itself in a rocky valley. Even then, he said, the morale was good, and there was no talk of surrendering. As a matter of fact, he said, the others would have shot him if he had tried to surrender. But then a couple of our planes spotted them, shot up their hideout, and dropped some napalm. When it was over, he found himself alone, a half mile from where he had been, with half his jacket burned off, and no sign of any of his company. A couple of hours later some of our tanks came along. And only then did the leaflet have an effect. He remembered it had told him to surrender with his hands up, and he did so.

In other words, the communication had no effect (even had an opposite effect from the one intended) so long as the situation, the personality, and the group norms were not favorable. When the situation deteriorated, the group influence was removed, and the personality aggression was burned up, then finally the message had an effect . . . [I]t is dangerous to assume any simple and direct relationship between a message and its effect without knowing all the other elements in the process (Schramm, 1960, pp. 17–18).

In the terms we have been using, the example shows that the verbal stimulus of the surrender leaflet cannot be considered to be the only determinant of the soldier's behavior—although the verbal stimuli can be considered to have had a direct effect upon him. Reading the leaflet had at least the effect of forming the simple verbal chain TO SURRENDER ONE MUST RAISE HIS HANDS, or some such sequence. However, although the communication stimulus had been effective in forming this verbal response chain, the motor response of surrendering was not elicited until a later time when other S^ps in the situation also supported this behavior. In the past, the soldier had no doubt been reinforced for "giving up" when in heavily unfavorable circumstances rather than persisting in oppositional behavior, and the stimulus situation in which he found himself was of that type. However, the verbal response resulting from the leaflet also determined the surrendering behavior.

The example perhaps illustrates that although a communication stimulus may have been effective in establishing verbal response sequences, this sequence may not mediate motor responses until some later time when other stimuli in the situation also tend to control the same motor responses. A communication stimulus may be only one of the multiple determinants of the individual's behavior.

It should be pointed out that in the example cited surrendering was not the only possible criterion of whether communication had taken place. When the verbal response chain had been formed as a result of texting the surrender leaflet, communication had occurred. The surrender situation served to elicit the chain, and communication was thus observed. Another situation in which communication might have been observed might simply have been to pose the question WHAT DID THAT LEAFLET SAY? This would then evoke the verbal response chain provided by the leaflet.

Efficacy of Communication

When the principles of some complex human behavior are set forth, as in the case of communication, the reader may question whether human behavior is actually a function of such principles. On first contact with such an analysis, he may feel that human behavior just does not occur in such an automatic manner as this. When a person is told TOM IS A THIEF he may or may not behave differently toward Tom. The communication may or may not be *effective*—it may be argued that the matter is not that cut and dried.

To suggest that additional complications may be involved, however, does not result in a rejection of S–R principles. In the previous examples, we might have pointed out some additional complications. However, as is so often the case in using naturalistic examples to demonstrate a point, more variables are involved than can be discussed easily. The result is usually an abstraction, the discussion of only a few principles and variables.

Such an analysis as this, however, does suggest where in the sequence of events the variables might be that would produce some result other than the desired effect of a communication. It may be pointed out, for example, that appropriate higher-order conditioning cannot take place unless the word stimulus of the sentence elicits the same meaning response in the listener as it does in the speaker. If THIEF elicits no meaning response, or even a positive evaluative meaning response in the listener, then the speaker in Mowrer's example will not communicate, that is, condition the listener in the same manner as himself.

In addition, other variables may be operative in the same situation. Because of the listener's past experience with the speaker, the speaker's statement TOM IS A THIEF may elicit in the listener covert sequences of verbal behavior that effectively "countercondition" the listener. He may respond covertly HE IS SAYING THAT BECAUSE HE DOES NOT LIKE TOM; ACTUALLY TOM IS A VERY HONEST PERSON; IN FACT IT IS LIKELY THAT THIS STORY IS UNTRUE. This learned verbal behavior would have the effect of conditioning this individual to negative evaluative meanings toward the speaker rather than toward Tom.

In terms of this interpretation, then, it would be thought that the effect of the communication could be in either direction and still be a function of the individual's learning history. This can also be said for communication that establishes word-response sequences. Even though the soldier in Schramm's example reads the surrender appeal, his instrumental and verbal behavior is multiply determined, as we have described. In response to the surrender appeal and the original supporting stimuli he may respond THEY ARE TRYING TO TRICK ME INTO SURRENDERING, ACTUALLY WE ARE GOING TO WIN, WE ARE IN BETTER POSITION, and so on. The message would thus not elicit the desired response.

In addition, communication may also fail even when the appropriate verbal response sequences are established by the message source. The listener simply may not have in his repertoire the appropriate motor behaviors the speaker wishes to elicit, so the verbal response sequences established cannot mediate the behaviors "demanded." A teacher may instruct a student, YOU MUST STUDY HARDER AND CONCENTRATE IF YOU ARE TO PASS THE COURSE. Unless the student has had a specific history of training, however, the appropriate behaviors of study and concentration cannot be elicited. Many communications may fail because although the verbal stimuli are received and the verbal response sequences are established, the instrumental behaviors are not there to be mediated. (See the next section for further discussions of the separability of such verbal and instrumental response sequences.)

REASONING AND PROBLEM SOLVING

The problems of modern man are not restricted to simple stimulus situations where single well-learned S–R mechanisms suffice, and psychologists have devoted considerable study to the behavior of man and other organisms in complex problem situations, where the correct response to the situation cannot be emitted immediately and automatically. Problem situations may be thought of as stimulus situations that require complex adjustments in order for a "satisfactory" outcome to occur (obtaining positive or negative reinforcement).

An early controversy in the study of problem solving concerned the importance of past experience. From one orientation, problem solution was considered to be dependent upon certain reorganizations of the problem situation taking place within the individual, rather than upon the effect of the individual's past experience on his problem-solving behavior. The implication of the first orientation is perhaps that problem-solving ability is a function of the nature of the problem situation and of the individual's "ability" to provide the correct reorganization of the elements in the situation—his ability to gain "insight." To illustrate, let us take an example from Wolfgang Köhler's ingenious early work on problem solving in primates. In one experiment a chimpanzee was enclosed within a cage and a banana placed outside the cage, easily visible but not within reach. A stick was available to the animal, however, and Köhler soon found that after some abortive attempts to reach the banana with his bare hands, the chimpanzee might survey the situation again and finally use the stick as an implement to secure the fruit (Köhler, 1925). This demonstration was interpreted by some psychologists as an indication that "insight" was the basis of problem solving. Successful response to the problem was thought to involve "perceiving" the stick, cage, and banana in the "correct relationships."

However, when used as an explanatory concept the term "insight" has serious shortcomings. Unless the determining conditions for "insight" are discovered, the term is empty of explanatory value. The questions remain open as to what conditions are required for an organism to solve a problem and for it to be unable to solve the problem. The term "insight" would not be explanatory if one must first wait until the problem has or has not been solved before he may infer that the organism did or did not have "insight."

Rather than relying upon "insight" as an explanation, the study of behavior principles suggests that critical in determining the solution of the problem is the animal's past experience. In the above example, the solution required that the chimpanzee take the stick and pull in the banana. Was the animal's past experience with respect to sticks important in its problem-solving behavior? From our general approach it would be thought so, and there is evidence to indicate that such is the case. Birch (1945) placed six chimpanzees in a problem which required that a banana be secured using a rakelike instrument which was lying adjacent to the banana. Since the animal was in a cage, it could obtain the food only in this way. Of the six animals, one had the previous experience of playing with sticks and responding to them in such a manner that the stick formed an extension of its arm. Another of the six had been in a prior experiment in which it had obtained food by pulling on a string to which food was attached. The other four animals had no experience of the type where responding to an object had the effect of extending the reach of the arm.

When placed in the problem situation, the animal that had previous experience with extending a stick solved the problem in 12 seconds. The animal with experience with the string as an extension solved the problem in 5 minutes. The other animals did not obtain the food; they did not solve the problem that day.

During the next three days, however, these four animals were given sticks to play with. They responded to the sticks in many ways, including extending the arm with the stick to touch something or someone. On the fourth day, they were again placed in the problem situation. On this occasion 20 seconds was the longest time required for any of them to solve the problem. It appeared that similar responses to the stick-stimulus of grasping and extending it had to have occurred in the past and had to have been reinforced through reaching some otherwise unattainable object. Unless this or some related responses to the stick-stimulus had been strengthened in this manner, the animals did not readily solve the problem.

Other experiments have shown the importance of past conditioning in human problem solving. In an experiment by Maier (1930) the problem was to build a structure, supported by the floor and ceiling of a room, from which could be hung two pendula. The problem-solving objects consisted of two short boards, a longer board, three clamps, and some string. Solution of the problem consisted of clamping the two short boards together making a longer one, which could be used to wedge the third board against the ceiling, thus forming a T. The pendula were suspended from the ends of the arms of the T, and the weights of the pendula came from the other two clamps tied on the ends of strings. The structure could be thought of as composed of three part structures, which when joined formed the complete structure: (a) making a long pole from two short ones by clamping them together, (b) making a pendulum from a string and clamp, and (c) using one board to wedge another one against a solid surface to make a self-supporting structure. It was shown that subjects who had received pre-problem demonstrations of the construction of these separate part structures were, in general, better able to solve the problem.

This is not to say, however, that all of an individual's past learning will be helpful in the solution of any particular problem. The strengthening of a particular response through past reinforcement of that response may be detrimental to the solution of a particular problem. Several investigators have experimentally shown this to be the case. The problem used by Birch and Rabinowitz (1951) was the Maier two-string problem, in which the subject had to tie together two strings which were too far apart to reach by hand. The solution required tying a weighted object to one string, and swinging it in a plane which would bring the object closer to the other string at the end of its arc, thus enabling the subject to grasp the object while holding the other string. The weighted objects available in solving the problem were an electrical switch and an electrical relay. Either could be used effectively. However, prior to the problem the subjects were introduced to a pretraining task in which an electrical circuit was to be completed using either the switch or the relay. For some of the subjects the pretraining involved the switch, for other subjects it involved the relay. It was found that regardless of which one of the objects was used in the pretraining task, it was the *other* implement which was used in the problem-solving task as a weight.

A closer analysis of the behavior principles involved in this experiment should be useful. Let us assume that prior to serving in this experiment, the subjects had hierarchies of responses to both the switch and the relay. As an example, let us take the case of a subject who had had no experience with either object. His response to the switch (or relay) would then be on the basis of stimulus generalization—he would respond in the same manner as he would to somewhat similar objects. Among these responses could be one of using the switch as a weight, as a door-stop, paper-weight, and so on. However, if in the pretraining he had been given the practice of using the switch to complete an electrical circuit, a new and strong response to the object would have been established. Thus, relative to this response, the other responses would be less likely to occur, in other words, strengthening the "electrical" response would make it the dominant response in the hierarchy, and other responses would occur only after this dominant response had extinguished. Now this subject, when placed in a situation involving both the switch and the relay, would be more likely to respond to the "unfamiliar" relay by using it as a weight. The strongest response to the switch would be to use it in electrical work. The reverse would have been true if the subject had been given preproblem training using the relay to complete the circuit and had no experience with the switch.

Thus, past experience, as it shapes or strengthens responses, could be thought to have a determining effect upon an individual's behavior in a complex situation. The situation may be such that although it elicits a number of responses, only some of these responses will result in reinforcement, that is, in solving the problem. If, by virtue of his past learning history, the individual has the "correct" response in his repertoire of responses elicited by the situation, he may "solve" the problem. How quickly he solves the problem would seem to depend upon the strength of the "correct" response relative to the strength of the other responses. If a number of "incorrect" responses are elicited by the situation more strongly than the "correct" response, it should take time for the incorrect responses to extinguish. If the correct response is too weak or is not present in the individual's repertoire he may never solve the problem. This interpretation of problem solving is based upon similar interpretations presented by Cofer (1954), Maltzman (1955), Osgood (1953), and Staats (1955), which will be summarized in a later section.

An individual's past experience may thus facilitate an adjustive response in a situation, or the past experience may have a detrimental effect by strengthening a competing and incorrect response. It should be remembered, however, that a response which is detrimental in one situation may not be detrimental in another. After having had the pretraining practice with a relay it might take longer to solve Maier's two-string problem, where it was necessary to use the relay as a weight. However, in a problem situation requiring the use of the relay to complete a circuit, this individual would do much better than if he had had no such experience.

Thus, simple problem solving may be regarded as involving situations that elicit not merely one response but a hierarchy of responses and in which only one of the responses will lead to reinforcement. The more nearly dominant that response is, the more quickly will the problem be solved. All the principles that apply to the strengthening and weakening of the various responses in the hierarchy should thus affect the course of problem solving.

Experimental studies of problem solving have included verbal problems. For example, Rees and Israel (1935) used anagrams as the problem-solving tasks. An anagram is a set of scrambled letters that can be rearranged to spell at least one word. In their study Rees and Israel had subjects work anagrams that could be solved only by rearranging the letters to form words of one particular class, such as "nature" words. After solving a number of these anagram problems the subject was given an anagram that could be solved by rearranging the letters either to form a nature word or to form a word of another class. Subjects who had been given practice forming nature words did this even when several solutions were possible. On the other hand, those subjects who had been given prior practice solving anagrams that formed "food" words later tended to give food-word solutions when the anagram could be solved in alternative ways. The instructions given to the subjects did not influence them to respond with either form of solution. Thus, when one class of response had been reinforced, it became the dominant problem solution.

Adamson (1959), again using anagrams as the problem task, has also shown that intermittent reinforcement has the expected effect upon the course of problem solving. In the training session, some subjects were given six anagrams in which the solution was to rearrange the four letters according to a 2-3-4-1 order, for example, ETYP when rearranged according to that formula spells TYPE. These subjects received six reinforcements for that response (a continuous reinforcement schedule). Another group of subjects received the same anagrams mixed in with six other anagrams that required other types of ordering solutions. Thus, these subjects had six reinforcements for the 2-3-4-1 ordering response interspersed with cases where this response was not reinforced. According to the relevant behavior principles, the subjects who had been on the intermittent schedule for the

2-3-4-1 solution should take longer to extinguish this response when it was no longer reinforced. This was measured by presenting all the subjects with a test series of anagrams, none of which could be solved by the 2-3-4-1 response. As expected, the intermittent reinforcement group took longer to solve the test anagrams.

These experiments, as examples, indicate that behavior principles may underlie these types of human problem solving. Although most human reasoning is more complicated than that which has been discussed, it is not unjustifiable to suggest that behavior principles would still be involved where the behavior, especially the language behavior, is much more complex. Skinner says, for example, "A better case can be made for identifying thinking with behaving which automatically affects the behaver and is reinforcing because it does so. . . . The speaker's own verbal behavior automatically supplies stimuli for echoic, textual, or intraverbal behavior, and these in turn generate stimuli for further responses" (1957, pp. 438–439). This suggests the importance of language behavior in problem solving and reasoning in the every-day life situation. The next section will attempt to extend learning principles to these types of examples.

A Learning Interpretation of Complex Problem Solving Involving Language

Both the language sequences involved in reasoning and the motor behaviors mediated in problem solving should be discussed more fully. Judson, Cofer, and Gelfand (1956) performed an experiment that can be used to illustrate the possible function of these mechanisms in actual problem situations. They used Maier's two-string problem as the task. Prior to introduction to the problem, however, the subjects received pretraining on an entirely separate learning task. The task was to learn lists of words in serial order. For one group of subjects the words *rope–swing–pendulum* were inserted in that order into the list. Thus, this group of subjects learned this sequence of word responses while other subjects learned these same words but not in serial order.

On encountering the Maier two-string problem, subjects in all groups should equally tend to respond with the word response STRING or ROPE to the cord presented in the problem. It would be expected, however, that subjects who had learned the response sequence ROPE–SWING–PEN-DULUM would respond with the latter two members of the chain after ROPE was elicited. The response ROPE would produce stimuli that would elicit the response SWING, and SWING would elicit PENDULUM. It might also be expected that the sequence ROPE–SWING–PENDULUM as a stimulus would mediate the motor response of making a pendulum out of the cord and swinging it. Thus, subjects who had learned this sequence of verbal responses should be more likely to solve the problem. In general, the results of the experiment substantiated this expectation. The problem solving is schematized in Figure 5.5.

A

$R_{\overline{ROPE}}$ S — — — — — $R_{\overline{SWING}}$ S — — — — — $R_{\overline{PENDULUM}}$ S

B

$S_{problem}$ — — — — $R_{\overline{ROPE}}$ S —— $R_{\overline{SWING}}$ S —— $R_{\overline{PENDULUM}}$ S —— $R_{making\ pendulum}$
(solves problem)

Fig. 5.5. In part A the subject learns in pretraining the verbal response sequence ROPE-SWING-PENDULUM. In part B, when the problem is presented, the presence of the string elicits the verbal response ROPE which in turn elicits the other members of the verbal sequence. Finally, the verbal response sequence would be expected to control (mediate) the behavior of making a pendulum and swinging it, thus solving the problem.

With this background the subject matter of every-day examples of more complicated problem solving can be more specifically considered to involve three behavioral mechanisms: tacting, verbal response sequences, and the mediated instrumental problem-solving behaviors.

Tacting

The experiment of Judson, Cofer, and Gelfand above may be examined more closely to clearly illustrate the three S–R mechanisms involved. First, in order for the pretraining to have been effective, the cord stimulus in the actual experiment must have been capable of eliciting the verbal response ROPE. The elicitation of the verbal response ROPE in the presence of the cord would depend upon a past (preexperiment) history of reinforcement for this verbal response in the presence of stimulus objects like a rope and the nonreinforcement of this response in "inappropriate" stimulus circumstances. Without this previous tacting training the subject would not emit the discriminated verbal operant ROPE (either implicitly or explicitly) in the presence of the cord stimulus, and the following responses SWING and PENDULUM would not be elicited. Anyone who had not had the previous tacting training would not profit from the establishment of the ROPE–SWING–PENDULUM verbal response sequence. A foreign-speaking individual would not have been aided in solving the problem through the establishment of the verbal sequence because the cord stimulus would not control the word-response ROPE to begin the problem-solving chain.

The general point is thus that much human reasoning and problem solving requiring responses to various environmental situations seems to depend upon the prior establishment of verbal discriminations. Unless the person has received the language training by which the environmental stimulus comes to elicit a particular verbal response, the problem will not be solved. This is one reason, as was pointed out in Chapter 4, why the language training given a child with respect to establishing a wide repertoire of verbal responses under the control of appropriate stimulus objects would be expected to be so important.

A systematic series of experiments by Kendler and associates (Kendler and D'Amato, 1955; Kendler and Karasik, 1958; Kendler and Mayzner, 1956; Kendler and Vineberg, 1954) have demonstrated the critical role of verbal discriminative responses in problem solving. Although the experiments are too complicated to describe fully here, their work suggests that adult human concept learning cannot be represented adequately without assuming that some verbal mediation occurs between the external stimulus and the overt responses. In an attempt to identify the nature of such verbal intermediaries, the experiments traced the development of a form of discrimination learning in which these verbal responses would be necessary. In the experiments, it was found, as expected, that the proportion of children who respond most effectively in the problem increased with age. Furthermore, when the younger children were required to tact the stimuli to which they were responding, they were found to require fewer trials to the criterion performance (problem solution) than children of the same age who had not made the verbal response or who had, rather, been trained in some irrelevant verbal response. Thus, it seems the solution of these problems was in some measure dependent upon the availability of tacts to the objects involved.

The importance of the tacting repertoire has often been pointed out by linguists and other social scientists. Consider for example, the significance of the difference between the English language and the Eskimo language with respect to the stimulus of snow. In English there is only the single word SNOW, which must be used in combination with adjectives to distinguish among differences in the snow, while in the Eskimo language there are a number of different words, one for each of the discriminated types of snow, such as falling snow, packed snow. Thus, in his discrimination training the Eskimo child is reinforced not for saying one word in the presence of all types of snow, but for making different verbal responses in the presence of the different types. Where it is important that different responses depend upon the different form of the snow stimulus present, the Eskimo would as a consequence be expected to be a better, or perhaps quicker, reasoner.

An experiment by Brown and Lenneberg (1954) also substantiates the assumption concerning the importance of tacts for later behavior. In their experiment subjects were shown simultaneously four colors that varied in what the investigators termed "codability" (actually this is largely the reliability of the tacting response among individuals who speak the same language). Then, after the four colors were removed, the subjects were asked to point to the colors just seen on a large chart of 120 colors. In general, the greater the codability—that is, the stronger the tacting response—the more likely was the recognition of the color. That is, in a situation with a number of complex stimuli present, the stimulus to which the individual responded seemed to be a function of his language learning—his tacting repertoire. It would be expected as a consequence that in a problem situation where responding to a particular stimulus was important, the tacting repertoire would be a significant determinant of the individual's ability to solve the problem.

The same principle is involved in naturalistic examples of problem-solving behavior. The mechanic who responds to the knocking of an engine with THE MAIN BEARINGS ARE GOING OUT and whose problem-solving behavior is mediated by this discriminated verbal operant may be considered to solve the problem in part on the basis of his past tacting training. The behavior of the physician who must first make a proper verbal discrimination—PNEUMONIA rather than LUNG CANCER—before he prescribes treatment may be considered to illustrate a more complex constellation of the same principles. The beginning of problem solution may often depend upon the correct elicitation by the environmental stimulus of a verbal response.

Verbal Response Chains

The S–R mechanism in the experiment of Judson, Cofer, and Gelfand that might most appropriately be called reasoning is the verbal response chain. Not only was it important that the cord stimulus elicit the verbal response ROPE, it was also necessary that ROPE elicit the subsequent verbal response SWING, and so on. The prior establishment of verbal response sequences may be crucial to problem solution.

An example from anthropology might most dramatically show how the same stimulus event may lead to widely disparate verbal response chains. The Jivaro Indians of South America are said to have no concept of death from infection or disease. In our terms we would say that the complex sequences of verbal responses regarding infection and disease, as we know them in Western societies, have not been developed in the Jivaro. Rather, on the death of a relative or friend, the Jivaro might respond, HE IS DEAD; DEATH IS CAUSED BY EVIL SPIRITS. THE SPIRITS MUST HAVE BEEN SET INTO HIS BODY BY A SHAMAN AT THE INSTIGATION OF HIS ENEMIES. This is, let us say, the type of verbal response sequence that has been established in his history.

An early Christian, on the other hand, after saying HE IS DEAD might have continued with the response sequence IT WAS THE WILL OF GOD. A person educated in our society today, however, would be likely to have had a still different language training, and he might respond IT WAS THE RESULT OF A FLU INFECTION COMPLICATED BY PNEU-MONIA BECAUSE HE GOT OUT OF BED TOO SOON. The differ-ences in this reasoning (word-association chains) may be thought to result from past training.

In the example of the mechanic, not only was it important that he emit the discriminated verbal operant (MAIN BEARING TROUBLE) to the stimulus of the knocking engine, it would also be necessary that this verbal response elicit other verbal responses, such as ON THIS CAR, REPLAC-ING THE MAIN BEARINGS STARTS WITH REMOVING THE PAN, and so on. The mode of communication by which this type of verbal response sequence could be established could vary from personal instruc-tion to reading a manual. As was discussed earlier, much of formal educa-tion is aimed at setting up such verbal response chains, which, once the first tacting response has been emitted, will result in an appropriate reason-ing sequence. In a course in physics or electrical engineering, for example, the following verbal response sequence might be established. THE CUR-RENT (AMPERAGE, OR I) THAT TRAVERSES A CIRCUIT IS EQUAL TO THE VOLTAGE (ELECTROMOTIVE FORCE, OR E) DIVIDED BY THE RESISTANCE (OHMS, OR R) OF THE CIR-CUIT. If after learning this sequence the student was asked to determine the current a circuit will yield and if he was provided with the voltage and resistance, the appropriate verbal sequence could be emitted to attain the solution.

Many investigators have pointed to the critical role of the verbal response sequence in controlling overt behavior, as will be summarized shortly. Luria and his associates give the following examples.

Already in 1929 Vigotsky showed that every time the little child of four to five years of age is confronted with a problem which causes some kind of difficulty, there arises external speech, not directed to the inter-locutor; the child states the situation that has arisen [tacting], takes from it "verbal copy" and then reproduces those connections of his past experience which may help him out of present difficulties. Vigotsky attempted to show that this was . . . the inclusion of speech to mediate behaviour by the mobilization of verbal connections which help to solve a difficult problem. His observations showed that the child first speaks aloud, to himself, but that his speech gradually dies away, passes into a whisper and finally becomes internal speech; and that the child of seven to eight years begins to solve complex problems with the aid of systems of internal verbal connections, which have arisen earlier in the course of verbal intercourse but have since become converted into his own individual mechanisms, enabling him to include verbal connections in the organization of his activity (Luria and Yudovich, 1959, pp. 19–20).

In the early stages of child development, speech is only a means of communication with adults and other children . . . Subsequently it becomes also a means whereby he organizes his own experience and regulates his own actions. So the child's activity is mediated through words (Luria, 1957, p. 116).

Several experiments may be cited that support this conception of the role of tacting and verbal response sequences in problem solving. For example, in another version of the two-string problem a screwdriver was used as the potential weight for the pendulum, and, in an attempt to measure the effect of a verbal response sequence on problem success, subjects were asked to list the possible functions of the screwdriver prior to the problem participation (Staats, 1957b). The results of this experiment were inconclusive in this respect; no relationship was shown between these verbal responses and problem solution. However, Maltzman, Bogartz and Breger (1958) later showed that the effect of verbal response sequences under the control of tacts to the screwdriver could influence successful problem solution. Saugstad (1952), using a somewhat different method and problem, also indicated that where the verbal response sequences concerning the function of the problem-solving objects were present, the subjects tended to solve the problems. Where these verbal response sequences were absent, problem solution tended not to be attained.

Experiments in other types of problem situations also give evidence to the importance of verbal response sequences in problem-solving behavior. Marks (1951) found a high correlation between performance and vocalization by subjects during problem solution. Gagne and Smith (1962) indicated in an experiment that requiring individuals to verbalize while practicing in a problem-solving situation was significantly related to superior performance. These authors suggest that "[t]he results appear to indicate that requiring Ss to verbalize during practice has the effect of making them think of new reasons for their moves, and thus facilitates both the discovery of general principles and their employment in solving successive problems" (p. 18).

Elicitation of Problem-Solving Behavior
by Word-Response Sequences

The third S–R mechanism which seems to be involved in the problem-solving experiment of Judson, Cofer, and Gelfand is the elicitation of motor behavior by the individual's own verbal responses, that is, the control of the actual problem-solving behaviors. We have discussed the importance of the cord stimulus controlling the response ROPE, and of the response ROPE producing stimuli controlling the verbal response sequence of SWING and PENDULUM. In addition, for the actual solution of the problem it would be necessary that the sequence of verbal responses mediate the behavior of tying a weighted object on one piece of cord and swinging it to form a pendulum.

Thus, solving problems of the type under discussion would seem also to require that the sequences of verbal "reasoning" responses serve as a discriminative stimulus mediating the motor behavior of manipulating the problem objects to attain solution. For example, the mechanic must not only tact the engine noise correctly, setting off a chain of appropriate word responses, but these word responses must elicit that sequence of motor behaviors which in effect repairs the problem engine. Establishing the skilled responses under the control of verbal directions may require long and arduous experience. Much of the training of the physician, engineer, mechanic, and so on, seems to involve the acquisition of manual skills under appropriate stimulus control.

Before correct problem-solving behavior can occur for the beginner on some tasks, the appropriate verbal response sequences must intervene. However, when an individual has completed a problem task a number of times the "reasoning" response sequences originally necessary may drop out. After a number of repetitions, the problem stimuli alone may come to elicit the appropriate behavior. The experienced mechanic, for example, upon hearing the engine knock may immediately begin work upon the car without further "thought" responses. At this point we say he does the task "automatically." That is, the motor responses are directly controlled by the situational stimuli, and the person may, in fact, be emitting other verbal responses (such as singing) while the task is performed. This should not obscure the fact, however, that the task may have originally been a problem in which the three types of learned S–R associations were involved.

A series of experiments by Verplanck and his associates (Verplanck, 1962) has indicated the manner in which the mediation of problem-solving behaviors by verbal response sequences may be manipulated by reinforcement. In one experiment Oskamp (1956) asked subjects to place cards (handed to him one at a time) either to the right or to the left. Of the 110 cards, half had representations of a single object or figure and half had two or more object pictures. Correct placement of the card depended upon the number of objects on the card. The subjects were also instructed to state before placing the card the rule that was involved in placement. The three responses of the chain of responses to a card might thus be (1) the tact ONE DOG, TWO DANCERS, and so on, (2) the mediating verbal response sequence BELONGS TO THE RIGHT, GOES ON THE LEFT, and so on, and (3) the motor response of actually placing the card.

One group of subjects was told RIGHT or WRONG on each trial according to whether the card was placed correctly. In another group the same social reinforcers were administered contingent upon the correct emission of both the tact to the card and the verbal response indicating where it should be placed (both together are called the rule-statement) regardless of where they placed the card. Thus, for the one group, a "correct" response was placing the card in the appropriate pile, while for the other group the "correct" response was a particular tact and verbal response sequence.

The data indicated that when reinforcement was contingent upon correct rule-statements, but not upon correct placement, 92.2 percent of the rule-statements were correct as compared to only 76.8 percent of the placing responses. In contrast, for those subjects for whom reinforcement was contingent upon correct placement, but not upon correct rule-statements, 71.8 percent of their placement responses were correct as compared to only 48.4 percent of their rule-statements. Thus, in the situation where reinforcement of the mediating verbal responses (rule-statements) and the problem-solving behavior (placement responses) was independently applied, the two behaviors were, at least to some extent, independently strengthened. This experiment seems to indicate that mediating verbal responses and problem-solving behaviors are distinct parts of problem-solving situations. As Verplanck states, "[t]he rule-statement, and the behavior for which it is presumably a discriminative stimulus [the behavior which the rule-statement mediates], have been dissociated by manipulating their contingencies of reinforcement" (1962, pp. 137–138).

Of course, while the experiment illustrates that these last two operants in the problem-solving chain can be dissociated, normally these two events are not so independent. An individual more frequently is reinforced only when he actually does what he says he is going to, or when the verbal response sequence is actually a discriminative stimulus for the motor behavior. This seems usually to be the case because the correct problem-solving behavior cannot occur without the mediation of the correct verbal response sequences. In Oskamp's experiment this would be analogous to reinforcement only after the correct rule is given and is followed by the correct problem-solving response.

Congruent Approaches to Problem Solving

It should be pointed out that other analyses of reasoning and problem solving have been made which are congruent with the present one in including the three phases of the process as outlined: tacting, mediating verbal response sequences, and final problem-solving responses. Verplanck (1962), for example, using another terminology, states the following about his problem-solving situation.

> The protocols of this and of similar experiments show that the monent is a chain composed of two responses, made up of a word or phrase descriptive of the card, the "notate," linked to an instruction, the "pred-ocent" such as "put to the right," or "goes to the right." A notate may not recur after a single unreinforced occurrence. If the subject says "people go to the right" and gets no reinforcement, he is not likely to try "people go to the left"; he is more likely to say something such as "cards with blue go to the right." The two parts of the monent thus may be separated; their initial strengths differ greatly, as does their resistance to extinction.
>
> A "notate" . . . is defined as follows: any word or phrase given in response to a stimulus or to an object incorporating stimuli. . . . They are synonymous, then with Skinner's (1957) "tact."
>
> The second part, "put to the right," "goes to left" termed the "pre-docent" . . . is defined as a verbal response that is an S^D for motor behavior (p. 140).

In addition, Dollard and Miller (1950) have made an analysis of reasoning in S–R terms that in principle is very similar to the present one and that also has implications for topics yet to be discussed. The following quotation illustrates their approach.

> Attaching the same . . . response to two distinctive stimulus objects gives them a certain *learned equivalence* increasing the extent to which instrumental and emotional responses will generalize from one to the other (Birge, 1941; Foley and Cofer, 1943; Miller, 1935). . . . To give another example, once a child has learned to be slightly afraid of objects that are labeled "sharp" and to handle them carefully, these responses can be generalized to a new object by the simple expedient of labeling it "sharp." The child thus may often be taught to fear the new object and be cautious without first being cut by it. Similarly, the label of "Doctor" tends to mediate the transfer of confidence and respect to anyone to whom it is attached.
>
> Conversely, attaching distinctive cue-producing responses to similar stimulus objects tends to increase their distinctiveness. To use the ex-ample of counting change again, an array of nineteen nickels is sufficiently

similar to an array of twenty nickels so that few people would be able to make the discrimination by merely looking. When the nickels are counted, however, they lead to the distinctive cue-producing responses "nineteen" and "twenty," so that the discrimination is easy. . . .

Similar results can be secured by nonverbal cue-producing responses such as images and perceptual responses, or by focusing the attention on the parts of complex stimulus objects that are similar or different. . . .

Part of the effectiveness of the verbal labels probably comes from the nonverbal cue-producing responses which are attached to them in the course of extensive social learning. As a result of this learning, words and sentences become able to direct attention toward relevant differences, to influence perception, and to elicit images and other nonverbal cue-producing responses. . . .

The verbal responses of labeling are especially important because language contains those discriminations and equivalences that have been found useful by generations of trial and error in a given society (Miller, 1948b). Common examples are "boy" vs. "girl," "big boy" vs. "little boy," "friend" vs. "enemy," "married" vs. "single," . . .

In our society, where discriminating different stages in the ripeness of cocoanuts is not important, we have only two phrases, "green" cocoanuts and "ripe" cocoanuts. Among the Cook Islanders (Hiroa, 1932) in Polynesia, in whose economy cocoanuts play a paramount role as source of food, drink, and fiber, there are 12 distinctive words and phrases, each describing a different stage in the maturity of this nut. Learning to use these words to describe correctly the state of the cocoanut is of great assistance in subsequent behavior where correct discrimination or generalization is important (pp. 101–103).

Kendler and Kendler (1962) discuss problem solving in terms that are very relevant for the account that has been developed herein. After making an analysis of their experiments in problem solving in S–R terms, they state that verbal behavior is very important to problem solving and that the problem-solving ability of the child depends upon the development of verbal behavior which mediates between the problem stimulus and the problem-solving behavior.

These observations . . . point to the complex interrelationships existing between verbal behavior on the one hand and problem solving on the other. If nothing else, they destroy the illusion that it is reasonable to describe an organism as verbal or nonverbal without considering the problem with which it is confronted. The terms verbal and nonverbal become meaningful—and fruitful—when related to specific problem solving tasks.

It would seem fruitful to investigate the cue function of words for children of two age levels. One possibility is that age influences problem solving only in so far as it leads to the acquisition of words (pp. 9–10).

The Kendlers also discuss an experiment they interpret as involving an orienting or attentional response that then results in the occurrence of a visual stimulus. The visual stimulus elicits a symbolic response and the cue this response produces then controls the response that solves the problem. They also showed that when one of the responses in the chain was in the subject's repertoire but not the other response, the advantage was negligible. They make, as a consequence, the following statement.

> The reason for this is that reinforcement is only achieved consistently when both the appropriate orienting and mediating responses are operating. This particular study points to the need for discovering laws associated with the strengthening and weakening of independent S–R units in a problem solving chain, as well as the principles governing their synchronization (p. 12).

In addition, other theorists (Cofer, 1954; Maltzman, 1955; Osgood, 1953) have developed models of human problem solving with which the present discussion is congruent. In doing so Cofer also draws attention to the role of verbal processes in human problem solving and states the following.

> We think that problem solving is carried on by response systems which become temporarily dominant because of (1) activation by the nature of the stimuli in the problem situation, (2) their high strength and wide availability as in the case of strongly held attitudes or other habits, or (3) their being subjected to special conditions of reinforcement or non-reinforcement with consequent changes in strength either before or during the course of problem solving itself (1954, pp. 8–9).

Maltzman has presented a theoretical interpretation which is based upon the conception that the elementary laws of behavior can be applied to human problem solving. He presents a detailed model that he feels can also take place on a symbolic level. In the model, stimuli have tendencies to elicit hierarchies of mediating responses, which in turn tend to elicit hierarchies of problem-solving behaviors. The originating stimuli may also be of a verbal nature, such as instructions. Maltzman also indicates that these behavioral mechanisms may be integrated into even more complex chains in the solution of a problem. Nevertheless, he sees their manner of functioning as being dependent upon the effects of conditioning, discrimination learning, deprivation variables, and other behavioral laws.

Osgood has also presented a model of human problem solving with which the present discussion is quite congruent, but which tends to emphasize the role of meaning responses in the reasoning sequence. (Dollard and Miller's previously quoted statement on reasoning mentions similar types of responses.) Briefly, he says that the object involved in a problem elicits a hierarchy of ways of perceiving the object (a hierarchy of meaning responses in the subject) and each way of perceiving the object will elicit a hierarchy of problem-solving (instrumental) behaviors.

If a subject is shown a STICK and asked to state its properties as they occur to him, he might respond as follows: "long, wooden, hard, flexible, round . . . ," later responses having longer latencies, i.e. being less readily available. In other words, subjects have hierarchies of ways of perceiving objects—a STICK, being more readily perceived as *long* rather than *thick*, is more likely to be utilized as a probing tool than as a wedge to separate objects. If we provide the subject with the meaning of *wooden* and ask him to state various potential functions, he might respond as follows: "build things, burn, strike, nail . . ." Again, evidence for a hierarchy of potential functions would be obtained. . . .

A subject for whom perceived *woodenness* of PENCIL is relatively available should be more likely to think of "burning" as a potential function —and he should be more likely to survive in a problem situation in which using pencils for kindling is the correct solution (1953, pp. 631–632).

See Figure 5.6 for an illustration of this example. This interpretation might be extended by suggesting that chains of meaning responses could constitute the reasoning mechanism which finally controls the overt problem-solving behavior.

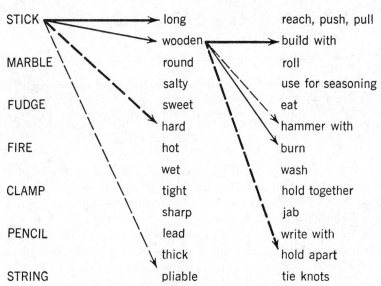

OBJECTS	WAYS OF PERCEIVING OR MEANING	POTENTIAL FUNCTIONS
STICK	long	reach, push, pull
	wooden	build with
MARBLE	round	roll
	salty	use for seasoning
FUDGE	sweet	eat
	hard	hammer with
FIRE	hot	burn
	wet	wash
CLAMP	tight	hold together
	sharp	jab
PENCIL	lead	write with
	thick	hold apart
STRING	pliable	tie knots

Fig. 5.6. Adapted from Osgood's mediational model of problem solving. Osgood states: "Objects . . . are associated with hierarchies of representational mediators (ways of perceiving objects or their significance) which in turn elicit readiness for executing a hierarchy of instrumental skills" (1953, p. 631).

It will be remembered that in Chapter 4 an effective stimulus was said to elicit sensory responses in the individual which themselves produce stimulus events. Whenever two such sensory responses occur in close contiguity the second sensory response is conditioned to the first (actually to the stimuli produced by the first). As an example, in the stimuli provided by a musical melody, each tone may be considered to be a stimulus that elicits a sensory response, that is, a particular "hearing" response. Since the tones form a sequence of stimuli, a sequence of sensory responses should result. Part of each sensory response would be conditionable to the stimuli of the preceding sensory response. The result would be a sequence of conditioned sensory responses. When the first sensory response occurs, the

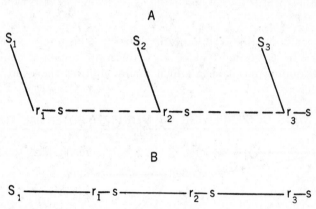

Fig. 5.7. In part A each tone elicits a sensory response. Since each response occurs in close contiguity with the next, the response is conditioned to the stimuli provided by the prior response, until finally, as in part B, the entire sequence may be elicited in the absence of the original eliciting stimuli.

second is elicited, it elicits the third, and so on. Thus, even though the actual stimuli are not present the sequence of conditioned hearing responses may be elicited; in common-sense terms, "the melody runs through his mind." This is illustrated in Figure 5.7.

As an illustration of the function of such responses in problem solving, let us suppose a person has performed a number of activities in various places in sequential order, only to find at some later time that he is missing some object he had been carrying at the beginning of the sequence. In terms of the preceding discussion, the sequence of activities would have resulted in a sequence of conditioned sensory responses (constituting what would be called his "memory" of the activities). The process of finding the missing object would then consist of the elicitation of the sequence of conditioned sensory responses. This alone may solve the problem since one of the conditioned sensory responses may be the visual response to the object sitting in one of the places the person had visited. Then his sensory response would mediate the motor response of going to that place and looking for the object. Or the sequence of conditioned sensory responses might mediate the retracing of each of the previous activities and searching for the object at each place. Again, problem solving would depend upon the sequence of reasoning responses, that is, the sequence of sensory responses.

One more point: the processes of reasoning and problem solving, as Dollard and Miller indicate, would seem to be the same whether the problem is a technical or a social one. The tacting and reasoning behaviors of the Jivaro Indian with respect to the death of a relative, as well as the problem-solving behaviors mediated under their control (such as killing the suspected evil-doer) may be considered to be the same type of behavioral process as those involved in solving a problem in physics. This emphasizes again how important our conceptions of man and his behavior may be, for these tacting and reasoning sequences may mediate many of our social problem-solving behaviors, ranging from how we vote on an issue like the use of capital punishment to how we train our children. Thus, such social-reasoning and problem-solving behaviors may also be considered to be a function of our complex past experiences (see Chapter 8 for further discussions of social reasoning).

Acquisition of the S–R Associations Involved in a Problem

It may now be helpful in concluding the discussion of reasoning and problem solving to present a detailed interpretation of the types of past learning thought to be involved in complex problem solving involving language behavior. Let us take the hypothetical example of an electronics engineer who is presented with the following problem. The manufacturer of a television set produces a transformer with a certain voltage output, tubes that require a certain current, and wires connecting them that have a certain resistance. He asks his engineer to CONSTRUCT A CIRCUIT FROM THE TRANSFORMER TO THE TUBE SO THAT THE CORRECT AMPERAGE WILL BE SUPPLIED TO THE TUBE. The transformer produces 220 E (volts), and the tube requires 20 I (current flow).

The problem requires, let us say, that the engineer respond to the instructions CONSTRUCT A CIRCUIT with the following verbal response sequences: (1) $I = E/R$ (CURRENT EQUALS VOLTAGE DIVIDED BY RESISTANCE), (2) BUT I MUST FIND WHAT THE RESISTANCE IS TO BE, (3) $I = E/R$ IS THE SAME AS $RI = E$ OR $R = E/I$,

(4) R EQUALS 220 DIVIDED BY 20 ($R = 220/20$), (5) 11 R (OHMS) RESISTANCE MUST BE PROVIDED. Following this sequence of language responses (reasoning) the engineer might connect the transformer and a set of wires and resistors that provide 11 ohms resistance to an ammeter (where the tube will finally be attached) to measure the amount of current—which should be 20 amps.

Basic to such a problem-solving task would be the relevant language responses established in the individual's past experience and the motor responses that are controlled by some of them. Let us briefly summarize a few probable highlights in such experience, starting from the beginning. First the vowel and consonant sounds in syllabic units were differentially reinforced in the child's home. In extensive language experience grammatical verbal response sequences were formed. Then in school these verbal responses came under the control of written verbal stimuli in the process of textual learning. Later in technical courses verbal responses (tacts) to tubes, transformers, wires, and so on, were acquired. The student learned in mathematics courses the verbal response sequences we call algebraic rules (such as $a/b = c/d$ is the same as $ad = bc$). He also learned the verbal response sequence $I = E/R$ and, because of the previous training of the algebraic response sequences, the variations of this electrical sequence. He also learned in arithmetic class the response sequences involved in such operations as 220 divided by 20 equals 11. The motor responses involved in attaching an ammeter have also been reinforced, and he texts the dial of the meter as 11 ohms because of early school texting training. The 11 reading of the dial and the 11 answer to these verbal sequences constitute a reinforcement because of his past "matching" training; they also form an S^D for ceasing the problem-solving behaviors and for sending his results to his employer.

Actually, of course, a more detailed analysis of this example of problem-solving behavior would be necessary to understand the behavior fully. The main purpose of the example, however, is to demonstrate the constituent experiences which could have molded the engineer's behavioral repertoire so that he would be able to "reason" successfully in this situation and solve the problem. Most importantly, it is suggested that his reasoning ability depended upon experiences which molded his behavior (especially his language behavior) through his entire history. Without any one of the constituent experiences and the response sequences they established, it would seem that individuals would not solve such problems. Thus, when we look for an understanding, for an explanation, of reasoning ability, it is suggested that we explore the principles of behavior in general and the specific manner of their involvement in the formation of language behavior and skilled manual responses.

It would be expected that the behaviors involved in complex human problem solving are exceedingly complex and established as a function of exceedingly complex training experiences. Because of this complexity experiments have not yet dealt analytically with the every-day case of such behavior. Nevertheless, an extension of behavior principles to such cases seems suggestive and has perhaps useful implications that will be pointed up in later discussions.

DEVELOPMENT OF MATHEMATICAL LANGUAGE SEQUENCES

Mathematics has been spoken of as a language: for example, ". . . mathematics is the language of *size* as opposed to English which is a language of *sort*" (Stevens, 1951, p. 2). Mathematics should be analyzable in the same manner as other language behavior involving tacting of objects and other verbal stimuli, verbal response sequences, and so on. This section will present a tentative interpretation of a limited mathematical repertoire and will consider in terms of learning principles how such behavior might be acquired.

Although the use of a learning analysis seems to be a fairly straightforward extension of previous behavioral analyses of language, there is little laboratory evidence to draw upon for support.[1] The genetic orientation of early investigations may be partially responsible for the lack of attempts to achieve laboratory control of mathematics learning. For example, Piaget, perhaps the best-known contributor to the theory of the child's mathematical development, states, "When adults try to impose mathematical concepts on a child prematurely, his learning is merely verbal; true understanding of them comes only with his mental growth" (1953, p. 2).

And Fowler (1962), after reviewing the literature on early learning of mathematics, concludes,

> Yet even contemporary research on the numerical abilities of preschool children . . . is still highly concentrated on merely registering the ages and order of normal development. It is as if the development of abilities does indeed evolve autogenously or through maturation alone. In fact no experiments were found which were directly concerned with how, or the degree to which, preschool children can learn quantitative relationships and numbers (p. 135).

---

[1] C. B. Ferster is conducting experiments in which he attempts to train chimpanzees in elementary counting and binary arithmetic response sequences using a behavioral analysis. At this time, however, his results have not been prepared for formal publication (lecture given at Arizona State University, April 1962).

Nevertheless, interest in demonstrating the importance of learning variables in acquisition of mathematics has been increasing. Fowler has also pointed to the arguments for such an approach.

> That long periods of learning are indispensable for the early acquisition of calculating and similar abilities is suggested by the following: case records, although often less complete than those on early reading, similarly point to years of exceptional, early stimulation and practice as the rule. . . . Second, there is much evidence to suggest that the preschool child's successful efforts to attain high abilities have frequently been early and liberally reinforced and channelized by such social role labels as "wizard" or "genius" calculator. . . . Finally, it is unreasonable to believe that even the "simpler" mathematical concepts, thousands of years in the attainment historically . . . , could emerge autogenously in untutored children . . . (pp. 134–135).

Although empirical support for the role of learning variables in this area is sparse, an analysis in such terms should prove to be worthwhile. Perhaps one way that research may be stimulated is through analyzing some simple mathematical behaviors in S–R terms. (See Chapter 10 on "Experimental Educational Psychology" for a fuller statement of the possibility of a behavioral analysis being productive in this manner.)

Counting Behavior

Counting behavior may be thought to develop in several different ways and come under the control of several stimuli even for the same individual. These different procedures may be discussed as tacting, number-response sequences, and extensions through redundancy.

Tacting

It is probable that several "number" responses are frequently established in the child on the basis of tacting training. In the same manner that a child is reinforced for saying BALL in the presence of the ball so that the stimulus comes to control that response, a child is trained ordinarily to tact singular objects with the verbal response ONE _____, to say TWO in the presence of two stimulus objects, and THREE in the presence of three objects. Perhaps even a few additional number responses come under the control of the appropriate number of objects.

The reader has probably recognized that these tacts are not simple discriminated operants. Rather, such number tacts are an example of the discrimination training that results in an "abstraction," as was discussed in Chapter 3. It will be recalled that an abstraction is a response under the control of a single isolated property of a stimulus, which cannot exist alone. "Number" is such an abstraction. "Twoness," for example, cannot exist in the absence of other stimulus qualities; it is simply one property of certain stimulus objects. The stimulus objects are different from time to time, for example, two oranges may be the discriminative stimulus on one occasion and two puppies the next. The term "two" applies to both of these but not to three oranges or one puppy. Thus, it would be expected that these tacts would not be acquired as easily as most simple nouns.

Many examples would have to be provided, each having the same property, but among the various examples there would have to be a wide range of other properties as well.

Number-Response Sequences

At the same time as, or soon after, the first few number responses have been formed, the child may receive another type of training that establishes a greater repertoire of number tacts as well as sequences or chains of number responses. In the presence of, let us say, eight objects the parent may say ONE and prompt the child to say ONE; then say TWO and prompt the child; then THREE, and so on. At the same time the parent may point in turn to each one of the eight objects. If the child has had the necessary previous training he will attend to—look at—the object to which the parent points.

On the basis of this training the child may be expected to acquire the combination of attentional responses, manual responses, and vocal number-response sequences of which counting is composed. That is, the general stimulus of a group of objects would be expected through such training to come to control certain eye movements, or observing responses. If the stimuli are in a line the child might look first, let us say, at the leftmost member of the group, because of his past training. This stimulus would then control the first number response ONE. The stimuli produced by this response, plus the stimulus of the leftmost object, would then come to control the response of looking at the second leftmost object. This object, plus the stimulus produced by the response ONE, would then elicit the response TWO, and so on. As the child counted further the particular number response to be elicited would be controlled both by the stimuli of the object and by the stimuli produced by the preceding number response. This chaining process is depicted in Figure 5.8. However, Piaget makes the following statement.

A child of five or six may readily be taught by his parents to name the numbers from 1 to 10. If 10 stones are laid in a row, he can count them correctly. But if the stones are rearranged in a more complex pattern or piled up, he no longer can count them with consistent accuracy. Although the child knows the names of the numbers, he has not yet grasped the

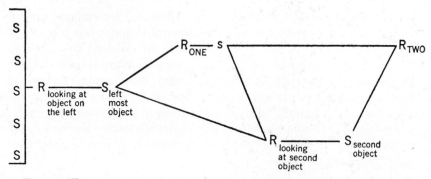

Fig. 5.8. Illustration of the chain of responses involved in counting. A group of stimulus objects is depicted as well as the already formed number responses of the child that control further counting responses. First, the group of stimuli elicit the orienting response, let us say, of looking at the leftmost object. This stimulus then elicits the number response ONE, as well as the response of moving the eyes to the next object. The next stimulus, plus the preceding response ONE, elicit the number response TWO, and so on.

essential idea of number: namely, that the number of objects in a group remains the same, is "conserved," no matter how they are shuffled or arranged (1953, p. 2).[2]

Piaget would be correct in arguing that in our above example, it would not be expected that the simple training of counting a row of objects would be sufficient experience to produce a complete repertoire of "number" behaviors. If the child had received training in counting a group of objects from left to right, as in the above example, then when these general position stimuli were removed it would be expected that control over the appropriate behavior would deteriorate. When controlling stimuli are eliminated, the behavior that is controlled weakens or disappears.

According to our interpretation, however, the child must receive training in counting groups of objects in many different arrangements before his counting behavior will come under the control of the different arrangements. Depending upon the arrangement, different observing responses

---

[2] From a methodological standpoint, it may be pointed out that the operations which define terms like "the essential idea of number" are the behaviors of the child with respect to counting objects. Understanding such behavior concerns knowledge of its determinants. Piaget, in contrast to the present approach, considers internal "maturational" changes to be the primary basis of the child's successful mathematical behavior. He states, for example, "It is a great mistake to suppose that a child acquires the notion of number and other mathematical concepts just from teaching" (1953, p. 2). (A fuller discussion of maturational approaches to child development will be given in a later chapter.)

must be elicited. The problem, however, is simply a more subtle example of "abstraction" in number training where the irrelevant aspects of the stimuli are their arrangements. In well-rounded training, many examples of the possible arrangements would have to be given, each requiring, let us say, "counting to ten" as the appropriate response. This is true of behavior other than counting as well. A child who has acquired a tact under the control of a stimulus object presented in one set of conditions will not "name" the object when it is seen under markedly different conditions. The child must often be reinforced for tacting an object with a single response under varying conditions of presentation.

Accordingly, the same number or counting responses on the part of the child, no matter how the single group of objects is arranged, would be expected to develop only after the child has been reinforced for emitting the same type of responses under the several different stimulus conditions. Actually, according to this analysis, it should be possible to train the child to make the same responses in the presence of the somewhat different arrangements of the same stimulus objects; or, indeed, it should be possible to train the child to make different responses in the presence of the different arrangements. Either one would involve a fairly complex training program. The fact is that in our culture children are trained to the former, and at the rate at which we train our children the training is ordinarily, according to Piaget's statements, not complete until about the age of six or seven.[3]

In addition, other types of experiences may be necessary before the child will emit number responses appropriately. Prior to training, a child who is asked, HOW MANY PIECES OF CANDY DO YOU WANT, ONE OR TWO?, might not respond appropriately even if he had been trained to count. Ordinarily, however, it would be expected that the child would have to be trained to make correct number responses in this and many different types of situations, for example, the grocer says YOU MUST HAVE FIVE PENNIES FOR *THAT* CANDY BAR. All these training situations and many more are the variables that would be thought to underlie the child's acquisition of appropriate number responses— "the idea of number."

Extensions of Counting and Redundancy

Once the child has acquired a rudimentary repertoire of number responses, under the control of stimulus objects rather than of their different arrange-

---

[3] Corroboration for this analysis is given by the repertoire of the authors' three-year-four-month old daughter, who can presently count any arrangement of objects up to thirteen in number. The behavior would indicate she "has the essential idea of number"; a result of the type of training program described in the analysis.

ments, the chain is probably extended solely on a verbal basis—through establishing further number-response sequences. Let us say, for example, that the child can count to twelve, that is, respond consecutively to twelve different objects. The parent or teacher may prompt the child to emit these number responses without counting objects and reinforce him each time the repertoire is emitted. He may then prompt the child to say THIRTEEN at the completion of the repertoire, and then FOURTEEN, and perhaps one or two more responses. Under the proper training and reinforcement conditions these number responses would thus be added to the child's repertoire.

Now, even though this training was purely verbal, it would be expected that when the child was counting a group of objects and came to twelve, he could continue on. His counting behavior would be under the control of the objects still left in the group, as well as the words emitted in the verbal chain: TWELVE, THIRTEEN, FOURTEEN, and so on. Thus, the child's "number tacting" repertoire might grow through purely verbal training. It seems apparent that most of our counting repertoires have been established through verbal training, yet we could actually count an indefinite number of objects should it be required; although most of us have never counted a group of, say, 1713 objects, we could do so on the basis of our verbal training and the general "counting" responses we have acquired.

Because of the redundancy in our number system it is relatively easy to extend the number-response sequences once a basic repertoire has been established. After acquiring a repertoire up to twenty, counting to thirty would seem to be easy to establish because there already are associations between the responses ONE, TWO, THREE . . . NINE. When the child says TWENTY–ONE, and then TWENTY–, the preceding ONE response tends to elicit TWO on the basis of the already learned chain. Thus, establishing TWENTY–TWO should take relatively few trials. This is, of course, also true for other number responses which follow— the 30's, 40's, 130's, and so on. Thus, the psychological mechanisms underlying redundancy (and therefore ease of extension) in the number system would seem to be the chains or verbal response sequences which have been previously established.

The Texting of Numbers

In the same way that the child learns to "read" and "write" other verbal material, he also learns to read and write numbers. Usually, as part of his formal school training, the child acquires vocal number responses under the control of visually presented printed number stimuli, that is, number textual responses. He may be taught through a "matching" technique to produce written numbers in response to visually presented number stimuli. Once these responses have been acquired much of his later acquisition of number sequences may then be based upon visually presented number stimuli. Figure 5.9 shows examples of the S–R sequences established in this type of texting training.

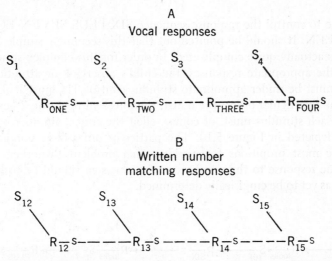

Fig. 5.9. The child will acquire vocal number responses under the control of visually presented number stimuli (part A), as well as writing number-matching responses under the same control (part B). Since the responses occur in close contiguity in both cases, chains of both vocal and written number responses become established.

Addition

The child may also acquire a rudimentary "addition" repertoire through what is essentially a process of "tacting." For example, he might be presented with two marbles and then another two and asked: HOW MANY MARBLES ARE TWO MARBLES PLUS TWO MARBLES? The child may then be prompted to say ONE–TWO–THREE–FOUR marbles, or the parent or teacher may simply prompt the child to say FOUR. From this training the number response sequence TWO PLUS TWO IS FOUR should eventually be formed.

Although the first "adding" number response sequences may be established as tacts to objects, additional sequences are probably ordinarily established on a purely verbal level. Perhaps the most important developments customarily await the formal training the child receives in school where he acquires sequences such as SEVEN PLUS TWO IS NINE,

EIGHT PLUS NINE IS SEVENTEEN, etc. In addition, he will ordinarily be trained to text addition stimuli. That is, the stimuli

$$\begin{array}{r} 6 \\ +\,7 \\ \hline 13 \end{array}$$

will come to control the response sequence SIX PLUS SEVEN EQUALS THIRTEEN. It should be pointed out that this seemingly simple S–R sequence is actually quite complicated. In order for this complex stimulus to control the appropriate responses, the child's observing or attentional responses must be under appropriate stimulus control. He must look at the stimuli in a particular order: the 6 first, the plus sign next, the 7 next, then the 13. Each stimulus must, of course, elicit the correct number response. This is depicted in Figure 5.10. The particular order of responding that would be most propitious for working such problems—whether, for example, the response to the numbers or the plus sign should be first in the chain—has yet to be empirically determined.

**Complex
stimulus**

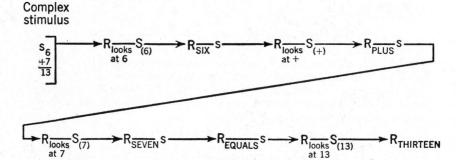

Fig. 5.10. A complex chain of observing and texting responses is involved in texting a simple addition problem. The child must observe the stimuli in the proper order and respond appropriately to them.

After such basic adding sequences have been established, plus the appropriate chains of observing and texting responses, the child may be presented with more complicated number stimuli (problems), such as

$$\begin{array}{r} 18 \\ +\,19 \end{array}$$

The prompting in this case, as in the preceding one, may require a fairly complex set of instructions involving the elicitation of both vocal and writing responses from the child.

Let us consider an example of a plausible chain in which a child might be trained in order to solve addition problems. Naturally, in this example, and all others considered in this chapter, the sequences established are not the only ones that will result in the "right" answer. Nor are we suggesting that the chains discussed are the most efficient. At each stage, the reader should remember that such questions must be answered through experimentation.

To continue, in the presence of the addition problem above, the instructor might say, TO ADD THESE TWO NUMBERS, FIRST ADD THE EIGHT AND THE NINE. HOW MUCH IS EIGHT AND NINE? When the child responds, SEVENTEEN, the instructor may continue, WRITE THE SEVEN UNDER THE EIGHT AND NINE, AND PUT A LITTLE ONE JUST TO THE LEFT SIDE OF THE SEVEN SO THAT YOU REMEMBER IT REALLY STANDS FOR SEVENTEEN. NOW YOU MUST ALSO PUT A LITTLE ONE JUST ABOVE THE ONE IN THE EIGHTEEN. THEN YOU JUST ADD THE ONE AND ONE AND ONE WHICH IS THREE AND WRITE IT UNDERNEATH.

These verbal stimuli provided by the instructor should elicit the correct behaviors of the child (provided the necessary basic responses—"attending"—have been acquired). In so doing a chain of responses to a more complicated addition problem begins to be formed. The response chain is depicted in Figure 5.11.

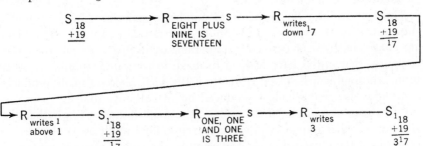

Fig. 5.11. An addition response sequence.

After the child has been prompted to respond in this manner to a number of these problems, the child's sequence of behavior might be expected to come under the control of certain *general* features of the complex stimulus, in the manner of "abstraction" learning, as well as of the specific features of the numbers involved. As in the previous example, the general features of the problem consist of the position of the stimuli and the observing responses which the position stimuli control. Ignoring the specific numbers involved, the stimuli have position characteristics as follows:

$$
\begin{array}{r}
XX \\
+\,XX \\
\hline
XX
\end{array}
$$

These position stimuli would be expected to come to control an appropriate sequence of observing responses. In a complex chain the child should come to look first at the upper rightmost stimulus, then the lower rightmost stimulus. The specific number stimuli would control the first adding response, then the writing response would occur, then the position stimuli would again control looking at the upper leftmost stimulus, and so on.

When correct observing responses to the general stimuli of position as well as the correct number responses to the specific number stimuli have been acquired, it would be expected that the child then would respond correctly and without prompting to any addition problem of the type just discussed. The necessary chains of addition responses should be acquired on far fewer trials than the infinite number of different possible problems made up of the various number combinations. Although never having added 78 and 83, as an example, the child who has the appropriate general responses, as well as the individual basic addition sequences should arrive at a correct final response. The motor and verbal responses acquired here are like a system in that the responses acquired are appropriate to a very large number of different stimuli.

Thus, we see how the sequence of number responses might come under the control of the appropriate stimuli. The responses to a new problem are considered correct or incorrect to the extent that they are the same responses that others have learned to make to the same stimuli. In other terms, the problem is solved correctly if the final response made produces a stimulus like that which is produced by an authority source.

Of course, in any practical problem, the final authority is whether the addition number responses produce the same final result as would tacting (counting) the objects directly; for example, the adding chain is reinforced by yielding a final response that is the same as that given by responding to the objects themselves. It seems reasonable to conjecture that it is because of the reinforcement of saving time and effort through emitting the verbal adding chain in contrast to simply tacting the objects, that the adding chain becomes more and more frequently emitted in situations in which either response chain would be finally successful.

Multiplication

To a large extent the acquisition of multiplication sequences would seem to involve the same forms of responses as those discussed under addition. Multiplication deals with a special class of addition problems where the same number is repeated, and added, more than once. To such problems as

$$
\begin{array}{r}
4 \\
4 \\
4 \\
\hline
\end{array}
$$

the child already has acquired number response sequences, such as FOUR PLUS FOUR IS EIGHT, AND EIGHT PLUS FOUR IS TWELVE.

In place of this chain, he may be trained on a new chain, consisting first of counting the number of fours, and then emitting the number response sequence THREE TIMES FOUR EQUALS TWELVE. The child may thus acquire another number response chain to these types of number stimuli (problems). It is interesting that in teaching, these new multiplication response sequences are not usually first brought under the control of stimulus objects in the same way that counting and adding responses are. The objects "tacted" in this instance are number stimuli—the child "counts" numbers. Later, the multiplication response sequences must be brought under the control of the appropriate stimulus objects, perhaps through the use of word problems. That is, in counting there is a stimulus object (or objects) which can control the verbal response. Also, for addition there is a stimulus event of combining two or more objects that can control an "adding" number response. There is no additional event to control multiplication responses, the event being the same combination that controls the adding responses. Perhaps, for this reason, multiplication tends to be originally acquired as a tacting response to number stimuli rather than through tacting objects.

Thus, the child may acquire his multiplication response sequences by responding to the number stimuli of the multiplication tables. In this case, the appropriate chains are acquired by making the responses in sequence (by texting or echoing the teacher). Problems might be given also in which the final response is absent and the child is correct if his response matches that of an authority source. Formation of the multiplication table sequences seems to be necessary for further multiplication learning just as a basic single-digit addition repertoire was necessary for more complicated addition problems in the procedure already discussed.

Although no new principles are introduced, an example of multiplication learning is presented in Figure 5.12 to illustrate the complex chain of responses involved in even a relatively simple multiplication problem. The specific responses are not important, of course, but the figure does show what sort of complex chain might be involved. It would be expected that all the attention, adding, writing, and verbal response sequences we have

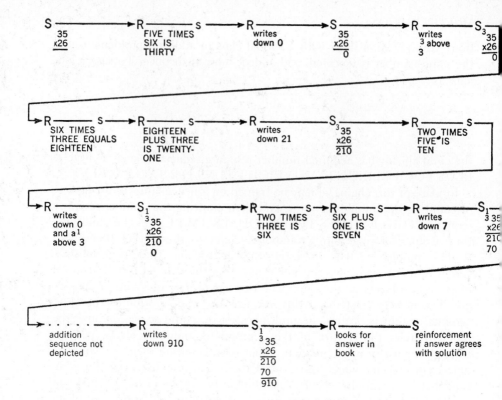

Fig. 5.12. The figure illustrates the complexity of a chain of responses that might be involved in training a child to complete the multiplication problem 35 × 26. The child might first be prompted to respond to the two right-hand stimuli with a multiplication sequence already acquired: FIVE TIMES SIX IS THIRTY. The instructor might then prompt the child to write a zero under the 5 and 6 and to write a small 3 above the 3 in 35. This writing response should thus come under the control of the stimulus produced by the preceding response, FIVE TIMES SIX IS THIRTY. The child might then be prompted to respond to the bottom right-hand number stimulus 6 and the upper number stimulus second from the right, 3, with the previously acquired multiplication response, SIX TIMES THREE EQUALS EIGHTEEN. This response produces a stimulus (visual, if it is written, or auditory) which with the 3 previously written ("carried"), and perhaps further prompts from the instructor, produces the addition response EIGHTEEN PLUS THREE IS TWENTY-ONE. In the presence of this stimulus, the child may be prompted to write 21 just to the left of the 0. The process might then continue with the pupil texting the number stimulus 2, second from the right in the bottom row, and the right-hand upper stimulus 5, and emitting the multiplication response TWO TIMES FIVE IS TEN. In the presence of this stimulus the child might then be prompted to write the 0 indented one space to the left of the right-most number stimulus in the preceding product and to write a small 1 above the 3. He may then be prompted to respond to

previously described would be included in such a multiplication chain, formed into more complex constellations such as depicted.

In problems requiring many steps in a certain order, as in Figure 5.12, the responses would probably be elicited first by both the number stimuli of the problem and the instructor's prompting. However, after many trials, the complex sequence of responses under the control of the general (position) and specific stimuli would be expected to become firmly established.

In problems as complex as this, it is easy to see that the multiplication response sequences would be more quickly reinforced and be less aversive in terms of effort expended than either addition response sequences or the direct counting response sequence in the presence of the actual objects, that is to say, multiplying 35 × 26 would be more reinforcing than adding 35 twenty-six times or directly counting 910 objects. The multiplication response sequence would thus, in appropriate situations, become a stronger behavior than either adding or counting.

Division

Long division does not present any new psychological processes in addition to those already discussed in this section. However, Gilbert (1962) has made an analysis of the behavior chain involved in long division for purposes of machine teaching of the sequence, that may indicate to the reader a practical utility of the various S–R analyses of mathematical sequences that have been made herein. Although, as has been stated, there is not yet much laboratory experimentation on the learning of mathematical behavior, the following example of Gilbert's as well as the experimentation that has been started by Ferster (1962) seem to indicate that this shortcoming will soon be remedied.

Consider a simple behavior chain such as performing long division. This behavior is represented in stimulus–response notation in Figure [5.13]. The behavior has been oversimplified for illustrative purposes and letters are used to represent actual numbers. We shall assume the

---

the 2 again and the number stimulus 3 (second from the right on the top row) with the number response sequence TWO TIMES THREE IS SIX. To the stimulus produced by this response and the 1 written above the 3 the child may be further prompted to respond with the addition response SIX PLUS ONE IS SEVEN, and to respond to this by writing 7 just to the left of the previously written 0. Addition responses then emitted would lead to the terminal response 910. The reinforcement for this complex sequence of events would normally be the matching visual stimulus of seeing 910 in the answer book (or hearing the instructor give 910 as the answer).

student knows short division, basic terminology, what to do with re-mainders and how to estimate quotients (p. 17).

$$S_1^D \longrightarrow R_2 \cdot S_2^D \longrightarrow R_3 \cdot S_3^D \longrightarrow R_4 \cdot S_4^D \longrightarrow R_5$$

$$\begin{array}{llll}
 & & q & q \\
d \div n & \text{set up} \quad n\overline{)d} & \text{estimate} \; n\overline{)d} \;\; \text{find} & n\overline{)d} \quad \text{subtract} \\
 & \text{problem} & \text{quotient} \qquad \text{product} & \underline{p} \quad \text{to get} \\
 & & \text{\& place it} \qquad \text{\& place it} & \text{remainder}
\end{array}$$

S^D = controlling stimulus   R = response of mastery
n = divisor   d = dividend   q = quotient   p = product

Fig. 5.13. "Long division as a behavior chain. (Simplified for this ex-ample.)" (Gilbert, 1962, p. 17.)

Then in actual lessons, Gilbert gives examples of how the behaviors described in the figure can be established. The following exercise (adapted from Gilbert, p. 18), for example, establishes the terminal operant in the chain.

Divide 45 by 11

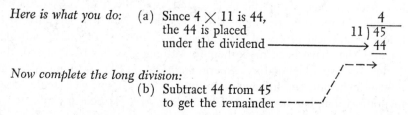

Here is what you do: (a) Since 4×11 is 44,
the 44 is placed
under the dividend ⟶ 44

$$\begin{array}{r} 4 \\ 11\overline{)45} \end{array}$$

Now complete the long division:
(b) Subtract 44 from 45
to get the remainder -----

In this exercise Gilbert points out that he has arranged three conditions for the operant $S_4^D \rightarrow R_5$.

First: We arrange for the student to observe the S^D (product in place under dividend). We do this by stimulating an observ-ing response: ($S^O \rightarrow R^O$). In the exercise, part (a) and the solid arrow together constitute the observing stimulus (S^O).

Second: Some stimulus existing at strength for the response is used to get the response made. Usually, a simple verbal instruction (S^I) is an adequate stimulus for this purpose. In [the] exercise . . . , part (b) and the broken arrow serve as an (S^I).

Third: The reinforcement factor should be inherent in the results of mastery performance itself; from the terminal operant comes the end-product of mastery. It is necessary that the student be able to recognize this end-product. It is assumed that the achievement of this end-product is reinforcing to the student, and it will be if mastery is an educational objective of the student (p. 19).

While Gilbert has presented a simplified analysis for his example, it can be seen that he has analyzed the chain into the same constituents we have pointed to in the previous examples, that is, he too indicates the importance of attention or observing responses, of the number response sequences (for example ELEVEN TIMES FOUR IS FORTY–FOUR), of the prompts or instructions of the teacher, and of course, of the reinforcement occurring when the student's answer matches the answer provided by some authority source.

Further Extensions of Mathematical Sequences

Although it is not within the scope of this book to analyze mathematics learning in detail, the processes will be considered just a little further. The acquisition of "exponent" responses would seem to follow principles similar to those already described. In this training, let us say, the child is prompted to text number stimuli with an additional response. For example, the vocal response TWO SQUARED or the written response 2^2 might be elicited in the presence of the visual S^D 2×2. Or, following upon the auditory stimulus WRITE TWO TIMES TWO, the student might be reinforced for writing either 2×2 or 2^2, and then, perhaps $2 \times 2 = 2^2$. This same process might then be extended to 2^3, 2^4, 6^2, 9^8, and so on.

When these various S–R sequences have been established, relevant "algebraic" responses might be acquired. That is, it is customary in high-school algebra to instruct the student in literal numbers. In behavioral terms this amounts to training in tacting arithmetic numbers with verbal letter responses. Thus, for example, to the stimulus 7 the student might be taught to respond a. When a student has been trained to respond to several arithmetic numbers with the response a in the manner described above, this response may be expected to generalize to all arithmetic numbers. That is, having been trained to tact 6 with the response a, 19 with the response a, 2 with the response a, and so on, he may be expected to tact also all other number stimuli in the same manner. (Actually, this probably is accomplished by verbal instructions as well as through stimulus generalization.) A hierarchy of specific number stimuli, each of which tends to elicit the response a, is illustrated in part A of Figure 5.14.

In addition, the student must also be trained so that a literal number comes to elicit all arithmetic numbers, in order for literal number sequences to serve their function. Thus, the response a must come to be made to a class of arithmetic number stimuli, and a as a stimulus must come to elicit a class of arithmetic number responses. The elicitation of a hierarchy of arithmetic number responses by the literal number stimulus a is depicted in part B of Figure 5.14.

When these convergent and divergent response hierarchies have been

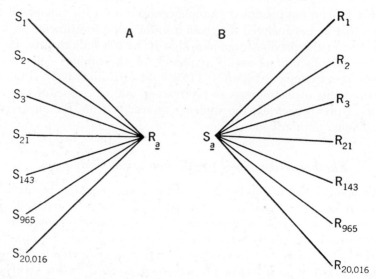

Fig. 5.14. Part A of the figure represents a hierarchy of specific number stimuli, each of which tends to elicit the literal number response a. In addition, a as a stimulus comes to elicit a class of arithmetic number responses. This is depicted in part B.

established for literal numbers, such sequences as $a \cdot a = a^2$ may serve as "general rules," that is, they may mediate an indefinite number of solutions to problems. As a simple example, let us say that the student has been given a problem, $219 \times 219 = ?$, and that this stimulus does not already control the response sequence of multiplying 219 by 219. Let us also say that he has the described repertoires concerning literal numbers and in addition has acquired the literal number sequence $a \cdot a = a^2$. The problem would then be solved by the mediation of the literal number sequence (the general rule). The arithmetic numbers of the problem would elicit the literal numbers $a \cdot a$ and this response would further elicit a^2. The response a^2 would in turn mediate the arithmetic response 219^2. This, let us say, could mediate the response of consulting a table of squares. This is depicted in Figure 5.15. Ordinarily, of course, by the time literal numbers are learned, the individual would directly respond with 219^2 to this particular problem, without the mediation of the literal number sequence. The next example, consequently, may better illustrate the function of literal numbers as mediating response sequences.

When this training has been complete—when the class of number stimuli will elicit a literal number response, and vice versa—then new sequences of number responses which hold for any number may be introduced simply by training the child in a literal response sequence. For example, when the

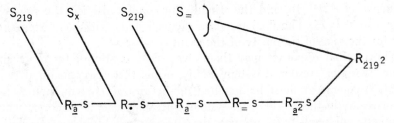

Fig. 5.15. The problem $219 \times 219 = ?$ may be solved, although the responses of multiplying 219 by 219 have not been acquired, if the problem stimuli elicit an appropriate literal number response sequence. In this example, the problem stimuli elicit the literal number sequence $a \cdot a =$, which in turn elicits a^2. Then through the combination of the final literal number stimulus, a^2, and the stimuli of the problem, the correct arithmetic number 219^2 is elicited.

child has acquired the literal response sequence $a^x \cdot a^y = a^{(x+y)}$ this sequence could mediate the addition of any exponent number stimuli in relevant problem situations.

It is true that the answer response to a new problem (such as $2^3 \cdot 2^7 = 2^?$) may occur less rapidly with the mediation of a literal number sequence than if the specific arithmetic number sequence had been strongly established. However, it takes far fewer repetitions to establish one literal response sequence than it does to establish an infinity of specific number sequences, and one literal response sequence will suffice. In addition, it is easier to retain a relatively few literal response sequences than a relatively large number of specific solutions (correct specific number response sequences).

Another example will show how literal number responses established in a beginning algebra course may be functional in problems which are met later. Let us say that a student in plane geometry has been conditioned to tact the hypotenuse of a right triangle with the response c, one leg of the right angle with the response a and the other with b. He is then prompted to emit the literal response sequence (or he may text the sequence) $a^2 + b^2 = c^2$. Later these tacts and literal number response sequence can mediate the solution to an infinite number of such arithmetic problems, or even environmental problems.

Thus, in the presence of the verbal stimuli (problem) FIND THE LENGTH OF THE HYPOTENUSE OF A RIGHT TRIANGLE WITH ONE SIDE OF 3 FEET AND THE OTHER SIDE OF 4 FEET, the responses c, a, and b are elicited. The stimuli RIGHT TRIANGLE, plus the stimuli produced by the above responses then elicit the response sequence $c^2 = a^2 + b^2$. The stimuli of the problem of 3 FEET and 4 FEET, plus the stimuli produced by the cited responses, then elicit the response sequence $c^2 = 3^2 + 4^2$. These stimuli then elicit the response sequence $c^2 = 9 + 16$, and the stimuli thus produced elicit the response sequence $c^2 = 25$. The final response then elicited (with some steps left out for the sake of simplicity of the example) is $c = 5$.

Thus, verbal responses may themselves serve as stimuli for more and more "abstract" response systems. This means that fewer manipulations (verbal sequences) must be acquired in the abstract system than would be necessary in the less abstract system; for example, $a^x \cdot a^y = a^{(x+y)}$ when acquired will mediate appropriate responses to all problems no matter what the specific number stimuli. But each new "abstract" level, since it is composed of tacts to other verbal stimuli, would seem to have depended, at least originally, upon the previous establishment of the lower level responses. However, whether it is best for the child to retrace in *his* particular training the various steps involved or whether the training could begin on a more abstract level might be a matter for empirical study.

The way in which literal number response sequences might enter into the development of novel number responses will be described in the next section. This could be the most important psychological aspect of a more "abstract" system of responses.[4]

ORIGINALITY

Analyses which treat an individual's behavior as a function of his experience, as does the present one, are frequently criticized on the grounds that while they can perhaps account for behavior for which the individual has been specifically trained, they do not indicate how the emergence of original or novel forms of behavior may occur. Certainly naturalistic observations of human behavior yield innumerable examples of the emission of original or novel behaviors. Cultural progress is a result of these. Although it might appear incongruous at first glance, it seems quite possible that certain specific trainings in verbal behavior, for example, could result in the emission of novel verbal responses under appropriate stimulus conditions. A few examples of how this might happen will be presented in this section.

As a first very simple example of novel responses, let us once again look

---

[4] It might be of interest to point out that the function of grammatical "rules," as well as algebraic "rules," may be described in terms of sequences of responses which mediate other types of responses. That is, when the individual has acquired a grammatical rule in learning a foreign language he may then be prepared to write correctly in that language through the mediation of the rule, for example, IN THIS LANGUAGE THE ADJECTIVE FOLLOWS THE NOUN could mediate the correct response sequence CASA BLANCA in Spanish, even though the correct word associations have not yet been established.

at complex tacts—verbal responses under the control of stimulus objects or events. Let us suppose that a child has been reinforced upon saying MAN, or THE MAN, in the presence of a man as a stimulus object. It would then be expected that he would tend to make this response in the future in the presence of such a stimulus. The same child might also be reinforced upon saying WALKS in the presence of certain "walking" stimulus objects and thus respond in appropriate circumstances with BABY WALKS, LADY WALKS, etc. In addition, this child might acquire the verbal response IT IS ON THE SIDEWALK to various objects occupying space on the sidewalk. These responses would simply be tacts and their occurrence would not involve novel forms of behavior. Through the child's past experience the stimuli would have come to control the specific verbal responses.

However, on the basis of this learning (as well as the development of grammatical associations to which we will refer again in a moment) and the appearance of new stimulus conditions, the child might emit a novel verbal response chain. That is, in the presence of the stimulus object of a man, the additional stimulus of walking motion, and the stimulus of a sidewalk, the child might, without further training, emit the response THE MAN WALKS ON THE SIDEWALK even though he had received no prior training on the complete word response sequence.

As a result of the emission of this response sequence and its reinforcement, the associations would be strengthened in the child. In the future, there would be a tendency for the stimulus produced by the response THE MAN to elicit WALKS and for the stimuli produced by this response to elicit ON THE SIDEWALK. There would also be an even slighter tendency for the first response to elicit the third one, and so on. And if this sequence were written, let us say for the first time, it would constitute a novel performance which could establish new verbal response sequences in other people. Dollard and Miller make a similar analysis of originality, as the following excerpt indicates.

> *How novelty is produced.* Once having learned, the person responds in a new way. But if the correct response must always occur before it can be rewarded, what novelty is added by learning? The new feature is that the particular response rewarded now occurs regularly to a specific cue, whereas previously its occurrence at just that time and place may have been exceedingly infrequent. The connection between cue and response is the new product of learning. Often a number of different response units are connected to cues so that they all occur together, either simultaneously or successively. Thus a new pattern of responses is produced; the responses are old, but the combination is new. Once this new combination occurs frequently, variations in it may be points of departure for still further learning (1950, p. 37).

Figure 4.24 in Chapter 4 shows in greater detail hierarchies of word-response sequences in which the separate links have been established, but for which some of the complete sequences might never have been emitted. These could also serve as other examples of novel verbal response sequences.

Although these are simple examples, they seem to have a good deal of significance as a model for the emergence of certain new forms of verbal behavior. They provide an interpretation of how individual verbal responses acquired in various stimulus situations might be elicited in new complex situations in novel combinations. They suggest that verbal sequences of responses may be extended by virtue of the individual's contact with environmental stimuli. Thus, this interpretation suggests that language learning may occur in two ways: it may take place on the basis of specific language training (including the processes of acquisition of tacts, communication, and texting) but in addition, *new language sequences might occur simply on the basis of the individual's experience with environmental events.* For this latter process to occur, however, the original tacts or verbal response sequences must have been acquired previously. It would be thought that novel behaviors are probably produced quite frequently in this manner, and, if they are significant, when they are recorded they add importantly to our cultural heritage.

Still, these examples may not seem world-shaking and do not begin to account for what we call originality. Another example, however, based upon the same principles may place the process in better perspective. The verbal response sequences in this case are more complex, and cannot be completely described in this space although the principles may be indicated. The example deals with an "original proof" in geometry and will attempt to show the types of experiences upon which such novel behavior might be based.

First, the following verbal response may be considered to be a complex tacting sequence under the control of appropriate stimulus objects and events: QUANTITIES EQUAL TO THE SAME QUANTITY ARE EQUAL TO EACH OTHER. This response might have been acquired, for example, in a situation where each of two bags of sugar were successively balanced with the same weight and then with one another, and the individual tacted the situation as IF THE TWO BAGS BALANCE WITH (EQUAL) THE SAME WEIGHT, THE BAGS EQUAL EACH OTHER. Further training would bring the verbal sequence under the control of many analogous stimulus situations involving numbers, angles, lengths, and so on.

Another verbal response, IF EQUAL SUMS ARE SUBTRACTED FROM EQUAL SUMS THE REMAINDERS ARE EQUAL, could also come under the control of appropriate stimulus situations through procedures comparable to those described above. Finally, a third verbal response can also be considered a complex tact to certain objects, in this case a tact to certain lines and angles: THE SUM OF THE ANGLES ABOUT A POINT ON ONE SIDE OF A STRAIGHT LINE IS EQUAL TO 180°.[5] This verbal response, just as the other two described, might have been acquired through experience in many diverse situations.

On the basis of these complex verbal responses, each of which is itself under the control of complex stimulus situations, the development of an even more complex language structure might be considered, that is, Thales' demonstration that vertical angles of two intersecting straight lines are equal (Shute, Shirk, and Porter, 1960). This example is clearly one of "originality" in verbal behavior but may be considered in terms of a number of previously acquired tacting response sequences that are controlled by specific situations and are emitted together in a novel manner when the individual is confronted with a complex situation that simultaneously tends to elicit all of them.

Figure 5.16 illustrates the problem showing the intersecting lines and the angles produced.

> To demonstrate that when two straight lines intersect the vertical angles in pairs are equal, Thales was given two straight lines, AB and CD intersecting at O, forming the vertical angles, $\angle 1$ and $\angle 2$, and the vertical angles, $\angle 3$ and $\angle 4$. Since AB was given a straight line, and since the sum of the angles about a point on one side of a straight line is equal to 180°, Thales knew that $\angle 1 + \angle 3 = 180°$. Similarly, since CD was given a straight line, he knew $\angle 3 + \angle 2 = 180°$. Applying the axiom, quantities equal to the same quantity are equal to each other, Thales obtained the equality: $\angle 1 + \angle 3 = \angle 3 + \angle 2$. Thales next applied the subtraction axiom by subtracting $\angle 3$ from both sides of the equation to get the equality: $\angle 1 = \angle 2$. In like manner, Thales proved that $\angle 3 = \angle 4$. Thus Thales proved that vertical angles in pairs are equal (p. 25).

The following will attempt a brief account of the "derivation" of the final statement in terms of the behavioral principles that have been discussed. Figure 5.17 which depicts the possible S–R processes involved in

---

[5] In these examples, the complex tacts or verbal response sequences are probably composed of simpler individual tacts. The response SUM is a tact, under the control of multiple stimuli which can be responded to singly or as a group, usually by making an arithmetic response. The response ANGLES is also a tact under the control of multiple "angle stimuli." The same is true for POINT, STRAIGHT LINE, EQUAL, and 180°. In addition, other S–R processes would be thought to be involved such as those discussed previously in the discussion of grammatical and mathematical response sequences. For the purpose of simplifying the example, these may, however, be described as complex tacts or tacting sequences.

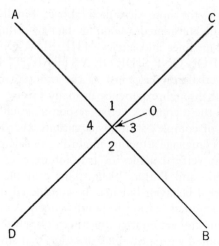

Fig. 5.16. Illustration used in demonstrating that when two straight lines intersect, the vertical angles in pairs are equal.

this example, is simplified for purposes of illustration and some steps have been omitted to conserve space.

The first S^D in the chain of reasoning might be part of the geometric form: Line AB is a straight line intersected at point O producing the angles $\angle 1$ and $\angle 3$, and producing another line OC. As S^D_1, this complex stimulus might control the verbal response sequence R_1, THE SUM OF THE ANGLES ABOUT A POINT ON ONE SIDE OF A STRAIGHT LINE IS EQUAL TO 180°. This response sequence could then be considered S^D_2, in the chain eliciting the writing response R_2: ANGLE ONE PLUS ANGLE THREE EQUALS 180°. Line CD with the line OB emanating from point O is also a stimulus (S^D_4), which elicits R_4, the same verbal response elicited by S^D_1, and thus the analogous writing responses with respect to angles $\angle 2$ and $\angle 3$, that their sum equals 180°.

The stimuli produced by the next two written responses (S^D_3 and S^D_6) combine because of the past history of training to elicit the verbal response sequence (R_6) QUANTITIES EQUAL TO THE SAME QUANTITY ARE EQUAL TO EACH OTHER; ANGLES ONE PLUS THREE EQUAL TWO PLUS THREE. This verbal response sequence produces S^D_7, which then elicits the next verbal response (R_7) EQUALS SUBTRACTED FROM EQUALS LEAVE EQUAL REMAINDERS; SUBTRACTING ANGLE THREE FROM BOTH SIDES LEAVES ANGLES ONE AND TWO AS EQUALS. This response might then be the S^D that would elicit the final statement WHEN TWO STRAIGHT

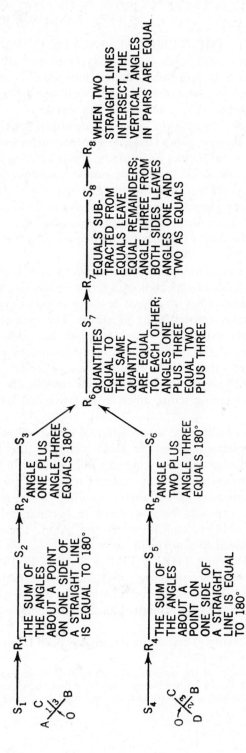

Fig. 5.17. An S–R sequence illustrating the elicitation of previously acquired responses to specific situations that, when elicited together in a situation that simultaneously tends to elicit all of them, results in a novel or "original" behavior.

LINES INTERSECT, THE VERTICAL ANGLES IN PAIRS ARE EQUAL. It thus seems conceivable that such types of original reasoning could be based upon S–R processes acquired individually through the individual's past experience and that without such previously acquired response sequences, the novel response could not occur.

Thus, in this example, the response sequences described could be called "original" reasoning because the extended sequence of responses that emerges has never occurred before. Each of the components as described, however, had been conditioned to a more simple stimulus, but in the presence of a more complicated stimulus the first response sequence produces stimuli which, in conjunction with the complex stimulus, elicits the next response and so on, until the final novel response occurs.[6] The final sequence might then become a complex tacting sequence to the geometric stimulus.

The authors do not intend to suggest that complex cases of mathematical originality are now capable of explanation in terms of learning principles. The example used oversimplifies what must be a very complex event, determined by other complex constellations of events. For example, Thales might have had specific experiences that resulted in his "looking for"— attempting—a solution to the problem, and many failures to obtain the "answer" might have occurred prior to eventual success. Nevertheless, it is perhaps advantageous to point out that even such complicated examples may be considered in learning terms, albeit in tentative and rudimentary form.

In some cases of originality, the immediate role of the stimulus object would seem more important, as in the above example (the geometric figure); in others the verbal response sequences might be further removed from immediate environmental stimulus control. Consider, for example, the verbal response sequences of arithmetic counting. These number responses, as described, may also be considered to become ordered into various chains called addition, multiplication, and so on. The individual child may then be trained to emit many such sequences, such as TWO PLUS THREE IS FIVE and THREE TIMES SEVEN IS TWENTY-ONE, under the control of the appropriate stimuli. However, each response may also be considered as a stimulus, and additional verbal responses may be formed as tacts to these verbal stimuli. This has already been described in the section on literal numbers.

Let us suppose, for example, that an individual has been trained to emit

---

[6] For simplicity, the stimulus of the geometric figure is not shown in Figure 5.17 at each step of the chain. It should be remembered, however, that the geometric figure could remain an S^D at each stage and might be quite important in eliciting the appropriate R.

many sequences of responses such as TWO PLUS FOUR IS SIX, SIXTY-NINE PLUS TWENTY-FOUR IS NINETY-THREE, ONE PLUS ZERO EQUALS ONE. Let us also say that the individual is trained to tact the stimuli of various such examples in the following way: WHEN TWO NUMBERS ARE ADDED THEY YIELD A THIRD NUMBER. This verbal response may be considered to be of a "higher order"; it is a tacting response to previous number responses and functions like the literal numbers shown in Figure 5.14 of the preceding section. Such a verbal response sequence could be called a general rule. In the terms developed herein, it could be said that the sequence could mediate many arithmetic number sequences in which the third term would indeed be a number.

Other equivalent verbal response sequences might also be acquired in the same way, or they might occur as consequences of grammatical response chains. For example, ANY NUMBER A ADDED TO A NUMBER X WILL PRODUCE A NUMBER B, and FOR ANY NUMBER B AND ANY NUMBER A THERE IS A NUMBER X WHICH WHEN ADDED TO A WILL EQUAL B, are also verbal response sequences that might have been acquired as tacts on the basis of the particular addition examples given.

However, consequences of the latter response sequence might well be seen as leading to another example of originality in verbal behavior: the origin of negative numbers. This could occur because this verbal response sequence would mediate some responses that at one time in the history of mathematics (prior to the time negative numbers were invented) did not match any previous number in the system. For example, if an individual were to respond to A with SEVEN and to B with FIVE, there is no positive number response that when added to A will allow the completion of the verbal response sequence in the manner in which the individual had been trained. Thus, either new number responses had to be introduced (negative numbers) or the sequence of verbal responses stating the "general rule" had to be rejected or qualified since it would not always mediate responses that match existing numbers. In behavioral terms, either the rule verbal response sequence would control the individual's behavior, in which case a new type of number response had to be introduced, or the customary number stimuli would control the individual's behavior, in which case the rule verbal response sequence had to be qualified.

What eventually happened was, of course, that negative numbers were incorporated into our number response sequences. The general rule holds, for example, when the sequence is completed in the following manner, SEVEN PLUS MINUS TWO EQUALS FIVE.

This example thus suggests that verbal responses to other verbal stimuli (tacts to verbal stimuli) can produce new verbal responses—numbers—

which were not acquired as tacts to environmental stimulus objects. It is interesting to note (see Stevens, 1951) that in the history of mathematics there seem to be many examples of new number responses elicited by other verbal responses which were originally acquired as tacts. Since the new responses were not tacts to environmental stimuli they were often not accepted as justified members of the number response sequences. In addition to negative numbers, other examples are irrational numbers such as $\sqrt{2}$ and imaginary numbers such as $\sqrt{-1}$. As in the case of minus numbers, however, after a verbal response has been elicited purely on a verbal level, environmental counterparts to which the new number response is a useful tact may be encountered. For example, minus numbers are useful tacts to debts (a minus bank account entry), and their use is probably reinforced through their efficiency in performing many calculations.

The important point here, which might also be significant for understanding "originality" in the extension of scientific theories, is that verbal responses which may be developed as tacts through experience with environmental stimuli may produce new verbal responses which may have no known environmental counterparts but which may lead individuals to look for environmental events not previously seen, and so on. An illustration of the possibility of discussing some of the functions of scientific theories in terms of behavior principles may be useful here.

In a science area a possible example might be the periodic table of elements in chemistry. As tacts to environmental events a table of the weights of different elements was formed, let us say. The table may be regarded as a description of the observations. The table itself, however, may be considered to have stimulus characteristics that can be tacted (described). The new set of verbal responses tacted, let us say, the systematic nature of the table, with the weights increasing in a certain fashion from element to element, even though there were gaps in the table. These verbal response sequences might then have elicited the final sequence that perhaps there were elements, yet unobserved, which would fill in the gaps. This verbal response sequence might then have controlled the behavior of making further observations, leading to the discovery of new elements, filling in the table, and so on.

It is possible that the function of many scientific theories, which may be considered verbal response sequences formed on the basis of observation (tacts) and past language learning, is to elicit further verbal response sequences (hypotheses). These new verbal response sequences may then control further observing behaviors which result in the acquisition of new "facts."

It may also be the case, of course, that scientific theories which are not adequately developed as tacts to environmental stimuli may result in further verbal response sequences mediating observing behavior which is unsuccessful and wastes time and effort. A discussion of good and poor theories and their development in terms of behavior principles is beyond the scope of this discussion. Some relevant matters, however, will be touched upon in the next section.

These examples and the interpretations in terms of learning principles are suggestive that even such complex behaviors as originality may involve learning. (See Skinner, 1953, Chapter XVI, for a congruent discussion.) The discussion given here may be considered in only very tentative terms; nevertheless, the principles applied did not seem inappropriate to the subject matter. The next section will discuss several other aspects of scientific behavior in terms of learning.

SCIENTIFIC BEHAVIOR

Some of the principles already discussed seem important for an interpretation of scientific activities in psychological terms. Of special importance are the sequences of responses discussed in the section on reasoning and problem solving and the section on originality, that is, tacts to environmental stimuli, the sequences of verbal responses they elicit, and the instrumental behaviors which are mediated.

Let us first review what we mean by "scientific" statements. It was suggested in Chapter 2 that an explanatory law in science can be characterized as one which states a relationship between an antecedent event, $event_1$, and a consequent event, $event_2$. From such a law, $event_2$ can be predicted if the value of $event_1$ is known. If $event_1$ can be manipulated, then $event_2$ can be controlled. Thus, such laws can yield the two important products of a science, prediction and control.

These, however, are logical statements and do not describe the principles of human behavior whereby such laws develop and the manner in which they function psychologically. In this section a rudimentary and tentative psychological analysis will be attempted. In brief, we will suggest that such laws develop when the following sequence has been completed: (1) observing responses to the two events have been made; (2) both events have been tacted; (3) the tacts have been recorded (responses have been emitted which constitute a description to which others can respond); and finally (4) the verbal response sequences which relate the two tacts have also been made. This cryptic statement must, of course, be elaborated. First, however, an example might be helpful.

Let us say that earthquakes as events have been observed and tacted. Tidal waves have also been observed and tacted. In addition, appropriate responses have also been acquired to tidal waves—for example, removing oneself and one's loved ones from the path of the wave. In recent times, the relationship between earthquakes and tidal waves has been tacted with appropriate sequences of responses connecting the tact to the first event with that of the second. Thus, the tact to an earthquake in the Aleutian Islands made by someone on the spot and transmitted to someone in the Hawaiian Islands who has the appropriate repertoire of behaviors will elicit a sequence of verbal responses that culminates in, perhaps, A TIDAL WAVE OF SUCH AND SUCH AN AMPLITUDE WILL STRIKE THESE ISLANDS AT SUCH AND SUCH A TIME. This verbal response sequence could then act as a stimulus that would mediate the behavior of responding appropriately to the impending wave. The verbal responses TIDAL WAVE and SUCH AND SUCH TIME, prior to the statement (discovery) of the lawful relationship, might only have been tacts to the actual tidal wave after it had happened. However, once the relationship between the earthquake and the tidal wave has been stated, the verbal responses alone might elicit responses appropriate to the actual events, that is, anticipatory responses of great adjustive value.

Prediction and Control

As the example indicates, prediction may result from the sequence of scientific verbal behaviors and the instrumental behaviors they mediate. Because the tact to event$_1$ and the connecting verbal response sequence can elicit the tact to event$_2$ in advance of the actual stimulus event that would otherwise control the second tact, the event may be responded to before it happens. Prediction may thus be considered in S–R terms as the case where a tact is elicited in the above manner prior to the event which ordinarily controls that verbal response.

Furthermore, in behavioral terms, it may be said that scientific control requires that in addition to the above verbal response sequences other response sequences must be developed with which to manipulate the first event. In the above example response sequences for manipulating earthquakes have not been developed. The responses involved in manipulating the first event may also be of a very complicated nature involving a constellation of verbal and motor behaviors of the various types already discussed as well as complicated instrumentation and apparatus.

Sources of Reinforcement

Skinner (1957) has stated that verbal behavior is behavior which is reinforced through the mediation of other people. While social reinforcement seems particularly important for much of the development of verbal behavior, classical conditioning procedures also appear to be involved, as has already been discussed. In addition, much verbal behavior may be maintained because it enables the individual to avoid events in the physical world that are harmful or aversive (the tidal wave) or because it enables the individual to secure or utilize the physical events that are positively reinforcing. This is the type of reinforcement that seems to underlie the development and maintenance of scientific statements.

This is not to say that other sources of reinforcement may not also be important in maintaining scientific behavior. Although the basic source of reinforcement may be gaining or avoiding various physical events, nevertheless in a complex society such as ours there seem to be many social reinforcers that affect the individual scientist's behavior—monetary rewards, honors, and so on—even though these may be backed up by the material reinforcers his work produces—the nuclear reactor, the new drug, or in psychology the contribution of automated teaching to training methods.[7]

Although the occurrence or avoidance of certain physical events may be particularly important sources of reinforcement for scientific behavior, much of every-day verbal behavior is probably also developed and maintained by this same reinforcement, and scientific verbal behavior may be considered in these psychological terms to be a special development of this form of behavior. Perhaps it would be helpful here to give an example of every-day verbal behavior that is maintained by physical events as reinforcers in contrast to an example of verbal behavior reinforced solely by social reinforcers. The statement, THE SKY HAS BEEN GETTING CLOUDIER ALL DAY, IT WILL PROBABLY RAIN TOMORROW SO WE'D BETTER CALL OFF THE PICNIC, is an example of the former. Basically, we would suggest, it is the occurrence of a natural event that is the source of reinforcement. That is, the verbal response sequence can be said to improve one's adjustment to one's physical surroundings to the extent that it actually "anticipates" what will happen. To this extent this statement has the properties of a scientific statement.

On the other hand, the sequence ONCE UPON A TIME THERE LIVED IN THE LAND OF XEH A GROUP OF ELVES, and so on, would be thought to be maintained by a different type of reinforcement. This statement, by virtue of the criteria to be discussed, does not seem to relate to environmental events nor enhance one's adjustment to these environmental events. This is not to say that this type of verbal behavior

---

[7] Actually the several variables are probably intertwined in a complex fashion. The scientist's behavior yields its products of prediction and control of natural events that are reinforcing to society, as well as to himself, and society maintains the scientist's behavior by supplying him with conditioned and primary reinforcers. (See Chapter 8 for further discussion of reinforcement principles and group behavior.)

(story telling) may not be heavily reinforced and thus maintained in good strength. However, this behavior would seem to be maintained because it is reinforcing to the audience, and the audience in turn reinforces the speaker.

Thus, while the principles of acquisition of both types of behavior are the same, the basic sources of reinforcement would seem to be different. Although it might not be proper to value one type of verbal behavior more than the other, the fact that the former may be of greater aid in adjusting to the physical environment seems possible.

It may also be suggested that scientific behavior as considered in the previous terms could come to be reinforcing of itself. If this type of behavior was followed by reinforcement, it would be expected that the behavior would itself become a conditioned reinforcer. Thus, this type of behavior would be maintained even in fields of study in which the consequences were not strongly reinforcing, that is, in fields where there were no "practical" applications. Perhaps it is because of the development of conditioned reinforcement that it may become reinforcing to conduct "pure" research. Therefore, to predict something—to emit a tact prior to the occurrence of an event—may be reinforcing even if that event has no other reinforcing value and thus is inconsequential in terms of the individual's adjustment.

Development of Stimulus Control
(Observing and Tacting)

The foregoing suggests a behavioral interpretation of why the scientific method is based upon observation. To develop the types of verbal response sequences just discussed the scientist must emit responses that bring him into "contact" with the events of the world. As a rule, the first "contact" made probably occurs on the basis of the observer's response to the object or event.[8]

In addition, it should now be clear why a discussion of the proper definition of terms (operationism) was necessary in the second chapter. Scientific activity does not consist exclusively of the observing behavior itself.

---

[8] In later developments of scientific behavior in a field, the emission of observing responses may depend upon complex verbal and motor sequences involved in constructing apparatus that will respond to environmental objects and events in a way the human apparatus cannot. The behaviors involved in construction and use of apparatus may be as complex as any discussed in this book. Since the principles would seem to be the same in this area as in others, however, a separate discussion may not be necessary—for present purposes at least.

The scientist's activity is ordinarily considered significant when he responds in some verbal fashion to the objects and events that are the subject of his observation and when these verbal responses serve as stimuli to other individuals. The section on operationism stressed the fact that one must be very careful about the terms he accepts, that they must be defined by observables, and that the term's scientific meaning is its observational referents. This account was a logical one, not a psychological one. But the injunctions of operationism can now be discussed in behavioral terms.

Without calling it operationism, Skinner (1957) makes the following statement on this topic.

> The scientific community encourages the precise stimulus control under which an object or property of an object is identified or characterized in such a way that practical action will be most effective. It conditions responses under favorable circumstances, where relevant and irrelevant properties of stimuli can usually be manipulated. To dispose of irrelevant controlling relations, it sets up new forms of response as arbitrary replacements for the lay vocabulary—not only the special vocabulary of science but graphs, models, tables, and other ways of "representing the properties of nature." . . . [T]he contingencies established by the scientific community work to prevent exaggeration or understatement, misrepresentation, lying, and fiction (pp. 419–420).

Skinner's statement can be considered a behavioral analysis of operationism, that is, the manner in which stimulus events precisely control the verbal responses (tacts) of the scientist. The procedures to establish such behavior in the scientist may include reinforcement by the scientific community (as Skinner implies), but in addition the logical statements about operationism may also play an important role. Even though these statements are "logical" rather than psychological explanations, the statements themselves may aid in determining the scientist's behavior, that is, control of behavior through communication mechanisms may be involved.

Individual Training to Stimulus Control

In addition to the reinforcement of the scientific community, as well as training received through communication, it might also be suggested that other more general experiences of the child, including his home experiences, might condition the precise stimulus control of the scientist's behavior. Consider, for example, the general characteristics of observing behaviors. Such general responses as turning the head from side to side and looking at objects from different angles, and so on, would be thought to be strengthenable through conditioning procedures so that they could become characteristic of an individual. The same is true of other responses that get the senses (such as hearing and touching) into good "contact" with environmental stimuli. Studies of "vigilance" in visual monitoring tasks indicate that this type of behavior may be developed and maintained by manipulating schedules of reinforcement (Holland, 1958).

It would also be expected that individuals with a history of reinforcement for observing behavior would emit these responses in many different situations, that is, generalization would occur. In addition, being observant—responding to subtle features of the environment—should become, after a time, reinforcing in itself when the stimuli produced by the responses involved acquire conditioned reinforcing value.

It is likely that to some extent everyone has such a history of reinforcement, because responses which bring one's sensory apparatus into position so that it may be stimulated by some portion of the environment are reinforced in many ways, from "finding" positive reinforcers to "avoiding" negative ones. Parents, however, may further "instruct" their children to observe with varying degrees of subtlety many aspects of the environment and reinforce them for doing so. That is, parents may present social reinforcers (such as praise) for more assiduous observing behavior than would ordinarily occur on the basis of the natural physical and social events themselves. For example, there may be little intrinsic reinforcement for a child in observing minutely varied physical aspects of plants. However, under the shaping by a parent who is a botanist, such behavior could become relatively strong. As a consequence of different reinforcement histories with respect to this general type of behavior, it would be expected that some people would be generally more "observant" or "curious" than others—they would display stronger, and perhaps more detailed, observing behavior.

It is possible, of course, that this strong and detailed observing behavior need not be entirely general; discrimination learning may also be involved. Some individuals could be conditioned to be better observers in some types of situations than in others. The example of the botanist's child was given above. On the other hand, a child raised in a merchant's family might have much contact with people in the course of business activities. In such situations reinforcement could be contingent upon slight changes in facial expression, tones of voice, and so on, and the child may be reinforced upon keenly observing everything that occurred in such interactions. Such a history might well produce an astute observer of people and their behaviors, thus one who might be said to be "a keen observer of human nature."

In either case, however, the child might not be reinforced for acute observing outside of the family "interests." The merchant's child, for example, might not be reinforced (or have opportunity) for observing plants. Thus, his observant behavior would be differentially astute.

In summary, then, it is suggested that certain generalized behavior important to the basic nature of scientific activity—observation—can be influenced by one's operant conditioning history.

The same procedures may also underlie the shaping of verbal responses under strict control of stimulus objects and events. To varying degrees parents probably condition in their children verbal behaviors which are under the strict control of stimulus events—that is, they may shape their children in such a manner as to "prevent exaggeration or understatement, misrepresentation, lying, and fiction." We may infer, also, that there are differences in the extent to which this training occurs, yielding differences in the child's behavior.

Many situations in the child's history probably determine the relative precision of the stimulus control of his verbal behavior. Consider, for example, a child conditioned to emit verbal responses such as BOGEY-MAN, ELVES, WITCHES, and a host of other terms referring to "imaginary" entities, as if they were tacts. It might be likely that this individual would accept verbal statements which were not under the control of explicit stimuli in the environment, in other words, respond to them as if they were tacts. Such an individual, in "logical" terms, might be less concerned about operational definitions than would an individual who had a history that included extensive training in making tacting verbal responses *only* to actual stimulus objects.

There have been many controversies in the history of science that apparently have involved the question of the acceptance of supposed tacts that were actually verbal responses not under the control of any stimulus, in other words, verbal responses to "fictional" or "imaginary" entities.

Development of "Logical" Response Sequences

The preceding discussion emphasizes the point that scientific statements require the tacting of two related natural events. In addition, the relationship between the events must be paralleled by a verbal response sequence that "connects" the two tacts. Two events, for example, could relate in different ways: "If A then B," "If A then no B," "the greater A the greater B," "The greater A the lesser B," or in the form of various complicated mathematical functions. The verbal response sequence, to yield prediction, for example, must coincide with or parallel the relationship between the events, whatever this relationship may be.

It would be expected that these logical or mathematical verbal response sequences would also be developed by the individual according to the principles of behavior already discussed. Skinner (1957) also discusses these types of verbal response sequences in a similar manner.

The logical and scientific community also sharpens and restricts verbal behavior in response to *verbal* stimuli. . . .

The logical and scientific community eliminates intraverbal responses [sequences of verbal responses] which interfere with a "logical train of thought." . . . The community guards against confusing or misleading collateral responses to verbal stimuli. . . .

Logicians and scientists have, of course, extensive repertoires of intraverbal behavior, but these are composed of items which have been found to have satisfactory practical results [are isomorphic with some relation between two natural events]. . . .

Rules of logical and mathematical thinking, Laws of Thought, forms of syllogisms, and so on, have a related use. . . . In engaging in verbal behavior which is logical and scientific the speaker slowly acquires skeletal intraverbal sequences which combine with responses appropriate to a given occasion. Just as the poet who has written many iambic pentameters finds it easy to "think" in that meter, so the logician who has emitted many responses having a given logical structure will find it easy to compose others on the same pattern. He is helped by the fact that fragmentary or skeletal operants combine with other responses in multiple causation and also by the fact that responses which do not have a customary pattern are speedily rejected as awkward and strange [or illogical] (pp. 420–422).

The logician, as well as the mathematician, because of his special training, may be said to emit verbal responses some of which will precisely parallel the relationship between natural events and thus mediate good problem-solving behaviors with respect to those events.[9] Because of differing past histories of training with respect to this type of behavior, however, people may be expected to differ in the extent to which they emit such verbal response sequences, that is, in the extent to which they are "logical." (See Dollard and Miller, 1950, and also Chapters 8 and 9.)

In addition to differences produced by scientific training, parents also seem to present to children verbal sequences that are "logical" or "illogical" in the sense discussed, and to varying degrees they probably also reinforce behavior of this type in their children. It would thus be expected that one's personal history of training, including the statements and reinforcements of parents and associates, school experience, and so on, would shape the individual's repertoire of logical responses as well as his repertoire of "illogical" ones. In addition, these repertoires would have general significance for the individual, as they might be expected to occur in many situations and in this way contribute to the success of later scientific training.

---

[9] Stevens (1951, pp. 1–2) states that the power of mathematical statements, verbal response sequences in our terms, is in their isomorphism or parallelism with events of the real world.

Evolution of Stimulus Control and "Logical" Verbal Behavior

Thus, there are probably differences among children in the extent to which strict stimulus control of verbal behavior and logical response sequences are developed. On the basis of the same types of training, it might also be expected that different groups of people would vary in these two respects. Indeed, in our own culture it seems that there has been a progressive development of this important type of behavior—the movement toward scientific verbal behavior seems to be making historical progress, in other words, to be an example of social evolution.

One has only to read some of the verbal behaviors supposedly relevant to our natural world that were common in the Middle Ages to find a dramatic illustration of this "evolution." Statements that are now generally unacceptable were then commonly accepted. In the Dark Ages terms such as "demons," "dragons," "spirits" of all kinds, strange animals with supernatural powers, and so on, were commonly emitted although there are no objects to act as controlling stimuli. A few quotations from a history of science by A. D. White (1899) will illustrate.

> . . . [T]he basilisk kills serpents by his breath and men by his glance . . .
> . . . "As to the ant-lion, his father hath the shape of a lion, his mother that of an ant . . . these bring forth the ant-lion, a compound of both and in part like to either . . ."
> . . . [T]he "cockatrice" of Scripture . . . ". . . drieth and burneth leaves with this touch, and he is of so great venom and perilous that he slayeth and wasteth him that nigheth him without tarrying . . ." . . . "The dragon is most greatest of all serpents, and oft he is drawn out of his den and riseth up into the air, and the air is moved by him, and also the sea swelleth against his venom, and he hath a crest, and reareth his tongue, and hath teeth like a saw, and hath strength, and not only in teeth but in tail, and grieveth with biting and with stinging. . . ."
> The phoenix rising from his ashes proves the doctrine of the resurrection; the structure and mischief of monkeys proves the existence of demons . . . (Vol. I, pp. 33–35).

This is not verbal behavior emitted as a jest or in creating fiction. Such verbal behavior was displayed by learned individuals as well as common folk and was only slowly replaced by verbal behavior under the control of environmental stimuli. It has already been suggested that this type of verbal behavior has not been completely replaced today. Even in a modern society like our own there seem to be wide differences among people in the extent to which they emit verbal behavior analogous to the above and the extent to which they will "accept" such verbal behavior in others.

When an individual studies in a scientific area he receives training in verbal responses that are precisely controlled by environmental stimuli. He also is taught a set of verbal response sequences that mediate the overt behaviors of observing certain objects and events. In addition, he may be taught a set of verbal response sequences (a philosophy of science) that "cautions" him to look for observables when he meets new terms and theories.

As in the observing behavior itself, this type of training may be restricted to the particular area of study. In this case the individual scientist may evidence a high-level behavior in one area but not in another area of science, where different particular verbal response sequences have been developed. Thus it is found that scientists well trained and respected in one area may use unacceptable terms in another area.

Just as more precise stimulus control of verbal behavior seems to have evolved, so also have logical sequences apparently changed. In the long history of language development, there are numerous examples of *sequences of verbal responses* that have shown varying degrees of utility to science. That is, here again there has apparently been a cultural development in which many "illogical" connecting verbal response sequences, once quite dominant for individuals and groups of individuals, have become much less evident. Further examples taken from A. D. White's history may illustrate this point.

> Philo had found for the elucidation of Scripture especially deep meanings in the numbers four, six, and seven; but other interpreters soon surpassed him. . . . Josephus argued that, since there were twenty-two letters in the Hebrew alphabet, there must be twenty-two sacred books in the Old Testament; other Jewish authorities thought that there should be twenty-four books, on account of the twenty-four watches in the temple. St. Jerome wavered between the argument based upon the twenty-two letters in the Hebrew alphabet and that suggested by twenty-four elders in the Apocalypse. Hilary of Poitiers argued that there must be twenty-four books, on account of the twenty-four letters in the Greek alphabet. Origen found an argument for the existence of exactly four gospels in the existence of just four elements. Irenaeus insisted that there could be neither more nor fewer than four gospels, since the earth has four quarters, the air four winds, and the cherubim four faces . . . (1899, Vol. II, p. 296).

The general logic here (these types of verbal response sequences) appears to have been to tact (with number responses) some stimulus object or event, this tact then eliciting a sequence of verbal responses culminating in the production of the final tact to another stimulus event. Frequently these intervening numerological sequences were quite complicated, as the following example indicates.

In the mystic power of numbers to reveal the sense of Scripture Augustine found especial delight. He tells us that there is deep meaning in sundry scriptural uses of the number forty, and especially as the number of days required for fasting. Forty, he reminds us, is four times ten. Now, four, he says, is the number especially representing time, the day and the year being each divided into four parts; while ten, being made up of three and seven, represents knowledge of the Creator and creature, three referring to the three persons in the triune Creator, and seven referring to the three elements, heart, soul, and mind, taken in connection with the four elements, fire, air, earth, and water, which go to make up the creature. Therefore this number ten, representing knowledge, being multiplied by four, representing time, admonishes us to live during time according to knowledge—that is, to fast for forty days (1899, Vol. II, p. 298).

This type of sequence of verbal responses is generally recognized today as unacceptable for mediating behavior that adjusts to natural events. Since the verbal sequences do not follow or parallel actual events they are not likely to mediate adjustive behavior. In contrast, other types of sequences of word and number responses have proved more "practical" in the sense of mediating such behavior. It is suggested that the "useful" verbal response sequences in this sense are of the type which tend to be developed in a scientific language and that these have also become more dominant in our common language because of their consequences.

Reinforcement and the Emergence of the Scientific Method

In spite of earlier conflicts, it may certainly be argued that the practice of science has emerged as a dominant behavior in our culture, in other words, it is characteristic of a large and active group of people. This development may perhaps be inspected as an important example of cultural evolution, taking place according to the principles of behavior we have discussed. In simplified terms, let us say, as an example, that there were two types of behavior which were extant in the beginning: scientific behaviors on the one hand, and behaviors controlled by statements of authority, tradition, dogma, and so on, on the other. When one of these two classes of behaviors was reinforced by successful problem solving (adjusting to natural events), it would be expected that this class of behavior would be strengthened and appear more frequently.

More explicitly, a class of behavior of this sort might perhaps become more frequent in a society in two ways. First, a reinforced behavior would be strengthened for one individual in his life time. In addition, however, the behavior might also be strengthened in the group. This might occur in the following manner. When some form of behavior that improves an individual's adjustment is strengthened, it makes him a more "successful" individual. If this behavior is also important to the group, the individual may also become more "successful" with respect to other members of the group. As a consequence, it might be expected that those persons with the most effective behaviors would emerge in a predominant position in relation to other individuals. The "successful" individual, further, may then be in a position to influence (through communication and reinforcement principles) a number of other people to behave in ways like his own. (See Chapter 8 for a fuller discussion of reinforcement in social interaction and social change.)

It is conceivable that there were many instances in history when different individuals emitted "competing" verbal statements and where those which were of a scientific nature in contrast to those of a dogmatic nature resulted in the success of one individual or group of individuals. Because scientific statements led to prediction and control, individuals behaving in this manner perhaps had more influence on other people.

Philosophy of Science

In time it might be expected that men would come to tact the above two types of behavior as well as the relative successes they mediated, since these too would be observable events. If certain behaviors of men are effective in adjusting to natural phenomena while other behaviors are not, then individuals who have been trained to observe might also tact these behavioral events. These tacts might finally culminate in general statements of methodology, or a philosophy of science. Stevens, in discussing certain aspects of the philosophy of science, called them "an empirical study of the actual doings of science-makers" (1939, p. 243). Thus, the behaviors of scientists, and their successes and failures, can be considered as observable events, descriptions of which could enter into statements that mediated the behavior of others in their approach to problem features of the natural world.

Again, however, these statements themselves might be in "competition" with each other in terms of the extent to which they were promulgated and the extent to which they were influential. A. D. White has also given many good examples of the "competition" between such general statements of method, and he suggests that many discoveries of the physical and biological sciences were arrested by dogma during the Middle Ages and even in many cases right up to the twentieth century.

The cause of this arrest was twofold: First, there was created an atmosphere in which the germs of physical science could hardly grow—an atmosphere in which all seeking in Nature for truth as truth was regarded as futile. The general belief . . . was, that the end of the world was at hand; that the last judgment was approaching; that all existing physical nature was soon to be destroyed: hence, the greatest thinkers . . . generally poured contempt upon all investigators into a science of Nature . . . (Vol. I, p. 375).

Then, too, there was established a standard to which all science which did struggle up through this atmosphere must be made to conform—a standard which favoured magic rather than science, for it was a standard of rigid dogmatism. . . . The most careful inductions from ascertained facts were regarded as wretchedly fallible when compared with any view of nature whatever given or even hinted at in any poem, chronicle, code, apologue, myth, legend, allegory, letter, or discourse of any sort which had happened to be preserved in the literature which had come to be held as sacred (Vol. I, p. 376). . . . . [T]oo much prying into the secrets of Nature was very generally held to be dangerous both to body and soul . . . In place of research came authority . . . (Vol. I, p. 32).

However, in the same way that the scientific behaviors themselves might be strengthened in a group, the statements of general methodology of science might also be expected to increase in frequency through the principles of reinforcement. An individual whose behavior was controlled by such general statements might solve problems better, and so on, and emerge as more "influential." Once these general statements became "accepted," for example, were taught in universities, they then could influence a greater number of people according to the principles of communication. As a result, the dominance of the more successful approach would be expected to accelerate.

In the first chapter it was said that the scientific method may be characterized in the following terms: (1) it is based upon systematic public observation; (2) it is deterministic, as it assumes that events in the world are determined by other natural events; and (3) it is skeptical of statements based upon authority, tradition, dogma, and so on. The reader may now recognize that these three statements may be considered complex facts to certain aspects of this most successful type of behavior—scientific behavior. That is, these statements may be considered as conclusions rather than as assumptions. For example, in the past when controversies occurred concerning natural or supernatural determination of an event, the former was shown to be the case many times, the latter never.

Cultural Differences in Scientific Behavior

We have discussed the individual and familial differences in language behavior that may have the effect of producing in the child behaviors more or less amenable to scientific training. In addition, it was suggested that our society has progressed considerably with respect to the dominance of scientific behaviors. It is also reasonable that societies would differ in the extent to which they have developed a language which parallels the physical and social events in the environment. In this respect, some linguists have suggested that there are differences in the "concepts" of the world held by different peoples, in other words, that the world is differently experienced and conceived in different linguistic communities. Benjamin Whorf (Carroll, 1956), for example, was influential in describing some of these differences. However, linguists have tended to stress the importance of describing these differences in nonevaluative terms, as is implied in the name for this approach, "linguistic relativity." That is, they might say that although languages differ, no one language could be said to be better than another. On the other hand, on the basis of the above discussion, we might suggest that languages may vary in ways which could lead to behaviors which are more or less adjustive. Thus, in this sense, one language might be said to be better than another. This is not to say that a language which mediates better behavior in one area will necessarily be better in other areas. The development might well be uneven.

The differences in the adjustive value of a language might also extend to social events, as Dollard and Miller (1950) indicate. Since other people and their behaviors constitute physical stimuli, there may also be differences in the extent to which these events and their determining events are tacted successfully and related to one another. Prediction and control of the behavior of organisms, just as for other events, could depend upon the adequacy of tacts and relating response sequences. Thus, people who have learned good scientific verbal behaviors in these respects might well adjust better to such social events. The same processes might also apply to different cultures as well as to individuals within a culture.

Another note of caution should be injected before concluding this section. It should be stressed that the preceding statements regarding the operation of learning principles in science are oversimplified, interpretive extensions into a very complex subject matter in a manner which may only be considered as tentative. The authors merely wish to suggest that behavior principles may be involved and that further exploration of these complex activities as learned behaviors may prove productive. For supplementary treatment of some of these topics the reader may be interested in some related discussions that consider scientific activity in psychological terms (Mandler and Kessen, 1959; Skinner, 1957).

6

Personality

In chapter 2 the manner in which descriptions of behavior can become specious explanations of behavior was discussed. Several different examples were given of terms that were incorrectly given explanatory value. As Skinner was quoted to say in that chapter, terms which start out as descriptions of behavior are turned into nouns and treated as the causes of behavior. The term *personality* has been used in ways that are analogous to this.

For example, personality in one type of popular usage is thought to stand for some internal entity or process that determines the behavior of an individual. If a person has one type of "personality" he will behave one way; if he has another kind this will be demonstrated through different overt signs. Thus, as an illustration, a child observed to behave in certain ways—for example, to hang around his mother a good deal, initiate activities infrequently, or often to ask for all kinds of directions, might be said to have a dependent personality. To one who considers the behavior a result of the inner "dependency," the behavior itself would not be thought of as the primary problem. Rather, basic to change in the behavior would be the means of effecting the "inner" personality. Changing the behavior would seem relatively superficial, since behavior would be thought to be only a manifestation of the inner man—and then only a partial and sometimes misleading manifestation. (See Chapter 9, for additional discussion on this topic.)

However, used in this manner, there are no independent observations of the "personality" as an internal process or entity. Furthermore, there may be little specification of the antecedent conditions that result in the development of the term. In certain cases, it might be suggested that biological variables were antecedent to the "personality." In other cases environmental variables might be thought to be the important antecedent conditions. In either case, it would not be enough simply to refer to biology and environment; their effects would have to be specified through observation.

In attempts to modernize the term and to bring it into alignment with a systematic empirical approach, it has been suggested that personality be considered an intervening variable (Kimble, 1956; Stagner, 1948). However, the term cannot be considered in this manner until specification both of the effects of antecedent conditions upon the intervening variable and of the relationship of the intervening variable to the consequent behavior of the individual have been established. That is, the characteristics of the term must be systematically established by this type of observation. Actually, the antecedent environmental variables and consequent behavior and the principles of their relation are so complex that a single term such as personality hardly seems to be adequate. Perhaps this is the reason that *personality* is usually broken into many subterms, such as, dependent personality, hostile personality, and immature personality, as well as needs, interest, instincts, beliefs, expectancies, and many others. In addition to these uses of personality terms, systematic attempts have been made to specify the "personality" with terms such as *ego, superego, id, self,* and *traits.* These attempts are usually treated under the heading of "personality structure." A few of these will be briefly mentioned as examples of personality theory. These examples by no means constitute a survey of the field of personality; there are excellent sources of such discussions available, (for example, Hall and Lindzey, 1957).

PERSONALITY CONCEPTS

The Self

The concept "self" has been considered predominantly in psychology in two ways (Hall & Lindzey, 1957): one, as the individual's "self-perceptions"; and the other as an inferred process that determines the individual's behavior. We will discuss the usage as self-perception first and return later to the self as an explanatory term.

Self-perception

According to this usage, the term has been defined as the "attitudes" and "feelings" of the individual about himself. Customarily, psychologists who have used this term in this manner infer that there are inner processes which determine what the individual will say about himself. These inner processes might at various times be called "attitudes," "feelings," "perceptions," "evaluations," and so on.

However, such internal processes are not observed. Rather, the observations from which such internal processes are inferred generally include largely the verbal statements of the individual, particularly that verbal behavior which is descriptive of himself and his actions. Considered in this manner, it would be appropriate to use *self* only as a descriptive term, to stand for the verbal behavior the individual emits concerning himself, not as an explanatory term standing for some inner psychic agent (see also Keller and Schoenfeld, 1950; and Stephenson, 1953).

Explanation of this type of behavior would only be obtained when the variables that determine the behavior, and the principles by which the variables have their effect, are established. Thus, one might ask the reasons why some people make positive statements about their physical appearance, their general behavior, and so on, while the statements of other people about themselves and their actions are derogatory.

A study by Nuthmann (1957) substantiates the descriptive view of the "self" as a set of verbal responses and at the same time indicates what certain of the determining variables might be. In this experiment, acceptance-of-self statements, from which the individual's self-concept is customarily inferred, were treated as a class of responses subject to the principles of operant conditioning. A test made up of 100 such items was administered to a large group of students and those students who scored in the lowest 15 percent of the acceptance-of-self distribution were selected for the experiment—to be conducted about two months later. The subjects were then matched on the basis of these scores and assigned to one of the experimental groups.

In the experiment, the individual acceptance-of-self items were successively presented to the subjects. For half the items, a response of TRUE to the item would indicate acceptance of self, while for the remaining half a response of FALSE would be appropriate to the self-acceptance class. In one of the groups to be conditioned, whenever the subject gave an acceptance-of-self response whether TRUE or FALSE, it was followed immediately by the reinforcing stimulus of the experimenter saying GOOD. In the control group, no reinforcement was given.

It was found that when subjects were reinforced for acceptance-of-self statements, the frequency with which they emitted such statements increased. Thus, Nuthmann's study indicates that at least certain of the independent variables which determine this class of behavior are the principles of learning. That is, behavior which constitutes the observations on which the concept of self is based is subject to the principles of operant conditioning.

Other psychologists who consider the self as the way the individual regards himself have also suggested learning variables as determinants. Sarbin (1952), for example, believes that the individual's conceptions of his social behavior are acquired through experience and emerge in a developmental process.

It might be suggested that the study of the class of verbal behavior which defines the term "self" will require a detailed examination of the manner in which the individual's history shapes the behavior and determines the types of stimuli which have come to control it. A discussion of this approach to the self by Keller and Schoenfeld describes in behavioral terms how this may come about.

> Of great importance . . . is the fact that human beings can discriminate their own actions, appearance, feelings, and successfulness. In the course of growing up, the child comes to "know" about himself; he becomes at least partially "aware" of his capacities and weaknesses, his likelihood of winning or losing in given situations, his physical and social attractiveness, his characteristic reactions. This is sometimes spoken of as the development or emergence of the "Self," a word that is meant to designate the ability to speak of (be "aware" of) one's own behavior, or the ability to use one's own behavior as the S^D for further behavior, verbal or otherwise. The sociologist Mead spoke of the "Self" as a social product, that is, it arises out of social interaction; but more specifically, we can say today that the individual is *taught* by his fellows to respond discriminatively to himself and his behavior. He can observe himself and judge himself with words like "good" and "bad." He can estimate his own efficacy as a social agent in pleasing people and in striving for social success; and if he discriminates what in his behavior is causing failure, he may switch to new responses, that is, "improve" or "snap out of it." The "Self," in short, is the person, his body and behavior and characteristic interactions with the environment, taken as the discriminative objects of his own verbal behavior . . . (1950, pp. 368–369).

More specifically, in Chapter 4 a section deals with the manner in which the child may be trained to make appropriate verbal responses to the stimuli produced by his own behavior. To various degrees he learns to tact responses such as his own movements of various kinds. In addition, it was suggested that a child also acquires tacts to his own social behavior. He will learn in various situations to respond to the stimuli produced by his own behavior, for example, I WAS KIND, I WAS AMUSING, I WAS SUCCESSFUL, I BEHAVED LIKE AN IDIOT, I WAS SOCIABLE, I WAS DISHONEST. It is this type of training that seems to be relevant to the development of the verbal behavior involved in the term *self-concept*.

Furthermore, the several variables of which these types of statements would be a function may also be suggested. First, the individual's statements should to some extent depend upon the physical properties of the individual and the behavior he emits—which itself would depend in part upon the individual's learning history. That is, one determinant of the individual's self-statements, though not by any means the only one, would seem to be the behavior of the individual itself. Whether a person will state that he is "unkind," for example, will tend to depend upon whether he behaves in a manner labeled as unkind in his community.

In addition, however, it has been suggested that the child's training to make statements about himself may be to some extent independent of what he is and does. Lundholm (1940), for example, has made a distinction between the discrepancies in the descriptions of a person by himself and by others. He does not use behavior principles to account for the distinction, but calls one's own self-description the *subjective self* and other descriptions the *objective self*. In behavioral terms, it might be said that this discrepancy arises when an individual who may have learned to behave in a certain way has not been trained to describe verbally—to tact—his behavior in commensurate terms, that is, as others do. In the above example, although the individual may behave so as to cause pain to others, he may never have been trained to describe his behavior as "unkind," and so on. The child of a despotic ruler might behave extremely cruelly to his father's subjects and yet never receive tacting training that would develop appropriate self-descriptive verbal behavior. This would be an unusual case; however, many other examples could be cited of discrepancies between self-descriptions and the behavior serving as the discriminative object for the description, the discrepancies being a result of the child's training in verbal behavior. A child might be reinforced for tacting his skills as low level, unintelligent, whereas they are really very capable. His verbal behavior would then be inappropriate and he would be said to have "low regard for himself," "to perceive himself as a person of no ability," and so on. On the other hand, it would seem equally possible to shape the converse discrepancy in a child—verbal behavior that would be an unrealistically flattering tact to himself and his behavior.

The same procedures may thus also operate with respect to the individual's physical characteristics. A commonplace-appearing child might be trained to tact his appearance in much more positive terms than others might. Or a child might be trained in the opposite manner; although the child was physically very attractive, he might be trained to emit derogatory self-descriptions to himself as the discriminative object.

Other discriminative stimuli besides those of the individual himself and his behavior seem also to determine statements about the "self." One's statements about oneself may vary from situation to situation. An adolescent, for example, might emit expansive self-statements in the presence of his peer group or his girl friend, in comparison to the more modest descriptions of self made in the presence of some authority persons. It is expected that the stimulus control exerted in such cases would also develop according to the principles of discrimination. That is, certain types of self-descriptions are reinforced in the presence of some people and not others. The people then as discriminative stimuli would be expected to come to control the verbal behavior involved.

In conclusion, it is suggested that children would differ in the types and extent of training they might receive with respect to tacting their own behavior. The discriminations might thus vary from relatively fine to gross. The degree of correspondence between self-tacts and the tacts of other people to the individual would also vary with the precision of the training. (This important type of training will be discussed further in Chapter 9 under the heading of "Social Reasoning.") It is suggested that this type of experience is in part what shapes the individual's self-descriptions, and that these descriptions form the observations from which the *self* or *self-concept* is inferred. To some extent, thus, the individual's self-statements seem independent of his other behaviors—they depend upon the way the individual is trained to respond to his own behavior.

Although the terms and principles used in this type of analysis are quite different, the account is actually congruent with statements made by self-theorists. For example, Rogers (1951) states the following.

> As a result of interaction with the environment, and particularly as a result of evaluational interaction with others, the structure of self is formed—an organized, fluid, but consistent conceptual pattern of perceptions of characteristics and relationships of the "I" or the "me," together with values attached to these concepts (p. 498).

It is suggested, however, that the behavior of the individual, largely verbal behavior, from which such terms as "self-structure" or "self-perception" are inferred is learned behavior. A productive analysis of such behavior should therefore be possible through a detailed consideration of the behavior involved as well as the types of learning conditions that could produce such behaviors.

The Self as an Independent Variable

The second way in which the term *self* is treated by some psychologists is as an explanatory term. Hall and Lindzey state, for example, that sometimes "it is regarded as a group of psychological processes which govern behavior and adjustment" (1957, p. 468). This means that the *self* is considered to be some unobservable internal process which determines the way the individual behaves. As such it would have the same status as the term "personality" which was discussed at the beginning of this chapter. In order for the term to have such explanatory value, its relationship to independent variables would have to be specified, as well as the relationship of the term to the behavior it determines, and this specification has not yet taken place.

In the preceding section, on the other hand, self-statements were considered as behavior that is acquired and functions according to the principles of learning. The paradigm was that of an S–R relationship, with the self-statements constituting the R and other stimuli the independent variables. However, it may be suggested that verbal statements produce stimuli which can be responded to by oneself as well as by others. In these terms one's self-statements, or the self, could be considered to be an independent variable that would control one's own behavior and the behavior of others.

First, it is suggested that the types of statements a person makes about himself, the things he can do, how well he can do them, and so on—statements to which we refer as self-confidence—may influence the way other people respond to the person. A person who makes deprecatory statements about himself is likely to be responded to in a manner appropriate to those statements. We have been trained so that when some object or event is labeled as "bad," for example, we respond to it in certain characteristic ways. The individual who describes himself in these terms may not, as a consequence, achieve the same sorts of success as a person who speaks more positively of himself. Other things being equal, an individual who states I AM NOT VERY GOOD AT THIS TYPE OF THING is hardly likely to get the "call" when in competition with someone who says SURE, I'LL DO IT; I AM PRETTY GOOD AT THIS TYPE OF THING.

In addition, the statements the individual makes about himself would be expected to function as a stimulus that would control his own behavior, as was discussed in Chapters 4 and 5. Thus, a distorted set of self-statements may mean that the individual behaves in accord with the statements. It would be expected that different reasoning sequences would ensue if the individual tacted his own behavior in positive rather than negative terms. For example, the individual who makes derogatory self-statements may "conclude" in a problem-solving sequence on the basis of these tacts not to attempt tasks at which he might otherwise be successful. He may thus not present himself for situations in which he might develop new skilled behaviors. On the other hand, the individual who makes "confident" self-statements may, other things being equal, attempt the task on the basis of his reasoning and be successful. As a consequence, these two individuals as they progress through life may have different opportunities to gain experience, and their behavior would be shaped accordingly. The self-confident individual might well have many more experiences (again, other things being equal) where he is reinforced for emitting certain skill behaviors. The former individual might not develop those skills in the same measure. The self-confident individual may also, because of his verbal behavior, tend to gain more attention, social approval, and social rewards such as raises and honors. These experiences could reinforce the verbal behavior and act as S^Ds for further "self-confident" self-description.

Of course, inappropriate self-confident statements in the face of little skill will customarily be responded to adversely, and the above processes would be reversed. In addition, it would be possible to discuss how various other statements about the "self" might influence the behavior of others and thus their responses to the individual, but this short section should suffice to suggest the general process.

At any rate, considered solely as behavior, without inferring any internal "self" process, it is suggested that the individual's "self-concept" may be a determinant of the individual's behavior and, further, of the stimulus conditions the individual will experience. If this is the case, it would seem productive to analyze in detail the manner in which this type of behavior is developed and the effects that the behavior has upon the individual's own behavior as well as upon the response of others to him. The principles of behavior would seem to offer a justifiable approach to dealing with such problems, since they seem to be problems of learning and stimulus control, and of the types of language principles that have been discussed.

Traits

Attempts to account for man's behavior in terms of typologies go far back into history. Hippocrates, for example, proposed that all human behavior resulted from a combination of four types, in various mixtures. The strength of each type, and thus the mixture, was determined by the relative strength of its "causative" agent, a body humor. According to this interpretation, if the body humors were in good proportion the individual's personality would be in good balance. On the other hand, if there was an excess of one humor, the individual's behavior would be extreme in the one type as a result.

However, no independent observations were made of such body humors; nor have investigations of physiology since that time turned up additional evidence in that regard. Thus, it may be suggested that Hippocrates' source of information, rather than residing in observations of some variables antecedent to the behavior, was actually the observation of the behavior itself. His term "body humor" could thus not be explanatory in the sense of establishing laws relating antecedent and consequent events.

It is recognized now that such an approach to understanding human behavior has not been productive in the manner intended. The method on which it is based has not proved successful and the elaboration of terms descriptive of the behavior in attempts to account for the behavior is now recognized as fallacious.

In contrast to these early beginnings, however, there are more modern and more systematically founded formulations that analyze human behavior in terms of types (Sheldon, 1940), or traits (for example, Cattell, 1946; Eysenck, 1947; Thurstone, 1947). One approach to the study of traits has been called the factor approach because its method utilizes statistical procedures called factor analysis.

In this method, as an example, a large number of items may be gathered that are descriptive of human behavior. An item from the Guilford-Zimmerman Temperament Survey (Guilford and Zimmerman, 1949) may be used to illustrate some statements of self description: "You find it easy to start conversation with strangers" (p. 1). The respondent indicates his description of his behavior by stating whether or not the statement is characteristic of him. When a group of people describe their behaviors by means of such items, the method of factor analysis can be used to discover which of their answers covary or are related. That is, people who answer one of the items in the set in a certain way tend also to answer other items in a specifiable way. Thus, the results indicate that certain descriptions of behavior (and, presumably, the behavior itself) tend to go together, or to constitute a factor. Various sets of descriptions of behavior have been found to covary in this manner, and yet to be relatively independent of other classes of descriptions of behavior.

On the other hand, individuals differ in the extent to which they display the behaviors in a factor. For example, on the Guilford-Zimmerman Temperament Survey trait of Sociability there are thirty related items. One individual might indicate that he behaves in a sociable direction on nineteen of the items, another individual on twenty-six, another on twenty-two, and so on. On the basis of their responses to the various items, it might be said that these individuals were more or less sociable or, rather, that their behaviors may be described as being more or less sociable.

The many investigators who have used factor analysis have tended to avoid the error of interpreting their descriptions of behavior as a basis for explaining behavior. Eysenck (1947), for example, treats traits as consistencies in behavior. Thurstone considers interpretation of factors to be assumptions which depend "on one's philosophical preferences and manner of speech, and on how much one already knows about the domain to be investigated . . ." (1947, p. 56). However, he prefers the approach where, "No assumption is made about the nature of these functions, whether they are native or acquired or whether they have a cortical locus" (p. 57).

Cattell (1946) has discussed the various interpretations of traits at some length and describes six types of interpretation. One of these six that Cattell discusses is congruent with an orientation such as the present one. This interpretation is that the environment molds a cluster of behaviors.

"[T]he elements of a social mold trait will covary . . . because a single external influence—e.g., family, school, national culture pattern—has impressed all of them, as from a single focus" (p. 66). Cattell also suggests, "Or, in the terms of one psychological school, the habits have been 'rewarded or punished' in common" (p. 64), and he adds to this the following.

> [T]rait elements formed under one environmental influence are likely to have in common other things than the common variance impressed at the time. Habits formed at the same place and the same age are likely to share reactivity to the same stimuli . . . to follow the same curves of extinction, etc. There are probably as yet unknown similarities through coincidence of place and age in habit formation . . . (pp. 90–91).

Lundin (1961) has also discussed traits as behaviors that have some "common descriptive characteristic" (p. 16). He states, "Traits are, then, not the causes of behavior but merely descriptive terms applied to a general class of responses which appear to have something in common" (p. 16).

The present authors and their associates (Staats, Staats, Heard, and Finley, 1962) have conducted an experiment which supports the following very similar interpretation.

> Individuals behave in characteristic ways in many different situations. These characteristic ways of behaving are commonly spoken of as reflecting underlying personality traits. Tests have been constructed to measure these traits (or, rather, the covariance of specific behaviors). It is suggested that such measured personality traits have psychological status in that they are functionally unified classes of responses which have been operantly conditioned in the life history of the individual. Following from this, it is suggested that responses to trait items found through factor analysis are such classes of responses. . . . Thus, strengthening the response to one item through reinforcement should strengthen this type of response to other items in the same trait (p. 102).

These authors used Nuthmann's (1957) procedure to test the possibility that responses to trait items would condition as a response class. Thirty items were taken from the Guilford-Zimmerman Temperament Survey's trait of Sociability and by composing similar items the number was expanded to 100 items. The original Guilford-Zimmerman items had been obtained through the methods of factor analysis. In the present experiment, depending upon how the subjects responded to the items when the scale was originally administered, two matched groups were formed. At a later time, each subject was again individually presented the items in an experimental situation. Whenever the subject in the experimental group answered the item in a "sociable" direction, the response was reinforced, that is, the experimenter said, GOOD, THAT'S FINE, VERY GOOD, and so on. No responses of subjects in the control group were reinforced.

The results showed that strength of response in the sociable direction was increased through response-contingent reinforcement for the experimental group relative to the control group. The difference in the strength of the sociable response for the two groups over the blocks of items is shown in Figure 6.1. The experiment was repeated using the Guilford-

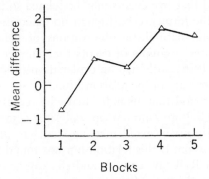

Blocks

Fig. 6.1. "The abscissa represents the order of the blocks of items presented to the subjects. The ordinate represents the difference between the means of the Experimental and Control groups. The increase in the difference scores indicates that Experimental subjects are responding to a greater extent than the Control subjects in the direction of Sociability." (Staats, Staats, Heard, and Finley, 1962, p. 105)

Zimmerman trait of General Activity. Again, it was found that such a class of responses could be operantly conditioned. In addition, Oakes and Droge (1960) have conditioned in a similar manner responses to social introversion items on the Minnesota Multiphasic Personality Inventory. In this case, subjects in one group were reinforced by the experimenter's saying GOOD following responses that would contribute to a high social introversion score while subjects in another group were reinforced for responses in the opposite direction. The difference between the scores of the two groups indicated that this type of trait behavior also constitutes a response class that can be operantly conditioned.

These experiments certainly do not account for all the observations (both formal and naturalistic) that have gone into trait descriptions. The results, however, do support the contention that what are called personality traits may be considered to be classes of responses which have developed according to the principles of operant conditioning. They also suggest that detailed application of these principles to the study of the behaviors involved might yield a deeper understanding of the determinants of the behavior. On the other hand, it may also be added that although traits have been spoken of as "mental structures," or as springing from physiological processes or organic structures (Allport, 1937), no observations have yet been made of such internal events.

Traits and Prediction

In Chapter 2 R–R laws and their potentiality for prediction were discussed. It was stated that two events may be related so that the latter may be predicted from the former, even though no determining relationship is involved. Formal and naturalistic observations of behavior of the type called traits are another example of events that may enter into R–R relationships (Kimble, 1956), although an explanation of the second behavior is not given by a knowledge of the relationship.

Thus, it may be found that an individual who scores low on the Sociability scale of the Guilford-Zimmerman will later demonstrate rather unsociable behavior. He might avoid meeting strangers, attending meetings, joining groups, and so on. If this relationship was found to hold in general, it could be that an R–R law existed, and the extent of one's sociability could be predicted on the basis of the test score.

It must be kept in mind in such cases, however, that the information yielded in this relationship does not indicate the determinants, either of the individual's response to the test times, or of the actual social behavior itself. This would demand independent observations of the antecedent conditions involved in each case.

Perhaps it is because verbal behavior is generally related to later behaviors that the inference is so often drawn from the verbal behavior that there are internal processes or structures which determine the later behavior. Such inferences, as has been stressed, cannot, however, yield new explanatory knowledge by which control of the consequent event (in this case behavior) can be obtained.

Freudian Determinism and
the Id, Ego, and Superego

Sigmund Freud is possibly the best known of all contributors to psychology. Upon the basis of his naturalistic observations, together with those he made in treating patients, Freud stimulated the study of complex human problems through methods consistent with science. He accepted man's behavior as a natural occurrence to be objectively studied, and he encouraged others also to break away from preceding dogma and orthodox taboos.

Freud's great contribution to Western thought has been described as the application of the principle of cause and effect to human behavior. Freud demonstrated that many features of behavior hitherto unexplained —and often dismissed as hopelessly complex or obscure—could be shown to be the product of circumstances in the history of the individual. Many of the causal relationships he so convincingly demonstrated had been wholly unsuspected—unsuspected, in particular, by the very individuals whose behavior they controlled. Freud greatly reduced the sphere of accident and caprice in our considerations of human conduct (Skinner, 1959, p. 185).

Freud's determinism is clearly revealed in the following excerpt from his writings.

As is known, many persons argue against the assumption of an absolute psychic determinism by referring to an intense feeling of conviction that there is a free will. This feeling of conviction exists, but is not incompatible with the belief in determinism. Like all normal feelings, it must be justified by something. But, so far as I can observe, it does not manifest itself in weighty and important decisions; on these occasions, one has much more the feeling of the psychic compulsion and gladly falls back upon it. (Compare Luther's "Here I stand, I can not do anything else.")

On the other hand, it is in trivial and indifferent decisions that one feels sure that he could just as easily have acted differently, that he acted of his own free will, and without any motives. From our analyses we therefore need not contest the right of the feeling of conviction that there is a free will. If we distinguish conscious from unconscious motivation, we are then informed by the feeling of conviction that the conscious motivation does not extend over all our motor resolutions. . . . What is thus left free from one side receives its motive from the other side, from the unconscious, and the determinism in the psychic realm is thus carried out uninterruptedly (McClelland, 1955, pp. 15–16).

This determinism contrasts markedly with the explanations of human behavior prevalent at the time of his writing.

The traditional procedure had been to invent an inner determiner, a "demon," "spirit," "homunculus," or "personality" capable of spontaneous change of course or of origination of action. Such an inner determiner offers only a momentary explanation of the behavior of the outer organism, because it must, of course, be accounted for also, but it is commonly used to put the matter beyond further inquiry and to bring the study of a causal series of events to a dead end (Skinner, 1959, p. 187).

While his approach was a great advance in the study of human behavior, Freud nevertheless did not break fully with traditional procedures. In developing his interpretation of human behavior, Freud included internal, unobservable processes, thinking that these would one day prove to be natural events capable of observational specification.

For Freud there were three primary structures that interacted in various ways to determine the individual's behavior. The *id* was thought to consist of the organism's biological inheritance and to include instinctual energies. The *id* operated according to the pleasure principle: any rise in tension (for example, any deprivation) would result in immediate action of some kind that would diminish the tension. Dreaming, hallucinating, and behaviors of this type, as well as reflex responses and "impulsive" behaviors were seen as adaptive actions of the *id*.

The *ego*, on the other hand, was thought to assume more responsibility for the personality (in some cases the terms *ego* and *self* are used synonymously). The *ego*, for example, was thought to determine most of the various complex behaviors that go into adjusting to the physical and social environment. This includes learning, thinking, problem solving, and all the complex language behaviors. Impulsive actions were interpreted as occurring where the *ego* has not been developed highly, as in young children. The development of the *ego*, thus, was thought to produce behavior that is controlled by stimuli other than merely the internal drive stimuli— to be controlled by other physical and social stimuli. However, the *ego* arises from the *id*, receives its energy from the *id*, and serves to satisfy the instinctual needs through its actions.

The *superego*, however, acts in a manner antagonistic to the impulsive strivings of the *id*. The *superego* is the last part of the personality to develop. It represents the cultural values, ideals, and morals acquired by the child through the experience of rewards and punishments imposed upon the child, especially by his parents. Freud thought of the *superego* developing through the influence of parents, teachers, and so on, to finally become "the representative of all moral restrictions, the advocate of the impulse toward perfection. In short, it is as much as we have been able to appreciate psychologically of what people call the 'higher things in life'" (Freud, 1949, p. 94).

Although he leaned heavily on such concepts in discussing behavior, as a determinist Freud still looked to the antecedent environmental and biological events in the history of the organism to account for these inner mental structures.

> Freud, himself, however, did not appeal to the inner apparatus to account for spontaneity or caprice because he was a thoroughgoing determinist. He accepted the responsibility of explaining, in turn, the behavior of the inner determiner. He did this by pointing to hitherto unnoticed external causes in the environmental and genetic history of the individual. He did not, therefore, need the traditional explanatory system for traditional purposes; but he was unable to eliminate the pattern from his thinking. It led him to represent each of the causal relationships he had discovered as a series of three events. Some environmental condition,

very often in the early life of the individual, leaves an effect upon the inner mental apparatus, and this in turn produces the behavioral manifestation or symptom. Environmental event, mental state or process, behavioral symptom—these are the three links in Freud's causal chain. He made no appeal to the middle link to explain spontaneity or caprice. Instead he used it to bridge the gap in space and time between the events he had proved to be causally related (Skinner, 1959, pp. 187–188).

However, it may be pointed out that the characteristics of the personality terms which Freud used were not specified sufficiently by observations of environmental conditions and of their effects upon behavior. And, in the light of what is known about human neuroanatomy, it is unacceptable to suggest that there might be anatomical structures which correspond to Freud's mental structures. Thus, adequate specification by systematic observation was not made of actual structures of the personality by which to gain explanation of human behavior, nor was the systematic observation of antecedent environmental events related to the intervening terms and then to behavior. Reasons why this systematic observation did not take place by Freud or his followers are suggested as follows by Skinner (1959).

> The important disadvantages of Freud's conception of mental life can be described somewhat more specifically. The first of these concerns the environmental variables to which Freud so convincingly pointed. The cogency of these variables was frequently missed because the variables were transformed and obscured in the course of being represented in mental life. The physical world of the organism was converted into conscious and unconscious experience, and these experiences were further transmuted as they combined and changed in mental processes. For example, early punishment of sexual behavior is an observable fact which undoubtedly leaves behind a changed organism. But when this change is represented as a state of conscious or unconscious anxiety or guilt, specific details of the punishment are lost. When, in turn, some unusual characteristic of the sexual behavior of the adult individual is related to the supposed guilt, many specific features of the relationship may be missed which would have been obvious if the same features of behavior had been related to the punishing episode. Insofar as the mental life of the individual is used as Freud used it to represent and to carry an environmental history, it is inadequate and misleading.
>
> Freud's theory of the mental apparatus had an equally damaging effect upon his study of behavior as a dependent variable. Inevitably, it stole the show. Little attention was left to behavior per se. Behavior was relegated to the position of a mere mode of expression of the activities of the mental apparatus or the symptoms of an underlying disturbance (p. 189).

In short, in this very brief discussion, it is suggested that Freud was a confirmed determinist and made many, many productive observations of human behavior and its environmental determinants. (The agreement between his deterministic position and a learning approach has led to various attempts to integrate the two sets of principles; see Dollard and Miller,

1950; Mowrer, 1950; Sears, 1951, as examples.) However, because of his preoccupation with the characteristics of his inferred mental terms, the attempt to make systematic observations of behavior and its environmental antecedents may ultimately have suffered.

It may be said, however, that when Freud commenced his theorizing, methods by which to experimentally establish the principles relating environmental events to behavior had not yet been developed and extended to the study of significant human behaviors. As a consequence, Freud's statements—as with most other interpretations of human behavior in terms of inferred, internal processes—were based for the most part upon naturalistic observations, especially those made in clinical interactions, in the course of treatment of an individual's personal problems. Because of the great dependency of personality theories upon such data, it is important to give some consideration to the strengths and weaknesses of such methods of observation.

CLINICAL METHODS OF OBSERVATION
AND PERSONALITY THEORY

The primary place of origin of many terms in personality theory has been the clinic. Individuals with problems have consulted physicians, psychiatrists, and clinical psychologists, and in the process of treating these individuals the therapists have developed terminologies that have frequently become "theories."

Most of the usual interaction between the patient and the therapist is of a verbal sort. The patient speaks to the therapist, the therapist speaks to the patient. It is the patient's behavior, especially his verbal behavior, which forms to a large extent the observations that make up the clinician's data and upon which his theoretical formulations are based.

> Most present-day theories of human personality and of the historical and dynamic causes of human behavior were originally formulated by individuals practicing psychotherapy. In fact, it was the memories and free associations of neurotic patients that led Freud to formulate his theory of psychosexual development. Similarly, the memories and free associations of patients talking to other such innovators have led to very different conceptions of the origins of human personality. Even though these personality theorists presumably began with the same raw verbal materials, however, it is apparent that they derived quite different formulations. . . . Moreover, the various schools have defended their positions mainly on the basis of further psychotherapeutic contacts with patients, with no resolution of the theoretical differences (Quay, 1959, p. 254).

To some extent, observations may be obtained from the reports of family or associates of the patient concerning the patient's experience and his behavior. The question, however, of the types of laws which can be founded upon such observations—and the probable reliability of such statements—must be raised. Is it possible to establish R–R laws on the basis of observations of the patient's behavior and reports given by associates? Can S–R laws be established by inferring causative factors from their reports of past or even current environmental events?

Clinical Observation and R–R Laws

Before discussing either type of law, it should be emphasized that the observation and description of behavior alone, as discussed in Chapter 2, constitutes an important source of knowledge. As in any other case where the concern is about observable events in the natural world, the first step is to make detailed, reliable observations of the occurrences and to record them systematically. Clinical observations may be considered significant in this respect alone. And the conceptions, such as Freud's, that have emerged from clinical observations have been great improvements over the notions that preceded them.

It is possible, in addition to simple observation and description, however, that R–R laws can be established by observing in the clinical situation relationships between behaviors. It might be found, for example, that patients who emit certain verbal statements when in psychotherapy may later recover more rapidly than usual, while patients whose verbal behavior is of another sort will require hospitalization, and so on. These could constitute R–R laws—if the observations were systematically made and the relationships noted. As with traits and the factor analysis of behaviors that has been described, detailed and systematic observations of behavior when related to other behaviors can enter into R–R laws. This could occur even without quantitative expression of the statement. Further, such laws would involve no assessment of the "truth" of the patient's statements. It might be found, for example, that patients who "recall" childhood difficulties while in therapy improve in their "life" behavior, even though their recollected events had never taken place. The law relating the verbal statements to prognosis would still be valid and useful.

Clinical Observation and S–R Laws

In addition, S–R laws might also be established on the basis of clinical observation. The behavior (R) of the individual might be found to be related to observations of the events that have occurred in the individual's history (S)—observations provided by associates or by the patient himself.

However, the question of obtaining S–R laws from clinical observations depends upon the reliability of the observations of the explanatory stimulus events. Thus, the status of the observations made by the family or associates as well as the reports given by the patient himself must be examined more closely for "truth" value. First, the reports of an untrained individual with limited knowledge of the principles of behavior probably should not be expected to supply observations with which a systematic account of human behavior may be constructed. It must be remembered that what the individual observes is a function of his discrimination training, especially the discrimination training involving his verbal behavior. If these discriminations had not been established in the observer, he might be present when occurrences significant in shaping the patient's behavior took place and yet not respond to them at all, or perhaps respond to them erroneously.

Let us take an example to illustrate this weakness of clinical observations for constructing a scientific set of principles. It has been firmly established in laboratory study that intermittant schedules of reinforcement (see Chapter 3) yield behavior which is different in certain important characteristics from behavior reinforced continuously. It is to be expected that each of us has certain characteristic behaviors which are a result of these extremely complicated conditions of reinforcement scheduling. However, the individual with usual training could not be expected to recognize such effective variables underlying someone else's behavior. This knowledge is only beginning to emerge from the science systematically concerned with human behavior. The complexity of the principles of behavior and the difficulty in establishing them even in the laboratory makes it certain that the untrained individual could never recognize them in naturalistic circumstances.

The same is true when the individual gives an account of conditions that supposedly have effected his own behavior. Not knowing what the relevant variables are (not having acquired verbal discriminations to the variables) he cannot be expected to describe them. For this reason alone, it would not be expected that clinical observations based upon the reports of untrained people would ever lead to the discovery of the simple, analytic principles which underly the complex acquisition and maintenance of human behaviors.

Furthermore, to the extent that the therapist-investigator relies upon the verbal statements of the patient to supply observations of the antecedent conditions which account for the patient's behavior, the therapist's principles may be built upon observations which are neither public nor repeatable. Many of the early experiences of the child are not accessible to anyone else, nor of course, could they be staged again to determine their

effects upon behavior, or duplicated with someone else with other determining variables controlled as would be necessary to establish the relationship reliably.

It might be argued, however, that while the reports of the untrained
might never illuminate *basic* principles, it might still be possible to establish the relationships between certain more obvious complex environmental
situations and complex human behaviors. Further, the generality or universality of these relationships might be supported by the fact that they
seem to be reported repeatedly. Nevertheless, although it may be possible
to establish such laws through naturalistic observation, precaution must be
taken in interpreting the reports of patients, even when the same events
seem to be reported again and again. As an example, it might be suggested
that the "Oedipal" situation was discovered in clinical interviews because
so many male adults reported their childhood experiences of disturbance
in the father's response to the love relationship between mother and child.
Must this occurrence be accepted as an influential determinant of the
individual's behavior simply because so many patients report it in their
background? The status of the verbal report of the patient as reliable evidence must be examined even more closely before we can answer this
question.

> *Control of Patients' Verbal Reports.* Logical analysis makes it evident
> that if psychoanalytic therapy, or any other form of psychotherapy, is to
> serve the hypothesis-testing as well as the hypothesis-finding role, it is
> absolutely necessary to assume that the verbal productions of patients are
> free of influence from the therapist. Suspicions that the psychotherapist,
> however unintentionally, does influence subtly the productions of his
> patients have already been voiced (Quay, 1959, p. 254).

These suspicions have arisen from the numerous experiments, some
of which were described in Chapter 4, in which the verbal behavior of the
subject of the experiment was operantly conditioned through making the
attention or approval of the experimenter contingent upon the behavior.
Krasner (1958) concludes as follows after reviewing such studies.

> If future results in this area confirm the indicated trends, it might be
> concluded that all psychotherapy is to some extent directive in nature.
> The therapist uses cues, often without his own awareness, to modify,
> control, guide, or manipulate the patient's verbal behavior. This mode of
> subtle communication can probably be offered as a means of understand-
> ing how the therapist's own theoretical explanation of the dynamics of
> personality and of psychotherapy are transmitted to the patient (p. 164).

As Krasner points out, the therapist does not knowingly condition verbal
behavior in his patients to support his theories. However, he may be conditioning verbal behavior without being aware himself of the principles

involved. It might be added that because of the therapist's own training certain of the patient's statements, such as those on the topic of familial relationships, may be S^Ds for the therapist's attention and approval. In common-sense terms, these may be the events which the latter considers "significant" and about which he "encourages" the patient to talk. In our terms, it may be said that the therapist responds to these statements of the patient in such a way that he operantly conditions the patient to speak on certain topics.

> In other words, even though the interviewer reinforces the interviewee's behavior unknowingly, he may still do so in a lawful way. To the interviewer who considers sex problems to be the core of abnormality, the interviewee's statements about these will constitute reinforcing events for the interviewer, since they will tend to confirm his theory; for the interviewer who believes social causes to be crucial for abnormality, statements concerning these factors will act similarly. Each kind of interviewee statement would in turn be reinforced by the respective interviewer. In this way, the theory or bias of a given interviewer will determine what reinforces him, what he reinforces, and therefore what theory he will confirm (Salzinger, Portnoy, and Feldman, 1962, pp. 3–4).

Several studies especially relevant to the qualification of patients' statements for discovering S–R laws may be briefly mentioned. For example, in a study reported by Verplanck (1956) the experimenter decided to shape one subject to say "close relative" words (to talk about his family). Successive approximation was used to get the subject to emit words, then words connected with home, then any "relative" words, and so on. In this particular instance the shaping was proceeding very well until the subject suddenly refused to continue. He explained his refusal by saying that he did not want to talk about his brother and the experimenter had influenced him to do so.

In another study (Quay, 1959), subjects were instructed to "recall events from their early childhood" in two half-hour experimental sessions. For one group of subjects, reports of early memories having to do with their families were reinforced, while for the other group early memories having to do with people and events outside the family were reinforced. The reinforcing stimulus made contingent upon the subjects' reports of their early experiences was the simple response UH–HUH spoken by the experimenter. The results showed that individuals' reports of early experiences could be manipulated using reinforcement procedures. Quay's conclusions were as follows.

> This study has demonstrated that highly personal and emotionally charged memories can be manipulated by another person in an interview with very minimal verbal participation selectively placed after certain classes of these memories.

While this process of subtle interpersonal influence has not been demonstrated within psychotherapy itself, several considerations lead one to predict that the effect would appear with even greater magnitude over a series of psychotherapeutic interviews. For example, a psychotherapist would have much more time in which to respond selectively, his verbal participation in psychotherapy would be considerably greater than the very minimal reinforcing verbalization used in this study, and it seems very likely that he would have more prestige . . .(p. 256).

In addition, Rogers (1958), in what he calls a quasi-therapy setting, has used operant conditioning procedures to shape individuals' self-reference statements. His conclusions follow.

Our data have clearly established that in a free-interview situation the interviewer can influence the self-reference verbalizations of the subject through simple reinforcement behavior—by responding selectively the interviewer can modify the frequency of particular classes of verbal response in the subject. This finding has considerable importance for both the theory and practice of psychotherapy since changes in patient verbalizations are characteristically adduced as proof of personality change via psychotherapy (p. 15).

Similar results have emanated from actual psychotherapeutic relationships. For example, Bach (1952) has observed that the human figures his patients draw in the process of psychotherapy are different from those drawn by patients under the aegis of psychotherapists of a different theoretical orientation. The differences were in the direction expected upon the basis of the therapists' theoretical orientation. Heine (1953) has also reported that patients who successfully completed therapy cite reasons for their improvement which correspond to the theoretical convictions of their therapists.

Along a similar line, it is interesting to consider some of these same factors as they contribute to the therapist-investigator's conviction of the validity of his theories. In addition to the therapist shaping the patient's behavior through reinforcement and thus influencing theory construction as described above, the patient may also be considered to be an influence through his more direct effect upon the behavior of the therapist. That is, the patient may also present certain reinforcers which in all probability strengthen the therapist's "beliefs" and theories about human behavior and the practice of psychotherapy. First, of course, the patient pays the therapist. But other behavior of the patient probably functions to shape the therapist's theories more precisely. The patient's verbal behavior, contingent on some statement of the therapist, may function as a reinforcing stimulus to increase the frequency of such statements by the therapist. As Krasner (1955) states, the "therapist learns what behavior on his own part is most effective with particular types of patients and behaves accordingly" (p. 20). Rogers (1958) also found in his "quasi-therapy" situation that many of his subjects' statements would constitute reinforcement to a therapist and thus effect his conceptions.

> The many testimonials offered as to the value the interviews had for the subjects—how greatly their understanding of themselves had been advanced—are identical with those occurring in actual psychotherapy. Certainly, statements like the following would hearten many a therapist: ". . . something new has been opened in myself. I mean that something that has never been explored before has been explored now, which is bound to make some little difference." "I feel that I have probably a more firm, more organized opinion of myself than I had before." "It's forced me to face up to my own shortcomings." "It's tended somewhat to clarify what I've thought about myself." "Maybe I can see where I might have fallen down a little bit more than I thought I had and maybe in this way I can straighten myself more." "I'm more aware of different things." "I believe I have possibly a little clearer insight into my own personality and myself." These depositions from our subjects constitute, in our opinion, substantial evidence of the need for healthy caution in utilizing such evaluations from patients as a measure of therapeutic progress or as a means of comparing the efficacy of one form of psychotherapy with another. . . .
> Although the experimenter clearly structured the experiment as a laboratory investigation concerned with generalizing about personality and not as a clinical study to help the individual subject, many of the subjects construed it as the latter, reacting very positively to the experience and wanting to continue their relationship with the experimenter. A number of them subsequently requested aid or advice on personal problems (p. 14).

Because of these considerations, it is suggested that the psychotherapeutic interview be approached as an interaction between two people, with the reinforcers delivered by each affecting the behavior of the other. (See Chapter 8 for a more general discussion of such social interaction.) One must therefore be cautious in concluding that because a particular therapy achieves positive results that the theory of human behavior which served as the rationale for the therapy has been substantiated. The successful case may be a result of the manipulation of events which change the behavior of the patient in a positive direction but which have no relation to the variables which the patient or therapist assumes are operative.

From this standpoint, it would seem that there may be limitations on the development of a system of general principles, a system of explanatory statements, which are based solely on the clinical method of investigation. It should be realized that explanatory statements which derive from this method will be no more valid than the observations on which they are based. Because of the cited types of limitations in interpreting clinical observations, it may be argued that the basic set of explanatory principles must come from laboratory research rather than from clinical observation.

Advantages of the Experimental Method

This is not to say, of course, that there are no errors or deficiencies in experimental observation or in the statements of the experimentalist which are based upon such observation. However, as a method it presents certain possibilities for establishing basic principles that clinical methods of investigation do not.

As discussed in the first three chapters, the methods of laboratory observation, in contrast to the clinical method, are direct—not dependent upon descriptions of untrained patients or their relatives. In addition, the methods of the experimental psychologist emphasize manipulation of independent variables (such as classes of environmental events) in order to observe their effects upon behavior. Conditions of study can thus be arranged that would not occur readily in naturalistic situations. Furthermore, the effects of interfering conditions that might obscure the function of some independent variable may be eliminated or controlled. When the principles of these environmental-behavior relationships have been established for simple organisms and simple responses, then more complicated behaviors can be studied experimentally in organisms that have a more complex history—in man. Thus, a systematic set of basic behavior principles could be expected to emerge from experimental investigation that would not develop from naturalistic and clinical observation—and this appears to be occurring.

Advantages of the Clinical Method

This is not intended to suggest that no progress has been made through the use of clinical methods of observation. The statements based upon the prolific observations by trained individuals may be considered a great advance over those based on prescientific methods; they pave the way for dealing with human behavior with even more precisely established principles and methods. Probably the most adequate descriptions of many aspects of human behavior, the manner in which people interact, the types of stimuli that control their behavior, the classes of stimuli that are effective reinforcers for the individual and the group, and so on, have been made in the clinic and form a valuable body of information.

In addition, as will be shown more fully in the next chapter, some observations may arise in a naturalistic setting that might be unlikely to occur in the laboratory. Concerning the clinical method, Dollard and

Miller (1950) state, "Observations made in the situation of psychotherapy are a kind of natural history. They have the advantage of locating significant problems in a realistic setting . . ." (p. 6). Complex interactions of variables might arise in such naturalistic settings which the experimentalist might not try to arrange because of his attempts at simplification or because of ethical restrictions (for example, cases of severe punishment of children can be found, but not arranged). Often, it seems, some facets of human behavior are also observed in every-day living, and these observations lead to speculation concerning the principles which may be involved. At that point, it may prove productive to return to the laboratory for the experimental principles and methods that may answer the questions raised.

As an example, clinical observations have called attention to the phenomenon of an individual who has already developed a particular behavior that is characteristic of adults "regressing" or reverting to a behavior characteristic of children. Such observations have led to experiments in which such "regressions" or reversions have been studied as one response in a hierarchy of responses, with the emission of the response a function of learning variables (Mowrer, 1940).

Combinations of Experimental
and Clinical Methods

Thus, it may be suggested that a combination of naturalistic observations with the principles based upon experimental observations might provide a productive interpretation of human behavior.

In addition, it may sometimes be possible to conduct carefully designed naturalistic studies based upon experimentally established principles. In the end, the experimentally established principles must be extended to actual problems of human behavior. When this first occurs the investigator may simply look for examples in naturalistic settings in which the principle occurs. That is, he may be alert for experiential circumstances involving a principle and see if the consequent behavior occurs. Thus, in the next chapter naturalistic examples of variations in the reinforcers used by different cultures in raising their children will be cited.

Verification of a principle on a naturalistic level will encourage further extension. Ultimately he will be interested in manipulating stimuli in the naturalistic or applied setting to *produce* benign changes in behavior. (Later chapters will provide examples of the application of learning principles to the solution of human behavior problems.) In these cases it can be seen that the growth of knowledge began with naturalistic observations, including those of the clinic, and returned to naturalistic observations, albeit ones which have been improved by stemming from experimentally established principles.

The present book may be considered such a combination of methods, though not the first, by any means. There have been a number of formulations that have utilized the basic principles of learning in conjunction with clinical and other naturalistic observations of human behavior (Dollard and Miller, 1950; Keller and Schoenfeld, 1950; Mowrer, 1950; Sears, 1951; Skinner, 1953; Whiting and Child, 1953, among others).

In conclusion, to the extent that a combination of the methods is necessary in understanding and dealing with human problems, it is suggested that experimental psychology cannot restrict itself to the laboratory. Much of the significance of the bare behavior principle is added when it is found to operate in the acquisition or maintenance of an important human behavior—in the clinic, the school, the home, in the breadth of every-day life. The importance of the principle in this respect cannot be found solely from laboratory observations.

It may also be concluded, on the other hand, that the applied psychologist (as well as other social scientists) must realize the explanatory limitations of his observations and, consequently, of his theories. He must be prepared to look to experimental psychology for his basic principles.

"PERSONALITY" CONSIDERED AS BEHAVIOR

In the preceding sections of this chapter several types of personality terms were briefly considered as learned behaviors. The *self* or *self-concept* was considered to be a series of tacts that the individual acquired to his own physical and behavioral stimulus qualities and to the responses that other people make toward him. The principles involved in the formation and function of such verbal behavior were discussed in Chapter 4. The term *ego* has been used (Dollard and Miller, 1950) to label higher "intellectual" behaviors. These too can be treated in detail as learned behaviors—as was described in the sections that have dealt with the various aspects of verbal behavior, reasoning, problem-solving, and so on. Personality traits have been considered also as classes of behavior acquired according to the principles of learning and brought under stimulus control. Later chapters will deal with still other behaviors that are usually considered within the province of "personality."

This approach to "personality," considered as complex human behavior acquired and maintained by learning variables, is put nicely in the following excerpt from Keller and Schoenfeld (1950).

While all human beings obey the same laws of behavior, each individual ends up with a unique behavioral equipment that defines his "personality." The emergence of uniqueness from uniformity is possible because of the variations in circumstance under which the basic processes are worked out. . . . Thus, persistence in the face of failure may vary greatly from one person to another, depending upon the amount and variety of periodic reinforcement one has had in the past. Again, one may be more or less dominant or submissive in the presence of friends and strangers, depending upon his experience with other people.

The fact that the individual's present personality is related to his biography leads to an interest in behavioral development from birth through infancy, childhood, adolescence, adulthood, and old age. . . .
. . . There is little reason to resist the conclusion that the personality development of the individual is a function of his own conditioning history.

After the time when the role of the family is at its peak, formative influences continue to work upon the maturing child through his friends and his school. The currents and counter-currents of conditioning and extinction that stem from social origins do not stop. Joined with the reinforcement history of an individual are such factors as his general health, physique, personal appearance, social and economic position. Other things equal, a strong and healthy child is more likely than a weak and sickly one to develop physical self-reliance through the success of his running and jumping and climbing and pushing. In our society, where "good looks" are highly prized, a handsome child can quickly acquire social suavity and self-assurance (or a "spoiled brat" character) because of the partiality and indulgence shown by his elders. Persons of high socio-economic status are often the victims of obeisance and flattery— and what is flattery but the indiscriminate use of positive reinforcement? Obstinacy and arrogance may be the result. The "cute" child who is encouraged again and again to recite, to tell jokes, or dance, may continue to do so as long as he wins approval, until he ends up making his living at it. With such examples, we do not, of course, intend to over-simplify the factors that contribute to any personality. The phrase "other things equal" seldom holds outside the laboratory where things are kept equal by experimental devices. It must be admitted at once that the detailed analysis of any personality is an extremely complex matter because of the multiplicity of co-acting variables, past and present. In broad outline, nevertheless, we can see how such variables exert their force by determining *when* reinforcement and extinction will be applied, *how often*, and by *what schedule*, and similar questions (pp. 366–368).

It may be concluded that the subject matter of interest in the study of "personality" is the behavior of human beings. Although many terms have been used to describe this behavior—and often these terms direct one's interest away from behavior and toward inferred internal processes and entities—the actual problems are those concerning the way complex human behavior is acquired and maintained. It is suggested that the applications of learning principles to the behaviors under discussion in the book are all dealing with "personality" behavior: social behavior, language behavior, intelligent behavior, problem-solving behavior, and so on. It would be of no use to separate "personality" behavior from these, since in our view the field of "personality" is made up of the study of the development and maintenance of all these behaviors.

7

Human
Motivation

THE TOPIC of human motivation has been dealt with in many different ways. A great many terms in our common language refer to, or purport to refer to, internal motivational variables and the effects of these variables on behavior. We speak of wishes, wants, desires, interests, instincts, needs, as well as conscious and unconscious motivations and drives. When these statements are examined in terms of the principles discussed so far, however, it seems that the observations labeled in motivational terms sometimes refer to behavior, or its strength or frequency, sometimes to reinforcing stimuli, sometimes to stimuli which exert a discriminative control over behavior, and less often are of the type made in the laboratory—as a relationship between deprivation and the strength of reinforcers, the activity of the individual, and so on. These various types of observations will be discussed in separate sections. The discussion will attempt to integrate concepts of human motivation based upon naturalistic observations from various behavioral sciences with the principles of motivation and learning derived from laboratory investigations as discussed in Chapter 3.

Motivation Inferred from Behavior

Many concepts concerned with aspects of man's behavior considered under the topic of motivation have been defined solely on the behavioral end. In fact, most of our common-sense motivational terms are of this type. In times past a widely used term was *instinct.* Any type of behavior that was observed with some frequency was attributed to some inner, unobservable, process called an instinct. Thus, since people lived in groups it was "because" they had a *gregarious instinct.* If they fought it was "because" they had an *aggressive instinct,* and so on.

In our present-day common language there are many such terms. A person is said to play the piano, build model airplanes, study hard, and so on, "because" he is interested in, motivated by, or "likes" the activity. The circularity of such terms can be seen by the question which asks, "How do you know he is interested in music?" The answer is, "Well look at how much time he spends playing the piano." It is apparent at this point that such a concept does not explain the behavior in which one is interested. Independently observed events and their relationship to the behavior in question have not been stipulated. At best these terms can be thought of as labels or names for the behavior—they tell nothing new about it, however.

Moreover, the use of the motivational term, if it is thought to be explanatory, may lead one away from looking for the variables that actually account for the behavior in question. To some extent this misdirection of interest has occurred even in professional fields of psychology. A few examples may better illustrate the misuse of internal, motivational terms in an explanatory way when they are actually only descriptions of behavior.

Murray has dealt extensively with the concept of "need," which he uses in an attempt to account for behavior. However, some of his descriptions of needs seem actually to be observations of behavior. For example, Murray (1938) describes the need of "aggression" in the following terms. "To assault or injure. . . . To murder. To belittle, harm, blame, accuse or maliciously ridicule a person. To punish severely. Sadism" (p. 82).

These seem to be only descriptions of behavior, rather than explanations. To account for the behavior, it may be, as we will discuss more fully in the ninth chapter, that it is necessary to look to the learning variables in the individual's history. If the child, for example, has had many experiences in which aggressive behavior has been reinforced, it would be expected that behavior of this type would become strong. At any rate, it would seem mistaken to infer an internal, unobservable, motivational process to account for behavior, in cases where the behavior may have been acquired and maintained with no reference to motivational variables. Even if the learning condition was not established, it would be of little value to infer some explanatory term from the description of behavior alone.

Freud also often attempted to infer motivations for behavior he observed. He too conceived of powerful internal forces and energies to be found in the so-called "unconscious region of the mind," which directed the behavior of the individual. Although he considered these instincts to be naturally determined through the individual's biology and learning history, as indicated in the last chapter, he made a great effort to infer the nature of these internal processes—to the detriment of specifying the environmental variables that might account for the behavior. An example of an inference by Freud of an unconscious motivational state is given in the following.

> In latter years, since I have been collecting such observations, it has happened several times that I have shattered and broken objects of some value, but the examination of these cases convinced me that it was never the result of accident or of my unintentional awkwardness. Thus, one morning while in my bathrobe and straw slippers, I followed a sudden impulse as I passed a room, and hurled a slipper from my foot against the wall so that it brought down a beautiful little marble Venus from its bracket. . . .
> This crazy action and my calmness at the sight of the damage are explained in the then existing situation. We had a very sick person in the family, of whose recovery I had personally despaired. That morning, I had been informed that there was a great improvement; I know that I had said to myself, "After all she will live." My attack of destructive madness served therefore as the expression of a grateful feeling toward fate, and afforded me the opportunity of performing an "act of sacrifice," just as if I had vowed, "If she gets well, I will give this or that as a sacrifice." That I chose the Venus of Medici as this sacrifice was only gallant homage to the convalescent. But even today, it is still incomprehensible to me that I decided so quickly, aimed so accurately, and struck no other object in close proximity (McClelland, 1955, p. 8).

Freud went on to recount the various destructive accidents in which he was involved (no mean number) and accounted for them after they had occurred in terms of an unconscious motivational force. In the terms of a behavioral analysis, however, it may have been that the accident behaviors would have been better accounted for in terms of learning variables. It is possible that a particular object would have come to gain discriminative control over a person's behavior such that the individual would destroy the object. An explanation of the action might thus include the learning history of the individual, specifically with reference to the motor behavior as well as the discriminative control of the behavior.

Various examples of the shaping of "impulsive," or "destructive" behaviors could be given. In Chapter 3, the manner in which temper tantrums can be shaped was discussed (see also Ferster, 1961). It is also common to see individuals erupt into "impulsive" behaviors under the control of certain situations, for example, the tennis player who throws his racket into the net when he loses a point. At any rate, the account of this type of behavior is not completed simply by inferring some motive thought to cause the behavior.

To some extent Freud is probably responsible for the general method of observing a patient's behavior and then searching about for an unconscious "motivation" which could have caused the behavior. Perhaps as a consequence it is not uncommon in applied psychology today in dealing with a patient's behavioral problems to conjecture about the underlying "unconscious dynamics." Thus, when a patient evidences some interesting form of behavior, verbal or other, the unconscious "motivation" of the behavior is frequently conjectured. An interesting example from the psychological literature is given in the following.

> Laffal, Lenkoski, and Ameen (1956), have recently reported the case of a schizophrenic patient demonstrating what they call an "opposite speech" syndrome. The authors state that the syndrome is basically a reversal in certain language usages, especially in the use of "yes" and "no." Feeling that the speech reversal is an expression of repressed hostility, they suggest that opposite speech copes with the hostile impulses by disrupting communication and rejecting other people or by allowing the "verbalization of ideas which the patient consciously rejects" . . . (Staats, 1957a, p. 268).

The description of this patient's behavior and of the way it was treated, however, suggested that at least in part it was a behavior which was being maintained by reinforcement. Because the therapists were particularly interested in this behavior, they made a good deal of attention contingent upon the behavior. Other reinforcers, such as cigarettes, were also presented when the patient said "No" instead of "Yes." It is possible in this case, as in the others, that the behavior involved was shaped and maintained as a consequence of a learning history rather than through motivational operations.

In all probability this is not an infrequent occurrence. For example, Ayllon and Michael (1959) described undesirable behavior of psychotic patients that was maintained by the unwitting attention and approval of ward nurses in their attempt to be understanding of the individual's "mental illness." Ayllon and Michael, on the other hand, found that these behaviors could be changed through the manipulation of reinforcement principles.

Perhaps it is in cases where some behavior is highly unusual or even bizarre and it is difficult to see under what circumstances the behavior could have been learned, that one is most tempted to infer inner, unobservable, "motivations" with which to account for the behavior. However, as has been described, highly unusual behaviors such as temper tantrums can be shaped through successive approximation. In addition, there are other learning variables, even more subtle and unlikely to be spotted in naturalistic clinical observations, that can produce very "unusual" behavior. Morse and Skinner (1957) have described reinforcement circumstances that will produce such behavior. In these studies it has been shown that reinforcing stimuli presented adventitiously, that is, not contingent on any behavior of the organism, can result in conditioning just because they coincidentally follow a response. The reinforcers, for example, could be delivered after certain intervals of time irrespective of what the animal does. As one illustration, a pigeon might be conditioned to "senselessly" pirouette frequently about a cage solely through the chance occurrence of reinforcement following the response. Furthermore the behavior could be maintained because it receives reinforcement adventitiously from time to time (on an intermittent schedule) because the behavior occurs so frequently.

> From these and other experiments there emerges at least one trend. The more complex the experiment—the more responses, stimuli, and types of reinforcement that are involved, and the more extensive the organism's behavioral history—the greater will be the likelihood of adventitious control over the behavior. The moral is evident, for what experimental situation involves more of these complexities than do the ordinary life situations of the behaving human? Because adventitious control is, in one sense, unrealistic control, its existence may give an impression of disorderliness in behavior, but the disorder is only in our interpretation, not in the behavior itself . . . (Sidman, 1962, p. 196).

In all probability there are many behaviors whose determinants lie in such adventitious reinforcement. It would seem that in psychotics there might be even greater likelihood that such circumstances would result in unusual behaviors. Particularly in a hospital setting, ordinary suppression of deviant behavior through social disapproval would be less likely to occur. Furthermore, reinforcement would probably not be contingent upon the emission of certain required customary behaviors to the same extent that it is in the normal environment. (Learning variables as determinants of behavior disorders will be discussed in Chapter 11.)

The above is only one example of learning principles underlying bizarre behavior. It is suggested, however, that it is not advantageous, even where the determinants of a behavior are difficult to imagine, to infer inner needs or motivations as explanations of behavior, unless the term is specified by observations which define a drive: deprivation operations for appetitive drives and the presentation of aversive stimuli for aversive drives. The necessary specifications for an explanatory account of behavior consist of the antecedent conditions related to the behavior, whether these be learning variables, motivational variables, or perhaps biological variables of various kinds. In each of these cases, explanation that yields prediction and control may be possible. However, inferring a motivational mechanism for each behavior without specification of the antecedent conditions may lead one away from searching for the actual determining conditions, or, in applied settings, may lead to unsuccessful handling of other people's behavior. The following sections will describe in learning terms some additional types of observations that are discussed in the field of human motivation. Although the motivational terms inferred from such observations do not seem productive, the observations themselves constitute important sources of information concerning human behavior.

The Role of Reinforcers in
Accounts of Human Motivation

Another set of observations related to human motivation concerns the nature of the reinforcers effective for an individual. In practice, these reinforcers can be very important to the behavior which the individual will develop and which will be maintained, for it is often the case that different reinforcers will be made contingent upon different behaviors. The behavior finally shaped will depend upon the type of reinforcer that is effective for the individual.

In school, for example, if the teacher's approval is reinforcing, one type of behavior—perhaps scholarliness and good social behavior—may be shaped up, since the teacher's approval will ordinarily be contingent only upon that type of behavior. On the other hand, if the approval of a group of rebellious students in a class is more reinforcing, actions of opposing the teacher may be strengthened since the group's approval will be made contingent upon such behavior. The behaviors of achievement in that situation, and the amount of learning which occurs, may thus be to some extent a function of the child's reinforcement system.

The same relationship may be observed in other situations. Where money and prestige are the strongest reinforcers, then one class of behavior has an enhanced opportunity to be conditioned. If someone else's gratitude and other consequences of helping another person are the strongest reinforcers, then quite another class of behavior may emerge as characteristic. Without further elaboration, it should be apparent that the constitution of the system of reinforcers has important effects upon the characteristics of the individual's behavior. Thus, perhaps a primary concern of an account of human motivation should be with the sources of reinforcement. For humans, this means for the most part, the discussion of conditioned reinforcers and the manner and mechanisms by which they are learned.

If it can be said that the nature of the effective reinforcers will to a large extent determine the class of behavior the individual will develop, where the reinforcers are common to many individuals the same principle may apply to a group of individuals, for example, to a society. If the reinforcers effective for a group have been described, then a good deal may be suggested about the typical behavior which will be displayed by the individuals in that group. For this reason, naturalistic and clinical descriptions of the reinforcers effective for an individual or a group of individuals may be very significant.

It is perhaps because of this importance for human behavior that reinforcers effective for individuals or cultural groups are frequently described by scholars from various behavioral-science disciplines. For example, theories of human behavior that have arisen in the clinic offer many descriptions of differences among people in the strength and type of various reinforcers that are effective for them. These are often treated under the rubric of some motivational term, such as needs (see Maslow, 1954; and Murray, 1938; for fuller accounts).

In sociological theory, on the other hand, the same types of observations are related to the prominent concept of "values." "People cherish certain ideas or beliefs which are often called their 'values.' These ideas contain or express the judgments which people have of the relative worth or importance of things . . . In America, for example, we characteristically value highly such things as success, beauty, a high standard of living, and education" (Cuber, 1955, p. 42). Homans (1961) has discussed the concept of value in terms of reinforcers.

> A man emits a unit of activity, however that unit be defined, and this unit is reinforced or punished by one or more units of activity he receives from another man or by something he receives from the non-human environment: he may give another man help and receive approval, or he may bait his hook and catch a fish. The *value* of the unit he receives may be positive or negative; it is the degree of reinforcement or punishment he gets from that unit (pp. 39–40).

> Men, like pigeons, inherit certain values from their genetic past: food, water, sex, shelter, and so on. Others they have acquired as part of the ancient social history of their race: perhaps, for example, a value put on an affection more general than sex. Since by the very fact of their humanity the social experience of most men has been to some extent the same, we assume that to some extent they hold similar values (p. 45).

As Homans also points out, economics has been concerned with concepts involving the reinforcing value of certain objects. The term *utility* can be thought to refer to the reinforcing value of an object or service. Ulmer, for example, defines the term utility as: "The satisfaction or pleasure obtained from use or consumption of a good . . ." (1959, p. 66). Homans refers the term *utility* to the reinforcing value of an object and considers it synonymous with *value*.

Social anthropological accounts of human societies also include important descriptions of the objects and events that are reinforcing or aversive to members of the society. Often prominent aspects of the comparisons between societies refer to differences in what is reinforcing for the members of the society.

As described in the accounts of reinforcers from these various behavioral-science disciplines, reinforcing stimuli can be objects such as different goods, dresses, cars, and so on; the behavior of others such as their manners, loyalty, or courage; verbal stimuli such as flattery, praise, criticism; or complex stimulus events such as the results of an election, the institution of education, success.

Some examples will be given in the next section of motivational terms applied to man that appear to be defined by important classes of *reinforcers* that shape human behavior.

Examples of Reinforcing Stimuli

In the first section of this chapter we attempted to show that sometimes motivational terms are used when only observations of behavior are involved. Although such observations may be important, addition of a motivational term implying an internal "cause" of the behavior is not useful. Now, several examples will be given of other important observations that are often labeled in motivational terms as "social needs." These observations, however, seem to involve only reinforcing stimuli that shape and maintain human behavior. Again, deprivation operations do not appear to be involved in the observations, and the motivational concept of need appears to be superfluous.

A type of reinforcement that has received a good deal of attention concerns the stimuli called "achievement." Murray's (1938) definition of achievement may be paraphrased in the following manner: "To accomplish something difficult. To master, manipulate, or organize physical objects, human beings, or ideas. To do this as rapidly and as independently as possible. To overcome obstacles and attain a high standard. To excel oneself. To rival and surpass others. To increase self-regard by the successful exercise of talent" (p. 164). This definition includes descriptions of behavior, but certain reinforcing stimuli are also implicitly described in the definition.

Consider the stimuli associated with attaining a high standard. Certainly in a naive organism, overcoming obstacles and doing something difficult is not itself originally reinforcing. Effortful behavior produces stimulation that is aversive (Azrin, 1961; Hull, 1943). Without some change in these aversive features, it is to be expected that an organism would escape from hard work, that is, the cessation of work would act as negative reinforcement (Azrin, 1961). The same might be true of working as rapidly as possible. Since rapid responding is not itself reinforcing, unless such behavior has been shaped in the individual's learning history, the behavior would not be expected to occur.

The same is true of accomplishment, attaining high standards, excelling oneself, rivaling and surpassing others, and so on. These consequences are not by themselves positive reinforcers. Prior to the appropriate training, there is no reason to suppose that surpassing others, matching standards, and so on, will be reinforcing. Such events only become reinforcing because they have in the past been paired with positive reinforcers. Children have to be trained to find "winning" reinforcing, to hold "standards," and so forth. Anyone who has attempted to instruct small children in group games finds immediately that those aspects of "competitive" events that are reinforcers for adults may be quite neutral stimuli for the children.

There are no doubt great differences in the extent to which these kinds of reinforcers are taught to children. This learning may continue throughout life and new "achievements" of various sorts may become conditioned positive reinforcers. For example, it is not unusual for undergraduate students in college to be surprised to find that a professor works hard for the reward of publishing an article when no pay or other obvious reinforcement is contingent upon such performance. Unless the "approval" of a select group of interested colleagues has become a positive reinforcer, it is difficult to see how one would "work hard and long" for such consequences.

For some children, working at certain tasks and meeting some end result may be heavily reinforced. Each new behavior the child acquires may be reinforced. The parents of such children may also reinforce excelling in comparison to other children. The conditioned reinforcement associated with the acquisition of standards may be developed by reinforcing the behavior of matching the stimuli produced by someone else.

Other children may not have such experiences. For these children the above sources of reinforcement will not be developed. The ramifications of this may be clearly seen in the educational situation. Briefly, it may be said that a child raised so that these objects and events have become reinforcers will have a more abundant supply of reinforcement in the school situation than will the child for whom these are not positive reinforcers (Staats and Staats, 1962; Staats, Staats, Schutz, and Wolf, 1962). The implications for education will be more fully elaborated in Chapter 10.

Rather dramatic examples of differences in social groups concerning the extent to which events such as surpassing others or winning are reinforcing may be obtained from anthropological sources. It has been observed, for example, that the Kwakiutl Indians expend a great deal of energy acquiring goods which have no functional value; the reinforcing effect is derived simply from having more of them than one's rival.

The Kwakiutl are a people of great wealth and they consider it honorable to amass a fortune. But it is not hoarding they are interested in. Wealth, such as blankets, boxes, and copper plates, is used in a game of rising in rank, or validating honorific titles and privileges. Upon the occasion of taking a name a man distributes a considerable quantity of blankets among the men . . . in the presence of the entire community. The recipients are obligated to accept the property and must be prepared to repay it at the end of the year with 100 per cent interest. Such men probably have property out at interest, which they call in at the end of the year to meet their payments. Should a man be unable to repay he is "flattened" and falls in social status. The victor, on the other hand, rises another rung in the social ladder. With each successful potlatch [1] a man accumulates more renown as well as more property with which to conduct even greater potlatches. With prestige the driving motive in Kwakiutl society and with the basic intent of the potlatch the crushing of a rival, these property bouts take on a fiercely competitive tone (Goldman, 1937, p. 188).

Among the Zuñi people, on the other hand, winning is not a positive reinforcer, nor is having a great deal more than someone else.

Strikingly characteristic of all social relations in Zuni is the relative lack of emphasis upon wealth. Property does not figure in marriage. Individuals do not compete for a fixed supply, and in terms of the prestige an individual may achieve, property in itself is not the determining factor. This does not at all imply that the Zuni are unmindful of the blessings of material comfort or that they are completely disinterested in the accumulation of wealth. But they do frown upon any undue interest in material possession, upon acquisitiveness, covetousness, stinginess, or sharp practice in economic transactions. If a material object has value, it has that only as a means toward a specific utilitarian end. But hoarding —the piling up of goods far beyond what is necessary for a comfortable existence—is practically unknown. Wealth circulates freely, and property rights are neither clearly defined nor strictly enforced. For one thing, material effects are never valued as a means to power and are only indirectly a source of prestige (Goldman, 1937, pp. 326–327).

It would be expected that a child born into one of these two cultures, simply as a result of the different reinforcing system, would have very different behaviors shaped than would a child born into the other culture. Since competitive behavior is normally critical to acquiring goods, for example, it is only to be expected on the basis of operant conditioning principles that, as the descriptions indicate, the Kwakiutl Indians would be a much more competitive people.

In addition, implications of this analysis for understanding certain dif-

---

[1] Broadly defined, a ceremonial assembly organized by an individual for the purpose of establishing a competitive social position.

ferences among social groups within a society may also be drawn. A child raised in a situation where middle-class achievement is not reinforced will not "work for these consequences." The individual who has been deprived of a history where "achievements" have come to be reinforcing, is frequently described as lazy, stupid, constitutionally inferior, and so on. Actually, however, this individual would not aspire to middle-class achievements—would not find them reinforcing—because he had not been so trained.

A study by Rosen (1956) describes the differences in "aspirations" (reinforcers) among high-school boys from different social classes. Using a test that was ". . . designed to detect and measure the degree to which a person thinks about and is emotionally involved in competitive task behavior that is evaluated against a standard of excellence," (p. 205) Rosen found that ". . . members of the middle class tend to have considerably higher need-achievement scores than individuals in the lower social strata" (p. 206). In the test, the middle-class boys tended to show more ". . . evaluation of individual performance in relation to and competition with a standard of excellence" (p. 205), as well as more "affect" connected with the evaluated performance. Thus, Rosen demonstrated that lower-class boys typically find achievement stimuli less reinforcing than middle-class boys.

Rosen goes on to interpret these findings by analyzing the different training practices of middle and lower-class parents.

> In the pre-school period the tendency for middle-class parents to make early demands upon their children is reflected in such practices as early toilet training and the intense concern with cleanliness. As the child grows he is frequently urged and encouraged to demonstrate his developing maturity (e.g., early walking, talking, and self care). Signs of precocity are signals for intense parental pride and often lavish rewards. It is precisely this . . . which provides . . . a most fertile environment for the growth of the achievement motive.
>
> When the child starts his formal schooling, the achievement oriented demands and values of his parents tend to be focused on the school situation. From the beginning of his school career the middle-class child is more likely than his lower-class counterpart to have standards of excellence in scholastic behavior set for him by his parents. In fact, the relatively higher position which scholastic attainment has in the middle-class than in the lower-class value system means that more frequently for the middle- than for the lower-class child parental demands and expectations, as well as rewards and punishments, will center around school performance (p. 211).

Other groupings in society may also receive different experience with respect to "achievement" events. If a group is discriminated against so that the individuals from the group cannot hold high positions which demand considerable educational background, then it is not likely that the individuals in that group will come to value educational achievement, that is, find educational achievement reinforcing. Specifically, if the skilled verbal and motor behaviors we call knowledge are not allowed to be paired with strong positive reinforcement (money, social approval, material possessions, and so on) then the consequence of these skills—achievement—will not become a conditioned reinforcer. Minority group members who face such discrimination would not be expected to acquire the necessary behaviors for achievement, *nor would they even acquire the reinforcers which ordinarily would shape-up that type of behavior.* In common-sense terms they would not even "desire" or "want" to achieve. They would appear unmotivated, lazy, disinterested, and so on. (Of course, this is only a description of a group in general—some individuals in such a group may have had an unusual history for the group and thus behave differently. This was true, for example, in Rosen's study of the "achievement motive" of boys in different social classes. Some boys from the lower classes measured high on this variable, while some from the higher classes measured low.)

There seems to be evidence to support these arguments in the *1950 Census of Population* reports: for example, in the relationship between minority group status and occupation. At one end of the continuum, an example of a group experiencing little discrimination might be English and Welsh second-generation male immigrants (that is, native-born Americans who have one or both parents born in England or Wales); at the other end, a group experiencing considerable discrimination in the U.S. is the American Negro. The marked differences in concentration of individuals from these two groups in occupational categories is illustrated in the following comparisons. Of the Negro sample, 78 percent were found in the occupations of service workers, laborers, and operatives; the same occupations included only 28 percent of the English-Welsh. At the other end of the occupational hierarchy, 49 percent of the English-Welsh fell into the professional-business and clerical-sales categories, while only 12 percent of the Negroes held such positions.

Since the positions are not equally filled by individuals from these two groups, it is to be expected that for Negroes there would be less opportunity for "achievement stimuli" to become conditioned reinforcers. For the Negro, then, weak achievement reinforcers would be expected to only weakly shape or maintain "achievement behaviors"; there would, for example, be little "motivation" for working hard or acquiring an education. This latter expectation is supported in the census statistics. While the English and Welsh males acquired a median of 12.3 years of education, the median for the Negro group was only 8.3 years. It is suggested that the shorter duration of school attendance behavior for many Negro youngsters may lie at least partially in the weakness of educational achievement reinforcers.[2]

The same general analysis might be made for several other "needs" in addition to achievement. *Order*, for example, listed as a "need" by Murray (1938) has been defined as follows: "To put things in order. To achieve cleanliness, arrangement, organization, balance, neatness, tidiness, and precision" (p. 201). As we have suggested with respect to other stimuli, cleanliness, arrangement, balance, and so on, may also be considered as stimulus conditions that can become conditioned reinforcers, if the individual has the requisite history of reinforcement. Reinforcement in the presence of these stimuli should result in their becoming reinforcers—in which case behavior that is followed by these stimulus conditions would be strengthened.

An individual raised and positively reinforced in the presence of filth and disorder, however, would, if he had no counteracting experiences, not be expected to develop cleanliness and order as conditioned reinforcers; in fact, uncleanliness and disorder, under certain conditions, could be expected to become positive reinforcers. As a consequence, such an individual would not develop behaviors that lead to clean stimulus conditions. To an individual with such a history, a habitual slum-dweller let us say, it might be "nonrewarding" as well as too bothersome to keep his new apartment in a housing project tidy. Blaming the person, however, would be irrelevant on the basis of this analysis. The conditions under which he was raised would be responsible—it is to those conditions that attention would have to be addressed to change such an individual's "cleanliness" behavior.

Another "need" described in the literature involves the same principles but this case illustrates more clearly how a behavior itself (or, rather, the stimuli the response produces) may acquire conditioned reinforcement value. Murray's definition of the *dominance* need has been stated as follows: "To control one's human environment. To influence or direct the behavior of [others] by suggestion, seduction, persuasion, or command. To dissuade, restrain, or prohibit . . ." (p. 152).

These seem to be descriptions of behaviors that could be developed through an appropriate history of reinforcement. Such behavior could be maintained because it results in the reinforcement of the other person doing what we "want"—what is reinforcing for us—or in obtaining objects that are reinforcers. In addition, however, it would be expected that they

---

[2] Of course, the relationship between occupation and education is not perfect, nor should it be assumed from this that the sole reason for Negroes acquiring less education is lower occupational opportunity. Other variables may also be important, such as lack of financial support to stay in school, parental urging to earn a living, and so on. However, it is probably often the case that the lowered opportunities are indirectly responsible for these latter conditions as well.

would become reinforcing themselves, through the stimuli they produced, to the extent that these stimuli were paired with reinforcers. In this event, they might be observed to be maintained only by the intrinsic reinforcement of "dominating," for example, a salesman might habitually "sell himself" even when there was no possibility of material gain involved.

This principle is particularly important because many "needs" and "values"—loyalty, courage, and so on—seem to be difficult to consider as reinforcing stimuli. "Values like pride, altruism, aggression—values that are, as we sometimes say, their own reward—are just the ones that give us most trouble in predicting and explaining the behavior of men" (Homans, 1961, p. 45). When some of these values are considered as response-produced stimuli that have reinforcing properties either for the individual who makes the response, or for some other person, at least part of the difficulty seems dispelled.

In these examples of descriptions of effective reinforcers we have so far mentioned only positive reinforcers. However, many stimuli that effect human behavior are aversive. Several of Murray's (1938) "social needs" seem to involve conditioned negative reinforcers. *Defendence:* "To defend the self against assault, criticism, and blame. To conceal or justify a misdeed, failure, or humiliation. To vindicate the Ego" (p. 194). *Infavoidance:* "To avoid humiliation. To quit embarrassing situations or to avoid conditions which may lead to belittlement: the scorn, derision, or indifference of others. To refrain from action because of the fear of failure" (p. 192). *Rejection:* "To separate oneself from a negatively cathected [object]. To exclude, abandon, expel, or remain indifferent to an inferior [object]. To snub or jilt an [object]" (p. 177).

These several "needs" seem to involve descriptions of various stimuli that have become aversive in the course of the individual's experience. Further, the definitions include descriptions of behavior acquired because the withdrawal of these conditioned aversive stimuli has been made contingent upon that behavior. Again, the difference in the effective negative reinforcers that are observed for individuals in the clinic seem also to describe differences between groups of people.

One of the prominent aspects of the description of the people of Alor, for example, concerns the use of aversive stimuli in controlling the child. The parents, rather than encouraging or praising their children for desirable behavior, tend to suppress undesirable behavior through the deliberate use of ridicule, shame, or intimidation. For example, the parent may frighten the child by threatening to kill him or to cut off his ears or hands (Du Bois, 1944). Such treatment would be expected to establish a very effective system of conditioned negative reinforcers for children raised in such circumstances.

In contrast to this procedure for controlling behavior (and establishing negative reinforcers), the Comanche Indians of our Southwest had a practice of using as many positive reinforcers in the treatment of the child as was possible. The parents imposed very few restrictions, used little punishment, and attempted to make life as pleasant as possible. The result was a society in which no corporal punishment was used (at least by the parents), but rather a ". . . strong factor of encouragement to do as the parent does, and a tendency to elaborate praise of achievement" (Kardiner, 1945, p. 86).

Observations from social psychology also reveal differences within sub-groupings of our society in the extent to which aversive stimuli are used and conditioned reinforcers presumably formed. In an important study contrasting child-rearing practices in the middle and lower classes in the Boston area, Maccoby and Gibbs found the following: (1) lower-class mothers were more severe in their toilet training methods, employing more punishment and scolding in connection with toilet accidents; (2) lower-class mothers were more severe in sex training, punishing the child for masturbation or sex play; (3) lower-class parents employed physical punishment, deprivation of privileges, and ridicule as techniques of controlling their children more commonly than did middle-class parents; (4) although these findings were not too consistent, it appeared that middle-class parents used reasoning and praise and possibly some forms of withdrawal of love more often as controlling techniques than they did physical punishment (Maccoby and Gibbs, 1954).

In each case, it would be expected that differences in the use of aversive stimuli would affect the individual's reinforcing system. Individuals with a history of abundant use of aversive stimulation would be expected to develop a greater number of conditioned aversive stimuli (or stimuli of a greater intensity of aversive value). The extent to which one's reinforcing system includes aversive stimuli would in turn be expected to affect one's behavior in the same way as was earlier described with other reinforcers.

In conclusion, this discussion is not meant to be an exhaustive or even systematic presentation of the types of reinforcers effective in shaping human behavior. (Such descriptions may be obtained elsewhere in the various disciplines concerned.) Its function is rather to indicate that descriptions of reinforcers given in various behavioral sciences are very important to knowledge about man's behavior. Thus, it appears at this point in the discussion that motivational terms, such as needs, as used in various behavioral sciences sometimes refer solely to the behavior of humans. At other times the referent for such motivational terms appears to be observations of reinforcers that have proven effective for people.

It may also be added that important practical consequences may be attached to the manner in which one describes the events under discussion. When a term, in this case a motivational term, is used that infers an internal process or entity accounting for man's behavior there is a greater tendency to consider the process or entity as a fixed personal attribute. On the other hand, consideration of the stimuli which affect that behavior as conditioned reinforcers, for example, contains the suggestion that advantageous conditions may be produced and undesirable ones changed. In addition, in this latter case, there is the implication that the individual is not himself personally *responsible* for either his desirable or undesirable reinforcers (motivations) or the behavioral characteristics the reinforcers shape.

The Discriminative Function of Reinforcers in Defining Human Motivational Terms

The reader will remember that in Chapter 3 a reinforcing stimulus was defined in terms of its strengthening effect upon behavior. If, when a stimulus follows a response, future occurrences of that response increase in frequency, the stimulus is called a positive reinforcer. If one wished to discover in a laboratory situation whether some stimulus was reinforcing for an animal, he might make the stimulus contingent upon some behavior and see if the frequency of emission of the response was increased.

One may then ask if this is the definition that underlies the descriptions of the types of reinforcers (values) presented in the previous section. If this is not the case—that is, if the observations are not based upon the strengthening effect upon behavior—can these events be termed reinforcers?

For the most part the first question can be answered in the negative: the observations of reinforcers that are common in the other behavioral sciences do not seem similar to the method that would be used in the laboratory. It is true that it might be possible to use the laboratory method to canvas the reinforcers effective for an individual. For example, Lindsley (1956) has shown with psychotic patients in an operant conditioning apparatus for humans that there is great diversity in the reinforcers which are effective for different individuals. Some patients' behavior was strengthened by money, some by cigarettes, some by candy, some by pictures of nude women, some by pictures of nude men; for one patient the most effective reinforcer consisted of seeing milk fed to a kitten—this complex stimulus would strengthen the behavior it followed.

There is little doubt that these laboratory methods would prove more reliable than the naturalistic methods more generally used. However, the laboratory method seems to have some serious disadvantages for the assessment of many reinforcers that are effective either for an individual or for a group of individuals. Although one might attempt to observe the effectiveness of such a stimulus as a reinforcer in every-day life by waiting until it followed a behavior and then seeing if the behavior occurred more frequently, such observations are normally inefficient and may even be impossible. Some events that have very strong reinforcing value occur only infrequently in a man's life, for example, graduation from college; observation of the effects such stimuli have upon the behavior of an individual could involve exorbitant longitudinal observations of behavior. Furthermore, objects and events that an individual has never experienced directly, and might never experience, might still act as strong reinforcers for him.

Perhaps this is a reason why the concept of the experimentally established reinforcing stimulus has not made as great an impact upon behavioral scientists as have concepts (such as values) which, although less precisely defined, include reference to observations more readily obtained than that of the strengthening effect of a stimulus on future occurrences of behavior. Nevertheless, these naturalistic observations of reinforcers may also be based upon valid principles of behavior, and as such may constitute important practical alternative means of assessing reinforcers. Examination of some of these observations reveals that many refer to the *discriminative* function of reinforcing stimuli. We will now attempt to show that it is to this function that many investigators refer when they talk about human motivation.

Reinforcers Become Discriminative Stimuli

It has been widely observed on a naturalistic level that people seem to "strive" for certain objects, events, or behaviors. For example, in discussing instincts, Freud stated that in addition to an instinct having an "impetus," an energizing or motivating function, an instinct has both an "aim" and a particular behavior for attaining the object which would satisfy the "aim," reducing the tension of the instinct.

Other theorists have similarly stressed the fact that the individual's behavior often seems appropriate to the reinforcers which are effective for him—that is, appropriate in the sense that the behaviors tend to obtain those reinforcers. Newcomb, for example, defines motive as a ". . . state of the organism in which bodily energy is mobilized and selectively directed toward parts of the environment" (1950, p. 80). Klineberg also concludes that "Motive would therefore include a state of drive and a direction of behavior toward some goal" (1954, p. 76). He further states,

> A drive . . . is probably never found without a direction of behavior toward some goal, except possibly in the diffuse, undifferentiated reactions of the new-born, and perhaps not even then. There is no simple way of separating a "hunger drive" in its pure state from a "food motive"

in which the drive is directed toward food. The relationship becomes even more complicated when the sight of food (the goal) induces hunger . . . , or the presence of a female rat in heat results in sexual excitement in the male (pp. 76–77).

In addition, we have already discussed the term "value," which may be thought of as the reinforcing property of a stimulus. A term frequently used in conjunction with value is "norm," which may be considered in an analogous fashion to concern the directing function of such stimuli.

A norm, then, is a rule or a standard that governs our conduct in the social situations in which we participate. It is a societal expectation. It is a standard to which we are expected to conform whether we actually do so or not. It is a cultural specification that guides our conduct in society. It is a way of doing things, the way that is set for us by our society. It is also . . . the essential instrument of social control (Bierstedt, 1957, p. 175).

The discriminative function of norms is put even more clearly by Homans. "A *norm* is a statement made by a number of members of a group, not necessarily by all of them, that the members ought to behave in a certain way in certain circumstances" (1961, p. 46).

These various terms—aim, direction, goal, norm, and so on—have not been developed from laboratory-established learning principles, such as have been presented herein; however, these naturalistic observations may be considered in terms of behavior principles. That is, they appear to share the implication that certain behaviors are appropriate for obtaining certain consequences, or, stated in another way, certain stimuli seem to exert control over behaviors which are appropriate to obtaining those stimuli. To consider these naturalistic observations, it is necessary to see how reinforcers as stimuli come to have controlling (discriminative) functions over the behavior that is likely to obtain these stimuli.

As an example, although food is a reinforcer for a baby, the sight of the food or its container, when it is first presented, is not. The visual stimuli are at first neutral with respect to reinforcing value. Nevertheless, after a certain number of trials where the sight of food is followed by food in the mouth, the sight of food becomes a reinforcer. Furthermore, these stimuli would also be expected to become an S^D for certain kinds of behavior. Thus, crawling or walking across the room and reaching up to a table are not reinforced unless the table includes on it the visual stimulus of some piece of food. Through experiences such as this it would be expected that food stimuli would become S^Ds and control appropriate "striving" behaviors (at least when the organism has been deprived of food).

More specifically, as a result of this type of training, certain complex patterns of behavior would be expected to develop. In the process of gaining food stimuli and then of being reinforced following the behavior, a good deal of motor and verbal behavior would normally occur and come under the control of the reinforcing stimulus. When the visual properties of food come to be reinforcing because the sight of food is followed by food in the mouth many times, the sight of food will also come to be an S^D that may control the behavior of locomoting toward it, taking it into the hand, inserting it into the mouth, and so on.

This same process of developing stimulus control would be expected to occur with most reinforcing stimuli, such as toys, reinforcing people, reinforcing activities, social approval, the class of reinforcing words, and perhaps even stimuli of a more complex and subtle nature, such as education, loyalty, cleanliness. It is suggested that after "striving" behaviors have been acquired in the presence of many different reinforcing stimuli, coming under the discriminative control of those stimuli, when new reinforcers are introduced they too would control "striving" behaviors without further training. The previous responses under the control of other reinforcers would be expected to generalize. As an example, after many food stimuli had come to control the "striving" behaviors of a child, a new food delicacy, to the extent that it shared stimulus characteristics with other food reinforcers, would be expected to exert the same kind of control upon the first presentation. The child would locomote towards the food stimulus without any further training.[3]

It is suggested that the generalization gradient might be primary—in terms of the physical characteristics of the stimulus situation—referring to the fact that the new food is presented on a plate, on the dining table, surrounded by fork and knife, and so on. Or mediated generalization might be equally effective—labeling the new stimulus a "food" after other foods have become strong reinforcers would also allow the new stimulus to gain discriminative control over the "striving" behavior.

Naturalistic observation would seem to indicate that this latter principle, where the controlling stimuli are verbal, may account for "striving" behaviors which become quite intricate, complex, and of long duration. Possibly even such complex behaviors as "striving to become president" of a corporation could be thought of as the discriminative control of a stimulus, the presidency, where verbal stimuli would play an important role.

It also appears that children are trained in making appropriate verbal

---

[3] As was stated in the footnote on page 76 (Footnote 1), some psychologists (for example, Keller and Schoenfeld, 1950) consider that the conditioned reinforcing properties of a stimulus are established in the process of making the stimulus an S^D. What is being suggested here, as discussed in Chapter 3, is that the conditioned reinforcing value of a stimulus may be established by classical conditioning, and, when this is done, the stimulus becomes an S^D which controls various types of "approach" behaviors.

responses to stimuli which have reinforcing properties. That is, reinforcing stimuli come to have discriminative properties for "striving" verbal behaviors. As an illustration, when the mother says to the child DO YOU WANT MILK OR ORANGE JUICE? in the presence of the two liquids and the child responds by saying MILK, reinforcement follows when he receives the milk, provided that of the two fluids milk is at that time the more reinforcing. In a similar fashion, it would be expected that children would be trained to indicate the absolute reinforcing property of an object: I LIKE THAT A GREAT DEAL, I HATE THAT, and so on, or to emit appropriate verbal responses comparing the reinforcing values of various stimuli: I LIKE THIS BETTER THAN THAT, and so on. Technically, it might be said that this training results in reinforcers (plus other supportive stimuli such as questions) becoming discriminative stimuli that control a class of verbal responses; the effect of these verbal responses is to indicate the reinforcing value of the stimuli. This repertoire of behaviors, at least in our society, generally becomes quite complex, and comparative statements are made under the control of fine differences in the reinforcing property of various stimuli.

It would seem that when individuals generally have been trained in these ways, the reinforcing value of stimuli for people could be observed without making the reinforcer contingent upon some aspect of their behavior to see if the behavior is strengthened. An anthropologist in the field might simply observe stimulus objects and events for which members of the group "strive," stimuli that serve as discriminative stimuli in controlling "striving" behavior. Or, they may possibly observe the verbal behavior of members of the group by asking the individual what he values, or what other members of the group value.

Perhaps the function of certain types of "tests" used by the applied psychologist is at least in part to assess the reinforcers that are effective for an individual or a group. Such tests might consist of items that control the appropriate verbal behaviors with respect to the reinforcing value of stimulus objects and events, such as the behavior of others and various activities. For example, more than half the items on the Strong Vocational Interest Blank (1952) ask the subject to state whether he likes, dislikes, or is indifferent to various occupations, school subjects, amusements, activities, and characteristics of people. This may be considered to involve a simple listing of reinforcers for the individual. A large part of the remainder of the test seems to concern the same thing. The subject is asked, for example, to choose from a group of ten factors influencing his work, the three most important to him; from ten renowned individuals, the three he would most like to have been; from ten official positions in a club, the three he would like to hold, and so on.

Items on the Study of Values questionnaire (Allport, Vernon, and Lindzey, 1951) may also be considered to be verbal questions that evoke responses under the control of the reinforcing properties of the described stimulus objects and events. The following items illustrate the stimuli the subject is asked to evaluate. No. 9: "Which of these character traits do you consider the more desirable? (a) high ideals and reverence; (b) unselfishness and sympathy." No. 29: "In a paper, such as the New York *Sunday Times*, are you more likely to read (a) the real estate sections and the account of the stock market; (b) the section on picture galleries and exhibitions?" No. 4: "Assuming that you have sufficient ability, would you prefer to be: (a) a banker; (b) a politician?"

It is to be expected, of course, that such verbal statements would not always yield the same results as direct observations of the strengthening effects of a stimulus as a reinforcer, or as a discriminative stimulus controlling actual "striving" behaviors. The individual's verbal behavior may be a function of factors other than the reinforcing value of a stimulus. Even though money or sex was an extremely strong reinforcer for a person, for example, he might not report this readily if describing this state of affairs had in the past been followed by aversive consequences.

Nevertheless, to the extent that a verbal assessment of an individual's reinforcers is accurate it may save a good deal of time as compared to the method of directly observing the strengthening effect of a stimulus on behavior it follows, or even of observing the effect of stimuli that control "striving" behaviors. When a person has been appropriately trained (as most of us probably are), the relationships among these three events should be quite high. When the person states that he values something highly it would be expected that receipt of it would strengthen the behavior which obtained it. In addition, it would be expected that the valued object or event would control "striving" behavior.

Because, as in the above case, "striving" behavior and verbal behavior usually come under the control of the same reinforcing properties of a stimulus, the spurious impression may be gained that a motive determines both classes of behavior. The person says I REALLY WANT THAT JOB and proceeds to "strive for" it. From such observations it might be concluded that the statement indexes an internal motivation which determines the behavior. As we have said, however, the job may be a reinforcer with S^D properties for both the verbal and the "striving" behavior. In this case, the explanatory variables would seem to lie in the conditions establishing conditioned reinforcers as well as discriminative control—rather than in some motivating force.

Thus, in summary, it is suggested that reinforcing stimuli also become discriminative stimuli which control the behavior of "striving to attain" the stimulus. The same stimulus has in this case two functions: the one of reinforcing behavior it follows, and the other of controlling certain behaviors in the manner of a discriminative stimulus. This dual function of a stimulus is seen in naturalistic accounts which discuss both the rewarding properties and the "goal-directing" nature of motivational objects and events.

Distinction of Reinforcing and Discriminative Functions of Stimuli

Referring back to some of the examples of reinforcers already given may be helpful. It has been stated, for example, following Murray's description, that achieving standards may become reinforcing—that standards may come to be reinforcers. It would also be expected that as standards became reinforcing, "standard stimuli" would become discriminative stimuli and control the behavior of striving toward those standards. The behavior would be reinforced when the standard was obtained. A similar situation might prevail with respect to the conditioned reinforcer of cleanliness stimuli. It would be expected that dirtiness would become a discriminative stimulus which would control cleaning behavior—the behavior reinforced by the change from dirty to clean conditions.

The fact that the same stimulus has two functions has probably been the cause of some ambiguity in naturalistic accounts referring to these functions. For example, although we earlier analyzed norms and values into discriminative and reinforcing properties of a stimulus respectively, the literature is not actually this clear on the dichotomy.

> Obviously values are closely related to norms—so closely that one might ask what the difference is. . . . In general, however, we shall use the term "norm" for a relatively specific pattern of expected behavior. . . . Values are general standards and may be regarded as higher-order norms. Norms themselves may be evaluated . . . (Johnson, 1960, p. 50).

It seems that such difficulty in distinguishing the functions of norms and values might be corrected if both reinforcing and discriminative properties were made explicit. Thus, when a norm is spoken of as a ". . . rule or a standard that governs our conduct" (Bierstedt, 1957, p. 175) or as a ". . . statement made by a number of members of a group, not necessarily by all of them, that the members ought to behave in a certain way in certain circumstances" (Homans, 1961, p. 46), the discriminative function of norms is being referred to.

On the other hand, "achieving the norm" may also have reinforcing properties. "When we get down to particular groups of people, a special kind of reward, the reward obtained by conformity to a norm, becomes important. . . . The members who make the statement find it rewarding that their own actual behavior and that of the others should conform to some degree to the ideal behavior described by the norm" (Homans, 1961, p. 46).

The same is true of value statements. The value "Education is good" has two functions. It indicates that education is a reinforcing stimulus in our society. On the other hand, since reinforcers come to have discriminative properties, education becomes something that people attempt to gain; education has discriminative properties that control "striving" behaviors.

Thus, the value statement, although referring specifically to reinforcing properties ("good"), also sets up a discriminative function. The norm, on the other hand, although referring specifically to discriminative properties —what a person should or should not do—also sets up reinforcing properties—what a person should do is made reinforcing.

Motivational Concepts Involving Deprivation

Although the preceding sections analyze "motivational" stimuli in terms of reinforcers and discriminative stimuli, nothing has yet been said about the type of independent variable, for example, the deprivation operation, that is characteristic of the definition of motivation in the laboratory. It will be recalled from Chapter 3 that an important part of the definition of motivation is the fact that deprivation of certain stimuli increases the reinforcing value of those stimuli.

However, outside the laboratory the opportunity for manipulating deprivation of certain stimuli so that the reinforcing value of the stimuli can then be assessed is not generally available. Nevertheless, some naturalistic accounts of human behavior have included conceptions of the effect of deprivation upon the reinforcing value of a stimulus. For example, the action of deprivation upon the strength of reinforcers has been recognized by some psychological theorists working in the clinic (Maslow, 1954; Sullivan, 1950). Maslow states that needs are ordered in hierarchical form in terms of strength. When the strongest needs are satisfied, then the next strongest become prepotent, and so on. The hierarchy he describes ranges from the strongest physiological needs such as hunger and thirst and ends with esthetic needs (for example, for works of art). As we noted earlier, Maslow's needs seem to deal with broad categorizations of reinforcers. The argument here may be interpreted to indicate that under the same deprivation conditions some reinforcers will be more effective than others, but that satiation of a particular reinforcer will allow for an increase in the relative strength of other reinforcers of which the individual is still deprived.

The same sort of effects could probably be observed for reinforcers within a category. For example, different foods have different reinforcing properties; even if deprivation is held constant some will be stronger reinforcers than others. However, if an individual is sated on one, the others of which the individual is still deprived will be relatively stronger (provided there is still some deprivation for food in general). Naturalistic observation would also indicate that total deprivation of food would raise the reinforcing value of even very weak food reinforcers, which is to a certain extent a corollary of Maslow's theory. This type of deprivation may be important in certain common situations. For example, when the sexes are segregated (as in military service, prison, or boarding schools) the customarily present "sex"-reinforcers may be absent and reinforcers of this category that are normally much weaker (less socially approved, perhaps) may increase in relative strength.

Other behavioral scientists have shown similar concern with the reinforcing value of stimuli and the effect of deprivation upon this reinforcing value. A good example in the area of economics is the law of "diminishing (marginal or extra) utility" (Samuelson, 1958, p. 430).

> According to this law, the *more* an individual has of some given commodity, the *less* satisfaction (or utility) he would obtain from an additional unit of it. Note that it is the additional (or marginal) utility obtained from each successive unit which diminishes. *Total* utility may go on increasing. Illustrations of the law are available at almost every hand. . . . [I]f pork were a rarity, the consumption of a small amount a week, say a quarter of a pound, might be the source of considerable satisfaction to a person with a taste for it. Now keep adding to his diet successive "doses" of a quarter of a pound of pork. Would not the added satisfaction from each new addition be less than that derived from the last? Assume that he finally obtains 10 pounds of pork per week so that he eats it at each of his three meals seven days a week. Now he is given an extra quarter pound. Is he overcome with tearful gratitude and unrestrained joy? Or with nausea? . . . It follows from this analysis that the more an individual has of a given commodity, the less he will be willing to *give* in exchange for an additional unit of it (Ulmer, 1959, pp. 319–320).

Homans, who discusses several sociological topics in terms of behavior principles (for example, values are described as reinforcers), also emphasizes the relationship of deprivation operations to the strength of a reinforcer in his description of human interaction.

> [W]hen we say that Person values help highly, we mean, first, that help is a reward, *a value*, to him, and second, that he has recently gone without help. In assessing the first component we need not necessarily ask him if he wants help. Often we need only look at his past history as it affects his present circumstances. If he is employed to do a job that

requires a certain amount of skill and through lack of either training or experience he has not got the skill, we may confidently say that help is a value to him. We may even say that he will value help relatively more highly than will a man like Other, who has already acquired skill at the job. Or better still, when he has been deprived for some time of both help and, say, social approval, and now he has a choice between getting one and getting the other, he will set a relatively higher value on help and a relatively lower one on social approval than will Other under the same circumstances (1961, p. 44).

Thus, it has been said that stimulus objects and events may gain differing amount of reinforcement value through variations in learning variables. In addition, differences in the individual's reinforcer systems may result from variations in deprivation levels. Two reinforcers could be of the same strength, but if the individual is sated on one and deprived of the other, then the latter will be preempting: it will have a greater reinforcing effect upon his behavior.

In our society, for example, sex reinforcers might be no stronger than food reinforcers (given some way to equate their deprivation levels). However, many people appear to face deprivation of sex reinforcers while there are few constantly suffering food deprivation. On this basis it would be expected that sex reinforcers would have a more potent effect in shaping up certain kinds of behavior. It is conceivable, for example, that it was the inhibiting nature of sex expressions (deprivation of sex reinforcers) in the milieu in which Freud worked that led him to place such great emphasis upon sexual factors in determining human behavior.

It could be said with as much justification, however, that in our present-day culture there are many reinforcing stimuli which most people are deprived of in good measure. Many social reinforcers (social approval, attention, money, fine clothes, expensive cars, prestigeful jobs and titles, entertainment, company of others) are not abundantly supplied to most people and they are in a state of deprivation for these reinforcers. For the usual married individual there is usually greater deprivation of these other reinforcers than of sex, and the effects of these reinforcers might then be of greater importance in molding the behavior of the individual. Some of these stimuli no doubt gain some of their reinforcing value from sex reinforcers but other reinforcers might play a more significant role even here.

These various social reinforcers may also be more significant because they are made contingent upon behaviors that are more integrally concerned with the adjustment of the individual than is the case for many sex reinforcers. Thus, they may be influential in conditioning many types of important behavior in probable contrast to the narrower range of effect of sex reinforcers.

This is not to say, however, that sex reinforcers are unimportant, for the various forms of such reinforcers (for example, the smile of a handsome member of the opposite sex) may also be made contingent upon many behaviors. In addition, different groups of people in our culture are subjected to different types and degrees of sex deprivation. Adolescents and young unmarried adults, as examples, are more strongly subjected to the deprivation of sex reinforcers than are other groups of people. As a consequence, sex reinforcers should be in a relatively stronger position in their reinforcer systems than for other people, and this should be reflected in the strength of certain of their behaviors. Naturalistic evidence supports this. Thus, for adolescents, the attention and approval of members of the opposite sex is very effective in shaping behavior. Behaviors such as grooming, smoking, "pretended" adultness and sophistication, and "masculinity" or "femininity" as the case may be, may emerge in good strength as the child enters adolescence. Various faddish behaviors and dress may also be shaped up under the reinforcement of the attention and approval of the opposite sex.

In general, in our society different groups seem to receive different deprivation conditions. For example, the different socio-economic classes should have different hierarchies in their reinforcer systems as a result of variations in deprivation. Restrictions on the accessibility of sex reinforcers for middle-class individuals has been noted when compared to individuals who are in the lower classes. According to the Kinsey report, for example, the frequencies of sexual behavior vary with the educational level to which an individual belongs.[4] The physically well-developed and mentally normal boys who never go beyond eighth grade in school are more sexually active than the boys of any higher educational level. The single males who have the lowest frequency of total sexual outlet are those who ultimately go on to college (Kinsey, Pomeroy, and Martin, 1948). Because of this deprivation, sex reinforcers should be stronger reinforcers for middle-class individuals, other conditions being equal (which they probably are not), although the only reinforcers that might be available were conditioned sex reinforcers.

On the other hand, members of the lower socio-economic levels, not deprived of sexual reinforcers, might be expected to be more deprived of many other reinforcers, such as money, fine clothes, prestigeful jobs, and social approval. Jeffery (1961), for example, suggests that young adult males who live in slum areas and are members of minority groups have a

---

[4] As in many studies of social class, educational level was only one of the more important criteria for determining social class. There is, however, sufficient correlation between measures of social class to justify the use of educational level as a rough index of social class level.

high incidence of criminal behavior because a characteristic of their living conditions is the deprivation of the important reinforcers of our economy. "A middle class person secures food, clothing, automobiles, money, and sex gratification by non-criminal responses; he does not develop criminal responses to obtain these reinforcers" (p. 17). For such an individual, reinforcers are obtained by responses less difficult and less dangerous than are the criminal responses. For the slum dweller, however, the same reinforcers are more commonly unavailable as a consequence of lawful behavior, while they normally follow upon unlawful behavior.

> Behavior theory takes into account the level of deprivation and satiation of the organism. . . . A person deprived of food will respond to a food stimulus in a manner which a satiated person will not. A sexually deprived person will respond to stimuli which will not arouse a sexually satiated person who has access to a sexual partner. In prison camps prisoners eat rats and commit homosexual acts; they do not behave in this manner when beefsteak and females are available (Jeffery, 1961, p. 17).

In summary, it might be stated that deprivation conditions would be expected to influence the behavior of individuals and of groups through determining the relative and absolute strengths of various conditioned and unconditioned reinforcers.

Conclusions

It is suggested that in the various social-science areas of study there are many important observations of human behaviors, reinforcing-discriminative stimuli, as well as of the relationship between the deprivation of a reinforcing stimulus and the strength of its reinforcing-discriminative value. Many times the importance of these observations seems to be lost because of a greater interest in inferring inner explanatory fictions, using a variety of motivational terms. It would seem that if these observations were described in terms of the principles of behavior this type of misleading emphasis would decrease, there would be greater emphasis on the observations, and the learning interpretation would lead to suggestions concerning the significance of learning conditions which account for the observations which have been made. This could lead also to new observations involving the effect of experience upon the development of "motivational" variables. One of the important things a learning analysis appears to suggest concerns the mechanisms by which various stimuli come to acquire their reinforcing-discriminative value—which will be the subject of the next section.

Mechanisms Involved in Establishing
Motivational Stimuli

In Chapter 3 we discussed how stimuli could *acquire* reinforcement value and become discriminative stimuli. Naturalistic descriptions in other behavioral sciences include similar concepts—concepts referring to the fact that stimuli may *acquire* motivational properties.

For example, according to Freud's theory of instincts, although the source of an instinct remains unchanged throughout the individual's lifetime, the means by which the instinct can be satisfied may vary considerably. If for some reason one object of an instinct is not available, the instinctive energy may be *displaced* to some other object. If this object is accessible, it can be used to satisfy the need. Thus, within this theory objects are often substituted for one another to satisfy the basic internal needs.

We may interpret Freud here as stating that many objects can become reinforcers during an individual's lifetime. However, in order to gain an explanation rather than a description of the fact that reinforcers may vary during the person's lifetime (or may vary for different groups), the concept of displacement must be defined in terms which specify the conditions under which it will take place. We have already suggested that such explanation lies in the principles of establishing conditioned reinforcers.

The same issue is apparent in discussions of changes in values over time or from one group to another. In the following quotation, Homans (1961) indicates that he considers learning principles to underlie the manner in which values (reinforcing stimuli) are acquired.

> More nearly alike than that of all mankind is the social experience of members of a particular society; they are apt to have acquired the same special tastes for the rewards they received at the hands of their mothers, fathers, and other members of their community, and they in turn may hand the same tastes on from generation to generation. This is what we mean when we say that certain values are characteristic of American culture, or that certain rewards are more highly valued in American culture than in Chinese. Still more similar are the values held by members of a subculture. If certain people are not just Americans but also Yankees —white, Anglo-Saxon, Protestants living in New England—we may have reason to believe that, while sharing many American or human values, they also hold certain values peculiar to themselves. . . .
>
> Finally, we reach the individual as such. Though he be a man, an American, a Yankee, and a Raytheon worker, his values, the things that reward him, are never wholly determined by circumstances like these, which he shares with others, but always partly by his unique experience. . . .

We have said that it may be hard indeed to answer the questions how and why mankind, or the members of a particular society, or an individual acquired the values they did acquire. In what has gone before we have not even tried to answer them, but have only pointed out where the answers are to be sought—in the past histories of the persons concerned (Homans, 1961, pp. 45–47).

It would seem, thus, that the principles discussed in Chapter 3 concerning the establishment of conditioned reinforcers and discriminative stimuli would be pertinent to the way in which values and norms (certain human reinforcing and discriminative stimuli) are established. In Chapter 4 it was suggested that verbal stimuli can become reinforcers and discriminative stimuli, and in Chapter 5 the manner in which the reinforcing properties of words (positive evaluative meaning responses) may be "transferred," that is, communicated, to other words was outlined. In this chapter, and elsewhere, it has been argued that the individual's own behavior (or the stimuli it produces) may become reinforcing. All these principles seem important in the establishment of a reinforcing system for the individual. Some of the mechanisms in every-day life that appear to play a role in the establishment of reinforcers will now be discussed.

Direct Experience in Establishing Reinforcers

Some stimuli may become reinforcers because the individual's behavior is reinforced in their presence. This has been discussed at length earlier, where we indicated that many stimuli—money, approval, attention, and so on—become conditioned reinforcers. In the same way it would be expected that the individual's own behavior could become reinforcing. Aggressive behavior, for example, may be directly reinforced: a child may successfully repulse through his own aggressive behavior the attempt of another child to take his toy. As a consequence of this experience, the S^Ds present when the behavior is reinforced, perhaps the other child's crying, may also acquire reinforcing value if the circumstance occurs frequently enough. Later on these stimuli can themselves serve as reinforcing stimuli and strengthen behavior. The stimuli produced by the aggressive behavior itself could also become conditioned reinforcers, and the behavior would later be intrinsically reinforcing. In addition, tacts to (descriptions of) the aggressive behavior would become reinforcers through mediated generalization, and norm and value statements might arise: ONE MUST DEFEND HIMSELF AGAINST ASSAULT, IT IS GOOD TO BE BRAVE.

It may be concluded that many of the individual's reinforcers are formed through his own direct personal experience, and these reinforcers (especially in the language form) may serve as discriminative stimuli and control the individual's behavior. (For the sake of brevity, in the following sections only reinforcing properties will usually be discussed. However, where a stimulus becomes a reinforcer, it is suggested that it also becomes a discriminative stimulus.)

Language Experience in Establishing Reinforcers

The same type of conditioning of reinforcement value should be capable of taking place entirely on a language level, however. A child could be told such things as A GOOD MAN STICKS UP FOR HIS RIGHTS. HE DOESN'T LET ANYONE TAKE THINGS WHICH ARE HIS, and so on. The reinforcing value of GOOD MAN would be conditioned to the words concerning the actions of defending one's possessions. The statement itself might be considered a norm; serving an S^D function it would act to direct the behavior of the individual with respect to his possessions. Whenever such actions of the child occurred, these words would be elicited as tacts and serve to reinforce the actions. The individual might then be thought to be "proud of" or "bragging" about his conformity to the norm.

Thus, once verbal reinforcers have been established, it is suggested that the individual may strengthen his own behavior when such responses are elicited as tacts to his own behavior. In general, a most important part of a child's training might be thought to be the formation of verbal reinforcers that as tacts have come under the control of his own behavior. For the child who has been told in many different ways that it is GOOD TO LEARN, the word stimulus LEARN will have become a positive reinforcer. Presuming he has also acquired correct tacts to his own behavior, he will provide his own reinforcement when he has learned something—and this will help maintain his studying behavior in good strength. More generally, as has been mentioned and as we will discuss further on, the nature of the words that are effective reinforcers for an individual is very important in shaping his behaviors. For the child for whom "good student" is a positive reinforcer, the statement YOU ARE A GOOD STUDENT will strengthen studying behavior.

Vicarious Experience in Establishing Reinforcers

Not all the individual's reinforcing "self-tacts" are learned on the basis of his own experience, it would seem. Observing someone else's experience may provide an analogous type of experience. The person who has acquired the appropriate verbal habits may "learn from example." Thus, if a child is punished for striking another child and is told THAT WAS VERY MEAN AND BAD, this will constitute a learning trial for that child. In addition, however, another child observing this incident might acquire similar responses. He might make an echoic response to the words of the

adult in the presence of the visual event including the sight of the blow
being struck and the crying of the recipient of the blow. This would establish an association between these stimuli and the word responses MEAN,
BAD, and so on. In the future if the child who was the observer strikes
another child, the stimulus situation will be similar to that on the preceding occasion and according to the principles of stimulus generalization the
similar stimulus situation should elicit the verbal responses WHAT I DID
WAS MEAN AND BAD, and so on. These verbal responses should then
function as aversive stimuli, the removal of which would be reinforcing.
And removal would be contingent upon good behavior.

Bandura (1962b) and associates have conducted a series of experiments
providing a number of general statements that indicate how reinforcers may
be acquired "vicariously." He states that the child learns behavior from
other individuals who act as models for the child. One of the ways this can
occur is for the model's behavior (as a stimulus) to acquire reinforcement
value. "Thus, once the model's behavior has attained positive valence, the
child can self-administer secondary reinforcers simply by reproducing the
desirable responses" (Bandura, 1962b, p. 9; see also the section on imitation
in Chapter 8).

To test this, Bandura and Huston (1961) consistently paired a model's
behavior with positive reinforcement for an experimental group of children
but not for a control group. The frequency with which the emitted behaviors of the children were like those of the model was then observed in both
groups.

> In the *nonreward* condition a female, who played the role of the
> model, brought the child to the experimental room. After instructing him
> to play with the toys that were spread on the floor, she busied herself with
> paper work at a desk in the far corner of the room.
> With children in the *reward* condition, in contrast, the model sat on
> the floor close to the child; she responded readily to the child's bids for
> help, approval and attention, and in general was positively demonstrative
> and rewarding to the child (Bandura, 1962b, p. 11).

The test situation followed. This consisted of a series of discrimination
games, in which the model always had the first turn and in which she was
always correct. During this "the model exhibited relatively novel verbal,
motor, and aggressive responses that were totally irrelevant to the discrimination problem." The child then took his turn and the number of the
model's responses he reproduced was recorded. When the two groups were
compared it was found that children who experienced the rewarding interaction with the model reproduced responses resembling those of the model
to a substantially greater extent than did children who were in the nonreward condition.

> The predicted facilitating effect of positive conditioning on imitation was clearly confirmed . . . Moreover, the evidence that a positively conditioned model enhances the production of partially imitative verbal responses suggests that exposure to a model possessing rewarding qualities not only facilitates imitation of the specific behavior exhibited by the model but also increases the probability of occurrence of responses of a whole response class (Bandura, 1962b, pp. 12–13).

It must be concluded upon the basis of this analysis that the "examples" set by a reinforcing agent with which the person is confronted act to condition him: these vicarious experiences will be very important in determining both the form of his behavior and the events which will be reinforcing for him.

For this reason, the examples set by such sources of reinforcement as parents, the child's companions, friends of the parents, as well as school associates, and so on, would be expected to affect the child in the manner described. As these factors vary, the child should acquire different reinforcers, and these would be elicited by his own behavior and thus shape his future behavior in different ways.

There also appear to be more formal sources of influence on the individual's reinforcer system which might be called mass communication media. These will be discussed separately.

Mass Communication and the Reinforcer System

The way in which verbal reinforcers can be conditioned through communication, as well as the manner in which the individual can acquire reinforcers by observing other individuals' experiences, have been described. It is suggested that mass communication sources provide analogous conditioning experiences for the individuals whom they reach. Newspapers, books, magazines, television, radio, and moving pictures would be expected to exert strong influences upon our behavior by determining the stimuli which will be reinforcing for us. "With the advent of audio-visual devices in the field of education, and cathode ray tubes in virtually every household, pictorial and symbolized models are coming to play an increasing role in the social learning process" (Bandura, 1962b, p. 15). About one sixth of children's nonsleeping time is spent watching television (Schramm, Lyle, and Parker, 1961).

The movies, as an illustration, provide many examples for the child that mold his reinforcer system—according to the same principles that explain the other effects of "vicarious experience." When characters in a movie experience reinforcement (positive or negative) contingent upon their behavior, this constitutes a learning trial for the child who watches the film. Consider, for example, the effects of some apparent trends in dramatic entertainment to show the "good guy," the hero or positive character, participating in the same type of brutality as the villainous character. When the hero is positively reinforced for this type of behavior this behavior would be expected, according to the principles discussed, to become more reinforcing for the observing child.

Using a methodology similar to the one already summarized, Bandura and associates have conducted additional experiments to discover whether reinforcement procedures would affect the behavior of the child, presumably through affecting the reinforcement properties of the model. In the experiment to be reported, the behavior of the child was observed for similarities to the model when the model was not present, and when the conditioning circumstances were presented through a mass communication medium (films).

In the study (Bandura, Ross, and Ross, in press), children were subjected to either an *aggressive* model-condition, or a *nonaggressive* model-condition. For some children the models were presented by film, with either realistic human models or cartoon models. Other children observed live models rather than films. After the film, the children were tested for their aggressive behavior in an experimental setting different from that shown in the film.

> Children who had been exposed to aggressive models performed substantially more aggression than did children . . . in the control group. The corresponding mean total aggression scores for subjects in the real-life, human-film, cartoon-film, control, and nonaggressive groups are 83, 92, 99, 54, and 42, respectively. While children who viewed the real-life and film-mediated models did not differ from each other in total aggressiveness, all three experimental groups displayed significantly more aggression than both the control subjects and those who observed the nonaggressive models. A similar augmenting of nonimitative aggressive responses following exposure to film-mediated aggression has been demonstrated recently with adults (Walters, Llewellyn-Thomas, and Acker, 1962) as well as with children (Lövaas, 1961; Mussen and Rutherford, 1961).
>
> The data furthermore indicates that exposure to nonaggressive models decreases the probability of aggressive reactions to subsequent frustration as evidenced by the fact that children in the nonaggressive condition exhibited considerably more nonaggressive behavior relative to the aggressive model groups, and significantly less total aggression and less imitative aggression than subjects in the control group (Bandura, 1962b, p. 226).

It is therefore to be expected that the sheer portrayal of violence in the dramatic arts would decrease the extent to which the verbal counterparts of violence would function as negative reinforcers for the audience. Let us say that a child has experienced many conditioning trials (mostly verbal) to the effect that fighting and other forms of aggression are unworthy and as a result the terms involved as well as aggressive behavior itself become aversive stimuli. This training would be expected to be counteracted by seeing films involving aggression. That is, presenting this child with a scene in which fighting occurs and it is not paired with aversive verbal or pictorial stimuli should result in some extinction of the previous training. "[T]he uninhibited expression by a model of behavior which is often negatively reinforced may serve to extinguish or to countercondition anxiety responses in the observing subject" (Bandura, 1962b, p. 69). The actual stimulus events concerned with aggressive behavior, as well as the words, should through such experience become a little less potent as aversive stimuli and negative reinforcers. A few of these conditioning or extinction trials might not seem too important. But where there is a constant diet of violence paired with neutral or positive stimuli—as occur in many war stories, boxing stories, gangster stories, private detective stories, western stories, and so on—it would be expected that considerable change would take place in the reinforcement value of the stimuli of violence.

It is possible that this process may be important for a culture as a whole. Where a society is bombarded by these conditioning experiences, it would be expected that the people in the society would as a group shift in the direction of that conditioning. Some people who already have strong "aggressive" operants, or for whom the results of aggression are positively reinforcing, should become even more disposed in this direction. The movies, and so on, might in this way push these people closer still to some aggressive act. While it is perhaps unrealistic to attempt to trace a crime or delinquent act to a specific movie or other source of conditioning, it is reasonable to suspect that a history of many, many such conditionings might well result in a response to stimuli of violence which was much less negatively reinforcing than would otherwise be the case. Again, whether or not the person's actual behavior will be violent may be a function of many other types of training as well—and of the S^Ds present in the situation in which the individual finds himself.

However, whether or not the person himself participates in violence may not be the only question of significance to a society. The individual's tacit acceptance, or approval, of other people's violence might also be important. In these respects it is interesting that social psychologists who have studied the content of Germany's mass communication products during the Hitler regime found that they included more violence than they had in previous times (Kracauer, 1947). It would be expected that this experience from the mass communication sources would have resulted in an average German citizen being relatively unappalled by violence inflicted upon the persecuted people in Germany. The conditioning received in the mass communication sources would have made violence, and the consequences, human pain and misery, less aversive.

This, however, is only an example of the types of reinforcers that seem to be conditioned by the mass communication media. It would seem that mass media have profound influences on general aspects of our reinforcing systems. When these avenues of experience portray, for example, in exaggerated proportion, athletes or movie stars as heroes, then these people as social stimuli, their actions, and words describing these events, may become inordinately strong positive reinforcers. When this does not occur for scientists, government servants, teachers, factory workers, and so on, their behavior may remain in relatively weak status as reinforcers—as "models," to use Bandura's terminology, they would be expected to have relatively little influence.

It may, then, be suggested that the reinforcement value of many everyday objects, events, people, and so on, is influenced through the mass communication sources. To the extent that reinforcers or values are determined in this way, we find ourselves in essential agreement with social commentators who argue that these media are in considerable control of the "motivations" of a society.

8

Social
Interaction

PERHAPS BECAUSE of the very great importance of social problems to scholars in various academic pursuits, social psychology has a long history as a field of study that has surveyed and analyzed many aspects of interactions between two or more individuals. As a division of the scientific study of behavior, social psychology might be considered to be concerned with the interactions of individuals in groups, both with the behavior of members of the group as a dependent variable, and with the behavior as an independent stimulus variable controlling the behavior of other members of the group.

However, any division of group behavior from the types of behavior already treated is naturally somewhat arbitrary; there seem to be no clear lines of separation of topics within general and social psychologies. The preceding chapters have discussed situations involving more than a single individual, and indeed, many of the topics covered might easily fit into the present discussions.

Nevertheless, there are many areas of complex human behavior normally treated within social psychology that can be profitably approached in learning terms, and samples of these will be discussed from the standpoint of the principles presented herein. And, more importantly, although specific group interactions have already been discussed in previous chapters, it should also prove productive to discuss some general features of such interactions.

LEARNING PRINCIPLES AND INTERACTION
IN THE GROUP

Functional Analysis of Authority

Adams and Romney (1959) have made an analysis of authority situations in general terms using operant conditioning principles. There are a number of general and specific implications of this analysis for understanding interaction in the group. This section will present a summary of their analysis and several later sections will elaborate on the principles.

The central idea in authority relations is that of the reciprocal control and reinforcement of behavior of two persons. Basically, the paradigm is that a response of one person, A, is reinforced by another person, B, and that, in turn, the reinforcing response of B is, itself, reinforced by A. Such an interaction will be called an *authority sequence*. An example is the situation in which Person A asks B for water and B complies by giving A water. Figure [8.1] gives an illustration of the process. The

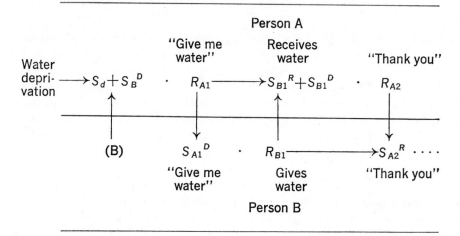

Fig. 8.1. "Authority sequence with initial response under control of deprivation." (Adams and Romney, 1959, p. 236)

figure is divided into two parts, the top half representing stimuli and responses directly related to Person A, while the lower half pertains to Person B. The interaction between A and B begins at the far left of the figure with A in a state of deprivation and in the presence of a discriminative stimulus, S_d and $S_B{}^D$. These stimuli set the occasion for the response R_{A1}, "Give me water." S_d is the stimulus, presumably physiological in the example, that results from water deprivation. $S_B{}^D$ is the discriminative stimulus resulting from B's presence in A's environment. $S_B{}^D$ is a discriminative stimulus with respect to R_{A1} in this illustration by virtue of previous conditioning. The response, "Give me water," would not occur unless A were thirsty; nor would it occur unless someone were present to give A water. In some sense, R_{A1} is "appropriate" only in the presence of S_d and $S_B{}^D$, and these stimuli may therefore be viewed as "setting the occasion for" and as having control over R_{A1}. As will be seen, this control is not exclusive, however, for it is the reinforcement of R_{A1} in the presence of the two stimuli that is crucial for the demonstration of authority.

Once the verbal command, "Give me water," has been emitted, it is a stimulus to B. Specifically, it is a discriminative stimulus, $S_{A1}{}^D$, in that it sets the occasion for a response by B that is later reinforced. . . . When B gives water to A, his response, R_{B1}, constitutes the reinforcement, $S_{B1}{}^R$ of response R_{A1}. In addition, R_{B1} is also a discriminative stimulus, $S_{B1}{}^D$, that sets the occasion for a further response by A. The response in this example is, "Thank you," R_{A2}. In turn, R_{A2} . . . constitutes a reinforcement of R_{B1}. . . .

In Fig. [8.1], A's initial response was partly under the control of deprivation. Instead it could have been under the partial control of aversive stimulation. For example, B might have been making some disturbing noise and this aversive stimulus might have set the occasion for the response, "Keep quiet!" It is also true that B's response, R_{B1} need not necessarily be reinforced by the presentation of a positive reinforcing stimulus. It could have been reinforced by the withdrawal of an aversive stimulus or conditioned aversive stimulus. Figure [8.2] shows how aversive stimuli might exercise control in an authority interaction.

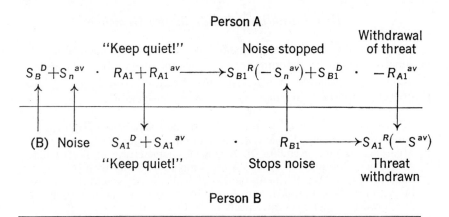

Fig. 8.2. "Authority sequence with initial response under control of aversive stimulation." (Adams and Romney, 1959, p. 237)

An aversive noise stimulus, $S_n{}^{av}$, and a discriminative stimulus, $S_B{}^D$, set the occasion for the responses R_{A1} and $R_{A1}{}^{av}$, constituted by the verbal response, "Keep quiet!" and an implied threat carried by the accentuation and intonation of the verbal response. Thus B is presented with a discriminative verbal stimulus, $S_{A1}{}^D$, and a conditioned aversive stimulus, $S_{A1}{}^{av}$. These stimuli set the occasion for stopping the noise, indicated in the figure as R_{B1}. This response consists of the withdrawal of the aversive noise stimulus, $S_n{}^{av}$, and constitutes a negative reinforcing stimulus for A, as well as a discriminative stimulus, $S_{B1}{}^D$, setting the occasion for a further response. The response, in this example, is the withdrawal of implicit threat and is labelled, $-R_{A1}{}^{av}$. This, in turn, is an appropriate negative reinforcing stimulus for B's response, R_{B1}. As in the previous example, the sequence of behavior is stopped at this point. Thus, we have here an interesting case of escape conditioning, with an implied threat as a conditioned aversive stimulus, as well as one of avoidance conditioning with respect to the negative reinforcing stimulus inferred from the threat (pp. 235–237).

Adams and Romney continue on to analyze in operant conditioning terms more complex constellations of such social sequences of stimuli and responses. The principles presented in the above analysis, however, provide a good deal of fodder for further consideration. While Adams and Romney addressed their analysis to authority interactions, there is much of significance in their arguments for understanding social behavior in general, as well as that specifically considered under the heading of authority. The basic principles upon which further analysis in the following sections will draw concern primarily (1) discriminative stimuli in the group, and (2) the reinforcing properties of stimuli in the group.

Discriminative Stimuli in the Group

In Adams and Romney's discussion of authority the operation of discriminative stimuli in determining the behavior of members of the group is explicitly formulated. The controlling effect of stimuli in the group seems very important and may be expanded considerably.

> Two general groups of discriminative stimulus variables controlling A's initial response may be considered, stimulus characteristics of B and situational stimuli, excluding B. A general characteristic of B that may serve as a discriminative stimulus is his being an organism with the potentiality of responding. Without another person's being present, a response by A cannot be reinforced, and A cannot exercise any authority. There are, however, other relevant aspects of B. One is B as a particular individual, i.e., the stimulus characteristics of a B who has previously reinforced A's response, as opposed to a B who has not. A second is B as the incumbent in a particular role, as an office boy or corporal for example. In this instance characteristics of B serve as discriminative stimuli for a comparatively narrow range of responses by A. In other instances characteristics of B may set the occasion for one class of responses only; for example, the elevator boy is a discriminative stimulus for the response, "Take me to the sixth," only. Thus we may think of B as having discriminative stimulus characteristics that exercise control over A's responses with different degrees of specificity. The specificity of control exercised is a function of the extent of differential reinforcement carried out in the presence of particular characteristics (Adams and Romney, 1959, p. 242).

This statement actually suggests several types of stimuli characteristic of the group situation which may function as discriminative stimuli and control the behavior of members of the group. First, the *behavior* of the individual may be a discriminative stimulus. Second, *physical characteristics* of the individual, aside from his behavior, may serve a discriminative stimulus function. In addition, other stimuli in the situation may exert this same type of control.

Behavioral Stimuli

Adams and Romney mention that the individual's role may serve as a discriminative stimulus and control restricted responses of other members of the group. The term role may be considered to refer to the behavior of the individual as it has discriminative stimulus value for other members of the group. For example, *role* is defined by Cottrell (1942) in the following terms. "A role [is] . . . an internally consistent series of conditioned responses by one member of a social situation which represents the stimulus pattern for a similarly internally consistent series of conditioned responses of the other(s) in that situation" (p. 617).

Thibaut and Kelley (1959) make a similar assertion: "Each subject's behavior is at the same time a response to a past behavior of the other and a stimulus to a future behavior of the other; each behavior is in part dependent variable and in part independent variable; in no clear sense is it properly either of them" (p. 2). And Sarbin (1954) states the following:

> A *role* is a patterned sequence of learned *actions* or deeds performed by a person in an interaction situation. The organizing of the individual actions is a product of the perceptual and cognitive behavior of person A upon observing person B. B performs one or a number of discrete acts which A observes and organizes into a concept, a role. On the basis of this conceptualization of the actions of B, A expects certain further actions from B. This expectation is covert, and is the equivalent of saying "locates or names the position of the other." Once having located or named the position of the other, A performs certain acts which have been learned as belonging to the reciprocal position; these actions are conceptualized as A's role. Although language imposes upon us the necessity for defining role in this rather deliberate way, the reader should bear in mind that this "locating the position of the other" may be placed somewhere on a continuum from deliberate to automatic, from witting to unwitting (p. 225).

Although the general conception of human behavior underlying some of these conceptions of role may derive from a somewhat different approach than the one in this book, in terms of learning principles it may be seen that the stimulus effects of one's behavior upon the behavior of other individuals in the group are considered an important determinant of social interactions. Several experiments and studies will be described to elaborate this type of interaction in the group, as well as to indicate the possibility of studying the phenomena using learning principles and experimental methods.

In Chapter 4 the manner in which the child comes to match (or echo) sounds made by the parent has been described. That is, producing a sound (or, for that matter, some other response) which matches a stimulus produced by an "authority" source comes to be reinforcing. This occurs because the child is ordinarily reinforced in the presence of such matching stimuli and not in the presence of "nonmatches." A more general description of such behavior might be "imitation," or imitative behavior. Miller and Dollard (1941) first performed experiments which indicated that the behavior of individuals may come to function as controlling stimuli for other individuals through the operation of learning principles. Using first animal subjects and then humans, they were concerned with an experimental analysis of the manner in which imitative behavior is acquired.

In an experiment to train imitation in the rat, one animal who was later to provide the model for imitation was first trained to run a T-maze. The animal was placed on the stem of the maze and would run the stem to the choice point, where a turn in the arm marked by a black card resulted in food as the reinforcement. A turn into the arm marked by a white card, however, resulted in no reinforcement. Thus, for this initial rat, the black card became a strong S^D (and the white card an S^Δ) for the behavior of turning in its direction.

After this training was completed, a new rat, one who had not received any discrimination training on the cards, was placed directly behind the model rat on the stem of the maze. The follower-rat received the food reinforcement if he turned into the same arm as the model rat, but no reinforcement if he turned into the other arm. If the imitative behavior was being learned, the behavior of the model rat should have become an S^D for the follower, just as the black card had for the model animal. That this was indeed the case was shown by the fact that, after training, the follower-rat nearly always made the same turn as had the model (with any possible influence of the cards controlled by not presenting them).

If later, other model rats were substituted in front of the follower, the imitative behavior was still exhibited, as the follower-rat continued to imitate the turn. Regardless of whether the S^D for the model's behavior was a black or a white card, or if he had simply been trained to go always to the right or always to the left, the follower-rat continued to make the same turn as the current model. Thus, as would be predicted on the basis of the principle of stimulus generalization, the follower later followed other new models, although the training of the rat had taken place with a single model as S^D.

Other experiments by the same investigators showed the feasibility of applying these principles to the study of the conditions under which imitation occurs in children. In one of these experiments, two identical closed wooden boxes were set in a room. Although the contents of both boxes were hidden, either one or both of the boxes (depending upon the condition being manipulated) contained some candy. Then two six-year-olds were brought into the room, and one of them (the model for the imitative behavior) was told in which box the candy might be found. Immediately after seeing the model child obtain candy from this box, the second child was told to choose a box so that he might find candy as well. At this point, most of the second children went to the other box, rather than to the same one in which the model child had already found his candy. The results this far would indicate, then, that there was a tendency toward nonimitative behavior, rather than toward imitation. The conditions under which this tendency had already been learned probably involve the fact that the reinforcement contingencies in the past social history of the child led to alternating behavior in general. For example, since two objects cannot occupy the same space at the same time, after having removed something from a single place, it is not possible to find a second object there. Or, on the social level, normally after someone else has eaten from a dish, drunk from a glass, etc., there is more food or drink to be gained by getting a fresh source rather than by using the same one.

In the experiment, after this first trial, the children were divided into two groups. One group received the reinforcer (candy) whenever it imitated, that is, whenever the members went to the same box as had the model child. For the other group, reinforcement was made contingent upon nonimitative behavior instead, in other words, these children found candy if they went to the box other than that which the model had chosen. Both groups' behavior quickly came under the control of the stimulus of the behavior of the model child. For the children who were reinforced for imitating, the behavior of the model child became an S^D for following; for the other children the behavior became an S^D for an opposite response.

In these cases, both imitative and nonimitative behavior are shown to develop under the control of reinforcement contingencies, and both are therefore patterns of behavior adjustive to the current environment. However, just as the follower-rats imitated models they had not seen before, so the principles of generalization would provide for children reinforced for imitating to follow along with the behavior of new models, even where this following might now be nonadjustive. It would be expected that a child who had an extensive history of reinforcement for following would later generally display this as characteristic behavior.

It is not necessary, of course, that the behavior of the individual must match that of the person whose behavior is the S^D, in order for the former's behavior to be discriminatively controlled by the latter. Other than imitative behavior may come under the discriminative control of another person's behavior as well. The leader's behavior may serve as a stimulus that controls the behaviors of his followers in many different ways. Thus, leadership in general may be considered in terms of the S^D properties of the leader's behavior.

> If following one person's suggestion is consistently rewarded and following another person's is consistently punished, a discrimination can be formed so that one will trust certain people but not others. Similarly, one can learn to trust a person for some things but not for others. . . . Such discriminations determine whose advice will be sought and the extent to which it will be followed; they are the basis for prestige (Dollard and Miller, 1950, p. 118).

It would not be hard to see how, in preliterate societies, the individual who was keen of scent and vision and swift of limb, who had acquired the skills necessary in hunting, might become a "leader." If this individual continually returned from the hunt with game, whereas others failed, it might be expected that "imitation" of his behavior would soon be acquired. By traveling with this person and using the same hunting techniques, the others in the group would also gain the crucial reinforcers and the pattern of following this man would be correspondingly reinforced. The behavior of the leader would thus become a discriminative stimulus for further following. On the basis of stimulus generalization, in addition to following his actions on the hunt, imitating or matching him would be expected to generalize to other modes of behavior. Others would be likely to respect his verbal statements pertaining to many spheres of activity, in addition to those involving hunting methods, construction of spears, organizing the hunt, and so on.

It is perhaps a little more difficult to analyze the development of leader-follower interaction in the more "abstract" realm of behaviors; for example, with reasoning and thinking. However, it would seem likely that the same principles are involved even here. The fact that verbal response sequences can act to mediate overt behaviors which may be more or less effective in solving problems of a physical or social nature, argues for the conception that certain verbal sequences are "better" than others. Certain sequences mediate behaviors that will be reinforced; others mediate behavior resulting in lack of reinforcement, or even in aversive consequences.

Thus, in many situations of modern living, a leader might emerge because his verbal responses mediate behaviors that are later reinforced. It would be expected then, that "educated" men, more generally than others, would become leaders in positions of distinction in the society. Or, in the educational institution, the leader in the classroom would be an individual whose verbal behavior had discriminative stimulus value controlling behavior that is later reinforced. The teacher of physics, for example, is in command of verbal response sequences that are unfamiliar to the students. When this instructor makes a prediction and it is later corroborated in an experiment, these verbal response sequences are strengthened for both teacher and student. Moreover, when the students can repeat (imitate) these verbal sequences under the control of appropriate physical stimulus conditions, their behavior—as scientists, engineers, and so on—is further reinforced by the society.

Many studies in social psychology on leadership are seemingly concerned with the phenomena we have described in this section, although they do not employ this terminology. The famous study by Whyte (1955) of the "street-corner gang" provides a good example of results found in such research. Whyte's study concerned the interaction patterns emerging in an informal group—a gang—when there was little initial differentiation among the members. Among the men in this group Whyte showed that a couple of members emerged as leaders, although they had not started out occupying any special position in the group. Before analyzing this situation in terms of the principles involved, it is worth while noting the description Whyte gave of the pattern of behavior in the group. For example, Whyte described the situation as involving a high rate of social interaction within the group, as well as a system of mutual obligations among the members. In this interaction, moreover, Whyte showed that one or two persons were "depended upon." Whyte defined this to mean that the other members looked to this person for advice and encouragement. When this person gave his word to one of the boys, he kept it. He received more of their confidences than did any other man, and consequently he knew more about what was going on in the gang than anyone else. In Whyte's terms, the leader is ". . . the man who acts when the situation requires action. He is more resourceful than his followers. Past events have shown that his ideas were right" (p. 259).

This description thus indicated the manner in which the leader might have acquired value as a discriminative stimulus for the following behavior of other members of the group. First, as in the simple imitation situation, because he acted when the circumstances required some action (while the others did not), his own behavior and that of his followers had an opportunity of being reinforced. As a consequence, the potential leader's behavior would come to be an S^D, since the behavior of the follower would be reinforced in the presence of the leader. But, furthermore, to say that the leader was more resourceful might well mean that, in addition, his verbal response sequences mediated behavior of other group members which led to a reinforcing state of affairs. The course of action he suggested would turn out to be more satisfactory to the members—he was "right."

His verbal response sequences might lead to reinforcers for others in still other ways. For example, Whyte says that the leader is depended upon by all members of the group—that when he gave his word to one of his boys he kept it. To keep one's word, however, simply means that the individual's verbal responses parallel his overt behavior. If he says he will be at the intersection of Main and Sixth at four o'clock, at the designated time he is indeed there. But most significant for maintaining this person's verbal behavior as an S^D is the fact that when this verbal sequence occurs, it mediates the behavior of the listener who himself appears at the corner at four o'clock. However, the listener's behavior is only reinforced if the speaker appears. If the verbal behavior of the speaker mediates behavior which is not reinforced, however, some extinction of the discriminative stimulus value of the speaker's behavior would be expected to occur.

Another way that a leader may retain his control as a discriminative stimulus is by dispensing reinforcement himself which is contingent upon appropriate following behaviors. As Whyte points out, he may share food with others, praise them, spend his money on them, and so on. When a person has reinforcers to dispense, he can arrange it so that he strengthens other people's behavior when it is under the stimulus control of his "directions."

It would be expected that the same discriminative control of other people's behavior, as has been discussed in this section, could be established on the basis of aversive stimuli. That is, where the leader has the power to apply aversive stimulation until his "directions" are followed, at which time the follower is negatively reinforced by the withdrawal of the aversive stimulus, his directions would be expected to acquire discriminative control. French and Raven (1959) discuss "social power" in terms of aversive control as well as of various types of positive reinforcement.

Physical Characteristics as Discriminative Stimuli

Adams and Romney also suggest that physical characteristics of the individual may serve as S^Ds for the behavior of other members of the group. This could be elaborated to include features of dress, grooming, office, title, and so on, which could be discussed in sociological terms such as status symbols, indicators of social class position, and role symbols. While such stimuli appear to exert important social control of behavior, they are somewhat difficult to separate from the discriminative stimuli produced by the individual's behavior—as the following discussion of "role symbols" indicates.

The building blocks of role perception, of course, are the overt acts of others. These acts may be defined as everything the other does. This includes his gross skeletal movements, his verbal behavior, what he wears, his facial expression, his posture, his gait, his accent and intonation, his adornments, visible emblems and tattoo marks, etc. The wearing of a uniform and a silver badge, for example, is part of the role of policemen. The perception of these objects on a person leads to predictable role behavior on the part of the perceiver (providing the system of role expectations of the perceiver is known). Perceiving the position of the other, then, becomes a matter of attending to and organizing cues (Sarbin, 1954, p. 230).

Thus, it is possibly arbitrary to separate the behavior of the individual from the physical stimulus properties of the individual, his dress, and so on. However, while in certain examples below the two classes of stimuli blend, it is useful for purposes of discussion to make this distinction.

First, specific individuals as physical stimuli may be considered to acquire discriminative control of behavior. Because the child is reinforced for certain behavior in the presence of his mother, her presence comes to control this type of behavior. He is reinforced for a different behavior in the presence of a playmate, who then comes as an individual physical stimulus to control this behavior. A study by Cohen (1962), for example, shows that under the same conditions of reinforcement, leader-follower behavior and competitive-cooperative behavior vary as a function of the past history of the individual with respect to his "partner." Thus, a young male subject when placed under exactly the same experimental conditions, emitted different behaviors depending upon whether his partner was his mother, sister, brother, friend, or a stranger.

It seems also to be the case that *classes* of "people" stimuli come to control certain types of behavior. For example, different behavior of a little boy is reinforced in the presence of little girls than is reinforced in the presence of other little boys. Thus, the different classes of "people" stimuli come to exert discriminative control over different aspects of his behavior on the basis of direct experience and primary stimulus generalization.

In addition, there seem to be many physical stimuli *associated* with people which can function as discriminative stimuli and control social behavior. Some of these conform to what was called mediated stimulus generalization in Chapter 3. Thus, although two individuals may be different on a primary stimulus generalization gradient, let us say a man and a woman, a title such as "Doctor" applied to both may equally function as a discriminative stimulus and the two people would control similar behavior.

It would be expected that titles gain a discriminative stimulus function because generally a certain type of behavior is reinforced in the presence of a person with a particular title. As an example, the child of a working class mother may be prompted to behave in certain ways when he is ushered into the home where his mother is employed and introduced to "Mrs. So-and-so." He is trained to behave differently here from when he accompanies his mother next door while she has a cup of coffee with a lady addressed by her first name.

Because of such differences in discriminative training, it would be expected that people would customarily respond differently to persons introduced with titles such as "Mr.," "Dr.," "Professor," "Judge," "General Manager," "Janitor," "Reverend," "Mayor," and "President."

> In societies where the differences of social class position are reinforced by ideologies that articulate the "basic" and "inherent" character of the differences, modes of address and titles of social position that correspond at least roughly to social class position are often formalized and elaborate. This has been true in societies with feudal nobilities, or where noble titles have persisted into modern times in what are on the whole democratic societies, such as England or France. A title indicates upper-class position, and different titles, such as duke, marquis, earl, viscount, baron, baronet, and knight, indicate roughly the differences of position within a range of the upper class (Barber, 1957, p. 141).

It would be expected that because of differences among individuals in their training histories, their responses to such social S^Ds would differ. Thus, a youngster from a poor family might be trained to respond differently with respect to individuals with titles such as "Mr.," "Dr.," "Judge," and so on, than would a child from a wealthy, educated family. The responses that these titles would control would thus be expected to differ.

Other events related to social class may also be considered as social discriminative stimuli.

> The style and quality of clothing for both men and women have been among the most obvious symbols of social class position in all societies. For this reason, we have a multitude of examples, especially on the dress of the upper classes, about whom—in this respect as in others—most has been written. In classical China, the upper-class Mandarin symbolized both his social class position and his abstention from manual labor by his close-fitting, ankle-length gown of fine silk and by his long fingernails. . . . In some parts of India, the use of gold and silver ornaments and of umbrellas and shoes was appropriate only for certain high-ranking castes, taboo for lower castes. . . .
> At the present time on the island of Trinidad in the British West Indies, wearing a coat and tie is an indispensable symbol for a middle-class colored man; otherwise, he is not marked off from lower-class colored people. . . .
> And even in communistic, equalitarian Soviet Russia, as a result of recent laws several million people now wear uniforms which indirectly

symbolize their position in the hierarchy of social evaluation. Employees of the railway and river-transport systems, of the iron-ore and coal industries, of the Ministry of Foreign Affairs, students in the State Labor Reserves Schools, and of course all who are in the military services now wear uniforms varying in color, quality, and insignia of rank. . . .

In the modern world, it is women's clothes that are the more esthetically brilliant and handsome and the more obviously symbolic of social class position. (Barber, 1957, pp. 146–149).

There are many additional S^Ds that seem to control other's social behavior that are not strictly part of the person. One's church and organizational affiliations may serve as social discriminative stimuli; the type, number, and quality of car; place and type of residence; one's club or recreational haunts, and so on.

Even less personal situational social discriminative stimuli come to control behavior in respect to another person, such as a football stadium, place of worship, school, movie, or physician's office.

The second group of discriminative stimulus variables are situational variables. They include virtually all relevant stimuli not directly pertaining to [group members]. Some situational variables are part of the purely physical environment. Thus, the request, "Take me to the sixth," has a low probability of being reinforced in the absence of an elevator. Similarly, "Give me water," will usually have a low probability of occurring without a source of water in the immediate environment. However, in an instance of this sort, deprivation may become so severe that it exercises almost exclusive control. The "Water, water!" of the wounded soldier on the deserted battlefield is an example. Other situational variables are of a more "social" character in that the presence of other persons, or of persons having particular types of interaction, has a controlling discriminative stimulus function. Certain kinds of commands or requests are not issued to one's wife at home in the context of a cocktail party (and would go unreinforced, if issued), though they are issued and reinforced when just family members are present. Orders may be successfully given to an employee at the office, though not at the country club (Adams and Romney, 1959, pp. 242–243).

Reinforcing Stimuli in the Group

By separating the discussion of social discriminative stimuli and social reinforcing stimuli, we do not intend to indicate that different stimuli are necessarily involved. In the preceding chapter it was suggested that the discriminative and reinforcing functions of a stimulus may be exerted by one and the same stimulus. Thus, for example, in addition to the discriminative function of such social stimuli as dress and titles as described in the previous section of this chapter, it would also be expected that these same stimuli could possess reinforcing value. Titles, style and quality of clothing, possessions of various types, as they become S^Ds in the course of the child's training, would also be expected to become conditioned reinforcers.

One reason possession of such "stimulus objects" can be reinforcing is that they control reinforcing behavior of other people. The title of "Doctor" is an S^D to most people that controls various types of "respectful" behaviors. Because of this function it would be expected that the title would be a reinforcing stimulus and would strengthen behavior which is followed by receipt of the title "Doctor." The same may be said of other social S^Ds. The following quotation concerning the usurpation of social class symbols in seventeenth-century France illustrates these dual functions: the reinforcing function of social symbols is indicated, as well as the discriminative function in controlling the behavior of striving for them.

> That Jansenist, Robert Arnault d'Andilli, son of a lawyer, ambitious to get the office of Secretary of State, a man who was a great bourgeois, expresses himself like a perfect knight. The bourgeois, shopkeepers and office-holders, called themselves "Sieur" and took the title of Squire. Their wives adorned themselves with the name of "Damoiselles." The husbands even placed helmets on their coats of arms, in spite of the prohibitions of the Ordinances of Orleans and Blois; they carried swords; and they decked themselves in the dress of gentlemen. Monchrestien lamented: ". . . these days it is impossible to make distinctions on the basis of external appearances. The shopkeeper is dressed like the gentlemen. . . . [w]ho couldn't see that this uniformity of dress was corrupting our ancient discipline? . . ." one woman told her friend: ". . . I was in very good company the other day when there appeared an elegant young man . . . dressed in a satin suit, his cloak lined with silk plush, wearing a beaver hat and silk stockings . . . they told me that he was the son of a surgeon-barber; but never in my life have I seen anything smarter, for he looked just like a courtier . . ." (Mousnier, 1945, p. 502).

This naturalistic example illustrates the reinforcing nature of the title, the dress, the speech, and so on, of the upper class in the period described. As S^Ds, however, these stimuli controlled the behavior of the lower classes in striving for them, apparently to the chagrin of the nobles they copied.

In addition, in the preceding chapter it was suggested that reinforcers generally come to have an S^D function simply because they have reinforcing value. It would be expected that this process would also function in social interaction. The following experiment of Bandura and Ross (Bandura, 1962b) illustrates how reinforcing stimuli that are not contingent upon the behavior of the subject can be manipulated in an experimental situation to produce S^D control of behavior. In this study, children were given certain experiences with two adults. The situation was arranged so that one of the adults had many reinforcers to dispense: toys, tasty drinks, and so on.

The other adult had none. In one group of children, the "potentially" reinforcing adult actually presented the child with some of the reinforcers. In another group the children only saw the adult present the other adult with some of the reinforcers, but did not receive any themselves.

Later the S^D characteristic (using our terms) of each of the two adults was measured in the following procedure. The children all observed the two adults play a complicated game. The two adults "played" the game in markedly different ways, putting on different hats, posturing differently, and emitting different verbal behaviors. When it was the child's turn to play, the extent to which his behavior *matched* either the adult with the reinforcers or the adult without the reinforcers was tabulated.

The results indicated that the adult with the reinforcers was "imitated" more frequently, whether or not the children had been reinforced by this adult. Thus, in terms of the present analysis, possession of the reinforcers made him a stronger discriminative stimulus, controlling the behavior of the children. That is, the behavior of the adult had greater discriminative stimulus value as it had greater reinforcing value.

Thus, it may seem only arbitrary to separate the reinforcing and discriminative functions of social stimuli. As the preceding section indicated, however, the discriminative value of social stimuli is independently important. Now an independent discussion of the reinforcing value of social stimuli will be given.

It might be said that one's social power or social control—one's ability to influence the behavior of others (see Maccoby, 1959; Mussen and Distler, 1959; Parsons, 1955; Raven and French, 1958 for related discussions) resides to some extent in the *reinforcement value* of one's behavior (and it might be added, in one's attributes as a physical stimulus, and the discriminative stimulus value of one's surroundings, titles, and so on). "Social power is generally defined as the ability of a person to influence the behavior of others by controlling or mediating their positive and negative reinforcement" (Bandura, 1962b, p. 250).

Adams and Romney (1959) derive a principle of authority relationships which also concerns influence through control of reinforcement.

> A further derivation is that A's probability of successfully developing or maintaining an authority relation over B will in part be a function of the amount and variety or range of reinforcers he has available. The person who can mediate reinforcements appropriate to several states of deprivation can exercise more authority than one who can, say, provide only food (e.g., a parent versus a neighbor). The person who has access to a large range of aversive stimuli can have more authority than one who has not (e.g., a company commander versus a corporal). From a similar consideration it also follows that the greater the amount and range of reinforcers available to A, the greater the range of B's responses he can

control, other variables remaining constant. Thus a parent can have wider authority than an older sister who can mete out limited punishment only and who has no money for material rewards (p. 240).

Homans' (1961) analysis of influence also emphasizes the leader as the source of reinforcement, although the following passage also includes a description indicating the S^D value of the leader.

> A man influences another when he asks the other to do something and the other does it. Each member of a group may have influenced, in this sense, every other member. We say that a man who regularly influences more members than another does holds higher authority than the other; and the man who holds highest authority we call the leader of the group. A man earns authority by acquiring esteem, and he acquires esteem by rewarding others. What he does for them often takes the form of giving them advice that, when taken, they find rewarding. Accordingly they come to recognize him as a man compliance with whose instructions is apt to be rewarding, and they get to be all the more prepared to comply with his instructions on some new occasion. This allows him the opportunity of giving them instructions when they have not asked for them, particularly instructions that, if obeyed, coordinate their activities toward the attainment of some group goal. Their obedience depends on the nature of the activities he orders and on the fact that it is he that has ordered them. If the followers do obey, and find the results rewarding, the leader has confirmed their confidence in him and reestablished the esteem he risked in giving the order. He will be still more ready to give them orders on the next occasion, and they will be still more ready to obey (p. 314).

At any rate, the reinforcing value of the individual's behavior itself, or the things the behavior presents, as well as the reinforcing value of the individual as a physical stimulus, seem important determinants of social interaction. These topics will now be discussed more fully.

Behavioral Stimuli as Reinforcers

To begin with, it might be said that the behavior of the individual in the group is to some extent a function of the reinforcing properties of his own behavior for the other party and of the other's behavior for him. An experimental illustration of how reinforcement principles operate to shape the behavior of group members will be presented.

The minimal social situation.—A series of experiments by Sidowski and associates attempted to evaluate the essential features of a social situation from the point of view of learning theory. They started by investigating the simplest situation that can be considered social within this framework. For these experiments the definition of a social situation included the following: (a) two or more persons must have at their disposal responses that result in reinforcement for other persons; (b) the principal sources of reinforcement for any person depend on responses made by other persons; and (c) the responses controlling reinforcement are subject to learning.

In an experiment to test these propositions two subjects, each of whom was wearing a pair of electrodes, were placed in separate experimental rooms containing two push buttons and an electrically operated counter. Pressing the right-hand button in one room resulted in the delivery of an electric shock to the electrode worn by the subject in the other room. Pressing the left-hand button resulted in a "point" being tabulated on the counter for the subject in the other room. Because of the instructions to the subject, each point could be considered to be a positive reinforcer (the subjects were told to try and make as many points as possible). The subjects were isolated from each other completely; they were each unaware of the other's presence or function in the experiment. The subjects were simply told the following:

> . . . You can press either of these buttons in any manner that you wish, and as frequently as you wish. Do not attempt to press both buttons at the same time and use only your right hand for pressing. . . . The object of the experiment is to make as many points as you can . . . (Sidowski, Wyckoff, and Tabory, 1956, p. 116).

Thus, unknown to each other the two subjects were in a social situation in which each had the "power" to both reward and punish the other. That is, each had a repertoire of behaviors (pushing the right or left button) some of which were aversive and some of which were positively reinforcing to his invisible "partner." Under such a situation, the question is how will the subjects behave; will their behavior be shaped (will they learn) to be reinforcing or aversive to the other person? Or, indeed, will learning take place at all? It should be remembered that neither subject could reinforce or shock himself, only the other individual.

The results showed that when the shock was strong the subjects' behavior was effected by the combination of the positive reinforcers and the aversive stimuli. Examination of the situation reveals the systematic variables that account for the learning. Most importantly, receipt of a shock following a particular response would suppress that response or lead to a change in that response while receipt of a point following a response would strengthen that response and lead to repetition. With that in mind, several social modes of maximizing positive reinforcement and minimizing aversive stimulation could occur.

> . . . Generally, we might assume random behavior by both Ss at the beginning of the experimental session. For example, let us suppose that

each S made a response that shocked the other. It is not unlikely that this event might occur by accident early in the session. However, it is clear that some shift away from this behavior would soon appear since neither S is receiving reinforcement and both are being punished. This shift would probably occur sooner under conditions of Strong Shock. The Ss might shift at the same time, or one might shift sooner than the other, resulting in at least two possible new patterns. If both shifted to the reinforcement button at the same time, both would now receive reinforcement and we would expect a tendency for this pattern to continue. (In fact, the same prediction would be made if Ss commenced to reinforce each other at any time.) . . .

It is suggested that under conditions of Strong Shock, the most probable stable pattern (end state) was that of both Ss reinforcing each other. Thus, Ss would tend to shift among patterns until they hit on this solution (p. 118).

The investigators also pointed out how alternation in button-pressing could occur and perhaps even reach a stable mode of adjustment. It might be added, however, that where two subjects had reached a state where they were both pressing the reinforcing button, one of them switching to the punishment button might not disrupt their previous maximization of reinforcement for long. That is, A switching to the shock button would aversively stimulate B and, as a consequence, B would be likely to also switch and begin pressing his shock button. This in turn would make it likely that A would return to his reinforcement button. B could then return to his reinforcement button, in which case a steady state would return, or if B continued pressing the shock button he would soon again experience shock; this would alter his behavior, and so on.

In conclusion, it might be said that the only way the subjects could maximize positive reinforcement and minimize aversive stimulation is through pushing the correct button and avoiding the incorrect one. There would be many possible ways that this "maximal social adjustment" could be shaped up in the situation. On the other hand, with so many of the usual cues not accessible to the subjects, it would also seem possible that less than maximal adjustments could result, for example, alternation could continue in both subjects so that sometimes they received shock and sometimes "points." It would be unlikely, however, that the least optimal behavior of the subjects would eventuate: that both would continue to press only the shock button and receive only aversive stimulation.

The study is important in showing how the reinforcing properties of one's behavior shapes the behavior of others in the social group and how this behavior in turn is shaped by the reinforcing properties of the others' behavior. It might be said that behavior which is aversive to others results in, or is likely to result in, reciprocal behavior which is aversive. This demonstration of reinforcing variables important to social behavior assumes no complex behaviors of the subjects (language, attitudes, and so on) and the variables important to the behavior of the participants reside only in the experimental situation. In fact, the experiment may be assumed to exclude almost entirely pre-experimental effects on the social behavior of the participants.

Additional experiments involving reinforcing properties of behavior.— The experiment of Sidowski, Wyckoff, and Tabory showing the reinforcing properties of behavior in the group situation had the artificial characteristics of laboratory studies that have been simplified to gain experimental control. There are several more lifelike studies of individual behavior in groups in which the properties of the behavior of the individuals determines the way the "group" will behave. In a study by Azrin and Lindsley (1956) reinforcement was arranged by the experimenter to be contingent upon certain social behaviors of two children. The study was concerned with cooperative behavior and the situation set up so that "playing together" and "sharing" were strengthened through reinforcement while other behaviors were not.

In the experiment, two children were placed at opposite sides of a table with three holes and a stylus in front of each. A cooperative response was defined as the two children placing their styli in opposite holes at the same time. Whenever this occurred a single reinforcing stimulus, a jellybean, fell into a cup that was accessible to both children. Although no specific instructions concerning cooperation were given, it was found that the children did learn to cooperate; the "matching" behavior of both yielded each reinforcement. By manipulating the reinforcement contingencies the experimenters were able to develop, maintain, and also to eliminate cooperation between the children.

In addition, of particular interest was the "sharing" behavior that developed. Since only a single reinforcer was delivered whenever a cooperative response was made by the pair of children, most of the children quickly learned to divide the candy. The reason for this can be seen by referring to the cases where sharing did not occur. In two of the ten pairs one member took all the candy. When this occurred the other member of the pair refused to cooperate in playing the game (that is, because of no reinforcement his "playing" behavior extinguished), thereby eliminating all possibility of reinforcement for the other child. Thus, in order for either child to obtain reinforcement, the behavior of the other child had to be maintained; *sharing* the reinforcement in the situation was necessary if reinforcement for a child was to be obtained at all. This demonstration of behavior principles is particularly important since the situation has great generality. Frequently, in interaction with other people, maintenance of the other's participation and cooperation depends upon sharing the reinforcers the situation has to offer. (A frequent personal problem of social interaction involves an insufficiency of "sharing behaviors.")

Another important point in this experiment concerned the children's language behavior. Unlike the subjects in the experiment of Sidowski *et al.*, the children in this experiment were able to interrupt their activity long enough to arrive at some verbal agreement as to how to divide the candy. The verbal behavior, which had been shaped in the past, provided for rapid shifts in behavior. That is, it was not necessary to go through a lengthy process of shaping the behavior of the two participants in the immediate task, as was the case in the Sidowski experiment where the reinforcement contingencies alone were the controlling variables.

The experiment of Azrin and Lindsley has implications for a consideration of competition, as well as for cooperation, in terms of learning principles. An outline of competition and cooperation in learning terms will help in showing what those implications are.

> People can hurt one another directly, as by trading blows, but they can also do so by depriving one another of rewards. They can either present negative reinforcers or withdraw positive ones. The first case is so obvious that we shall not bother with it further, but consider only the second. So far we have been mostly concerned with cooperation between men. Cooperation occurs when, by emitting activities to one another, or by emitting activities in concert to the environment, at least two men achieve a greater total reward than either could have achieved by working alone. . . . The situation usually contrasted with cooperation is competition. The contrast need not lie in the fact that the two men now work alone. It means rather that each emits activity that, so far as it is rewarded, tends by that fact to deny reward to the other. The activity, if reinforced, withdraws reinforcement from the other (Homans, 1961, p. 131).

The experiment of Azrin and Lindsley thus provides a paradigm for competition as well as for cooperation. Since competition refers to that situation in which the delivery of available reinforcers to one person is at the same time the withdrawal of potential reinforcement for another, one individual gaining a reinforcer constitutes an aversive stimulus for the other. When one child took the single jellybean, the other child received no candy, at least for a while. The fact that in the experiment the children learned to divide the reinforcers means, of course, that the actual contingencies were shaping cooperation and not competition; but it can be seen that, with only slight changes in the situation, competitive behavior might have been shaped instead. If, through some extrinsic control, for example, the member of the pair who did not get the candy was forced to continue playing the game, there would have been no "pressure" (no reinforcing contingency) for the other member to share. The possibility of gaining additional reinforcers would not have been withdrawn and there would have been no environmental restrictions to taking all the candy for himself.

To summarize, then, in this study the behavior of each member of the group had reinforcing properties for the other member. Cooperative behavior (playing together) and sharing were made positively reinforcing. The opposite behavior was made aversive (resulted in loss of reinforcement for the other member as well as for the individual himself). The results of the experiment suggest that the type of behavior the individual displays in the group is a function of reinforcement conditions in the group.

An experimental study by Simpkins (1962) further contributes to an understanding of social interaction from the standpoint of reinforcement variables. The experiment shows how an individual A can effect the behavior of individual C indirectly by effecting through reinforcement the behavior of an individual B who interacts with C and whose behavior is reinforcing for C. In the experiment, A (the experimenter) manipulated the behavior of C by manipulating the behavior of B, without himself ever being in contact with C.

The experiment was conducted in the following manner. One of the subjects in each pair was the "reader." He was shown a series of sets of three words and his task was to compose a sentence using one of the three words. Each of the three words in each set was from a different class, such as "animal" words.

The other subject in the experiment was the "critic." He was instructed to comment upon each of the reader's sentences. He was limited to one of two comments (responses) for each sentence, either THAT'S A GOOD ONE or THAT'S A BAD ONE.

Both subjects were aware of the participation of the other and were told that they were competing for points in the task. The points may be considered to be the reinforcers operating in the experiment. Neither was told how the other subject was to get points, only the circumstances under which he would get points. The reader was told his points depended upon whether the critic stated that his sentences were good or bad (he gained one point if the sentence was called GOOD and lost one when it was called BAD). The critic's score was obtained in a somewhat more complicated manner; however, essentially he gained a point when he said GOOD following a sentence of the reader that used one of the particular class of words from the set which the experimenter had previously decided was "correct." That is, the experimenter reinforced the critic-subject if *he* reinforced the reader-subject for using the class of words previously decided upon by the experimenter.

The results indicated that it was possible to condition one subject (the critic) to condition another subject (the reader) in the manner desired by the experimenter. This study seems to be an experimental analogue for leadership situations in which the leader does not have face-to-face contact with some of his followers; where he manipulates the behavior of "lieutenants" or "disciples" who do have contact with the followers. Many life situations of large group interaction probably involve such principles.

Reinforcing Value of Members of the Group

In the preceding section the way in which the individual's behavior may be reinforcing and thus affect group phenomena was described. In addition, it seems that as a static object the individual may gain reinforcement value and this variable may itself affect social interaction.

For example, when an individual has aversive properties for others, behavior that "escapes" the presence of the aversive individual will be negatively reinforced. In essence, the individual as a physical stimulus will serve to strengthen behavior of others which in effect removes him from their presence.

On the other hand, when an individual has become a positive reinforcer for others, behavior that is followed by the presence of the individual will increase in probability of occurrence. Thus, associating with the positively reinforcing individual will be reinforced.

The reinforcing value of the individuals in a group may thus be considered to effect the extent to which these individuals tend either to "cluster" or to "escape" from one another. The characteristic of groups in terms of the members tending to "hang together," or to "attract" each other has been dealt with widely in social psychology under the label of "group cohesiveness."

> One of the key concepts, which has been the subject of much experimental investigation, is that of *cohesiveness*. Intuitively, cohesiveness refers to the forces which bind the parts of a group together and which, thus, resist disruptive influences. Hence, the study of conditions affecting group cohesiveness and of the effects upon group functioning of variations in group cohesiveness is at the heart of the study of group life (Deutsch, 1954, pp. 214–215).

Thus, cohesiveness refers to the general degree of "attractiveness" of a group for its members. Such a definition, however, serves to provoke the important question, "how?" What are the processes through which group activities and other members operate to keep an individual in a group? A series of studies by Lott and Lott (1960) are addressed to answering this question within a general S–R framework. They suggest the following principles to account for the attractiveness of a group for its members.

1. Persons may be conceptualized as . . . stimuli to which responses may be learned.
2. A person who experiences reinforcement or reward for some behavior will react to the reward . . . [in the terms used in this book, we might say that a positive evaluative response will be elicited—see Chapters 4 and 5].
3. This response to reward will become conditioned, like any other response, to all . . . stimuli present at the time of reinforcement (p. 298).

On the basis of these premises, it would be expected that a person (group member) who is present at the time another individual is rewarded will in a later situation elicit this positive evaluative response. We would simply state, within our framework, that the group member becomes a conditioned reinforcer through the principles of respondent conditioning, eliciting the response previously associated only with the reward. Thus, the primary condition underlying the formulation is the receipt of reinforcement in one another's presence.

On the basis of this analysis, Lott and Lott generated an experiment to study the possibility that members of a group who are rewarded in the presence of their fellow group members will more likely develop an attraction toward those individuals than will members of such groups who are not rewarded.

Prior to the experiment, each child was asked to select two other classmates with whom he would prefer to travel, or to whom he would like to return if he were to go on an extended trip. On the basis of the responses, groups of three children were formed so that a group was made up of children who had not chosen each other. A game was then introduced to be played in the group of three. The objective was to land a "rocket ship" on a planetary objective. By having the children take turns, the experimenters arranged to have some children succeed and others fail in the task. Half of the children were permitted to succeed, while half were prevented. Some time after the game was played the children were again asked to select two others with whom they would care to take a long trip. The results of this last test indicated that the reinforced or successful subjects chose a significantly higher proportion of the others with whom they had played the game than did the nonreinforced subjects. In terms of cohesiveness, the subjects reinforced in the presence of others showed greater "attraction" to the other members of the group than did nonreinforced subjects. It might be said that for the reinforced subjects the other group members had become secondary reinforcers by coming to elicit the positive evaluative responses. This did not occur for the nonreinforced subjects.

Many studies have also produced results which support the conception that the behavioral principle involved in group cohesiveness is the acquisition of reinforcement value by the members of the group as a consequence of the receipt of positive reinforcement within the group. Thibaut (1950) has shown that "cohesiveness" is produced to a greater extent in a high-status group than in a low-status group; in the present terms a high-status group may be considered to be one which receives more conditioned positive reinforcers of various kinds. Schachter (1951) produced higher cohesiveness in groups formed of members expressing high interest in their activities than in groups formed of members expressing low interest; when "interest" in an activity is considered in terms of the reinforcing value of the activity, it can be seen that the high-interest group is the group experiencing the greatest reinforcement, and its members should become conditioned reinforcers for one another. French (1941) found that groups of higher cohesiveness were formed from individuals who had played together on athletic teams versus groups formed of unacquainted subjects; again, individuals who have "played" together have experienced positive reinforcement in each other's presence and would be expected to become conditioned reinforcers. Back (1951) found that he could produce higher cohesiveness by verbal means, that is, by stressing to the subjects how much they would like each other, by stressing the importance of the task, or the "prestige" of the group. All these procedures appear to involve the application of verbal reinforcers in the presence of the group, thus making the individuals conditioned reinforcers for one another by verbal means.

Homans (1961) also has pointed out in making a learning analysis of social interaction that frequency of interaction is a variable which is related to "liking," or cohesiveness. "That is, Person's liking for Other varies directly as the frequency of his interaction with him" (p. 182). This occurs, Homans states, because sheer interaction provides an opportunity for group members to experience positive reinforcement in each other's presence.

On the other hand, at the beginning of this section it was pointed out that when an individual as a physical stimulus has aversive properties, the response of avoiding him will be reinforced in other persons. In terms of group interaction, it also would be expected that if the members experienced aversive conditions in each other's presence they would become for each other conditioned aversive stimuli. Instead of group cohesiveness, then, they would display group "disintegration."

Thus, Homans states that although the more frequently people interact, other things being equal, the more will they become conditioned positive reinforcers for each other, there are conditions which "prevent the proposition from holding good. When a man interacts with another and the other's activity punishes him, but he is not free to break the interaction off—under this condition frequent interaction is not associated with much liking" (1961, p. 203). One way for individuals to be aversive to each other involves participation in competition for positive reinforcers. "People who compete with one another are not rewarding one another, and, therefore, except for the expression of the hostility itself, their frequency of inter-action will be low unless the form of competition requires interaction. . . . As for competition between groups, it is, for the reasons already given, likely to increase the hostility members of one group express toward members of the other" (Homans, 1961, p. 144).

In conclusion, it is suggested that an important aspect of social inter-action, group cohesiveness, is the extent to which the individuals in the group elicit as stimuli, positive or negative responses in the other members of the group, or, in synonymous terms, the extent to which the individuals serve as reinforcers. As the next section will describe, the terms *positive reinforcer, positive meaning response,* and *positive attitude* may all be con-sidered to refer to the same characteristics that some stimuli possess. And the same is true of negative reinforcing stimuli.

Group Attitudes (Cohesiveness) Established by Communication

It has already been suggested that the reinforcement value of a stim-ulus can be established or changed through language. It was stated in Chapters 3, 4, and 5 that some stimuli are positive reinforcers because they elicit certain "positive meaning" responses in the individual, and that aversive stimuli have their function because they elicit "aversive mean-ing" responses in the individual. These responses may be conditioned to other stimuli, including verbal stimuli. When a word has been paired with a positive reinforcer it comes to elicit part of the same response the positive reinforcer does, and the word thereby becomes a conditioned posi-tive reinforcer. When this word is paired with other words, or other non-verbal stimuli, these also come to elicit the positive meaning response and thus acquire reinforcing value.

It has been suggested (Doob, 1947) that attitudes are implicit, mediat-ing responses. Others (Osgood and Tannenbaum, 1955; Rhine, 1958; Staats and Staats, 1958; Staats, Staats, and Heard, 1960) have considered attitudes as meaning responses that have an evaluative aspect—are either "positive" or "negative." Following this rationale, it may be suggested that the study of attitudes involves the various principles concerned with the nature of positive reinforcing stimuli and aversive stimuli, both conditioned and unconditioned. Thus, for example, a positive reinforcing stimulus may be considered as one that elicits a positive evaluative meaning response or a positive attitude.

On this basis everything that has been said about the establishment and change of conditioned reinforcers through language should apply also to attitudes. Thus, once the word BAD has through classical conditioning become a conditioned negative reinforcer, it may function to further condition the individual to negative attitudinal responses to various other stimuli. By saying NEGROES ARE BAD, for example, it would be expected that the negative meaning of BAD would be conditioned to the word NEGROES. See Figure 8.3 for a schematization of both of these conditionings.

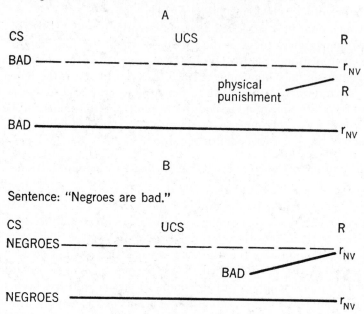

Fig. 8.3. "The diagram depicts first-order conditioning of word meaning. After a number of pairings of BAD, the CS, with punishment, the US, BAD comes to elicit the conditionable (i.e., "detachable") components of the responses elicited by the punishment (symbolized as r_{NV} because of the negative value). The components of the total response which are not stably conditioned are symbolized as R. Diagram B depicts higher-order conditioning of meaning. The negative meaning responses now elicited by BAD are conditioned to NEGROES through contiguous pairing of the two words in the sentence." (Staats, Staats, and Heard, 1960, p. 339)

That attitudes to social stimuli may be formed through this type of language conditioning was shown in an experiment by the present authors (Staats and Staats, 1958). In a classical conditioning procedure, negative meaning words were paired for some subjects with certain national names, such as DUTCH; positive meaning words were paired with another name, such as SWEDISH. For other subjects the group-name–word-class relationship was reversed; SWEDISH was paired with negative meaning words and DUTCH with positive words. Later the subjects rated the national names in terms of their pleasantness–unpleasantness. The results indicated that the subjects' attitudes had been affected by the language conditioning. The name paired with negative words was rated unpleasant, while that paired with positive words was rated pleasant.

While this conditioning applied only to the national name, it would be expected that the attitude would have generalized to a member of the national group involved—to a Dutch or Swedish person. This would be another example of mediated generalization. Thus, if the word DUTCH elicited a negative attitude response, then when a person was labeled DUTCH the negative attitude response would be elicited, mediated by the word. That such mediated generalization of attitude responses occurs has been shown by Eisman (1955) and more recently by DiVesta and Stover (1962).

The model of attitude learning developed above may be considered to account, at least in part, for the development of attitudes of individuals in a group towards each other (group cohesiveness) as well as attitudes of individuals within a group toward members of another group. That is, it is suggested that attitudes toward other people may be acquired on a purely vicarious level, through verbal means, and in the absence of any direct experience. The influence of various media of communication in the formation of attitudes, and thus group cohesiveness, seems important. (See also Chapter 7 for related discussions.)

The fact that the mass media often aid the process of learning the prevailing attitudes has been well documented. Through a procedure called "content analysis," Berelson and Salter (1946) showed that in short stories published in widely read magazines in the United States there is a substantial difference in the presentation of "Americans" as contrasted with that of minority groups or foreigners. The foreign and minority group individuals were described in terms we would consider as negative reinforcers—Italians as gangsters, Negroes as ignorant, Jews as sly and shrewd, whereas "American" was more often paired with words of positive meaning.

A number of studies of the effects of moving pictures have also suggested that exposure to such material conditions the individual. For example, in one of the first of such studies, films favorable to and films unfavorable to certain ethnic groups and other topics were shown to high-school students. Attitude questionnaires administered before and after seeing the films showed relatively large shifts toward the attitude developed by the movie (Peterson and Thurstone, 1933).

Doob (1935) has characterized propaganda as "a systematic attempt *by an interested individual (or individuals) to control the attitudes of groups of individuals . . ."* (pp. 75–76). This would suggest that certain aspects of propaganda may be considered in terms of the conditioning of attitude responses through communication. Perhaps a learning analysis could be productive in studying these aspects of propaganda. For example, a great deal of data has been gathered concerning the question in propaganda of whether a persuasive communication is more effective when it concentrates exclusively on the arguments supporting the communicator's position or when it includes some discussion of the opposing arguments. This question can be referred to the relevant principles of learning that have already been presented earlier in the book and that have shown to be effective in analyzing many of the problems of attitude development. An important principle for dealing with this immediate question is that concerning the *effect of schedule of reinforcement on the conditioning of responses.* Specifically, basic studies of human learning have shown that intermittent reinforcement results in less conditioned response acquisition than does continuous reinforcement. The way in which this principle can be shown to underlie the problem of one-sided versus two-sided propaganda arguments is demonstrated in another study of attitude acquisition by Staats, Staats, and Heard (1960). Using the procedure of the earlier studies, it was shown that the intensity of an acquired attitude is also a function of the percentage of reinforcement. A nonsense syllable was presented visually a number of times, each time paired with the auditory presentation of a different word. Three reinforcement conditions (100 per cent, 50 per cent, and 0 per cent) were employed, in which a reinforced trial consisted of a nonsense syllable paired with a word of positive or negative meaning, while a nonreinforced trial consisted of a nonsense syllable paired with a word of no systematic meaning. The results agreed with the basic research findings on the principles of conditioning, that is, attitude intensity was significantly greatest in the 100 per cent group, intermediate in the 50 per cent group (although the number of reinforced trials was equal in the two groups), and least in the 0 per cent group.

Extending the result to the propaganda question would lead to the prediction that one-sided communication (the continuous reinforcement situation where one side of a controversial issue is favored) would be more effective in developing strong attitudes than the two-sided communication (the intermittent reinforcement situation where arguments of both sides are presented).

On the other hand, it will be remembered that basic research has shown that responses acquired under intermittent reinforcement are much more resistant to extinction than are those acquired under continuously reinforcing conditions. Thus, it would be expected that, although more intense attitudes are acquired under the continuous reinforcement condition, the attitude would be more resistant to change if acquired under intermittent reinforcement. In propaganda, it would therefore be predicted that two-sided arguments (intermittent reinforcement) would lead to greater resistance to change.

Experiments on the effects of communications in the propaganda situation seem to confirm these predictions. For example, the results of Hovland, Janis, and Kelley (1953) substantiate the prediction that one-sided communication is more effective than two-sided communication in establishing strong attitudes. They conclude on the basis of a number of studies that one-sided communication presenting only positive arguments will tend to sway the audience farther in the direction advocated by the communicator than will two-sided communication.

In another study, analogous to the intermittent reinforcement situation, Lumsdaine and Janis (1953) found that a two-sided communication was markedly more effective than a one-sided argument when the audience was subsequently exposed to counterpropaganda; that is to say, attitudes learned in this way were more difficult to change. This would confirm the hypothesis that attitudes learned under intermittent reinforcement should be more resistant to extinction.

The Discriminative Function of Attitudes

In order to discuss more fully the importance of the study of attitudes in understanding group interaction, it is necessary to digress from the reinforcing function and return once again to the discussion of the discriminative function of reinforcers. The discriminative function was discussed, in part, in Chapter 7 as well as earlier in this chapter, where it was suggested that because the child is reinforced for "striving" toward positive reinforcers, positive reinforcing stimuli come generally to exert discriminative control over "striving" behaviors. Thus, it may be said that positive reinforcers customarily function also as discriminative stimuli. Actually, reinforcing stimuli may be considered to come to control a whole hierarchy of responses, including the class of "striving" responses.

Moreover, in the previous section, it was pointed out that reinforcers are stimuli which elicit positive attitudes or positive meaning responses, and they thus influence the cohesiveness of a group as well as other interactions in the group. But stimuli that elicit positive attitudes or meaning also come to control a class of word responses having positive meaning—GOOD, FINE, NICE, and so on. (See Chapter 4 for this discussion.) Thus, any stimulus that has positive reinforcing value may generally be considered to control a class of both verbal and nonverbal responses.

The same line of reasoning would apply to negative reinforcers; these stimuli would control negative meaning words, as well as nonverbal responses that would remove oneself from the presence of the negative reinforcer, or remove the negative reinforcer. Thus, ordinarily it may be assumed that a person learns a hierarchy of responses to people who are negative reinforcing stimuli. He learns to escape or avoid them and the things they say and do, by various means; by arguing, by castigating, by running away, by attacking, and so on.

It is also suggested that it is because we learn hierarchies of verbal and nonverbal responses to reinforcers that attitude tests (observations of verbal behavior) may be used to predict actual behavior toward an object. The R–R law between an attitude test score and some other behavior is then simply a result of the fact that both are under the control of the same attitude. A positive evaluative response to one political party should control, for example, both obtaining a score toward one extreme on a scale of attitudes toward the party and voting for the candidates of that party. The test is then said to be predictive of the actual overt behavior, but it would be more correct to say that the two overt behaviors (answering the items on the attitude scale and voting) are both a result of the single attitude response elicited by the political party, and this a result of the conditioning history.

In certain cases, of course, a person could have acquired verbal behaviors that did not "agree" with the nonverbal behaviors he had learned. In this case the score obtained on the attitude test would seem to be unrelated to the other overt behavior. Another and more common reason for an apparent discrepancy between the way an individual talks (or how he responds on an attitude test) and how he acts, may be the introduction into the situation of additional stimuli that are also related to the overt behavior. A negative attitude towards one political party might for one individual control the behavior of tearing down the billboards advertising that party. Should a policeman be standing nearby, however, the overt behavior of the same person might well be quite different. The policeman is an S^D for behavior incompatible with that normally elicited by the attitude.

At any rate, it can be seen that many significant social behaviors may be considered to be under the control of the reinforcing value of stimuli, or, in other terms, of the attitude response elicited by the stimuli.

LEARNING PRINCIPLES AND CULTURE

The previous sections have dealt with attempts to extend learning principles to some of the complex phenomena of social behavior. Other investigators have applied learning concepts in dealing with additional social phenomena. For example, Davis and Havighurst (1947) have discussed the differences between social classes in terms of S–R reinforcement principles. Whiting and Child (1953) have utilized learning principles in an analysis of differences in training methods by different cultures and the effects of this training upon characteristic behaviors in the culture. Bachrach (1962) has made an analysis of superstitious and ritual behaviors in terms of reinforcement principles. Gillen (1948) and Miller and Dollard (1941) have integrated learning principles into discussions of other anthropological problems. Sears (1951) has analyzed two-person interactions in terms of learning principles and suggests that such an analysis can serve as a basis from which to consider all social interaction and personality development.

Skinner (1953) suggests that even the most complex aspects of human affairs (including some of the types of social interaction already discussed) are to be understood in terms of reinforcement principles. Thus, he describes various social institutions, such as education, religion, and government, as mechanisms for the control of human behavior through the application of aversive stimuli and positive reinforcers. Skinner considers culture for the individual to be "[i]n the broadest . . . sense . . . all the variables affecting him which are arranged by other people" (p. 419).

Elaborating upon this, we might assume that learning variables would be operative in two ways in this process. The behavior of the person arranging the variables for others would have been learned, and as he imposes these variables upon others (perhaps especially upon children) they would result in learning. In the same way that culture transmission may be considered to occur through learning variables, it might be supposed that changes in cultures are also a resultant of learning variables, as Skinner (1959) has suggested in abbreviated form.

The slaves in a quarry cutting stone for a pyramid work to escape punishment or death, and the rising pyramid is sufficiently reinforcing to the reigning Pharaoh to induce him to devote part of his wealth to maintaining the forces which punish or kill. An employer pays sufficient wages to induce men to work for him, and the products of their labor reimburse him, let us say, with a great deal to spare. These are on-going social systems, but in thus analyzing them we may not have taken everything into account. The system may be altered by outsiders in whom sympathy with, or fear of, the lot of the slave or exploited worker may be generated. More important, perhaps, is the possibility that the system may not actually be in equilibrium. It may breed changes which lead to its destruction. Control through punishment may lead to increasing viciousness, with an eventual loss of the support of those needed to maintain it; and the increasing poverty of the worker and the resulting increase in the economic power of the employer may also lead to countercontrolling action (p. 36.07).

We change our cultural practices because it is in our nature as men to be reinforced in certain ways (p. 36.11).

Thus, it might be expected that the extent to which a social event is positively reinforcing or aversive will affect its stability as a cultural practice. In addition, Skinner suggests that cultures may be compared to one another on the basis of reinforcement principles.

> We have seen that in certain respects operant reinforcement resembles the natural selection of evolutionary theory. Just as genetic characteristics which arise as mutations are selected or discarded by their consequences, so novel forms of behavior are selected or discarded through reinforcement. There is still a third kind of selection which applies to cultural practices. A group adopts a given practice—a custom, a manner, a controlling device—either by design or through some event which, so far as its effect upon the group is concerned, may be wholly accidental. As a characteristic of the social environment this practice modifies the behavior of members of the group. The resulting behavior may affect the success of the group in competition with other groups or with the nonsocial environment. Cultural practices which are advantageous will tend to be characteristic of the groups which survive and which therefore perpetuate those practices. Some cultural practices may therefore be said to have survival value, while others are lethal in the genetic sense (1953, p. 430).

In addition, it might be suggested that where two behaviors (two cultural practices) were extant side by side, if one resulted in much greater reinforcement for the individuals involved than did the other, it would produce much stronger and more vigorous "striving" and "maintaining" behavior with respect to the practice. In this manner, in many situations of conflict, the more reinforcing cultural practice—or even culture—might be expected to survive, or to "win out" over the other in terms both of the number of its adherents and of the strength of their "supporting" behavior. (See the discussion of the evolution of scientific methods in Chapter 5 for a more specific example of cultural change in terms of reinforcement principles.)

If certain cultural practices lead to greater "satisfaction" in man, as well as to greater survival value of the practice, and if these events are determined according to the principles of reinforcement, then an understanding of those principles should enable man to design cultural practices that meet behavioral criteria. Perhaps more propitious conditions for man could be arranged by consideration of the principles of man's behavior and of the conditions which would produce more desirable behaviors. Skinner (1953) suggests that this is indeed the case and that advantageous cultural practices could be arrived at by design.

Why should the design of a culture be left so largely to accident? Is it not possible to change the social environment deliberately so that the human product will meet more acceptable specifications?

In many cultural groups we observe practices which might be described as "making changes in practice." The great religious books supply many examples of the deliberate construction of a social environment. The Ten Commandments were a codification of existing and proposed practices according to which, henceforth, behavior was to be reinforced or punished by the group or by the religious agency. The teachings of Christ were more clearly in the nature of a new design. In governmental control, the enactment of a law usually establishes new cultural practices, and a constitution is a similar undertaking on a broader scale. Experimental curricula in schools and colleges and books on child care which recommend substantial changes in family practices are attempts to manipulate important parts of a culture. The social environment is changed to some extent when a new technique of psychotherapy is derived from a theory or from an experimental study of human behavior. Social legislation creates an experimental environment in which behavior is more often reinforced with food, clothing, housing, and so on, and in which certain kinds of deprivation are less likely to occur. Planning the structure of a large industry or governmental agency is an experiment in cultural design. These are all examples of the manipulation of small parts of the social environment; what is called "Utopian" thinking embraces the design of a culture as a whole (pp. 426–427).

When we speak of the "deliberate" design of a culture, we mean the introduction of a cultural practice "for the sake of its consequences" (p. 428).

Skinner's approach suggests, however, that our culture's most accepted practices and cherished beliefs be reviewed in the light of the principles of learning and the methodology of a scientific psychology. Involved in this, it might be added, is a "general conception of the nature of man," or a "philosophy of man's behavior." As such it might be expected that considerable opposition would be engendered by such a suggestion. Not only are different conceptions of man deeply rooted and strongly held in our culture, but many of our dearly valued practices for dealing with problems of behavior are mediated by the conceptions. However, to the extent that cultural practices are formulated on the basis of an inadequate conception of man and man's behavior, it might be expected that more advantageous practices could stem from an improved conception.

It seems evident, however, that acceptance of a conception of man in terms of learning principles, as well as the utility of the conception in designing a culture, will require a more complete behavioral analysis of social and cultural practices, and of man's complex behavior in general, than has been available. The development and change of significant human behaviors will have to be treated systematically, and the science of behavior extended in greater detail to see if the statements that spring from a learning analysis check with the naturalistic observations collected throughout the history of man. At present, the suggestion to design a culture in terms of behavior principles and experimental methods can only be considered programmatic, a suggestion that the foundation be laid through the extension of laboratory principles to analyses of complex human behaviors.

Such analyses might appear to be to a large extent the job of social theorists and other behavioral scientists—anthropologists, sociologists, historians, economists, and so on. The use of psychological conceptions of man by other social scientists is not unusual today. Much of the work done in other behavioral sciences is based upon a "psychology," a conception of man's behavior. For example, much of anthropology in recent years has utilized psychoanalytic terms and principles in an approach to many problems of analysis. As yet, however, an integrated set of learning principles has not been comprehensively applied in the various fields of social science. It is suggested that a learning conception of human behavior is now available for this purpose.

A program of behavioral analyses of complex human practices would not necessarily imply experimentation. It might be expected that experimentation would lag considerably behind theoretical extensions of behavior principles to formulate a general conception of man. Behavioral analyses might instead be judged by their ability to incorporate naturalistic observations. Many psychologists tend to be opposed to such extrapolations, which go far beyond their laboratory support. It is only fair to say, however, that *any* general conception of man we adopt must now be accepted without direct experimental support of its more complex aspects. No currently available conception of man's behavior in its broader social phases is based upon actual experimentation. Our most widely accepted conceptions of man were founded under much less stringent standards than those of learning principles. Perhaps the closest one can get at this time to a scientific conception of man is through the type of approach under discussion, in which basic principles are anchored in the laboratory, as well as through some laboratory extensions to complex human behavior, but where major extensions are made to encompass naturalistic observations.

After an acceptable analysis has been made to produce a conception of man's cultural behavior in terms of behavior principles, the propositions involved might be subjected to empirical test—albeit, perhaps, not laboratory test. Skinner suggests that an experimental orientation is perhaps the most important contribution the methods and principles of learning can make to designing a culture.

> Perhaps the greatest contribution which a science of behavior may make to the evaluation of cultural practices is an insistence upon experi-

mentation. We have no reason to suppose that any cultural practice is always right or wrong according to some principle or value regardless of the circumstances or that anyone can at any given time make an absolute evaluation of its survival value. So long as this is recognized, we are less likely to seize upon the hard and fast answer as an escape from indecision, and we are more likely to continue to modify cultural design in order to test the consequences (1953, p. 436).

9

Child Development
and Training

EVEN THE most casual observation reveals the marked changes in behavior that occur in the course of any individual's personal history. He goes from an organism with an extremely limited response repertoire to an organism that responds in exceedingly complex and detailed ways.

As might be expected, there have been many attempts to account for this progression in the behavioral repertoire as a function of age. It is important to describe briefly a few of the relatively contemporary interpretations of behavior development; first because they are important systems of thought about human behavior, but also because they point out some of the topics of development that must be handled within the system of principles presented in this book. To a large extent Chapters 4 through 8, as well as those to follow, include material that is part of a psychology of child development. However, there are additional forms of behavior not yet covered that are important to this topic.

SOME THEORIES OF DEVELOPMENT

Psychoanalytic

Freud was one of the first systematists to be interested in the effects of early events upon human development. He attributed paramount importance to these early experiences, discussing their effects upon the "personality" and "character" of the individual. Actually, Freud thought of the personality and character structures as the resultants of the impact of the child's experiences upon the progressively changing internal instinctual sources of energy. In general terms, many psychoanalytic theorists today conceive of development as an instinctual unfolding that is influenced markedly by external occurrences.

This instinctual psychological development is thought to take place in stages. The principal instinctual investments of energy occur first in certain organs and then later in others. Depending upon how the child is treated in these stages the energy will either flow normally from one organ system to another, or be "fixated" at one stage, crystallizing the character of the individual at that level.

The first hypothetical stage is the "oral," when the primary energy investment is in the mouth. This stage lasts for about a year, during which satisfaction of the child's instinctive energy impulses comes from oral activities through the feeding process. Either from overindulgences or from deprivation, the child may fixate at this level of development and the extent to which he is so fixated will determine the later primacy of oral energy —that is, oral needs. The behavior thought to result from deprivation of oral satisfaction includes greediness, verbal aggression, and depressions; while "dependence" and insecurity mark the behavior of the orally overindulged. Actually, a large investment in oral impulses is thought to result in a wide variety of character structures.

In the "anal" stage the instinctual energies shift to the anal regions of the body and satisfaction is then attained through eliminative activities. The instincts will be differently affected and produce different behaviors, depending upon how these activities are handled and how toilet training is pursued. For example, if the child is too strictly treated the energies may be "fixated" at the anal stage and his character so shaped that his behavior would typically be excessively dependent, methodical, neat, and stingy. Or the child might express his resentment at the harsh treatment by later "blow ups" in different destructive ways.

After about a year at this stage, the child passes into the next stage of development—the "phallic"—in which the genital regions receive the heaviest investment of instinctual energy. Stimulation of the genitalia satisfy the impulses of this instinct. At this time a process described as the "development of the Oedipal complex" is thought to occur; the mother becomes the object of the instinct for the boy, and the father becomes the competitor for the mother's affections. (The opposite relationships are thought to occur between the girl and her father.) Depending upon how this Oedipal situation is handled, the child's sexual behavior is determined. If the Oedipal conflict is successfully resolved the child identifies with the parent of the same sex and acquires a superego with inhibitions concerning incest, and so on. If the child is fixated at this stage, later sexual aberrations —including homosexuality, frigidity, and impotence—are thought to be in store.

After a period of inactivity in development, in pubescence, the last developmental stage, the "genital" occurs. During this stage the instinctual energies become directed toward bodies of other individuals. Thus, the individual becomes interested in other activities and objects that will be important in his adjustment to adult life, acquires the capacity for loving others, doing things unselfishly, and so on.

The type of person the individual finally becomes, according to this view, depends upon the manner in which the various stages are traversed. Thus, Freud assumed that the internal biological energy forces which undergo a complex development in interaction with parents and siblings affect the most complex behaviors of the individual.

Freud's interpretations were an extremely important step forward in many respects. In addition to his many insightful observations of behavior, he suggested that the early environmental experiences of the child influenced later behavior in certain lawful ways. As a philosophy of behavior the theory led to concern about the experiences of the child. But perhaps even more important, the approach was consistent with a scientific causality in that the events of behavior were seen as determined by other natural events. This aspect of the theory has had great impact upon attempts to understand human behavior.

While recognizing the great contributions, it may be argued that the approach suffered from its circular instinctual theories, as was shown for other examples of such terms in Chapter 2. In addition, the explanations of the important behaviors were inadequate in terms of the specification of determining events; the importance of the principles by which environmental events effect behavior, the principles of learning, was never recognized. More importantly, perhaps, psychoanalytic theory, based upon a clinical method the limitations of which have already been described, had no explicit, built-in procedures for correcting its inadequacies. As a result, progress in the development of psychoanalytic theory has not been so great as the original advance might have led one to expect.

Self-actualization

Another philosophy of human development is offered by a number of theorists in the areas of abnormal and clinical psychology (such as Maslow, 1954; Rogers, 1951; Snygg and Combs, 1949), who also suggest internal forces as determinants of behavior. These theorists argue in addition, however, that the forces are beneficent; left alone to unfold in their natural benign way they would result in healthy, normal, and desirable behavior. In contrast, the maladjustments of behavior are seen as the effects of an interfering and evil environment. If these negative events could be eliminated, the growth forces would unfold in their naturally beneficial way. The following quotation from Maslow (1954) illustrates the approach.

First of all and most important of all is the strong belief that man has an essential nature of his own, some skeleton of psychological structure that may be treated and discussed analogously with his physical structure, that he has needs, capacities and tendencies that are genetically based, some of which are characteristic of the whole human species, cutting across all cultural lines, and some of which are unique to the individual. These needs are on their face good or neutral rather than evil. Second, there is involved the conception that full healthy and normal and desirable development consists in actualizing this nature, in fulfilling these potentialities, and in developing into maturity along the lines that this hidden, covert, dimly seen essential nature dictates, growing from within rather than being shaped from without. Third, it is now seen clearly that psychopathology in general results from the denial or the frustration or the twisting of man's essential nature. By this conception what is good? Anything that conduces to this desirable development in the direction of actualization of the inner nature of man. What is bad or abnormal? Anything that frustrates or blocks or denies the essential nature of man. What is psychopathological: Anything that disturbs or frustrates or twists the course of self-actualization. What is psychotherapy, or for that matter any therapy of any kind? Any means of any kind that helps to restore the person to the path of self-actualization and of development along the lines that his inner nature dictates (pp. 340–341).

Thus, this philosophy suggests that environmental events can either impede or facilitate the inner development which determines man's behavior. On the whole, however, because the approach emphasizes the genetic nature of man and the importance of actualizing this nature, it tends to deny the importance of environmental variables in shaping behavior. The result is a diminished interest in a systematic examination of the principles by which environmental conditions have their effect. In contrast, from the present orientation the term "self," as discussed in Chapter 6, refers to learned behavior acquired according to the principles of learning.

Maturation

The next approach to be discussed is similar to the previous one, but it derives from extensive controlled observations and experimental evidence rather than from clinical observations. In general, however, its major conceptual interest is also in inferred inner processes.

This conception of human behavior development has led to a wide number of observations that have contributed greatly to a practical understanding of child behavior by parents, educators, pediatricians, and so on. In this view, age is the most important dimension, and the observations are primarily of the types of behavior that characterize a particular age level. From these observations, the nature of internal maturational processes is inferred.

For example, Gesell indicates the consistency in the appearance of supine behavior patterns by such observations as (1) nearly 100 percent of four-week-old children evidence predominance of head rotation, (2) nearly 80 percent of twenty-eight-week-old children have their hands predominantly open, and (3) about 30 percent of twenty-week-old children mutually finger their hands (1954, p. 350).

Developmental norms are available for a wide range of ages. As an illustration, the following behaviors are described as characteristic of nine-month-old children: sits alone, raises self by chair, walks with help (ten months), creeps (ten months), says DA–DA or its equivalent, waves bye-bye (Kimble, 1956, p. 180).

Some investigations have focused on the progressive changes in some behavior across age. The example of supine behavior above illustrates this approach. As another example, it has been found that there is considerable "stability" in the "IQ." That is, observations of the child's behavior on intelligence tests over a period of years indicate that his score remains in about the same relationship to other children's scores (Bayley, 1940a, 1940b; Honzik, 1938).

It is these sorts of data which have led to the inference that an internal developmental process of some kind must be the underlying determinant.

> The conclusion to be drawn from such data is that there is considerable stability of the individual patterns of development. Certainly the consistency is sufficiently marked that it must be explained by any theory of development. . . . This conformity in the development of children is the most solid basis for the assumption of a maturational process. The growth of the abilities of the child seems—to some extent at least—an unfolding of innate potentialities. Such consistency of development is very difficult to explain in terms of the child's experience . . . (Baldwin, 1955, p. 368).

In terms of the principles discussed in this book, such a conclusion does not seem warranted; the absence of an explanation of a behavior in learning terms cannot be used as evidence that the behavior is due to an internal development.

In any event, however, the actual observation and description of child behavior has made a most important contribution, yielding very useful knowledge and practical understanding. For example, most pediatricians today consult the work of these investigators when they look at charts or norms describing some of the behaviors displayed by children of a certain age. A mother worried about the progress of her child in acquiring behavior may consult a pediatrician or child psychologist and discover that the behavior of her child either is, or is not, what would be expected on the basis of wide and systematic observations of other children of the same age. If a problem exists, perhaps certain steps can be taken to meet it. Or, in other cases, unnecessary anxiety may be allayed and steps that might be inimicable to the child's welfare can be prevented.

This use of the observations of child behavioral development follows the logic described in Chapter 2: that simple observation and description may allow prediction of the individual case from a knowledge of the general class. In the above example, the general class is a description of the behavior that occurs in a certain age group. The individual case is the description of the behavior of the individual child. From comparing the two descriptions, it is possible to ascertain whether or not the individual case can be considered to be a member of the general class. Then, on the basis of this comparison, predictions about future development may be made.

Intelligence tests (and other tests) may also be considered to be quantified observations that permit a general description of a class of behavior. Thus, the test given to a representative (or random) sample of children (of various ages) produces a description of the general class of behaviors of the children on the test for each of the different ages. Then the behavior of the individual child on the test can be compared to the description of the general class, and a quantified comparison of the individual case with the general case may again result.

On the other hand, it must be remembered that simple description does not constitute explanation. Observation of how the individual's intelligence score relates to the general class does not explain either the observation of the individual or that of the general class. Nor does the observation that most children develop in a certain fashion—first creep, then crawl, then walk, then run—justify the inference of some inner maturational process to explain the progression. To make an explanatory statement of this type it would be necessary to observe the inner processes independently. Such a statement relating the two independently observed events could then perhaps lead to more refined prediction as well as potential control of the behavior involved. Without the independent observations of maturational processes, however, the explanatory statement is only circular, and may even be misleading by suggesting that the behavioral event has been accounted for.

Thus, the importance and utility of such observation and description of behavioral development should be distinguished from the approach of using the data to *explain* the development of behavior. Although the observations of behavior form an important source of information, they do not provide an explanation and, consequently, do not offer the possibility of the control of the behavior. Thus, a mother who is told that the behavior of her child is behind that of other children of that age (that her child is retarded) has no information by which to change the child's behavior.

In addition to simple observation and description of behavior, other types of evidence have been offered as support for the maturational conception of the development of behavior. One type of experiment that bears upon this interpretation has been conducted with lower animals to indicate the relative importance of nonlearning factors in the acquisition of behavior. For example, Carmichael (1926) showed that tadpoles prevented from gaining any experience in swimming (through the use of a depressant drug) swam as well after the drug had worn off as tadpoles of the same age with experience in swimming. Such findings have been thought to suggest that man's behavior also would develop without training experiences. This generalization has a major flaw, however, as the following example will show. When the eye of a frog is surgically rotated, or its eye transplanted to the other side of the head, the frog continues to respond as though the eye were in its original position. No learning takes place (Sperry, 1951). On the other hand, when Stratton (1897) performed an experiment in which the same type of optic change was induced by means of lenses in humans, appropriate responding to the new stimulus conditions was learned (Kimble, 1956).

Thus, interpretations that learning is relatively unimportant in the development of man's behavior, based upon experiments showing that a specific behavior in a lower organism is not altered by experience, do not seem justified. Although the principles of learning appear the same from lower species to man, learning appears to be much more important in the repertoire of behaviors displayed in man. "The higher one goes in the phylogenetic scale, the more behavior depends upon learning, and consequently the more modifiable it is" (Kimble, 1956, p. 173).

Studies with human subjects have also been designed to ascertain the comparative importance of learning and nonlearning factors.

Another type of study that has given convincing evidence of some predetermination of development is called the method of *co-twin control*. Gesell and Thompson (1929), for example, studied the modifiability of developmental patterns by giving one of a pair of identical twins special training on such activities as climbing stairs and building structures with cubes. Twin T (for trained) was given daily practice over a six-week period, whereas the control twin C was given no opportunity to practice these activities. After T had been trained for six weeks, C was then given two weeks' training. The results of this study are typical of others also. When C was first allowed to perform any of the activities in which T was trained, she did better than T had done on her first attempt six weeks earlier but not as well as T was doing at the moment. In the two-week period of delayed training, C improved almost as much as T had in six weeks . . . (Baldwin, 1955, pp. 385–386).

The results are interpreted as demonstrating the relatively minor role of training as compared to maturation. Fowler (1962), however, concludes after reviewing this and other studies that, "Often underplayed . . . is the fact that specific training has invariably produced large gains, regardless of whether training came early or late in development" (p. 118). He continues with the following argument.

In addition, partly as a result of the maturational bias, there have frequently been methodological shortcomings. These have further lessened awareness of the influence of experience upon development. In the first place, most studies have dealt with simpler skills for which there is evidence of ability "ceilings" or physiological limits. For example, in Hilgard's (1932) experiment on teaching 10 2–3 year old children buttoning, climbing, and cutting with scissors, the experimental children's learning curve tended to fall off toward the end of their 12-week training program. Such a ceiling limits the relative advantage possible from longer training (p. 118).

Fowler also points out that the control children in such studies are customarily exposed to a certain amount of training in their natural environments during the time the twin is undergoing the experimental program, as well as prior to that time. "It appears, then, that maturation and general experience have been confounded" (p. 119). He concludes that the importance of this training has been generally underestimated.

In addition to such studies of motor-behavior development, studies of language behaviors have been conducted to demonstrate the relative contribution of maturation and training. It has been found for example, that while children trained in repeating a series of digits improved somewhat over a control group of children, after a period of nonpractice the differences between the groups disappeared (Gates and Taylor, 1925). This type of evidence cannot be interpreted as demonstrating that learning is unimportant, however. If the experiment had included training of skilled behaviors, which then permitted training of a later skill to successfully take place, and this training in turn provided the basis for additional learning, then important effects of the training could perhaps be traced. In contrast, the experiment involved, on the one hand, behavior that cannot be much affected by training; and on the other, the experimenter did not continue to reinforce the behavior in his experimental subjects. It would be expected that under such conditions of nonreinforcement, the behavior would not be maintained at its experimental level.

As another example, Strayer (1930), using the co-twin control method, first trained one twin (eighty-four weeks old) for a period of four weeks on word–object associations and word usage. At the end of this period the second twin was given the same training. The results showed that the second twin learned a few more words than the first in the training period —a result which could be interpreted as due to the greater "maturational" development of the second. However, closer scrutiny shows that the results are actually not unequivocal, for example, the total vocabulary at the end of the period was slightly larger for the twin trained first.

However, the defect in the experimental design is obvious; there was still opportunity for learning by the second twin during his control period. In addition, the progress of both twins was clearly associated with their training. Most importantly, however, as in many of these studies, the training periods were far too brief to produce the profound differences in language behavior produced by normally lengthy language training (Fowler, 1962).

Fowler has reviewed a number of studies concerned with the development of various aspects of behavior, such as mathematical behavior and reading, and draws the following conclusions regarding the maturational approach and the various observations that have been used to support the interpretation:

> In research, this view has led to a concentration on empirical studies organized cross-sectionally for collecting normative data. For the most part, these norms have been linked sequentially to chronological age levels. . . . The use of longitudinal studies has been, logically, an important additional derivative of this view. But a maturationally oriented developmental framework has so dominated long range investigations made under its jurisdiction, as to cloud evidence which might have led to alternate conclusions. In addition, there are other important research errors and orientations which have tended to feed this bias. These include the frequent omission of adequate controls; the experimental fusion of variables; an emphasis on sensory-motor and social-emotional development to the relative exclusion of complex, perceptual-cognitive processes; and, above all, the simple omission of (antecedent) experiential data.
>
> An important group of better controlled studies has probed the maturation versus learning issue. These studies have, in the main, continued subordinate to maturationally oriented hypotheses; have failed to separate general experience from maturation; and have too often designed training programs with only simple material and/or have covered too short a time span. These limitations have aborted opportunities for impressive gains to accrue in cognitive learning (1962, p. 143).

As Fowler indicates, there have been all too few experiments, from whatever orientation, that have dealt with the learning of complex behaviors over an adequate period of time. Although there is a vast store of well-controlled studies of learning in lower animals and men, many more studies of learning of complex behaviors in children must be conducted. The possibility of conducting research on the acquisition of complex behavior, while maintaining the precision of laboratory experimentation, will be discussed in Chapter 10. At this point, however, it must be stated that the type of evidence collected to verify maturational hypotheses does not justify either the conclusion that learning variables are not important in the development of human behavior, or the conclusion that there are maturational processes which have a major effect upon the development of complex human behavior.

In any event, there are so many studies with both humans and animals which indicate the significant effects on behavior which can be produced by manipulation of learning variables that it is impossible to ignore the importance of experience. Naturalistic observations corroborate this. Studies which attempt to indicate negligible effects of experience on language behavior development, for example, are more than countermanded by such simple observations as the fact that children raised in France speak French, children raised in Turkey speak Turkish, and so on.

Maturational concepts have been discussed in such detail because the philosophy of developmental processes has significant practical implications. Acceptance of the view that the development of behavior is internally determined directs one's attention away from the environmental events involved, whether one is a behavioral scientist, a parent, a teacher, or a medical or psychological practitioner. Since internal maturational processes cannot be reached and manipulated, this philosophy may lead one to take a passive attitude toward the development of the child's behavior. For example, the parent who has this conception will tend to wait passively until a "developmental stage" is attained or passes. Or the parent may be loving and accepting toward anything the child does, believing that the behavior springs from the child's inner developing nature and that the only thing he can contribute is a general atmosphere conducive to this growth. Similarly, the educator who observes that a child's behavior is severely retarded may conclude simply on the basis of the behavior that defective internal processes of some kind are involved when actually the child's behavior is a function of impoverished training conditions.

It is suggested that these are but examples of unfortunate derivations of a maturational approach to behavior development. Even if environmental events did not account for tremendously significant aspects of human behavior, but were of lesser import, it would still be worthwhile to systematically study the "minor" effects of these events on behavior. Only when the principles have been established would the parent, educator, or practitioner be able to make the most benign use of these environmental conditions, in other words, to manipulate the conditions so that they have maximal effect upon the adjustive behavior of the child or adult. Since there is evidence that indicates the great importance of environmental occurrences, systematic specification of the relevant principles is *essential* in solving some of the problems in the relationships among people, child and adult.

A BEHAVIORAL CONCEPTION
OF CHILD DEVELOPMENT

It must first be stated that the present approach does not deny the importance of individual, biologically based, differences among men. Certainly persons vary in strength, in speed, and so on, as a result of biological variables. It is quite likely, moreover, that such variables play an important role in learning. Thus, the rate of behavior acquisition under identical circumstances is likely to differ among individuals. As a result, two organisms who differ in this rate would be expected to develop repertoires different in complexity if they were presented with the same environmental circumstances, provided each was allowed to move at his own speed. Or, as another example, the same stimulus may have somewhat different reinforcing effects upon various individuals; for example, withdrawal of an aversive stimulus may not have as great a reinforcing effect for one individual as for another. There might possibly also be specific behaviors that have biological determinants. However, before any statements concerning such hypothetical biological contributions to behavior can be useful in prediction and control of behavior, independent observation of the biological determinants must be made and related to behavior. All the research possible should be encouraged in this area. However, inference that internal maturational processes are involved does not provide such information.

Moreover, in view of what is known about how behavior can be conditioned, it would seem that even some possibly biologically based differences in behavior could be affected by training variables. As has been discussed earlier, the rate of acquisition of behavior, the reinforcing value of a stimulus, the speed and strength of an individual, and so on, may all vary over wide values on the basis of training variables alone. And although the rate of learning or the value of various reinforcers, and so on, may vary for different children, the principles of learning—reinforcement, scheduling, extinction, and so on—would seem to be the same over a wide range of individual and species differences.

In addition, the specific behaviors acquired appear to be a function of one's learning history. One infant organism reacts to the same stimuli and is capable of making similar responses as other human infants; whether he becomes a socialized human adult or a criminal, for example, would seem to be a function of training.

It should be pointed out again, because of its practical implications, that whatever biological determinants of behavior exist in the child may be largely inaccessible. There are a few manipulations which can presently be made to improve individual children in this respect, such as corrective glasses and drugs to "tranquilize" the hyperactive child. When empirical laws have been established between the child's genetic parentage and the behavioral repertoire he would be able to acquire, it might also be possible to control the future behavior of the child by selecting his parents. But as yet such precise laws have not been found, and the task, in any event, is not one of picking parents but rather of doing the best with the fruit of the "choices" the parents themselves make.

Thus, at least for the present, for the intact child there is little that can be done of a biological nature to produce the important complex behaviors of the human, or even to affect such basic variables as learning rate. No one who is concerned with the problems of shaping a child into an acceptably behaving adult can rely upon the manipulation of biological factors to produce a desirable behavior of some kind, or to eliminate an undesirable one. Environmental conditions, on the other hand, are accessible and the important variations in behavior that they determine are subject to benign manipulation.

Dollard and Miller (1950), to continue, have considered child development predominantly in learning terms. In their approach, the child has at birth only a limited repertoire of responses. Development of complex adult behaviors is seen to involve the acquisition of control of responses by new stimuli, extinction of stimulus control, the development of new responses, and new reinforcers.

It is suggested that this formulation may be put in even stronger terms to state that the child learns all his socially important skills: his language, thinking, and reasoning; his reinforcing system, values, and morals; appropriate responses to complex stimuli; in short, the infinitely complex set of behaviors we term personality.

It is not possible to survey the many experiments which have extended the learning principles found with simple organisms, situations, and responses to learning in children. In general, however, the various *principles* of learning have been validated with children (see Spiker, 1960). For example, as early as 1925 it was shown by Krasnogorski that classical conditioning principles held with children. Many other studies have extended classical conditioning principles to simple behaviors of children (see, for example, Razran, 1949).

A number of studies have also demonstrated that the principles of learning determine children's behavior in a characteristic manner in operant conditioning situations. Several examples can be mentioned.

In one of the early experiments that applied operant conditioning procedures to child learning, the response of taking a ball from the bottom hole of a two-holed box and placing it into the top hole was conditioned in two groups of preschool children. Using trinkets as reinforcers, one group was placed on a continuous reinforcement schedule, the other on a variable-ratio schedule. The results indicated that the responses of those children reinforced on the variable-ratio schedule were more resistant to extinction than the responses of the children under continuous reinforcement (Bijou, 1957b).

Orlando and Bijou (1960) have shown that the principles of discrimination learning function in a somewhat more complicated operant conditioning procedure with children. The response involved in this study was a simple manipulation. In the presence of one stimulus the response was reinforced on one schedule of reinforcement while under another stimulus condition the response was reinforced on another schedule. Some of the children were on only one schedule of reinforcement, while for other children the two schedules were alternated during the experiment. The results indicated that with this procedure the stimuli could acquire sensitive control over the responding of the child; each stimulus controlled the behavior appropriate to the schedule with which it had been presented. Figure 9.1 shows the record of such stimulus control for one subject. (Further extensions of the principles of operant discrimination and scheduling in the acquisition of complex behavior in children will be discussed in Chapter 10.)

Although the types of naturalistic examples of child training to be discussed in this chapter involve more complex constellations of variables, and the behaviors have not yet been subjected to experimental investiga-

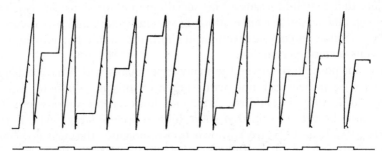

Fig. 9.1. Multiple-schedule performance of a developmentally retarded child in a lever pressing task. During one component of the schedule an edible reinforcer (piece of candy) was presented for every 100 depressions of the lever, on the average (VR100); in the other component no reinforcers were provided (extinction). The two components alternated every three minutes, as indicated by the fluctuating lower line of the graph. Delivery of a reinforcer is noted by the slash mark on the record. This record shows well-developed discrimination performance, in other words, periods of rapid responding alternate with nonresponding in accordance with the changes in the reinforcement contingencies. (Adapted from Orlando and Bijou, 1960, p. 346)

tion, the finding that learning principles hold for simple responses of children may be tentatively generalized to their more complex behaviors, as the following statement of Bijou and Baer indicates. The statement refers to the type of study just summarized.

> It would be easy to point to the artificiality of such studies and suggest that the relationships found need not be typical of child behavior in vivo. Certainly it is correct to say that few if any of a child's everyday discriminations will be formed under conditions like those established in the laboratory. Real life discriminations are not made to such regular alternations of stimuli, the cues and the responses are more variable and more complex, the reinforcers differ from occasion to occasion, the reinforcement schedule is more complex, and the entire process is probably not pursued systematically.
>
> A laboratory study of discrimination is ideally suited to a study of any of these variables acting in a pure and simple form. Despite the fact that a child will rarely encounter a pure and simple case of any such variable, this information is of value. The history of science suggests that the complexities of the child's real world are probably only multiple combinations of pure and simple processes. Hence the complexity of child behavior in vivo may result only from the large number of factors involved; yet each factor by itself may operate in a simple manner, readily and completely understandable in a laboratory setting.
>
> Since this supposition has served other sciences well in the past, no other justification will be offered (1960, pp. 142–143).

This rationale suggests that the learning of children in everyday situations is composed of complex constellations of variables which have been singly studied in the laboratory. This is supported by naturalistic observations of the differences in behavior found as a function of societal, class, and familial circumstances (all include learning variables), as well as those observations which indicate that normal and abnormal behaviors may be learned. Many of these behaviors and stimulus variables are discussed elsewhere in the book. The next section of this chapter will tentatively consider, in terms of laboratory established learning principles, some of the common training problems that face the parent.

Sensory-Motor Development

As was mentioned earlier, there has been a good deal of observation of the child's sensory-motor development. Because a large proportion of children of a particular age develop certain skills, it has been concluded that maturational processes must become functional at that age. However, little attention has been paid to the influence of experience on the development of many of these skills (Fowler, 1962).

Locomotion is a form of behavior in which there is a certain progression in the behavioral development of the child; for example, usually creeping first, then crawling, then walking. Walking, as an example, appears to be a complex behavior consisting of sequences of different muscular responses that must be emitted in the correct order. It would seem that each response, through the stimuli it produces, must come to elicit the next response in the sequence in order for a smooth response chain to occur. This means that the necessary muscular and nervous system must be present, intact, and adequately developed.

In addition to an adequate neural and muscular system, however, the development of "walking" responses involves learning variables. First, reinforcing stimuli appear to have their characteristic function. In the acquisition of the skill, reinforcers are obtained by the child when he locomotes to another part of a room and obtains a toy, trinket, morsel of food, or other object. When the various responses in the chain occur in the proper order, the child attains the reinforcer, or he attains it more quickly than he does when some "incorrect" order of the responses is emitted. In addition, an "incorrect" variation in the order of responses may be followed by aversive stimulation—falling, bumping furniture. Thus, differential positive reinforcement is customarily available for the appropriate response chain, and aversive stimulation contingent upon an inappropriate chain.

Stimulus control seems also to be another important variable in walking. First, it would be expected that the sequence of responses involved in walking would have to be formed, so that the stimuli produced by one response would come to elicit the next. In addition, other perceptual-motor skills (stimulus–response sequences) seem to be involved. That is, in addition to proprioceptive stimuli, other (sensory) stimuli must come to control responses involved in the skill of walking. Visual stimuli would be expected to control certain "walking" responses. For example, in the presence of some visual stimuli reinforced locomotion may occur, whereas in the presence of other stimuli (such as the sight of approaching walls, doors, and furniture) aversive stimuli such as knocks and bumps might be produced by the behavior.

Balance is another example of the importance of stimulus control. Appropriate "righting" responses to the "off-balance" visual stimuli should also be learned according to the principles of reinforcement. Thus, in the presence of visual cues of the room deviating too far from the vertical, if certain responses occur, aversive stimulation of falling is avoided. Without those responses the child falls. The visual cues, as discriminative stimuli, should in this way come to control the appropriate responses.

The same would be true of the stimuli of balance that arise in the semicircular canals of the inner ear. These canals, which extend in three planes, contain fluid. Any movement of the head results in movement of the fluid with respect to the walls of the canal. Extending from the walls into the fluid are hairlike organs that are activated by movement of the fluid, and this results in some of the stimulation of "balance." Since being off-balance (a certain pattern of stimulation from these sources) would frequently be paired with the aversive stimulation of knocks and bumps, it would be expected that the off-balance stimuli would become negative reinforcers. Any "righting" response would be reinforced by eliminating these stimuli. In common-sense terms, it could be said that it should become "unpleasant" for the child to be off-balance, and it would be expected that this source of negative reinforcement would be a factor in learning to make the correct walking responses.

Thus, even from this oversimplified description, it may be seen that a complex set of stimulus controls, including chaining, would seem to require development, based upon the individual's history of reinforcement. Looked at in this light, the regularity in the development of locomotion skills could be considered to involve learning processes as well as muscular and neural development. This regularity might be partially explained by the fact that the system of events which reinforce the development of walking, as well as the way the reinforcers shape behavior, are much the same for most children. That is, the reinforcing system customarily depends upon the physical principles of the world in which the child lives. Similar movements would be expected to come to be made when the child is off-balance, because the reinforcing contingencies are the same—one movement restores the balance and is reinforced, another results in sharp contact with the ground and aversive stimulation. Chains of walking responses that lead the child to locomote in a straight line are more immediately reinforced than chains that result in curved or variegated paths. The development of stimulus control in these behaviors also should progress in a regular manner because the determining conditions (the reinforcers) are to some extent a result of invariant physical principles.

Observations of other sensory-motor developments of the child suggest that responses which one may feel are naturally present in the human actually have to be acquired in childhood. For example, a child must *learn* to lower his head upon walking under an object, such as a table, when he grows too tall to walk under it upright. Many trials that result in aversive stimulation may be required to complete this visual discrimination involving the sight of the object toward which the child is walking. If the child does not duck his head, aversive stimuli follow. Then, if the child lowers his head sufficiently, aversive stimulation ceases. It would therefore be expected that through a number of negatively reinforced head-lowering responses, the child would finally acquire the discrimination, and the approach of visual objects on the level of one's eyes would control the ducking response. This coordination seems so automatic for an adult that it is somewhat surprising to observe a child going through a long course of training before it is acquired.

The same variables also appear to play a role in simple "eye-hand" coordinations. Stimuli in various positions with respect to the body must come to be S^Ds for various hand movements. Prior to training, the child does not respond appropriately to such visual stimuli. He cannot without training reach unerringly for objects he sees. However, in the presence of an object in a certain position a particular movement will be reinforced by the consequence of obtaining the object, whereas other movements will postpone reinforcement. After a number of trials in which differential reinforcement is contingent upon these responses, the child should finally come to quickly reach in any required direction and obtain the reinforcing object. Stimulus control would then be considered complete.

Again, this class of behavior should develop in roughly similar patterns for all children because the physical principles of the world (as well as the psychological principles of behavior) are the same for all. On the other hand, these interpretations also suggest how some individual differences in locomotor development would arise as a function of training variables. For example, parents may provide different opportunities for the discriminations and chains of behavior to occur and be reinforced—thus influencing the speed of behavioral development. Some parents, when the infant makes a slight movement toward an object, or looks at an object and emits a vocal response, obtain the object for the child; others allow the infant to fend for himself when the task is not too great, to make struggling movements toward an object within his reach. The latter procedure would allow locomotor movements to be followed by reinforcement in the presence of the appropriate stimuli. It would be expected that a systematic training program in which reinforcing objects were gradually placed further and further from the child and were gradually placed in different positions as well, would result in more rapid locomotor development.[1] At any rate, it would seem that individual differences in this behavior could be generated by varying treatments, and a long-continuing program which reinforced increasingly complex motor behaviors could lead to a superior individual in this sphere of activity. Of course, in order to produce large differences in

---

[1] Although the study is not yet complete, K. A. Minke and W. G. Heard, graduate students at Arizona State University, have extended such an analysis to a problem in training a brain-damaged child. The child, who has defective motor control of one arm, has been presented with the task of touching a target stimulus (S^D). Maintaining the child's behavior by response-contingent reinforcement, the target has been gradually reduced in size in a training program extending over a number of days, requiring increasing accuracy. The training program has thus far been successful in producing increasing sensory-motor discrimination.

such behaviors the program would require great duration, in which very complex behaviors would be built upon previously acquired skills (Fowler, 1962). Examples of such complex sensory-motor skills might be seen in such activities as expert dancing, athletics, and singing.

Feeding Problems

The classes of child behavior that can be analyzed in terms of experimentally established learning principles in one chapter cannot be exhaustive. However, some problems of development and training are probably general enough to be included. Feeding is certainly one of these. In addition, some problems of training should be included in this analysis because they have assumed critical significance in well-known psychological theory. For example, as was shown at the beginning of this chapter, Freud's interest in various stages of instinctual development and in the manner in which the child is treated by the parent during these stages resulted in several areas of child training gaining importance to psychoanalytically oriented thought and research.

For example, since in psychoanalytic theory the personality is thought to be formed in part depending upon the way the oral needs are satisfied, there has been a great interest in the problems of feeding. Investigators have been concerned with the sucking and weaning experiences of the child, with breast vs. bottle feeding, small vs. large-holed nipples, time and manner of weaning, and so on, and with the consequent effects upon the "personality" of the child.

What may we say of the early oral experiences of the child in terms of learning principles? Although there is little systematic evidence to show that early feeding experiences involving these variables directly shape later complex behaviors, it may nevertheless be suggested that there are some important events in the feeding situation.

First, the feeding situation is generally one of the first to provide circumstances for development of conditioned reinforcement. Since food is a primary reinforcer, through pairing the ingestion of milk with other stimuli (social stimuli especially) the latter should become conditioned reinforcers for the infant. It would therefore be expected that differences in the reinforcing value of the milk or in its presentation would have effects upon this type of conditioning. In addition, it would be expected that differences in the milk, in the amount ingested, and so on, could have effects upon the health of the child and on the child's consequent behavior, and thus upon the response of parents and others to the child. Naturally such differences in response to the child would also be expected to shape differences in the behavior of the child.

It would seem that overconcern with the infant's feeding might also lead to problems. Some parents might feel that any cry of the child denotes hunger, and quickly give the child a bottle, not wishing to "frustrate" oral needs. Since feeding comes to have conditioned reinforcing value, it might be expected that a child would take a bottle even if the condition underlying the crying had no relation to food deprivation. If the child was fed often under these conditions, it would be expected that learning would result which would "mold" the child to this feeding schedule. Evidence that such learning occurs is given by an experiment by Marquis (1941) in which it was found that the behavior of infants just a few days old could be modified in accordance with feeding schedules. One group of infants was put on a four-hour feeding schedule for the first ten days of life. Another group was on a three-hour schedule for their first eight days, but was shifted to four-hour schedules on the ninth. Both groups became somewhat restless and active shortly before their regular feeding time. However, when the three-hour infants were shifted to the four-hour schedule, they became extremely restless—apparently these infants had learned to respond to deprivation stimuli at the end of three hours and failure to receive food at that time produced considerable activity.

It would therefore be expected that feeding the child more frequently than necessary would condition the child to this type of schedule. To what extent the child's feeding schedule will constitute a problem for the parent would as a consequence depend somewhat upon the parent's own method of feeding the child. Whatever the parents do with respect to the scheduling of feeding probably conditions the child to that pattern, and crying would then occur toward the end of the usual period. If the feeding is every four hours, the child's behavior could be expected to conform to that schedule, just as it would to another schedule. (Naturally, there may also be physiological considerations relevant to propitious scheduling.)

At any rate, since it seems that the parent himself manipulates the child's feeding habits, thought might be given to imposing a schedule which is reasonable both to parent and child. For it would seem in many cases that conditions which result in more work and effort for the mother may in the end have an adverse effect on the child. If the mother is impatient, irritable, or tired at feeding time, she may not impose the most benign learning conditions possible. The extent to which she is tired and irritable, however, depends partially upon her ability to train reasonable behaviors in the child concerning feeding, as well as other functions.

Some psychologists have recognized this effect and offer the following advice, which is quite consistent with that derived from the present extension of learning principles.

Of course, there are situations where the mother cannot feed her child on a strictly demand schedule because of the pressures of family or work duties. If she attempts to do so, she may become irritable and inadvertently handle the child roughly, thereby making the feeding situation unpleasant. Since babies soon develop fairly regular schedules of their own, a modified demand-feeding regimen may provide a good compromise. Under such a system, the mother can anticipate approximately the proper time to feed her child (Mussen and Conger, 1956, p. 161).

Another important aspect of feeding training is weaning. From the standpoint of learning principles, it would seem wise to undertake this change gradually and without the use of aversive stimuli, since, as has already been suggested, the extent to which the parent becomes a secondary reinforcer depends upon the amount of positive stimulation the child receives in the presence of the parent.

Again, this training may have implications for other behavior. If the change is attempted abruptly, following a long history of only bottle feeding, so that the child cries and is finally reinforced with the bottle, then a conditioning trial has occurred which will result in an increase of the child's crying behavior. On the other hand, in a gradual program of weaning, solid foods might be introduced early but tentatively and piecemeal. Each bite should constitute a reinforcer to a hungry child, and the sight and feel of the solid food should gradually acquire reinforcement value. It might be expected to take a long period of training before various consistencies and tastes of food become reinforcing for the child.

As the child grows older, there continue to be important variables connected with the manner in which feeding is handled. One example is the child with feeding problems—the child who does not eat enough, refuses many foods, is overdemanding in terms of the kind of food, its preparation and its presentation, and so on. It is suggested that these problems may also be a product of the child's reinforcement history. It should be quite easy to condition a child *not* to eat at dinnertime. This could be done simply by reinforcing the child with an abundance of attention when he does not eat, and, on the other hand, by feeding the child snacks between meals, especially if they are delicacies. It would seem that in this manner very extreme difficulties with eating could be shaped which would continue into adulthood.

For example, a not-infrequent behavior of hospitalized psychiatric patients is their "refusal" to eat under ordinary conditions of feeding for an adult. Ayllon and Michael (1959) and Ayllon and Haughton (1962) have demonstrated that such extreme deviations in eating behaviors are subject to the principles of conditioning. Their behavioral analysis suggested that this behavior was maintained by the social-reinforcement consequences of

"noneating" behavior. On the basis of this interpretation, social reinforcement was withdrawn for noneating behavior, and in two cases (Ayllon and
Michael, 1959) slight aversive stimulation was paired with spoon-feeding.
On the other hand, proper eating was paired with the primary reinforcement of food, and in some cases with social reinforcement. Appropriate
eating behavior was produced and maintained under this treatment. (See
Chapter 11 for a fuller discussion of these experiments.)

Food preferences may constitute another problem. Since foods may vary
in reinforcing value prior to training, and the child's first foods are liquids,
food preferences upon the part of the child may be expected as soon as
new tastes and consistencies are introduced. Certain foods, however, are
customarily consumed in a particular culture, and it is necessary that the
child come to find most of these foods reinforcing. In addition, even
though a particular food has no inherent aversive qualities, the child may
be inadvertently trained to avoid it in a manner similar to that described
above—coaxing and attention may serve to strengthen the behavior of
rejecting the food. If the child does not eat the food there will be no
opportunity for it to gain conditioned reinforcement value from its pairing
with other foods and social reinforcers. If the parents scold the child or
administer punishment, the food may in addition become a conditioned
aversive stimulus. On the other hand, manipulation of deprivation conditions so that edibles in general become strong reinforcers, and gradual
presentation of the new food with scant competition from other foods, as
well as social reinforcement contingent upon *eating* the food, would be
expected to yield the conditioning desired, with no negative side-effects.

A study by Lövaas (1961) illustrates the operation of learning principles
in establishing food preferences. Three four-year-old nursery subjects were
given four foods during a snack-time as part of their nursery-school routine.
Records were kept of the amount of each food consumed. Then conditioning was commenced, consisting of presenting reinforcement (such as
trinkets and words of praise from a puppet) contingent upon the child
voicing the name of the food that had been selected by the experimenter
for manipulation. The food selected was one that the child had been rejecting in the snack period. The results indicated that the intake of a specific
food (food preference) could be manipulated by reinforcing the verbal
response referring to that food. It might be expected that direct reinforcement of the eating behavior itself would have accomplished the same
result.[2]

---

[2] In addition to demonstrating the training of eating habits according to the principles
of reinforcement, the study also shows the relationship of verbal and motor behavior.
When the verbal behavior was reinforced, the appropriate nonverbal (motor) behavior
was also strengthened.

In conclusion, it is suggested that various eating behaviors, some having significant consequences for health, may be shaped up according to the principles of learning. This conditioning may take place on a verbal level, as well as by directly manipulating reinforcing conditions for the actual eating behavior.

Toilet Training

Psychoanalytic theory has also been especially interested in the way toilet training is conducted. This interest stems from the concept that in the anal stage of development the primary instinctual investment is in the processes of elimination. However, it may be suggested that toilet training has importance unrelated to such theories of instinctual development.

The child in our society must be toilet trained within some reasonable period and, other things being equal, the smoother and earlier it takes place the easier it is for the parent and the child. In this area, as in many others, it is sometimes assumed that the acquisition of appropriate toilet behavior takes place upon the basis of some maturational process. However, the simple fact that most children in our culture become toilet trained in roughly the same period of their lives does not constitute evidence for such an assumption. This could occur because there are training practices involved that take roughly the same number of trials. It would also follow that differences in training procedures might produce important variations in the time and efficacy of the training.

On the behavioral level, a description of a "bowel-movement" may include the responses of going to a particular place, and in the presence of the appropriate situational, internal, and time cues, of assuming a particular postural response, and emitting certain other operant behaviors (such as straining and relaxing sphincters), which will expedite the respondent behaviors of the lower intestine that function in evacuation.[3] On the basis of this behavioral description, the acquisition of toilet control may be considered as a complex learning task for the child and a formidable training task for the parent—and one that is capable of all kinds of variations and consequences. In these terms it would be expected that to cope most efficaciously with this training problem the parent should be armed with a series of explicit instructions, rather than the instruction to wait for development to occur.

Although there is no formal research on the application of learning principles to toilet training, application of this method has yielded observations which conform to the analysis, and the tentative analysis itself should suggest further systematic investigation.

---

[3] Chapter 11 discusses analogous problems concerned with the control of bed-wetting.

First, in accord with the principle of successive approximation, and gradualness in training, it is suggested that the training should begin considerably prior to the time the parent expects the child to be completely trained. This seems necessary to enable all the S–R relationships to be developed without undue haste or stringent training methods. The parent must also expect very slow progress at first, and then only in simple general behaviors that set the stage for the specific training.

A first step might be to observe the usual times of bowel-movement of the child. When this has been ascertained, the child could be placed upon the "pottie-chair" at a likely time. Without some source of reinforcement, however, the child may attempt to escape or start to cry. This means that not only should the sitting period be short at first, but that some reinforcers—games with the parent, play with toys, and so on—might profitably be introduced.

Through this procedure, a necessary adjunct to successful total toilet behavior, sitting in the appropriate place, may be brought under the control of the stimuli of the toilet situation through the use of positive reinforcement. The time of sitting on the toilet may also be gradually increased through reinforcement procedures and the child can then be trained to spend periods upon the toilet without being attended by the parent.

In addition, the behaviors involved in evacuation must undergo conditioning—but this should happen as a by-product of the above procedure. If the child sits on the toilet each day at a propitious time, a certain proportion of "successes" should occur. Specific reinforcement of this behavior by the parents would then be expected to bring the operants (such as straining) under the control of the situational cues. The respondents involving the lower intestines should also through classical conditioning tend to be elicited on future occasions by the stimuli of the situation.

Verbal training may also play an important part in the process of toilet training. The verbal training may commence long before the other toilet-training procedures. For example, the parents may simply say B–M (or some such term) whenever they see the child in the act of evacuation. By pairing the auditory stimulus with the respondents involved, the word B–M should to some extent come to be a conditioned stimulus that elicits these respondents. This verbal stimulus may then be used in the child's training to increase the probability that he will evacuate during the time he is on the "pottie."

In time, in accord with the relevant principles of language learning, the child should come himself to say B–M. After he learns to say the word and the parents prompt him to say it as he evacuates, the child's response of saying B–M should start to come under the control of the stimuli produced by the distended bowels, and so on, until finally it occurs sufficiently prior to the act for the parent to have time to take him to the "pottie" before elimination begins. This will improve the efficiency of the type of training previously discussed.

Verbal training of a slightly aversive nature may also be used when the appropriate verbal repertoire has been established. If the parent says, DON'T GO B–M UNLESS YOU ARE SITTING ON THE TOILET this will have the effect of making the act aversive unless the child is on the toilet. Thus, the act of evacuation in the absence of the toilet should become a conditioned aversive stimulus on the basis of language conditioning.

Dollard and Miller (1950) discuss some other advantages of language for training the child in these behaviors.

> [T]he reinforcement of the act of defecation itself will fix the correct series of responses into place. This will happen whether the course of the training has been stormy or smooth. However, in the case of the smooth, verbally aided learning there is much less danger of arousing furious anger or of creating maladaptive habits such as retention of feces and lack of control. Extremely strong anxiety reactions do not occur and feelings of excessive worthlessness are less likely. The end result is the same so far as mere cleanliness training is concerned. The difference lies in the fact that the . . . verbally aided method of getting out the response has much less risk of violent side reactions and character distortions (p. 140).

The above may thus be considered part of a program that is consistent with established learning principles and that would involve a minimum of aversive stimulation.

However, as can be seen from this description, with a task of this complexity there is a good deal of leeway for accomplishing a pretty poor job of training. Certainly, a philosophy of behavioral development through maturation that leads to the absence of training would hardly seem adequate. Furthermore, it may have negative effects if the parent who postpones toilet training on these grounds is finally socially embarrassed by the child's behavior and then commences the training too abruptly.

Even if the training is begun at an appropriate time, the mother may find the lack of quick success to be aversive. If as a consequence she then uses punishment, there is an opportunity for much improper training to take place. The inappropriate use of punishment might condition both the mother and the child with respect to one another in a manner that will produce future difficulties for both. As with feeding, discussed previously, the extent to which the parents (and consequently other people as well) will become positive reinforcers will depend upon the smoothness with which toilet training takes place, and the extent to which aversive stimuli are used.

Crying Behavior

In this class will be included all of those behaviors ranging from mild whinings to full-blown temper tantrums, since they share several important characteristics.

As a stimulus the sound of crying is aversive to most people. The child who cries frequently is consequently frequently aversive to other people, including parents, siblings, and playmates. Any circumstance that increases the frequency of inappropriate crying would thus seem to make the child's social adjustment more difficult. Other children might respond with behavior aversive to the child, they might tend to avoid the child, and so on; adults probably also tend to treat the whining, crying, child in a different, less felicitous, manner than they would other children. In addition, the parents of such a child might be exposed to criticism, and in other ways receive less social reinforcement from adults concerning the child, and this in turn would be expected to affect the parents' response to the child.

However, as a stimulus, it is apparently just the aversive quality of crying that accounts for its functional attributes. Because crying is aversive it serves to arouse the tending adult to action, which is then reinforced by the cessation of crying. This negative reinforcement maintains the parent's behavior as a response to the child's crying.

As a response, crying appears to be an unlearned respondent to aversive stimulation—at least at first. When the aversive stimulus is removed, the crying ceases. Later, crying seems to become an operant that is subject to strengthening through reinforcement.

> *After* a hungry infant begins crying, he is fed; soon he cries regularly when hungry. Feeding is said to have reinforced crying which has now become conditioned. A psychologist fed her son when he emitted a faint "cooing" sound. The rate of "cooing" when hungry was expected to (and did) increase as a result of this reinforcement. . . . The psychologist fed the baby when he emitted "coos," but *not* when he cried. We should expect that crying when hungry would be . . . extinguished because of the withholding of . . . food (Holland and Skinner, 1961, pp. 47–51).

It would seem that such operant behavior might be widely extended in terms of the frequency with which it would occur, as well as the stimuli which would control it, on the basis of the training history of the child.

For example, naturalistic observation suggests that crying may be learned as a type of "striving" behavior—analogous to the class of verbal operant I WANT IT. If the parent frequently reinforces crying in the presence of a reinforcing stimulus toward which the child is making incipient movements, then crying as an operant will come under the control of reinforcing stimuli in general. It may then be observed that whenever the child sees a reinforcing stimulus, especially if it is out of reach, he will cry and this response may become one of the strongest "striving" behaviors in the child's repertoire. The success of this behavior, if it is frequently reinforced, also may make unlikely the development of other striving verbal and nonverbal behavior that might be acquired under better training conditions. The result would be a child who makes undifferentiated whining or crying responses to many reinforcing stimuli, sometimes with accompanying gestures that "aid" the parent in "determining" what reinforcing stimulus he must obtain for the child.

As the example illustrates, wide differences in the training conditions for such behavior are possible, and, as would be expected, there are consequently wide differences in the incidence of the behavior. Although reinforcement of crying would in learning terms appear to be undesirable, it seems customary among many groups in our society to respond to a child's crying with some response that is intended to terminate the crying, which in fact constitutes a reinforcement for crying. Failure to provide such reinforcement is considered callous whether the crying arose as a result of injury or was an unjustified response that one would not want to see repeated.

Certainly there are circumstances when the response to the child should include removal of aversive stimulation, and perhaps other attention and comfort. (As a matter of fact, as a by-product of such care, the parent may add to his value as a conditioned reinforcer.) Although such treatment is necessary, and crying may be immediately decreased, even this would be expected to strengthen the behavior. In other than the necessary situations, however, it would seem better from the standpoint of the child's adjustment for the parent to extinguish crying behavior. Whenever the child's crying behavior is not justified—crying when put to bed, as a "mand" for some reinforcing object, and so on—nonreinforcement would seem indicated.

In addition, it may many times be possible to avoid reinforcing crying by responding to the child's first request and providing the requisite relief, rather than by waiting until crying commences. As this implies, correction or prevention of crying behavior may involve shaping of more effective "striving" behaviors. Since the incidence of crying should depend also upon the strength of competing responses, one way of decreasing the crying operant is to train the child to functional behaviors that remove aversive conditions more effectively than crying does. For example, the child deprived of water who has not learned to say WAH–WAH may cry, when the more verbal child will emit the appropriate vocal response. The earlier the child acquires verbal behavior and other adjustive behaviors, other things being equal, the less often should crying occur.

On the other hand, since crying itself may be a response to aversive stimuli, it is paradoxical to attempt to stop the behavior through punishment. Sometimes parents will punish a child for crying, prompted by the aversive quality of the crying, but this can only result in further crying.

Dependent Behavior

As was pointed out earlier, Freudian theory has also called attention to the importance of early experiences in determining dependent behavior, or as it is often called, "emotional dependence." Here again, some important behaviors seem to be involved that may be discussed in learning terms.

For example, children differ in the extent to which they (1) cling to their mothers in the presence of strangers; (2) resist separation from their mothers for even short periods of time and are upset when this is necessary; (3) insist upon having only their mothers care for them in feeding, dressing, and cleaning; (4) display few behaviors for entering a situation on their own and behaving appropriately, and so on. Later in life it may be observed that people differ in the extent to which they "make decisions" by themselves, behave appropriately on their own, depend upon others for initiating and carrying through any action, or are too closely attached to relatives or friends, and so on.

This is only a thumbnail sketch of the class of behavior labeled dependent. However, several learning principles would appear to be involved in the acquisition of any of these behaviors. First, it could be said that individuals differ in their repertoires of "adjustive" behavior (behaviors reinforced in the society) that are under the control of different physical and social stimulus situations. Some individuals with wide experience, yielding a large repertoire in many different situations, are never "helpless." There are relatively few entirely novel situations for these individuals, since stimulus generalization from the wide range of previous experiences will cover almost any eventuality. On the other hand, an individual with sparse experience in this respect will more frequently "be at a loss." It would be expected that all sorts of behavior would be important in this sense—motor and verbal behaviors, as well as both direct experience with stimulus situations and vicarious contact through verbal experience, as in reading.

In addition, individuals seem to differ in the range of stimuli which for them are effective social reinforcers, that is, they may differ in the number of people who become strong conditioned reinforcers for them. A child could be raised, at one extreme, by a solicitous and loving widow who was uneasy except with her own close relatives. The child would thus have positively reinforcing occasions with his close relatives, but would have uncomfortable (aversive) experiences with other people. It would be expected from this discriminative training that for this child a few people would come to have strong reinforcing value and other people would tend to be somewhat aversive. If the child also had little experience with other children, this condition might be aggravated. The restricted nature of these social reinforcers would shape up "dependent" behavior in the sense that the behavior of clinging to the mother or close relative would be strong.

On the other hand, a child could be raised in a situation involving many adults and children in positively reinforcing circumstances. This would be expected to produce a different set of social reinforcers, and consequently a different set of behaviors.

The behaviors acquired by the child may also determine later whether other social interactions are reinforcing. For example, a child might be treated in the family in such a manner as to shape "spoiled," "unreasonable," "demanding" behavior, including frequent crying and temper tantrums, as well as aggressive and destructive behaviors. With a repertoire like this, the experiences of the child with other children could hardly be anything but aversive for him. Such experiences would have the effect of shaping a dependent child, since they would be expected to result in people other than the close family members becoming conditioned aversive stimuli, and thus would prevent the acquisition of adjustive social behaviors and social reinforcers.

Dependence might also be produced by keeping the behavior under the exclusive control of "directions" by the parent. If in a wide variety of situations the child is punished unless he does just what the parent does, or what the parent instructs, then his behavior will be largely under the control of these stimuli. In a new situation, this child will look to the parent for S^Ds—his behavior will be "dependent" upon cues produced by the adult. Parents who do everything for the child, or who instruct the child how to do everything, might be expected to set up this type of dependent behavior.

Thus, independent behavior would seem to depend in part upon having certain skills and upon the appropriate stimulus control of these skills. Even in such intellectual skills as independent "decision making," these variables seem to be involved. Decision making may be considered to consist of complex sequences of reasoning responses that culminate in some overt instrumental behavior. In order, then, for decision making to occur, the sequences must be established under the control of various situations. A child who has not been trained in the constituent behaviors involved, as well as the emission of these behaviors in actual problems, but who has, rather, been reinforced in such situations for asking instructions from parents, will be unable to make decisions for himself, or when he does make them, the decisions may be poor and turn out badly.

The counteracting experience for such dependence in decision making would thus seem to involve social and physical reasoning sequences, as well as opportunities for these responses to be emitted and reinforced in problem situations. When the child responds and is reinforced in the presence of stimuli other than those produced by the parents, it could be expected that his behavior would be brought under the control of those new stimuli. These various types of training would be expected to influence the "independence" of the child. (See Gewirtz, 1956, 1959, for a more extended learning analysis of emotional dependence.)

Socially Controlling Stimuli

If a response is reinforced in the presence of a stimulus, S^D, but not when another stimulus is added, the S^Δ stimulus situation, then the response will occur when S^D is present alone, but not when S^Δ occurs. It could be said that S^D would control responding and S^Δ would control "nonresponding." This type of training and the concept of S^Δ seem to be important for considering certain aspects of child training.

Previously we have discussed classes of behavior that have aversive qualities and that therefore are not desirable to shape up. There are other behaviors, in addition, that are not aversive when they occur under appropriate conditions but that may be aversive unless they are controlled by certain social stimuli.

As was pointed out in the preceding chapter, children are ordinarily exposed to conditions where when they emit various types of "striving" behaviors in the presence of a reinforcing stimulus they obtain the stimulus. For example, the child may reach up on a table and grasp a cookie. When this occurs, a cookie—or to some extent, any reinforcing object—becomes an S^D that will control the behavior of reaching for it, moving toward it, grabbing it, and so on. Other behaviors, such as crying "for" something, could be strengthened in the same sort of situation. A child seems through such experience to acquire a hierarchy of behaviors of a "striving" nature that would be under the control of various "discriminative-reinforcing" stimuli. Without additional training of the type to be discussed, these "striving" behaviors would be emitted in the presence of any reinforcing stimulus, even if the behavior is not appropriate when considered in other terms. A child who has had many reinforced trials of reaching for objects will also reach up and get a knife, a lamp, a wrist watch, and so on, or reach out and take a reinforcing stimulus away from another child, pull off an adult's glasses, and so on.

Since some "striving" behaviors may be aversive or harmful to other persons, as well as to the child himself, it is important that training which leads to appropriate control of such behaviors take place. One way of achieving this kind of control would seem to be through forming social S^As that control "nonstriving" (or, in general, "cessatory") behaviors. The child would have to experience situations in which in the presence of a discriminative-reinforcing stimulus (S^D-S^R) *and* another social stimulus, seeking behaviors will not be reinforced by obtaining the object. For example, suppose when a child reached for a piece of candy, the parent said NO, YOU MAY NOT HAVE A PIECE OF CANDY NOW. If this situation was followed by the parent preventing the child from obtaining the candy, this would constitute a learning trial in which in the presence of the S^D-S^R stimulus *plus* the verbal stimulus, the seeking behavior underwent extinction. Ordinarily, a child receives many trials where in the presence of such verbal stimuli as STOP THAT PLEASE; I'M SORRY, I'M USING THIS NOW; I AM ALREADY PLAYING WITH THIS TOY; YOU WILL HAVE TO BE QUIET NOW; LEAVE THAT ALONE; DON'T TOUCH THAT; THAT BELONGS TO ME he will not be reinforced for the on-going behavior.

It is suggested that it is through this kind of training that many social stimuli, verbal and otherwise, come to control "cessatory" responses so that behavior which would otherwise be inappropriate does not occur. In addition to the verbal stimuli of social control already described, some others that must gain the same kind of control may be briefly mentioned. For example, the visual stimuli of another child playing with a particular toy will come to be an S^A if the behavior of seeking that toy in the presence of those stimuli is not reinforced, while the toy *alone* can still be a stimulus in the presence of which seeking behavior is reinforced. More broadly, the child must receive analogous, nonreinforced training in many situations in which a discriminative-reinforcing stimulus occurs in the presence of additional stimuli which indicate that the reinforcer "belongs to someone else."

As another example, the child must come to respond with "cessatory" behavior to social stimuli such as frowns and other facial and verbal expressions which indicate that another person is suffering aversive stimulation. In other words, the child must learn to cease behavior that is painful to others. A child who has not been so trained will be *solely* under the control of the cues of the reinforcing object or event rather than the social stimuli, and may therefore persist in behavior that is aversive to others. People who have had the more appropriate training will find it difficult to accept such "unrestrained" behavior.

Since many of the stimuli described are rather complex and subtle, extensive discriminative training may be required to achieve the desired social control. It would thus seem reasonable that this training should start early and be conducted in a gradual manner. Rather than waiting until the child has acquired many strong behaviors under no social control and then attempting to bring the child rapidly under such control, it would seem better to deal with social learning from the beginning so that the training is neither abrupt in onset nor intensive. It is when a behavior has become quite strong and is noxious to others that extinction procedures may not seem adequate to the parent, and he is more likely to use punishment to achieve the social control. To the extent that social control can be established through the procedures of S^Δ training, however, the need for punishment would be reduced.

Social Reasoning

In Chapter 5, in discussing reasoning and scientific prediction, it was suggested that tacts under the control of certain environmental stimuli can elicit sequences of verbal responses which mediate problem-solving behaviors (or predictions of future events). However, the examples used pertained almost entirely to physical problems, although it was indicated that the principles might also apply to social and personal problems. Dollard and Miller (1950), in discussing human behavior in learning terms, give a central role to reasoning and planning involving the above types of behavior.

> While learning to talk the child receives training in matching words, sentences, and descriptive paragraphs with important features of the environment. He is trained not to call the sky "green" or the grass "blue." . . . He is also taught to distinguish between . . . the situations in which sentences that do not run parallel to sequences in the environment will be tolerated and those in which they will not. He is taught to discriminate between his own private dreams, images, and phantasies, and the perceptions that can be verified by cross-checking with other senses and that agree with the reports of other people. . . .
>
> We believe that this training serves to provide motivation against hallucinations and delusions. The strength of this motivation is shown by the anxiety that a normal person will show if through some unexpected illusion he seems to be seeing things that others do not see.
>
> The training in matching words to important features of the environment applies to the social as well as the physical environment. The child is trained to give an accurate account of social events and to make his statements about the probable social consequences of acts match the cultural pattern. He is also trained to be fair and not to blame others when it is his own fault, although blaming others is sometimes inadvertently rewarded. This training, imperfect as it often is, tends to operate against

showing behavior of the types called displacement, projection, and rationalization (p. 119).

That is, it is important that the child acquire a veridical language system with regard to social events—one which is isomorphic with the events involved. Such a system may be considered to include tacts to social events (including the events of one's own behavior) that are under precise stimulus control; intervening response sequences that parallel acceptable principles of behavior; and effective social behaviors (behaviors that gain positive reinforcers) mediated by the verbal response sequences.

It might be expected, following previous discussions, that the individual's solution of his social-personal problems will depend upon his language system in the above respects. Yet it would seem that there are large individual differences in the manner in which training is conducted in all three of these links in social behavior. Thus, variability is possible at each one of these parts of social reasoning, and as a result wide differences in social behavior are only to be expected.

An example, albeit a hypothetical and extreme one, may illustrate the function of such social-reasoning sequences in the social adjustment of an individual. One morning, let us say, an individual walking along the street suddenly whips out a revolver and shoots several businessmen who are standing on a street corner talking in a group. Later, under questioning, the individual states that people are plotting against him, that he has been under surveillance, and that the group of men talking were part of the movement to kill him. Although seemingly "senseless" when only the final behavior is considered, such a behavior might be seen as the culmination of experiences all involving the operation of established principles of learning. Before suggesting a history which could lead to such bizarre behavior it will be useful to restate the extreme behavior in terms of the three links in social reasoning. First, suppose because of this individual's highly unusual personal history he tacted the businessmen as PART OF THE GROUP WHO IS AFTER HIM. This complex tact then elicited the sequence THEY ARE GOING TO KILL ME, BUT I'LL GET THEM FIRST. This sequence finally mediated the instrumental responses of drawing and firing the gun.

It may be difficult to see how such unusual tacts, mediating response sequences, and instrumental behaviors could arise. That is, it is difficult to see how normal training processes could shape up such deviant behavior. Let us suppose, however, that this individual as a child acquired behaviors in the home which were aversive to other children and adults—unreasonable, demanding, aggressive behavior. To the extent that the child's behavior was aversive, other children would respond with aversive behavior in return. Let us say also that when the child reported how other people had mistreated him, the parents said that other children were jealous of him, were wrong to treat him in that manner, and so on. The child thus had many experiences in which such events were tacted in terms of the other individual's jealousy, perversity, and so on. The child was never trained to tact correctly his own behavior as aversive and other people's unpleasant behavior as a response to his own behavior.

Let us also say that the child acquired, in addition to tacts, verbal sequences such as PEOPLE ARE EVIL, YOU CAN'T TRUST ANYONE, IF YOU HAVE SOMETHING THEY WANT THEY WILL TRY TO TAKE IT FROM YOU, WATCH OUT FOR PEOPLE AND BEAT THEM TO THE PUNCH IF THEY TRY TO GET THE BEST OF YOU. Suppose, furthermore, as this individual grew older, violent behavior to others who did not "treat him right" had been reinforced. In this process, not only might fighting with other children be reinforced, but he might also acquire the verbal sequences FIGHT TO PROTECT YOUR-SELF; IF SOMEONE MISTREATS YOU THE BEST WAY TO HANDLE HIM IS TO FIGHT, and so on.

Let us also say that because of this individual's aversive behaviors, verbal and nonverbal, he has many aversive interactions with people as he grows older. For example, when someone else is promoted over him (actually as a consequence of his behavior) he responds with aversive verbal behavior about and to the other person. Further, adding to the cycle, since he is aversive to many people, people may indeed "organize" against him, talk about him, get him fired from jobs. Thus, his social experiences may continue to be generally aversive. He cannot hold a job, thus many other primary and social reinforcers are withdrawn, and so on.

The individual tacts each one of his "social conflicts" as he has been trained to do: THEY ARE JEALOUS OF ME, THEY ARE ALL AGAINST ME. People in general could in this manner become very aversive for this individual and he might respond to everyone—his land-lady, the grocer, his casual associates—in verbal and other ways that are aversive. Again, these people would respond aversively to him, talk with each other about him, plan retaliations against him, laugh at him, and mistreat him. In reality, because they are a group they could be more aver-sive to him than he could be to them.

With this history, it might not be unreasonable that the individual would tact his accumulated social experience by saying EVERYONE IS AGAINST ME AND IS OUT TO GET ME, THEY HATE ME SO THEY WANT TO HARM ME, THEY ARE PLOTTING TO HURT ME. In such a history, the gradual road to extremely abnormal aggressive behavior might be seen. It could be the operation of behavior principles, and principles of language behavior in particular, that account for such a development.

The behavior in this example is, of course, highly unusual, although such abnormal behaviors (called delusions of persecution) do occur from time to time. (See Chapter 11 for further examples of learned abnormal behaviors.) More importantly, this illustration includes behavior that is relevant to the less extreme variations common in everyday life. It is suggested that children may be trained to tact their own behavior, as well as others' responses to their behavior, in different ways. To the same action one individual will come to respond HE WAS KIDDING ME, while another says HE IS JEALOUS OF ME; another says HE WAS MEAN TO ME; and yet another says nothing, the action controlling no specific verbal response.

In addition, different individuals may be taught different sequences of behavior ranging from MEN ARE EVIL through MEN LEARN TO BEHAVE THE WAY THEY DO, to MEN ARE GOOD. There are widely different "conceptions"—verbal sequences—concerning the "principles" of human behavior. For example, some individuals still think in terms of supernatural forces that determine man's behavior, others of biological instincts, others in terms of environmental conditions; and these verbal response sequences might be expected to determine how the different individuals will respond to other people's behavior.

Finally, men are taught different motor behaviors to the same sequences elicited by the same social situations. One man, when told by his son, THE NEIGHBOR TOLD ME NOT TO CROSS HIS YARD ANYMORE will "tell the neighbor off." Another will engage in physically aggressive behavior. Another will tell the boy to respect the neighbor's property rights.

This interpretation of the importance of language behaviors in one's social behavior extends beyond present research. Nevertheless, as has been pointed out, this kind of interpretation is consistent with principles of learning established in the laboratory. The interpretation has a close relationship to several clinically derived conceptions customarily included under the term "ego defense mechanisms," but which have here been discussed in terms of language learning. (See also Dollard and Miller, 1950.) Several of these language behaviors will now be described.

Rationalization

A description of the behavior of rationalization is given in the following.

> Rationalization . . . helps us to justify what we do and what we believe, and . . . aids us in softening the disappointment connected with unattainable goals.

Typically, rationalization involves thinking up logical, socially approved reasons for our past, present, or proposed behavior. With a little effort we can soon justify to ourselves the absolute necessity of purchasing a new car, or going to a show instead of studying, or even marrying someone with whom we are not in love. Carrying matters a step further, we may find it equally easy to justify most selfish and antisocial behavior. "Why should we yield the right of way to an oncoming motorist? He wouldn't yield it to us if he could help it, so why should we show him any consideration either?" "Suppose we did misrepresent the facts in making a sale—the other fellow has to learn sometime not to be so gullible and this provided a cheap lesson." "Yes, we did cheat on the test, but so would everyone else if he thought he could get away with it" (Coleman, 1950, pp. 86–87).

Rationalization has been discussed previously in terms of behavior principles (for example, Dollard and Miller, 1950; Holland and Skinner, 1961; Lundin, 1961). Rationalization may be considered to concern the way we talk about our behavior, rather than the behavior itself. Children customarily experience a number of situations in which their different tacts to the same behavior will have different consequences. Thus, a child who has broken a vase may be treated differently if he says I DIDN'T MEAN TO BREAK THE VASE rather than I BROKE IT BECAUSE I DIDN'T LIKE IT. There are certain tacts to our own behavior that are ordinarily followed by aversive consequences, whereas the same behavior may go unpunished if tacted with other verbal responses. "If we report that our friend has benefited from our criticism it is not punishing to report having criticized him. . . . Claiming that bumping a rival on the dance floor was an 'accident' is attributing the behavior to reasons for which bumping is not usually punished" (Holland and Skinner, 1961, p. 313). It would be expected that through such training the child would ordinarily acquire a repertoire of verbal behavior which helps to avoid possible aversive consequences of his behavior.

From these considerations, rationalization may appear to be a rather adjustive type of behavior; it removes or prevents the presentation of aversive stimuli that would otherwise be contingent upon the behavior. However, it must be remembered that the individual's own tacts and verbal response sequences also have an important function in mediating his own problem-solving behavior—and if they are too distorted, the behavior mediated may be maladjustive. For example, the struggling student may say that a college degree is really not important to him, that his interests are in other activities, and so on. This verbal behavior may prevent the aversiveness entailed in more accurate tacts that he himself or his associates might otherwise emit. In addition, however, his rationalization verbal behavior may also mediate the behavior of withdrawing from the university. Here, of course, is the drawback to rationalization. If the tacts and verbal response sequences of the rationalization are not accurate the behavior they mediate may not lead to reinforcing consequences for this individual.

In the preceding discussion of social reasoning, a hypothetical case of a man who states that people are "out to get him" was described. His tacts and mediating verbal response sequences culminated in a violent act. While this example includes verbal behavior more extreme than what is ordinarily called rationalization, in terms of learning principles the behaviors are quite analogous. As Dollard and Miller state, "a delusion is only quantitatively different" (1950, p. 178) from a rationalization. Thus, although rationalizational (or delusional) verbal responses may remove or prevent conditioned or unconditioned aversive stimuli, the behavior that is mediated by the distorted verbal behavior may later be the cause for even more aversive treatment, or the loss of considerable positive reinforcement— either of which may be much graver than the aversiveness that was avoided initially.

It seems, however, that most people develop, at least to some extent, two types of verbal behavior as a consequence of differential training. On the one hand, the verbal behavior emitted in the social situation leads to the removal of aversive social stimuli and gains social approval. In addition, however, verbal behavior of a different sort may be emitted when the individual is alone or with confidants in the process of "decision making." Thus, the individual who says in public that he took advantage of the other fellow because the other fellow planned the same thing, may in privacy emit the response sequence I ACTUALLY WAS WRONG IN TREATING HIM IN THAT MANNER. I GUESS HE WILL BE AGAINST ME NOW. I MUST NOT DO THAT IN THE FUTURE. If this verbal response sequence mediates his future behavior, this individual might gain the positive consequences of both classes of verbal behavior in a manner unlike what is typically called rationalization.

While it is not suggested that this particular illustration is exemplary behavior, it would seem that it is necessary that the individual's tacts and reasoning sequences of behavior be differentially controlled by social circumstances. It would be expected that discrimination training would be necessary to establish such discriminations—in other words, that the individual must have had a history where socially acceptable verbal behavior was reinforced under the social circumstances while other verbal behavior was reinforced under other circumstances. Through such discrimination training, the individual's verbal behavior would come under the control of, and be appropriate to, different social circumstances.

What proportions of "public" and "private" verbal repertoires lead to the best adjustment cannot be stated, of course. It would seem important that the individual's language system be veridical enough so that the "reasoning" sequences in which he engages will mediate effective behavior. On the other hand, if his behavior were completely "veridical" in all social situations, either much social disapproval would be incurred or the individual would be behaving in a rather restricted fashion in comparison to other people.

As is implied in the foregoing discussion, there are differences among people in the extent to which they evidence rationalizing behavior, and it would be expected that these differences would be determined by the history of training. It will be helpful to recall here the previous discussion of stimulus control in scientific behavior. It was suggested that parents may give their children more or less training to emit verbal responses under the strict control of a stimulus. In part, rationalization may be considered to involve the manipulation of the same classes of variables except that it consists of tacting one's own behavior (or the behavior of one's family, friends, or community) as a stimulus event in a different manner than one would tact the same behavior emitted by someone else. Still, this behavior would seem to be subject to the same type of training as are other verbal tacts. Whether the individual displays consistent verbal behavior (stringent stimulus control) or inconsistent verbal behavior with respect to his own behavior should depend upon his conditioning history.

Projection

Projection is a defensive reaction by means of which we (1) transfer the blame for our own shortcomings, mistakes, and misdeeds to others, and (2) attribute to others our own unacceptable impulses, thoughts, and desires.

Projection is perhaps most commonly evidenced in our tendency to blame others for our own mistakes. The student who fails an examination may feel sure the examination was unfair, the erring husband may blame his moral lapse on the girl "who led me on." "It wasn't my fault, he hit me first" or "If I hadn't taken advantage of him he would have taken advantage of me," and so it goes (Coleman, 1950, p. 86).

The way in which aversive social stimuli are removed by these types of tacts and verbal response sequences, and the apparent inconsistencies in tacting, are clearly very similar to those involved in rationalization. Again, although the behavior may be considered "adjustive" because it reduces immediately aversive stimuli (which accounts for the maintenance of the behavior), it may have the same detrimental consequences if it later mediates inappropriate behavior. Thus, the response, "If I hadn't taken advantage of him he would have taken advantage of me," may be strengthened by the removal of social disapproval. However, this kind of verbal behavior may at a later time mediate a response to someone that is highly inappropriate to the circumstances, and so result in strongly aversive consequences.

Repression

Repression is another class of behavior that seems to involve escape from aversive stimulation. It is described as a defensive reaction by means of which painful or "immoral" thoughts or impulses are excluded from "consciousness." The individual has certain experiences, for example, but does not "remember" them. In other terms, it may be said that the individual has had certain responses in his repertoire but that they are no longer controlled by the usual stimulus conditions. It has been suggested, moreover, that behavior principles can account for this occurrence without recourse to such concepts or processes as "exclusion from consciousness."

Dollard and Miller have pointed out that when any verbal response has been conditioned to elicit an anxiety response (is a conditioned aversive stimulus), replacement of that verbal response by the emission of another response will be strengthened. These authors give as an example the fact that people will change the topic of conversation because it elicits anxiety; "people tend to learn to avoid unpleasant topics of conversation" (1950, p. 199). In addition, Eriksen and Kuethe (1956), in an experimental situation, have tested the principles whereby word responses may be "repressed." The subjects were presented with stimulus words and instructed to say aloud their first response. After making an aversive stimulus, an electric shock, contingent upon the emission of a particular response word, the experimenters found that this response was no longer elicited by the stimulus word. It is interesting to note that this could occur without the subjects' awareness of the determinants of the change in their behavior.

Thus, when "repressive" training has occurred, rather than the response coming under the control of different social circumstances, the verbal responses are simply no longer available to the individual. Of course, as Dollard and Miller point out, to the extent that these verbal responses are important to the individual's adjustment (are social problem-solving) the individual is handicapped when they are absent from his repertoire; in their terms, he is "stupid."

Accordingly, it might be said that the individual is handicapped in social reasoning when certain verbal responses become extremely aversive. However, while aversiveness should not be so great that the response is avoided entirely, in the next section of this chapter it will be suggested that it is also important to the child's adjustment that he develop a number of words in his repertoire which do have aversive qualities.

Fantasy

One more "defense mechanism" will be described. "The person who finds his frustrations more than he can handle will often get around them in his imaginings. The commonplace examples of fantasy behavior are daydreams and night dreams" (Kimble, 1956, p. 352). In terms of behavior principles, it might be said that there are occasions when verbal behavior ordinarily under the control of environmental stimuli or textual stimuli (printed or written stimuli) will be emitted in the absence of these stimuli, as well as the absence of external reinforcing stimuli.

Thus, the reinforcement seems intrinsic to the verbal responses themselves, that is, they seem to have reinforcing properties. These verbal behaviors could be positively reinforcing themselves, as when the individual daydreams of some pleasant occurrence. Or the reinforcement could be negative—the fantasy verbal behaviors could provide escape from other "realistic" behaviors (behavior under environmental stimulus control).[4]

The individual who has a great deal of reinforcement for his every-day behavior, on the other hand, should display strong behavior of this type and fantasy behavior would not compete successfully. On the other hand, it is suggested that a life situation in which there are few reinforcers contingent upon the individual's "realistic" behavior would not be expected to maintain "realistic" behavior in good strength, and the relatively small reinforcers of fantasy might serve to strengthen fantasy behavior until it becomes much more dominant (further discussions of this principle in abnormal behavior will be presented in Chapter 11). A child, for example, for whom there are few reinforcers in a schoolroom situation and for whom the work is aversive would be more likely to emit fantasy behavior. The fantasy would bring the cessation of the aversive activity and also provide weak positive reinforcement.

Fantasy behaviors, however, since they are not problem-solving in nature, would not ordinarily contribute much to the adjustive behaviors the individual must emit in society. Thus, a preponderance of behavior of the fantasy type would have drawbacks for the individual's adjustment.

Use of Aversive Stimuli in Child Training

When the use of aversive stimuli in training was first described in Chapter 3 it was pointed out that rather complex learning is the result.

---

[4] Customarily, fantasy or daydreaming is thought also to involve imagery, a form of behavior that could also be considered in learning terms utilizing the concept of the conditioned sensory responses suggested in Chapter 4.

Although a response may be weakened by making an aversive stimulus contingent upon the response, this training has the additional effect of making all the other stimuli present in the situation become, at least to some extent, conditioned aversive stimuli and potential negative reinforcers. Thus, the parent in punishing a child would be expected to become somewhat of an aversive stimulus, and to the extent that his own stock of positive reinforcement value would be depleted he would lose his effectiveness as a trainer.

Furthermore, Azrin (1960) has shown that aversive stimuli lose their effect with continued use. Thus, it might be expected that parents who depend upon punishment too much in training would become less effective as trainers in two ways: on the one hand, they would be a poor source of positive reinforcement; on the other, their control through negative reinforcement would also weaken.

Perhaps, however, there are situations where attempts to train the child through the use of positive reinforcers only would be cumbersome and relatively ineffective, yet where appropriate behavior must be developed quickly if more extensive aversiveness or injury is to be prevented. For example, playing with electrical outlets and electric appliance plugs is potentially harmful. These stimuli should be avoided; however, they also constitute positive reinforcers for a young child. When the child heads for an electrical outlet, the parent could offer him an alternate reinforcer and so strengthen moving away from the outlet. However, the parent has a limited supply of reinforcers that are more effective than the electrical outlet, and sooner or later the outlet will control the child's approaching behavior. Even if it were possible to reinforce moving away from the outlet positively so that the child would never approach it, such training might be cumbersome. (Of course, this case should only be considered an example of the problem since safety devices can be obtained for electrical outlets.)

To take another example, the parent might wish to train the child not to take toys away from other children. Thus, whenever the child took a toy from another child the parent could insist the toy be returned and reinforce in some manner the behavior of returning it. In addition to the possibility that the positive reinforcement might strengthen *both* behaviors this type of training has the same limits as the previous example: "selfish" behavior is itself positively reinforced by what it obtains, and it is difficult to use positive reinforcement to weaken such behavior. In this example, as well as the one above, if the positive reinforcement fails and the required behavior is not learned, the child may be faced with considerable aversive stimuli later on. Injury in the first example might be an obvious consequence. In the second, if the child is not trained to behave "socially" he may be faced with aversive social consequences.

For these reasons, as well as those yet to be discussed, it is suggested that aversive stimuli have a place in child training, although it seems advisable that they be used judiciously, in the minimal amount necessary to achieve the required results, and only under the most effective training conditions.

One way of doing this is to use the primary, or corporal, punishment predominantly to produce *verbal stimuli* that are aversive and can take the place of the primary punishment. This can be done by pairing the verbal stimulus with punishment, as outlined in Chapter 4.

It is suggested that where even few primary punishments are administered to the child, if in each case the verbal stimuli are paired with the punishment, these words will become effective aversive stimuli and negative reinforcers. This type of training could be supplemented by the use of aversive stimuli that occur naturally, as in an accident. For example, when a child falls and receives a bump, if the parent says HURT, or WHEN YOU DO THAT YOU GET HURT, or THAT HURTS, DOESN'T IT, or some such thing, the relevant verbal stimuli will become aversive.

It would be expected also that these types of training could be, and customarily are, extended on the basis of communication in line with the principles discussed in Chapter 5. For example, by saying THAT'S DANGEROUS, YOU WILL GET HURT, the aversive meaning of HURT would be conditioned also to DANGEROUS. This verbal stimulus would now also be effective in controlling the child's behavior, and through the statement that an activity was dangerous, further appropriate avoidant behavior could be produced. Another example would be the statement WHEN SOMEONE IS UNKIND IT HURTS THE OTHER PERSON, which would make UNKIND a conditioned aversive stimulus. Appropriate behavior could then be produced by saying IT WOULD BE UNKIND TO DO THAT.

The formation of conditioned aversive stimuli through communication should also extend to nonverbal stimuli. Provided that in his training DANGEROUS has come to be an aversive stimulus, when an individual is told DRIVING FAST IS DANGEROUS, this would make driving fast an aversive stimulus.

When a word has become an aversive stimulus through any of these procedures, control of behavior should be possible through the use of the word as through the use of any unconditioned aversive stimulus. Thus, following some behavior with the aversive word should weaken the behavior. In addition, "withdrawal" of the word contingent upon some behavior should serve to strengthen that behavior. With a child for whom BAD is an aversive stimulus, the statement THAT WAS A BAD THING TO DO would be expected to weaken the behavior involved. On the other hand, if the child does something else which ameliorates the situation and is told THAT IS BETTER, it would be expected that this "removal" of the aversive stimulus BAD would strengthen the new behavior. (In this example the latter statement might also have positive reinforcement value.) The same should also be true of nonverbal stimuli. Following the example already used, when driving fast has become an aversive stimulus through communication, escape from driving fast (driving more slowly) would be negatively reinforced.

In addition to taking the place of primary punishment, aversive verbal stimuli are also important general shapers of behavior for the child. Thus it is important in our society, if the child's behavior is to be controlled, that he respond appropriately to a variety of aversive verbal stimuli. The words DON'T, DANGEROUS, BAD, STOP, FORBIDDEN, MEAN, UN-KIND, UNLAWFUL, and so on, must come to elicit "escape" responses and weaken behavior, or the individual may encounter harmful or socially aversive consequences of far greater severity than that involved in the aversive verbal stimuli. The child who does not respond appropriately when told by a teacher YOU ARE FORBIDDEN TO DO THAT AGAIN, by the policeman THAT IS UNLAWFUL, by the older child or adult THAT IS DANGEROUS, is likely to suffer later aversive stimuli of a social or physical nature.

It might therefore be expected that one's verbal training in this respect would affect the degree to which the individual is cautious, responsible, prudent, and so on, in behavior.

The establishment of aversive verbal stimuli seems to have even greater significance for the adjustment of the child. When the child learns reasoning sequences in addition to verbal aversive stimuli, he then has a means of avoiding behaviors that would be followed by punishment without requiring the administration of controlling stimuli by others. He thus becomes largely independent of control from others. In Chapter 5 the manner in which the individual's behavior can be mediated by reasoning sequences was discussed. The preceding section also suggested that reasoning sequences of behavior could be important to the individual's social adjustment. It would seem that the efficacy of one's reasoning in certain situations would depend in part upon the existence of verbal stimuli in the individual's repertoire which were of an aversive nature. That is, if the individual emits a set of reasoning responses relevant to carrying out some action at a later time and the verbal response in the sequence relevant to the action is an aversive one, then the action will tend to be avoided, whereas if the terminal response is a positive reinforcer, the action will be likely to occur. For example, the student may reason, IF I DON'T STUDY TONIGHT I WILL FAIL THE EXAMINATION. For the individual for whom the verbal stimulus FAIL is strongly aversive, nonstudying behavior will tend to be avoided. The student who does not reason in this manner, or for whom FAIL is not an aversive stimulus, will be less likely to avoid "non-studying."

As has been suggested, although a future event cannot determine behavior that precedes it, verbal response sequences may precede other behavior and determine it. An important aspect of this effect of verbal behavior is the existence of verbal aversive stimuli that control avoidant behavior. The cautious man who "anticipates" the aversive consequences of certain actions, the socially sensitive man who "anticipates" socially aversive consequences of certain actions, and so on, would seem to do so, at least in part, because of training that had established for them effective verbal aversive stimuli, as well as the necessary reasoning verbal response sequences. From this interpretation it would seem to follow that the over-cautious, timid man's behavior may be, in part, a function of a superabundance of this type of training. The irresponsible, reckless, wild individual, on the other hand, may suffer from a deficit in the relevant training. This could occur because he had never received aversive stimulation in training, or because the aversive stimulation was never applied in such a manner that it produced an aversive verbal repertoire which could function in "prudent" reasoning. (See Chapter 11 for examples of abnormal behavior that seem to involve deficits in this type of repertoire.)

This interpretation does not justify heavy punishment, such as spanking, whippings—or for that matter the frequent use of punishment of any kind. If considerable punishment seems required to control the behavior of a child it suggests that proper training methods are not being followed.

In conclusion, it could be said that where—for reasons of safety, for example—the training must be rapid, or where positive reinforcement is ineffective, punishment may play a part in training. Such occasions should constitute a small percentage of parent-child training interactions. When punishment is employed, it would seem advisable that it be infrequent, as slight as is necessary to be aversive, immediately contingent upon the undesirable behavior, and paired with appropriate words so that they can become effective conditioned aversive stimuli. It seems necessary that effective aversive words be developed for the child so that his behavior can be shaped by others through verbal negative reinforcement, rather than only through primary punishment. In addition, aversive words seem to function in the individual's own reasoning sequences and influence prudent actions.

Training Involving Sex Behavior

Stemming from psychoanalytic theory, there has been considerable interest in the manner in which sexual behavior and sexual training are handled in childhood. Certainly, it would seem that this is an important area of human behavior. Aside from the biological function of the behavior, sexual stimulation is an important source of reinforcement, both primary and learned. In addition, the individual is handicapped in many ways if he cannot make a satisfactory sex adjustment—he may find it more difficult to obtain many of the other important reinforcers in life.

It also appears to be generally accepted that the individual's personal experience determines the type of adjustment he will make in this area of behavior—sex behavior appears to be largely learned (Ford and Beach, 1951).

> There is nothing inherent in the undifferentiated sexual potentialities of the infant which guarantees beforehand whether he will develop a "normal" heterosexual pattern or a deviant one. Theoretically, under various educational conditions, almost any pattern could be produced— from complete abstinence to homosexuality or rape. There is almost infinite variety both in the situations which are potentially stimulating sexually, and in the patterns of discharge that an individual may develop (Coleman, 1950, p. 402).

As a consequence, it might be expected that very complex learning tasks would be involved in the development of adjustive sex behavior and that there are very complicated training problems for the parent. For one thing, sexual behavior seems to involve very fine discriminations. Some people should come to function as discriminative stimuli and control sex behaviors, other people must not. In addition, married couples must engage in a complex series of responses where both individuals must supply reinforcers contingent upon the behavior of the partner which is reinforcing to him —a complicated type of interaction behavior that may require much learning. Thus, to develop these behaviors it would seem that appropriate constituent behaviors would have to be acquired, and that appropriate reinforcing stimuli and discriminative stimuli must become effective. It is to some of the latter variables that we will first turn our attention.

In Chapter 7 it was suggested that very important to the behavior an individual will display is the system of reinforcers which is effective for him, and that sexual stimuli are an important class of such reinforcers. Although tactile stimulation of the genitals is an unlearned reinforcement, neutral stimuli that are paired with genital stimulation should acquire reinforcing value, in other words, become conditioned "sex" reinforcers. Thus, the sight, sound, and smell of various stimulus objects might be expected to become sex reinforcers in the course of the child's history.

> In the higher mammals, including the human, tactile stimulation is the chief mechanical source of arousal; but the higher mammal, especially the human, soon becomes so conditioned by his experience, or by the vicari-

ously shared experience of others, that psychologic stimulation becomes the major source of arousal for many an older person . . . (Kinsey, Pomeroy, and Martin, 1948, p. 157).

It might also be expected with respect to genital stimulation that children might have different experiences with a variety of stimulus objects. For example, farm animals are more accessible to farm boys and apparently, as a consequence, these stimuli are more apt to acquire sex reinforcement value than is the case with city boys. Kinsey *et al.* list twenty-three types of physical stimulations that are nonsexual sources of erotic responses in preadolescent boys, for example, "friction with clothing," "taking a shower," "riding horseback," and "motion of a car or bus" (p. 164).

Since there is close physical contact within a family in the processes of caring for the child and in play, some of which results in inadvertent genital stimulation for the child, it might be expected that the family members as stimulus objects would be most likely to become conditioned sex reinforcers. Perhaps, also, because of customs in our culture there is more contact between mother and son, and between father and daughter, than between parent and child of the same sex; this to some extent might account for the acquisition of reinforcement value by members of the opposite sex.

This experience is not completely one-sided, however, since there is in our society much interaction between children of the same sex, some of the experience inadvertent, some frankly sexual in nature, which could result in acquired sex reinforcement value. "About half of the older males (48%) and nearer two-thirds (60%) of the boys . . . recall homosexual activity in their pre-adolescent years" (p. 168). But, again in adolescence, through various heterosexual activities—parties, dancing, kissing games, or even direct sexual contact—there appears to be a better opportunity for establishing members of the opposite sex as reinforcers. As with most other experience, there is considerable difference in this sex training among individual children as well as among social classes, as was discussed to some extent in Chapter 7.

Chapters 5 and 7 suggested that the strength and breadth of one's reinforcers are markedly effected by communication experiences. This seems to be true also of one's system of sex reinforcers. The reinforcing value of sex stimuli might be established by means of language, or, on the other hand, it might be weakened by means of language. Language experience could involve verbal interaction with friends, reading materials, or mass communication media. Bandura and McDonald (Bandura, 1962b), for example, have shown that children may be trained to make moral judgments through vicarious experience, through observing a model (adult) being reinforced for making the judgments.

On the basis of the foregoing interpretation it would be expected that the wide experiences of any individual, both of a direct and of a language nature, would establish various stimulus objects as sex reinforcers. Ordinarily, members of the opposite sex would become the strongest reinforcer, some members gaining more value than others. In addition, members of the same sex as well as other stimulus objects could also to some extent become sex reinforcers (as in self-stimulation), and in aberrant cases, objects of various kinds might become reinforcing (see Chapter 11 for a case in which baby carriages and ladies' handbags acquired sexual reinforcement value for an individual).

Thus, the individual's personal experience might be expected to yield a hierarchy of sex reinforcers, ranging from those with very strong reinforcing value to those with very weak value. However, under most conditions, judging only from the overt sexual behavior of the individual, it might seem that only one stimulus object or type of stimulus object was reinforcing for the individual. On the other hand, in a situation where there was no access to this reinforcer, it is possible that the relative value of other reinforcers in the individual's hierarchy would increase. Individuals in a situation where there is no access to members of the opposite sex would be more likely to engage in behavior under the control of other reinforcers, as is shown by homosexuality in prisons and other sexually segregated living situations.

Even in terms of this abbreviated discussion, it can be seen that learning variables would play an important role in determining the stimuli that would become conditioned sex reinforcers. It would also be expected that the nature of the effective sex reinforcers would to some extent determine the type of sex behaviors which would be acquired. For example, if members of the same sex were strong reinforcers for an individual, different behaviors might result in reinforcement and thus be acquired than would be the case if members of the opposite sex were strong reinforcers. The behavior of the homosexual might have a tendency to show differences from that usually acquired by a member of his sex.

To continue, various types of social behaviors must be acquired if the individual is to "obtain" the customary sex reinforcers. The young person must acquire social behaviors of dating, courting, recreational and sports skills with both sexes, work behaviors, and so on. The requisite behaviors may vary from individual to individual depending upon life circumstances For example, the following is a description of such differences.

By the time the [lower-class child] becomes an adolescent, he has learned that it is possible to josh any passing girl, ask for a simple social date, and, inside of a few minutes, suggest intercourse. Such financial resources as will provide a drink, tickets for a movie, or an automobile ride, are at that level sufficient for making the necessary approaches. . . . The average college male plans repeated dates, dinners, expensive entertainments, and long-time acquaintances before he feels warranted in asking for a complete sexual relation (Kinsey, Pomeroy, and Martin, 1948, pp. 265–268).

In summary, the problems of training thus seem to involve at least the following: (1) how to arrange conditions so that appropriate sex reinforcers will be established, (2) how to encourage the child to gain experience which will establish the social behaviors (dating, for example) propaedeutic to the acquisition of sex behavior. To those a third point should be added: the problem of preventing the occurrence of the sex behavior itself until appropriate additional conditions have been satisfied, such as marriage. Thus, the problem of providing good training is complicated by the fact that sex behavior which is considered appropriate and necessary at one stage of life, may result in aversive social responses at another.

When the concern is mainly with preventing the occurrence of premature sexual behavior, the parent may use various methods of discouragement. For example, the child might be told that SEX IS EVIL, SEX IS SINFUL or BOYS (or GIRLS) ARE EVIL, and the like. Other things being equal, this training would be expected to markedly diminish the reinforcing value of members of the opposite sex, even perhaps resulting in the opposite sex becoming aversive as sex reinforcers. Or the development of sexual behavior of any acceptable kind might be largely prevented. Sexual exploration, including dating and other heterosexual activities, might be punished. Again, if the appropriate behaviors do not develop, it may be impossible for the individual to gain access to heterosexual reinforcers. In this case, as well as in the former case, he may be forced into a situation of effective sexual segregation that may lead to the development of aberrant sexual reinforcers.

Perhaps a way of leaving heterosexual reinforcers effective, but of preventing the emission of the sexual behavior, would be to develop controlling discriminative stimuli of a social nature. As an example, instructions that SEX IS FINE, BUT ONLY IN THE PROPER CIRCUMSTANCES, and so on, might be expected to have an effect different from SEX IS EVIL, even though both types of training might restrain the immediate overt practice of sex. In the former case, it might be easier to remove the controlling discriminative stimuli after marriage than in the latter where the sex reinforcers would have been changed in value.

On the basis of this analysis, it would seem that there are several potentially difficult aspects to the training. Many children apparently acquire improper sex reinforcers; some acquire none. The same is true of the sex behaviors. Other children may acquire strong reinforcers and well-developed sex behaviors but under inappropriate control, and the behavior would thus occur under circumstances considered deviant.

While this discussion must be considered both as limited and tentative, it is suggested that further consideration of the above problems within the framework of behavior principles might well prove valuable.

Working Behavior

In our society achievements of various kinds are extremely important and requisite to the acquisition of various social and material reinforcers. As a consequence work behaviors are generally critical to the individual's adjustment.

> If we return to the question of why men work, we find the answer only in many motives. Men work not only to secure food and shelter, but also because work means prestige and self-realization, and because work is applauded by society while idleness is scorned. Men also work because they thus secure the approval and the well-being of individuals to whom they are love-conditioned. To a young man, work means income and therefore money for dates and the possibility of marriage. Work thereby involves the sexual motive (Shaffer and Shoben, 1956, pp. 90–91).

In view of the importance of work behaviors, it seems justified to spend a moment on the topic. The manner in which "achievement" stimuli can become reinforcers was discussed in Chapter 6; however, there are several other points that might be made. First, vigorous and continued activity appears to produce stimuli that are aversive in character. Thus, it is negatively reinforcing to cease such activity. The greater the number of responses required per reinforcer the more aversive the activity appears to be (Azrin, 1961).

It might be expected, in view of the above, that it would not be effective to *introduce* an organism to a work schedule which required many responses with infrequent reinforcement. The findings of the effects of schedules of reinforcement upon behavior yield the same conclusion. As was discussed in Chapter 3, an organism cannot be placed immediately upon a schedule that produces a reinforcer only after a large number of trials. In such a case, the response may extinguish before the reinforcer is acquired—or the behavior may remain weak and irregular for a long period.

On the basis of such findings it might be expected that the child's history with respect to work behaviors, and the manner and type of reinforcement made contingent upon such behavior, will markedly affect the extent to which he is capable of sustained and effective work behaviors. A history of gradually increasing work demands in the sense of the delay of reinforcement, and under the action of effective reinforcers, would be expected to produce greater work productivity than a history deficient in these variables.

> An optimal schedule of reinforcement of a repertoire is essential at an early stage of development if a strong disposition to engage in the performance is to be maintained later under less optimal schedules. The genesis of avid gamblers illustrates the importance of the schedule of reinforcement during the initial acquisition of the repertoire. Professional gamblers, for example, will arrange a high frequency of reinforcement for the beginner in order to provide conditions under which the beginner will continue to gamble later when the schedule of reinforcement is less adequate. Similarly, at least a part of the difference between the person who continues to gamble, and those who failed to continue after a brief exposure, lies in the initial "luck." . . .
>
> The community maximizes the frequency of reinforcement during the educational phase of an individual by providing reinforcement for rough approximations to the ultimately effective forms. . . . Thus, in the early stages of development of the repertoire a higher frequency of reinforcement is more easily achieved than later . . . (Ferster, 1958, p. 111).

It might be expected that a program of training which provided opportunity for increasingly longer and more effortful sequences of productive behavior, always providing adequate reinforcement to maintain the behavior in good strength, would be desirable for producing a hard-working, productive individual. It would be expected that such a program would culminate in reducing the aversive aspects of work behavior to some extent at least, and might possibly make the behavior positively reinforcing.

This latter result might also be achieved on a verbal level through statements such as HARD WORK IS GOOD, HONEST, and so on. In addition, upon the basis of such language conditioning, the individual may come to tact his own working behavior by saying I DID A GOOD DAY'S WORK TODAY, and so on. Such tacts would function as reinforcers for the individual and help maintain work behavior.

Thus, it is suggested that both direct reinforcement of working behaviors, as well as one's language experience, may be important determinants of the individual's work capacity.

Intelligent Behavior

Intelligence is a term widely used in both common and technical languages. Customarily, it is given explanatory value and it is felt that the individual's "intelligence" *accounts* for certain of his behaviors. If he is "intelligent" he behaves intelligently, solves problems well, learns academic material easily, and so on. If his "intelligence" is low or weak he behaves stupidly. A child who behaves subnormally is seen as being "mentally retarded," and as having a stunted development of "intelligence."

Furthermore, most people would feel that this development depends upon variables internal to the individual himself—probably on his biological make-up, his inherited qualities. Although they might recognize that the individual's experience may also affect him, nevertheless the development of the "intelligence" would be seen as primarily a personal, biological process.

Notwithstanding such strong convictions, there have been no independent observations of any internal processes or structures (or faculties) which could be labeled by our common concept of "mental development," "intelligence," or what have you. There are no observations of internal events ("intelligence") that correlate with the normal differences in people's intelligent behavior. Thus, any characteristics that are attributed to an internal structure or process of "intelligence" must have been established upon the basis of other types of observation.

As is customarily the case when the characteristics of a term are not tied to explicit observations, these characteristics are relatively free to vary and many inconsistent and sometimes conflicting definitions of the term may result—which is what seems to have occurred with the term "intelligence." "The somewhat confusing thing is the multitude of definitions which have been offered for intelligence. There are almost as many definitions as there are psychologists to make them" (Kimble, 1956, p. 51).

Many of these definitions unfortunately follow the same methodology of inferring inner processes to account for the external behaviors observed. In addition, however, it has been suggested that the term "intelligence" may be operationally defined as the behavior observed when an intelligence test is given; thus we may define "intelligence" as intelligent behavior, as measured by tests (Boring, 1923). Used in this way the term would be a descriptive label for a certain type of behavior.

Furthermore, it has been suggested that "intelligence" may also be operationally defined as the intelligent behavior the individual demonstrates in his everyday life, in school success, in work success, and so on (Kimble, 1956). Again, used in this way the term would be a descriptive label for a certain type of behavior.

Naturally, these two definitions are related. Intelligence tests were constructed to aid in identifying children who were, and would be, training problems in school. As a result, the success of school behavior should be predictable from intelligence test behavior. Intelligence test behavior should also be related to success of behavior in certain types of work situations.

Because of this relationship between the two types of intelligent behaviors, it has been suggested that the relationship $(R_1 \rightarrow R_2)$ may be used in identifying "intelligence." Accordingly, the term "intelligence" could be considered to be an intervening variable defined on the one side by test behavior and on the other side by performance in school and work situations (Kimble, 1956).

However, as was discussed in Chapter 3, R–R laws are not explanatory in the sense that the antecedent event R_1 is a determinant of R_2, the consequent event. Although one could predict R_2 from R_1 (or vice versa), control of R_2 could not be gained from manipulating R_1, the individual's intelligence test behavior. The antecedents of both R_1 and R_2 must be sought if explanatory understanding is to be gained. Without these antecedents specified the term intelligence would still be only a descriptive label with no explanatory value.

This is not to say, of course, that the R–R laws found between intelligence test behaviors and school behaviors are not important. It is very useful, as an example, to be able to observe children under standard conditions for the intelligent behavior they display, in comparison with other children. From these observations important predictions can be made of the probable success of the child in school, the types of educational tasks for which he is prepared, and so on. Thus, the field of intelligence test construction and use has included some of psychology's most systematic work, has yielded many technical skills, and has made many practical contributions. The present discussion of intelligence will not be able to survey this area of study and the technical knowledge involved in test construction and use. For this material there are excellent sources available.

If, on the other hand, one is interested in accounting for intelligent behavior on a test, or in school or work situations, the conditions that determine such behavior must be found. It is of no use whatsoever, and may be quite misleading, to infer some internal, unobservable process that is identified only by the behavior of the individual.

As was mentioned in Chapter 2, there are two general types of determining conditions that may be investigated to account for some behavior—the biology of the individual and the environmental conditions that have impinged upon him. Early in the development of the study of intelligent behavior questions arose concerning the relative contributions of these two types of determinants. Many studies were conducted to correlate environmental factors with IQ tests or to correlate closeness of genetic structure, as measured by closeness of familial relationship, with such tests (see Fowler, 1962, for a review of such research). Customarily these studies attempted only to demonstrate either that environmental factors did or did not play an important role in learning. The necessary experimental work to establish the determinants of intelligent behavior, whether learning or biological, has not yet been conducted—nor has a detailed specification been made of the behaviors included in the category "intelligence."

The largest amount of work has consisted of cross-sectional studies of children and adults of all ages. In these studies, investigators have correlated IQ test performances and environmental indices (amount of education; parents' educational, occupational, and social class level; urban-rural differences; etc.). A multitude of relationships of this kind, often important, have been found. Their value may be considered only partially attenuated by the discovery of other associations which concede greater importance to heredity (e.g., between IQ scores of parents and their children). *The basic problem stems from the fact that broad, background correlations throw insufficient light on particular environmental ante-cedent-consequent relationships* [italics added]. . . .

The extensive work done on intelligence in relation to the nature-nurture problem has been the subject of vigorous discussion and conflicting findings over many years (cf. Anastasi, 1958). But one regrettable consequence has been the manner in which arguments over the relative importance of heredity and environment have obscured the fact that the environment does perform an *essential* role in development. It is difficult to argue, considering all the evidence, that environment has a *negligible* role in producing mental test variations or in developing intelligence and conceptual abilities, however important genetic factors may also be. The dispute has seriously retarded interest in experimental work on pre-school cognitive learning. It also has discouraged long range educational programs aimed at developing each child to near the maximum level of his capacities (Fowler, 1962, pp. 125–128).

In summary, it would seem that an interest in accounting for the development of intelligent behavior must lead to a detailed consideration of the behaviors involved and to the way that this behavior is acquired—as Fowler states, discovery of the "particular environmental antecedent-consequent relationships." It may be suggestive in indicating the possibilities of such an approach to analyze some of the behaviors included on a child's intelligence test in terms of the types of learning principles described in earlier chapters. Such an analysis will not, of course, take the place of research to find the particular environmental determinants of intelligent behavior, but it may demonstrate what sort of explanatory statements are required, as well as what some of the determinants may be.

Intelligence Test Behaviors Considered as Learned

There are a great many items on an intelligence test such as the Revised Stanford-Binet (Terman and Merrill, 1937), test items from which will be considered here, and it would be prohibitive in terms of space to attempt to discuss each one as a learned behavior. In addition, many of them are quite complex and would require a very involved analysis. For these reasons only samples of the items that seem to fit some of the types of learned behavior discussed in prior sections of this book will be analyzed. These types of items, however, do compose a good percentage of the test.

Tacting items.—Tacting responses, as well as the appropriate response to the instructions (verbal stimuli) presented by the examiner, constitute a considerable proportion of the behavior required on the Stanford-Binet with items testing these types of behavior occurring at a number of age levels. Thus, the child is shown pictures of a common object and asked, " 'What's this?' 'What do you call it.' " (p. 77) The child must tact the picture appropriately.

On the basis of the detailed discussion of the development of a repertoire of tacts presented in Chapter 4, it would be expected that the success of the child on such test items would be a function of his training in this area of behavior. In addition to training involving stimulus objects, it would be expected that training of observing and responding to pictures would be important, since a pictured or schematized object is quite different from the object itself.

Discriminated tacts.—At the three-year-old level two match sticks of different lengths are placed before the child in several parallel positions and the child is asked, " 'Which stick is longer?' 'Put your finger on the long one.' " (p. 84) The child may respond by tacting the two matchsticks with THIS IS THE LONGER ONE, or something to that effect. Such a response would involve the same type of training as is involved in responding to matching stimuli (as discussed in Chapter 4), except in this case it is the "mismatch" which is the controlling stimulus. On this item the response need not be verbal, however; the child may correctly respond by pointing.

Number tacts.—Several items involve counting responses that are largely tacts. However, the type of number response chaining described in Chapter 5 could also be involved. At the five-year level, for example, the examiner is instructed to test the child in the following manner.

> Present the objects [blocks, beads, or pennies] in a row, one series at a time, first the 4 blocks, then the 4 beads, and then the 4 pennies. Remove each preceding series before presenting the next in order. Ask for each series, "How many?" S. is not asked to count or to point, but it is permissible for him to do both (p. 93).

Thus, the child may successfully respond to the item if he has been trained to respond FOUR in the presence of 4 objects. Or, he may be successful if he has acquired the number response sequence ONE–TWO–THREE–FOUR with each response under the control of the single stimulus object plus the stimulus produced by the preceding verbal response.

Echoic behavior and word association items.—There are a number of items involving echoic behavior, where the subject must emit a response which matches that already produced by the examiner. Thus, at age three the child is told to "echo" three digits pronounced by the examiner. This involves the emission of three verbal responses in sequence and success would also seem to involve prior establishment of word associations between the verbal responses.

Prior word associations would seem to be even more critical to the later echoic items. For example, an item at age five instructs the child to repeat sentences ten words in length. As was discussed in Chapter 4 in the section on grammatical sequences, it would be expected that one's "memory" in such tasks would be a function of the strength of the associations between word responses.

Words associations which do not involve echoic behavior are also included on the test. At age two, for example, the child's spontaneous use of word-response sequences in his conversation with the examiner is tabulated. The extent to which the child uses multiple words in his vocalizations determines the score. Examples of multiple words are " 'Mama bye-bye,' 'All gone,' 'See man,' etc." (pp. 77 and 198).

Responses under the control of verbal stimuli, and matching behavior.— The first item on the test for young children includes a board with insets for a circle, square, and triangle. The instructions for administration state: "Present the board with the blocks in place. Place the board so that the base of the triangle will be towards the subject. Say, *'Watch what I do.'* Remove the blocks, placing each before its appropriate recess on the side toward S. . . . Then say, 'Now put them back into their holes' " (p. 75).

The first important behavior is the appropriate response to the verbal instruction, that is, the verbal stimuli as an S^D must control the appropriate observing response of the child. The second statement of the examiner must control an even more complex behavior, that of replacing the objects in their holes. To do this requires rather complex matching skills (see Chapter 4, p. 123). The hole and the object are both of a certain form. The child must respond to the matching stimuli by taking one and inserting it into another, but not do this with disparate forms. (Actually, these matches do not have to be well established for this item. As long as the verbal stimulus controls the appropriate behavior of attempting to insert the blocks in the holes, continued attempts, even if at first unsuccessful, can eventuate in success within the time limit.)

Another item at the two-year-old level of this intelligence test involves both matching and the control of the child's observing responses by verbal stimuli presented by the examiner. In this case the child must build a tower of blocks after the examiner has demonstrated this. The child must match his responses and his final product to those produced by the examiner.

Also at the two-year level is an item on which the child is instructed to point to various objects (button, cup, engine, spoon) and is scored for the appropriate pointing response. The child is presented the miniature objects and the examiner says "Show me the kitty," "Put your finger on the kitty," "Where is the kitty" (p. 75). The verbal stimuli (instructions) and the specific object must, as S^Ds, control the response of looking at the various objects and pointing to the referent object. The kind of discrimination training that would produce success on this item was also discussed in Chapter 4.

Another item at this age-level also involves the same type of behavior and presumably the same type of training. For this item the child must point to the parts of a doll's body as the parts are named by the examiner. Again, it would be expected that children would have varying experience with respect to training in which in the presence of WHERE IS YOUR TOE, for example, the child is socially reinforced for pointing to his toe. A number of other items seem to involve essentially the same types of behavior.

Reasoning response sequences.—A number of items seem to involve reasoning sequences such as were discussed in the section on problem solving and reasoning in Chapter 5. A clear-cut example of reasoning involving number response sequences is given in an item at the Average Adult level. The subject must read the problem on a card and respond without the use of paper and pencil. A sample problem is: "If a man's salary is $20 a week and he spends $14 a week, how long will it take him to save $300?" (p. 122).

Vocabulary items.—There are items that commence at year six and continue to occur throughout the test that ask the child to define words. An appropriate response could involve some of the complex processes discussed in Chapter 4. Meaning responses elicited by the word presented might thus mediate the elicitation of a word in the same verbal habit-family (Staats, 1961). For example, the word ORANGE could elicit the "fruit" meaning-response component that had been conditioned to it. This meaning-response component would also tend to elicit a number of other "fruit" words including the word FRUIT itself.

On the other hand, successful response to the vocabulary item could occur on the basis of word associations. For example, the word ENVELOPE could elicit the response FOR A LETTER on the basis of previous explicit instruction in the sequence AN ENVELOPE IS FOR A LETTER.

At any rate, it would be expected that the types of variables underlying language learning discussed in Chapters 4 and 5 would to a large extent underlie the acquisition of a vocabulary repertoire. Besides training procedures, it would be expected that personal experience, such as amount and type of reading, would affect the vocabulary repertoire.

Implications of a Learning Interpretation of Test Behavior

This interpretation of test behaviors in learning terms suggests that the behaviors usually used to index "intelligence" are learned behaviors. If we are interested in the determinants of these test measurements, we must describe the behaviors involved and look for the learning variables that could function in their acquisition.

More broadly, it may be suggested that intelligent behavior in general is learned behavior, largely of a verbal nature, which includes the following: tacts, reasoning sequences, and communication behaviors; reading, arithmetic, and mathematical repertoires; attentional, observing, and discrimination behaviors; and various skills under verbal control. Many of these behaviors would constitute a basic repertoire for the preschool child on which further acquisition of behaviors important in school would rest. Without the appropriate repertoire, the child would indeed be "retarded."

This interpretation also suggests that many of the variables which determine "intelligence" are accessible to manipulation. This, in turn, suggests not only that wide differences in intelligent behavior are a function of experience, but also that children could be trained to be "intelligent." What the limits are of this training cannot be established on the basis of conjecture, however. Such questions are empirical and will only be answered by attempts to manipulate, under controlled research circumstances, those learning variables that will lead to intelligent behavior. (See the next chapter for a discussion of a relevant research methodology.)

The Parent as a Trainer

In the various preceding chapters we have attempted to show how significant complex human behaviors are acquired according to learning principles. In these discussions it has also been suggested that the parent plays a most important role in the training of these complex behaviors. As a consequence, for a parent faced with the task of providing propitious learning conditions, a simple analysis of behavior leading to very general instructions for child care may be insufficient, if not actually harmful. For example, a philosophy of developmental stages or maturational processes, while it may at times serve various purposes, such as quieting the mother's fears, is not sufficient in the many training tasks where the parent must take positive action.

Or, to take another example, it is also frequently suggested that specific training is unnecessary and that it is the parent's attitude which is crucial to acquisition of behavioral skills (see McCandless, 1961, pp. 86–87), that the parents must be loving and warm and comforting and not rejecting or frustrating. However, it would seem that this is not sufficient as an instruction to a parent, nor would it necessarily provide a good learning atmosphere for the child. Within the pattern of a loving mother widely different training practices leading to widely different behaviors of the children could occur.

On the other hand, there are aspects of the parents' love for the child that would seem to be affected by their ability as trainers. Much has been said of the cold, loveless, rejecting mother. Little has been said of the fact that there are great differences in the "attractiveness," or positive reinforcing qualities, of the behavior of their children. Some children are "lovable," their behavior has many positive features and few aversive ones. The child whose behavior has aversive aspects—the whining, crying, complaining child; or the overshy, dependent, nonresponsive child; or the aggressive, cruel, hostile, demanding child, and so on—will not acquire positive reinforcing value (be lovable) as a function of this type of behavior.

As was discussed in the previous chapter, the social interactions of individuals and the extent to which they are "attractive" to others depend to an important extent upon the reinforcing value of their behavior. It would be expected that this would hold as well for the parent-child relationship. In order for the parent to be a positive reinforcing stimulus object for the child, the child has to receive positive reinforcement in the presence of the parent. It is suggested that the same is true in reverse, however, and that one of the important sources of reinforcement for the parent is the behavior of the child. It would be expected that the degree to which the parent is loving will depend to some extent upon the behavior of the child.

Thus, the fact that a mother cares for a child as a duty without enthusiasm, or is cold, loveless, and rejecting, may be secondary. That is, her behavior may be a result of the fact that she does not have the skills as a trainer with which to shape behavior in her child which is reinforcing to her and to others. As a consequence she receives relatively little positive reinforcement from the child, as well as relatively little positive reinforcement from other people concerning her child.

In summary, a learning analysis of the acquisition of behavior leads to a focus upon the parent as a *trainer*. Whether the parent intends to or not, he manipulates many conditions of learning that will determine to a large extent the behaviors the child will acquire. As long as the child's behavioral development consists of innumerable training experiences, many of which occur in the home, then the parent has many of the controlling variables in his hands and cannot relinquish them regardless of his philosophy of child development.

This suggests that the parent could be an active participant in arranging circumstances to most efficaciously produce an abundant, rich, adjustive, behavioral repertoire using a minimum of aversive stimulation and a maximum of positive reinforcement. Good working behaviors, good studying behaviors, the ability to work without immediate reinforcement; reasonable, cooperative, not overselfish behavior; a good language system about the world, his own behavior, and that of others; a good system of reinforcers, including words of positive and negative reinforcement value; social stimuli that appropriately control striving and nonstriving behavior; social behaviors that reinforce other people as well as oneself; these seem to be some of the behaviors that the parents help determine by the conditions they present to the child. Thus, to a large extent the learning conditions that occur in the home would seem to determine whether the child will grow into a "well-adjusted," "happy," "productive" individual.

Faced with a training task of such imposing responsibilities, it would seem that the parent would need an understanding of the principles of behavior by which children learn. In addition, it would seem that the parent would require an analysis in terms of those principles of the various specific training problems he faces. The parent needs to know how not to shape undesirable behaviors, or, when they have developed, how to decrease them benignly; and he needs to know how to shape the many adjustive behaviors the child will require.

Some of the discussions of training tasks in the present chapter represent a theoretical extension of behavior principles to naturalistic observations of the stimuli and behaviors involved—some of the observations made by the authors themselves. It is thus evident that much research is necessary to clarify the problems of training in order to provide the knowledge needed by the parent with which to deal with those problems. Such research should cover the problems discussed in the present chapter as well as many others which are important. Certain aspects of the type of research which might produce such information will be discussed in the next chapter. The need for knowledge concerning child learning is well expressed in this statement by Dollard and Miller.

> The slowness, the labor, and the expense of psychotherapy are evident to all, especially to patients and therapists. Analysis of the forces involved does not make it seem likely that therapists will hit on swift, economical techniques for treating neurotic patients. The important inference from this fact is the following: neurosis must be prevented, not cured; its waste and loss must be avoided, not repaired late in life. Since we hold that neurotic behavior is learned, we also hold that it is taught—taught unwittingly by the confused practices of child rearing in our culture. As of today, there is no science of child rearing (Dollard, 1949). Fad after fad sweeps the field. The parents of today weep at the thought of the pseudo-science they practiced yesterday on their beloved children. Neurotic behavior in children is dismissed as a mere incident of growth.

Research is conducted in the clinic—and the home, where all happens, is neglected. Advice given to parents is mainly "ad-libbed." It lacks the pattern and ordering which it might have were it derived from a powerful scientific theory. It lacks the power to prevent or to predict the disaster of a severe behavior disorder.

Further research in psychotherapy will teach ever new things about the higher mental life of human beings. But though such research is urgently needed and will contribute greatly to human welfare, it will never solve the problem of neurosis. That solution can come only by such a powerful and systematic knowledge of how children learn in our culture as to enable us to change those culture patterns which produce neurosis. We now know how to go about the needed research. New developments in learning theory offer a powerful systematic basis for development. The zeal and the resources to launch the research on child learning must be found (1950, p. 428).

10

Experimental Educational
Psychology

THE FOLLOWING statement, although addressed to the fields of child psychology and development, is equally cogent in this introduction to the field of educational psychology.

> Much if not most of the energy in child psychology and development in late years has been concentrated on the child's personality, perceptual motor, and socioemotional functioning and development. Originating primarily as a reaction to historically inadequate and stringent methods, fears have generalized to encompass early cognitive learning per se as intrinsically hazardous to development. As legitimate areas of study, the contributions of studies on perceptual-motor and socioemotional problems are obvious. But in the field of child guidance, interest in these areas has come to permeate and dominate work in child development almost to the exclusion of work on cognitive learning. In harking constantly to the dangers of premature cognitive training, the image of the "happy," socially adjusted child has tended to expunge the image of the thoughtful and intellectually educated child. Inevitably, in this atmosphere, research (and education) in cognition has lagged badly, especially since the 1930s, not only for the early years of childhood but for all ages (Fowler, 1962, p. 145).

Consistent with this, educational psychology has been in late years primarily interested in the child's personality, attitudes, socioemotional adjustment, and interpersonal skills. Its methods have relied heavily upon testing the child's achievements and abilities, and child-guidance techniques. While these topics continue to be of great concern in the educational situation, in the present book most of these topics have been considered in preceding chapters, or will be in the following one. The present chapter, on the other hand, will be concerned with learning principles and methods applied to the study and solution of problems involving the acquisition of various types of motor and intellectual skills related to formal education.

This type of application received its impetus from B. F. Skinner, as part of his general conviction that the principles of operant conditioning have wide application to the understanding of human behavior and the control of its problems. Perhaps the best known application of learning principles to problems in educational psychology has been in the area called variously programed teaching, teaching machines, automated instruction, and so on. Although this is only one representative possibility of the importance of the application of learning principles to educational psychology, its significance is major in terms both of its particular accomplishments and of the general methodology involved in the approach.

AUTOMATED INSTRUCTION

Skinner has stated that the "advances in the experimental analysis of behavior suggest that for the first time we can develop a true technology of education. This technology, following the practice of the laboratory, will use instrumentation to equip students with large repertoires of verbal and nonverbal behavior. Even more important, the instrumentation will be able to nurture enthusiasm for continued study. The instruments that will help our schools to accomplish all this are called teaching machines" (Skinner, 1961, pp. 91–92).

The major components of this educational technology taken from experimental psychology include, in addition to the instrumentation, (1) an assumption that the behaviors to be established are operants, (2) which must be gradually shaped, (3) through the application of experimental methodology.

The last of these, the experimental approach to the development of appropriate teaching methods, is probably the most important and is involved in the others. It should be emphasized that the automated instruction movement has, from the beginning, been an attempt to approach educational tasks as experimental problems. Thus, training programs have been slowly and systematically studied.

The tentative programs have been administered to single subjects and the behavior of each individual has been studied. On the basis of the degree of success of the program in producing the desired criterion behavior, parts of the program are retained, others altered. Slowly, experimentally, a program is developed that will produce certain explicit and observable behavior. As will be discussed more fully later, this process has usually involved working for a long period of time with a single subject, rather than with testing the relative merit of two methods with two groups of subjects.

The application of experimental methods has included the development of equipment to control the presentation of the training program—the widely known teaching machine. The teaching machine assures that the stimulus materials to be presented, as well as the other variables to be manipulated, occur as planned—are not subject to the vagaries of the individual student's and teacher's behavior.

Another primary principle of the automated-instruction approach is the consideration of the behavior as acquired according to operant conditioning principles. Reinforcement is considered necessary to the maintenance and acquisition of behavior. Principles of discrimination learning are extended to the establishment of new discriminations, and so on. Furthermore, following upon a stimulus–response approach, the attempt has been to break the complex behaviors into simpler components. The program then attempts to establish the constituent behaviors in the subject.

A derivation from both the definition of training as the acquisition of operant behavior and the experimental approach of analyzing behavior into its constituents has been to design "programs" that progress gradually in a step-by-step manner.

With this as the introduction, the following sections will elaborate on some of these points.

Stimulus Materials—the Program

It was said that the orientation of an experimental approach to teaching has involved the method of analyzing complex behaviors into simpler constituents. "Programing" is the part of educational technology concerned with the precise selection and arrangement of educational content.

Programing begins with an analysis of the complex behaviors to be taught and arranges them in a sequence so that the constituents eventually build into the final behavior. It has thus been suggested that the programer start from the teaching objective and work back. "The programer has to begin by identifying . . . the specific responses that constitute criterion behavior. . . . Once each task has been analyzed, it is necessary to determine as best as one can, the capability of the learner at the beginning of training. Between these two levels the transition or modification requirement is located. . . . The main point is that once the criterion behavior is identified, then the plan can be made to move the learner to that point" (Stolurow, 1961, p. 85).

The various responses to be acquired in much material are related in such fashion that one response must be learned before the next can be. Learning in mathematics, the physical sciences, many aspects of language, and so on is of this type. An example of what is meant by programing in general

PART OF A PROGRAM IN HIGH-SCHOOL PHYSICS

The machine presents one item at a time. The student completes the item and then uncovers the corresponding word or phase shown at the right.

SENTENCE TO BE COMPLETED	WORD TO BE SUPPLIED
1. The important parts of a flashlight are the battery and the bulb. When we "turn on" a flashlight, we close a switch which connects the battery with the _____.	bulb
2. When we turn on a flashlight, an electric current flows through the fine wire in the _____ and causes it to grow hot.	bulb
3. When the hot wire glows brightly, we say that it gives off or sends out heat and _____.	light
4. The fine wire in the bulb is called a filament. The bulb "lights up" when the filament is heated by the passage of a(n) _____ current.	electric
5. When a weak battery produces little current, the fine wire, or _____, does not get very hot.	filament
6. A filament which is less hot sends out or gives off _____ light.	less
7. "Emit" means "send out." The amount of light sent out, or "emitted," by a filament depends on how _____ the filament is.	hot
8. The higher the temperature of the filament the _____ the light emitted by it.	brighter, stronger
9. If a flashlight battery is weak, the _____ in the bulb may still glow, but with only a dull red color.	filament
10. The light from a very hot filament is colored yellow or white. The light from a filament which is not very hot is colored _____.	red
11. A blacksmith or other metal worker sometimes makes sure that a bar of iron is heated to a "cherry red" before hammering it into shape. He uses the _____ of the light emitted by the bar to tell how hot it is.	color
12. Both the color and the amount of light depend on the _____ of the emitting filament or bar.	temperature
13. An object which emits light because it is hot is called "incandescent." A flashlight bulb is an incandescent source of _____.	light
14. A neon tube emits light but remains cool. It is, therefore, not an incandescent _____ of light.	source
15. A candle flame is hot. It is a(n) _____ source of light.	incandescent
16. The hot wick of a candle gives off small pieces or particles of carbon which burn in the flame. Before or while burning, the hot particles send out, or _____, light.	emit

Fig. 10.1. Excerpt from a program in high-school physics (Skinner, 1958, p. 973)

17. A long candlewick produces a flame in which oxygen does not reach all the carbon particles. Without oxygen the particles cannot burn. Particles which do not burn rise above the flame as _____.　　smoke

18. We can show that there are particles of carbon in a candle flame, even when it is not smoking, by holding a piece of metal in the flame. The metal cools some of the particles before they burn, and the unburned carbon _____ collect on the metal as soot.　　particles

19. The particles of carbon in soot or smoke no longer emit light because they are _____ than when they were in the flame.　　cooler, colder

20. The reddish part of a candle flame has the same color as the filament in a flashlight with a weak battery. We might guess that the yellow or white parts of a candle flame are _____ than the reddish part.　　hotter

21. "Putting out" an incandescent electric light means turning off the current so that the filament grows too _____ to emit light.　　cold, cool

22. Setting fire to the wick of an oil lamp is called _____ the lamp.　　lighting

23. The sun is our principal _____ of light, as well as of heat.　　source

24. The sun is not only very bright but very hot. It is a powerful _____ source of light.　　incandescent

25. Light is a form of energy. In "emitting light" an object changes, or "converts," one form of _____ into another.　　energy

26. The electrical energy supplied by the battery in a flashlight is converted to _____ and _____.　　heat, light; light, heat

27. If we leave a flashlight on, all the energy stored in the battery will finally be changed or _____ into heat and light.　　converted

28. The light from a candle flame comes from the _____ released by chemical changes as the candle burns.　　energy

29. A nearly "dead" battery may make a flashlight bulb warm to the touch, but the filament may still not be hot enough to emit light—in other words, the filament will not be _____ at that temperature.　　incandescent

30. Objects, such as a filament, carbon particles, or iron bars, become incandescent when heated to about 800 degrees Celsius. At that temperature they begin to _____ _____.　　emit light

31. When raised to any temperature above 800 degrees Celsius, an object such as an iron bar will emit light. Although the bar may melt or vaporize, its particles will be _____ no matter how hot they get.　　incandescent

32. About 800 degrees Celsius is the lower limit of the temperature at which particles emit light. There is no upper limit of the _____ at which emission of light occurs.　　temperature

33. Sunlight is _____ by very hot gases near the surface of the sun.　　emitted

34. Complex changes similar to an atomic explosion generate the great heat which explains the _____ of light by the sun.　　emission

35. Below about _____ degrees Celsius an object is not an incandescent source of light.　　800

Fig. 10.1. (Continued)

which also demonstrates this need for planned sequencing is given by an excerpt from a program in high-school physics as shown in Figure 10.1.

It can be seen from this short excerpt that because the technical terms, facts, laws, principles, and examples are arranged in a plausible developmental order, the student moves from a largely unverbalized acquaintance with such objects as flashlights and candles to an understanding of the subject, including new facts, vocabulary, and so on.

The excerpt illustrates another aspect of programed instruction that results from the analytic approach. The items progress in small steps, and therefore the training the subject has already received within the program should guarantee that the correct response will be made to each item—which is the subject's reinforcement.

Besides the order of the items in a program, behavioral analysis of the behavior to be taught may suggest other means of establishing the necessary repertoire. Often this involves bringing a response under the control of new stimuli, as the following example will illustrate. In the Holland-Skinner program in psychology the subject is shown a graph depicting stimulus generalization where a particular stimulus has through conditioning come to control a response. The graph shows that when similar stimuli are presented, there is a gradual decline in number of responses as a function of the distance of the new stimulus from the stimulus present during reinforcement. In the program the student is asked to complete the statement: "As the wave length changes in either direction from the wave length present during reinforcement, the number of responses _____" (Holland and Skinner, 1961, p. 150). The answer is, of course, "decreases."

This example illustrates the use of one S^D, the graph, which already controls a particular verbal response, to bring the verbal response under the control of another S^D, in this case a verbal statement (the item). Thus, the S^D of the item is paired with the graph that elicits the tact "decreases." When the new S^D (the item) controls this response, the subject may be said to have acquired the verbal "principle of stimulus generalization."

There are other techniques of programing that involve stimulus control of a sort called "vanishing," or "fading." For example, in teaching the geography of the United States, a fully labeled map might be placed before the student while he works with a large set of items pertaining to the spatial relations among the various mountains, rivers, and so on shown on the map. The student would complete several items in this way. Then another map would be placed before him as he works on the next set of frames, but on this map the sites would be labeled only with initials. After completing these items he would then go on to another set and its accompanying map, but this time the map would not be labeled at all—the controlling S^Ds are "faded" further. These items would be followed by still another set of new frames, but now the map would be entirely removed. The student should finally be able to discuss the geographical relations without an accompanying map. It is expected that if the material has been well programed, the student will be able to progress through these various stages with few if any errors.

In this example, the labels and the map first serve as controlling discriminative stimuli for the responses, but after repeated pairings of the verbal items with the map, the items themselves acquire discriminative control of the responses.

Other techniques of presentation of stimulus materials can also be derived from a behavioral analysis of the material to be acquired, supplemented by an analysis of the student's history of conditioning to indicate what behavior on the part of the student can be assumed. Formal prompts refer, for example, to textual stimuli that can be used to evoke a response so that it can be brought under the control of a new S^D. Echoics can be used in the same manner. Skinner and Holland (1960) suggest several ways that echoic and textual discriminative stimuli can be used to produce new terms. The most common is probably the "definition" or "example." The following frame from a psychology program illustrates the technique.

> A technical word for "reward" is reinforcement. To "reward" an organism with food is to _____ it with food (p. 165).

All students gave the correct response "reinforce" to this item. Since the definition was given within the frame, the response would be said to be evoked by a *textual prompt*.

Another more complex example of prompting as a programing technique is the "ruleg" system of Homme and Glaser, who suggest that *all* verbal statements in a program of verbal knowledge of a subject matter can be shown to belong to one of two categories: They are all either rules or examples. Both rules and examples, they suggest, can function as extremely powerful prompts.

In the following illustration, in frame (1) the first sentence is a "rule" that acts as a prompt for the example in the second sentence. In frame (2) the example is given again, but this time the prompting rule is withdrawn.

1. To "emit" light means to "send out" light. For example, the sun, a fluorescent tube, and a bonfire have in common that they all send out or _____ light.
2. A firefly and an electric light bulb are alike in that they both send out or _____ light.

(These frames are from the Skinner High-School Physics Program reconstructed according to the ruleg system; Homme and Glazer, 1960, p. 491.)

This system is not theoretically different from the "vanishing" system, but does show that in going from the learning model to its implementation in programing, several technical variations are possible. Each of these methods will also have to be tested empirically before decisions on their relative merits can be made.

Another set of techniques also derived from a behavioral analysis of the material is called *thematic prompting* (Skinner and Holland, 1960).

> The thematic prompt is a specialized form of interverbal dependency. . . .
> [One] example of the exploitation of interverbal dependencies is in the construction of items containing parallel grammatical constructions. Strong tendencies exist for humans to emit synonyms or antonyms to verbal stimuli. For example, in studies of free association, many common responses to verbal stimuli are the opposite or the antonym of the verbal stimulus. One may exploit this tendency in the verbal behavior of students. Consider the example "With increased food deprivation the response rate of the organism increases and with decreased food deprivation the response rate _____." Not only does the tendency to emit opposites determine the response in this item, but the parallel construction strengthens the tendency to echo the word "decrease." In the first half of the statement "increase" is repeated; the parallel construction determines the repetition of "decrease" (Green, 1962, p. 153).

Since in any of these cases one trial may not result in the acquisition of a response in sufficient strength for it to be reliably emitted under the appropriate conditions, it is often necessary to program repetitions into the materials. This is illustrated in the set of frames that were designed to shape a correct spelling response of "manufacture," as shown in Figure 10.2.

Many other examples could be cited. However, this discussion attempts only to illustrate some of the general methods of programing for automated instruction, without fully describing either the results of the approach, or its full armamentarium of specific methods and techniques. It should be pointed out that, utilizing this general approach, programs have been constructed in such diverse fields as spelling, grammar, mathematics, foreign languages, shape discrimination, inductive reasoning, a "sense" of rhythm and pitch, and chess playing, to mention a few examples.

Reinforcement Principles in Automated Instruction

The major behavior principles, in addition to those already mentioned, that are involved in the "automated teaching movement" concern reinforcement. First and foremost is the conception that behavior is acquired and maintained through the action of reinforcing stimuli. Without adequate reinforcement new behaviors are not acquired and old ones weaken in strength.

A SET OF FRAMES DESIGNED TO TEACH A THIRD- OR FOURTH-GRADE PUPIL TO SPELL THE WORD "MANUFACTURE"

1. **Manufacture** means to make or build. *Chair factories manufacture chairs.* Copy the word here:

   ☐ ☐ ☐ ☐ ☐ ☐ ☐ ☐ ☐ ☐

2. Part of the word is like part of the word **factory**. Both parts come from an old word meaning *make* or *build.*

   m a n u ☐ ☐ ☐ ☐ u r e

3. Part of the word is like part of the word **manual**. Both parts come from an old word for *hand*. Many things used to be made by hand.

   ☐ ☐ ☐ ☐ f a c t u r e

4. The same letter goes in both spaces:

   m ☐ n u f ☐ c t u r e

5. The same letter goes in both spaces:

   m a n ☐ f a c t ☐ r e

6. **Chair factories** ☐ ☐ ☐ ☐ ☐ ☐ ☐ ☐ ☐ ☐ ☐ **chairs.**

Fig. 10.2. Frames designed to shape the correct spelling of the word "manufacture" (Skinner, 1958, p. 972)

A most important aspect of this general conception is the process of successive approximation discussed in Chapters 3 and 4. It was shown in detail how an organism may be trained to emit a new response by first reinforcing very gross approximations to the response, then reinforcing only progressively better and better approximations to the criterion while the poorer approximations are allowed to extinguish. In this process, it was pointed out, the "trainer" must not raise his standards too rapidly, reinforcing only those responses which represent large improvements. If the "steps" are too large, few of the organism's responses will be reinforced—and the behavior of generally participating may become too weak to keep the organism in the training situation. If that occurs, tuition ceases.

This paradigm may be extended to human learning, and the same principles applied to the construction of programs to train repertoires in various fields of study. An interesting example is in the teaching of rhythm. In this program a device is used that produces a rhythmic pattern; the student's task is to reproduce the pattern by tapping a key. "At first the student is allowed a wide margin of error. He can be early or late with each tap, but these specifications are gradually sharpened until the student's performance reaches a satisfactory level of precision" (Skinner, 1961, p. 102).

However, as the preceding section illustrated, the programing task is not strictly one of successive approximation when dealing with verbal behavior. Most of the constituent verbal responses are already in the subject's repertoire; what is required is to form the responses into new sequences, to bring them under the control of new stimuli, and the like.

Nevertheless, even in these tasks the general principles of reinforcement involved in successive approximation are important, since plenty of reinforcement must be assured if general participation and the basic behaviors of reading and study are not to extinguish from lack of reinforcement. The analogy from the process of successive approximation is the gradualness of the behaviorally designed program. The steps must be small, and there must be sufficient repetition so that the subject rarely experiences "failure" in responding to the items. This means that the material must introduce new information or new concepts only at the rate at which the individual can proceed without making errors.

Another principle of behavior already discussed involves the delay of reinforcement. Greatest behavioral strengthening occurs when the reinforcer follows the response immediately. When the time lapse is too great the reinforcement is ineffective. At this point, however, the reader may be wondering just what reinforcing stimuli are available in the automated instruction situation.

Holland suggests that the only reinforcement necessary is the correspondence between the student's response and the answer which is immediately given. "With humans, simply being correct is sufficient reinforcement . . ." (1960, p. 278). It might be said that if the student writes his response and then immediately reads the correct answer, reinforcement occurs when he sees that the two match. A comparable source of reinforcement that has been suggested is moving on to the next item when the previous item has been completed successfully.

Porter (1957), in reviewing the literature, indicated that exploratory and manipulative activities have also been suggested as reinforcers but that these weaken through satiation. He commented that alternative reinforcers could be used; Skinner has mentioned social reinforcers, desired activities, and aversive stimulation, and Pressey has indirectly suggested candy. For the most part, however, the exclusive reinforcement obtainable in the automated instruction programs has been that of being "correct," "moving on," or other types of "achievement," or perhaps "explorations." It is suggested, however, that restriction to these sources of reinforcements seems to be one of the primary weaknesses of contemporary applications of learning principles to the problems of education—a topic which will be discussed in a later section of the present chapter.

The "Teaching Machine"

One general requirement of experimental methodology is to gain control of the independent variables which may affect a particular event so that the independent variables can be manipulated and their relationship to the event ascertained. Unless this can be done while other irrelevant independent variables are controlled, the relationship may be obscured. This is equally true in the experimental analysis of behavior. To find how a particular condition will affect behavior, other conditions that also may affect the behavior have to be controlled.

Often it is only possible to gain precise control through the use of various mechanical and electronic devices. For example, delay of reinforcement is a critical variable in operantly conditioning behavior. To test a procedure for shaping behavior it would be important that the delay of reinforcement not be allowed to vary freely—this alone could distort the results. Thus, laboratory apparatus would be used to control precisely the delay of reinforcement.

The teaching machine represents the same sort of control in the automated instruction movement. In the preceding sections it was stressed that the items in a program must be ordered properly (that is, stimulus presentation must be controlled), reinforcement must be immediate, and so on. The teaching machine is a method of controlling some of these important variables. A short description of one of the machines that has been designed to achieve this control will illustrate these points.

In the Skinner machine shown in Figure 10.3 the visual materials to be presented to the student are stored under the locked cover of the machine. These materials are so arranged that each piece of information is separately presented in a single "frame," and only the single frame is exposed to the student at a time. When the top portion of the frame appears in the left-hand window of the machine, the student composes his response and writes it on the strip of paper appearing on the right. He then lifts a lever that moves his answer under a transparent cover and at the same time exposes the correct answer given on the frame. In the machine shown here, the student would compare his response with the answer given and if the two correspond, he would record his correct response by moving the lever to punch a hole opposite his response. In this machine, once the student has called his response to a frame "correct" in this way, the frame would not reappear on successive presentation of the material. Whether the student's response was correct or not, however, when he moves the lever again, another frame appears in the left-hand window and the entire process is

Fig. 10.3. A typical teaching machine (Skinner, 1958, p. 971)

repeated. In this way the student works through the full set of materials, until he completes successfully all the frames.

Several modifications of this machine are available. For example, for use with younger children the response may be composed by moving sliders with numbers or letters into different positions (to give an answer to an arithmetic problem or to spell a word). Then the machine automatically compares the setting with a coded response. If the two correspond, the next frame is presented, but if they do not, the machine clears, and another response must be composed. Many other modifications have been designed, but the description of these Skinner machines should suffice to indicate the basic equipment used to implement most of the work on automated teaching.

It can be seen how the machine provides some of the experimental control required. First, with the machine described above, by incorporating the feature of repetition of all frames until they are correctly answered and by demanding a response before new material is presented, the machine requires the student to thoroughly understand each and every point considered to be important. The student cannot gloss over some critical point as he might in reading the material. He is not allowed to believe he has adequately comprehended the material until his emitted responses correspond to those set by the preparer of the material.

Yet because each student works alone at his own machine, each learns the material at his own rate. He can neither miss new material because he is not ready for it when it is introduced, nor waste his time waiting for classmates to catch up before new material is introduced. To the extent that individual automated instruction work is incorporated into the school, the usual classroom problem of the teacher moving too rapidly for many and too slowly for most of the rest would be eliminated.

Secondly, the use of the machine requires that the student proceed through the material in the predetermined order. He cannot skip on to more advanced material before he masters the elementary material. Nor can he reverse the order in responding to any single frame. He cannot find the correct answer until he has made a response himself and lifted the lever to expose the prepared answer.

Thus, the machine obviously prevents the lack of control called "cheating" in the sense that the student cannot change his answer, because although it is still visible it cannot be altered under the transparent cover. Furthermore, the order of emitting the response first, then confirming it by comparing it with the answer to the frame, preserves the observance of the crucial principle associated with teaching machines devised on an operant conditioning model—the emission of a response followed immediately by reinforcement. By preventing the student from finding the answer before he composes his response (as when the student first looks up the answer in the back of the arithmetic book, and then tries the problem), reinforcement is made contingent upon the appropriate response.

While the various types of teaching machines are too numerous to be described, the alternative to a machine for presenting a program, a *programed textbook*, must be briefly mentioned, if only because they are even more common than the machines. This is simply a program without an auxiliary device for presentation. The textbook may merely present the frames one beneath the other with the correct answer at the side of the frames. The answers are covered with a slider, e.g., a sheet of paper which the student slides down after he writes each of his answers. Or the textbook may present a frame on one page and its answer on the next page.

There has been some argument over the relative merits of the machine and the textbook, but little research to compare their effectiveness. However, with respect to the arguments above concerning the necessity for experimental control, Green points to the following obvious fact.

The teaching machine potentially gives more adequate control over the sequence of the learning process than does the programed textbook. It may well be that this additional control is not particularly important, but until more evidence is available, we shall not assume that it is unimportant (1962, p. 134).

Experimental Method in Automated Instruction

Each of the preceding discussions has included mention of the application of the experimental approach to automated instruction. There are a few remaining points that should be added concerning the experimental approach, however.

First, after the analysis in terms of learning principles of the behavior to be trained, and the tentative selection of items with which to develop the repertoire, the succeeding steps are largely of an experimental nature. An experimental subject, or subjects, is obtained, the program is administered to the subject, and the program's effectiveness in gradually shaping a complicated repertoire of behaviors and maintaining the behavior by frequent reinforcement is evaluated.

The philosophy underlying this empirical method of constructing a program is that the subject is always right—he is behaving according to the "laws" of behavior. The problem is to find that set of conditions which will shape his behavior to the desired outcome. Moreover, as is true of science in general, this methodology insures that the outcome will be explicit and observable. Under circumstances where attention is focused upon the behavior of the subject, the experimenter is under some "pressure" to continue until the explicit result is reinforcing to him, in other words, is "successful." Where the reigning philosophy of education is that it is the *student's* responsibility to learn, attention may not be directed to the inadequacy of the program of training even in the face of many educational failures. Thus, merely the act of accepting an experimental framework for some human problems results in an orientation of placing the responsibility on the trainer and the training situation, and on explicitness —valuable contributions to progress in themselves.

The final objective of producing an adequate program can only be accomplished by presenting the subject with the program and then observationally ascertaining where the program is at fault; where the principles of behavior in the program are incorrectly applied, where the necessary preceding repertoire of the subject has not been established, where the stimuli of the item do not control the necessary behavior, where the sequencing of the items is poor, where the steps are too large, and so on. If the program is inadequate in any of these aspects, it will be reflected in the improper responses of the subject. Mistakes will be made on the faulty item or on succeeding items. Or, as Brooks (1961) has shown, the time to respond to the item may increase as a function of item difficulty.

When such weaknesses have been found in a program, it may be revised in line with further analysis of the items. Each revision, however, demands further experimentation, or assessment, concerning the effect of the program in shaping the behavior to be trained. Ultimately, the simple extension of this experimentation to the construction of teaching programs should considerably enhance the precision of the product. Each of the specific aspects of the program can be individually subjected to experimental evaluation. For example, earlier it was pointed out that the size of steps in the program should be such as to minimize errors. At one time it was thought that the best way to accomplish this was to make the size of the steps as small as possible. However, as Green points out, "The optimal step size now is recognized to be a matter of experimental determination. It is a function of the ability level of the student population with which the program is to be employed" (1962, p. 164).

Another empirical question concerns the schedule of reinforcement that is optimal for automated instruction procedures. The schedule of responses to reinforcer is normally of great significance. In the development of automated instruction, however, there has been to this point an attempt to insure reinforcement upon the emission of every response. Holland seems to believe that this continuous reinforcement schedule is most efficient for automated teaching procedures. He says,

> Not only is reinforcement needed for learning, but a high density of correct items is necessary because material which generates errors is punishing. Laboratory experiments (Azrin, 1956) have shown that punishment lowers the rate of the punished behavior. In our experiments with teaching machines, we have also observed that students stop work when the material is so difficult that they make many errors. Furthermore, they become irritated, almost aggressive, when errors are made (Holland, 1960, p. 279).

Of course, Holland is describing the effects of punishment rather than of a schedule of reinforcement alone. However, the problem of whether errors should be permitted in a program should be subject to experimentation as well. As Skinner says, "Whether we should try to design material that will be error-free . . . or whether there is an optimal percentage of error will have to be decided by experimentation" (Skinner, 1961, p. 96).

Another approach to incorporating reinforcement schedules would be to confirm only a portion of the student's responses on some schedule, rather than to generate errors. How scheduling might be implemented in a program is suggested by Green in the following.

Repetition of particular items provides us with an opportunity to employ . . . the scheduling of reinforcement. We cannot schedule reinforcement in the early stages of learning because the most effective acquisition of a response repertory during the differentiation phase is accomplished with continuous reinforcement. To impose a schedule of reinforcement upon the initial differentiation procedure might in the long run result in a more firmly established repertory, but it would decrease the speed with which the repertory was acquired. The spacing of reinforcement, although it contributes to resistance to extinction, also decreases the rate of initial conditioning. . . . Therefore, if we were to make use of variable ratio reinforcement in a conventional program, it would almost have to be used only in review sections where material is presented for a second or third time (Green, 1962, pp. 160–161).

Green points out also that a variable-ratio schedule may be imposed upon the acquisition of a verbal repertory almost from the beginning where the fading of textual materials is used. He suggests that the first couple of times a term is required as a response, the program would provide the answer as usual. Then the third time through, the answer would be withheld. The next time the answer was required, it would again be provided, and so on.

In any case, whether or not to build in errors and in what proportions, whether or not to reinforce on a continuous schedule or only intermittently, what step size is most appropriate, and so on, are examples of research questions that should be solved in the future.

Although all these proposed methods are derived very clearly from laboratory-established procedures, it must be emphasized again that they must be verified within the context of automated instruction before they can be accepted as valid for this field. However, "[p]rogrammed instruction offers the possibility of making more extensive use of powerful laboratory techniques than is true of conventional instruction because the stimulus-response and response-reinforcement contingencies are explicit and are therefore amenable to manipulation" (Green, 1962, p. 161).

General Implications of the
Automated Instruction Movement

In a paper entitled "The Need for Simplicity in Research in Child Psychology" Terrell (1958) has suggested that research in child psychology be concentrated on basic variables and principles rather than on complex constellations of each. He recommends against studies that attempt to deal with such complex and vague variables as child-rearing practices or to assess their effect on such equally complex and vague variables as personality. He suggests, rather, that research in child psychology take the principles of learning already established in basic experiments and extend them to the study of children, still in basic experiments dealing with simple behaviors. By means of such study it should be possible to establish a basic set of behavior principles relevant to child learning.

This strategy is certainly congruent with the step-by-step development of science. Thus, it is to be expected that early in its development the science of behavior would attempt to establish principles using only simple organisms, simple stimulus situations, and simple responses. In moving on, the science would then include extensions of the principles to the more complex organisms that are of special interest (such as children), perhaps still in simple situations and involving only simple responses. This must be done to determine whether the principles hold for this organism, as well as to develop methods and techniques for working with this organism.

At some point in the advancement of the science of human behavior, however, a further extension to experimental studies of more complex behavior is necessary. It is suggested that the great message of the automated teaching movement for educational psychology is that there are learning principles and an experimental methodology which are now available for solving some of the problems of educating the child—that the science of behavior has reached this more advanced stage. Abstracting further, the movement suggests that we do not have to wait until all the details of the basic principles of learning are worked out in simple experiments in the laboratory before the findings can be extended to more complex human behaviors. We have empirical laws now that when suitably applied can provide better solutions to problems of human training than those developed through other methods. The teaching machine movement extends learning principles and experimental methods to complex problems of training, and in so doing opens up a vast area of study to "attack" through these procedures.

Present Limitations in Automated Instruction

Nevertheless, the movement does not by itself constitute a complete technology of education that will solve all of the problems encountered in the field. Indeed, the present authors suggest that the automated instruction movement may be valuable more for what it offers as a *methodology* of experimental educational psychology than for its present solutions to problems in education. Thus, it seems that programed instruction and teaching machines have great significance as applications of learning principles and experimental methods, and constitute a basic methodology for studying problems of complex human learning, even though there are certain limitations which characterize the effort at present. Although most of these limitations are probably a product of the relative recency of the developments rather than an inherent feature of them, it may be worthwhile to indicate some of the gaps that should be filled in establishing an experimental educational psychology.

Need for Further Analysis of Learning Variables

The most important learning principle applied in automated instruction is that of strengthening a response through reinforcement. But even here the application is somewhat weak and incomplete. As already described, the reinforcers involved are mainly those of producing a stimulus which matches that given by the machine or programed textbook, and the reinforcement involved in moving on. (To some extent these reinforcers are also available in traditional methods of study—for example, mathematics books give answers to which the student can match his solutions.)

The extensive reliance upon being "correct" and moving on to the next frame as the reinforcing stimuli should be reevaluated and an analysis made of the assumption that these events may justifiably be considered sufficient reinforcement for maintaining the studying behavior of the subject.

The observables which define "correctness" are that the response of the subject produces some record, a stimulus, which matches the stimulus of the "answer" to the item. As was discussed in Chapter 4, children ordinarily are trained to match their behavior to the behavior of an "authority" source—parents, other adults, and older children. As a consequence of this training in which they are reinforced in the presence of matching stimuli (those produced by the authority, as well as those produced by themselves), producing a stimulus that matches a standard becomes reinforcing.

This analysis has certain implications for the general use of being correct as a reinforcer for the maintenance of studying behavior. Since the reinforcing strength of the matching stimulus, the stimulus of being "correct," depends upon the past experience of the individual, it would be expected that its strength would vary within a wide range. For some individuals being correct would be a very strong conditioned reinforcer and would be expected to maintain strong studying behaviors. For others, this might be a relatively weak source of reinforcement. It should be pointed out that "the younger the child, the fewer matching conditioning trials he would be expected to have received. In addition, special populations such as mental retardates or lower-class children would be expected to be weakly trained in this manner. Being 'correct' would thus be expected to be a weak (if not absent) reinforcer for many people, and especially for very young children in their first learning tasks" (Staats, Staats, Schutz, and Wolf, 1962, p. 34).

The same is true of the reinforcement supposedly inherent in moving on to the next frame in the program. Moving on, covering material, "achievement" of educational goals of various kinds, and the like, would only be expected to be reinforcing if the individual has had an extensive history in which this type of achievement has been reinforced. (See Chapter 7 for a discussion of achievement as a conditioned reinforcer.)

Research is needed to assess appropriate reinforcers for different age groups, different socioeconomic groups, indeed to capitalize upon any differences in individual histories that would affect the adequacy of reinforcers. In addition, as was pointed out earlier, various ways of utilizing reinforcers, such as scheduling, must be studied. (A fuller discussion of the types of research needed will be made in a later section of this chapter.)

Another necessary area of analysis of learning variables involves the behavior to be trained. Kendler (1959) has pointed out that "[u]ltimately we will have to develop better theories of behavior, particularly those of transfer and symbolic processes, in order to make the best use of teaching machines" (p. 184). In general, it could be said that although the automated instruction movement is based upon the application of learning principles, too few of the complex behaviors to be dealt with have been analyzed in terms of learning principles. Detailed analyses of the acquisition and function of the behaviors to be trained have not been made even though most programers recognize the need for identifying the specific responses that constitute criterion behavior. Although there are a number of programs already in existence in mathematics, for example, the specific behaviors involved have not yet been described in terms of learning variables. (There are signs that this situation is beginning to be changed, however; for example Gilbert (1962), indicates that a behavioral analysis is prerequisite to programing and gives several illustrations, including the analysis of long division presented in Chapter 5.)

Another example may be seen in the task of teaching a foreign language. In terms of learning principles, what is the function of grammatical response-sequences (grammatical rules) in the acquisition of new language? Certainly, natives acquire grammatical language habits before they are taught grammatical rules. Nevertheless, in foreign language instruction, it is customary to teach rules. A behavioral analysis of the function of grammatical response sequences in the acquisition of a language would aid in the construction of programs for teaching languages. It would be expected that such an analysis also would require a great deal of experimentation.

Need for Applications to Additional Areas of Study

Related to the preceding discussion of the limited learning analysis of the types of behavior to be dealt with is the fact that the automated instruction movement has not yet attempted to deal with many important content aspects of human learning in any depth. There has been little study of original learning, or the learning of basic skills. The learning of algebra, for example, rests upon prior establishment of basic verbal behaviors, reading, the acquisition of counting and various number response sequences, and so on. However, for the most part, the acquisition of these repertoires has not been studied or programed.

As such, the programed teaching movement constitutes a "leapfrog" strategy. The work is being carried out on very complex behaviors even before research has been conducted on the more basic but still complex skills that form the foundation for the secondary skills. The principles and methods of the experimental study of learning have not yet been adequately applied to experimentation with various aspects of original language learning, reading acquisition, the learning of counting and other arithmetic behaviors, for example. Kendler (1959) makes the same point with respect to application to the areas of problem solving and creativity.

This is not to say that complete study of the basic behaviors must precede application of learning principles to the more advanced skills. It is quite possible that the latter as an area of study presents less difficult problems than the study of original language learning, and need not come second. Nevertheless, the procedures and principles involved in these areas are most important and deserve considerable attention.

Need for Further Application of
Available Experimental Methodology

In the automated instruction work there has been a great deal of emphasis upon experimentation in writing frames of programs. Experimental methods have also been used in the evaluation of the complete program constructed. In all, however, in the same way that the principles and fields studied have been restricted, so also has there been limited employment of experimental methods in problems of education. As will be pointed out in greater detail in later sections of this chapter, it would seem that a full-blown experimental educational psychology will require greater borrowing of the methods of operant conditioning available from the laboratory, as well as adaptation of these and other methods for use in dealing with complex human learning problems. (See Zeaman, 1959, for a related discussion.)

Conclusion

It is suggested that the development of teaching machines and programed instruction constitutes a major movement in the fields of psychology and education. It represents, at least in part, the stage in the development of a behavioral science when its basic principles and methods have begun to be applied to practical and important problems. The movement generally suggests that the principles and methods of learning, as well as the laboratory methods by which they were discovered, can be applied to problems of complex human learning and yield improvements over other approaches. The implication is that such applications can now successfully be made to many areas of behavior (see the next chapter for additional examples).

Nevertheless, there are many problems in educational psychology that have not, and may not, be attacked through programing and related machine developments. Some of the possibilities for enlarging the scope of the application of learning principles and methods to an experimental educational psychology will be dealt with in the following sections. As an example, a fairly detailed description will be given of a research program applying the principles and methods of operant conditioning to the acquisition of reading behavior.

READING RESEARCH AS AN EXTENSION OF EXPERIMENTAL EDUCATIONAL PSYCHOLOGY

Many studies have drawn from the body of learning principles to test the applicability of the principles to the learning of children. Some of these studies relevant to reading were discussed in the last chapter (for example, studies in stimulus discrimination and generalization). The following experiment indicates that even very young children can be used as experimental subjects in studying "reading-type" behavior.

Jeffrey (1958) performed an experiment designed to test the facilitative effect of attaching simple motor responses to stimuli differing in spatial (left-right) orientation on the subsequent tacting of these stimuli. Four-year-old children were used as subjects. The experimental treatment consisted of learning to press buttons oriented in the directions the stick figures used as stimuli were pointing. This task was readily learned by all subjects in the experimental group, and the training was found to have a significant effect on subsequent learning of the tacts.

> At a practical level, these data can be interpreted as having fairly direct implications with regard to specific instruction, such as teaching reading. Davidson (1935) has indicated that children are not normally capable of discriminating "b" from "d" until 7½ years of age. The present data indicate that a child incapable of performing this discrimination at a given time can be taught it very quickly, even as early as four years of age, if conditions are properly arranged (p. 274).

As discussed in Chapter 4, reading may be considered as the emission of verbal responses under the control of visual verbal stimuli; in Skinner's terms, as textual responses. Considered in this way, reading acquisition can be seen as discrimination training where certain verbal responses are reinforced in the presence of certain visual verbal stimuli; this immediately suggests the application of operant conditioning principles and methods to the study of the acquisition and maintenance of reading behavior. Furthermore, the analysis of the acquisition of reading in comparison to the acquisition of speech suggests that the use of immediate reinforcement and a gradual program of training could result in a more effective training than ordinarily occurs (see Chapter 4). The problems remain of arranging a specific laboratory situation in which the application of operant conditioning principles to this type of behavior can be experimentally studied.

Other investigators have devised reinforcing systems for work with the simple responses of young children (see, for example, Bijou, 1957a; Bijou and Sturges, 1959; and Orlando and Bijou, 1960). The reinforcers have generally consisted of edibles—peanuts, potato chips, candy, and so on, and trinkets, such as plastic rings and puzzles. A first step in a project to study the development of reading might be to test both the applicability of such a reinforcing system and the principles of operant discrimination training to new subjects and the new behavior to be studied. Successful extension of these principles would encourage further study using the methods suggested. In addition, the first study might serve to gather information concerning apparatus and procedural needs.

It should be pointed out at the outset that the systematic study of the principles and variables involved in the acquisition of reading cannot be accomplished with short-term studies using groups of children. Fowler (1962) has argued this point very convincingly.

> Reading a language, number calculation, playing a musical instrument, and conceptualizing physical causality are all processes organized in terms of complex systems of interrelated verbal symbols and concepts. Learning such systems inevitably becomes a long-term, increasingly complex, and cumulative process. Each series of steps is integrally related to and founded on lower orders of information. As a result progress demands that material be broken into simplified components and presented systematically, step-by-step in a long, shallow gradient (p. 144).

Accordingly, the research strategy adopted was to study the learning of individual children over a longer period, so that conditions which affect the learning of reading could be assessed.

The first study (Staats, Staats, Schutz, and Wolf, 1962) formally tested the effect of reinforcement in the original training of children to read. For this purpose, a system of reinforcers as well as a device for the automatic delivery of the reinforcers was devised. A preliminary reading program was designed that included the presentation of twenty-six single words, later combined into sentences and stories.

Six four-year olds were used individually as subjects in the experiment. These children had had no prior training in reading. Three of the subjects were given a No-Reinforcement condition first, where correct responses were not followed by reinforcers. They were switched to the Reinforcement condition as soon as they wished to discontinue participation in the activity. The sequence of treatment for the other three children was Reinforcement (two sessions)–No-Reinforcement (until participation ceased)–Reinforcement. In addition to the mixed edibles and trinkets, tokens were used as reinforcers that could be exchanged for small plastic toys on a 1:24 ratio. The children were in the experiment for nine forty-minute training sessions.

The measure of learning was the number of new words the child could read as a result of the prior day's training. In addition, qualitative observations of the vigor of each child's attentional and working behaviors in the learning situation were made. Since all children experienced both experimental conditions (Reinforcement and No-Reinforcement) it was pos-

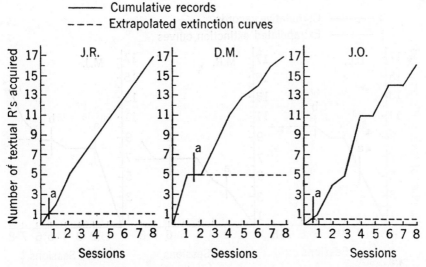

Fig. 10.4. "The curves shown here were generated under a beginning period of no 'extrinsic' reinforcement. When S would no longer remain in the experimental situation, reinforcement was instated as indicated by the mark on the curve. The dotted line commences at the point S would no longer remain in the experiment, and indicates the curve which would have resulted if reinforcement was not introduced" (Staats, Staats, Schutz, and Wolf, 1962, p. 37).

sible to determine the effect of this experimental condition on each child, that is, each child's reading learning was compared under the two conditions.

The cumulative records of the No-Reinforcement–Reinforcement sequence are shown in Figure 10.4. Under the No-Reinforcement condition, working at the task quickly weakened and children asked to leave the situation. When reinforcement was instituted the reading behavior became strong and subjects continued to learn throughout the remaining sessions and no longer wished to discontinue the activity. The dotted lines show projected learning curves for a continued No-Reinforcement condition, or what would have occurred if the Reinforcement treatment had not been introduced.

Figure 10.5 shows that each of the three children first under the Reinforcement condition learned to read words well initially, but when the treatment was changed to No-Reinforcement, the reading behavior weakened, the learning of new words decreased, and the children said they wished to cease their participation. When reinforcement was reinstated, two of the three children decided to continue participation and both working in the situation and learning new words improved.

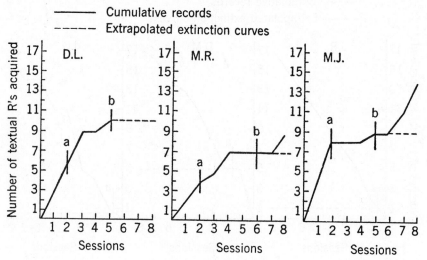

Fig. 10.5. "For these Ss, the first condition included reinforcement, which was discontinued at the point of the first mark on the curve. When S would no longer remain in the experimental situation, reinforcement was reinstated, as the second mark on the curve indicates. The dotted line commences at the point the S would no longer remain in the experiment and depicts the curve which would have resulted if reinforcement was not reinstated" (Staats, Staats, Schutz, and Wolf, 1962, p. 38).

The results indicated the importance of response-contingent reinforcement in the learning of young children. The work and attentional habits of four-year-olds deteriorated under conditions of No-Reinforcement, and learning ceased, whereas under Reinforcement conditions strong work and attentional habits were maintained within the period studied.

> The [children] acquired totals of 16, 17, and 17 texts, tested out of context. Thus, the operant-conditioning procedures, in these few sessions, proved to be very successful compared with the reading achievement which these [children] would make in their *next* year's work in kindergarten. The length of time these young children worked at a task ("attention-span") was directly a function of the reinforcing properties of the situation (Staats, Staats, Schutz, and Wolf, 1962, p. 37).

In addition, this study also pointed up certain leads and problems for further research on the educational psychology of reading. The study indicated that further developments should be made in (1) the response measure indexing the learning of reading, (2) the apparatus for the controlled presentation of stimuli, (3) a system of reinforcers for maintaining strong working behavior over a long period of time, and (4) the reading materials themselves. Each of these topics of study will be discussed separately.

Work and Attentional Responses as a Measure of Learning to Read

The qualitative observations of the children's behavior in the learning situation indicated that basic to learning to read are the minute-to-minute attentional and working behaviors of the child. When the child attends to the material and works at a high rate, he rapidly learns to read. The major variation in learning seems to be a function of these basic behaviors. The more "reading responses" emitted, the more reading learning occurs. In contrast to the gross measure of the number of new words learned, a record of these actual reading behaviors would result in a much more sensitive tool for testing the effects of different variables on the learning. The next step in the project was thus to develop a procedure and apparatus for observing and recording all the reading responses made by the child during the training sessions.

Accordingly, the experimental procedure was changed so that each "reading" response was automatically and cumulatively recorded. Each time the child was presented with a stimulus and made a response an electronic device (which will be further described) recorded the response, providing a continuous record of the child's curve of learning to read. The record produced is the cumulative type described in Chapter 3, which is used in standard operant conditioning procedures. The pen movement from left to right represents time. As each response is made the pen takes a step upward. Thus, the more frequent the steps (the greater the rate of responding), the steeper the slope of the line. (See Figure 10.7.)

Reading Materials

In the procedure initially developed for the study of reading acquisition, the reading materials were of diverse kinds. Sometimes the child was presented with a single word, sometimes with a sentence consisting of previously presented words, sometimes with a short "story" composed of previously presented sentences. In addition, many of the words differed in length, and so on.

It would be expected that such a set of reading materials would not produce a homogeneous rate of response. If the stimuli differed in difficulty they would affect the rate of response. The appearance of a group of words in a sentence, rather than a single word, would also be expected to affect rate of response. Thus, the type of "reading response curve" produced would be expected to vary as a function of the vagaries of the stimulus materials presented. If left uncontrolled, this would interfere with experiments in which the goal was to find the effects of certain other experimental (independent) variables on the reading response curve.

For this reason, a new set of reading materials was designed to remove much of the response variation to be expected from variability in the stimulus materials. This was done simply by presenting single letters.[1] Although the letters still differ somewhat in stimulus complexity or distinguishability from other letters, response variability was markedly decreased.

In devising this program attention was also directed to a preliminary analysis of the learning to be achieved, that is, the type of stimulus discriminations which must be made and the responses which have to be controlled. This analysis, as will be discussed, by no means solves the problems, but it does begin to confront them. Many investigators concerned with reading have pointed out that in the English language the same letter stimuli often must come to control different speech sounds when the letters are in different contexts. The letter *a* is responded variously to, as in *father, fate, fast,* and so on. One stimulus must thus come to elicit several responses depending upon the context in which it occurs. This represents a complex type of learning. Although there are some general consistencies or rules according to which the stimuli of context can come to control the correct one of the several responses, there are many exceptions, and even the consistencies of context form a very complex learning task.

---

[1] Actually, in the case of the consonants, the verbal stimulus was composed of consonant-vowel combinations.

There have been various suggestions for overcoming such problems in the training of reading, for example, (1) the English spelling may be altered and new symbols introduced, but this may make the transfer to normal English spelling quite difficult; or (2) in order to retain the actual English spelling, the system may deal with only a limited number of words, not including the many exceptions; however, this limits the generality of the learning.

In a preliminary effort to overcome some of these problems, the research project developed a method that retains the letters used in English. However, a different identifying mark appears in conjunction with the letter for each different sound the letter must come to elicit, for example, $\bar{a}$ controls the "a" response in *father*, and $\dot{a}$ controls the "a" response in *fate*. As a result, each letter with its symbol (when necessary) controls only one response, a method consistent with a preliminary behavior analysis of the learning involved. Once the child acquires such a letter repertoire he should be able to read any word including these letters. As the learning progresses, and the context stimuli have come to assume control over the correct response, the supplementary identifying stimuli could be "faded" gradually from the reading materials.

Apparatus for Stimulus Presentation

In addition to the reading materials constituting variable stimuli, the manner of presentation also involved complex variation. In the first experimental study the word stimuli were presented by the experimenter by hand, and the action sometimes included pointing to other words, directing the child's attention to "pictures of the words," and so on. Again, this could be the source of a good deal of variation in the children's behavior.

To improve the experimental control for further studies an apparatus was designed for a standard presentation of the phonetic letter stimuli. (The apparatus is schematized in Figure 10.6.) The stimulus presentation apparatus consists of the panel with four plastic covered windows. One of the windows is centered above the other three. Pressure on any of the plastic covers activates microswitches which lead to various experimental contingencies.

The verbal stimuli are presented to the child in a discrimination procedure. The top stimulus is "matched" by one of the three stimuli in the bottom row of windows. The task of the child is to select the stimulus that matches the one in the top window. In the procedure the stimuli are presented, and the experimenter, who is not visible to the child, "names" the top stimulus. The child must repeat the name—text the stimulus—and then press the plastic cover over the top window. Then he must select the matching stimulus from among the bottom windows, press the plastic

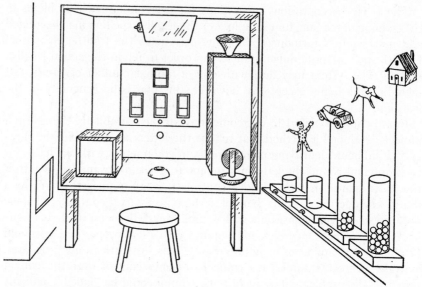

Fig. 10.6. Drawing depicting the experimental chamber utilized in the study of reading development.

cover, and again "name" the phonetic stimulus. When this response occurs, and the match is correct, the child is automatically and immediately reinforced. If the child correctly "names" the stimulus before the experimenter does so reinforcement immediately follows—it is then not necessary to go through the matching task.

The development of the apparatus was found to be crucial in insuring that only the *correct* behavior is learned. For example, the apparatus insures that the attentional responses of the child are under experimental control; he must be looking at the visual verbal stimulus while emitting the response. The apparatus also insures that *errors* in performance are not rewarded—for example, to eliminate "guessing" the electronic control was designed so that an error requires repetition of the task from the beginning. Reinforcement is thus contingent only on a correct response.

The System of Reinforcement

While the reinforcement described was adequate for the early studies, the experimental results over the nine training sessions indicated that the effect of the reinforcers was weakening. For longer-term studies, a reinforcer system of greater effective duration was required. It was thought that perhaps the limited variability of the first reinforcers accounted for their weakening. The system was consequently modified to a "self-selection" method with a great deal of variability in the reinforcers available to the child—analogous to the way that money becomes a stable conditioned reinforcer.

Central to the system is the use of tokens, contingent upon correct responses. Each time a correct response is emitted a token, a marble, is ejected from the tube into the dish in the right corner of the table in front of the child, as shown in Figure 10.6. The tokens are backed up by reinforcers of different value, the difference in value determining the number of tokens that must be accumulated before the tokens may be exchanged for the reinforcer. One class of reinforcers, the small edibles and trinkets, may be exchanged for the token on a 1:1 ratio. Small toys are exchanged for 10 tokens, larger toys (or toys of higher quality) for 35 tokens, yet larger toys for 80 tokens; and the largest toys for 150 tokens. None of the toys are expensive; each token averages about one cent in value.

In the procedure, the child selects a number of toys from a large class of each value, before he commences the training program. A toy from each class is then hung in the experimental room (see Figure 10.6), each above a plastic tube. The size of the plastic tube indicates the number of tokens required to obtain the reinforcer. The child may thus "work" for any of the back-up reinforcers; he may obtain an edible or a trinket by depositing the token in the funnel shaped opening in the right upper corner; he may consecutively deposit 10 tokens in the smallest plastic tube and obtain the reinforcer above it, and the same with the other plastic tubes; or he may work for several different back-up reinforcers at the same time.

The child can thus use his tokens to obtain four different classes of reinforcers (or trinkets or edibles) that are available to him. As soon as he obtains a toy, another that he has previously selected from the same class is placed on display so that he always has a choice among four "for which to work."

Further Results in the Experimental Analysis of Reading

The next step in the experimental analysis was to test the combined apparatus and procedure for the laboratory study of reading acquisition. Although each phase had been subjected to experimentation, it was important to determine whether the entire system would maintain the child's behavior for a long enough period to study significant variables in the learning process.

Two of the children used in the laboratory procedure will be described. They were run under continuous reinforcement conditions in twenty-minute training sessions, five days a week, for eight weeks—a total of forty sessions for each (Staats, Minke, Finley, Wolf, and Brooks, in press). The learning curves of the two children are shown in Figure 10.7.

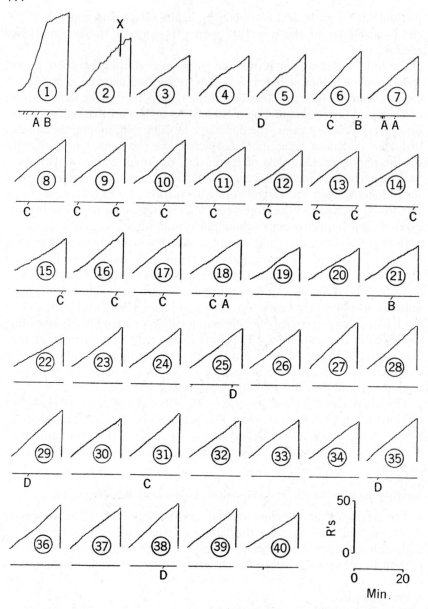

Fig. 10.7. Learning curves by 20-minute sessions of two children engaged in the reading acquisition task under conditions of continuous reinforcement. The 40 sessions are numbered. Reinforcement is indicated on the line underneath the curves by the slash marks; a slash mark lettered A stands for the delivery of a reinforcer in exchange for 10 tokens, a slash mark lettered B by a reinforcer in exchange for 35 tokens, a slash mark

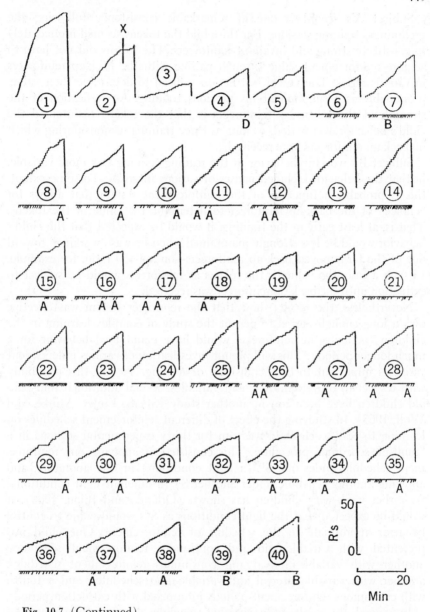

Fig. 10.7. (Continued)
lettered C by a reinforcer in exchange for 80 tokens, a slash mark lettered
D by a reinforcer in exchange for 150 tokens, and an unlettered slash
mark for the delivery of an edible or trinket in exchange for 1 token. The
working behaviors of both 4-year-old children were maintained in good
strength over the 40 days with infrequent pauses. Each of them emitted
over 1300 reading responses in this period.

Subject A's record is one of remarkable consistency following the preliminary training sessions. For this child the tokens seemed immediately to constitute strong and invariant reinforcers. The tokens did not have to acquire reinforcement value through pairing with the back-up reinforcers in various ratios. The verbal instruction sufficed to determine their value, presumably as a function of his previous training. An indication of the strength of the tokens as reinforcers is that the tokens maintained the child's behavior over periods as long as three training sessions during which no back-up reinforcers were received.

Subject B's working behavior in the reading training was more variable, in that the behavior included pauses of various intervals. To some extent, this is probably a function of the reinforcement system that allows for "choice" of the back-up reinforcer to determine the value of the tokens. That is, at least early in the training, it would be expected that the child's behavior would be less strongly maintained when he was "working" toward one of the far-removed back-up reinforcers—on a 1:150 ratio, for example. In such a case, the value of the tokens as reinforcers would be subject to extinction until the back-up reinforcer was received.

Nevertheless, the results show that the reinforcer system was effective over a long enough period to permit the study of complex learning in the children (actually the reinforcers would have maintained behavior for a much longer period). This will permit investigation of various independent variables important to the acquisition of reading. To test this possibility with respect to other reinforcement variables, several additional four-year-old children have been run in another study (Staats, Finley, Minke, and Wolf, 1963). In studying the effect of different reinforcement schedules on learning to read, each child was run for thirty experimental sessions in a "multiple-schedule" procedure. This consisted of applying one reinforcement schedule under one S^D (a light condition) in the laboratory, and applying another schedule under another S^D (a different light condition). As earlier work with children has shown (Orlando and Bijou, 1960), it would be expected that the light conditions as S^Ds would come to control behavior appropriate to the schedule of reinforcement. One child was presented with variable-ratio and continuous reinforcement schedules; another with variable-interval and continuous reinforcement schedules; another with variable-interval and variable-ratio schedules; and a fourth with continuous reinforcement periods intermixed with extinction periods.

In general, the results indicated that schedules do affect the strength of behavior in the reading situation in an expected manner, although they are not entirely analogous to results from studies with animals or with simpler responses in children. This would be expected, since the behavior involved in the reading procedure is actually a chain of responses in contrast to a simple response such as pressing a bar or pulling a knob.

The record for the child presented with alternate periods of continuous reinforcement and periods of extinction, under different light conditions, is shown in Figure 10.8. The discriminative stimulus control of the child's behavior is striking. Under the light condition in the presence of which his behavior is not reinforced, "non-working" largely comes under control. Under the light condition in the presence of which reading behavior is reinforced, the reading behavior occurs in good strength.

This study indicated the importance of reinforcement conditions on shaping complex learning of children. It showed the importance that stimulus conditions may acquire in controlling the child's learning behavior. It also suggested the possible applied functions of schedules of reinforcement. Thus, for example, the child who was presented with both continuous reinforcement and variable-ratio reinforcement showed *more* vigorous working behavior under the *intermittent* reinforcement. This has many implications for further experimental study of the important basic variables involved in learning to read, as well as for the design of a program for teaching children to read with maximum effectiveness and with minimum cost.

An additional finding in this study concerns the experimental method. Each child was used as his own control to assess the effect of the different experimental conditions; the child's behavior under one condition was compared to his behavior under another condition. It was thus possible in this experiment to gain reliable results using single children studied over a long period of time rather than groups of children studied over a short period of time. This is an important point in establishing an experimental educational psychology, as will be discussed further.

Implications for the Experimental Analysis of Reading

These studies by no means solve the problems of teaching children to read, nor do they provide a completed behavioral analysis of such learning.[2] They do seem, however, to suggest both a method for gaining such knowledge that approaches the precision of the laboratory, as well as further studies that should lead to these ends. Perhaps a brief description of a few possible extensions of this research would be helpful in this respect.

---

[2] However, A. W. Staats has since applied the principles involved in the actual task of devising a reading-training program. The first subject, at the age of three years and three months, has a reading vocabulary of 41 of the 52 lower- and upper-case alphabets, as well as 32 words read singly or combined into sentences and stories. The procedure is now being extended in research with additional children of four years of age.

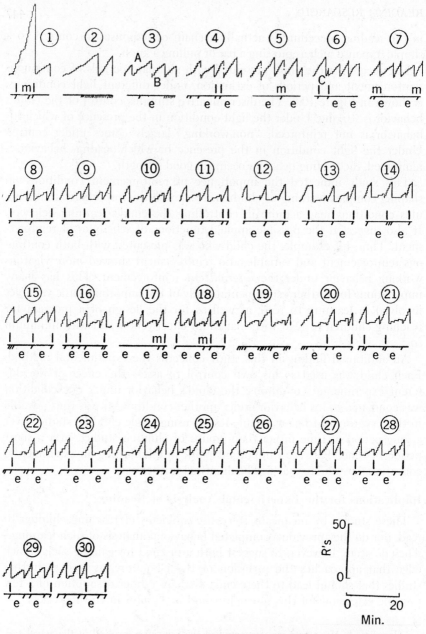

Fig. 10.8. Learning curve by sessions of a child engaged in a reading acquisition task under alternating conditions of continuous reinforcement (CRF) and nonreinforcement (extinction). A change from one condition to the other is indicated by a return of the recording pen to the base line. From Session 4 on, each session commenced under a continuous

For example, utilizing the experimental methods, later studies should be able to determine the effect of different procedures of presentation of the reading stimulus materials, which has been a problem for education for some time. The program of reading materials tentatively developed for experimentation was based upon a "one stimulus–one response" conception; only one verbal stimulus served as the S^D for each verbal response. This is not the only possible method for training reading. For example, each verbal stimulus could be presented so that it would control a hierarchy of verbal responses—the letter *a* might control the responses *ah*, *ay*, and so on. Such alternative methods of training could be studied using the methodology developed.

In addition to experimentation on the reading materials, further knowledge of the most effective schedules of reinforcement must be gained. The preliminary results of the last experiment described above indicate that intermittent schedules of the variable ratio type may be the most effective in several ways, for example, in producing stronger behavior as well as in conserving the value of the reinforcing system. However, this study does not scratch the surface of the information needed to understand the acquisition of reading as well as to design an improved and practical reading training program. Other reinforcers and modes of application of the reinforcers must be studied (as will be discussed in a later section), as well as other scheduling variables.

Further developments of the reading procedure to make it fully automatic, eliminating the presence of the experimenter, would have experimental significance as well as immense practical potentialities. Such an automatic reading procedure might ultimately lead to direct application in the schools.

---

reinforcement condition followed by an extinction condition, then a reinforcement condition and so on. The extinction conditions are labeled by the *e* underneath the curve, the CRF condition is unlabeled. The occurrence of the various reinforcement events are indicated on the line underneath the curves by the slash marks; a slash mark lettered with an *l* stands for the delivery of a reinforcer in exchange for 10 tokens, a slash mark lettered with an *m* for the delivery of a reinforcer in exchange for 35 tokens, and an unlettered slash mark for the delivery of an edible or trinket in exchange for 1 token. The A, B, and C indicate slight procedural deviations which do not require discussion. As can be seen from the record the light condition (S^D) in the presence of which the child is not reinforced for reading clearly begins to control "not working" behavior by the eighth training session; while the light condition in the presence of which the child is reinforced for reading comes more strongly to control working behavior.

ADDITIONAL AREAS TO STUDY
IN HUMAN LEARNING

The rationale for the application of experimental learning principles and methods to educational problems involved in the automated teaching movement, supplemented by the methods described in the laboratory study of reading, has additional significance for the experimental study of other educational areas. Some of the possibilities will be briefly described here.

Early Language Learning

Even more basic than the experimental study of original learning of reading is the study of the first learning of vocal language. "One of the basic drawbacks in the available research literature is that it is based mainly on observations in naturalistic settings. Theories of language learning cannot ultimately be tested unless an experimental approach is adopted. Oddly enough, one never seems to think of 'teaching' a child to learn language in the early phases, or of investigating the effects of specific practices in such teaching" (Carroll, 1961, p. 335).

The possibilities for systematic experimental study of this type of behavior development have been illustrated in the study of Rheingold, Gewirtz, and Ross (1959) with three-month-old infants described in Chapter 4. However, this was just one short-term study and therefore represents a *demonstration* that the principles and procedures are applicable, rather than a systematic exploration of the independent variables underlying the acquisition of speaking.

It is thus suggested that further studies of speech acquisition, possibly constituting a continuing series dealing with individual children over a long period of time, are necessary. In a manner similar to the reading research experiments, procedures for shaping up vocal responses and bringing them under stimulus control might be developed.[3] Experimental apparatus already available (see Rheingold, Stanley, and Cooley, 1962) could be adapted for this purpose.

It would seem possible to study experimentally the various forms of verbal behavior described in Chapter 4, the importance of which was suggested in the discussion of intelligent behavior in Chapter 9. Thus, bringing the child's behavior under the control of verbal discriminative stimuli, the establishment of a wide repertoire of tacts and mands, the establishment

---

[3] Salzinger and Salzinger are conducting a research project studying operant conditioning of continuous speech in preschool and first-grade children (see *Research Relating to Children*, 1961).

of echoic behaviors and other matching responses, are processes that are accessible to the methods of an experimental educational psychology.

The procedures developed could be employed in even longer range studies with individual children. Institutionalized retarded children would make ideal subjects and the training would contribute to their welfare. Systematic treatment of a child's early language learning should promote accelerated progress in this area of behavior and contribute to the later adjustment of the child as well. In this respect it is interesting to note that Luria has conducted such a long-term study, which demonstrates many of the characteristics of the research suggested, although his methods did not appear to be based upon a full analysis of language in terms of learning principles or indeed upon an experimental methodology. The subjects of the experiment were twins with retarded language development. According to Luria and Yudovich the retarded behavior of the two children was due in part to the restricted experience resulting from their very close relationship. They did not, for example, experience the usual "demand" for communication through language. With one another they could rely largely on pointing and gestures and idiosyncratic exclamations. The investigators further suggest that because of their primitive speech, the twins attentional behaviors were undeveloped, and they could not reason adequately or formulate plans and aims for activities. Consequently, their behaviors could not be mediated by language. "Therefore, even at the age of five to five and a half years our twins could not master skills nor organize complex play of a kind proper to children of this age, and were unable to engage in productive, meaningful activity. Their intellectual operations thus remained very limited; even such operations as elementary classification were beyond them" (Luria and Yudovich, 1959, p. 121).

In treating and studying this problem of speech development, the twins were separated by placing them in different kindergarten groups so they would obtain experience necessary to shape their speech; one twin was additionally treated as a subject in an experiment to train him systematically in various speech functions—experience which in our terms would establish verbal stimuli as discriminative stimuli, would establish extended verbal response sequences, and so on. Both twins improved under this change in environment, with the twin who was systematically trained surpassing the other both in speech and in thinking. Luria and Yudovich indicate also that the experience which improved the twins' speech improved those general behaviors which would commonly be called intelligence.

Even more significant was the fact that the whole structure of the mental life of both twins was simultaneously and sharply changed. Once they acquired an objective language system, the children were able to formulate the aims of their activity verbally and after only three months we observed the beginnings of meaningful play; there arose the possibility of productive, constructive activity in the light of formulated aims, and to an important degree there were separated out a series of intellectual operations which shortly before this were only in an embryonic state.

In the course of further observations we were able to note cardinal improvements in the structure of the twins' mental life which we could only attribute to the influence of the one changed factor—the acquisition of a language system (pp. 122–123).

The progress that might be expected under informed and systematic tutelage deriving from learning principles is not now known. Studies on the early development of speech utilizing learning principles and methods, especially if conducted on institutionalized children, could lead directly into further studies of intellectual behaviors and other training using the same subjects in even longer term studies.

Original "Mathematical" Learning

Similarly, the analysis of the acquisition of counting, addition, multiplication, and so on, in Chapter 5, together with the methodology developed for studying reading, suggest that original mathematics learning could be studied with the precision of the laboratory. A behavioral analysis should suggest methods of stimulus presentation that could be subjected to experimentation.

By controlling the mathematical repertoires established in the laboratory, it might also be possible to study experimentally how such repertoires function in the problem-solving behavior of the child.

Early "Music" Learning and Other "Artistic" Behavior

Certain aspects of "artistic" behavior should also be susceptible to experimental study. For example, at least parts of music learning may be considered discrimination learning involving the process of differential reinforcement. Skinner (1961) suggests the possibility of training certain skills important to music and other behavior.

> [T]here is much else that could be done to increase the behavioral repertories of children, even those who are younger than school age. Consider, for example, the temporal patterning of behavior called rhythm. Behavior is often effective only if properly timed. Individual differences in timing skill (often thought to be almost entirely innate) affect the choice of career and of artistic interests, as well as participation in sports. Presumably a "sense of rhythm" is worth teaching, yet nothing is done at present to arrange the necessary contingencies of reinforcement. The skilled typist, tennis player, lathe operator or musician is, of course, subject to non-educational reinforcing mechanisms that generate subtle timing, but many people never reach the point at which these natural contingencies take over.

We have been experimenting with a comparatively simple device that supplies the necessary contingencies . . . [See Figure 10.9]. The devise produces a rhythmic pattern that the student reproduces by tapping a key. He may tap in unison with the device or echo it during intervals provided for his responses. The machine scores a tap as being correct by flashing a light and a complete correct sequence by ringing a bell. At first the student is allowed a wide margin of error. He can be early or late with each tap, but these specifications are gradually sharpened until the student's performance reaches a satisfactory level of precision. The programing techniques here are exactly parallel to those used in animal research (pp. 101–102).

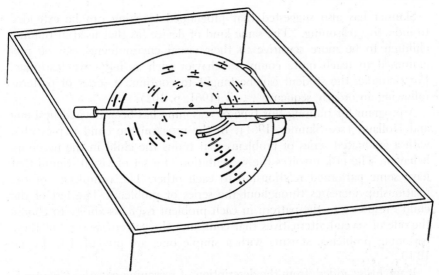

Fig. 10.9. "Rhythm-teaching machine requires a student to tap in unison with or echo a pattern of beats. To be reinforced by a light and a bell his response must fall within time limits set by a device that both generates patterns and monitors responses" (Skinner, 1961, p. 92).

Learning to echo or match a given sound, note, or melody may also be considered to involve complex discrimination training. There are people who can not sing on key, or reproduce a melody, even though their vocal and sensory apparatuses are quite functional. The formation of such discriminations could be studied in young children as well as in subjects of other ages through the application of human operant-conditioning experimental techniques.

Skinner discusses also the possibility that other artistic behaviors may be taught through operant conditioning methods.

Another kind of teaching machine presents a variety of shapes of patterns from which the student is to select a pattern related in some way to a sample displayed. This is a multiple-choice procedure, but it is justified in this case because what is learned is a process of selection from an array. The objective is to teach children to be more sensitive to the visual properties of their environment (1961, p. 102).

Implicit in these analyses is the suggestion that research in these areas start with simple discriminations of these kinds and then progress in a long term research project to deal with the more and more complex behaviors related to music and art.

Inductive Reasoning

Skinner has also suggested that programed teaching can be extended to inductive reasoning. "The same kind of device [as that used in training children to be more sensitive to their visual environment] can be programmed to teach quite complex behavior such as inductive reasoning. For example, the student can be taught to continue a series of patterns following an orderly sequence . . ." (1961, p. 102).

A program for training this type of reasoning has been devised by Long and Holland (see Skinner, 1961). In the program the child is presented with a graduated series of problems that trains the child in the necessary behavior. The task involves the presentation of a set of visual stimuli that have some patterned relationship to each other. The complexity of the relationship increases throughout the series of problems. The test of the child's response to the pattern in each problem is of his ability to choose the one of several alternatives that continues the pattern. Several of these reasoning problems, starting with a simple one, are presented in Figure 10.10.

It might be added, from the description of reasoning given in Chapter 5, that this area of behavior would appear to be quite complex and would seem to require long-term experimental study to determine the principles involved.

Attentional Behaviors

Further studies should also be conducted of even more basic behaviors in learning situations. Holland (1960) has discussed, for example, the importance of adequate observing behavior in the classroom and the advantage of machine teaching in producing this "attention" behavior.

In the classroom the student is often treated as though he were some kind of passive receiver of information, who can sop up information spoken by the teacher, written on the blackboard, or presented by films. But all of these are effective only insofar as the student has some behavior with respect to the material. He must listen carefully or read carefully, thus engaging in usually covert echoic behavior. Ineffectiveness of class-

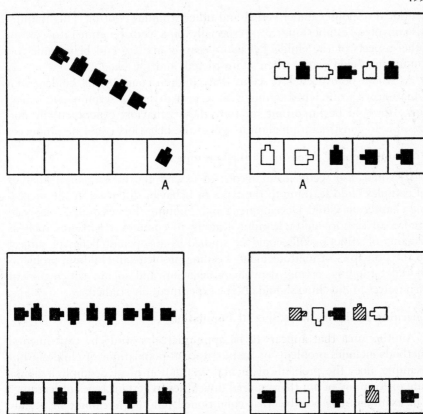

Fig. 10.10. Four frames from the inductive reasoning program of E. R. Long and James G. Holland are schematized. The child's task on each frame is to select the one of the alternatives shown at the bottom that continues the series commenced in the sequence of figures at the top of each frame. The correct response is shown by the A underneath the appropriate alternative. (Adapted from B. F. Skinner, 1961, p. 90.)

room techniques is often credited to "inattention" or poor "concentration." It has been shown (Reid, 1953; Wyckoff, 1952) that if a discrimination is to be learned, adequate observing behavior must first be established. We have further found that observing behavior, or speaking loosely, "attention," is subject to the same forms of control as other behavior (Holland, 1958). This control of observing behavior is of prime importance. When the student becomes very "inattentive" in the classroom, the teaching material flows on; but with a machine, he moves ahead only as he finishes an item (pp. 281–282).

Observation of kindergarten classes indicates also that a large proportion of the training provided by the teacher involves getting the children's attentional responses under verbal and other stimulus control. This training also involves establishing S^Ds (especially of a verbal nature) to control other aspects of the child's behavior—ceasing activity and being quiet on command, being seated when so instructed, and the like.

As would be expected, it seems that children come to the kindergarten situation with different training with respect to such discriminative behaviors. It would be important to study these behaviors experimentally and possibly to construct a program in which the behaviors could be produced.

"Nonintellectual" Areas of Child Learning

It would also seem advantageous to extend the experimental analysis of complex child learning to the types of behavior discussed in the preceding chapter on Child Development and Training. For example, long-term studies of sensory-motor learning leading to complex repertoires such as dancing or athletic skills could be studied as an operant behavior subject to the principles of reinforcement. Feeding problems in children, problems of toilet training, crying, dependent behavior, and so on, which present themselves to the clinic should also be experimentally studied.

Learning Problems with Special Populations

Another area that appears to be appropriate for study by experimental methods includes problems of training special populations of children. For example, does the problem of mental retardation involve simply a slower rate of learning, or are there special difficulties in certain types of learning? For example, it is possible that conditioned reinforcers cannot be readily established in retardates. Or, perhaps, the fine and detailed discriminations required in complex training materials (like language) cannot be made by the retardate. On the other hand, it appears from naturalistic observations that many children labeled as mental retardates or autistic children are only victims of poor training conditions. We simply do not know at this time what learning disabilities, if any, are involved with such children.

Such questions should be studied in experimental situations where the children are learning complex behavioral repertoires, such as reading and mathematics. It would be interesting, for example, to observe systematically how retarded children would respond to the use of extrinsic reinforcers in learning to read, to take continuous records of the children's learning curves in such an experimental situation as has been described, and to devise a reading program for their special needs, if any.[4]

The special problems involved in teaching language to deaf children also

---

[4] It is interesting to note in this respect that R. L. Sprague and A. M. Binder are studying automated arithmetic instruction for the retarded (see *Research Relating to Children*, 1961).

present a challenge to ingenuity in the application of learning principles, perhaps especially in the invention of apparatus that can successfully manipulate the variables essential to a teaching program.

Reinforcement Variables and Applications

Cutting across all the areas of study we have discussed are the major variables and principles of child learning. These too must be a focus of systematic study within educational psychology. For example, the research on the original acquisition of reading indicated that reinforcement contingent upon the "reading" behaviors is crucial. With adequate response-contingent reinforcement the reading behaviors were maintained in good strength; without reinforcement reading behaviors decreased in strength and were replaced by other competing behaviors.

Of course, the problem of inadequate reinforcement in the school has been recognized for a long time. Progressive education, for example, among other things attempted to introduce positive reinforcers into the school situation by making the activities more practical or more "game-like." However, there has been little systematic study of the possible sources of reinforcers in early school training or of the potential ways in which these reinforcers may be made contingent upon the learning behavior of the child.[5]

As an example, consider the nursery school or kindergarten situation. Some of the reinforcers present in these school situations have been described—games, recesses, toys, snacks, rest periods, television, desirable activities of various kinds, and social approval. These are potent reinforcers but for the most part they are not made contingent upon the individual behaviors to be strengthened. Since most of these reinforcers occur only infrequently in the school day, however, even if they were made contingent upon a specific learning behavior, very few could be provided and thus only a few behaviors reinforced.

These reinforcers might prove to be very effective, however, if they were incorporated into a procedure involving a token system. For example, a recess could be exchanged for 100 tokens, and the tokens could be made contingent upon 100 appropriate responses. Through employment of such a token system effective use could be made of many reinforcers that are a natural part of early school training.[6]

---

[5] Although publications are not yet available, J. A. Myers and N. A. Myers are conducting a research project on kindergarten and preschool children to evaluate variables influencing secondary reinforcement of children's learning (*Research Relating to Children,* 1961).

[6] Although the back-up reinforcers were of a material nature, rather than activities or social reinforcers, a remedial reading program based upon a token system has already

The development of such a system of reinforcers might necessitate some changes in school organization. For example, one way to use a token system might be to have a "work" room for the learning activities and other rooms for dispensing the "primary" reinforcers. It is to be expected that soon only behaviors appropriate to the different situations would be emitted in the different rooms. The child would stay in the work room until he accrued a given number of tokens and then go to one of the "reinforcer" rooms to receive his primary reinforcers. The child might thus have optional reinforcing activities, all of them dependent, however, upon the emission of certain working behaviors.

These speculations are, of course, too unsubstantiated experimentally to be the basis for a revision of any existing school program. However, they could be incorporated into a systematic study of potential reinforcers and their use. A situation similar to a nursery school could be set up for experimental purposes within which to study the reinforcing variables involved.

This example is not intended to suggest that material reinforcers or pleasant activities are the only reinforcers available, or even the best available in the school situation. In Chapter 4, as in the present discussion, various other sources of reinforcement in the acquisition of school learning were mentioned. For example, if the child has had a fortunate history, acquiring new skills may itself be reinforcing. The approval of the teacher may serve as another source of reinforcement.

However, these and other traditional reinforcers are ineffective for some children and in such cases would not be expected to maintain behaviors requisite to school learning. It is suggested that inadequacies in reinforcement conditions lie at the root of many educational failures.

In this context, it may also be productive to point out that the issue of what reinforcers to use in education is for some "emotionally charged." As indicated in Chapter 4, some people feel that "learning should be its own reward," and that a self-conscious application of reinforcement to behaviors involved in learning has some self-evident disadvantageous quality. However, a priori judgments such as these are not justified. There is certainly adequate evidence to suggest that some type of reinforcement is involved in much, if not all, of the learning which occurs in school. Before practical circumstances can be adequately evaluated, and statements made as to the type of reinforcers that should be used and those that should not, it will be necessary to gather empirical results on which to base decisions.

---

been successfully demonstrated by Corke and Toombs (1962) at the University of Houston. In addition, Birnbrauer (1962) of the University of Washington has described an effective classroom set-up for the application of reinforcement principles to teaching educable retarded children that employs a token system backed up by trading stamps that have a monetary value.

Strong opinions excluding the use of certain reinforcers are not at this time capable of support. What *is* necessary is the study of reinforcement variables in school learning as well as the study of practical means of implementing the findings.

Conclusions

While the foregoing is not intended to be an exhaustive exploration of the possible problems in educational psychology which should be approached experimentally, it is suggested that the automated teaching movement, supplemented by other experimental applications to complex learning, indicates that the experimental application of learning principles and methods to some of the other problems of education should be highly productive.

The possibilities for such an educational psychology as well as the significance of studying various areas of learning have been suggested to some extent by Skinner.

> Motor skills such as rhythm, perceptual skills such as matching and intellectual skills such as inductive reasoning are seldom taught directly. It is expected that students will rise to their best level of competence indirectly through the teaching of subject matter. It is also usually assumed that the large individual differences seen in an adult population are due to differences in natural endowment. But we have by no means explored the possibility that they are due to large differences in environmental circumstances, particularly in the early lives of students. The environment of the young child contains poor contingencies to shape and sustain rhythmic and musical abilities, pattern discrimination and so on. Until we have remedied this environmental defect we are in no position to assign differences to genetic limitations. It is quite possible that wide difference in abilities will still survive, including the difference now measured crudely as one of intelligence, but that the whole population can be moved upward in competence and achievement (1961, p. 102).

METHODOLOGY IN AN EXPERIMENTAL EDUCATIONAL PSYCHOLOGY

Looking again at the developments in psychology that have led to the fields of programed teaching and automated instruction, as well as the possibilities of further experimentation as exemplified by the research on reading, we may abstract several general points of methodology.

Behavioral Analysis

In some cases, the behavior of interest may be very poorly specified by prior naturalistic observations. This might occur because the behavior is particularly subtle or complex. Before research can begin to establish the relationship between the determining events and the behavior, systematic observations may be required.

For example, in a discussion of problems of rehabilitation, Meyerson, Michael, Mowrer, Osgood, and Staats (1963) recommended that psychologists trained in learning principles and experimental methods be given an opportunity to spend enough time in rehabilitation facilities to observe the problems of training behaviors in the rehabilitation facilities. They might then set about applying learning principles to these problems. It might be suggested, thus, that in order to approach various problems of behavior, the behavior involved must first be carefully observed; then the determinants may be sought and procedures commenced to bring the behavior under experimental control.

In other cases, the behavioral analysis may be of a more "theoretical" nature. When the behavior of interest is more explicit and has already been described, at least on a naturalistic level, but there is uncertainty regarding the determinants of the behavior, the first step may be to consider the behavior in terms of the principles of learning so that some of the possible determining variables may be suggested. Skinner's analysis of verbal behavior may be considered such an exercise, as might the analyses of other investigators, such as Dollard and Miller (1950), Mowrer (1954), and Osgood (1953). Based upon naturalistic observations of language behavior, these learning analyses suggested how such behavior develops and what the controlling stimuli, reinforcers, and so on may be. It was Skinner's analysis that induced other investigators to begin the experimental manipulation of operant verbal behaviors, as well as to apply the principles in the field of automated instruction.

The importance of prior behavioral analysis was also suggested when it was said earlier that the programer must start with the behavior to be learned and then work back from this to the initial behaviors to be trained. This methodology, however, has greater significance than solely in its application to constructing programs—it seems generally applicable to experimental educational psychology.

It may thus be concluded that research into a new area of complex human learning may often profitably commence with an analysis of the behavior involved (as well as the stimuli, the reinforcers, the schedules of reinforcement, and so on). Such analysis may well have to precede research, to further stimulate the interest of other investigators in the area.

Experimental Precision in Studying
Complex Human Learning

When learning principles and experimental methods are taken out of the laboratory situation and applied to actual problems of training complex behavior it is to be expected that often the initial work will lack the precision associated with laboratory experimentation. Considerable work with the training problems may be necessary before experimental procedures and apparatus are devised to make the research more precise. In some cases the research might never approach laboratory precision, and yet the general application of learning principles could be an improvement upon methods deriving from nonlearning approaches.

Although precision is a goal of all experimentation, for it is through laboratory procedures that the most reliable observations may be obtained, criteria that are too strict with respect to the applications of learning principles and experimental methods could, it would seem, be inhibiting. "Preoccupation with precision and accurate measurement has induced many behavioral researchers to cling to high control animal experimentation of the laboratory. This has meant a comparative neglect of experimentation on learning in children" (Fowler, 1962, p. 144). While the control of irrelevant variables obtainable in the laboratory is a goal well worth striving for, the approach of the methodological purist can prevent research on significant human behaviors from beginning—and thus leave the field of study to others who may be less well prepared to deal with the problems involved.

Long-term Studies

It has been suggested that many of the problems of training in educational psychology, especially those of early learning, may well involve long-term experimental studies. As previously noted, Fowler (1962) points out that reading learning, mathematical learning, musical learning, and so on, all involve the acquisition of complex behavioral repertoires and must as a consequence be studied over relatively long periods.

On the other hand, possibly because of the deficiencies in methodology, the psychology of human learning has for the most part been restricted to short-term studies. "Learning processes, where studied, have embraced problems whose solution depends only upon a few simple operations acquired over a restricted number of trials. Little attention has been directed toward longitudinal work on the antecedent-consequent relations of basic cognitive dimensions" (Fowler, 1962, p. 144).

The deficiencies may have in the past sprung from the fact that traditional experimental designs have rested upon group studies to compensate for the interference of variables the experimenter cannot control. As an example, let us say that it is suspected that the more often a child is presented with the paired-associates learning task such as CANDY–SWEET, the more likely he will be to respond with SWEET when CANDY is presented. To test this, two children could be given varying amounts of training and the relative strength of their word associates tested. Unfortunately, the results would be meaningless since the experience of each child *prior* to the experimental training might have determined his response. It would be possible, however, to test the hypothesis by randomly selecting two groups of children and subjecting the two groups to different experimental conditions. If the groups differ originally in experience only in a random fashion, and if after experimental treatment there is a difference in the average behavior of the groups beyond the random difference, it can be concluded that a lawful relationship exists between the experimental condition and the observed behavior.

Since with human subjects past experience has so great an effect, it has frequently been necessary to use group studies to establish or extend principles of learning to humans. Often the experimentally manipulated variable, as the number of pairings of CANDY and SWEET in the above example, are much weaker than the effect of uncontrolled variables, such as the number of times CANDY and SWEET have been presented to the child in his own personal history. In such a case, a very large number of subjects may be required to test the effect of the experimental variable. Large groups, however, do not lend themselves to long-term studies. The expense would be prohibitive. Thus, group research design may have contributed to the restriction of experimental study of learning to the laboratory and to avoidance of research on complex human behavior.

The sometimes prohibitive cost of group research is discussed by Skinner in the following statement.

> [Our research] is usually single organism research. Any other experimental method is often impossible. When an experiment on one pigeon runs to thousands of hours, it cannot be repeated on even a modest group of, say, ten subjects—at least if one wants to get on with other matters. Fortunately, a statistical program is *unnecessary*. Most of what we know about the effects of complex schedules of reinforcement has been learned in a series of discoveries no one of which could have been proved to the satisfaction of a student in Statistics A (1959, p. 140).

As the above statement mentions, methods that do lend themselves to applied research involving long training periods have been developed and refined. Skinner has for some time encouraged the use of single organisms in research and has developed methods for obtaining reliable observations by this method. Research designs for work with individual subjects have been formally explicated by Sidman (1960a). As has been shown, these methods are relevant for dealing with actual problems of child learning. The method involves gaining experimental control of the important conditions affecting the organism's behavior rather than using methods of group, or statistical, control. Thus, in contrast to using many subjects for a short period of time, it might be preferable in the above hypothetical example to give only a few subjects long-term training on CANDY–SWEET to make the experimental experience much stronger relative to the nonexperimental life experience of the subjects.

Since individual subjects, rather than groups, may be used to study the effects of experimental variables, these research designs lend themselves to long-term studies of complex behaviors. Thus, it was possible to begin the study of a complex behavior such as reading acquisition with methods analogous to those used in the operant conditioning laboratory by working with individual subjects; this methodology should be extensible to the study of other complex behaviors.

Other Experimental Methods

Although the application of experimental principles to the practical problems of education have come almost entirely from operant conditioning methods, it seems quite feasible that other experimental methods and learning principles may have a good deal to contribute. For example, Palermo and Jenkins have instituted a research project "To establish norms for 200 words of various parts of speech; to determine the developmental characteristics of word associations obtained in written form from children of fourth grade through college level inclusive; to allow for a basic understanding of language or word habits for use in the study of verbal learning and language development in children" (1961, p. 15). Norms such as these could be used in the development of a reading program according to S–R principles. The use of word-associations in programing has already been discussed. These principles could also be used in training of other skills as well, such as reading. Let us say, for example, that it was found that there was a strong TABLE–CHAIR word association for children. In constructing a reading program, if CHAIR was to be introduced to the child and he already could read TABLE AND, it might be wise to introduce CHAIR in the phrase TABLE AND CHAIR. The two preceding words would contribute to the stimuli tending to elicit the vocal response CHAIR and make it a more probable occurrence. (This may be recognized as a form of "prompt" discussed earlier.) Thus, a reading program could be constructed to incorporate word association norms.

Perhaps, as another example, grammatical response sequences in their development and function could be studied using the technology and principles established in the field of verbal learning. As was pointed out in Chapter 4, there has been a great deal of experimentation on the acquisition of word associations (serial and paired-associate learning). The methods and principles of this research may have application to educational problems (see Zeaman, 1959).

Conclusion

A major contribution of the automated instruction movement has been in suggesting a method for an experimental educational psychology. The implication is that experimental methods and learning principles have reached a stage of development where they can be applied to the study of more complex human learning—especially learning in childhood. An experimental educational psychology based upon this general approach seems capable of attacking a wider range of problems than has so far been undertaken within the automated instruction movement.

In the light of the success already shown in the field of automated instruction, and in the other studies mentioned herein, it would seem that a major effort in psychology and education will in future years be allocated to an experimental study of complex human learning problems. The next chapter will summarize another area of psychology in which the application of learning principles to the study of human behavior problems has been accelerating rapidly.

11

Behavior Problems
and Treatment

IN PREVIOUS chapters we have argued that explanation in terms of internal events is often fallacious and misleading. Now, in dealing with abnormal behavior, it should be recalled that the same arguments apply once again. While intelligent laymen no longer believe that evil spirits and demons are responsible for deviant behavior, there are still other concepts of inner events as determinants. The terminology today is most frequently taken from the field of medicine. The individual's behavior is considered but a symptom of some "mental," "personality," or "nervous" process that is "disordered." Cure the real, underlying disorder and the problem behaviors that are its manifestations will disappear, so the conception might conclude.

Psychoanalytic theory is also characterized by this view of behavior problems as only symptoms of underlying "psychic" disorders. As Eysenck (1960) has pointed out, "According to psychoanalytic doctrine, there is a psychological complex, situated in the unconscious mind, underlying all the manifest symptoms of neurotic disorder. Hence the necessity of therapy for the psyche" (pp. 10–11). "Freudian theory regards neurotic symptoms as adaptive mechanisms which are evidence of repression; they are 'the visible upshot of unconscious causes' " (pp. 8–9).

In contrast, a number of psychologists, in applying learning principles to understanding maladjustments, have considered them to be behavior patterns acquired according to the same principles as are any other behaviors. Dollard and Miller (1950), Eysenck (1947), Mowrer (1950), and Skinner (1953), to mention only a few examples, have all dealt with so-called "personality disturbances" as learned behaviors.

> Human behavior is learned; precisely that behavior which is widely felt to characterize man as a rational being, or as a member of a particular nation or social class, is learned rather than innate. We also learn fears, guilt, and other socially acquired motivations, as well as symptoms

and rationalizations—factors which are characteristic of normal personality but show up more clearly in extreme form as neurosis (Dollard and Miller, 1950, p. 25).

Other investigators have added to the formulation of maladjustment as learned behavior. Eysenck (1960) has suggested that there are two types of learning disorders which contribute to maladjustive behavior.

> On the one hand we have *surplus conditioned reactions,* i.e. reactions acquired . . . where the reaction is unadaptive, even though originally it may have been well suited to circumstances. On the other hand we have *deficient conditioned reactions,* i.e. reactions normally acquired by most individuals in society which are adaptive, but which . . . have not been acquired by a particular person (p. 7).

To this dichotomy, another distinction important to an account of behavior problems should be added. It has been suggested in abbreviated form that the reinforcing stimuli which shape or maintain behavior and the discriminative stimuli which control behavior must also be examined.

> In order to distinguish . . . [normal and maladjustive] behavior we must look to the stimulus conditions surrounding the expression of the neurotic behavior and compare these with those surrounding a similar response in the normal. These conditions refer both to the *discriminative* and *reinforcing* stimuli. This may not tell us the whole story, since an individual's neurotic behavior is going to be a function of many variables in his past conditioning history. However, it will give us some knowledge of the occasions under which neurotic behavior is emitted and the peculiar reinforcement contingencies that happen to be operating (Lundin, 1961, pp. 338–339).

Actually, all the principles that have previously been described [1] would seem to be potential contributors to abnormal behavior as well as to normal behavior. Nevertheless, in an abbreviated description of abnormal behavior it seems useful to organize the discussion in terms of behavioral deficits, surplus or inappropriate behaviors, improper stimulus control, and inadequate reinforcing systems. This is not meant to suggest that any deviant behavior pattern actually fits into merely *one* of these categories. Most of the behavior deviations to be discussed will not be pure examples in any case; most involve several categories. For example, although an abnormal behavior may be discussed in terms of a behavioral deficit, it might also involve lack of development of the control normally characteristic of the stimuli present in a situation. However, where the importance of the controlling stimulus is not obvious, the following discussion might be limited to the behavior deficit alone. The same sort of overlap occurs with the

---

[1] For example, those involved in speech learning, "self-tacting," reasoning, learning social discriminative stimuli, and so on.

other categories as well, although only one quality may be abstracted for discussion in the various examples.

Behavioral Deficit

Many adjustive difficulties may be attributed to the absence of behaviors when circumstances call for them. Certainly, it is easy to see in problem-solving and reasoning situations that an individual who does not have the requisite behaviors will not gain reinforcement, or may even receive punishment for his failure. It will be recalled that we already discussed deficiencies in social reasoning in Chapter 9. These and other behavior deficits are equally significant in the area of "abnormal" behavior, and a few such examples will be cited as illustrative.

Ferster (1961), in discussing autistic children (children with severe behavior problems) in terms of operant conditioning principles, states that many of the behaviors of these children seem to be like those of normals except that in the autistic child the normal behavior occurs much less frequently and abnormal behaviors much more frequently. He continues, however, by stating that the "major performance deficits of the autistic child are in the degree of social control: The kinds of performances which have their major effects through the mediation of other individuals" (p. 439).

> The main avenue of social control in a normal repertoire is usually through speech, a kind of performance that is unique because it produces the consequences maintaining it through the mediation of a second person. . . . Autistic children almost always have an inadequately developed speech repertoire, varying from mutism to a repertoire of a few words. Even when large numbers of words are emitted, the speech is not normal in the sense that it is not maintained by its effect on a social environment. When normal speech is present, it usually is in the form of a *mand*. . . . This is a simple verbal response which is maintained because of its direct reinforcement, e.g., "Candy," "Let me out." The main variable is usually the level of deprivation of the speaker. It lacks the sensitive interchange between the speaker and listener characteristic of much human verbal behavior, as for example, the *tact*. . . . In contrast to the mand, the tact . . . is almost completely absent. This form of verbal behavior benefits the listener rather than the speaker and is not usually relevant to the current deprivations of the speaker. This is the form of verbal behavior by which the child describes his environment, as, for example, "This is a chair"; "The mailman is coming." This latter kind of verbal control is generally absent or weak, as with other kinds of verbal behavior except an occasional mand (pp. 439–440).

The example of defective tact development involves a problem of stimulus control as well as of the deficit in the verbal responses. It is important to note that it is this type of verbal behavior which, as discussed in Chapter 5, ordinarily becomes for the child an essential constituent of reasoning and problem solving, enabling him to make a complex adjustment to his physical and social environments. As Dollard and Miller state, when language behavior that is ordinarily involved in such reasoning is defective, the individual is in essence "stupid."

Ferster suggests that behavioral deficits of an autistic child result from deficits in the conditioning history of the child. The following describes the influence of a behaviorally deficient adult in producing a deficient conditioning history.

> Any severe disruption of the parental repertoire will severely affect the frequency with which the parent reinforces the behavior of the child. Consider, for example, the depressed parent whose general level of behavior is very low. One consequence of this low level of behavior will be a lessened frequency of reacting to the child. Therefore, many items in the child's repertoire will be less frequently reinforced in the depressed than the normal parent. The verbal responses, "May I have some bread" or "I want to go outside," might go unreinforced or be emitted many times without reinforcement. Various kinds of somatic disturbances, such as alcoholic "hangover," drug addiction, severe headache, somatic diseases, etc., could also produce large changes in the over-all reactivity of the parent to a child. To the extent that the child's performances occur because of their effect on the parent, the severely weakened parental repertoire may correspondingly weaken the child's behavior. If the parental extinction of the child's behavior is systematic and periodic, much of a child's behavior could be eliminated (p. 444).

Punishment may also play an important role in explaining behavioral deficits. In general, it may be said that when children develop adjustive behaviors later than usual, they are subject to aversive social stimuli of various kinds, such as derision. The child who does not develop independent toilet habits, who does not speak well enough, who stutters past an acceptable age, who lacks motor skill, and so on, receives much social punishment as a consequence. This state of affairs would be expected to continue throughout life. As the individual approaches adulthood, the loss of positive social reinforcers of various kinds—money, prestige, jobs, companionship—may provide an even more critical aversive contingency. At any rate, it might be said that a child or adult with noticeable behavioral deficits can expect to receive more aversive stimulation and less positive reinforcement. These are poor conditions for further shaping adjustive responses or maintaining those which were already developed. A vicious cycle may thus be engendered.

Ferster suggests that a behavioral analysis is also relevant to adult maladjustments analogous to those of the autistic child.

The same kind of functional analysis can be made for the performance of the adult psychotic although the specific deficits observed in autistic children and their manner of occurrence may not be relevant. In particular, the analysis of the adult's behavior would be more concerned with the factors which weaken behavior already in the repertoire rather than the development of new repertoires as with the analysis of the autistic child's behavior. Maintaining already-established behavior is more at issue in the adult than the initial development of a performance as in the case of the child . . . (p. 455).

This suggestion that behavioral deficits are involved in serious behavior problems of adults seems to receive support from some descriptions of "abnormal" behavior. Consider, for example, the grossly disturbed behavior called simple schizophrenia.

In simple schizophrenic reactions, the patient evidences a gradual narrowing and waning of interests, loss of ambition, emotional indifference, and withdrawal from social relations. He no longer cares whether he passes or fails in school and is no longer concerned about his friends or family. He may show periods of moodiness and irritability, but becomes increasingly emotionally indifferent and seclusive. Conversation becomes scant and trivial, personal appearance and hygiene are neglected, there is little or no interest in the opposite sex, and the patient has difficulty in concentrating on anything outside of his fantasy world. He makes no effort to work or to assume responsibility and seems content to lead a simple, irresponsible, indifferent, parasitic existence.

Lecturing, pleading, and encouragement by well-meaning family members are of no avail and often lead to obstinate, negativistic, evasive behavior (Coleman, 1950, p. 245).

The type of behavior at issue here—studying and doing well in school, taking care of one's personal appearance, conversing and behaving in a socially successful manner, ambitious hard-working behavior—may be considered to develop and to be maintained through reinforcement, of which social reinforcement is an important form. However, the description of the simple schizophrenic's behavior indicates that his repertoire does not include a sufficient supply of such adjustive behaviors—behaviors which will result in positive reinforcement in our society. This type of deficiency could thus be interpreted as resulting from inadequate training of the necessary skills, including social and work responses.

The deterioration described could be laid to the increasing demands made upon the individual in terms of extended sequences of work and social behaviors as one grows older, and to the corresponding delays in reinforcement he experiences. For an individual whose behavior is not maintained in good strength even in the less demanding condition of childhood, a point may be reached for the adult when the reinforcers his poor behavioral repertoire can gain may be totally inadequate. (Although this analysis includes mention of the fact that the reinforcers are inadequate, they may be inadequate because his defective behavioral repertoire does not allow him to obtain a more adequate supply. That is, to some extent at least, the inadequacies of reinforcement are a result of the behavioral deficit, as well as the converse.)

As already noted, because of the individual's deficient behaviors he may also suffer aversive stimulation that will act as a further handicap for the maintenance and development of his behavior. Thus, not only are the lectures, pleadings, admonishments, and the like of no avail, they may backfire and, in the manner of aversive stimuli, lead to suppression or deterioration of the few adjustive behaviors that have been acquired.

Lundin (1961) has suggested that in addition to the severely disturbed "psychotic" behavior already described, behavior disorders included under the general heading of "neurosis"—a wide class of milder behavior disorders —involve deficits in behavior.

> The first step in explaining the persistence of a behavior that is apparently unreinforcing and punishing as well (neurotic paradox) is to realize that the neurotic is somewhat limited in the behaviors that can achieve reinforcement. When placed in a situation of frustration where reinforcements are blocked or withheld, a normal person with an adequate behavior repertoire will find some alternate solution by making use of some previously acquired responses. . . . [The neurotic] suffers from a learning deficit, one which he is unable to correct. In other words the neurotic lacks adequate behavior which would allow him to resolve his conflicts and overcome his frustrations (pp. 362–363).

Another group of behavioral deficits in addition to the class labeled "abnormal" concern those deficits occurring as a result of some special physical disability of the individual—disabilities resulting from birth defects, disease, or injury. A broad range of problems concerning the special circumstances in which an individual must learn or relearn some behavioral skills is included under the term rehabilitation. "[T]he disabled person often has to learn new tasks, or he has to relearn to perform an old task in the same way he originally did it, or he has to learn to accomplish an old task in a new or different way. The tasks cover the whole range of sensory, motor, perceptual, emotional, motivational, cognitive, and social learning. In behavioral terms, the problems of the disabled person require the acquisition of some new behaviors, the maintenance of adequate behaviors, and the extinction of inadequate or deficient behaviors" (Meyerson, Michael, Mowrer, Osgood, and Staats, 1963, pp. 69–70).

Thus, as one example, behavioral deficits may occur because of impaired sensory processes. As an illustration, the child who is deaf from birth does not acquire ordinary language facility under the same methods of training given hearing children. As a result severe deficits in general behavior may result (Bowers, Clement, Francis, and Johnson, 1960, p. 67).

The problem of deficit may also be a product of loss of function from disease or injury. The individual who has suffered such a loss may have to learn entire repertoires of various kinds. The carpenter who has lost his legs may have to acquire a new class of walking behaviors and perhaps a whole new repertoire in terms of work and family relations, recreation, and so on.

Inappropriate Behavior

It is perhaps the unusual, bizarre behaviors of individuals, rather than their behavioral deficits, that are customarily the object of most interest and that seem to typify "abnormal" behavior. The behaviors may seem so deviant and their causes so enigmatic that it is easy to conclude that different principles must be operating with individuals so "afflicted." The unusual posturings and facial contortions, the "word salad" verbalizations, mumblings, shoutings, compulsive countings; the destructive and violent episodes; the immobility and lack of movement; all seem inexplicable by usual standards although they are common features of hospitalized psychotic patients.

The fact that behavior is bizarre, however, does not by itself imply that the principles by which it was acquired and is maintained are different from those underlying "normal" behaviors—although such an argument seems to be implicit in many interpretations of abnormal behavior. "Experimental and clinical psychologists alike seem to equate the two terms *abnormal* and *disorderly*. . . . Neither worker seems to give much thought to the possibility that maladaptive behavior can result from quantitative and qualitative combinations of processes which are themselves intrinsically orderly, strictly determined, and normal in origin" (Sidman, 1960b, p. 61).

An example may be used to illustrate how learning contingencies may underlie behaviors that seem inexplicable in terms of ordinary training. This case, reported originally by Lidz, Cornelison, Terry, and Fleck (1958), concerned the belief of two schizophrenic brothers that "disagreement" meant constipation. Although such an example might suggest an explanation in terms of the symbolic value of this bizarre meaning, looking into their learning histories, it was found that whenever the sons disagreed with their mother she informed them that they were constipated and proceeded to give them an enema. Bandura, in commenting on this case, points out that the procedure most certainly must have dramatically conditioned an unusual meaning to the word "disagreement." While this example deals primarily with deviant stimulus control (to be discussed in the next section), it does illustrate that extreme and unusual behavior may be learned directly. According to Bandura, this and other cases "provide ample evidence that delusions, suspiciousness, grandiosity, extreme denial of reality cues, and other forms of 'schizophrenic' behavior [are] frequently learned through direct reinforcement and transmitted by parental modeling of unbelievably deviant behavior patterns" (1962a, p. 4).

In discussing the acquisition of some of the bizarre behavior of the autistic child described earlier, Ferster (1961) also points out that differential reinforcement may be involved.

> The same factors in the parental repertoire that tend to produce non-reinforcement of the child's behavior—general disruption of the parent or other behaviors prepotent over the child—correspondingly produce reinforcement of large-order-of-magnitude tantrums. The parent whose total repertoire is severely enough disrupted . . . will also react only to tantrums that are of large order of magnitude of aversiveness. A range of sensitivity of the parent to aversive control by the child produces ideal conditions for progressively increasing the intensity or frequency of tantrums. A high sensitivity to aversive control guarantees that some tantrums will be reinforced at least periodically. A low sensitivity differentially reinforces tantrums of large orders of magnitude. At one extreme, the parent may be hypersensitive to the child and, at other times, so depressed that only physical violence will produce a reaction. The schedule by which the parent's behavior terminates the tantrum is a second factor which will increase the range of reactivity of the parent. As more behavior is required of the parent to terminate the tantrum, the parent's inclination to do so will fall. When the parent is less inclined to reinforce a given intensity of tantrum, any variation in tantrum intensity is tantamount to differential reinforcement of extreme forms, if the parent now reacts to the larger-order-of-magnitude tantrum (pp. 446–447).

Other so-called abnormal behaviors may in themselves be common and adaptive, but because they occur with great frequency they are considered inappropriate, deviant, or nonadaptive, such as overly frequent handwashing, counting, and so on. Such behaviors are customarily called compulsions. Dollard and Miller (1950) suggest that such responses may be acquired through the action of negative reinforcement.

> Similarly, the anxiety-reducing effects of a particular act, such as handwashing, are often due to social training. Then the act of washing the hands may have a direct reassuring effect because it has been so frequently associated during childhood with escape from criticism for having dirty hands. Stated more exactly, the cues produced by the act may elicit responses that inhibit fear (p. 164).

Dollard and Miller also suggest that in other cases the ". . . compulsive act may have an anxiety-reducing effect because it serves as a distraction"

(p. 164). Thus, counting, or some other form of compulsive verbal behavior could be negatively reinforced in replacing aversive verbal behavior of various kinds. For example, an individual who ruminates continually on his complete failure or who thinks in sexual terms that are aversive (anxiety-producing) will be negatively reinforced by verbal behaviors that replace the aversive ones. Whatever particular verbal behaviors replace the aversive stimuli would, additionally, be expected to be a function of the individual's reinforcement history.

Two experiments of Ayllon and Michael (1959) seem to indicate that compulsive behaviors may also be maintained in their unusual frequency through positive reinforcement procedures. One study concerned a hospitalized patient who made such frequent visits to the ward office that she interrupted and interfered with the functioning of the ward personnel. This behavior had persisted for two years at the time the study began. "Frequently, she was taken by the hand or pushed back bodily into the ward" (p. 326). Upon the basis of the analysis that this treatment constituted positive reinforcement for this patient, the nurses were instructed to pay no attention whatsoever to her when she entered the ward office. The results of this extinction procedure are shown in Figure 11.1. The frequency of the behavior dropped over eight weeks of extinction from an average of sixteen office visits per day to two per day.

The other illustration is of four hospitalized patients who displayed "compulsive" collecting and hoarding of papers, rubbish, and magazines. This material was carried beneath their clothing next to their skin and resulted in skin rashes in one patient. Again, it was thought that a good

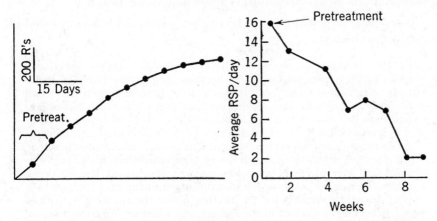

Fig. 11.1. Extinction of the response "entering the nurses' office" (Ayllon and Michael, 1959, p. 327). The graph at the left is a cumulative record; the right-hand graph is a conventional record.

deal of the reinforcement maintaining this behavior was the attention of being "dejunked" from time to time by the nurses. The experimental procedures consisted of extinction for the behavior (withholding the attention) and also of satiating the patients for magazines by making an abundance of magazines available. The results of this procedure on the compulsive hoarding are shown in Figure 11.2, which indicates a gradual decrease in the frequency of the behavior.

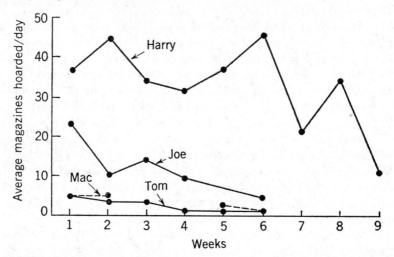

Fig. 11.2. Satiation and extinction of magazine-hoarding behavior for four hospitalized patients (Ayllon and Michael, 1959, p. 333).

Inappropriate Behavior Resulting from Behavioral Deficit

It has been suggested that the occurrence of unusual behaviors is linked to behavioral deficit.

Much of the schizophrenic's behavior exemplifies very weak performances which appear strong simply because most of the normally maintained behavior is weak. . . . If this analysis is correct, then the actual form of the behavior observed in psychotic patients is much less important than the absolute amount of behavior and, particularly, the levels of activity controlled by an effect on a social or socially derived environment. An analogous situation occurs frequently in normal individuals when they are placed in situations in which few of their currently available performances are relevant. Some examples are: experiments on sensory deprivation; waiting for someone to keep an appointment in a relatively isolated place; attending a formal meeting where the speaker's activity is not sufficiently important to the listener, but where at the same time, no behavior other than listening is appropriate. Under these circumstances, many individuals emit performances that are very similar to those of psychotic persons, such as rubbing the table constantly, scratching a particular part of the body, doodling, or some kind of oral activity. All of these activities have the common feature of not being supported by the external environment, particularly the social environment (Ferster and DeMyer, 1961, pp. 343–344).

Thus, certain psychotic behavior would appear to be a result of a behavior deficiency. The problem of treating this type of behavioral disorder would seem best framed in terms of training of adequate behaviors to good strength, as well as diminishing the psychotic behavior. This will be discussed in the latter portions of this chapter. At this point, the reciprocal nature of deficiencies in adequate behavior and the development of bizarre forms of behavior can be demonstrated in the following experiments.

In an extended research program conducted at the Metropolitan State Hospital in Massachusetts, Lindsley (1956) developed an operant conditioning chamber in which the behavior of chronic schizophrenic patients could be observed and manipulated in much the same way that the behavior of lower organisms has been studied. Each room was furnished simply with a chair, a plastic ash tray, a manipulandum, and devices for presenting discriminative stimuli and for dispensing reinforcers. The manipulandum was a plunger like that on a cigarette or candy vending machine, which could be pulled up to 10,000 times per hour. The reinforcements which have been used are quite varied, including money, candy, pictures of nude figures, and cigarettes. Using the standard operant conditioning paradigm, reinforcers were delivered contingent on pulls of the plunger according to a particular schedule of reinforcement. In another room, common operant conditioning devices regulated the presentation of stimuli and the schedule of reinforcement, recorded the rate of responding on the plunger, and so on.

The following results, based upon an analysis of some sixty records of chronic psychotic patients, indicate the relationship between deficits in adequate behavior and the appearance of bizarre behavior.

There was a direct relationship between the severity of the psychosis and the irregularity of the rate of responding. Normals tended either to respond at a fairly steady rate or leave the room. In contrast, the more disturbed the patient, the longer the pauses seemed to be between the more regular rates. Similarly, when a single patient was in a period of severe disorder with respect to the psychotic behavior, the pauses were longer; when his adjustment appeared better outside the experimental chamber, the pauses were correspondingly shorter.

It is interesting to note that this relationship is between irregularity and *degree* of the disorder and not between rate and psychiatric classification —for example, schizophrenic or paranoid. However, when the patient was observed through a one-way screen during the periods of pausing the topography of this behavior was found to correlate with the particular psychiatric diagnosis. The patient might be hallucinating, engaging in violent behavior, and so on, in such periods.

The relationship between this bizarre behavior and the pausing was important for another reason. Lindsley showed that during fixed-ratio reinforcement the psychotic behavior appeared only during the pauses after reinforcement—no psychotic performance was exhibited while under the control of the fixed-ratio schedule. This would substantiate the suggestion that the bizarre behavior of the psychotic may appear strong simply because the normal behavior is weak. Furthermore, when the normal behavior is reinforced on a fixed-ratio schedule, it may become quite strong—sometimes displacing the psychotic behavior entirely. Only when the schedule has been completed to where pauses normally occur does the bizarre behavior return. Sidman (1962) also argues for such an interpretation.

> The first, and perhaps the most striking observation, was that each patient engaged in his characteristic psychotic symptom during the pauses in plunger pulling. "For example, the pacer paced, the hallucinator berated the empty room, the destructive patient tore his clothing, the compulsive patient made patterns out of his candies on the floor, the depressed patient just sat, etc." (Lindsley, unpublished report). This observation suggests that psychotic processes function as competing response systems in the operant testing situation; that the frequency and duration of pauses in the patient's operant performance can be used as an index of the frequency and duration of discrete psychotic episodes or incidents (p. 202).

The work of Ferster and DeMyer with autistic children led to a very similar conclusion. They point out that the atavistic and tantrum behaviors are operants in competition with those responses required in the conditioning situation. Where the plunger pulling came under good control, the inappropriate behaviors decreased correspondingly. When control was lost for some reason, the severe tantrums and atavisms again occurred (Ferster, 1961; Ferster and DeMyer, 1961).

Thus, psychotic behaviors may be considered as operants that compete with other operant behaviors. Only when the environment is such that the other operant behaviors are strong will the aberrant behaviors be replaced. However, when the other operant behaviors are not strong, then the psychotic behaviors are displayed. (In view of this interpretation, it is perhaps worthwhile to speculate upon the deficiencies in the type of reinforcing environments, including hospital environments, which must exist to allow behaviors that would compete with the psychotic behaviors to remain so weak.)

In addition to the schizophrenic behaviors in adults and the autistic behaviors in children already mentioned, there are other "surplus" nonadaptive behaviors of a verbal nature that also may be thought of as replacing normal verbal behavior. For example, among the "ego-defense" verbal behaviors, rationalization was discussed in an earlier chapter as a nonadaptive behavior that might be positively or negatively reinforced for the individual. When there is too great a deviation from others' descriptions of events, the verbal behavior may mediate other behavior harmful to the individual himself or to others, and finally lead to his hospitalization.

That this type of verbal behavior (called delusional) is subject to the principles of behavior and can be manipulated in the hospital environment is suggested by the results of Ayllon and Michael (1959). In the case at issue, a delusional female patient was found to be spending a great deal of time speaking about her illegitimate child and the men she claimed were constantly pursuing her, and relatively little time in speech that paralleled real events as reported by other people. Consistent with the view that delusional speech was replacing the relatively weak normal speech, treatment for this patient consisted of extinction for this delusional talk. All the ward personnel were instructed not to pay attention to the patient when she emitted this type of verbal behavior. On the other hand, they were to reinforce (by their attention) talk of the patient that was nondelusional, or "reality-oriented." Prior to the extinction and reinforcement procedures the patient's delusional talk amounted to 91 percent of her total conversation. After extinction of delusional conversation and reinforcement of nondelusional conversation the percentage was reduced to 25. Near the end of the experiment the patient was contacted by someone who again reinforced the delusional speech and the percentage rose almost to the preexperimental level.

Inadequate or Inappropriate Stimulus Control

Another class of "abnormal" or nonadaptive behavior is made up of those cases in which the behavior under appropriate circumstances is not unusual, but is nonadaptive when elicited under inappropriate stimulus conditions.

The classic experimental example of this with respect to a "phobia" (an abnormal fear), was given by Watson and Rayner (1920). Through respondent conditioning, the response to animals of an eleven-month-old boy called Albert was changed from fondness to a strong aversion. A loud noise (as the UCS) was presented each time the child reached for a white rat (the CS). As would be expected, the white rat became an aversive stimulus for the boy and it could be said that the rat stimulus elicited a "fear" or "anxiety" response; the child responded in a way which would be described as "fear of" the animal. Moreover, as would be expected from the principle of stimulus generalization, other furry animals also elicited the "phobic" response from the boy although they had never been paired with the aversive sound stimulus. The "phobic" response to these animals could be regarded as inappropriate since the stimuli were not harmful to the child and did not normally elicit such extreme responses.

Dollard and Miller (1950) also discuss phobias as unusual conditioned responses to initially innocuous stimuli. They describe the case of a four-year-old boy punished by the maid for masturbating. The boy subsequently displayed reluctance and fear of going to bed. They suggest that the response-produced cues of masturbation became conditioned stimuli that elicited a fear response (the phobic response).

> In this case it seems fairly evident that punishment and disapproval from the maid had attached fear to the response of masturbation. The child seems to have been more strongly tempted to masturbate when he was alone in bed. Thus the fear was aroused in bed. . . . Whenever the child approached the bed or was told to go to bed, his fear was increased; any response that took him away from bed was reinforced by a reduction in the strength of this fear. He learned a variety of such responses (p. 160).

As Jones (1961) has pointed out, the anxiety response itself may be the nonadaptive symptom, or the symptom may be the overt behavior that is acquired in escaping from the anxiety-producing stimulus. The escape behavior may be considered in some cases as analogous to the compulsive behaviors already described. However, in each of the cases discussed here, the behavior is nonadaptive, particularly in the sense of its unusual stimulus control.

Another example of these problems of stimulus control may be seen in the disturbances often categorized as "psychosomatic illnesses," which may be described as follows: "[I]t has been repeatedly demonstrated that psychological factors, such as anxiety, fear, anger, and other emotional conditions, seriously affect the general resistance of the organism to disease, and in some instances may even bring about actual tissue pathology . . . for example, peptic ulcer, high blood pressure, asthma, acne, migraine, overweight, and even the common cold" (Coleman, 1950, p. 205).

It is suggested that some psychosomatic illnesses may be problems of stimulus control in that a response has been conditioned to an inappropriate stimulus, or to a wide variety of inappropriate stimuli.

> There is . . . a recent tendency in psychosomatic medicine to regard many somatic disorders such as allergies, peptic ulcers, mucous colitis, hypertension, etc. as conditioned response patterns of hidden origin. . . .
> The wide variety of body functions which are capable of being readily conditioned has caused several workers to attempt to induce specific

psychosomatic disorders by experimental means. There are for example, many indications that bronchial asthmatic attacks can be provoked by means other than direct contact with the specific noxious agent, i.e. various conditioned stimuli may be effectively substituted for the original agent . . . (Franks, 1961, p. 477).

Extensive research in Russia (reviewed by Razran, 1961) has also indicated that visceral responses can be conditioned in the laboratory to many stimuli, and that the visceral responses can themselves produce stimuli to which other responses can be conditioned. Razran describes for example, an experiment in which the response of vascular constriction (constriction of blood vessels) was conditioned to another response (breathing).

Razran also presents evidence of six types of conditioning with humans where internal responses were conditioned to external stimuli: "sensory (report of sensations), motor (respiratory changes), and visceral (vascular and electrodermal reactions), in response to both sensory and verbal CSs" (p. 92). Such studies may be interpreted as demonstrations of the basic ways that responses important to psychosomatic illnesses may be learned.

The foregoing have been problems in inappropriate stimulus control, that is to say, of a response controlled by the wrong stimulus. There are other problems of behavior that involve the lack of stimulus control, in other words of the responses usually under the control of some stimuli failing to occur. For example, an analysis of enuresis (bedwetting) has been made (Jones, 1960; Mowrer and Mowrer, 1938) in terms of classical conditioning. According to this view enuresis may be considered to be a deficit in stimulus control in which the stimuli produced by the bladder distension have not come to elicit waking, so the child can go to the bathroom. This rationale has been applied to a procedure for appropriately training the child. In the training, whenever the child in his sleep has an extended bladder (the CS) and begins to urinate, an electric circuit embedded in his bedclothes is activated, which in turn causes a bell to ring loudly (UCS) waking the child (UR). Soon the extended bladder comes to elicit the waking. Thus, nocturnal enuresis may be considered a problem of inadequate stimulus control and attempts to remedy it should be aimed at gaining such control.

A large class of behavior problems seems to involve defective stimulus control where the situation appears to involve operant learning rather than respondent learning. The following section will deal with examples of such deficits in discriminative stimulus control.

Defective Discriminative Stimulus Control of Behavior

The importance of verbal stimuli in controlling appropriate behaviors has been pointed out in several earlier chapters. When this control is defective, even when the necessary behaviors are in the individual's repertoire, his adjustment may be poor. In ordinary living, it is necessary that visual and auditory verbal stimuli of many kinds—signs, laws, directions, requests, and so on—come to control certain behaviors. An interesting example of the lack of such control in hospitalized patients as well as of the behavior principles involved in gaining such control is given by Ayllon and Haughton (1962).

The verbal stimulus deficient in control for the group of psychotic patients was the announcement of mealtime. Many patients would not respond at all; others responded to the call in a dilatory fashion. Accordingly, and in the interest of illustrating the utility of discrimination training and successive approximation techniques, the following procedure was initiated. If the patient responded to the call to the meal by going to the dining hall within thirty minutes, he was reinforced by securing a meal. If, however, he did not respond until after that time, he found the dining room locked. Under this contingency of reinforcement, it was found that the call to meal quickly gained control over the behavior of the patients; they responded within the time limit. Later the time between the presentation of the verbal discriminative stimulus and the locking of the dining hall was reduced to twenty minutes, then to fifteen minutes, and finally to five minutes; each time the verbal stimuli came to exert the stronger control necessary. In this manner the call to mealtime was given discriminative control over this required behavior. It may be concluded that the original lack of control of the verbal stimulus for these patients was a result of faulty training circumstances.

It seems likely that this general class of defective verbal control of behavior plays a part in other forms of maladjustment. As was discussed in Chapter 9, an important training of the child involves the development of verbal and nonverbal stimuli that act as S^Δs controlling "desisting" behavior. It is important that the words, NO, DON'T DO THAT, YOU ARE HURTING ME, THAT BELONGS TO ME, and so on come to control the appropriate class of behavior. It is to be expected that where such controlling stimuli have not been established, the individual's behavior would be inadequately socially controlled.

Many instances of criminal behavior are probably examples of this type of poor stimulus control. It will be recalled from Chapter 7 that Jeffery (1961) has made an analysis of criminality and delinquency in terms of reinforcement principles. He emphasizes the fact that many prominent reinforcers are not available to lower-class individuals through "law-abiding" behaviors. Thus, they are under greater deprivation for these reinforcers, which consequently have more reinforcing power for them, and thus shape up "law-breaking" behaviors. Jeffery uses this greater strength of the reinforcers, plus the fact that the criminal has no legal behaviors in his repertoire that will get him the reinforcers, to explain the criminal behavior.

> A person . . . is reinforced by automobiles. If an automobile is available to a teen-ager, either because he can afford to own one or because his father has one, then there is no need to steal automobiles. However, if access to automobiles is only by a response which society labels stealing, then he steals automobiles (p. 13).

To this analysis we might add that another variable which differentiates individuals who steal from those who do not may be quite independent of the potency of the reinforcers. For two individuals who are equally deprived, a reinforcer may have the same value; however, one will unlawfully obtain the reinforcer while the other will remain deprived. The difference could lie in the presence or absence of appropriate stimulus control. The social control over such behavior may be established through a history in which certain reinforcers that are labeled in a variety of ways as "one's own property" come to have S^D properties for "striving" behaviors, while other reinforcers that are labeled as "belonging to someone else" acquire S^Δ properties for these behaviors.

The necessity for establishing this social control may be extrapolated from observations of young children before they are trained in this respect. Such children ordinarily do not respond in a conventional manner with respect to others' belongings. A visiting child may toddle over to another, take the other's toy from his hand, and insist on taking it home. For him, any reinforcing stimulus is an S^D that controls the behavior of attempting to obtain the stimulus. Normally, however, the child experiences many training situations where in the presence of some reinforcing stimulus, but also of certain additional stimuli—for example, the other child's mother, the verbal stimuli THAT BELONGS TO SO AND SO, THAT IS NOT TO BE PLAYED WITH, and so on—striving behaviors go unreinforced. These additional stimuli, as S^Δs, would thus be expected to control "leaving the object alone." Ordinarily, children are given extensive training of this sort and many social stimuli (some of these may be nonverbal) come to act as S^Δs controlling this behavior.

Where such control is weak or absent the individual's behavior may be expected to be inappropriate. He may obtain reinforcers that are not considered by the society to be rightfully his due. The important variables in such cases would include the lack of control by the social stimuli, in addition to the reinforcing value of the stimulus taken. (The reinforcing nature of the stimuli may also determine *which* articles will be stolen.) It is suggested that there would be wide differences in the extent to which such "socializing" training had taken place and thus wide differences in behavior. When the training has been too stringent and too comprehensive the result might be described as very constricted behavior. Compared with other persons in the same stimulus situation, this individual might not "claim" reinforcers of which he might be thought deserving. On the other hand, decided deficiency in such training might produce an individual who was extremely unrestrained in this sense—controlled almost entirely by the reinforcing value of objects, and perhaps only by the obvious restraints of coercive forces such as the presence of policemen.

Another form of defective verbal control underlying abnormal behavior is also important to note. The manner in which verbal stimuli can become aversive and "socially" control the individual's behavior was outlined in Chapter 9. It is suggested that individuals who have not received training on the basis of which they would learn to avoid situations tacted by most people as DANGEROUS or UNLAWFUL, or to avoid behaviors which most people tact as CRUEL, UNKIND, SINFUL, VICIOUS, and so on, may not respond in socially approved ways or even self-protective ways.

Two factors appear to be involved here: One is acquiring tacts to such stimuli; the other is the developing of these tacts into aversive stimuli.

As an example, the business man preparing his income tax return who states that IF I INCLUDE THIS EXPENDITURE AS A LEGITIMATE COST OF MY BUSINESS, EVEN THOUGH IT IS A PERSONAL EXPENSE, I WILL SAVE A GREAT DEAL OF MONEY may have a different final response from another business man who emits the same sequence followed by the tact BUT THAT MIGHT BE DANGEROUS SINCE IT IS UNLAWFUL. Then, to the extent to which DANGEROUS and UNLAWFUL have become aversive stimuli for the individual, we would expect the behavior under question to be avoided.

The following description of "antisocial" behavior seems to include reference to the absence of discriminative stimuli that provide social control for the individual, as well as to the absence of verbal reasoning sequences that might culminate in words aversive enough to prevent impulsive and socially unacceptable actions.

> Upon brief acquaintance they [the antisocial personalities] usually make an excellent impression. However, closer acquaintanceship reveals a deficiency in moral and ethical values. Conscience is poorly developed and the individual seems completely unable to understand and respond to accepted human values. Related to this trait is a further inability to forego present pleasures for future gains or worth-while, long-range goals. All these propensities, coupled with immaturity and impulsiveness, frequently lead to sexual irregularities, lying, excessive use of alcohol, drug addiction, and criminal behavior.
> The antisocial personality has the happy faculty of completely ration-

alizing and projecting any responsibility for his unacceptable behavior, and despite the pleading of his family, exhortations from the clergy, and punishment by the law, he seems quite unable to profit from his mistakes in a socially acceptable manner. He frequently shows superficial regret for misdeeds and may even promise in a very convincing manner to reform. . . . It is of vital significance to note that such undesirable behavior is frequently impulsive and unplanned, and is executed with a complete disregard for consequences, even though the likely consequences, such as imprisonment, are well known to the individual. It is almost as though he lives in a series of present moments without real consideration for past or future, and with a callous disregard for the happiness of others (Coleman, 1950, pp. 383–384).

This, of course, is a description that seems complicated by the inclusion of inappropriate behavior, a deficit in social reasoning and tacting behavior (as discussed in the previous chapter), as well as the lack of control by verbal stimuli that normally are considered aversive and by stimuli that normally control "desisting" behavior.

In conclusion, it would be expected that deficits in the controlling properties of various social and environmental stimuli (both in over- and in undercontrol) could result in various types of problem behaviors. This section can only hint at the wide variety of such problems.

Inadequate or Inappropriate Reinforcing Systems

Another determinant of "abnormal" behavior may be found in the inadequacies and inappropriateness of the individual's reinforcing system. It is suggested that because of these inadequacies, some responses necessary to successful adjustment may fail to develop; or because of inappropriate reinforcers, a behavior which interferes with normal adjustment may become strong. Several examples of nonadaptive behavior involving defects in the individual's reinforcing system will be discussed in this section.

Ferster (1961) has stressed the significance of the failure to develop conditioned reinforcers for the progressive behavior deficit of the autistic child. He points out that the normal repertoire of a child consists almost entirely of sequences of behavior that are maintained by conditioned reinforcers, of either a physical or a social nature. When the child's over-all activity is drastically diminished, however, these same stimuli may not have the opportunity to become reinforcers.

Parental responses, such as smiling, "Good," or "Right," can have little effect on the child if there is not a history by which many different forms of the child's performance have produced various reinforcers on these occasions. Without parental generalized reinforcement, educational processes and positive parental control are all but impossible. This control is normally carried out by the use of praise and parental attention, coupled with mild forms of threats of discontinuing the reinforcers (p. 449).

Where the customary reinforcers are not adequately developed, then, there is little opportunity for maintaining behavior or for adding to the behavior repertoire. The proverbial vicious cycle thus sets in: partially because the child's behavior is limited in the first place he does not learn the normal reinforcers; but not having acquired reinforcing value, these stimuli are ineffectual for training the child in new or stronger adjustive behavior with which to gain reinforcement.

Another type of nonadaptive behavior pattern which seems to involve inadequacies in the reinforcer system is that called neurasthenia. This disturbance, most common in young adults and housewives, may be described in the following terms.

> The patient's primary complaint . . . is that of physical and mental fatigue. He has difficulty in concentrating, is easily distracted, and lacks the vigor required to carry activities through to successful completion. . . . These patients usually spend a great deal of time sleeping in an attempt to counteract their fatigue, yet regardless of the amount of sleep they get, they still feel unrefreshed and awaken tired. In fact, the more the patient sleeps, the worse he often seems to feel when he awakens.
> . . . The fatigue gets worse as the day wears on, although by evening he may feel somewhat better and may go to movies or parties without experiencing anything like his usual degree of exhaustion.
> In fact, one of the most significant things about the neurasthenic's fatigue is its selective nature. Many of these patients show ample energy and good endurance in playing tennis, golf, or bridge or in doing anything else which really interests them. In the face of occupational and other routine activities, however, they are usually monuments of listlessness, lack of enthusiasm, and general "tiredness" (Coleman, 1950, pp. 168–169).

The fact that the fatigue and listless behavior is related to the kind of activity and the situation, immediately suggests that the problem may lie in the reinforcers which are effective in maintaining this individual's behavior. When the situation involves social or "game" reinforcers, the behavior is maintained in normal strength. On the other hand, when work is involved, that is, when effortful behavior must occur with little reinforcement, the behavior weakens. The behavior might then be described as listless, unmotivated, lackluster, perhaps as lazy and disinterested, or, by the individual himself, as fatigued.

Of course, everyone has had some such experiences. For example, in any situation in which the reinforcers are inadequate, behavior is not generally maintained in customary vigor. Many people have gone through periods when they have been separated from the important reinforcers in their lives—separations from family and pleasant activities due to business, military duty, ill health, retirement, and so on—and listless, depressed behavior may result. And everyone has in more ephemeral situations of limited reinforcement experienced the listless, tired behavior we describe as boredom. (Note here again Ferster and DeMyer's suggestions presented on pages 474–475 that behavior similar to that of the psychotic often occurs when normal behaviors are not being supported by the external environment.)

Nevertheless, two people in the same situation will not necessarily be similarly affected since the same stimuli may have different reinforcing potencies for them. A situation lacking in reinforcers (a boring situation) for one individual may maintain another's behavior in good strength and be described as interesting or exciting. However, if in many situations, or in situations which constitute a large portion of the individual's life, the reinforcers are not adequate for the individual, then his behavior will be nonadaptive in that it too frequently has the listless, nonproductive character described. When this behavior occurs in the same situations found reinforcing for most people, then the individual's behavior is likely to be considered as "abnormal."

The question arises, however, as to why the usual reinforcers are not effective with these individuals. Likely possibilities lie in the individual's past history both with respect to the classes of conditioned reinforcers formed, and to the schedules of reinforcement with which his behavior has customarily been maintained. The first of these principles may be illustrated with a history of a hypothetical housewife. Suppose that as a young girl, people and their behavior, the activities of attending school, social affairs of various sorts, and so on, had all become conditioned reinforcers, whereas she had had no history in which work (for example, housework) had been reinforced. When she married, suppose, however, that the situation changed rapidly and her customary reinforcers were largely withdrawn. As a housewife, she had to spend much of her time cleaning her house and caring for her children, activities that might involve little positive reinforcement and much aversiveness. Until some social reinforcers were made available in this new situation, it is quite possible that a housewife with this history might be listless, tired, and depressed.

On the other hand, the individual's past history with respect to schedules of reinforcement might be the more important variable in determining later "neurasthenia." An individual with a history of a largely continuous reinforcement schedule for his behavior may experience a marked decrease in the strength of his behavior when the schedule is relatively abruptly raised to a more intermittent one. Thus, an individual who has not been through a gradual program of increasing output prior to reinforcement may become terribly "fatigued" when the demands are suddenly increased—as so often occurs in work situations, starting college, military service, and so on.

Perhaps, however, in both types of cases, if the reinforcers were strong enough to maintain the individual's behavior in some strength, the situation might be expected to improve. Although the behavior was at first weak, the individual might eventually come under the control of the new schedule, and his behavior would become stronger. New stimuli might acquire reinforcing value through pairing with other reinforcers and through language conditioning. Perhaps this is why "neurasthenic" behavior is characteristic of young adults—as the person grows older, he probably has opportunities to establish a more adequate reinforcing system. On the other hand, if the schedule of reinforcers for the individual, and the reinforcers themselves, were too far out of line with the individual's past experience, his behavior might continue at the low level—or even deteriorate more severely.

It should be pointed out here that in this case, as in many others involving nonadaptive behavior, the behavior itself may bring about various secondary disturbances. First, the behavior might contribute to an individual's failure, further diminishing his chance to acquire primary and conditioned positive reinforcers (especially social reinforcers). In addition, such behavior is likely to be labeled by oneself and by others in aversive terms, and further limit the amount of positive reinforcement the individual might gain. These events could thus have several consequences. In the present case, the already weak reinforcement circumstances would become even more inadequate for maintaining productive behaviors. In addition, the aversive social stimuli could provide negative reinforcement for nonproductive escape behaviors—rationalization, projection, compulsions, as well as the imagined ills of hypochondriasis that are so often associated with "neurasthenic" behavior.

We may also point out some other classes of behavior difficulties that seem also to involve deficits in the effective social rewards and punishments for an individual. The source of the problem behavior of the delinquent and the "antisocial personality" may lie to some extent in the absence of effective negative reinforcers, as has already been mentioned. Bandura (1961) mentions that for schizophrenics many social stimuli have not acquired their customary reinforcing values, and primary reinforcers may thus be necessary in treatment. (A later section of this chapter will present a fuller discussion of reinforcers in the treatment of schizophrenics.)

The behavior of schizophrenics is also customarily described as indifferent, lacking in interests, ambition, and so on.(See the earlier quoted description from Coleman, 1950, on page 469.) It is suggested that these descriptions refer to the inadequacies of the individual's reinforcing system —with respect to social reinforcers of various kinds, achievement reinforcers, sex reinforcers, and so on—as well as to the weak behavior which is consequently engendered.

Sex reinforcers are worth considering as another example, for it would seem that many forms of sex deviation are based upon stimuli which have become inappropriately effective reinforcers for the individual. In discussing child training, it was suggested that the child's experiences might condition various classes of sex stimuli as reinforcers for him. When these reinforcers are unique, or markedly different from those most individuals in a society find reinforcing, the behavior shaped up under the action of these reinforcers is likely to be considered "abnormal" or sexually deviant. In descriptive terms, this behavior has been classified as "sexual patterns which are considered abnormal in regard to the choice of sexual object, such as homosexuality and sadism" (Coleman, 1950, p. 404).

More specifically, in this society the individual is considered sexually aberrant if his sex reinforcers include persons of the wrong sex, wrong age, wrong social relationship (brother-sister, father-daughter, and so on), or perhaps even more extreme, sex reinforcers made up of stimuli such as pain, the sight of others in pain, articles of clothing, or animals. If such stimuli become reinforcers, moreover, it might be expected that they would control behavior relevant to obtaining the stimuli. The adult for whom children are sex reinforcers, unless restrained by other discriminative social stimuli, might well acquire behavior necessary to obtaining such sexual "objects." The person for whom painful stimuli are sexually reinforcing might in the same way acquire behavior whose consequence was punishment. Behaviors appropriate to gaining usual heterosexual reinforcing objects would be less likely to occur for such individuals, unless, of course, these stimuli were also reinforcing.

Another class of behavior problems associated with the reinforcement system may occur in cases of physical disability. Here, however, it is not that the individual has learned inadequate or unusual reinforcers, but rather that the customary reinforcers are not obtainable for some reason. Consider, for example, the young child with a hearing loss. As was pointed out in Chapter 4, one of his difficulties is related to the fact that language stimuli will not acquire reinforcing properties. The adult who suffers a severe physical handicap may also face many difficulties in obtaining his customary reinforcers. An athletic individual who finds physical exercise and prowess reinforcing may have these withdrawn because of disease or accident. The social reinforcers contingent upon this behavior may be eliminated. His friends, his wife and children, may have been acquired during the time when he was strong and healthy, and as a consequence of the injury he may lose these sources of reinforcement in part or even completely. If his liveli-hood is connected to these activities, he may even suffer the loss or dimi-nution of reinforcers connected with income.

The result would be that in the face of the task of acquiring many new behaviors the individual might have available a very inadequate source of reinforcement with which to maintain the attentive, hardworking behavior required for the relearning (rehabilitation). Furthermore, responses when originally acquired may be provided with certain reinforcers that are not effective if the behavior must be relearned at a later time. The child when learning to walk has the reinforcement of attaining objects more easily and more quickly; in addition, social reinforcers may be contingent upon the first walking behaviors of the child. Thus, walking behavior is strengthened more than crawling behavior. On the other hand, when an adult has to learn to do something that is far inferior to his previous level of perform-ance (such as learning to walk with a prosthesis), his behavior may be aver-sive to him, rather than positively reinforcing. (For further examples of the problems of reinforcement in relearning elementary skills, see Meyerson, Michael, Mowrer, Osgood, and Staats, 1963.)

TREATMENT

Treatment and the Concept of Maladjustment

We have discussed previously the fact that interpretations of behavior, the statements made about behavior, mediate the way that behavior is treated. Thus, in the area of behavior disorders, when abnormal behavior was considered to be the work of internal demons and spirits, treatment consisted of attempts to exorcise those supposed internal devils.

In the same manner, it is also to be expected that strategies of treatment would differ depending on whether the abnormal behavior was considered to be the result of an internal "mental illness," inner personality disorder, and the like, or whether the behavior itself was thought to be the problem. In the latter case, treatment would be oriented toward achieving a change in behavior; in the former case there would be greater interest in diagnos-ing the behavior in terms of the inner disturbance so that this inner dis-turbance could be treated, and the behavior improved as a by-product.

Bandura summarizes this "mental illness" approach and its implications in the following terms.

[T]he inner disturbing agents comprise a host of unconscious psycho-dynamic forces and psychic complexes—warded-off ego-alien impulses, Oedipal, castration and inferiority complexes, ancestral unconscious and primordial images, latent instinctual tendencies, self dynamisms, counter-instinctual energies, wills and counter-wills, and ego instincts and apparatuses—somewhat akin to the hidden demonic spirits of ancient times. Thus, the prevailing theories of psychopathology essentially employ an amalgam of the medical and demonology models, which have in common the belief that the underlying pathology and not the symptomatic manifestations must be treated. Consequently, therapeutic attention is generally focused not on the deviant behavior itself, but on the presumably influential internal processes. Indeed, direct modification of so-called symptomatic behavior is considered not only ineffective, but actually dangerous, since the removal of the symptom may lead to even more serious forms of symptom substitution (1962a, pp. 2–3).

A number of other investigators—for example, Eysenck, 1957; Wolpe, 1958; and Wolpe and Rachman, 1960—have also contrasted these two different approaches to abnormal behavior.

As we suggested earlier, it may be that the approach of invoking inner "explanatory" agents in attempting to understand and treat behavior disorders represents to some extent lack of knowledge of the actual determinants of the behavior. Once the learning determinants of a behavior are known, pseudo-explanation in terms of "psychodynamic" causes may be recognized as superfluous.

As an example, we may cite Bandura's analysis of the case of the four-year-old boy (Albert) whom Watson and Rayner classically conditioned to fear animals by pairing the sight of a white rat with a loud sound.

> If Albert were referred to a modern psychiatric clinic for a diagnostic assessment, it is very likely that projective tests, observations of free play, and depth interviews with family members would be utilized in order to uncover the psychodynamic process mediating the phobia. It is highly improbable that the diagnostician would conclude from his exhaustive search that Albert's phobia simply represented a learned response resulting from paired presentation of a rat and a loud noise, and that the fear elicited by this pairing had generalized to other fur-like stimuli. It is much more likely that the diagnostician would assume that the phobia was a symptomatic manifestation of more basic underlying psychodynamic agents, the contents of which would be almost entirely dependent upon the diagnostician's theoretical predilections (1962a, p. 7).

This example also demonstrates how the two differing views of abnormal behavior may determine different treatment approaches. From the learning interpretation one would attempt to treat the problem fears through some conditioning procedure, rather than in an analysis of the internal mechanisms responsible for the behavior.

> According to social learning theory, so-called symptomatic behaviors are viewed not as emotional disease manifestations but as learned reactions which can be modified directly by the application of appropriate social

learning procedures. Once the maladaptive behavior is altered, it is unnecessary to modify or to remove an underlying pathology (1962a, p. 10).

A Learning Approach to Treatment

In Chapter 2 we stated that when an antecedent event (independent
variable) has been found to be lawfully related to a consequent event
(dependent variable) in such a way that manipulating the former changes
the latter, an empirical law which may yield prediction and control has
been demonstrated. It was stated that psychology as a science seeks such
laws.

It has been suggested that a learning approach to psychotherapy is based
upon these laws, whereas the "mental illness" approach generally is not.
In psychotherapy from a behavioral approach, the treatment objectives,
behavior change, constitute the dependent variable. Many other schools
of psychotherapy do not specify the dependent variable except in very
vague terms, such as "self-actualization," "enhancement of ego-strength,"
"achievement of emotional maturity," and so on (Bandura, 1962a). The
objectives are discussed in terms of improvement in these supposed internal
processes. Still, however, attainment of such objectives can only be ascertained by observing the behavior of the individual being treated.

> The client's behavior is the only reality that can be modified through
> psychological procedures and, therefore, it is the only meaningful subject
> matter of psychotherapy. Similarly, independent stimulus variables are
> the only reality events that the therapist can manipulate and control in
> effecting changes in the client's behavior. Psychotherapy, like any other
> social influence enterprise, is thus a process in which the therapist
> manipulates independent stimulus variables that covary with the desired
> dependent behavioral variables in the client. If, for instance, a psycho-
> therapist introduces variables that increase the frequency of behaviors
> from which ego strength is inferred, the client will have acquired in-
> creased ego strength as a function of treatment. On the other hand, if the
> frequency of ego strength behaviors has been reduced in the course of
> psychotherapy, the client has suffered a loss in ego strength. Clearly, ego
> strength is simply a hypothetical abstraction while its presumed behavioral
> referents are the only dependent modifiable reality available to the
> psychotherapist (1962a, p. 13).

In summary, it could be said that a learning approach to psychotherapy
is interested in effecting a change in behavior by the manipulation of the
conditions of learning. In this section we will present examples of how such
procedures have been applied to the treatment of behavior disorders.

Again, although the categories are by no means clearly separable, it seems
helpful to organize the examples in terms of the essential features of the
problems as presented in the first part of this chapter.

Behavioral Deficit

This category includes cases in which certain normal behavior has never been acquired as well as those in which the behavior has been allowed for some reason to diminish markedly in frequency or intensity. To illustrate treatment of the latter, Isaacs, Thomas and Goldiamond (1960) present a most significant report of the application of conditioning procedures to the treatment of mutism in a psychotic patient. The patient was a forty-year-old male classified as catatonic schizophrenic who had been mute since his hospitalization nineteen years earlier. The basic behavioral principle used in reestablishing speech was shaping through successive approximation. It will be remembered that with this method, available behavior is "shaped" into the desired form by successively reinforcing those parts of a selected response which are in the desired direction and extinguishing those which are not. The shaping process in this case involved a succession from eye movements which brought into play occasional facial movements, then movements of the mouth, lip movements, vocalization, word utterance, and finally verbal behavior. The following excerpt gives a more detailed account of the procedure.

Weeks 1, 2. A stick of gum was held before S's face, and E waited until S's eyes moved toward it. When this response occurred, E as a consequence gave him the gum. By the end of the second week, response probability in the presence of the gum was increased to such an extent that S's eyes moved toward the gum as soon as it was held up.

Weeks 3, 4. The E now held the gum before S, waiting until he noticed movement in S's lips before giving it to him. Toward the end of the first session of the third week, a lip movement spontaneously occurred, which E promptly reinforced. By the end of this week, both lip movement and eye movement occurred when the gum was held up. The E then withheld giving S the gum until S spontaneously made a vocalization, at which time E gave S the gum. By the end of this week, holding up the gum readily occasioned eye movement toward it, lip movement, and a vocalization resembling a croak.

Weeks 5, 6. The E held up the gum, and said, "Say *gum, gum,*" repeating these words each time S vocalized. Giving S the gum was made contingent upon vocalizations increasingly approximating *gum*. At the sixth session (at the end of Week 6), when E said, "Say *gum, gum,*" S suddenly said, "Gum, please." This response was accompanied by reinstatement of other responses of this class, that is, S answered questions regarding his name and age.

Thereafter, he responded to questions by E both in individual sessions and in group sessions, but answered no one else. Responses to the discriminative stimuli of the room generalized to E on the ward; he greeted E on two occasions in the group room. He read from signs in E's office upon request by E.

Since the response now seemed to be under the strong stimulus control of E, *the person,* attempt was made to generalize the stimulus to other people. Accordingly, a nurse was brought into the private room; S smiled at her. After a month, he began answering her questions. Later, when he brought his coat to a volunteer worker on the ward, she interpreted the gesture as a desire to go outdoors and conducted him there. Upon informing E of the incident, she was instructed to obey S only as a consequence of explicit verbal requests by him. The S thereafter vocalized requests. These instructions have now been given to other hospital personnel, and S regularly initiates verbal requests when nonverbal requests have no reinforcing consequences. Upon being taken to the commissary, he said, "Ping-pong," to the volunteer worker and played a game with her. Other patients, visitors, and members of hospital-society-at-large continue, however, to interpret nonverbal requests and to reinforce them by obeying S (pp. 9–10).

Notice that while the method of successive approximation was basic to the treatment, two other principles were also clearly involved. Both generalization of speech to the stimuli of people other than the experimenter, and extinction of nonverbal attempts at communication (hospital personnel were instructed to obey the subject only as a consequence of his explicit verbal requests) appear to have been critical in bringing the verbal behavior under good control.

Robertson (1958) has also worked with the limited speech of schizophrenic patients using operant conditioning techniques, and he too was able to shape generally improved verbal behavior.

Salzinger, Portnoy, and Feldman (1962) also report treatment of a speech deficit through the use of learning methods, but in their case, the four-year-old behaviorally deficient boy had never acquired speech.

[O]perant conditioning techniques were applied to the vocalizations of a four-year-old boy who had never learned to say any words at all and who had been hospitalized initially for autism and later rediagnosed as mentally defective. In daily conditioning sessions over nearly nine months, we were able to increase his rate of vocalizations in general and, by reinforcing successive approximations, were able to shape the articulation of at least a dozen words (pp. 4–5).

Deficient eating behavior has also been the focus of treatment through learning principles. Bachrach, Erwin, and Mohr's (to be published) treatment of a case of anorexia nervosa (noneating with no obvious physical cause) provides a most dramatic illustration. The treatment included the use of deprivation of social reinforcers to insure their effectiveness and then the administration of the same reinforcers contingent upon eating behavior. The patient, who was in the final stages of starvation when treatment started, improved markedly under this treatment.

Ayllon and Michael (1959) also describe the treatment of a female psychotic patient whose eating behaviors were so poorly developed that she had to be "spoonfed" in bed. The experimenters' problem was to increase the frequency of self-feeding. Treatment consisted of the manipulation of two basic variables. First, because the patient was fastidious about her clothing, it was decided to use escape from an aversive stimulus (food stains soiling her clothing) as an important source of negative reinforcement for independent eating. Positive social reinforcement was also made contingent upon independent eating.

> The following instructions were given to the nurses: "Continue spoon-feeding the patient; but from now on, do it in such a careless way that the patient will have a few drops of food fall on her dress. . . . As the patient likes having her clothes clean she will have to choose between feeding herself and keeping her clothes clean, or being fed by others and risking getting her clothes soiled. Whenever she eats on her own, be sure to stay with her for a while . . . talking to her, or simply being seated with her. We do this to reinforce eating on her own . . ." (pp. 330–331).

Figure 11.3 shows the number of meals per week the patient ate independently and the number she was fed during the course of the treatment. As the figure indicates, the treatment may be considered successful in developing self-feeding. Moreover, it apparently had an added by-product in needed weight gain. The course of the treatment is described as follows.

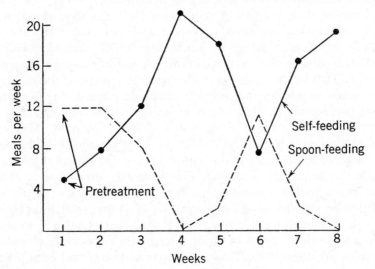

Fig. 11.3. Number of meals per week that the patient ate independently and the number she was spoon-fed during treatment (Ayllon and Michael, 1959, p. 331)

During the 8-day pretreatment study, the patient ate 5 meals on her own, was spoonfed 12, and refused to eat 7. Her weight at this time was a 99 pounds. Her typical reaction to the schedule was as follows: the nurse would start spoonfeeding her; but after one or two "good" spoonfuls, the nurse would carelessly drop some food on her dress. This was continued until either the patient requested the spoon, or the nurse continued spoonfeeding her the entire meal. The behaviors the patient adopted included (a) reaching for the spoon after a few drops had fallen on her dress; (b) eating completely on her own; (c) closing her mouth so that the spoonfeeding was terminated; or (d) being spoonfed the entire meal. Upon starting the schedule, the most frequent of all these alternatives was the first; but after a while, the patient ate on her own immediately. . . . Her weight when she left the hospital was 120 pounds, a gain of 21 pounds over her pretreatment weight (p. 331).

Inappropriate Behavior

A number of classes of what we have called inappropriate behaviors have been treated through the application of behavior principles. (See Eysenck, 1960, for treatment of stammering, compulsive behaviors, bronchial asthma, and other disorders, according to these methods.)

As an example of one of the techniques used, we may refer to Yates' report of the treatment of several severe tics in one individual. The tics included ". . . a complex stomach-contraction breathing tic, a nasal 'explosion' (expiration), a coughing tic, and an eyeblink tic" (1960, p. 238), which varied markedly from time to time in frequency.

Because of their histories of acquisition, these tics were considered as simple conditioned avoidance responses. The treatment consistent with this interpretation consisted of reinforcing "no-tic" behavior with rest periods after the tic had become aversive to perform because of repeated emission. That is, the subject was instructed to reproduce one of her tics as accurately as possible and to repeat it without pause during the practice period (five minutes), after which she might rest for one minute. After some 300 sessions, each of about forty-five-minute duration, there was a dramatic decline in the patient's ability to tic voluntarily in the laboratory conditions; in addition, she also reported considerable clinical improvement outside the immediate situation. "The percentage decrement in the frequency of voluntary responding for each tic was as follows: nasal, 84.14; throat, 68.83; stomach, 63.42; eyeblink, 51.47." (Yates, 1960, pp. 244–245).

A case of compulsive scratching provides another example of treatment of an excessively frequent behavior through the application of behavior principles (Walton, 1960). A young woman of twenty had been suffering from neurodermatitis on the nape of the neck for nearly two years. Although treatment had included ointments, pills, lotions, and x-ray therapy, she still scratched the irritation constantly, often bringing about bleeding.

An analysis of the patient's life situation indicated that the illness had led to more attention from her parents and friends than she had ever received before. Her fiancé, who was most solicitous over the condition, even rubbed her ointment on for her. These factors were thought to be important determinants of the compulsive behavior.

> It was considered that the skin condition may well have originated because of physical considerations, though its *continuance* might have been perpetuated by psychological factors, the understanding and treatment of which could be formulated in terms of learning theory. It was considered, for example, that the rewards initially associated with the continuance of the neuro-dermatitis had reinforced the scratching until it had become a powerful compulsive habit and it was this which had therefore directly perpetuated the skin condition. Until this compulsion came to an end the dermatitis would show little improvement (p. 273).

Consistent with this interpretation, the treatment was directed at decreasing the frequency of scratching through extinction procedures. The members of the patient's family were told not to discuss her skin condition with her, in fact to observe, as far as possible, a complete silence on the subject. The patient's fiancé was also instructed to stop applying the ointment for her.

These relatively simple procedures of treatment produced entirely successful results. Over a period of two months the scratching decreased until it was completely eliminated. The skin condition was correspondingly improved, until at the end of three months it too had completely disappeared. A follow-up four years later indicated no recurrence of the neurodermatitis, of any other skin disorder, or of any alternative psychiatric symptom. The success of behavior therapy was in marked contrast to the failure of the several physical methods of treatment over the previous two years.

Another case of treatment of inappropriate behavior using the principle of extinction, this time with a child, is described by Williams (1959). During a period of the child's illness the parents and an aunt engaged in training practices that produced very undesirable tantrum behaviors. Through reinforcing screaming, raging, and crying at bedtime they finally shaped this behavior to the point where it took from one-half to two hours each bedtime to get him to sleep. "If the parent left the bedroom after putting S in his bed, S would scream and fuss until the parent returned to the room" (p. 269).

Upon medical reassurance concerning the child's health, extinction procedures for the tantrum behavior were instituted. "After bedtime pleasantries, the parent left the bedroom and closed the door. S screamed and raged, but the parent did not re-enter the room" (p. 269). The duration of time was tabulated from the time the door was closed until the tantrum behavior ceased. Figure 11.4 shows the results of the treatment.

It can be seen that S continued screaming for 45 min. the first time he was put to bed in the first extinction series. S did not cry at all the second time he was put to bed. This is perhaps attributable to his fatigue from the crying of Occasion 1. By the tenth occasion, S no longer whimpered, fussed, or cried when the parent left the room. Rather, he smiled as they left. The parents felt that he made happy sounds until he dropped off to sleep.

About a week later, S screamed and fussed after the aunt put him to bed. . . . The aunt then reinforced the tantrum behavior by returning to S's bedroom and remaining there until he went to sleep. It was then necessary to extinguish this behavior a second time.

Figure [11.4] shows that the second extinction curve is similar to the first. Both curves are generally similar to extinction curves obtained with sub-human subjects. The second extinction series reached zero by the ninth occasion. No further tantrums at bedtime were reported during the next two years (p. 269).

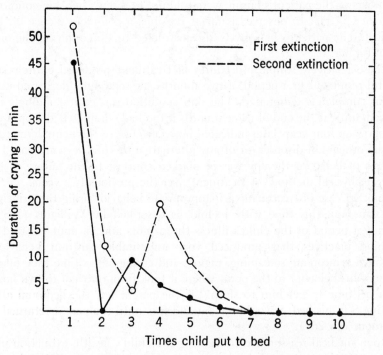

Fig. 11.4. Elimination of tantrum behaviors in a young child (Williams, 1959, p. 269)

Ayllon and Michael (1959) treated an even more disrupting form of inappropriate behavior by strengthening a competing behavior. The case involved the behavior of unprovoked violence. Both before and during her hospitalization, this patient had a history of frequent attacks of violence upon other people. She had received electroconvulsive shock treatments as well as psychosurgery (detachment of the frontal lobes from the rest of the brain in an operation called leucotomy) in an attempt to control this violence. At the beginning of the experiment the patient's behavior was so bad that ". . . at the least suspicious move on her part the nurses would put her in the seclusion room. She spent from 3 to 12 hours daily in that room" (p. 329). In order to decrease the frequency of these attacks, the experimenters decided to strengthen a response incompatible with the violence.

A 5-day pretreatment study, at 15-minute intervals, indicated that one of the nonviolent behaviors exhibited fairly often was "being on the floor" in the dayroom. The response included lying, squatting, kneeling, and sitting on the floor. Strengthening this class of responses would control the violence and, at the same time, permit the emotional behavior of other patients and nurses toward her to extinguish. To strengthen the patient's own social behavior, her approaches to the nurses were to be reinforced. The response "approach to the nurse" was defined as spontaneous requests, questions or comments made by the patient to the nurse. Ultimately, the plan was to discontinue reinforcing being on the floor once the patient-nurse social interaction appeared somewhat normal. Presumably, this would have further increased the probability of approach to the nurses.

For the duration of the program, continuous social reinforcement was to be available for her approach to the nurses. Social reinforcement was to be available for the first 4 weeks only, on a fixed interval of 15 minutes, contingent on the response being on the floor. For the last 4 weeks, social reinforcement was to be withheld for being on the floor. . . .

During the period of reinforcement, as shown in Figure [11.5], the relative frequency of the response being on the floor increased from the pretreatment level of less than 0.10 to a value of 0.21. During the succeeding 4 weeks of extinction, the frequency of being on the floor returned to the pretreatment level.

It was clear that being on the floor was incompatible with the fighting behavior and that the latter could be controlled by reinforcing the former. During the period of reinforcement for being on the floor, she attacked a patient once; but during the period of extinction, she made eight attacks on others. Her approaches to nurses increased over-all during the 4 weeks of reinforcement, but they decreased during the last 4 weeks, even though they were still being reinforced. This decrease paralleled the decrease in being on the floor. While being on the floor was undergoing extinction, attacks on the patients and nurses increased in frequency, and the nurses decided to return to the practice of restraining the patient. The program was terminated at this point (p. 329).

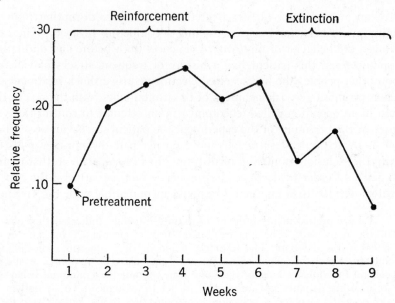

Fig. 11.5. Reinforcement and subsequent extinction of the response "being on the floor" (Ayllon and Michael, 1959, p. 330)

Thus, while the treatment had been successful in controlling the violent behavior by shaping incompatible behavior, the experiment did fail to condition normal social behavior because of ". . . errors in strategy."

> The patient's failure to make the transition from being on the floor to approaching the nurses suggests that the latter response was poorly chosen. It was relatively incompatible with being on the floor. This meant that a previously reinforced response would have to be extinguished before the transition was possible, and this, too, was poor strategy with a violent patient (p. 329).

It may be concluded, at any rate, that the unprovoked violence, a form of psychotic behavior, could be considered an operant behavior and manipulated by conditioning procedures in a treatment-oriented program.

In general methodology, this study is similar to that of Lindsley (1956) for working with psychotic adults as well as to the Ferster and DeMyer (1961) procedure for working with autistic children. Although the goals of these latter investigators were not those of treatment, they too demonstrated that the frequency of inappropriate behaviors could be reduced through strengthening other, incompatible, behaviors.

Change in Stimulus Control

Many cases in which a response originally elicited by one stimulus comes to be elicited by a new stimulus through the procedures of classical conditioning may be used to illustrate treatment through changing stimulus control. For example, classical conditioning procedures have been widely applied in an attempt to control alcoholism (Franks, 1960).

In terms of behavior principles, it might be said that for the alcoholic the stimulus of alcohol is clearly a discriminative stimulus which too strongly controls the response of obtaining the stimulus—in this case, imbibing the stimulus. For the alcoholic, then, alcoholic beverages have excessive reinforcing and controlling properties.

It would follow from this analysis that a means of obtaining more appropriate control of the alcoholic's drinking behavior would be to change the reinforcing properties of the sight, smell, and taste of alcohol, and in doing so change those discriminative properties of the stimuli which control the response of drinking. This change should be possible to achieve through classical conditioning procedures, by pairing these stimuli with an aversive unconditioned stimulus. As an example, if these stimuli were simply paired with some noxious drug or with electric shock it would be expected that they would become aversive stimuli themselves, and would negatively reinforce the behavior of avoiding them.

> Although the most usual way of producing a conditioned aversion is by the application of some nausea inducing drug, this is by no means essential. Bachet . . . was able to produce conditioned nausea to the sight or taste of alcohol without using any drugs, and as far back as the last century it had been suggested that alcoholism should be treated by associating a painful stimulus with the taking of alcohol. . . . More recently there has been an accumulation of evidence to show that all kinds of conditioned aversions may be readily produced in both animals and man by the application of electric shock as the unconditioned stimulus. . . . Using this technique, Kantorovich . . . was remarkably successful in producing a conditioned aversion not only to the taste of alcohol but also to its smell and sight and even to a photograph of the bottles. There is clearly a need for research into methods other than drugs of producing a conditioned aversion to alcohol (pp. 285–286). A frequent conclusion is that conditioning therapy is merely "symptomatic treatment" which fails to eliminate the underlying cause. . . . However, such critics merely present acceptable evidence in support of their assertions and ignore the possibility that a symptom may itself be as harmful as the disease. . . . Conditioning therapy may help the alcoholic to break his habit of drinking and thus enable him to find more socially acceptable ways of solving his problems (Franks, 1960, p. 284).

Conditioning procedures have been used in other cases in which the goal is the diminution of the reinforcing and controlling value of a stimulus. Raymond (1960) reports the case of a patient who was repeatedly hospitalized and convicted in court because of his behavior of injuring or soiling perambulators (baby carriages) and sometimes their occupants or the women who were pushing the prams. The patient derived sexual reinforcement from these actions.

> The patient said that he had had impulses to damage perambulators and handbags since about the age of 10, and that, although the police knew of only 12 perambulator attacks, the number of times he had so indulged was legion. He had sometimes made several attacks in one day, but he estimated the average at about 2 or 3 a week, fairly consistently. With the handbags he was usually satisfied if he could scratch them with his thumbnail, and as this could be done unobtrusively, a handbag had only once led him into trouble with the police (p. 304).

He had undergone extensive psychoanalytic treatment, the result of which was his report of several incidents in his childhood when he damaged a perambulator and had been admonished and another where he had been sexually aroused in the presence of his sister's handbag. His behavior, however, was not changed as a result of this treatment.

Finally, conditioning procedures were commenced with this patient in an endeavor to make the two classes of stimuli aversive.

> In reflecting upon this man's plight, the despair of his family, and his poor response to treatment previously given, the idea was conceived that he might benefit from aversion therapy similar to that used in the treatment of alcoholism. . . .
>
> A collection of handbags, perambulators and coloured illustrations was obtained and these were shown to the patient after he had received an injection of apomorphine and just before nausea was produced. The treatment was given two-hourly, day and night, no food was allowed, and at night amphetamine was used to keep him awake. At the end of the first week, treatment was temporarily suspended and the patient was allowed home to attend to his affairs.
>
> He returned after 8 days to continue the treatment, and he reported jubilantly that he had for the first time been able to have intercourse with his wife without use of the old fantasies. His wife said that she had noticed a change in his attitude to her, but was unable to define it (pp. 305–306).

In terms of the discussion in the preceding chapter of hierarchies of sex reinforcers, it might be expected that as the sexual reinforcing value of the purses and perambulators was reduced through conditioning, the reinforcing value of other stimuli—for example, the patient's wife—would show a relative increase. In addition, the patient's state of deprivation would be altered since the purses and perambulators would no longer be reinforcing; in this manner other sex reinforcers might be expected to increase in value.

At any rate, the conditioning treatment was continued until perambulators and handbags became aversive stimuli that controlled escape and avoidance behavior rather than the former "approach" behaviors. ". . . [H]e said that the mere sight of the objects made him sick." After further treatment, the patient gave up a number of photographic negatives of perambulators, ". . . saying that he had carried them about for years but would need them no longer" (p. 306).

Nineteen months after he first had been treated by means of conditioning he was still doing well. It is interesting to note that the patient attributed his improved behavior to the maturing of his "will power" rather than to the principles of conditioning or to the independent variables actually manipulated.

Unusual fear responses constitute another class of maladjustive behavior that has been successfully manipulated through respondent conditioning procedures. The object of the treatment would be for the conditioned stimulus which elicits the fear to be changed in such fashion that it controls instead either no response or an "approach" response. For example, Lazarus (1960) describes several cases of phobias which were treated through conditioning, one of which we may cite here.

> John D., 8 years of age, developed a fear of moving vehicles 2 years after he and his parents had been involved in a motor car accident. He refused to enter any vehicle and on one occasion when his father had unwisely forced him into his car, the child became panic-stricken and hysterical. Therapy consisted of first talking to John about trains, aeroplanes, buses, etc. Even this "mild exposure to the stimulus" tended to evoke anxiety in the child, but whenever he volunteered a "positive" comment, he was casually offered his favourite chocolate. During the third interview, John willingly spoke at length about all types of moving vehicles and there was no longer any evidence of overt anxiety. A series of deliberate "accidents" with toy motor cars constituted the next phase of the treatment project. The child evidenced a fairly high level of initial anxiety. After each "accident" he was given chocolate. His anxiety was soon dissipated and he entered into the full spirit of the game. The next step in the therapy programme consisted of sitting with the child in a stationary motor car while discussing the accident in which he had been involved. He was provided with liberal helpings of chocolate throughout this discussion. Thereafter the child was taken in a car for short distances. At the 17th session (less than 6 weeks after therapy had commenced) he willingly entered a car and accompanied by a complete stranger, he set off for a shop 1½ miles away where he bought chocolate. At first, he refused to go motoring with his parents unless he was given chocolate, but he soon began to enjoy motoring for pleasure (p. 116).

This example incorporates treatment through operant conditioning as well as respondent conditioning procedures. The child's operant behavior of talking about, as well as sitting or riding in a car was reinforced with chocolate. In the same procedures, the various conditioned stimuli such as the toy motor vehicles were paired with the unconditioned stimulus of candy. This UCS would have elicited "positive" responses so that these new responses were conditioned to the vehicle stimuli. As a result the conditioned stimuli should have become positive reinforcers controlling "approach" responses.

Manipulation of Reinforcing Stimuli in Treatment

In the previous section where we discussed behavior problems associated with inadequate or ineffective reinforcers it was suggested that certain behavior may be "abnormal" in that the stimuli contingent upon such behaviors have unusual reinforcing values for that individual. Thus, the sex deviant's behavior problem may lie in the fact that deviant stimuli are reinforcing for him. Or the converse may be true; stimuli that are generally considered reinforcing and that customarily act to maintain and strengthen adjustive behavior may not be reinforcing, or may even be aversive for an individual because of his early training.

The reader probably recognized that the cases presented in the section just preceding this, in addition to dealing with the controlling properties of stimuli, also were examples of "abnormal" reinforcing properties of stimuli. The cases of the alcoholic and of the deviant sex behavior of the man who attacked prams and handbags were examples of the "abnormal" reinforcing value of these stimuli. The examples were discussed in the previous section, however, because the deviant behavior exhibited illustrated that the reinforcing stimuli had gained an S^D function. Rather than continuing here with examples of this sort, we will devote this section not to treatment by changing the reinforcing nature of the stimuli (as was involved in the examples of the previous section) but rather to treatment using reinforcers normally considered "extrinsic" to the behavior at issue. We will discuss examples of reinforcing stimuli that are introduced by the experimenter-therapist to be contingent upon some response in order to strengthen or weaken that response. The problem in the cases to be discussed in this section will thus concern finding stimuli that are reinforcing for the individual and applying them as reinforcers to effect the response in an operant conditioning procedure.

For example, several investigators have pointed out that in working with psychotics, effective reinforcers must be available for manipulating behavior. Lindsley (1956) has shown that reinforcers which are effective for one psychotic individual may not be effective in general use. Robertson (1961) conducted a study specifically to determine the relative efficacies of different classes of reinforcers for modifying the verbal behavior of disorganized schizophrenics. The five reinforcers he used were neutral comment, praise, reproof, tokens (with no back-up reinforcer), and concrete rewards (patients preselected cigarettes, candy, or money as back-ups for five "points" accumulated). While Robertson did find that the most generally potent reinforcers were praise and the preferred concrete reward, he, like Lindsley, found that the reinforcer effective for one patient was not necessarily effective for another. Furthermore, the response to the reinforcer appeared to have no relation either to the severity of the disturbance or to the psychiatric symptom.

Nevertheless, Ayllon and Haughton (1962) suggest that a reinforcer powerful enough for general application to the manipulation of the behavior of psychotics is required. They argue that food is such a reinforcer and they tested its efficacy in a series of studies. The purpose of their first experiment was to determine if food alone could be used as a strong enough reinforcer to control normal eating behavior in schizophrenics, including patients with histories of chronic eating problems. In the past, refusal to eat had been interpreted in many of these cases in terms of various internal "dynamics" of the individual's "mental illness" and treated by spoonfeeding, tubefeeding, intravenous feeding, and electroshock. All these treatments had turned out to be relatively ineffective. Ayllon and Haughton discontinued these procedures, and in addition, the patients were no longer coaxed, reminded, led, or escorted to eat. All social reinforcements for refusal to eat were thus eliminated. The patients were simply required to respond to a call to a meal within a specified time limit, as has already been described. The results indicated that food could be a powerful reinforcer and could be used to shape behavior effectively.

The next experiment attempted to use food as a reinforcer for the acquisition of a new response, the motor response of dropping a penny into the slot of a collection can. Pennies were distributed to the patients before mealtime. In order to gain admittance to the dining room, each patient was required to place his penny in the can. With entrance to the dining hall the only reinforcement, the patients soon learned this new response.

Having established that schizophrenics can be conditioned to execute a motor response, in the third experiment the attempt was to condition the patients to cooperate with one another. Now receipt of the penny necessary for dining room admission was made dependent upon a cooperative response on the part of two patients. A table with two doorbell buttons seven and a half feet apart was placed outside the dining room shortly before and during the period of access to the meal. When the two buttons were pressed simultaneously by two people (one person could not reach both buttons) a buzzer and a light were set off, and a nurse handed a penny to each "partner." Some verbal instructions like "push the button and see what happens," or "It takes two people to make the buzzer go," were also given during the first week. At the end of this period, all but one patient gradually learned the simple social response. The authors conclude the following.

> These findings indicate that food is indeed a powerful reinforcer which may be used experimentally and therapeutically to develop or strengthen a wide range of normal behaviors. Contrary to the fears manifested by various psychiatric personnel, the patients were able to learn all the responses required in order for them to eat.
>
> Medication, severity of illness, length of hospitalization, and age were not significantly related to the acquisition or maintenance of the behaviors studied. Likewise, subnormal IQ presented no great problems in establishing the desired performance (p. 352).[1]

These studies had limited therapeutic affects upon the patient's behavior, but their implications for the treatment of psychotic patients are of much greater significance—as will be discussed further on.

Other forms of response-contingent reinforcement may also be used to shape behaviors significant to the adjustment of psychotic patients. May and Robertson (1960) report considerable success with a procedure called "habit training." An experimental group were given a six-month full program of social activities and entertainment that included training in dress and personal habits. Patients who did well in any respect were systematically reinforced. In contrast, a control group was given no special activities and no systematic reinforcement. There was considerable clinical improvement of the experimental group in comparison to the control group with respect to care of personal appearance.

Peters and Jenkins (1954) administered injections of insulin to chronic patients in order to increase the reinforcing value of sugar. Over a three-month period, the patients were presented a graded series of tasks with successful behavior followed by presentation of fudge. In the first few weeks of the project, the tasks included increasingly difficult multiple-choice and verbal-reasoning problems, while reinforcement was delivered personally by the experimenter. After a few weeks the insulin was discontinued and only social reinforcers were made contingent upon the solution of a new class of interpersonal problems. The behavior of patients treated in this manner, as compared to a nonreinforced control group, showed that

---

[1] It should be pointed out here that although the use of food in treatment may at first seem unusual, such procedures may be necessary where the patient's training history has not produced adequate conditioned reinforcers, especially social reinforcers, for the learning tasks involved.

the reinforced patients had improved significantly in their social relationships.

In another study by King and Armitage (1958) schizophrenic patients were reinforced with candy and cigarettes for the acquisition and maintenance of increasingly complicated behaviors, including motor, verbal, and interpersonal responses. In comparison to a control group of subjects who received traditional psychotherapy, the reinforced patients showed significant clinical improvement.

On the basis of some of these experiments Bandura states, "If the favorable results yielded by these studies are replicated in future investigations, it is likely that the next few years will witness an increasing reliance on conditioning forms of psychotherapy, particularly in the treatment of psychotic patients" (1961, p. 150).

Judicious use of extrinsic reinforcement may, of course, find application with forms of deviant behavior other than that of hospitalized psychotics. In discussing criminality Jeffery (1961), for example, criticizes penological institutions for the manner in which they apply reinforcement, and also offers some suggestions for improvement.

> The implication of behavior psychology for treatment and prevention of delinquency is that the focus of attention must be shifted from the organism to the environment. Rather than altering the self or ego of the criminal . . . the consequences of such responses must be changed in order to eliminate criminal behavior.
>
> To eliminate criminality (1) we can alter the consequences of the behavior, that is, we can remove the reinforcement or we can present an aversive stimulus in its place, (2) we can alter the discriminative stimuli controlling the response, (3) we can alter the variables of deprivation and satiation. . . .
>
> Our correctional institutions are now administered in such a way as to reinforce behaviors desirable to the prison administration. Prison authorities reinforce prisoners for obedience to prison rules and security measures by giving them better jobs, better food and clothing, and a quick release. Prisoners soon discover what verbal responses are reinforced by prison sociologists and parole boards. These behaviors are not involved in the rehabilitation of prisoners, however. The reason such institutions do not rehabilitate is because they reinforce the wrong responses. Recidivism can be regarded as a product of conditioning. . . .
>
> Many reinforcers are available within the prison: food, clothing, cigarettes, movies, reading materials, tickets to athletic events, week-end leaves from the institution, visiting privileges, and the like. These reinforcers are not immediately available, but points can be given to or taken from inmates, and these points can be exchanged for other reinforcers at a later date. In this way reinforcement is immediately presented, contingent upon a given response. . . . Cigarettes and coffee serve as special items in such communities, and are very strong reinforcers which could

be used to great advantage by a behaviorally-oriented prison staff (pp. 19–20).

Slack (1960) has actually applied reinforcement principles to delinquent boys in handling the problem of maintaining "attendance in treatment." Delinquents have usually been extremely difficult to work with because they will not present themselves for treatment with psychiatrists, psychologists, social workers, and the like. Slack's method provided reinforcement contingent upon their participation to solve the problem of maintaining contact.

> Following the initial contact, the boy may arrive at any time during the day. Whenever he arrives and for whatever reasons, his attendance is immediately reinforced by the sharing of food such as cokes, fruit, or sandwiches. Immediately after his talking into the recorder he is paid in cash. He may then help to build electronic equipment, listen to music, take driving lessons, or participate in other rewarding activities. When his hour or so is up, a time convenient for him is set for the next day. At first the experimenter is not particular about his early or late arrival. Only after attendance becomes dependable is there an attempt to get him to arrive on time. This is done by paying the boy more the nearer he arrives to the correct time or by using unexpected bonuses. Gradually, then, a time more convenient for the experimenter is set. Within 15 to 30 meetings the boys generally arrive very dependably, on time, and at the experimenter's convenience (Schwitzgebel, 1960).

In time the social reinforcement value of the experimenter-therapist increases so that interview therapy becomes possible. "The work is still in an early stage, but there are strong indications that once the initial hostility and suspicion are overcome the delinquent is as capable of accepting therapy as is the ordinary middle-class neurotic" (Sidman, 1962, p. 201).

These studies and analyses seem to indicate that where the reinforcers which are applied in the individual's natural habitat have failed to maintain, or shape up, behaviors necessary to his adjustment, an important aspect of the treatment of such behavior problems may involve the introduction of "extrinsic" reinforcers. These are but examples of the types of cases that might be expected to profit from manipulation of such reinforcers. Additional fields of application might include rehabilitation (Meyerson, Michael, Mowrer, Osgood, and Staats, 1963), mental retardation (Staats and Staats, 1962), and educational problems (see Chapter 10).

Further Implications for a Learning Psychotherapy

As the preceding chapters have attempted to show, adjustment to life in our society demands extremely complex behaviors. The individual must acquire intricate language behaviors, complicated social behaviors, work skills, and so on, in order to gain the reinforcers available in our society. Moreover, these behaviors must be under complex stimulus control, and the consequences of these behaviors must have customary reinforcing value for the individual if his adjustive behavior is to be acquired and maintained. Otherwise, competing and perhaps inappropriate behaviors may replace the adjustive behavior.

As has been suggested, an analysis of complex human behavior in terms of learning principles leads readily to the view that behavioral difficulties may best be explained and manipulated through the application of the laws and procedures of learning. As the preceding relatively brief citation of examples indicates, this approach to treatment gains support from the success that has been encountered so far.

Nevertheless, the formulation of a learning psychotherapy cannot be considered complete by any means. The work of application to deviant behavior has only begun. For the most part, the various examples of learning psychotherapy have dealt with obvious and specific behavior disorders —not the comprehensive behaviors of the individual that together are called "personality." Although there are cases in which a single response is the problem, a general restructuring, or the effecting of general changes in behavior, often seems to be demanded—especially for the many severe and deteriorated cases who do not benefit from other treatments and spend their lives making a marginal adjustment or vegetating in the back wards of mental hospitals.

Perhaps in order to deal with these general aspects of human behavior disorders, a learning psychotherapy that is based upon a more comprehensive rationale than has heretofore been presented may be necessary. A detailed and comprehensive set of learning statements accounting for human behavior may be a necessary foundation from which treatment methods for cases of general behavioral disorders may be derived.

An example may be helpful here. Consider the treatment devised by Isaacs, Thomas, and Goldiamond (1960) for restoring speech to the mute schizophrenic. As significant as this treatment was, it would seem that it was nevertheless of a limited and specific nature. Although an extremely important aspect of his adjustment, his speech, had been restored, it is quite possible that many of his general behavioral difficulties still remained. For example, one might ask about the quality of his language. Perhaps it would still be inadequate for mediating solutions to many of the social and physical problems the patient would encounter inside and outside of the hospital. It is possible that the speech would still not perform the functions of communication necessary for social intercourse or for the various learning tasks which this patient would have to successfully complete. The adequacy of his language in providing positive and negative reinforcers in his reasoning might also be questioned.

In addition, there might be many other aspects of such an individual's behavior that would remain defective even after regaining speech. For example, it is likely that the individual's work habits would be poor. He might be incapable of extended effort on an intermittent schedule of reinforcement, as is required in life; or perhaps he might never have acquired a basic repertoire of work skills or of various other social behaviors. Possibly the stimuli of social events might have acquired inappropriate reinforcing and controlling qualities for him.

Successful treatment of such a hypothetical, but probably common, case would thus seem to involve profound changes in all the various behaviors necessary for adjustment, rather than merely in a single response class. In the most serious cases, it might be expected that the learning or relearning would be of the same order of magnitude and complexity that each child must go through in the process of becoming a socialized human adult. For these reasons, it would seem that treatment which involved profound changes in the behaviors necessary to adjustment would require a general analysis of human behavior in learning terms. The possible forms of human behavior deviations that may contribute to lack of adjustment in life, as well as the types of training involved in changing those deviations, must be outlined.

Eventually, from such a rationale, *programs* of treatment analogous to the programmed instruction discussed in the last chapter might be devised for dealing with behavior disorders. Thus, if a person exhibited a deficit in social behaviors, a gradual program for training such behaviors might seem appropriate. A program for establishing work skills and general work habits might be another. In many cases the development of, or change in, the functional language might be indicated, and so on. The problems of behavioral disorders when described in learning terms seem to involve many areas of training, and the types of learning programs that would seem necessary to solve those problems might eventually be large in number. The methods for developing such therapeutic "learning programs" appear to be already available; some of the studies cited previously seem to be limited programs of training (such as the changes in feeding behaviors, the successive approximation training of the mute schizophrenic, etc.)

Perhaps a rationale for learning psychotherapy will also have to include some method for the assessment of behavior. In order to discover the behavioral deficiencies, the required changes in the reinforcing system, the circumstances in which stimulus control is absent, and so on, evaluational techniques in these respects may have to be devised. Certainly, no two individuals will be alike in these various characteristics, and it may be necessary to determine such facts for the individual prior to beginning the learning program of treatment.

Such assessment might take a form similar to some of the psychological tests already in use. It is possible, however, that a general learning rationale for behavior disorders and treatment will itself suggest techniques of assessment.

Verbal Learning Psychotherapy

Before concluding this chapter, it may be worthwhile to discuss briefly the place of the traditional method of psychotherapy, the clinical interview, in this framework. Traditional treatment generally takes place in the form of the psychological practitioner and the patient interacting on a verbal level. A variant of this is where one practitioner and several patients interact—a process called group therapy. Various investigators have discussed this verbal form of psychotherapy in learning terms (for example, Shoben, 1949; Dollard and Miller, 1950). While it may not be necessary in a book of this nature to consider the details of such treatment, it is perhaps important to point out that it should be possible for psychotherapy, in any of the areas of behavioral maladjustment discussed herein, to take place on a verbal level. Deficit behaviors, inappropriate behaviors, stimulus control, the reinforcer system, should all be accessible to change through verbal means. Thus, as was suggested in Chapter 4, language sequences may be used to control other motor behaviors or to establish new motor sequences. In this manner behaviors in which the individual was deficient could be acquired through verbal means, or inappropriate behaviors could be changed. Stimulus control could also be established in the same manner; and, reinforcers could be changed, extinguished, or established through communication.

Through verbal psychotherapy, reasoning sequences appropriate to physical and social events could be established, as was discussed in Chapters 5 and 9. Dollard and Miller (1950) have also emphasized the importance of establishing or re-establishing a verbal repertoire concerning one's own behavior, one's own needs (in our terms, important reinforcers), experiences, and so on. Without these verbal responses, the individual could not engage in the reasoning and problem-solving of which he would otherwise be capable. His behavior would thus be "stupid" or maladjusted in the areas involved.

Another function of verbal therapy is the extinction of avoidance or anxiety responses. Dollard and Miller (1950) point out that the verbal repertoire of the patient may be defective because the responses involved have been punished and are thus aversive. The individual does not emit the response, and his reasoning is consequently hampered. Part of therapy consists of extinguishing the "anxiety" responses elicited by the verbal responses so that the verbal responses are again emitted by the individual rather than avoided. In addition, the clinical interview may also be an opportunity for conditioning the individual positively toward the same verbal responses (see Bandura, 1961; Shoben, 1949). Both of these methods may restore verbal responses to the individual's repertoire and aid his reasoning.

However, although verbal therapy might be appropriate for some, the interview type of treatment would depend upon the patient having already acquired an adequate language system so that it could be used to manipulate his behavior in these various respects. Without the basic type of language repertoire discussed in Chapters 4 and 5, for example, it would not be expected that psychotherapy could occur on a language level. The following statement, using a somewhat different terminology, illustrates one way in which a defective language repertoire would vitiate attempts at psychotherapy on a verbal level.

> Wherever the therapist uses verbal cues to mediate responses he is taking advantage of what the patient has already learned. Unless the patient has already learned approach habits to the word "safe," the therapist cannot effectively make use of this word, and similarly for . . . other examples. . . .
>
> The long (and long-seeming) years of childhood are required to attach the correct emotional responses and habits to verbal cues. This all-important learning, without which no individual seems human, occurs largely within the family in the course of "teaching the child to talk." If the therapist finds that the patient cannot be motivated and reassured by ordinary verbal means, if the common verbal instructions do not have the correct approach and avoidance responses attached to them, the difficulties involved in therapy are grave. The therapist is essentially an operator in this field of language, exciting learned drives and administering learned rewards, eliciting adequate sentence chains to guide instrumental responses (Dollard and Miller, 1950, pp. 311–312).

Of course, many cases are not accessible to treatment through verbal means because the individual's behavior disorder *involves* his basic language learning. The "antisocial," or "psychopathic," individual may not have acquired "symbols" (verbal responses) which "stand for punishing consequences" (see Shoben, 1949). If the individual has not been exposed to training in which certain verbal stimuli, when produced by others or oneself, have acquired aversive properties, the restraint of behavior through the use of such stimuli may not be possible. Other individuals have even greater deficits in language. The psychotic's speech may be merely a jumble of incoherence and be unable to serve the various roles requisite to establishing or changing the individual's behavior. For such individuals, and others with language deficits, the direct shaping of behavior, including the language behavior, might first be necessary.

In conclusion, the methods and principles of learning seem to offer the possibility for dealing with disorders of complex human behavior in a more profound manner than is currently available. However, it is suggested that great advances still lie ahead in the application of learning methods and principles to behavior problems. In this task, because the general method of a learning psychotherapy is based upon the manipulation of observable independent and dependent variables, the method should have advantages characteristic of other applied sciences—one of which is their "self-corrective" nature. That is, when working with observable events, it is evident when something has been accomplished and when it has not, where principles hold and where they do not, where development is still necessary, and so forth. Since learning psychotherapy is based upon a set of experimentally established principles, a development consistent with that occurring in other applied sciences can be confidently predicted.

Index to References[*]

Adams, J. S., and Romney, A. K.   A functional analysis of authority. *Psychol. Rev.*, 1959, *66*, 234–251   **321, 322, 323, 324, 333, 335**

Adamson, R.   Inhibitory set in problem solving as related to reinforcement learning. *J. exp. Psychol.*, 1959, *58*, 280–282   **203**

Allport, G. W.   *Personality: A psychological interpretation.* New York: Holt, 1937   **270**

Allport, G. W., Vernon, P. E., and Lindzey, G.   *Study of values* (rev. ed.). Boston: Houghton Mifflin, 1951   **306**

Anastasi, A.   *Differential psychology* (ed. 3). New York: Macmillan, 1958   **407**

Ayllon, T., and Haughton, E.   Control of the behavior of schizophrenic patients by food. *J. exp. anal. Behav.*, 1962, *5*, 343–352   **375, 480, 503**

Ayllon, T., and Michael, J.   The psychiatric nurse as a behavioral engineer. *J. exp. anal. Behav.*, 1959, *2*, 323–334   **289, 375, 376, 473, 474, 477, 492–493, 497, 498**

Azrin, N. H.   Sequential effects of punishment. *Science*, 1960, *131*, 605–606   **395**

Azrin, N. H.   Time-out from positive reinforcement. *Science*, 1961, *133*, 382–383   **137, 293, 403**

Azrin, N. H., and Lindsley, O. R.   The reinforcement of cooperation between children. *J. abnorm. soc. Psychol.*, 1956, *52*, 100–102   **339, 429**

Bach, G. R.   Some diadic functions of childhood memories. *J. Psychol.*, 1952, *33*, 87–98   **279**

Bachrach, A. J.   An experimental approach to superstitious behavior. *J. Amer. Folklore*, 1962, *75*, 1–9   **351**

Bachrach, A. J., Erwin, W., and Mohr, J.   The control of eating behavior in an anorexic by operant conditioning techniques. (To be published.)   **492**

Back, K.   The exertion of influence through social communication. *J. abnorm. soc. Psychol.*, 1951, *46*, 9–23   **344**

Baldwin, A. L.   *Behavior and development in childhood.* New York: Holt, 1955   **360, 362**

Ball, R. S.   Reinforcement conditioning of verbal behavior by verbal and non-verbal stimuli in a situation resembling a clinical interview. Unpublished doctoral dissertation, Indiana Univer., 1952   **121**

Bandura, A.   Psychotherapy as a learning process. *Psychol. Bull.*, 1961, *58*, 143–159   **486, 505, 510**

---

[*] Boldface numerals after each entry indicate the pages on which the reference is cited.

Bandura, A. Psychotherapeutic objectives. In *Behavioristic psychotherapy*. New York: Holt, in press (mimeographed reprint, 1962a)   **471–472, 488–489, 490**

Bandura, A. Social learning through imitation. In M. R. Jones (Ed.), *Nebraska symposium on motivation*. Lincoln: Univer. Nebraska Press, 1962b   **316, 317, 318, 319, 334, 335, 400**

Bandura, A., and Huston, A. C. Identification as a process of incidental learning. *J. abnorm. soc. Psychol.*, 1961, 63, 311–318   **316**

Bandura, A., Ross, D., and Ross, S. Imitation of film-mediated aggressive models. *J. abnorm. soc. Psychol.*, in press   **318**

Barber, B. *Social stratification: A comparative analysis of structure and process.* New York: Harcourt, 1957   **332, 333**

Bayley, N. Mental growth in young children. *Yearb. Nat. Soc. Stud. Educ.*, 1940a, 39, 11–47   **360**

Bayley, N. Factors influencing the growth of intelligence in young children. *Yearb. Nat. Soc. Stud. Educ.*, 1940b, 39, 49–79   **360**

Berelson, B., and Salter, P. J. Majority and minority Americans: An analysis of magazine fiction. *Public Opinion Quarterly*, 1946, 10, 168–190   **347**

Bergmann, G., and Spence, K. W. Operationism and theory construction. *Psychol. Rev.*, 1941, 48, 1–14   **4**

Berko, J. The child's learning of English morphology. *Word*, 1958, 14, 150–177   **178**

Bierstedt, R. *The social order: An introduction to sociology.* New York: McGraw-Hill, 1957   **303, 307**

Bijou, S. W. Methodology for the experimental analysis of child behavior. *Psychol. Rep.*, 1957a, 3, 243–250   **436**

Bijou, S. W. Patterns of reinforcement and resistance to extinction in young children. *Child Develpm.*, 1957b, 28, 47–54   **368**

Bijou, S. W., and Baer, D. M. The laboratory-experimental study of child behavior. In P. H. Mussen (Ed.), *Handbook of research in child development.* New York: Wiley, 1960   **369**

Bijou, S. W., and Sturges, P. T. Positive reinforcers for experimental studies with children—consumables and manipulatables. *Child Develpm.*, 1959, 30, 151–170   **436**

Birch, H. G. The relation of previous experience to insightful problem-solving. *J. comp. Psychol.*, 1945, 38, 367–383   **200**

Birch, H. G., and Rabinowitz, H. S. The negative effect of previous experience on productive thinking. *J. exp. Psychol.*, 1951, 41, 121–125   **201**

Birge, J. S. Verbal responses in transfer. Unpublished doctoral dissertation, Yale Univer., New Haven, 1941   **212**

Birnbrauer, J. S. The Rainier School programmed learning classroom. Mimeographed paper, 1962   **458**

Boring, E. G. Intelligence as the tests test it. *New Republic*, 1923, 35, 35–37   **405**

Boring, E. G. *A history of experimental psychology* (ed. 2). New York: Appleton, 1950   **5**

Bousfield, W. A., and Barclay, W. D. The relationship between order and frequency of occurrence of restricted associative responses. *J. exp. Psychol.*, 1950, 40, 643–647 **164**

Bousfield, W. A., Cohen, B. H., Whitmarsh, G. A., and Kincaid, W. D. The Connecticut free associational norms. *Tech. Rep. No. 35*, under Contract Nonr-631 (00) between Office of Naval Research and University of Connecticut, 1961 **163–164**

Bowers, J. E., Clement, J. Francis, M. I., and Johnson, M. C. *Exceptional children in home, school and community*. Don Mills, Ont., Canada: Dent, 1960 **471**

Braithwaite, R. B. *Scientific explanation*. Cambridge: Cambridge Univer. Press, 1955 **1, 28, 30**

Brooks, L. O. Response latency in programmed learning: Latency related to error rate. Unpublished doctoral dissertation, Univer. of Houston, 1961 **429**

Brown, R., and Berko, J. Word association and the acquisition of grammar. *Child Develpm.*, 1960, 31, 1–14 **170, 172**

Brown, R., and Fraser, C. The acquisition of syntax. Paper delivered at the Second ONR-New York University Conference on Verbal Learning, June 1961, Dobbs Ferry, New York **170, 174, 177**

Brown, R., and Lenneberg, E. H. A study in language and cognition. *J. abnorm. soc. Psychol.*, 1954, 49, 454–462 **207**

Carmichael, L. The development of behavior in vertebrates experimentally removed from the influence of external stimulation. *Psychol. Rev.*, 1926, 33, 51–58 **362**

Carroll, J. B. (Ed.), *Language, thought, and reality*. New York: Wiley, 1956 **258**

Carroll, J. B. Language development in children. In S. Saporta (Ed.), *Psycholinguistics*. New York: Holt, 1961 **450**

Cattell, R. B. *Description and measurement of personality*. London: Harrap, 1946 **267, 268**

Cofer, C. N. The role of language in human problem solving. Paper presented at the Conference on Human Problem Solving, sponsored by the National Science Foundation, New York University, April 1954 **214**

Cofer, C. N., and Foley, J. P. Mediated generalization and the interpretation of verbal behavior: I. Prolegomena. *Psychol. Rev.*, 1942, 49, 513–540 **149**

Cohen, B. D., Kalish, H. I., Thurston, J. R., and Cohen, E. Experimental manipulation of verbal behavior. *J. exp. Psychol.*, 1954, 47, 106–110 **121**

Cohen, J. D. Justin and his peers: An experimental analysis of a child's social world. *Child Develpm.*, 1962, 33, 697–717 **331**

Coleman, J. C. *Abnormal psychology and modern life* (ed. 2). New York: Appleton, 1950 **4, 5, 390, 392, 399, 469, 478, 482–483, 484, 486, 487**

Corke, P., and Toombs, S. The use of "extrinsic" reinforcement in a remedial reading classroom. Manuscript copy, 1962 (in preparation for publication) **458**

Cottrell, L. S. The adjustment of the individual to his age and sex roles. *Amer. sociol. Rev.*, 1942, 7, 617–620 **325**

Cuber, J. F. *Sociology: A synopsis of principles.* New York: Appleton, 1955 **292**

Davidson, H. P. A study of the confusing letters d, b, p, and q. *J. genet. Psychol.*, 1935, 47, 458–468 **435**

Davis, A., and Havighurst, R. J. *Father of the man.* Boston: Houghton Mifflin, 1947 **351**

Deese, J. On the prediction of occurrence of particular verbal intrusions in immediate recall. *J. exp. Psychol.*, 1959, 58, 17–22 **164**

Deutsch, M. Field theory in social psychology. In G. Lindsey (Ed.), *Handbook of social psychology:* Vol. I. Reading, Mass.: Addison-Wesley, 1954 **342**

DiVesta, F. J., and Stover, D. O. The semantic mediation of evaluative meaning. *J. exp. Psychol.*, 1962, 64, 467–475 **347**

Dodge, J. S. A quantitative investigation of the relation between meaning development and context. Unpublished doctoral dissertation, Univer. of Illinois, 1955 **187**

Dollard, J. Do we have a science of child rearing? In *The family in a democratic society.* Anniversary Papers of the Community Service Society of New York, pp. 41–55. New York: Columbia Univer. Press, 1949 **413**

Dollard, J., and Miller, N. *Personality and psychotherapy.* New York: McGraw-Hill, 1950 **7, 53, 91, 92, 98, 112, 212, 237, 252, 258, 281–282, 283, 328, 367, 379, 386, 389, 390, 391, 393, 413, 465, 466, 472, 478, 509, 510**

Doob, L. W. *Propaganda: Its psychology and techniques.* New York: Holt, 1935 **347**

Doob, L. W. The behavior of attitudes. *Psych. Rev.*, 1947, 54, 135–156 **345**

DuBois, C. *The people of Alor.* Minneapolis: Univer. Minnesota Press, 1944 **299**

Dubos, R. Scientist and public. *Science*, 1961, 133, 1207–1211 **3**

Eisman, B. J. Attitude formation: The development of a color preference response through mediated generalization. *J. abnorm. soc. Psychol.*, 1955, 50, 321–326 **347**

Eriksen, C. W., and Kuethe, J. L. Avoidance conditioning of verbal behavior without awareness: A paradigm of repression. *J. abnorm. soc. Psychol.*, 1956, 53, 203–209 **393**

Ervin, S. M. Grammar and classification. Paper delivered at the American Psychological Association Symposium: "Language and the child's formation of concepts." New York, 1957 **174**

provement resulting from practice in a mental function. *J. Educ. Psychol.*, 1925, *16*, 583–592   **363**

Gesell, A.   The ontogenesis of infant behavior. In L. Carmichael (Ed.), *Manual of child psychology* (ed. 2). New York: Wiley, 1954   **360**

Gesell, A., and Thompson, H.   Learning and growth in identical infant twins: An experimental study by the method of co-twin control. *Genet. Psych. Monogr.*, 1929, *6*, 1–124   **362**

Gewirtz, J. L.   A program of research on the dimensions and antecedents of emotional dependence. *Child Develpm.*, 1956, *27*, 205–221   **112**

Gewirtz, J. L.   A learning analysis of the effects of normal stimulation, privation and deprivation on the acquisition of social motivation and attachment. In B. M. Foss (Ed.), *Determinants of infant behavior*. New York: Wiley, 1959   **384**

Gewirtz, J. L., and Baer, D. M.   Deprivation and satiation of social reinforcers as drive conditions. *J. abnorm. soc. Psychol.*, 1958, *57*, 165–172   **113**

Gilbert, T. F.   Mathetics: The technology of education. *J. Mathetics*, 1962, *1*, 7–73   **231, 232, 433**

Gillen, J.   *The ways of men*. New York: Appleton, 1948   **351**

Goldiamond, I.   Perception. In A. J. Bachrach (Ed.), *Experimental foundations of clinical psychology*. New York: Basic, 1962   **89**

Goldman, I.   The Kwakiutl Indians of Vancouver Island. In M. Mead (Ed.), *Cooperation and competition among primitive peoples*. New York: McGraw-Hill, 1937   **295**

Goldman, I.   The Zuni Indians of New Mexico. In M. Mead (Ed.), *Cooperation and competition among primitive peoples*. New York: McGraw-Hill, 1937   **295**

Green, E. J.   *The learning process and programmed instruction*. New York: Holt, 1962   **422, 428, 429, 430**

Greenspoon, J.   The effect of verbal and nonverbal stimuli on the frequency of members of two verbal response classes. Unpublished doctoral dissertation, Indiana Univer., 1950   **121**

Guilford, J. P., and Zimmerman, W. S.   *Guilford-Zimmerman temperament survey*. Beverly Hills: Sheridan Supply Co., 1949   **267**

Hall, C. S., and Lindzey, G.   *Theories of personality*. New York: Wiley, 1957   **260, 264**

Heine, R. W.   A comparison of patients' reports on psychotherapeutic experiences with psychoanalytic, non-directive, and Adlerian therapists. *Amer. J. Psychother.*, 1953, *7*, 16–23   **279**

Hilgard, J. R.   Learning and maturation in preschool children. *J. genet. Psychol.*, 1932, *41*, 31–56   **363**

Hiroa, T. R.   Ethnology of Ranihiki and Rakahanga. *Bishop Museum Bull.* 99, 1932   **213**

Hogan, B.   *Ben Hogan's five lessons of the modern fundamentals of golf*. New York: Barnes, 1957   **195**

Holland, J. G.   Human vigilance. *Science*, 1958, *128*, 61–67   **250, 455**

Holland, J. G. Teaching machines: An application of principles from the laboratory. *J. exp. anal. Behav.*, 1960, 3, 275–287 **424, 429, 454**

Holland, J. G., and Skinner, B. F. *The analysis of behavior.* New York: McGraw-Hill, 1961 **56, 75, 77n., 83, 98, 380, 390, 420**

Homans, G. C. *Social behavior: Its elementary forms.* New York: Harcourt, 1961 **292, 299, 303, 307, 308, 309, 313, 336, 340, 344, 345**

Homme, L. E., and Glaser, R. Problems in programming verbal learning sequences. In A. A. Lumsdaine and R. Glaser (Eds.), *Teaching machines and programmed learning.* Dept. of Audio-Visual Instruction, National Education Association, 1960 **421**

Honzik, M. P. The constancy of mental test performance during the preschool period. *J. genet. Psychol.*, 1938, 52, 285–302 **360**

Hovland, C. I., Janis, I. L., and Kelley, H. H. *Communication and persuasion.* New Haven: Yale Univer. Press, 1953 **349**

Howes, D., and Osgood, C. E. On the combination of associative probabilities in linguistic contexts. *Amer. J. Psychol.*, 1954, 67, 241–258 **164**

Hull, C. L. Knowledge and purpose as habit mechanisms. *Psychol. Rev.*, 1930, 37, 511–525 **86, 153**

Hull, C. L. Simple trial-and-error learning—an empirical investigation. *J. comp. Psychol.*, 1939, 27, 233–258 **102**

Hull, C. L. *Principles of behavior.* New York: Appleton, 1943 **40, 52, 53, 108, 111, 293**

Irwin, O. C. Infant speech: Development of vowel sounds. *J. speech hearing Disorders*, 1948, 13, 31–34. **118**

Irwin, O. C. Speech development in the young child: 2. Some factors related to the speech development of the infant and young child. *J. speech hearing Disorders*, 1952, 17, 269–279 **118**

Isaacs, W., Thomas, J., and Goldiamond, I. Application of operant conditioning to reinstate verbal behavior in psychotics. *J. speech hearing Disorders*, 1960, 25, 8–12 **491, 507**

Jeffery, C. R. Behavior theory and criminology. Paper presented at the annual meeting of the American Association for the Advancement of Science, Denver, 1961 **311, 312, 480, 505**

Jeffery, W. E. Variables in early discrimination learning: I. Motor responses in the training of a left-right discrimination. *Child Develpm.*, 1958, 29, 269–275 **435**

Johnson, H. M. *Sociology: A systematic introduction.* New York: Harcourt, 1960 **307**

Jones, H. G. The behavioral treatment of enuresis nocturna. In H. J. Eysenck (Ed.), *Behaviour therapy and the neuroses.* New York: Pergamon, 1960 **479**

Jones, H. G. Learning and abnormal psychology. In H. J. Eysenck (Ed.), *Handbook of abnormal psychology.* New York: Basic, 1961 **478**

Judson, A. J., Cofer, C. N., and Gelfand, S. Reasoning as an associative process: II. "Direction" in problem solving as a function of prior reinforcement of relevant responses. *Psychol. Reps.*, 1956, 2, 501–507 **204, 207, 210**

Kardiner, A. *The psychological frontiers of society.* New York: Columbia Univer. Press, 1945 **300**

Keller, F. S., and Schoenfeld, W. N. *Principles of psychology.* New York: Appleton, 1950 **7, 56, 76n., 77n., 84, 87, 261, 262, 283, 304n.**

Kendler, H. H. Teaching machines and psychological theory. In E. Galanter (Ed.), *Automatic teaching: The state of the art.* New York: Wiley, 1959 **433, 434**

Kendler, H. H., and D'Amato, M. F. A comparison of reversal shifts and non-reversal shifts in human concept formation behavior. *J. exp. Psychol.*, 1955, 49, 165–174 **206**

Kendler, H. H., and Karasik, A. D. Concept formation as a function of competition between response produced cues. *J. exp. Psychol.*, 1958, 55, 278–283 **206**

Kendler, H. H., and Kendler, T. S. Vertical and horizontal processes in problem solving. *Psychol. Rev.*, 1962, 69, 1–16 **213**

Kendler, H. H., and Mayzner, M. S. Reversal and non-reversal shifts in card-sorting tests with two or four sorting categories. *J. exp. Psychol.*, 1956, 51, 244–248 **206**

Kendler, H. H., and Vineberg, R. The acquisition of compound concepts as a function of previous training. *J. exp. Psychol.*, 1954, 48, 252–258 **206**

Kent, G. H., and Rosanoff, A. J. A study of association in insanity. *Amer. J. Insanity*, 1910, 67, 37–96 **164**

Kimble, G. A. *Principles of general psychology.* New York: Ronald, 1956 **23, 24, 260, 360, 362, 394, 405, 406**

King, G. F., and Armitage, S. G. An operant-interpersonal therapeutic approach to schizophrenics of extreme pathology. *Amer. Psychol.*, 1958, 13, 358 (abstract) **505**

Kinsey, A. C., Pomeroy, W. B., and Martin, C. E. *Sexual behavior in the human male.* Philadelphia: Saunders, 1948 **311, 400, 402**

Klineberg, O. *Social psychology.* New York: Holt, 1954 **302**

Köhler, W. *The mentality of apes.* London: Routledge, 1925 **200**

Kracauer, S. *From Caligari to Hitler: A psychological history of the German film.* Princeton, N. J.: Princeton Univer. Press, 1947 **319**

Krasner, L. The use of generalized reinforcers in psychotherapy research. *Psychol. Rep.*, 1955, 1, 19–25 **279**

Krasner, L. Studies of the conditioning of verbal behavior. *Psychol. Bull.*, 1958, 55, 148–170 **155, 277**

Krasnogorski, N. I. The conditioned reflex and children's neuroses. *Amer. J. Dis. Child.*, 1925, 30, 753–768 **367**

Kumata, H. A factor analytic investigation of the generality of semantic structure across two selected cultures. Unpublished doctoral dissertation, Univer. of Illinois, 1957 **155**

Kumata, H., and Schramm, W. A pilot study of cross-cultural methodology. *Pub. Opin. Quart.*, 1956, *20*, 222–237 **155**

Lachman, R. The model in theory construction. *Psychol. Rev.*, 1960, *67*, 113–129 **28, 29**

Laffal, J., Lenkoski, L. D., and Ameen, L. "Opposite speech" in a schizophrenic patient. *J. abnorm. soc. Psychol.*, 1956, *52*, 409–413 **289**

Lazarus, A. A. The elimination of children's phobias by deconditioning. In H. J. Eysenck (Ed.), *Behaviour therapy and the neuroses*. New York: Pergamon, 1960 **501**

Leuba, C. Images as conditioned sensations. *J. exp. Psychol.*, 1940, *26*, 345–351 **143**

Lidz, T., Cornelison, A. R., Terry, D., and Fleck, S. Intrafamilial environment of the schizophrenic patient: VI. The transmission of irrationality. *A. M. A. Arch. Neurol. Psychiat.*, 1958, *79*, 305–316 **471**

Lindsley, O. R. Operant conditioning methods applied to research in chronic schizophrenia. *Psychiat. Res. Rep.*, 1956, *5*, 140–153 **301, 475, 498, 502**

Lipton, L., and Blanton, R. L. The semantic differential and mediated generalization as measures of meaning. *J. exp. Psychol.*, 1957, *54*, 431–437 **143**

Lott, B. E., and Lott, A. J. The formation of positive attitudes toward group members. *J. abnorm. soc. Psychol.*, 1960, *61*, 297–300 **342**

Lövaas, O. I. Effect of exposure to symbolic aggression on aggressive behavior. *Child Develpm.*, 1961, *32*, 37–44 **376**

Lövaas, O. I. The control of food intake in children by reinforcement of relevant verbal behavior, 1961 (mimeographed reprint) **318**

Lumsdaine, A. A., and Janis, I. L. Resistance to "counterpropaganda" produced by one-sided and two-sided "propaganda" presentations. *Pub. Opin. Quart.*, 1953, *17*, 311–318 **349**

Lundholm, H. Reflections upon the nature of the psychological self. *Psychol. Rev.*, 1940, *47*, 110–127 **263**

Lundin, R. W. *Personality: An experimental approach*. New York: Macmillan, 1961 **268, 390, 466, 470**

Luria, A. R. The role of language in the formation of temporary connections. In B. Simon (Ed.), *Psychology in the Soviet Union*. Stanford: Stanford Univer. Press, 1957 **209**

Luria, A. R., and Yudovich, F. Ia. *Speech and the development of mental processes in the child*. London: Stables, 1959 **209, 451**

McCandless, B. R. *Children and adolescents: Behavior and development*. New York: Holt, 1961 **411**

McClelland, D. C. *Studies in motivation*. New York: Appleton, 1955 **271**

Maccoby, E. E.   Role-taking in childhood and its consequences for social learning. *Child Develpm.*, 1959, 30, 239–252   **335**

Maccoby, E. E., and Gibbs, P. K.   Methods of child-rearing in two social classes. In W. E. Martin and C. B. Stendler (Eds.), *Readings in child development.* New York: Harcourt, 1954   **300**

MacCorquodale, K., and Meehl, P. E.   On the distinction between hypothetical constructs and intervening variables. *Psychol. Rev.*, 1948, 55, 95–107   **15n.**

Maier, N. R. F.   Reasoning in humans: I. On direction. *J. Comp. Psychol.*, 1930, 10, 115–143   **201**

Maltzman, I.   Thinking: From a behavioristic point of view. *Psychol. Rev.*, 1955, 62, 275–286   **214**

Maltzman, I., Bogartz, W., and Breger, L.   A procedure for increasing word association originality and its transfer effects. *J. exp. Psychol.*, 1958, 56, 392–398   **209**

Mandler, G., and Kessen, W.   *The language of psychology.* New York: Wiley, 1959   **13**

Marks, M. R.   Problem solving as a function of the situation. *J. exp. Psychol.*, 1951, 41, 74–80   **209**

Marquis, D. P.   Learning in the neonate: The modification of behavior under three feeding schedules. *J. exp. Psychol.*, 1941, 29, 263–282   **374**

Maslow, A. H.   *Motivation and personality.* New York: Harper, 1954   **292, 308, 358**

May, A. R., and Robertson, J. P. S.   The efficacy of habit training in chronic schizophrenia. *J. clin. Psychol.*, 1960, 16, 359–361   **504**

May, M. A.   Experimentally acquired drives. *J. exp. Psychol.*, 1948, 38, 66–77   **113**

Meyerson, L., Michael, J. L., Mowrer, O. H., Osgood, C. E., and Staats, A. W.   Learning, behavior and rehabilitation. In L. Loftquist (Ed.), *Psychological research in rehabilitation.* Washington: American Psychological Association, 1963, in press   **460, 470, 488, 506**

Miller, N. E.   The influence of past experience upon the transfer of subsequent training. Unpublished doctoral dissertation, Yale Univer., 1935   **91, 212**

Miller, N. E.   Studies of fear as an acquirable drive: I. Fear as motivation and fear reduction as reinforcement in the learning of new responses. *J. exp. Psychol.*, 1948a, 38, 89–101   **49**

Miller, N. E.   Theory and experiment relating psychoanalytic displacement to stimulus response generalization. *J. abnorm. soc. Psychol.*, 1948b, 43, 155–178   **213**

Miller, N. E., and Dollard, J.   *Social learning and imitation.* New Haven: Yale Univer. Press, 1941   **7, 117, 326, 351**

Morse, W. H., and Skinner B. F.   A second type of superstition in the pigeon. *Amer. J. Psychol.*, 1957, 70, 308–311   **289**

Mousnier, R.   *La vénalité des offices sous Henri IV et Louis XIII.* Rouen: Editions Mauguard, 1945   **334**

Mowrer, O. H.   An experimental analogue of "regression" with incidental observations on "reaction-formation." *J. abnorm soc. Psychol.*, 1940, 35, 56–87   **282**

Mowrer, O. H.   *Learning theory and personality dynamics.* New York: Ronald, 1950   **7, 53, 98, 117, 465**

Mowrer, O. H.   The autism theory of speech development and some clinical applications. *J. speech hearing Disorders*, 1952, 17, 263–268   **118**

Mowrer, O. H.   The psychologist looks at language. *Amer. Psychol.*, 1954, 9, 660–694   **115, 141n., 149, 185**

Mowrer, O. H.   *Learning theory and behavior.* New York: Wiley, 1960a. **52, 96n., 97, 98, 108n.**

Mowrer, O. H.   *Learning theory and the symbolic processes.* New York: Wiley, 1960b   **53, 141n., 143**

Mowrer, O. H., and Mowrer, W. M.   Enuresis: A method for its study and treatment. *Amer. J. Orthopsychiat.*, 1938, 8, 436–459   **479**

Murray, H. A.   *Explorations in personality.* New York: Oxford Univer. Press, 1938   **287, 292, 293, 298, 299**

Mussen, P. H., and Conger, J. J.   *Child development and personality.* New York: Harper, 1956   **375**

Mussen, P. H., and Distler, L.   Masculinity, identification, and father-son relationships. *J. abnorm. soc. Psychol.*, 1959, 59, 350–356   **335**

Mussen, P. H., and Rutherford, E.   Effects of aggressive cartoons on children's aggressive play. *J. abnorm. soc. Psychol.*, 1961, 62, 461–464   **318**

Newcomb, T. M.   *Social psychology.* New York: Holt, 1950   **302**

Nuthmann, A. M.   Conditioning of a response class on a personality test. *J. abnorm. soc. Psychol.*, 1957, 54, 19–23   **261, 268**

Oakes, W. F., and Droge, A. E.   Operant conditioning of responses to social introversion scale items on the MMPI. *Psychol. Rep.*, 1960, 6, 223–225 **269**

Orlando, R., and Bijou, S. W.   Single and multiple schedules of reinforcement in developmentally retarded children. *J. exp. anal. Behav.*, 1960, 3, 339–348   **368, 436, 446**

Osgood, C. E.   *Method and theory in experimental psychology.* New York: Oxford Univer. Press, 1953   **40, 52, 53, 97, 111, 112, 118, 119, 141, 144, 149, 215**

Osgood, C. E.   A behavioristic analysis of perception and language as cognitive phenomena. In *Contemporary approaches to cognition.* Cambridge: Harvard Univer. Press, 1957   **90n., 141n., 169**

Osgood, C. E., and Suci, G. J.   Factor analysis of meaning. *J. exp. Psychol.*, 1955, 50, 325–338   **155**

Osgood, C. E., and Tannenbaum, P. H.   The principle of contiguity in the prediction of attitude change. *Psychol. Rev.*, 1955, 62, 42–55   **345**

Oskamp, S.   Partial reinforcement in concept formation: "Hypotheses" in human learning. Unpublished Master's thesis, Stanford Univer., 1956 **210**

Palermo, D. S., and Jenkins, J. J. Word association norms: Grade school through college. In *Research relating to children*, Bull. 14, Children's Bureau, U.S. Dept. Health, Educ. and Welfare, 1961 **463**

Parsons, T. Family structure and the socialization of the child. In T. Parsons and R. F. Bales (Eds.), *Family, socialization, and interaction process.* New York: Free Press, 1955 **335**

Peters, H. N., and Jenkins, R. L. Improvement of chronic schizophrenic patients with guided problem-solving motivated by hunger. *Psychiat. Quart. Suppl.*, 1954, 28, 84–101 **504**

Peterson, R. C., and Thurstone, L. L. *Motion pictures and the social attitudes of children.* New York: Macmillan, 1933 **347**

Phillips, L. W. Mediated verbal similarity as a determinant of the generalization of a conditioned GSR. *J. exp. Psychol.*, 1958, 55, 56–62 **143, 150**

Piaget, J. How children form mathematical concepts. *Sci. Amer.*, 1953, 189, 74–79 **219, 221**

Porter, D. A critical review of a portion of the literature on teaching devices. *Harvard educ. Rev.*, 1957, 27, 126–147 **424**

Quay, H. The effect of verbal reinforcement on the recall of early memories. *J. abnorm. soc. Psychol.*, 1959, 59, 254–257 **274, 277, 278**

Raven, B., and French, J. R. P., Jr. Legitimate power, coercive power, and observability in social influence. *Sociometry*, 1958, 21, 83–97 **335**

Raymond, M. J. Case of fetishism treated by aversion therapy. In H. J. Eysenck (Ed.), *Behaviour therapy and the neuroses.* New York: Pergamon, 1960 **500**

Razran, G. H. A quantitative study of meaning by a conditioned salivary technique (semantic conditioning). *Science*, 1939a, 90, 89–90 **37**

Razran, G. H. The nature of the extinctive process. *Psychol. Rev.*, 1939b, 46, 264–297 **37**

Razran, G. H. Stimulus generalization of conditioned responses. *Psychol. Bull.*, 1949, 46, 337–365 **37**

Razran, G. H. The observable unconscious and the inferable conscious in current Soviet psychophysiology: Interoceptive conditioning, semantic conditioning, and the orienting reflex. *Psychol. Rev.*, 1961, 68, 81–147 **479**

Rees, H., and Israel, H. An investigation of the establishment and operation of mental sets. *Psychol. Monogr.*, 1935, 46, No. 6 (Whole No. 210) **203**

Reichenbach, H. *The rise of scientific philosophy.* Berkeley: Univer. of California Press, 1951 **9, 10**

Reid, L. S. The development of noncontinuity behavior through continuity learning. *J. exp. Psychol.*, 1953, 46, 107–112 **455**

Research relating to children, Bull. 14, Children's Bureau, U.S. Dept. of Health, Educ. and Welfare, 1961   **456n., 457n.**

Rheingold, H. L., Gewirtz, J. L., and Ross, H. W.   Social conditioning of vocalizations in the infant. *J. comp. physiol. Psychol.,* 1959, 52, 68–73   **116, 450**

Rheingold, H. L., Stanley, W. C., and Cooley, J. A.   Method for studying exploratory behavior in infants. *Science,* 1962, *136,* 1054–1055   **450**

Rhine, R. J.   A concept-formation approach to attitude acquisition. *Psychol. Rev.,* 1958, 65, 362–370   **345**

Robertson, J. P. S.   The operant conditioning of speech and drawing behavior in chronic schizophrenics. *Swiss Review of Psychology and Its Applications,* 1958, 17, 309–315   **492**

Robertson, J. P. S.   Effects of different rewards in modifying the verbal behavior of disorganized schizophrenics. *J. clin. Psychol.,* 1961, 17, 399–402   **502**

Rogers, C. R.   *Client-centered therapy: Its current practice, implications, and theory.* Boston: Houghton Mifflin, 1951   **264**

Rogers, J. M.   Operant conditioning in a quasi-therapy setting: The influence of interviewer behavior upon subjects' self-reference verbalizations. Mimeographed adaptation of a doctoral dissertation, Stanford Univer., 1958. (An abridged article appears in *J. abnorm. soc. Psychol.,* 1960, 60, 247–252.)   **279, 280**

Rosen, B. C.   The achievement syndrome: A psychocultural dimension of social stratification. *Amer. Sociol. Rev.,* 1956, *21,* 203–211   **296**

Russell, W. A., and Jenkins, J. J.   The complete Minnesota norms for responses to 100 words from the Kent-Rosanoff word association test. *Tech. Rep. No. 11.* Contract No. N8 onr-66216 between the Office of Naval Research and University of Minnesota, 1954   **164**

Russell, W. A., and Storms, L. H.   Implicit verbal chaining in paired-associate learning. *J. exp. Psychol.,* 1955, 49, 287–293   **167, 169**

Salzinger, K.   Experimental manipulation of verbal behavior: A review. *J. gen. Psychol.,* 1959, *61,* 65–94   **155**

Salzinger, K., Portney, S., and Feldman, R. S.   Verbal behavior of schizophrenic and normal patients. Mimeographed paper, 1962   **278, 492**

Samuelson, P. A.   *Economics: An introductory analysis* (ed. 4). New York: McGraw-Hill, 1958   **309**

Sarbin, T. R.   A preface to a psychological analysis of the self. *Psychol. Rev.,* 1952, 59, 11–22   **261**

Sarbin, T. R.   Role theory. In G. Lindzey (Ed.), *Handbook of social psychology,* Vol. I. Reading, Mass.: Addison-Wesley, 1954   **325, 331**

Saugstad, P.   Problem solving as dependent upon availability of functions. Unpublished doctoral thesis, Univer. of Chicago, 1952   **209**

Schachter, S.   Deviation, rejection and communication. *J. abnorm. soc. Psychol.,* 1951, 46, 190–207   **344**

Schramm, W. *The process and effects of mass communication.* Urbana: Univer. of Illinois Press, 1960 **197**

Schramm, W., Lyle, J., and Parker, E. F. *Television in the lives of our children.* Stanford: Stanford Univer. Press, 1961 **317**

Schwitzgebel, R. A new approach to understanding delinquency. *Fed. Probation,* March 1960 **506**

Sears, R. R. Social behavior and personality development. In T. Parsons and E. A. Shils (Eds.), *Toward a general theory of action.* Cambridge, Mass.: Harvard Univer. Press, 1951 **283, 351**

Shaffer, L. F., and Shoben, E. J., Jr. *The psychology of adjustment* (ed. 2). Boston: Houghton Mifflin, 1956 **403**

Sheldon, W. H. (with the collaboration of S. S. Stevens and W. B. Tucker). *The varieties of human physique: An introduction to constitutional psychology.* New York: Harper, 1940 **267**

Shipley, W. C. An apparent transfer of conditioning. *Psychol. Bull.,* 1933, 30, 541 **100**

Shirley, M. *The first two years: III. Personality manifestations.* Minneapolis: Univer. of Minnesota Press, 1933 **119**

Shoben, E. J. Psychotherapy as a problem in learning theory. *Psychol. Bull.,* 1949, 46, 366–392 **509, 510**

Shute, W. G., Shirk, W. W., and Porter, G. F. *Plane and solid geometry.* New York: American Book, 1960 **239**

Sidman, M. *Tactics of scientific research.* New York: Basic, 1960a **28n., 43, 463**

Sidman, M. Normal sources of pathological behavior. *Science,* 1960b, 132, 61–68 **471**

Sidman, M. Operant techniques. In A. J. Bachrach (Ed.), *Experimental foundations of clinical psychology.* New York: Basic, 1962 **290, 476, 506**

Sidowski, J. B., Wyckoff, B., and Tabory, L. The influence of reinforcement and punishment in a minimal social situation. *J. abnorm. soc. Psychol.,* 1956, 52, 115–119 **337**

Simpkins, L. Conditioning and extinction effects in a restricted verbal interaction. Mimeographed paper, 1962 **341**

Skinner, B. F. *The behavior of organisms.* New York: Appleton, 1938 **44**

Skinner, B. F. *Science and human behavior.* New York: Macmillan, 1953 **7, 15, 26, 43–44, 57, 78, 143, 245, 351, 352, 354, 465**

Skinner, B. F. *Verbal behavior.* New York: Appleton, 1957 **124, 125, 126, 127, 129, 135, 162n., 204, 246, 249, 251**

Skinner, B. F. Teaching machines. *Science,* 1958, 128, 969–977 **418, 423, 426**

Skinner, B. F. *Cumulative record.* New York: Appleton, 1959 **271, 273, 351, 462**

Skinner, B. F. Teaching machines. *Sci. Amer.* 1961, 205, 90–102 **416, 423, 429, 452, 453, 454, 455, 459**

Skinner, B. F., and Holland, J. G. The use of teaching machines in college instruction. In A. A. Lumsdaine and R. Glaser (Eds.), *Teaching machines and programmed learning*, Dept. of Audio-Visual Instruction, National Education Association, 1960 **421, 422**

Slack, C. W. Experimenter-subject psychotherapy: A new method of introducing intensive office treatment for unreachable cases. *Ment. Hygiene*, 1960, 44, 238–256 **506**

Snygg, D., and Combs, A. W. *Individual behavior*. New York: Harper, 1949 **358**

Spence, K. W. The nature of theory construction in contemporary psychology. *Psychol. Rev.*, 1944, 51, 47–68 **15, 22, 24, 26–27, 28**

Spence, K. W. *Behavior theory and conditioning*. New Haven: Yale Univer. Press, 1956 **108, 111**

Sperry, R. W. Mechanisms of neural maturation. In S. S. Stevens (Ed.), *Handbook of experimental psychology*. New York: Wiley, 1951 **362**

Spiker, C. C. Research methods in children's learning. In P. H. Mussen (Ed.), *Handbook of research methods in child development*. New York: Wiley, 1960 **367**

Staats, A. W. *A behavioristic study of verbal and instrumental response hierarchies and their relationship to human problem solving*. Unpublished doctoral dissertation, Univ. California, Los Angeles, 1955

Staats, A. W. Learning theory and "opposite speech." *J. abnorm. soc. Psychol.*, 1957a, 55, 268–269 **289**

Staats, A. W. Verbal and instrumental response-hierarchies and their relationship to problem-solving. *Amer. J. Psychol.*, 1957b, 70, 442–446 **209**

Staats, A. W. Verbal habit-families, concepts, and the operant conditioning of word classes. *Psychol. Rev.*, 1961, 68, 190–204 **153, 191**

Staats, A. W., Finley, J. R., Minke, K. A., and Wolf, M. Reinforcement variables in the control of unit reading responses. Tech. Rep. No. 23. Contract No. Nonr 2794 (02) between Office of Naval Research and Arizona State University, 1963 **446**

Staats, A. W., Minke, K. A., Finley, J. R., Wolf, M., and Brooks, L. O. A reinforcer system and experimental procedure for the laboratory study of reading acquisition. *Child Develpm.*, in press **443**

Staats, A. W., and Staats, C. K. Attitudes established by classical conditioning. *J. abnorm. soc. Psychol.*, 1958, 57, 37–40 **114, 345**

Staats, A. W., and Staats, C. K. Effect of number of trials on the language conditioning of meaning. *J. gen. Psychol.*, 1959a, 61, 211–223 **187**

Staats, A. W., and Staats, C. K. Meaning and m: Correlated but separate. *Psychol. Rev.*, 1959b, 66, 136–144 **161**

Staats, A. W., and Staats, C. K. A comparison of the development of speech and reading behaviors with implications for research. *Child Develpm.*, 1962, 33, 831–846 **294, 506**

Staats, A. W., Staats, C. K., and Crawford, H. L. First-order conditioning of meaning and the paralleled conditioning of a GSR. *J. gen. Psychol.*, 1962, 67, 159–167 **142**

Staats, A. W., Staats, C. K., Finley, J. R., and Heard, W. G. Independent manipulation of meaning and m. *J. gen. Psychol.*, in press **161**

Staats, A. W., Staats, C. K., Finley, J. R., and Minke, K. A. Mediating responses in the operant conditioning of word classes. *Tech. Rep. No. 21.* Contract Nonr-2794 (02) between Office of Naval Research and Arizona State University, 1961 **164**

Staats, A. W., Staats, C. K., and Heard, W. G. Language conditioning of meaning to meaning using a semantic generalization paradigm. *J. exp. Psychol.*, 1959, 57, 187–192 **189**

Staats, A. W., Staats, C. K., and Heard, W. G. Denotative meaning established by classical conditioning. *J. exp. Psychol.*, 1961, 61, 300–303 **187**

Staats, A. W., Staats, C. K., Heard, W. G., and Finley, J. R. Operant conditioning of factor analytic personality traits. *J. gen. Psychol.*, 1962, 66, 101–114 **268, 269**

Staats, A. W., Staats, C. K., Heard, W. G., and Nims, L. P. Replication report: Meaning established by classical conditioning. *J. exp. Psychol.*, 1959, 57, 64 **186**

Staats, A. W., Staats, C. K., Schutz, R. E., and Wolf, M. The conditioning of textual responses using "extrinsic" reinforcers. *J. exp. anal. Behav.*, 1962, 5, 33–40 **294, 432, 436, 437, 438, 439**

Staats, C. K. Meaning acquisition and communication. *Tech. Rep. No. 11.* Contract No. Nonr-2794 (02) between Office of Naval Research and Arizona State University, 1959 **191**

Staats, C. K., and Staats, A. W. Meaning established by classical conditioning. *J. exp. Psychol.*, 1957, 54, 74–80 **186**

Staats, C. K., Staats, A. W., and Heard, W. G. Attitude development and ratio of reinforcement. *Sociometry*, 1960, 23, 338–350 **345, 348**

Stagner, R. *Psychology of personality.* New York: McGraw-Hill, 1948 **260**

Stephenson, W. *The study of behavior: Q-technique and its methodology.* Chicago: Univer. of Chicago Press, 1953 **261**

Stevens, S. S. Psychology and the science of science. *Psychol. Bull.*, 1939, 36, 221–263 **2, 8, 9, 11, 256**

Stevens, S. S. *Handbook of experimental psychology.* New York: Wiley, 1951 **219, 244, 252n.**

Stolurow, L. M. Teaching by machine. U. S. Office of Education, *Cooperative Research Monograph No. 6,* 1961 **417**

Stratton, G. M. Vision without inversion of the retinal image. *Psychol. Rev.*, 1897, 4, 341–360, 463–481 **362**

Strayer, L. C. Language and growth: The relative efficacy of early and deferred vocabulary training, studied by the method of co-twin control. *Genet. psychol. Monogr.*, 1930, 8, 215–317 **363**

Strong, E. K., Jr. *Vocational interest blank for men: Manual.* Stanford Univer. Press, Stanford, 1952 **305**

Suci, G. J. A comparison of semantic structures in American Southwest culture groups. *J. abnorm. soc. Psychol.*, 1960, 61, 25–30 **155**

Sullivan, H. S. Tensions interpersonal and international: A psychiatrist's view.

In H. Cantril (Ed.), *Tensions that cause war.* Urbana: Univer. of Illinois Press, 1950   **308**

Terman, L. M., and Merrill, M. A.   *Measuring intelligence.* Boston: Houghton Mifflin, 1937   **407**

Terrell, C.   The need for simplicity in research in child psychology. *Child Develpm.*, 1958, 29, 303–310   **430**

Thibaut, J. W.   An experimental study of the cohesiveness of underprivileged groups. *Hum. Relat.*, 1950, 3, 251–278   **344**

Thibaut, J. W., and Kelley, H. H.   *The social psychology of groups.* New York: Wiley, 1959   **325**

Thurstone, L. L.   *Multiple factor analysis: A development and expansion of the vectors of the mind.* Chicago: Univer. of Chicago Press, 1947   **267**

Toulmin, S.   *The philosophy of science.* London: Hutchinson's University Library, 1953   **29n.**

Triandis, H. C., and Osgood, C. E.   A comparative factorial analysis of semantic structures in monolingual Greek and American college students. *J. abnorm. soc. Psychol.*, 1958, 57, 187–196   **155**

U. S. *census of population: 1950.* U.S. Bureau of the Census, Vol. IV, Part 3, Chapter A, Nativity and parentage, Table 20; and Vol. II, Part 1, Characteristics of the population   **297**

Ulmer, M. J.   *Economics: Theory and practice.* Boston: Houghton Mifflin, 1959   **292, 309**

Underwood, B. J.   Verbal learning in the educative processes. *Harvard educ. Rev.*, 1959, 29, 107–117   **158**

Verplanck, W. S.   The operant conditioning of human motor behavior. *Psychol. Bull.*, 1956, 53, 70–83   **80, 122, 123, 278**

Verplanck, W. S.   Unaware of where's awareness: Some verbal operants—notates, monents, and notants. In C. W. Eriksen (Ed.), *Behavior and awareness.* Durham: Duke Univer. Press, 1962   **84, 210, 211, 212**

Walters, R. H., Llewellyn-Thomas, E., and Acker, C. W. Enhancement of punitive behavior by audio-visual displays. *Science*, 1962, 136, 872   **318**

Walton, D.   The application of learning theory to the treatment of a case of neurodermatitis. In H. J. Eysenck (Ed.), *Behaviour therapy and the neuroses.* New York: Pergamon, 1960   **494**

Watson, J. B., and Rayner, R.   Conditioned emotional reactions. *J. exp. Psychol.*, 1920, 3, 1–14   **477, 489**

White, A. D.   *A history of the warfare of science with theology in Christendom,* 1899 (1955 ed., New York: Braziller)   **2, 253, 254, 256**

White, S. H.   Generalization of an instrumental response with variations in two attributes of the CS. *J. exp. Psychol.*, 1958, 56, 339–343   **71**

Whiting, J. W. H., and Child, I. L.   *Child training and personality: A cross-cultural study.* New Haven: Yale Univer. Press, 1953   **283, 351**

Whyte, W. F. *Street corner society: The social structure of an Italian slum* (ed. 2). Chicago: Univer. of Chicago Press, 1955 **329**

Wickes, T. A., Jr. Examiner influence in a testing situation. *J. consult. Psychol.*, 1956, 20, 23–26 **121**

Williams, C. D. The elimination of tantrum behavior by extinction procedures. *J. abnorm. soc. Psychol.*, 1959, 59, 269 **495, 496**

Wilson, W. C., and Verplanck, W. S. Some observations on the reinforcement of verbal operants. *Amer. J. Psychol.*, 1956, 69, 448–451 **121**

Wolpe, J. *Psychotherapy by reciprocal inhibition.* Stanford: Stanford Univer. Press, 1958 **489**

Wolpe, J., and Rachman, S. Psychoanalytic "evidence": A critique based on Freud's case of Little Hans. *J. nerv. ment. Dis.*, 1960, 131, 135–148 **489**

Woodrow, H., and Lowell, F. Children's association frequency tests. *Psychol. Monogr.*, 1916, 22, No. 5 **173–174**

Wyckoff, L. B. The role of observing responses in discrimination learning. *Psychol. Rev.*, 1952, 59, 431–442 **455**

Yates, A. J. The application of learning theory to the treatment of tics. In H. J. Eysenck (Ed.), *Behaviour therapy and the neuroses.* New York: Pergamon, 1960 **494**

Zeaman, D. Skinner's theory of teaching machines. In Galanter, E. (Ed.), *Automatic teaching: The state of the art.* New York: Wiley, 1959 **464**

Zimmerman, D. W. Durable secondary reinforcement: Method and theory. *Psychol. Rev.*, 1957, 64, 373–383 **49, 67, 76**

Index of Subjects

531